Spring/Summer
75

Studies in
COMPARATIVE COMMUNISM

An International Interdisciplinary Journal

Spring/Summer
1975

Studies in Comparative Communism
is published quarterly by the
Von KleinSmid Institute of International Affairs
School of International Relations
University of Southern California

Studies in Comparative Communism is indexed in the *Social Sciences Index; Public Affairs Information Service; ABC POL SCI; Social Science Citation Index;* and *Current Contents, Behavioral, Social & Management Sciences.* Articles are listed in the *American Historical Review* and abstracted in *Historical Abstracts* and *International Political Science Abstracts,* abstracted and indexed in the *Universal Reference System,* and analyzed in the computer-based *United States Political Science Information System.* US ISSN 0039-3592

Studies in

COMPARATIVE COMMUNISM

An International Interdisciplinary Journal

Vol. VIII, Nos. 1 & 2

Spring/Summer 1975

CONTENTS

SPECIAL ISSUE ON FOREIGN POLICY

SYMPOSIUM ON THE COMPARATIVE STUDY OF COMMUNIST FOREIGN POLICIES

Area Studies and International Relations: Introductory Remarks
Charles Gati 5

What Should We Compare, Why, and How?
David D. Finley 12

Is Comparison Useful or Possible?
Roger E. Kanet 20

Some Undone Jobs
Henry Krisch 28

Does the Comparative Approach Merit High Priority?
Arnold L. Horelick 36

Comparison or Confusion?
Alvin Z. Rubinstein 42

Foreign Policy Issues Within Conceptual Frameworks
Jan F. Triska 47

The Plausibility and Utility of the Study of Comparative Communist Foreign Policies
Lawrence L. Whetten 52

Comparison as a State of Mind
James N. Rosenau 57

Level and Context of Analysis: Concluding Remarks 62

Détente and Soviet-American Trade: An Approach to a Political Balance Sheet
David D. Finley 66

Intra-Alliance Politics and European Détente: The Case of Poland and Rumania
Jeanne Kirk Laux 98

An International Anomaly: The United States and the Communist Parties in France and Italy, 1945–1947
Simon Serfaty 123

Soviet Decisionmaking and the Czechoslovak Crisis of 1968
Jiri Valenta 147

The Soviet Invasion of Czechoslovakia and the Limits of Kremlinology
Dimitri K. Simes 174

Rejoinder
Jiri Valenta 181

RESEARCH NOTE

China and the Rise of Khrushchev
Victor Baras 183

REVIEW ARTICLE

Political Power: USA/USSR **Ten Years Later—Comparative Foreign Policy**
William Taubman 192

CONTRIBUTORS 206

Symposium on the Comparative Study of Communist Foreign Policies

This symposium originated in a panel discussion at the Northeastern Slavic Conference of the American Association for the Advancement of Slavic Studies, held in Montreal in May 1971. The panel was organized and chaired by Charles Gati, who subsequently assisted in preparing the original three papers for publication. The papers were meant to complement the " Symposium on Comparative Politics and Communist Systems," which appeared in the March 1967 issue of *Slavic Review*. That symposium—edited by Robert Sharlet, with contributions by John Armstrong, Alfred Meyer, John Kautsky, Dan Jacobs, and Sharlet—has since been extensively cited in books and journals and reprinted in Frederic J. Fleron's methodological reader, *Communist Studies and the Social Sciences* (Chicago: Rand McNally, 1969).

When the panel papers were submitted to this journal, the Editors decided to circulate them for comments among selected specialists on Communist foreign policies, as well as among generalists in international relations. To stimulate the exchange, a special seminar meeting, co-sponsored with the California Arms Control and Foreign Policy Seminar and the Southern California Seminar on Communist Systems, was organized on May 14, 1974, in Marina del Rey, California. At that meeting the original papers, as well as comments solicited from Alvin Z. Rubinstein and Jan F. Triska, were discussed by Arnold L. Horelick of the Social Science Department of The Rand Corporation and James N. Rosenau of the School of International Relations, University of Southern California. These two discussions are included in this symposium, along with comments by Lawrence L. Whetten. (In addition, a specially commissioned paper by Judy Bertelsen and Charles A. Powell, " Macro and Micro Approaches to the Comparative Study of Foreign Policy: An Inventory for the Study of Communist Foreign Policies," was circulated and discussed at the meeting.) The seminar produced useful exchanges between the specialists in Communist foreign policies and the generalists in international relations.

We hope that this symposium—consisting of the original panel papers, as well as the comments—will stimulate further discussion of this important topic.

With the symposium as the nucleus, we have decided to devote this entire double issue to foreign policy. The second part of the issue contains a number of articles, a graduate student essay, a research note, and a review article, all dealing with foreign policy issues.

Ed.

CHARLES GATI

Area Studies and International Relations: Introductory Remarks

Another prescription

The papers that follow constitute a sophisticated kind of pleading for comparative studies of Communist foreign policies. As such, they may be regarded as companion pieces to the 1967 *Slavic Review* symposium whose contributors wanted the political science profession to be more scientific, to go beyond the " area studies " approach, and to attempt systematic comparison of Communist and non-Communist polities. Interestingly, no contributor to the symposium extended his analysis or pleading to the external conduct of the Communist countries. The question was not even raised, let alone answered, whether it was feasible or desirable to compare Communist foreign policies. One possible reason for the exclusion of foreign policy from serious consideration on that occasion had to do with timing: students of international relations had begun to turn to the comparative study of foreign policy only in the second half of the 1960s; theirs was the second wave of methodological experimentation and innovation. Another possible reason, suggested by Henry Krisch in the following pages, was the prevalent assumption that, while the post-Stalin era had opened the door to domestic diversity in the Communist world, the foreign policies of the Communist countries remained hopelessly appended to those of the Soviet Union and thus the comparative analysis of foreign policies was both unnecessary and potentially meaningless.

Accordingly, the integration of Communist studies with comparative politics has been far more evident in recent years than the integration of Communist studies with international relations. For better or worse, not only have the younger scholars of Communist domestic politics adopted the language, techniques, categories, and theoretical apparatus of modern social science, but so have some of their senior mentors as well (Armstrong, Barghoorn, Meyer, and Tucker in particular). By and large, this has not been the case with students of Soviet and East European international behavior; for better or worse, "traditional" approaches are still dominant there. A recent study by Horelick, Johnson, and Steinbruner [1] can point to only one full-length experimental-behavioral work on Soviet foreign policy, written by Triska and Finley.[2] Of the ten more senior writers on Soviet foreign policy (Aspaturian, Brzezinski, Dallin, Dinerstein, Rubinstein, Shulman, Triska, Ulam, Wolfe, and Zimmerman), only Triska and to a lesser extent Zimmerman can be said to be intrigued by modern social science. The most widely used anthology on Soviet foreign policy,[3] despite its editors' methodological preferences, is an essentially traditionalist reader. My knowledge does not permit me to comment on the Chinese field, but in the generally underdeveloped study of the international relations of East Central Europe there are only two methodologically different, though not entirely inspiring, works; [4] the rest, so far as methodology is concerned, is clearly old-fashioned.

Hence this symposium. Finley, Kanet, and Krisch were asked to consider some of the newer approaches in the area of comparative foreign policy and then address themselves to three specific questions in regard to the study of Communist foreign policies: *what* should

1. Arnold L. Horelick, A. Ross Johnson, and John D. Steinbruner, *The Study of Soviet Foreign Policy: A Review of Decision-Theory-Related Approaches* (Santa Monica: The Rand Corporation, December 1973), R-1334.

2. Jan Triska and David Finley, *Soviet Foreign Policy* (New York: Macmillan, 1968). For an appraisal, see my "History, Social Science, and the Study of Soviet Foreign Policy," as reprinted in Erik P. Hoffmann and Frederic J. Fleron, Jr. (eds.), *The Conduct of Soviet Foreign Policy* (Chicago: Aldine-Atherton, 1971), Chap. 1, pp. 11–17.

3. Hoffmann and Fleron, *op. cit.*

4. William R. Kintner and Wolfgang Klaiber, *Eastern Europe and European Security* (New York: Dunellen, 1971), and Jan F. Triska (ed.), *Communist Party-States: Comparative and International Studies* (Indianapolis: Bobbs-Merrill, 1969).

we compare, *how* should we compare, and *why* should we compare? In other words, they were asked to consider questions of substance, method, and purpose in the study of comparative Communist foreign policies.

Area Studies as the Enemy

The authors of the three papers, as well as the discussants, tend to differ as to the kinds of comparative studies that are needed or can be done, the level of generalizations that can be attained, and the uses to which theorizing can be put. On the other hand, the authors accept the premises of comparative analysis, reaffirming at the same time the need for the type of research usually identified with area studies.

Yet, in these papers as elsewhere, I sense a defensive tone whenever area studies are discussed. Even Rubinstein's eloquent comment below is a " defense " of what is widely believed to be an intellectual orientation of the past. Let us face it. To some, area studies have been the enemy for a decade or so, viewed as a reactionary approach that stands in the way of progress and precision, a deviation that some Communist specialists have denounced with fervor no doubt inspired by familiarity with the subject of their interest. Indeed, in the present professional climate it takes extraordinary courage for a younger scholar in particular to identify with or engage in non-theoretical or non-statistical research; for his work would receive little or no attention and he would be labelled a historian, an essayist, or even a journalist. It should be emphasized, therefore, that without the oft-criticized " idiographic " studies there would be no comparison, model-building, or theorizing.

While I certainly do not take a negative view of the promise of modern social science and its selective application to Communist studies, I find myself in substantial agreement with Rudolf L. Tökés, who recently concluded that " the introduction into Soviet studies of semantic, culture-bound neologisms and intellectually barren model-building exercises [has] thus far produced neither the kind of new evidence nor original insight that their proponents have claimed." [5] What I find disturbing, moreover, is that critics of area studies seem to forget that the most outstanding contributions to the Soviet and East European field have come from such unmitigated area specialists

5. Rudolf L. Tökés, " Introduction," in Henry W. Morton and Rudolf L. Tökes (eds.), *Soviet Politics and Society in the 1970's* (New York: Free Press, 1974), p. xxiii.

as Brzezinski, Hazard, and Moore, whose methods of research may fail to satisfy certain scientific standards yet the import of whose work cannot, and should not, be denied.

To advocate an eclectic and more tolerant approach—indeed *many* approaches—to scholarship, as I do, means that there must be no other criterion than quality, defined subjectively, I suppose, by one's peers. That means, in turn, that some may wish to pursue their work with the objective of making small but testable contributions on which others can subsequently build. Others may prefer the grand approach, tackling larger issues and topics and conceding that because of the nature of their work their conclusions will often flow from the information they present as much as from circumspection and intuition. Still others can, and I think should, take a *l'art pour l'art* approach to Communist studies, by which I mean experimentation for its own sake. For an informed and effective essay, for example, with or without footnotes, tables, or statistical calculations, can lead to insights that one may not gain in any other way. Should I say that extremism in the pursuit of knowledge is no vice?

In the final analysis, it is a question of how seriously we take ourselves as scientists, or how narrowly we define science. Without entering into a discussion of definitions, I view many aspects of politics, including especially Communist international politics, as areas of importance and interest that do not readily lend themselves to a strictly scientific inquiry; however, they should be explored by professional students of politics. I suspect that this view may not be rejected by most members of the profession; paradoxically, its acceptance would seldom be explicit or genuine in practice. For the methodologically old-fashioned—however well grounded he may be substantively—is tolerated only grudgingly these days, and his place is assured only if he has tenure or is otherwise a " nice guy." At times I wonder if we do not take ourselves a bit too seriously when we plead for scientific precision, or if we do not actually overcompensate for the very deficiencies of our work. I use the psychologically loaded term of " overcompensation " because the critics of area studies have produced so little in the way of substance, so much in the way of polemics.

In fact, much of that criticism has nothing to do with the methodological weakness or insufficiency of area studies. Instead, criticism is directed against the Cold War mentality that has presumably pervaded the profession and against its apparent corollary, the undue emphasis on the uniqueness of Communist political behavior (internal and external). But that criticism, however well taken, is not directly related to methodology. It has to do with the unfortunate impact of high politics on American scholarship, and that problem is not going to be remedied by methodological innovation or sophistication. Indeed, one likely consequence of methodological perfectionism is that by " approving " work that deals with the strictly " researchable " questions of politics only—those based on hard and verifiable evidence—we will effectively reduce policy-related research and stifle academic contributions to political controversy. Therefore, I share Finley's view, expressed in the following pages, that our objective should be to produce both theory-related and policy-related studies, to which I would hasten to add that that objective can be reached in many ways, including " old-fashioned " area studies that rely on traditional analysis of political culture, history, ideas, and so on. Although my own preference happens to be for less descriptive and more theoretically informed work in Communist studies, I think the profession has gone too far in discouraging and even denouncing the case study approach. Another way of putting it would be to say that if the subjects of our inquiries are so broad-minded as to speak of different roads to socialism, we should surely outdo them by insisting on different roads to sound scholarship!

The High Jumper's Dilemma

My plea for a corrective—for a more tolerant view of methodological diversity—stems from two additional considerations.

The first has to do with what I call the high jumper's dilemma. It is probably most applicable to graduate students who are so intimidated by the prevailing aura of methodological perfectionism that they often cannot produce at all. They cannot jump as high as they are advised they can and should, and they are encouraged to think it demeaning to lower the bar. Alas, they can always become methodologists and set high standards for others—a useful, but I would think not entirely satisfying, preoccupation.

The second consideration is more familiar: it has to do with the uses and misuses of statistical data in the methodologically more ambitious projects in the field. Rubinstein puts it well: " The salience of this data needs to be demonstrated; that which can be counted does not always count." In the study of Communist international behavior in particular, we deal with " indicators " of behavior—but what do they indicate?

Let me use an illustration. The *Midwest Journal of Political Science* published an article in 1970 on " Distance in Foreign Policy Behavior:

A Comparative Study of Eastern Europe."[6] Studying "the relationship between the foreign policies of Eastern European nations and that of the Soviet Union," the authors identify three indicators of foreign policy "distance," one of which is the deviation between the number of foreign embassies maintained by the East European countries and the Soviet Union. When I first read this otherwise competent and interesting article, I was intrigued by this particular indicator, partly because I thought it *was* meaningful and partly because I had tried to do the same sort of thing a few years earlier. I had given up, however, because I could not find reliable and comparable data; several of the East European countries for many years failed to disclose the number of embassies they had abroad, or published contradictory or confusing information, and I could not obtain good data from the receiving countries either. Unfortunately, the authors of this article "resolved" the data problem by using a single source, the *Statesman's Year-book*. When I worked with this most convenient British source, I discovered that its data on diplomatic exchanges were highly inaccurate. Comparing the information it gives with national (i.e., East European and Soviet) information whenever I could, I found a margin of error of up to 50 percent! Seeing the article in print, I wondered then, as I wonder now, why one should accept the authors' analysis of Soviet and East European foreign policy behavior based on such flimsy evidence and consider it a methodological advance in Communist studies.

The point is *not* that this particular article used poor data. Irrespective of approach or methodology, most of us sin at least some of the time. The point is that while there is normally sufficient questioning of the kind of information which area specialists use—and that is how it should be—there is little or no concern about the reliability of what we euphemistically call hard data. It would be useful to remind ourselves not only that it is easy to lie with statistics, but that the value of the statistics we must use, *especially in the comparative studies* advocated in this symposium, ought to be handled with caution if not outright skepticism.

Let me say in conclusion that those of us who have done some behaviorally oriented work and can read at least some of what is published in the *American Political Science Review* have a particular obligation to press for methodological pluralism. A "party line" can erode the necessary diversity of American scholarship on the Com-

6. Barry Hughes and Thomas Volgy, "Distance in Foreign Policy Behavior: A Comparative Study of Eastern Europe," *Midwest Journal of Political Science*, XIV, 3 (August 1970), pp. 459–492.

munist countries. Once it was a subtle form of the Cold War mentality; now it is the harmful trend toward methodological uniformity. Hence the kind of dialogue that follows is intended to provoke further discussion and debate, paving the way (it is to be hoped) for the synthesis, though not necessarily the integration, of the traditional and the modern in Communist studies.

DAVID D. FINLEY

What Should We Compare, Why, and How? *

A sympathetic reviewer of Frederic Fleron's book *Communist Studies and the Social Sciences* wondered whether the editor might not have contributed more to his discipline by devoting the time to a substantive piece of research rather than to a methodological exegesis.[1] I think the answer in that case is no, but the question raised is legitimate. It can properly be raised in the case of this symposium also, so I want to devote a few introductory comments to it. Why should we not dispense with these hybrid questions about what we ought to be doing, and get on with doing it instead?

My answer comes in three parts. In the first place, the bulk of substantive studies produced about Communist foreign policies is enormous, and there is little sign of abatement. While the coverage is disproportionate, principally because the lingering " satellite " stereotype has denied any point to many comparisons, the real problem lies not in the quantity of activity but in the quality. The events of 1972 and 1973 removed all doubts about the need for comparisons in the case of Eastern Europe as well as of Asia. Methodological critique seems the best way by which to filter this volume and to direct the efforts of the future.

* I am indebted to my fellow panelists and to Professor James Bruce of Marshall University for helpful comments on an earlier draft.

1. Frederick C. Barghoorn in *Slavic Review*, Vol. 29, No. 3 (September 1970), pp. 539–542. Review of Frederic J. Fleron, Jr. (ed.), *Communist Studies and the Social Sciences* (Chicago: Rand McNally, 1969).

Second, the literature on Communist foreign policies is more divided in the matter of interpretation than other subject matters. Leaving aside the obvious polemics pro and con, scholars aspiring to objectivity remain deeply split. So long as men of intelligence, dispassionate purpose, and good will continue to come up with such contradictory conclusions about the same subjects, there is good reason for us to continue to cut into these differences by concerning ourselves with the logic of the inquiry employed.

Finally, the natural history of American Slavic studies commends a special attention to continuing methodological *samokritika*. As Alfred Meyer has pointed out,[2] the great impetus for these studies emerged from the cold war. For some time they might have been described as academic handmaidens of cold-war policy. Together with the lack of data available to scholars in the fifties, this cold-war genesis made and perhaps continues to make the lines between journalistic speculation, political polemic, and scholarship difficult to define.

As William Welch has argued convincingly, the record is not good. In terms of explicitness of assumptions, clarity of conceptualization, and adequacy of evidence to conclusions (all elementary enough standards), American scholarship on Soviet foreign policy has on balance been wanting.[3] I would add that those studies focused on Eastern European foreign policies have suffered equally on the infrequent occasions when distinction has been drawn between these states and Moscow.

It is to be hoped that we could agree, then, that while we should not allow methodological debate to paralyze substantive inquiry, its pursuit remains a healthy and needed activity.

I

Turning to the questions presented to our symposium, I propose to deal rather summarily with the first two and at somewhat greater length with the third. It is not that I feel that the *what* and *why* questions are less important. It is just that I personally believe the answers to be pretty clear-cut and that the more problematic questions are properly subsumed under *how*.

The answers to what we should compare, and why, depend on what we need to know and what comparative method affords a good chance

2. Address to the Conference on Communist Studies, "Theories of Convergence," American Political Science Association, 66th Annual Meeting, Los Angeles, September 9, 1970.

3. William Welch, *American Images of Soviet Foreign Policy* (New Haven: Yale University Press, 1970).

of finding out. I contend that we justify our existence and the attention of readers and students, first, by making valid statements of contingent probabilities of use to policymakers [4] and, second, by making valid explanatory statements that contribute to an empirical or a normative theory of politics. That is to say, we must be either *policy-relevant* or *theory-relevant*—and preferably both.

Comparative method presents, it seems to me, some unique advantages to these ends, advantages that we can and should exploit. For theory-building, systematic comparison allows differences of consequence to be correlated with differences of process and circumstance. It allows us to identify crucial variations of structure and process and to separate them from incidentals, this to a degree of confidence which the case study, no matter how refined, cannot logically be expected to do. Through comparative study we can obtain bases for generalization. At the same time, comparison implicitly puts to the test the general category of "Communist states" with all the attendant temptations to deduce from principle which have so long imprisoned us in stereotypes. Further, because of their different ages and the different problem-clusters facing various Communist states, comparative study can suggest the developmental probabilities of Communist foreign policies, so far as domestic politics determine or condition them.

These advantages of comparative analysis obligate us to abstract and refine models of Communist state foreign policy as points of reference, to exploit the as-yet undefined potential of such techniques as factor analysis for identifying and analyzing covariance, and to design our comparisons across time as well as across geography.

Finally, what questions we should try to answer with the aid of comparative method depend significantly on the available data. This is a delicate point and is subject to misinterpretation. For we should neither cease searching for imaginative conceptualizations and transfers of knowledge and technique that promise to increase our explanatory power, nor delude ourselves that we can go much beyond conjecture and hypothesis where the necessary data are, through force of circumstances, simply not accessible. This point is discussed at greater length in the second part of this paper.

In concluding my attention to *what* and *why*, let me say a word about what my formulation seems to me to *exclude*, some things I think we should not be doing in comparative Communist foreign policy. We should not be exploring questions of intrinsic historical interest only; and we should not be squirreling away aggregate data

4. As contrasted to the pretensions of policy-scientism, which I regard as a dangerous delusion.

merely because they are available. I think that these are the respective pitfalls and self-deceptions of historians and political scientists—understandable dangers but ones to be guarded against more carefully just because they are understandable. One can always say that history is a seamless web, that no part is intrinsically insignificant. And one can say that these data should be collected because they may be of use later. But I contend that, at the present stage of knowledge and theory about Communist foreign policies, we need the direction afforded by self-discipline and attention to the criteria of theory-relevance and policy-relevance which I have advanced above.

II

Let me turn now to the question of *how* we should compare Communist foreign policies.

My first plea is on behalf of social scientific conceptualization of foreign policy behavior. I refer in particular to the conceptual approaches subsumed generally under systems analysis and decision-making: analysis of organizational behavior, role relations, communications nets, interaction of social strata, group interaction, coalition formation, and developmental phases. None of these terms, to my mind, really warrants the addition of the term " theory " at this point. By themselves they explain nothing. They are coherent perspectives (not mutually exclusive) for looking at political behavior. They have afforded hypotheses, some of which have been tested in some contexts sufficiently to generate partial theories. But, with that important caveat, I contend that such conceptualizations provide a basis for hypothesis formation far richer than the alternative historical conceptualization of unique, sequential, causally related events. Also, being less focused upon personalities or national entities, they tend to be less susceptible to distorted applications as a result of the emotional attachments of the investigator. At a minimum they provide the investigator with a checklist of variables which ought in some manner to be reckoned with before he makes causal interpretations, thus protecting him against the unarticulated eclecticism of much historical analysis in this controversial field.

But social scientific conceptualization cannot in most cases carry us beyond hypothesis formation. At the point where we ask ourselves, " How can I discover whether my hypothesis is valid? " we find it essential frequently to resort to historical modes of explanation. The aggregate data necessary for convincing social scientific explanation are very often nonexistent or inaccessible, whereas specific sequences of events can often be searched out and inferred with some confidence.

Just as importantly, the questions that we want ultimately to answer are frequently not amenable to social scientific answers alone. Aggregate data treated by social scientific techniques afford us predictive capacity only for statistical universes. Such theory as we can generate must therefore be a partner to historical extrapolation when we have to formulate premises for some sorts of policy choice. When we concern ourselves with contributions to empirical political theory, our reliance upon social scientific explanation may legitimately be far greater than when we aspire to project contingencies for the policy-maker. The significance of idiosyncratic factors can come only from historical interpretation of specific context, where social scientific theory has provided expectations based on the generic character of the situation and at best pointed out what idiosyncratic factors must be evaluated.

My second plea, then, is for complementary application of social scientific and historical explanation *after* hypothesis formation.

I think that the relationship between social scientific explanation and historical explanation is at heart the relationship between a disciplinary approach and an area-studies approach to comparative Communist foreign policy. Thus let me dwell a little more on what I feel that relationship should be.

The core of any area study is a unique shared characteristic of the objects of study, whether it be geographic (as in Eastern European studies) or ethnic (as in Slavic studies) or ideological (as in Communist studies), rather than a common method of attack—which would comprehend the application of a particular body of theoretical (nomothetic) knowledge, particular concepts, and particular instruments of analysis (such as disciplines of economics or linguistics or political science) to any area of subject matter. The contribution of the area specialist, then, is the product of a variety of applied disciplines, which cumulatively afford a rich idiographic knowledge.

Historical explanation is, to my mind, idiographic explanation; thus the natural form of contribution by the area specialist to understanding of political life is historical. For example, the contribution of the area specialist to understanding Bulgarian foreign policy is naturally the idiographic history of Bulgarian foreign policy. The stress is upon the distinctive, the unique.

Science has often been called a search for hidden likenesses. The phrase aptly contrasts the social scientist's (here, the political scientist's) thrust to that of the area specialist. Bringing to bear his concepts and techniques for manipulating data, the social scientist seeks the regularities of political behavior across areas. His explanation is a process " by which singular events (explicanda) are related to other events through the use of appropriate general statements."[5] I would argue that these two enterprises are dependent upon one another in order to produce maximum understanding of the subject.

The area specialist without the social scientist is likely to exaggerate the uniqueness of his subject, to obscure essential functional similarity beneath superficial differences of institutional form or style, hence to reject regularity beyond his area and define his subject *sui generis*. Also, he loses the creative input of hypotheses stimulated by associations and analogies to different subject matter from which more sophisticated theoretical knowledge may already have been developed. In short, he loses both a standard with which to compare his subject for its uniqueness and the benefit of transfer knowledge from other contexts. Strictly speaking, because ideographic knowledge does not logically permit extrapolation beyond its immediate context, the area specialist loses as well the predictive power associated with nomothetic theory. What predictions he may be nevertheless tempted to permit himself often imply social scientific generalization without scientific foundation—hence the stuff of competing polemics is generated.

The political scientist without the area specialist, on the other hand, lacks the historical knowledge upon which to judge the plausibility of hypotheses in the specific context of the area. Historical understanding is essential to parsimony in hypothesis formation and to the appropriate modification of broader-gauge social scientific theory to take account of the idiosyncrasies of an area. The latter afford a basis for predictive interpretation of scientific theory in that margin beyond the power of scientific explanation where we must draw conclusions before we can take positions among policy alternatives. The language of politics is imprecise and varies by area, whereas the language of science is precise. Misinterpretation is a likely consequence, one that can lead to distortions of understanding not inherent in the quality of scientific theory and that can be mitigated by the cultural grasp of the area specialist. Further, it is often the cumulation of the area specialist's data, categorized generically rather than by causal or temporal sequence, which provides the aggregate data needed for application of social scientific techniques. Finally, the evolutionary change in the nature of his variables across time—a constant threat to the confidence that one may lodge in any social scientific theory's continuing usefulness—may be mitigated by conscious historical tracking.

The conclusion to which I am necessarily drawn by the considerations advanced above is that area studies and social science are

5. Eugene J. Meehan, *The Theory and Method of Political Analysis* (Homewood, Ill.: Dorsey, 1965), p. 90.

mutually dependent in the rational effort to extend our systematic understanding of all political life in Communist states, and more particularly our policy-relevant and theory-relevant understanding from the comparative study of Communist foreign policies.

III

Before drawing these remarks to a close, let me be more specific and concrete than I have been heretofore and cite some objects of inquiry likely to yield useful findings to the sort of comparative study I am advocating.

A first aim of comparative Communist foreign policy might well be a definition of the contemporary relationship of domestic versus international factors as determinants of foreign policy across Communist states. The policy-relevance of such a study need not be belabored at a time when one tries to predict, for example, responses to various sorts of " bridge-building " between the United States, the Federal Republic of Germany and other North Atlantic states, and Eastern European states. The implications for theory are equally clear when we note the contemporary efforts by political scientists to discern patterns of linkage between domestic and international political life, given different forms of government. This effort has produced considerable conceptualization which has yet to be applied to the comparative study of Communist states, of which I will cite James Rosenau's *Linkage Politics* as just one example.[6] One reason why not much has been done with this approach among Communist states is the difficulty of obtaining the sort of aggregate data the social scientist would like. As Sidney Ploss has suggested with respect to the U.S.S.R., this may be the place where recourse to the Kremlinological history identified with Borkenau or Nicolaevsky may be used along with such aggregate data techniques as quantitative content analysis.[7] As I have argued above, such a combination would in no way be a mismarriage. I cite William Zimmerman's excellent study of *Soviet Perspectives on International Relations* [8] as a successful combination of social scientific conceptualization with historical explanation. It seems to me that such elite data as Beck, Farrell, Zaninovich, Bialer and others have generated could

6. James N. Rosenau (ed.), *Linkage Politics* (New York: The Free Press, 1969).

7. Sidney Ploss, " Studying the Domestic Determinants of Soviet Foreign Policy," mimeographed for the Interuniversity Research Colloquium on Russia and Eastern Europe (n.d.), pp. 12–13.

8. William Zimmerman, *Soviet Perspectives on International Relations* (Princeton: Princeton University Press, 1969).

be used in conjunction with historical analysis to refine a model of linkages in Communist state foreign policymaking as a datum from which to compare the policymaking of individual states.

A second and related aim of comparative Communist foreign policy might be time-series comparisons of the foreign policy of Communist states among themselves and with non-Communist states. For example, I am currently trying to explore the mutual impact of trends of regional integration and disintegration in Eastern and Western Europe on one another. There is policy relevance here for officials who must orchestrate regional and transregional policy. Implications also exist for integration theory. Quantitative indices of state foreign policies can be correlated with trends in integration or disintegration.

Both of these suggestions for commitment of energies in comparative Communist foreign policy are very sketchily described here. I introduce them only to try to clarify the thrust of effort which I have advocated above. Both deal, it seems to me, with policy-relevant and theory-relevant questions. Both take as a starting point conceptualization that has grown out of social science rather than area studies. Both promise to require employment of the historical method of area studies and the quantitative techniques of data manipulation characteristic of modern social science in order to reach any satisfactory goal. And both are designed to yield explanations with the aim of adding to our meager body of knowledge about comparative Communist foreign policy.

Roger E. Kanet

Is Comparison Useful or Possible?

During recent years a number of scholars, notable among them James Rosenau,[1] have advocated the development of a comparative approach to the study of foreign policy. Many of their arguments closely parallel those developed more than a decade ago in support of the comparative method in the analysis of domestic politics—in particular, stressing the benefits to be derived for both hypothesis formation and hypothesis testing.

1. See the following articles by James N. Rosenau: "Pre-Theories of Foreign Policy," in R. Barry Farrell (ed.), *Approaches to Comparative and International Politics* (Evanston, Ill.: Northwestern University Press, 1966); "Toward the Study of National-International Linkages," in James N. Rosenau (ed.), *Linkage Politics* (New York: Free Press, 1969); "Comparative Foreign Policy: Fad, Fantasy, or Field?" *International Studies Quarterly,* XII (1968), pp. 296–329; "Foreign Policy as an Issue-Area," in James N. Rosenau (ed.), *Domestic Sources of Foreign Policy* (New York: Free Press, 1967); "Foreign Policy as Adaptive Behavior: Some Preliminary Notes for a Theoretical Model," *Comparative Politics,* II (1970), pp. 365–389; and *The Adaptation of National Societies: A Theory of Political System Behavior and Transformation* (New York: McCaleb-Seiler, 1970). A number of these articles are reprinted in James N. Rosenau, *The Scientific Study of Foreign Policy* (New York: Free Press, 1971). In addition, see David C. Wilkinson, *Comparative Foreign Relations: Framework and Methods* (Belmont, Calif.: Dickenson, 1969); Wolfram F. Hanreider, "Compatibility and Consensus: A Proposal for the Conceptual Linkage of External and Internal Dimensions of Foreign Policy," *American Political Science Review,* LXI (1967), pp. 971–982, 1096–1098, and "International and Comparative Politics: Toward a Synthesis?" *World Politics,* XX (1968), pp. 480–493.

In addition, a number of political scientists interested in Communist political systems have attempted to respond to the call of Gordon Skilling, first made in 1960, to use the Communist states of the world as a "laboratory of comparative study of immense and hitherto neglected value for the student of comparative politics." [2] Some truly comparative studies of Communist political systems, such as Ghita Ionescu's *The Politics of the European Communist States,* have appeared where concepts, approaches, frameworks, and hypotheses, developed originally in comparative politics, have been increasingly employed in studies of Communist political systems.[3] More recently a number of students of the foreign policies of Communist countries—particularly that of the Soviet Union—have tried to introduce the comparative approach into their analyses.[4] Although the earlier efforts

2. H. Gordon Skilling, "Soviet and Communist Politics: A Comparative Approach," *Journal of Politics,* XXII (1960), pp. 300–313, reprinted in Frederic J. Fleron, Jr. (ed.), *Communist Studies and the Social Sciences* (Chicago: Rand McNally, 1969), p. 43. See also Robert C. Tucker, "On the Comparative Study of Communism," *World Politics,* XIX (1967), pp. 242–257.

3. For a few examples see Fleron, *op. cit,*; Roger E. Kanet (ed.), *The Behavioral Revolution and Communist Studies* (New York: Free Press, 1971); R. Barry Farrell (ed.), *Political Leadership in Eastern Europe and the Soviet Union* (Chicago: Aldine, 1969); and Jan F. Triska (ed.), *Communist Party-States: Comparative and International Studies* (Indianapolis: Bobbs-Merrill, 1969). More recent substantive studies employing methodological approaches drawn from contemporary comparative politics include Kenneth Jowitt, *Revolutionary Breakthroughs and National Development: The Case of Rumania, 1944–1966* (Berkeley: University of California Press, 1971); Dennis Pirages, *Modernizations and Political-Tension Management: A Socialist Society in Perspective—A Case of Poland* (New York: Praeger, 1972); Charles Gati (ed.), *The Politics of Modernization in Eastern Europe: Testing the Soviet Model* (New York: Praeger, 1974); Brian Silver, "Social Mobilization and the Russification of Soviet Nationalities," *American Political Science Review,* LXVIII, 1 (March 1974), pp. 45–66; and "Levels of Sociocultural Development Among Soviet Nationalities: A Partial Test of the Equalization Hypothesis," *American Political Science Review,* LXVIII, 4 (December 1974), pp. 1618–1637.

4. The comparative studies of Communist foreign policy completed to date can be divided into two basic groups according to subject matter. First are those studies that attempt to compare Soviet and U.S. foreign policy. See e.g. Leo Tansky, *U.S. and U.S.S.R. Aid to Developing Countries: A Comparative Study of India, Turkey, and the U.A.R.* (New York: Praeger, 1967); Karel Holbik, *The United States, the Soviet Union, and the Third World* (Hamburg: Verlag Weltarchiv, 1968); Zbiginew Brzezinski and Samuel P. Huntington, *Political Power U.S.A./U.S.S.R.* (New York: Viking Press, 1966); Robert S. Walters, *American and Soviet Aid: A Comparative Analysis* (Pittsburgh: University of Pittsburgh Press, 1971); Wynfred Joshua and Stephen P. Gibert, *Arms for the Third World: Soviet Military Aid Diplomacy* (Baltimore: Johns Hopkins Press, 1969), Ch. 8; Anatol Rapoport, *The Big Two: Soviet-American Perceptions of Foreign Policy* (New York: Pegasus, 1971); and Roger E. Kanet,

at comparative analysis suffered from a lack of rigorous conceptualization and adequate supporting data, several articles have now been published which go beyond the rather intuitive approach to comparison by employing "hard" data as the basis for comparative analysis of foreign policy outputs.[5]

The focus of the roundtable discussion for which the first version of these comments was prepared lay on the question of the value (and possibility) of employing a comparative approach in the study of the foreign policies of the Communist states. In the following pages, I shall attempt to deal with three basic questions related to this topic: (1) Why should comparison be attempted? (2) Assuming that comparison is useful, what should be compared? (3) How can we go about the task of comparing?

I

One of the major differences between the social sciences (including political science) and history/area studies is that the former attempt to discover regular patterns in human behavior, while the latter focus on the unique, the particular. The social scientist is concerned with what is common to a class of actions or processes, while the historian/

"Soviet and American Behavior Toward the Developing Countries: A Comparison, *Canadian Slavonic Papers,* XV (1973), pp. 439–461. All of these studies employ traditional historical research techniques.

A second category of studies attempts to compare various aspects of the foreign policies of Communist countries. Those employing traditional historical research techniques include Kurt Müller, *Die Entwicklungshilfe Osteuropas: Konzeptionen und Schwerpunkte* (Hannover: Verlag für Literatur und Zeitgeschehen, 1970); Jacques Lévesque, *Le Conflict Sino-Soviétique et l'Europe de l'Est: Ses incidences sur les conflicts soviéto-polonais et soviéto-roumain* (Montréal: Les Presses de l'Université de Montréal, 1970), esp. pp. 257–281.

5. Some early efforts to employ quantitative data in comparing the foreign policies of Communist states are reprinted in Triska, *op. cit.* More recent studies include Vilho Harle, "Actional Distances Between the Socialist Countries in the 1960's," *Cooperation and Conflict,* VI (1971), pp. 201–221; Kenneth S. Hempel, "Comparative Research on Eastern Europe: A Critique of Hughes and Volgy's 'Distance in Foreign Policy Behavior'," *American Journal of Political Science,* XVII (1973), pp. 367–394; Barry Hughes and Thomas Volgy, "Distance in Foreign Policy Behavior: A Comparative Study of Eastern Europe," *Midwest Journal of Political Science,* XIV (1970), pp. 459–492; Barry Hughes and Thomas Volgy, "On the Difficult Business of Conducting Empirical Research in a Data-Poor Area," *American Journal of Political Science,* XVII (1973), pp. 394–406; and William R. Kintner and Wolfgang Klaiber, "East European Conformity to Soviet Policy," Ch. 13 of their *Eastern Europe and European Security* (New York: Dunellen, 1971), pp. 219–268.

area specialist desires to understand fully the background and development of one event or series of events.

For the most part, studies of the foreign policies of the Communist states (including those of the author) have tended to be historical-descriptive in nature. Little effort has been made by students of Communist foreign policy—at least until quite recently—to bring into their analyses the hypotheses concerning foreign policy behavior which have been developed in the broader field of international politics. In addition, as Richard Brody and John Vesecky have pointed out in their survey of Western hypotheses about Soviet foreign policy, serious disagreement continues to exist among analysts of Soviet foreign policy concerning the factors that influence or determine that policy.[6] Many of these hypotheses stress the uniqueness of the Soviet political system, and their proponents have seemingly been unaware of the existence of similar behavior patterns in the policies of other countries that do not share with the Soviet Union a comparable ideology, social structure, or whatever else supposedly explains Soviet foreign policy.[7] If students of the foreign policies of Communist countries were more aware of the foreign policies of other countries—both Communist and non-Communist, both historical and contemporary—and of the theoretical innovations of scholars outside the field of Communist studies, the task of formulating and testing hypotheses to explain foreign policy behavior would be greatly facilitated. Few studies of the foreign policies of the Communist countries, for example, really *analyze*—rather than merely mention—the relationships between domestic and foreign policy.[8] What impact do differing domestic conditions—whether cultural, socio-economic, geographic, or political—have on the foreign policies of Communist states? What is the relative importance of ideology and national interest in Communist foreign policy? These and other similar questions can best be answered by a comparative analysis of the policies of several Communist states with those of non-Communist states.

6. See Richard A. Brody and John F. Vesecky, "Soviet Openness to Changing Situations: A Critical Evaluation of Certain Hypotheses About Soviet Foreign Policy Behavior," in Triska, *op. cit.*, pp. 354–359. See also William Welch, *American Images of Soviet Foreign Policy* (New Haven: Yale University Press, 1970).

7. For an excellent discussion of the comparability of Communist and non-Communist systems, see John H. Kautsky, "Comparative Communism Versus Comparative Politics," *Studies in Comparative Communism,* VI (1973), pp. 135–183.

8. See Sidney I. Ploss, "Studying the Domestic Determinants of Soviet Foreign Policy," *Canadian Slavic Studies,* I (1967), pp. 44–59.

In his study of the impact of the Sino-Soviet dispute on Soviet relations with Eastern Europe, Jacques Lévesque presents an interesting framework for comparing the reactions of East European countries to the split between the two Communist giants and the possibilities for " independence " of the popular democracy. The framework is based primarily on domestic socio-economic and political factors (e.g., the origin of the power of the Party) in Eastern Europe.[9] The question raised by Lévesque—as well as those questions raised in the studies by Barry Hughes and Thomas Volgy—would hardly have arisen had the author not engaged in comparative analysis. The country approach to the study of Communist foreign policy permits the scholar to amass large amounts of data, but it also leads him to overemphasize the uniqueness of Communist foreign policies. By focusing on this uniqueness, the scholar is not likely to pose some of the important questions concerning decisionmaking procedures and methods of policy implementation.

In sum, the major arguments in support of a comparative approach to the study of Communist foreign policy are the following. (1) Comparison will help us gain a broader understanding of the foreign policy process in general, since international relations theorists have tended to leave out information on Communist countries when formulating their theories. (2) Comparison will help us better understand the ways in which the policies of Communist countries both differ from and are similar to those of other states, both Communist and non-Communist. (3) Comparison will provide us with deeper insights into the policies of individual Communist states by raising questions concerning the relationship between domestic and foreign policy, as well as other matters that might not arise in specifically country-oriented studies.

II

If comparison is valuable for the reasons outlined in the first portion of this paper, an obvious second question concerns those factors or aspects of foreign policy which should be compared. In addressing this question, we must first ask what it is that influences a country's foreign policy behavior. Geographical location, level of socio-economic development, economic and military strength, size of population and territory, spectrum of domestic political systems, political culture, international political environment, quality of diplomatic per-

9. Lévesque, *op. cit.*, pp. 259 ff. See also Kintner and Klaiber, *op. cit.*, where they employ domestic data to measure the deviation of East European foreign policies from those of the Soviet Union.

sonnel, leadership, and a host of other factors have been considered important by students of foreign policy.

In applying a comparative approach to the analysis of the foreign policy of Communist states, the scholar can study any of these variables, depending upon the goal of his research. Studies of the relations of Communist countries with the developing nations indicate that domestic requirements in the former influence their transactions with the countries of Asia and Africa—for example, Rumania's requirements for oil imports and its need for markets for industrial production. East Germany's search for markets, as well as its desire to obtain international acceptability in order to bolster the government's domestic support, has apparently influenced its policies. In his study of Yugoslav relations with Afro-Asia, Alvin Rubinstein has emphasized the importance of domestic Yugoslav political factors in influencing the decision in the early 1950s to expand contacts with the developing world.[10]

How and to what extent do the policies of the Communist states toward Asia and Africa differ? How are differences in internal needs related to these differences in policy? To what extent does size influence policy with developing countries? These questions, which are important for an understanding of the policies of the Communist states, can be answered only by the use of a comparative approach.

In another area of research, most studies of CMEA have indicated that such factors as nationalism and level of economic development are important in explaining the varying responses of the East European countries to Soviet plans for economic integration over the past decade.

Although there are problems in obtaining the data required to carry out comparative analysis, they are not insuperable. Data on economic performance, foreign trade, joint economic projects, and economic assistance, for example, are fairly easily obtained. Defense information—at least estimates—can be acquired from Western sources. Information on elites and internal policies can be found. One major problem is the unavailability of survey research data on elite and popular attitudes toward foreign policy; however, content analysis can, in part, correct this deficiency by supplying alternative data.

In general, the student of the foreign policies of the Communist countries can compare the same variables as the student of the foreign policies of other countries, even though in certain areas data are difficult to obtain—occasionally impossible. Most important, however, is

10. Alvin Z. Rubinstein, *Yugoslavia and the Nonaligned World* (Princeton: Princeton University Press, 1970).

the need for more rigorous conceptualization than has been employed to date.

In an article published in 1967, Robert Tucker distinguished four levels of comparison in Communist studies:

1. " Aggregative comparison "—which juxtaposes studies of different Communist systems but is low in analytic content.
2. " Empirical comparison "—in which particular institutions, policies, and economic processes are studied.
3. " Generalizing comparison "—in which the object is " not just to compare societies or aspects of them, but to build on such empirical comparisons a structure of generalizations concerning the characteristic tendencies of Communism as a form of society, economy, polity, ideology, or cultural system."
4. " Model-building and the study of Communist societies in relation to the theoretical models." [11]

A fairly large body of literature on Communist foreign policy already exists which fits into the first two levels. Very few studies of Communist foreign policy, however, attempt to develop a system of generalizations or models of foreign policy behavior. Above, in discussing the question of what should be compared, I have referred to ways in which one might compare the policies of the Communist states. Most important, I believe, is the need to introduce into studies of Communist foreign policy some of the concern for precise, rigorous methods of analysis which is evident among students of general international relations,[12] and the development and testing of generalizations concerning foreign policy in Communist politics. But this can be accomplished only by analyzing the different ways in which Communist—and non-Communist—political systems respond to the international environment, how they organize their decisionmaking processes, and the like. Rather than continuing to be satisfied with descriptive studies of the policies of one Communist country or another, some scholars need to begin linking the study of Communist foreign policy with theoretical advances—however meager and halting—which have been made in general international relations.

11. Tucker, *op. cit.*, pp. 52–54.

12. I do not mean to imply that studies of Communist foreign policy are totally devoid of rigor. See, e.g., M. George Zaninovich, " Pattern Analysis of Variables Within the International System: The Sino-Soviet Example," *Journal of Conflict Resolution*, VI (1962), pp. 253–268; Jan F. Triska and David D. Finley, *Soviet Foreign policy* (New York: Macmillan, 1968), and a number of other books and articles, including those mentioned above.

III

It is very well to argue, as I have in the preceding paragraphs, that the comparative analysis of foreign policy is useful and that various internal and external factors which presumably affect foreign policy decisionmaking and implementation might usefully be compared. Far more difficult is the problem of delineating precisely those aspects of foreign policy which might be examined comparatively and those questions which one needs to confront.

Comparative analyses of non-Soviet Communist countries' foreign policies which have employed quantitative research techniques have focused almost exclusively on their convergence with or divergence from Soviet policies. This focus has meant an emphasis on policy outputs, for clear and understandable reasons. While we have relatively few data concerning the inputs into the policymaking process, information on policy outputs, whether of a verbal, an economic or a military nature, is more readily available.

For the foreseeable future it will probably continue to be most profitable, in approaching the development of studies of Communist foreign policy, to concentrate on policy outputs and on comparisons of the orientations of Communist countries on specific international issues. This will require, first of all, supplementing the existing data base for such analyses—in particular, by the development of time-series data on factors relevant to the foreign policy behavior of Communist regimes. Such data already exist for certain of these factors—e.g., trade data—but they are sketchy on other possible indicators of foreign policy behavior, such as tourist and communication flows.

The recent work of Vilho Harle, Hughes and Volgy represents a serious effort to systematize the analysis of the foreign policy behavior of Communist states. Although one might well criticize various aspects of their analyses, they have added to our understanding of the degree of conformity that exists in the foreign policies of the Communist countries and the relationship of the international environment to foreign policy behavior. William Kintner and Wolfgang Klaiber have added a dimension to our understanding of conformity and divergence in the foreign policies of Communist countries by relating foreign policy behavior to a variety of internal and external variables, such as the level of socio-economic development of the various countries and the level of economic relations with the non-Communist world. It is to be hoped that these authors, and others, will expand the scope of this research and make the efforts necessary to improve the measures employed in analyzing the foreign policies of the Communist states.

Henry Krisch

Some Undone Jobs

In recent years, the field of Soviet studies has undergone, in Robert Dahl's evocative phrase, a "successful revolution." The broad thrust of this upheaval has been to infuse Soviet studies with concepts originally generated within social and political science. Two developments in particular have been prominent. One is the assumption of *conflict* as a working hypothesis for the analysis of Communist politics, both internally and externally. The other is the increasing employment of a *comparative* mode of operation in the conduct of such analysis. This displacement of intellectual commitment away from historical, exegetical, and polemical approaches has been a desirable development, not only because it allows for the conversion of exotic "Sovietologists" or "China watchers" into "mainstream" social scientists, but precisely because comparative and conflict-oriented perspectives make possible a clearer understanding of what (if anything) is new, or revolutionary, about the political processes bequeathed to the world by the Bolshevik revolution.

Over the past decade and a half, the recognition of conflict as an essential if not inevitable component of Communist interstate relations has spread throughout the Soviet and Communist studies profession, even, as noted below, in the Communist countries themselves. This recognition was evoked primarily by the *facts* of conflict; the result has been an extensive and familiar literature on Sino-Soviet, Soviet-Rumanian, and other Communist interstate relations.

Comparison of Communist foreign policies, however, is rarely found in the literature of Communist studies—or in the general international relations literature, for that matter. A stimulating and widely noted collection of papers published in 1967[1] largely ignored questions of foreign policy, as did Alfred Meyer's list of suggestions for further research. Similarly, Paul Shoup, while "Comparing Communist Nations,"[2] did not extend his comparison to foreign policies. Although there are signs that this situation may be changing,[3] the complaint of Helen Desfosses Cohn in a recent issue of this journal that "future directions [in the study] of comparative Communism have generally been restricted, explicitly or implicitly, to the study of domestic aspects of Communist systems"[4] is justified.

The lack of comparisons of the foreign policies of Communist states may, in part, be a reflection of a more general dearth of such studies. James Rosenau and his collaborators have recently noted that the "theoretical and empirical basis" for comparative foreign policy texts does not exist.[5] A 1970 survey overlooked comparative foreign policies, neglecting Communist foreign policies entirely.[6] A collection of theoretical essays on "Comparative Foreign Policy" is similarly deficient.[7]

1. "Symposium on Comparative Politics and Communist Systems," in Frederic J. Fleron, Jr. (ed.), *Communist Studies and the Social Sciences* (Chicago: Rand McNally, 1969), pp. 188–214. See also Alfred G. Meyer, "The Comparative Study of Communist Political Systems," *ibid.*, pp. 194–195.

2. Paul Shoup, "Comparing Communist Nations: Prospects for an Empirical Approach," in *ibid.*, pp. 64–93. For an exceptional comparative work, see R. Barry Farrell, "Foreign Policy Formation in the Communist Countries of Eastern Europe," *East European Quarterly*, I, 1 (March 1967), pp. 39–74. There is a group of what may be called "semi-comparative" studies of intra-Bloc politics, many of which are primarily historical-descriptive. For a more general approach, see Vernon V. Aspaturian, *The Soviet Union in the World Communist System* (Stanford: Hoover Institution, 1966). Also of interest are some of the studies collected in Jan F. Triska (ed.), *Communist Party-States: Comparative and International Studies* (Indianapolis: Bobbs-Merrill, 1969).

3. Note, for example, some recent items in this journal: the review article "Chinese and Soviet Policies in Southeast Asia," by Charles B. McLane, *Studies in Comparative Communism*, VI, 1 & 2 (Spring/Summer 1973), pp. 196–201; Paul F. Langer, "The Soviet Union, China, and the Revolutionary Movement in Laos," *ibid.*, pp. 66–98.

4. Helen Desfosses Cohn, "The Study of Communist Powers in Africa," *ibid.*, VI, 3 (Autumn 1973), p. 302. See also the scattered remarks of Paul Langer in his "North Korea and North Vietnam," in Adam Bromke and Teresa Rakowska-Harmstone (eds.), *The Communist States in Disarray 1965–1971* (Minneapolis: University of Minnesota Press, 1972), pp. 269–272.

5. James N. Rosenau, Philip M. Burgess, and Charles F. Hermann, "The Adaptation of Foreign Policy Research: A Case Study of an Anti-Case Study Project," *International Studies Quarterly*, Vol. 17, No. 1 (March 1973), p. 127.

6. Norman D. Palmer (ed.), *A Design for International Relations Research: Scope, Theory, Methods and Relevance* (Philadelphia: American Academy of Political and Social Science, 1970).

7. Wolfram F. Hanrieder (ed.), *Comparative Foreign Policy: Theoretical Essays* (New York: David McKay, 1971).

Rosenau's call for comparative treatment of the initiative, implementive, and responsive aspects of national policy—of the phenomena that " reflect an association between variations in the behavior of national actors and variations in their external environments " [8]—has not evoked any notable spate of such studies. In the context of concern with Communist foreign policies, his article is remarkable for its failure to discuss Communist states and their foreign policies.

Nonetheless, the comparative study of the foreign policy of Western countries has produced a number of studies, such as the recent and excellent work of Karl Kaiser and Roger Morgan on society and foreign policy in Britain and West Germany.[9] One cannot think of a comparable work on Communist foreign policy.

Even the periodical sources are of little help here. Standard journals such as *World Politics* or *Problems of Communism* lack *comparisons* of Communist foreign policies. An examination of two recent annual volumes of the Soviet *Mirovaia Ekonomika i Mezhdunarodnye Otnosheniia* and the German Democratic Republic's *Deutsche Aussenpolitik* shows the same result. And to bring matters closer to home, the *Newsletter on Comparative Studies of Communism* was noticeably devoid of articles on foreign policy themes.

How shall we account for this state of affairs? I would argue that many of us have been operating under a semi-explicit hypothesis about Communist politics: that while the ebbing of Stalinism might allow increasing diversity in domestic policies, Soviet hegemony over the foreign policies of other Communist states would remain largely intact. Thus either the obvious, and noted, exceptions to this generalization were treated as a unique case (" the Sino-Soviet dispute "), or emphasis was placed on the failure of efforts at autonomous Communist foreign policy formulation (Hungary 1956, Czechoslovakia 1968).

In response to such criticism of scholarly omissions, it might be argued that the *fact* of Soviet domination over the foreign policies of the other Communist states was sufficient reason for not treating those policies as comparable entities, to be subjected to scholarly analysis. Such a position does not seem to be substantiated by the evidence of autonomous foreign policy formulation (as in the cases of China, Albania, Rumania, Cuba, Yugoslavia, North Korea—i.e., roughly half

8. James N. Rosenau, " Comparative Foreign Policy: Fad, Fantasy or Field? " *International Studies Quarterly,* Vol. 12, No. 3 (September 1968) pp. 308, 311.

9. Karl Kaiser and Roger Morgan (eds.), *Britain and West Germany: Changing Societies and the Future of Foreign Policy* (London: Oxford University Press [for RIIA], 1971).

of the states in question apart from the U.S.S.R. itself); moreover, I believe that latent, incipient, and possibly unsuccessful divergence of foreign policies from a Soviet "norm" can be usefully studied as well.[10]

I believe that a comparative investigation of Communist foreign policies can serve a number of useful scholarly purposes, a non-exhaustive list of which is presented herewith. First and most broadly, such research aids in clarifying general propositions in the area of international relations analysis, by allowing these propositions to be tested in different settings. Examples that come readily to mind include propositions as to the relationship of hegemony and autonomy in alliance systems, the effect of novel diplomatic style on the conduct of diplomacy, the organization of foreign ministries, and the nature of internal and external linkages.[11]

Speaking more generally, I would argue that the comparative study of Communist foreign policies can help to illuminate our own perceptions of international politics as well as those of scholars and participants in the Communist states themselves.

Thus the comparison of Communist foreign policies can be especially helpful in testing such concepts as those of penetrated systems, linkages (particularly party and ideology as "initiating" factors), integration theory, regional and hegemonic relations, and variations in external (geographic, nationality, partition) circumstances.[12]

It is characteristic of recent Communist (Soviet and East European) analyses of foreign policy matters that comparing the foreign policies of Communist ("socialist") countries has a low priority. Basically, this stems (on a theoretical level) from conceptualizing *integrative development* as being the main tendency of Communist foreign policy. Nonetheless, variation in foreign policy is admitted to be an important (if transitory) aspect of the contemporary situation. Thus at a June 1971 conference organized by the journal *Problems of Peace and Socialism*, G. K. Shakhnazarov declared that "the fact that the fundamental interests of the peoples of the Socialist countries coincide did not rule out differences, contradictions, and the like. . . . We know all too well that even the best of friends may fall out," [13] and the Hun-

10. Henry Krisch, "The GDR and Soviet Policy in Germany: Interest Assertion in an Unequal Alliance," paper delivered to the A.A.A.S.S. Meeting, Denver, Colorado, March 26, 1971.

11. Here I disagree with Rosenau's exclusion of linkage relations from the comparative study of foreign policy (Rosenau, *op. cit.*, p. 309).

12. Kaiser and Morgan, *op. cit.*, pp. 8–13.

13. "Laws Governing Development of Socialist World System," *World Marxist Review*, Vol. 14, No. 10 (October 1971), p. 34.

garian J. Berecz added that the "concrete situation of the Socialist countries in the world arena varies. Their means of influencing world politics are different." [14]

The GDR scholar Siegmar Quilitzsch goes somewhat further and lists some likely factors that produce these interstate variations. These factors may include the level of economic development, class structure, maturity of Socialist social relations, historical and national traditions, and, as especially aggravating factors, subjective actions and perspectives of national egoism.[15]

These rather typical observations suggest that the comparative study of Communist foreign policies may lead to an important, if limited, parallelism of research approaches between Western and Communist scholars which may give their work great mutual interest.

Turning to the field of Communist foreign policy studies itself, I would maintain that insofar as we focus on intra-Communist relations, we help to increase the precision of the analysis of regional systems, a growing and, I believe, important aspect of the field. In fact, the development of general propositions about the foreign policies of Communist states may serve the very useful function of casting doubt upon the research utility of the category "Communist," as opposed to non-Communist, states as generators of foreign policies (as contrasted with such other categories as great and small powers, developed and non-developed countries, and so forth).

Only a comparative approach can move us beyond the level of understanding reflected in the plethora of descriptive single-country studies. One thinks of attempts to conceptualize Soviet foreign policy under such varied headings as "Muscovite," "Slavic," "Eurasian," "continental," "great power," "international Communist," and so forth.

Finally, one may ask whether the historically developed pattern of state relations has been changed in any substantial way by the emergence of Communist states. (The assertion that it has is a staple Communist claim.) This question could not logically be answered on the basis of an examination of the foreign policy of a single Communist state (or of that state and its satellites). Only the emergence of comparable Communist foreign policies allows us to consider anew, in an international setting, that perennial problem of Soviet studies, the influence of a revolutionary ideology on political practice. From an empirical perspective, a reliable proposition on this point would be

14. *Ibid.*, p. 36.

15. Siegmar Quilitzsch, "Zu einigen theoretischen Fragen der Entwicklung des sozialistischen Weltsystems," *Deutsche Aussenpolitik*, Vol. 17, No. 3 (March–April 1972), pp. 442, 446.

an invaluable datum for understanding the nature of revolutionary change in societal patterns. From a normative perspective, it might well be argued that the traditional interstate order is not so conducive to peaceful human life that a possible alternative order is of no interest. Western normative theorizing about war and peace, when it does not take into account Communist theory and practice, is thereby deficient.

The content of such comparative studies must be left, to a considerable extent, to the interests and inclinations of the individual researcher and the availability of data. In the light of the purposes discussed above, however, some suggestions as to subject matter can be made. It would be useful to focus on a comparison between the foreign policies of Communist states *other than* the Soviet Union. While the unique position of the Soviet Union in its relations with other Communist countries will always be deserving of study, it seems proper to compare more nearly comparable state-actors: e.g., Balkan states, divided states, ethnically or historically related states. Through careful specification of the characteristics of states to be compared, " natural experiments " may be set up. By thus holding many variables constant, some tentative probabilistic statements may be made regarding the effect of the " Communist " variable upon state behavior.

As a case in point, let me mention the case of the partitioned states: Germany, Korea, Vietnam, China. It would be useful to compare the " unification " policies of East Germany, North Korea, North Vietnam, and the People's Republic of China, as well as their relationship to the United States (its hostile military presence in West Germany, South Korea, South Vietnam, and Taiwan) and to the " interior " of the Communist world.[16] (Similarly, comparing East European Communist policies toward the Federal Republic of Germany, or East Asian Communist policies toward Japan, might be instructive.)

It may be fruitful to examine patterns of non-state interaction, such as ties among ethnic groups split by state frontiers, social and economic organizations (e.g., trade unions), and intellectual contacts. The linkage of social change (e.g., the Great Proletarian Cultural Revolution) to foreign policy is also significant. Let me add a plea for more comparative studies of individual foreign policy makers, both through time within a single polity (e.g., Stalin-Khrushchev-Brezhnev) or on a cross-polity basis (e.g., Ho-Mao-Tito).

How shall Communist foreign policies be compared? Reviewing past scholarship in this area almost compels me to begin with a

16. There will be papers and discussion materials comparing GDR and North Korean foreign policies in a forthcoming volume edited by Ilpyong J. Kim and the author. See also the special issue on " Political Integration of Multi-State Nations," *Journal of International Affairs,* Vol. 27, No. 2 (Fall 1973).

negative stricture: no single country studies, and no double or triple country studies masquerading as comparative studies, are sufficient. Just as five chapters on five domestic political systems do not add up to one comparative analysis, so parallel foreign policy studies are not a comparative treatment. Only by means of genuinely comparative studies can we hope to distinguish between the particular and circumstantial, as opposed to the general, in the foreign policies of Communist states. The implication of this dictum is clear: as in comparative politics generally, investigations of comparative foreign policy should be organized around concepts and problems rather than around specific countries or their policies.[17] Moreover, while a great deal of data will continue to be developed by scholars with traditional interests, it behooves comparative analysts to attempt the organization of research in the light of their needs in filling conceptual containers.

Comparative investigations should be undertaken at various levels of analysis. Single country comparisons, subsystem and system activity, and intersystemic comparisons (NATO-WTO, etc.) all offer useful possibilities. Similarly, the focus of comparative investigation may be shifted from internal to external relationships, or from system-standard to system-deviant behavior.

A strong plea must also be made for research that makes greater use of the time dimension. Here I include both the successive phases of a single polity's history and the attempt to identify and compare foreign policies of different states at chronologically different but functionally equivalent periods of their histories. Here we attack the problem of whether the foreign policies of Communist states also pass through developmental stages; the developmental slant of Communist analysis comes to mind here.

Comparison of Communist foreign policies should be undertaken on the basis of the environmental parameters of the states concerned. It might be useful to enrich and expand those portions of general surveys of international relations actors (Banks and Textor, Russet, Rummel) which apply to Communist states, both to permit their foreign policies to be compared in their social, geographic, and other settings, and to facilitate comparisons across the boundaries of the "Communist states" category. The importance of resources and general economic factors in world affairs increases the need for such approaches. What are the energy needs and resources of various

17. A comparative rather than just parallel study is Alexander Dallin, "Soviet and Chinese Communist World Views," in Donald W. Treadgold (ed.), *Soviet and Chinese Communism: Similarities and Differences* (Seattle: University of Washington Press, 1967), pp. 367–374. Rosenau stresses this point—and quite rightly (*op. cit.*, p. 308).

Communist countries, and how may their foreign policies be affected thereby?

I have indicated that the field of comparative Communist foreign policy studies has thus far seemed to me to be little developed. Perhaps for that reason, I believe that a great deal of useful work lies at hand. For a useful body of knowledge to accumulate, the comparative study of foreign policy must become " normal science " for a larger number of scholars than is now the case. The emergence of a comparative analysis of Communist foreign policies will allow us to increase our understanding of international relations in general, of the Communist group of states in particular, and of the historical significance of the major revolutionary transformation of our times as well.

Arnold L. Horelick

Does the Comparative Approach Merit High Priority?

As I understand it, the 1971 regional A.A.A.S.S. symposium for which the papers presented here were originally prepared asked the authors to address themselves to three questions with regard to the comparative study of Communist foreign policies: (1) *why* should we compare, (2) *what* should we compare, and (3) *how* should we compare? The papers before us are long on " why " arguments, are short on " what " recommendations, and tell us almost nothing about " how " to do it. That is perfectly consistent with the difficulty of the questions. Unfortunately, the future of the comparative Communist foreign policy enterprise depends on the soundness of an integrated, rather than a sequential, answer to those questions.

Roger Kanet's approach to the " why " question is unobjectionable, but also not terribly useful. To argue against the reasons he advances for developing Comparative Communist Foreign Policies as a field would be like arguing against Motherhood. Study might broaden our understanding of the foreign policy process in general; might improve our understanding of how Communist policies differ from and are similar to the policies of non-Communist states; and might offer deeper insights than we might otherwise achieve into the foreign policies of particular Communist states. But while the virtues of Motherhood are unassailable in the abstract, it is necessary to arrive at puberty before getting pregnant; impregnation should be avoided when there is a high risk of miscarriage; and one ought to think about whether having a baby is the most useful or sensible *next* thing to do anyway. These caveats apply also to the enterprise advocated in the Kanet paper.

David Finley's discussion of "why" we should do comparative Communist foreign policy research provides, in my view, a much more useful point of departure; he at least makes a start in the direction of distinguishing among objectives to be served by such comparative studies. The utility of the comparative approach depends in the first instance on what it is we need or want to find out. Having determined that, we can then explore what comparative advantages the comparative approach might offer regarding the things we most want to learn about, given the present state of the comparative politics art and the accumulated body of knowledge about the formulation and implementation of foreign policy in Communist-ruled states.

Finley invites us to assess the utility of the comparative approach to Communist foreign policies by asking whether it can improve our ability to make valid statements that are *policy-relevant, theory-relevant,* or both. His answer, as I read it, is that if comparison of Communist foreign policies permits us to achieve what comparison theoretically can achieve by organizing and interrogating data in a comparative way, then it will contribute positively to both theory building and policy-relevant analysis. While I believe that Finley fails to provide credible justification for his optimism, his approach at least suggests that the comparative approach may be more useful and workable for some purposes than for others. I find his argument somewhat more persuasive on the theory-building than on the policy-relevant side.

Indeed, for the theory-building enterprise a comparative approach is indispensable. Comparison is at the very heart of scientific inquiry. For theory building, the "why" question virtually answers itself: because comparison is what it's all about. But *what* to compare depends on what kinds of theory one wants to build. In the international politics field, one can compare either all actors, which is unwieldly for most purposes; or the most powerful or influential actors, measured in a variety of quantifiable ways; or subsystems of actors, defined according to common membership in an alliance system, geographical propinquity, similarities in size, population, language group, political system, and so forth. One can study aspects of the behavior of all of these sets of actors. One can also study foreign policies comparatively without comparing the policies of more than one national actor. One can, for example, study comparatively the foreign policies of, say, the Kennedy and Nixon Administrations in this country, or the Khrushchev and Brezhnev regimes in the Soviet Union. It is not clear to me that the subset "Communist foreign policies" taken as a whole is of such great interest or contains enough burning issues of comparative foreign policy studies to make a large investment in the field an urgent matter of business. The authors make no effort to define that subset, so I assume that they are talking about the foreign policies of states that are ruled by Communist parties, or at least by parties that claim derivation from a common Leninist source. That is a crisp enough criterion, and I do not fault the authors for not trying to complicate it by Talmudic hair-splitting. The trouble is that the range of substantive foreign policies now embraced by units sharing that particular common denominator is so wide that the most interesting theoretical question seems to me to be "What difference does rule by parties that call themselves Communist make for the formulation and implementation of foreign policy by those national actors?" And that question in turn requires comparison with non-Communist foreign policies.

On the other hand, certain theoretical issues can be usefully explored by comparing subsets of the set of Communist-ruled states' foreign policies. If one is interested in exploring how subordinate members of an alliance system dominated by a hegemonal power attempt to assert distinctive national interests, the East European members of the Warsaw Treaty Organization make a promising group for comparison.

At the very high level of generality and aggregation at which comparative foreign policy theory building aims, I suppose it is possible that comparative Communist foreign policies, as a subfield, can contribute something to moving the theory-building enterprise closer to the capability to make statements about foreign policy that have universal validity. The trouble is that the kinds of statements about international politics that I see in the social science literature which can lay any claim to universal validity I just don't find very useful or intrinsically very interesting. I doubt that incorporating into that body of statements the kinds of propositions about *Communist* foreign policies that can be validated will increase its utility or enlarge its substantive scope.

I hope that what I have said so far does not simply expose my biases, but also makes clear that my judgments about utility are conditioned by my own research interests. Of the two criteria proposed by Finley for judging the utility of comparative Communist foreign policy research, my own interest centers on its potential contribution to policy-relevant research. Here my expectations regarding payoff have to be quite modest. It's not at all that comparative work *per se* is irrelevant to policy research; it's just that, with respect to what I believe needs most to be done to improve our analytical work on the foreign political behavior of Communist states, the kinds of comparative research that can be done and that are being proposed seem to me to have very little to offer.

Kanet puts his finger on the problem when he notes that all of the quantitatively orientated comparative analyses of Communist foreign policies produced so far have focused almost exclusively on foreign policy *outputs,* virtually ignoring the input side. The reason for this, as he points out, is that we have reasonably good information on some conventional policy outputs—like U.N. voting—and very little, especially not " hard " or quantifiable data, on inputs to the policy-making process in Communist countries. I agree with this, but not with Kanet's inference about what should be done next.

Kanet concludes that in the foreseeable future, in comparative Communist foreign policy studies as well as in country studies, it will continue to be profitable to focus on the analysis of policy outputs, making use of such quantitative data as can readily be obtained—he specifically mentions trade data and tourist and communications flows—and developing time series for the kinds of quantitative output data that are available. From my perspective, this simply means leaping over the research issues of highest salience—those having to do with the foreign policymaking process and inputs to it—and projecting into the comparative area the substantively thin, often trivial, quantitative, output-orientated country studies that are at best only marginally relevant to policy issues.

Given the limited resources available for the study of Communist countries' foreign policies, this does not seem to me an endeavor of sufficiently high value to warrant much priority. What needs most to be done in our field now is to improve our understanding of the foreign policy decisionmaking process in Communist states and of the most critical inputs to it. This is a prerequisite to developing a capability for making contingent predictions about foreign policy outputs under specified conditions, which is of interest both to theory and to policy. We have barely scratched the surface here, even in our studies of the most important, the most consequential, and the most thoroughly researched of the Communist states, the U.S.S.R.

The authors of these papers are wrong, I think, to speak about the state of Communist foreign policy research as if there were a vast and highly developed country literature standing behind it. Compared with the literature on both non-Communist foreign policy and the domestic politics of Communist states, the Communist foreign policy field is grossly underdeveloped. This is particularly true of the case-study literature, the building blocks that must provide the essential data base for purposes of theory building or other generalizations about the foreign policy behavior even of single states. There is nothing, for example, in the Soviet case-study literature—which, incidentally, is very small—to compare with the best of the case studies of U.S. foreign and military policy decisionmaking of recent years. The truth is that scholars of Soviet, not to speak of Chinese or other Communist country, foreign policies lack a sufficiently detailed or authoritative data base from which to write the most elementary, strictly journalistic, account of governmental behavior on any major foreign policy issue or crisis comparable in verifiable accuracy to, say, what a team of *New York Times* investigative reporters are ordinarily able to piece together within weeks of a major U.S. foreign policy decision.

Because the data are so poor, few of us try to do anything comprehensive or detailed. We look for manageable research problems, and the more manageable they are the less interesting or, if you will, policy-relevant they tend to be. The relatively few who do try—for example, Robert Slusser in his recent Berlin study [1]—are obliged to construct intricate pyramids of inferences derived from data that are several times removed from "hard" evidence. What is produced, often ingeniously, by such efforts, is seldom persuasive enough to command wide acceptance in the field, so that the storehouse of established knowledge from which new studies may draw grows very slowly and unevenly.

For all the talk we have heard about bringing Communist studies into the mainstream of social science, the Communist foreign policy field, on the plane of country studies, has barely been touched. *Techniques* of modern social science have been introduced into some studies, but on an ad-hoc basis with little regard for a theoretical or conceptual framework. For example, the application of models and concepts derived from decision theory is perhaps the most promising new development in the field of the U.S. foreign policy studies. But almost nothing has been done to adapt, refine, and operationalize those concepts or models to the context of foreign policy decisionmaking in Communist countries.[2] We should not expect to make dramatic improvements in Communist foreign policy studies simply by plugging in these models, which have been derived from the study of rather different decisionmaking systems on the basis of access to incomparably better and richer data than we have at our disposal. But still less can we expect to improve our performance significantly by leaping from our primitive country studies of Communist foreign

1. Robert M. Slusser, *The Berlin Crisis of 1961* (Baltimore: Johns Hopkins University Press, 1973).

2. See the report by Horelick and others cited above, p. 6, fn. 1.

policies to comparative studies on the same set of substantive issues which are bound to be still more primitive.

The most important immediate priority, in my view, is to improve and enlarge the established knowledge base about the context of foreign policy decisionmaking in Communist countries in ways that will render that knowledge more susceptible to disciplined inquiry, and to formulate and test theories in the middle range which are specific to what is known or can be learned about the foreign policy decisionmaking contexts of the countries that are the targets of our investigation.

Now I believe that a comparative approach to the solution of some of the problems associated with these objectives could be useful. For example, comparisons that permit us to experiment with extrapolations in foreign policy functions from structurally similar cases that are relatively data rich to cases that are data poor might be helpful. These comparisons could be between foreign policymaking in different Communist countries, between Communist and non-Communist countries, or across different regimes or policy issues in a single country. The selection of the most useful comparison would depend on the problem to be worked.

Given the limited range, uneven quality, and generally underdeveloped state of our storehouse of knowledge about the foreign policies of Communist states, a carefully discriminating problem-oriented approach to the selection of research issues that can be best, or better, treated comparatively appeals to me more than a wholesale endorsement of comparative Communist foreign policy research that is justified on the assumption that there is bound to be useful fallout—somehow—from such an effort.

ALVIN Z. RUBINSTEIN

Comparison or Confusion?

According to Professors Finley, Krisch, and Kanet, foreign policy is the last frontier of Communist studies, and the time has come to exploit the terrain. Equipped with theories, methodologies, and collections of data, social scientists should venture forth into the labyrinthine by-ways of Communist foreign policy behavior, bringing order and setting matters into comparative perspective. The authors suggest that the landscape is not so forbidding or formidable as has generally been assumed, that it can be charted and readily traversed; and they wave in the general direction that we are to take.

I do not believe that the skeletal papers under review help very much in determining what we should compare, how we should compare it, or even why we should compare it. Indeed, given the current underdeveloped condition of Communist foreign policy studies and the data that behaviorally oriented researchers have thus far produced in this field, I question whether it is possible to make many meaningful comparisons. The three papers talk about the insights that behavioral research has brought to our understanding of international relations in general, but nowhere do they spell them out or show precisely how these insights are to be applied to the comparative study of the foreign policies of specific Communist countries. They postulate anticipated benefits but fail to explain what exactly they will be. They exhort us to move ahead, but we willing recruits are left at the starting line not a little bewildered by the ambiguity of the means we are to use and the directions we are to follow in the journey ahead.

My reservations stem not only from uneasiness with what they advocate, but from disagreement with the assumptions underlying many of their arguments, which seem insufficiently thought through. At the risk of diverging from the central thrust of their case, let me make several points that I deem important and that contravene the essentials of the argument they have tried to make for this important research area.

First, I disagree that there is a spate of substantive studies dealing with the foreign policies of Communist countries. To begin with, we do not have all that many exhaustively researched studies of the foreign policy of the Soviet Union; and we have far fewer of that of the People's Republic of China, and still fewer of the foreign policies of Yugoslavia, Rumania, Poland, Hungary, Bulgaria, North Vietnam, or North Korea. Far from being deluged, we suffer from a paucity of detailed, thoroughly researched, systematic treatments of the actual behavior of these countries. I know of only a dozen or so that definitively examine specific aspects of Soviet foreign policy with the diligence and skill of, for example, Robert Slusser's *The Berlin Crisis of 1961*, Robert Legvold's *Soviet Policy in West Africa*, or Richard Ullman's *Anglo-Soviet Relations, 1917–1921*, 3 volumes. The neglect is due not to the nonavailability of data, but to the apparent unwillingness to undertake the kind of time-consuming intensive research which, regrettably, the profession depreciates as idiographic, overly "historical-descriptive," and atheoretical, while rewarding work that is conspicuously methodological or theoretically oriented.

True, many studies on Soviet foreign policy have appeared in the past decade or so, but most of these are broadly conceived political-strategic studies, tending to focus on motivations and aims rather than on the actual behavior or effectiveness of Soviet policy. The best of them are insightful, stimulating, indispensable, and more like them would be welcome. They are, however, no substitute for investigations of specific functional, topical, bilateral, or regional aspects of Soviet foreign policy. We need, not fewer, but more case studies of this type, dealing not only with the foreign policy of the U.S.S.R. but with that of other Communist countries as well.

Second, the authors seem confused over what it is they want compared. Is it decisionmaking processes? Domestic determinants of foreign policy? The actual policies themselves? Or the effectiveness of these policies? Interrelated, yet distinct and separable, these foci require very different research strategies, data, and hypotheses. Treating them as if they were one and the same thing results in a fuzziness of outlook, an uncertainty and ambiguity in formulations, and an insensitivity to the interrelatedness of hypotheses and data—all of which raises questions about the validity of the authors' key arguments.

Third, a list of researchable and significant hypotheses would be very useful, but one will not find it in these papers. Professor Kanet says that we can carry out comparative analyses using "data on economic performance, foreign trade, joint economic projects, and economic assistance." But what it is that we should hope to learn about Communist foreign policies from such data is never made clear. The salience of these data needs to be demonstrated; that which can be counted does not always count. As conventionally compiled, measures of direct interaction shed little light on the key questions that interest students of foreign policy. For example, crucial to the significance of data on economic aid is information on where in the recipient's political system the aid goes, who benefits from it, and how the donor seeks to influence the policies of the recipient as a consequence of the aid; instead of comparisons of foreign trade flows, we ought to know about the terms of trade and the efficacy of aid and trade for the elites in the recipient country. We must differentiate between aid and trade that facilitate Soviet influence and aid and trade that do not. To paraphrase George Orwell, "Some data are more equal than others." The importance of these distinctions is nowhere noted.

Before devising hypotheses for testing, it would be useful first to reach some agreement on the substantive topics that should be researched, on the kinds of data that can be brought to bear to explicate them, and on the information and insights that we hope to glean from the results. Then, and only then, can appropriate hypotheses be formulated. Most of the themes proposed in the subject papers would probably yield outcomes that are obvious or inconsequential. Surely we have advanced beyond such questions as "What is the relative importance of ideology and national interest in Communist foreign policy?" (Kanet).

Fourth, the authors cast so large a net so widely that they are not likely to catch the fish we're really interested in. One can wholeheartedly concur in Professor Finley's call for greater "explicitness of assumptions, clarity of conceptualization, adequacy of evidence to conclusions" and still find unsatisfactory the vagueness of the theories and propositions that he offers for investigation. One hears his plea for "analysis of organizational behavior, role relations, communications nets, interaction of social strata, group interaction, coalition formation and developmental phases," and one wonders how these

" coherent perspectives " are to be implemented with the behavioral data that are available to students of Communist foreign policies. In actual fact, the research of the behaviorally inclined has not figured prominently in enhancing our substantive knowledge of Communist foreign policy behavior.

It is necessary to de-mystify comparative study, theory-building, statistical computations, and the like; no matter what the concept or method, the final product will be no better than the boldness, precision, and sensibleness with which it is applied.

Fifth, comparative study (unlike idiographic research) is severely hampered by the paucity of data relevant for comparison of Communist decisionmaking or foreign policies. Too often, data are used only because they are available and lend themselves to comparison and hypothesis-testing, though neither characteristic brings with it the assurance of utility. And that which is at hand may mislead as often as inform—for example, U.N. voting statistics. On most of the issues that come before the U.N. General Assembly or Security Council, the statistics do not tell us who voted with whom. For example, they are not informative on whether India voted with the Soviet Union because of Soviet pressure, because it independently preferred the same outcome as the U.S.S.R., because it wanted to be on the winning side on a popular issue, or whether it was perhaps the Soviet Union which voted for the resolution out of a desire to align itself with India (and other non-aligned countries) and not the other way around. Voting studies rarely reflect the political dynamics attending the alteration of antecedent resolutions on which, after much bargaining, the final resolution is based. Until data are available which are appropriate to illumining the substantive questions in need of research, it is premature to push comparative studies of Communist foreign policies too far.

Finally, talk about the " social scientist " versus the " area specialist " is counterproductive. It is time we stop pretending that there is such an animal as a " social scientist "—meaning thereby one who transcends the parochial confines of a mere discipline or narrow geographic area and who, in so doing, is presumed to reach a higher stage of enlightenment. No one seriously interested in the study of foreign policy, Communist or non-Communist, is flimflammed by such pretentiousness. As an ACLS/SSRC report suggests, the dichotomy between area studies and academic disciplines is more apparent than real.

Inevitably, the researcher is going to use the tools and materials of his craft as best as he can to fashion a final product that he hopes will find a respected place in the profession. What can be done to improve the quality of the output is to specify in concrete and constructive terms how its value can be maximized, and to suggest the kinds of work that should be undertaken in the decade ahead. A symposium on priorities could serve a valuable professional purpose. If the priority areas and topics in need of further study are compiled, if the data available are identified, if the advantages of the various methodological approaches are examined and spelled out, if research strategies are operationalized, if a series of testable and germane hypotheses is drawn up, and if the results of such seminal deliberations are widely circulated, then perhaps we may get on with the challenging problems before us.

Jan F. Triska

Foreign Policy Issues Within Conceptual Frameworks

The three thoughtful essays under review argue forcibly and well for studies of comparative foreign policy, both of Communist states only and across the board. I agree with the thrust of the arguments. Comparison is useful, enlightening, and productive; it is also challenging and important. In fact, we have been doing it for years in political science in comparative politics, and the tempo is accelerating and the field is growing. Hence the Charles Gati idea for a panel is not so surprising. The time has come to ask the question, and he is right to raise it. The problem is, what to compare and, especially, how to compare it. In this respect, judging from the slow progress of comparative politics to date, we have a long, dusty way to go.

To start with, I agree with David Finley that we should compare when comparison is useful, interesting, or productive. I would not care to compare the foreign policies of, say, Costa Rica and Bulgaria, unless I found the exercise intellectually stimulating, needed, or in some way productive. Fishing expeditions have their limits. Neither would I be excessively enthusiastic about comparing foreign policy processes within one country over time. To be sure, area specialists can, because of their precise training, their special skills, and their sustained familiarity, analyze a single country's foreign policies much better when they take into account the myriad peculiarities that such cases present. Although in these efforts I would prefer that authors draw on relevant social science conceptualizations—in turn, greatly facilitating comparative foreign policy studies—I would certainly not want these authors to abandon their valuable efforts. Their work is irreplaceable. (The Brecher study of the foreign policy of Israel is a good illustration of such social science–single country foreign policy mutualism.[1])

Instead, I would propose that would-be students of comparative foreign policy turn their attention to the parts rather than to the whole of the foreign policy process. Assuming that issues determine interest, and keeping in mind past comparative foreign policy research efforts,[2] I submit that not comparative foreign policy as such but comparative policy *issues* settle the actual direction of research. The stimulus may come either from interactional behavior, whether conflictual (the Cold War, the Sino-Soviet conflict, the Communist coalition crises), cooperative (Comecon and the Warsaw Pact, U.S.-U.S.S.R. relations in World War II, arms control and disarmament, foreign trade), or both (the U.S.-U.S.S.R.-China triangle, nations' behavior in international organizations, East European coalition maintenance); or from interest in, need for, and anticipated productivity of comparison *per se* (comparative studies of decisional processes, of risk-taking, of domestic-foreign policy linkages, of group influences, of communication systems). Hence, unlike Finley, I would retain the idiosyncratic variable as a useful topic for comparison. In fact, comparative study of leadership in its many rich aspects has not been neglected in the past in spite of the disparate environmental and historical settings (e.g., studies of comparative Communist political leadership, of leadership of the U.S.S.R. and Eastern Europe, of the European administrative elites).

Thus, the subject matters for foreign policy comparisons are many and inviting. How to compare them is a bit more ticklish, however. Surprisingly, the three papers show a considerable amount of agreement in this respect. They propose that the studies "be organized around social science concepts" (such as decisionmaking, nation-building, interaction flows, communication problems). They stress "the concern for precise, rigorous method of analysis." And they recommend "development and testing of generalizations" in the process. Thus they argue for borrowing relevant social science mental

1. Michael Brecher, *The Foreign Policy System of Israel: Setting, Images, Process* (New York: Yale University Press, 1972).

2. Here I have in mind comparative foreign aid, comparative foreign and arms policies directed to non-committed nations and the Third World, comparative foreign policy perceptions of leaders, Chinese and Soviet policies in Eastern Europe, comparative distance in foreign policies, comparative foreign policies of divided nations, and comparative foreign policies in international organizations.

constructs applicable to substantive research issues for the purpose of obtaining generalizations as bases for hypothesis formulation, development, and testing. After all, as Finley rightly maintains, the social sciences and foreign policy studies have a great deal to offer one another. We tend to forget that. American politics and their many subfields, for example—which is but another area politics study—have profited from sustained, close association with the social sciences, proving in turn that area politics studies may indeed contribute to the social sciences. What matters, in my opinion, is the *fit* between the two, between the conceptual generalizations derived from the social sciences and the foreign policy concerns on hand. That, I submit, is the crux of the matter. Adoption of conceptual frameworks for comparative foreign policy issues, when successful, is bound to benefit both the social sciences and substantive knowledge. The question is how to do it, and how to do it well.

Obviously, as the field of comparative politics abundantly shows, there are no easy remedies and no short cuts. But we can learn from the mistakes of comparative politics. Take, for example, the ethnocentric notion that comparative politics have been known to foster. It emanates from the widely held opinion that the West, particularly the United States, should be the model against which all other political systems should be measured. As Mark Kessel recently put it, "... much scholarly literature [in comparative politics] is permeated by an implicit belief in the superiority of American values, institutions and processes. ... At the extreme, one may discern a continuity in perspective between scholar and policy maker. ..."[3] Is this not one of the arguments that have been persistently leveled against students of Communist party-state politics?

My advice would be to start at the beginning: first, to select a general pivotal issue, and then to look for conceptual frameworks that best fit the issue. This is a trial-and-error period, one of collecting alternative possibilities, testing them against the issue, and discarding misfits. Once the possible fit is found, the empirical investigation begins. If the selected concept turns out to be deficient, the search may continue even in this phase. But, in any case, I would tend to limit the intellectual effort to a single-country foreign policy. Only when the fit has been tested empirically to the satisfaction of the investigator would I proceed, holding the general pivotal issue constant, to add other countries' foreign policies to the investigation.

I would thus build upon what has already been accomplished. To arrive at the comparative aspects, I would start with those foreign

3. Mark Kessel, " Order or Movement? The Literature of Political Development as Ideology," *World Politics*, Vol. 26, No. 1 (1973), p. 153.

policy studies that attempt to show how to marry conceptualizations derived from the social sciences with empirical research. In Soviet foreign policy, a field with which I am acquainted, I would suggest emulating (and in the process improving upon) comparative level studies such as the correlation of defense spending with actual problems posed by international politics [4]; application of game-theoretic conceptualization to intervention [5]; quantitative analysis of risk-taking [6]; quantitative study of expansionism [7]; interaction of socio-psychological and economic variables as they affect nuclear deterrence decisionmaking [8]; quantitative study of ideology as an input into decisionmaking [9]; study of decisionmaking in terms of changing attitudes of decisionmakers [10]; foreign-domestic policy linkages and their importance for decisional outcomes [11]; attitudinal analysis of elite groups [12]; elite perception of international regions [13]; general foreign-policy decision models [14]; and many others.

4. Raymond Hutchings, "Soviet Defense Spending and Soviet External Relations," *International Affairs,* Vol. 47 (1971), pp. 518–531.

5. William A. Welch, "A Game-Theoretic Conceptualization of the Hungarian Revolt: Toward an Inductive Theory of Games," in Frederic Fleron, Jr. (ed.), *Communist Studies and the Social Sciences: Essays on Methodology and Empirical Theory* (Chicago: Rand McNally, 1969), pp. 454–459.

6. Jan F. Triska and David D. Finley, *Soviet Foreign Policy* (New York: Macmillan, 1968), Ch. 9; Hannes J. Adomeit, "Risk-Taking, Crisis, and Conflict Behavior in Soviet Foreign Policy After World War II: An Empirical and Theoretical Analysis," unpublished Ph.D. dissertation, Part I, Department of Political Science, Columbia University, 1972.

7. William Welch, "Soviet Expansionism and Its Assessment," *Journal of Conflict Resolution,* Vol. 15, No. 3 (1971), pp. 317–327.

8. David C. Schwartz, "Decision Theories and Crisis Behavior: An Empirical Study of Nuclear Deterrence in International Political Crises," *Orbis,* Vol. 9, No. 2 (Summer 1965), pp. 459–490.

9. Rita M. Kelly and Frederic J. Fleron, Jr., "Personality, Behavior and Communist Ideology," in Erik P. Hoffmann and Frederic J. Fleron, Jr. (eds.), *The Conduct of Soviet Foreign Policy* (Chicago: Aldine-Atherton, 1971), pp. 191–221; Triska and Finley, *op. cit.,* Chaps. 2–4.

10. Richard A. Brody and John F. Vesecky, "Soviet Openness to Changing Situations: A Critical Evaluation of Certain Hypotheses About Soviet Foreign Policy Behavior," in Jan F. Triska (ed.), *Communist Party-States: Comparative and International Studies* (Indianapolis: Bobbs-Merrill, 1969), pp. 353–385.

11. David W. Paul, "Soviet Foreign Policy and the Invasion of Czechoslovakia: A Theory and a Case Study," *International Studies Quarterly,* Vol. 15, No. 2 (June 1971), pp. 159–202; Thomas-Fingar, *Issues, Interest Groups and Linkages Between Foreign and Domestic Policy in the Soviet Union,* unpublished paper, Stanford, 1973; William Zimmerman, *National-International Linkages in Yugoslavia,* paper read at the 1973 Meeting of the American Political Science Association in New Orleans.

12. Milton Lodge, "Groupism in the Post-Stalin Period," *Midwest Journal of Political Science,* Vol. 12, No. 3 (August 1968), pp. 330–351.

From the single-country foreign policy studies I would move on to comparative-level analysis. Examples here would be the studies cited by Roger Kanet—aid to developing countries, arms for the Third World, foreign policy concepts, instruments of foreign policy implementation, foreign policies of East European nations, and Sino-Soviet conflict, as well as comparative studies of coalition members [15] and states' interactional comparative behavior.[16]

I would recommend that we restrict our investigation to the frontiers of middle-range-level analysis. Experience shows that, certainly in the field of Soviet foreign policy, the richer the theory the fewer the validated results. As I wrote recently elsewhere,[17] it appears that a general empirical theory of Soviet foreign policy—an overall, empirically tested framework for analyzing and explaining Soviet foreign policy behavior—is well-nigh impossible to construct and perhaps not very useful. Middle-level theories of decisional processes—avoiding the pitfalls of simple explanatory mechanisms, excessively rational explanations, and purely statistical analog modeling—are in their aggregate preferable to one grand over-arching theoretical framework. Given the present trend, I expect that we will be seeing such empirically tested theories with greater frequency and with high-quality results.

Flexibility and hop-scotching from issues to concepts and back again promise results. Imaginative search for variety appears to suit our needs. Yes, we do need to be on top of our data; but we need conceptual frames of reference to collect and organize the data, and a comparative approach to gain a better understanding and to offer a more meaningful explanation.

13. Charles Gati, "Soviet Elite Perception of International Regions," in Roger Kanet (ed.), *The Behavioral Revolution and Communist Studies* (New York: Free Press, 1971), pp. 281–299.

14. Erik P. Hoffmann and Frederic J. Fleron, Jr., "The Study of Soviet Foreign Policy," in Hoffmann and Fleron (eds.), *The Conduct of Soviet Foreign Policy*, pp. 5–10.

15. Terrence P. Hopman, "The Effects of International Conflict and Detente on Cohesion in the Communist System," in Kanet, *op. cit.*, pp. 301–338.

16. See studies by Ole R. Holsti, Maurice D. Simon, Bruce R. Sievers, Charles D. Cary, David D. Finley and Edward L. Miles with John S. Gillooly in Triska, *Communist Party-States*; William Ekhardt and Ralph K. White, "A Test of Mirror-Image Hypothesis: Kennedy and Khrushchev," *Journal of Conflict Resolution,* Vol. 11, No. 3 (September 1967), pp. 325–332; William A. Gamson and Andre Modigliani, *Untangling the Cold War* (Boston: Little, Brown, 1971).

17. "Soviet Foreign Policy Analyses in the 'Sixties and 'Seventies," an unpublished paper, Stanford, 1973, pp. 36–37.

Lawrence L. Whetten

The Plausibility and Utility of the Study of Comparative Communist Foreign Policies

All the contributors to this symposium agree that the comparative approach is valuable, if not indispensable, in arriving at valid insights and generalizations with respect to foreign policies of Communist states. But they disagree on what is to be compared with what, in what depth, and for what purpose, and on the plausibility and utility of focusing greater scholarly attention on such comparative studies.

Jan Triska is the most optimistic of the group about the feasibility of the proposal. Indeed, he seems to presume that the comparative study of Communist foreign policies is a logical, if not already existing, extension of the comparative study of Communist domestic studies. He bases this assertion on the suggestion that comparative foreign policy studies should be focused on the parts rather than on the whole of the foreign policy process. " Assuming then that issues determine interest . . . I submit that not comparative foreign policy as such but comparative policy *issues* settle the actual direction of research. He lists some issue-areas where substantial case work has already been achieved, and submits an itemization of additional areas for future work. Thus Triska stresses output and action rather than input and decisionmaking.

Alvin Rubinstein is more pessimistic, questioning the depth of the single-country studies submitted to date, not to speak of that of cross-national studies. There is a dearth not only of empirical data and accurate analyses, but also of standards or norms upon which a series of single-country studies might be organized. Finally, little effort has been made to interpolate between criteria commonly referred to in Western comparative politics and the unique features that seem to persist within Communist societies. Until the general data base is greatly expanded, correlations between the nomothetic and idiographic approaches to foreign policy analyses will only compound the problem of establishing agreed-upon principles for the study of comparative Communist foreign policies.

William Welch's work comparing the standard American histories of Soviet foreign policy is devastating evidence affirming Rubinstein's charge. Not only were many of the scholars guilty of subjectivity and indeed ideological prejudice, but they varied sharply on interpretation, emphasis, and even the facts. But even more critical in the light of Rubinstein's argument, few could provide substantiating empirical evidence to support their contending viewpoints.

Of the three commentators, Arnold Horelick is the most critical of the overall scheme. He condemns the piecemeal approach of accumulating data on actions in issue-areas as research leapfrogging over the most salient problems in foreign policy—the decisionmaking process and the inputs into it: "What needs most to be done in our field now is to improve our understanding of the foreign policy decisionmaking process in Communist states and of the most critical inputs to it." He cites the need

> to improve and enlarge the established knowledge base about the context of foreign policy decisionmaking in Communist countries in ways that will render that knowledge more susceptible to disciplined inquiry, and to formulate and test theories in the middle range which are specific to what is known or can be learned about the foreign policy decisionmaking contexts of the countries that are the targets of our investigation.

This is certainly a laudable aspiration, but it falls short of criticizing the charge placed on the three original contributors by failing to provide workable suggestions about how to move the project off dead center, as Triska does. How does a researcher accumulate data and analyses and then test hypotheses among societies that manipulate and release arbitrarily the data he needs, and control access to the process he requires to test suppositions? Horelick does succeed, however, in bringing the discussion back to the central point raised by Finley—i.e., should the purpose of the new undertaking be to improve our insight into policy-relevant or into theory-relevant foreign policies of Communist states, or into both?

Whatever the objective, it seems appropriate to refine the possible goals in each category as the first step toward resolving the problem of appropriate data-bases. If the purpose is to be policy-relevant, several subtargets might be suggested: (1) Ascertain the degree of deviation within the Soviet system in order to exploit a political adversary. (2) Gain greater insight into the Soviet alliance maintenance mechanisms. (3) Establish appropriate levels for bilateral relationships, à la *Ostpolitik*. (4) Develop increased understanding about the nature of great-power interaction and behavior. (5) Reduce, conversely, the levels of individual and mutual misperceptions. And (6) ascertain individual values and interests on issues of mutual concern.

If the objective comprehends all of the above, could it also incorporate the goal of determining differences in overall Communist policy objectives on specific issues that can tell us more about the nature of adversary relationships, about the opponents themselves, and about specific principles and interests that may or may not be compatible with ours? The difficulties in applying such sweeping objectives have been all too apparent in the past. American misperceptions of Soviet intentions during discussions of strategic arms limitation and mutual balanced force reduction, not to mention the "great grain robbery," present a bewildering assortment of erroneous judgments about the Soviets' principles and interests on each issue.

Further, Albert Wohlstetter has convincingly demonstrated in the summer and fall 1974 issues of *Foreign Policy* that until the mid-1960s the U.S. government grossly overestimated Soviet strategic nuclear capability, not just their political intentions as it did in SALT I. Despite the enormity of these miscalculations, it is generally agreed that by the nature of the empirical evidence available it is relatively easier to determine the physical capabilities than the political intentions of Communist states. But the errors on the capability side strengthen the arguments of those, like Horelick, who insist that the appropriate bridge should be to improve our grasp of Communist intentions.

The prospects for improving our knowledge of intentions are not quite so gloomy as Rubinstein implies, for two reasons. First, there is an increasing tendency among scholars on both sides, including specialists on East Germany and North Vietnam, to shift the emphasis of policy-relevant inquiries from the top of the suggested list of goals toward the bottom. Second, because this has been a mutually perceived process, it has afforded the various Communist states a greater degree of confidence and has resulted in a limited increase in the flow of relevant information. But such marginal improvements are insufficient to alter the picture for the theory-relevant objectives.

Can the theory-relevant objectives be refined to more tangible goals, such as the following? (1) Up-grade Kremlinology (the art of divining Soviet intentions by factoring the equation of who is on top, using Byzantine methods to cope with Oriental patronage practices) by introducing sophisticated model-building techniques and methodological explanations for otherwise abstruse phenomena. (2) Expose weaknesses in selected Western concepts by comparison with the harsher manifestations of reality often associated with the Communists' application of *Realpolitik*. (3) Generate new sources of data to supplement gaps and explain variants in existing Western theory. (4) Cultivate new empirical bases and models for testing accepted Western social science theory. And (5) make a genuine attempt to overcome previous barriers to the integration of nomothetic and idiographic approaches to social science theory. This is an area of unique challenge because of the diverse standards against which existing data have been compiled.

There may indeed be enough in the above to tempt Western scholars to emphasize the theory-relevant approach. As in the case of the policy-relevant approach, there are abundant instances of misjudgment by the West of the theoretical context and nomothetic implications of Communist behavior, such as our imperfect application of linkage politics to civil unrest in Eastern Europe. The most intriguing problem, from my viewpoint, is reconciling the principles and values upon which the respective societies have predicated data, policies, and foreign policy concepts. In the past, differences on the theoretical plane were regarded as either completely divergent or somewhat convergent; both positions now appear extreme. As we find with the policy-relevant approach, scholars on both sides are gradually shifting emphasis from the top to the bottom of my intentionally structured list of priorities.

On the Communist side, this reorientation has been due to the de-Stalinization process, the recognition that Marxism requires supplemental theoretical underpinnings relevant to post-industrial societies, and the grudging acceptance that capitalist societies have been more responsive to this phenomenon in creating a new body of theory appropriate to Marxist development.

Moreover, the seeming mutual interest in societal development has stimulated Communist interest in participating in Western social science theory. Indeed, national Marxism has produced a wide range of theoretical variations on societal development, often based on Western innovations. This seeming imitation by the East of Western concepts has nurtured the persistent notion of the inevitable convergence between the two.

Both of these generalizations about the relevance of the theoretical approach must be highly qualified in the specific area of foreign policy. It is in this area that the issues of systemic stability, national security, and domestic legitimacy are most sharply focused for Communist regimes. Foreign policy will remain for the foreseeable future an area of much greater sensitivity than it is for most Western societies.

Thus the expectations of the advocates of the theoretical approach must be severely restricted. The various Communist regimes will retain firmer control over the foreign policy (including defense) formation processes than over any of the numerous social functions. The prospects of testing one's hypotheses on high policy matters are so limited, then, that a meaningful contribution to comparative political theory is difficult to envision. The degree of control likely to be exercised by Communist states, however, should not reduce the importance of attempting to exploit the Communist area for the integration of nomothetic and idiographic analyses, especially in comparative foreign policies within the area. Western failures to interpret accurately the international behavior of various Communist states may be blamed largely on this lack of interdisciplinary integration, or an overemphasis of one or the other. Thus, one may conclude with Finley that it is plausible to gain greater perspective into Communist foreign policies from both the policy- and the theory-relevant approaches, but only to the extent that a greater degree of integration between the two is achieved.

James N. Rosenau

Comparison as a State of Mind

Let me begin by emphasizing that comparison is as much a state of mind, a predisposition, an impulse, as it is a method. What is involved is an interest in recurring patterns at rather abstract levels. If one has a comparative state of mind, instead of asking how various things converge to produce a certain set of outcomes in a given society, one asks what are the similarities and differences between this outcome and this process in this situation as against an outcome and a process in another situation. The comparative impulse predisposes one to look for similarities and differences across cases. The presence of the comparative impulse is signified by the kinds of questions one considers. If one is interested in how at a moment in time, or at a place in space, things converge to produce a given outcome, one does not have a comparative state of mind.

As you may know, a few of us in political science and international relations have gone off the deep end and in this regard, driven (some might say distracted) by the comparative state of mind to seeking out recurring patterns across 130 nations. Indeed, we have formed one of the more interesting organizations in which I have ever had the pleasure of participating (since it is not really an organization), the Inter-University Comparative Foreign Policy Project, otherwise known as the ICFP. It has been in existence since early 1967, has held four or five conferences, has consisted of members from ten different universities, and has somehow still managed to persist. ICFP has been the vehicle for two books and some 100 papers.[1] It has yielded some 145 hypotheses for which empirical data are now available. It has even contributed to the advent of a yearbook for foreign policy studies.[2] It has a history recorded through 1972 [3] and has since continued to grow as a community of scholars interested in comparing foreign policy.

The ICFP reminds me of Kuhn's description of a normal science in that this group of scholars spend their time elaborating upon and refuting each others' hypotheses and findings concerning foreign policy behavior across a number of systems. At its heart is a commitment to tough, hard empirical data, especially those types of data which have come to be called events data. Several events data sets relevant to the comparative study of foreign policy have been created, one at Ohio State, another at U.S.C., another at North Carolina, and still another at Syracuse. All of them involve a reconstruction, on a day-by-day basis, of what nations do with respect to other nations, based upon global sources like *The New York Times* or *The Times* (London) as well as several regional sources. I am not sure whether those of you who are specialists in Communist systems are aware of these data sets, but if you are not, I commend them to your attention for your own possible use. You will find that all of them contain data on the daily international behavior of a number of Communist countries.

Let me say with respect to the ICFP that I do not think that it is an empire-building group. Its members do not want to convert people. They long ago came to appreciate that conversion is neither desirable nor possible. They are interested only in unraveling the mysteries of foreign policy and building on each others' studies. There is, however, some annoyance at the progress which the ICFP has enjoyed, I think; and the differences between the Rubinstein and Triska papers are reflective of this annoyance, of the regretable tendency toward intellectual conflict between those who tend to be specialists in an area and those who are impelled by a comparative state of mind. To be sure, some specialists are also comparativists,

1. I am the editor of both books, which together contain 32 papers by ICFP members written expressly for meetings of the ICFP. The two books are *Comparing Foreign Policies: Theories, Findings and Methods* (New York: Wiley, 1974) and *In Search of Global Patterns* (New York: Free Press, forthcoming).

2. Patrick J. McGowan (ed.), *Sage Yearbook of Foreign Policy Studies* (Beverly Hills: Sage Publications, Vol. I, 1973; Vol. II, 1974).

3. James N. Rosenau, Philip M. Burgess, and Charles F. Hermann, "The Adaptation of Foreign Policy Research: A Case Study of an Anti-Case Study Project," *International Studies Quarterly*, Vol. 17 (March 1973), pp. 119–144.

but in my view a tendency toward intellectual conflict often pervades our deliberations.

Triska mentions in his paper that the comparative study of foreign policy has a variety of problems, just as, he says, ". . . the field of comparative politics has in political science." His paper does not make clear what the problems of comparative politics are. I suppose he basically means that people have been studying politics comparatively for some time and that they have little to show for it. I do not know whether comparative Communist studies are so bad off as comparative studies in general, but perhaps it is useful to note that to some extent those who study comparative foreign policy have an easier time of it. Persons who study comparative politics compare across cultures, legislatures, parties, or whatever institution or process interests them. In so doing they focus on entities that do not have final authority and that are always subject to inputs from and control by their external environment; whereas students of foreign policy have the advantage of at least focusing on entities that have, if not the final authority, close to final authority. The latter thus have the advantage of being able to hold a variety of important variables constant.

Although Rubinstein says in his paper that we should not talk about it, I might point out that most area specialists are not of a comparative frame of mind. So while I agree with Rubinstein's call for more case studies, I would argue that area specialists would probably benefit by looking at comparisons within their areas. This is a naïve statement, because I do not know that they do not. It seems to me extremely important that case studies be undertaken in such a way that others can use each case as one among many. Those who write case studies in Communist affairs thus ought to try to converge upon common problems and common variables so that others, either in the area or outside it, can use the variety of case studies for comparative purposes. I regret to say that, at least in the area of foreign policy analysis, the number of studies that allow for comparison with other case studies can be counted on the fingers of one hand—and that might come down to just the thumb and Glenn Paige's study of the Korea decision.

I have asked myself what one who thinks of himself as a student of comparative foreign policy can say that might be useful to one who is a student of the Communist world. This, in turn, leads to three questions: Why compare the foreign policies of Communist societies? What variables might a student of comparative foreign policy be interested in if he is also interested in Communist systems? If a student of Communist politics has a comparative state of mind, what variables might be of interest to him? I think the answer to all three of these questions is roughly the same. One compares the foreign policy of Communist systems because there are characteristics of such systems which can be clarified by comparing their behavior. That is, certain variables are central to Communist systems which can be better grasped through observing their operation in several such systems, and which, if this is accomplished, can serve the intellectual interests of both the student of comparative Communism and the student of comparative foreign policy. Three such variables come quickly to mind. One is ideology, since it remains static for some countries and varies for others. Another variable is one-party rule, or what might be called authoritarian or closed regimes—in which one looks for commonalities and differences across different systems that show the quality of having one-party rule. The third variable could be that of East European culture, wherein one compares the Communist states of that region with other Communist states that do not have a common geographic locale and shared historical experiences. To be sure, East European culture is extraordinarily diverse; nonetheless, a distinction can surely be drawn in terms of geography and history compared with Africa or Asia.

Now I would ask those of you who are students of the Communist world (even if you do not have a comparative state of mind, but would be interested in seeing where it might lead you) what kind of variables interest you? My test for the appropriateness of a variable would be to play a mental game along the following lines: If you want to test your interest in ideology as a variable, ask yourself whether the idea of comparing, say, Bulgaria and Cuba along other dimensions excites your imagination and whets your theoretical appetite. If your answer is that this is really a dull question, then ideology is not a variable that interests you. At least to an outsider it would seem that if you are interested in the potency of ideological considerations as dynamics in the foreign policy of Communist systems, the idea of comparing Bulgaria and Cuba would be a very legitimate one. If it does not seem very central to you, but if the idea of comparing Bulgaria and Rumania *does,* then your interest would seem to be in cultural variables—those having to do with Eastern Europe, making Bulgaria and Rumania more worth comparing than Bulgaria and Cuba. For myself, I would want to find out the relative strengths of different variables in different systems. The advent of a Communist regime in Cuba or China is, from a comparative perspective, a great event. It allows one to see what happens when one relaxes cultural variables.

Such a mental game yields an answer to the question, asked by Kanet, whether there is more to be gained from comparing the foreign policy systems of Communist states than from comparing Communist states with non-Communist states. My impulse is that it would be preferable to start out, not by comparing Communist and non-Communist systems, but by comparing the inputs and outputs of the former on the grounds that in this way one can hold a number of important variables constant and thus develop more incisive analyses.

Level and Context of Analysis: Concluding Remarks

What do the preceding papers and comments add up to? And what can be added to this timely and lively discussion? To start with the second question, two points come immediately to mind: the level and context of analysis.

It seems strange that, with respect to the level of analysis, hardly anything has been said in this symposium to imply the existence of another level than that of the nation-state. In fact, I believe that the original framework for the discussion panel was in the main rather too narrowly focused on a comparison of Communist nation-states. Even if we disregard Marxist theoretical strictures about the eventual withering away of the state, the most obvious fact of life about the Communist movement is that it is composed not only of nation-states, but of many subnational units—i.e., Communist parties. Up to the successful Russian revolution in 1917, the Communist movement was a grouping of exclusively subnational organizations; between 1917 and 1944 it was essentially a number of organizations grouped around one nation-state.[1] And while during the Comintern days Communist parties were treated as—and were indeed little more than—appendages of the international organization and thus tools of Soviet foreign policy, such is obviously not the case now. One cannot really study, for example, the Sino-Soviet dispute on the basis of bilateral or even multilateral state relations; one has to take into account the role played by non-ruling Communist parties. Indeed, the Italian Communist Party under the leadership of the late Palmiro Togliatti has thrust itself into the conflict with consequences for both sides. Another example is the special relationship between the Soviet Union and the Japanese Socialist Party which developed as a result of the one-time pro-Peking stand of the now " neutral " Japanese Communist Party. Soviet relations with Japan cannot be studied adequately only on the basis of government-to-government relations; an important role is played by relations with subnational units. Moreover, students of international relations have of late

1. The celebration of the fiftieth anniversary of the Mongolian People's Republic in 1971 notwithstanding, Outer Mongolia was for all practical purposes a protectorate and except for external trappings had no more latitude of action in the international arena than, say, the Byelorussian S.S.R.

exhibited an interest in the non-state nation, of which the Palestinian Arabs are perhaps the best known for their impact upon the international community, and hence are of importance to the two Communist superpowers.[2] This interest points to a further retreat from an exclusive nation-state perspective in international relations, something that most specialists in foreign affairs of the Communist countries do not seem to appreciate.[3] The lack of interest in nation-state relations with subnational units or non-state nations is matched (with very few exceptions) by a lack of concern with macro- and supranational levels of analysis. (The few exceptions are studies of the Comecon and the Warsaw Treaty Organization.) This is my second point, the context of analysis.

As I have argued elsewhere some years ago,[4] there is a distinct need for a middle level of analysis in international relations between the macro-level of studies of the international system, with their erstwhile emphasis on bipolarity, and the micro-level of studies of the foreign policy of individual states. Here I followed the lead of Leonard Binder [5] and Michael Brecher,[6] who have argued for an intermediate, *regional* level of analysis in their articles dealing with the Middle East and South Asia. Brecher saw in this approach a kind of a meeting ground between area specialists and theorists in international relations. Both of them and several others who have treated other areas of the world, however, have thought only in terms of geographical regions and nation-states. I see the need to extend such contextual analysis in two directions: first, to think of the " region " in subsystemic terms (i.e., where groupings are not necessarily geographically determined) and, second, to extend the units of analysis from nation-states to subnational, supranational, and non-state units.

2. For a recent survey, see Judy Bertelson and Charles A. Powell's paper cited in the introduction to this symposium, p. 4.

3. I will venture a guess that very few Soviet and East European specialists are members of the International Studies Association or of its regional organizations who participate in annual conventions or in various workshops, internets, or projects. Furthermore, at meetings of the American Political Science Association I can usually recognize area colleagues at the various panels sponsored by the Comparative Politics–Communist Areas section, but not at the International Politics section.

4. " International Subsystems—A Submacro Approach to International Studies," *International Studies Quarterly*, XIII, 4 (December 1969), pp. 3 *et seq.*

5. " The Middle East as a Subordinate International System," *World Politics*, X, 3 (April 1958), pp. 408–429.

6. " International Relations and Asian Studies: The Subordinate State System of Southern Asia," *World Politics*, XV, 2 (January 1963), pp. 213–235.

To give a concrete example, the invasion of Czechoslovakia could be studied on the micro-level from the point of view of the Soviet decisionmaking process (see, e.g., Jiri Valenta's article in this issue); on a bilateral level (Soviet-Czechoslovak relations); on a multilateral level (all the invading Warsaw Pact countries and Czechoslovakia, or the same actors plus Rumania and Yugoslavia); on the level of all Communist party-states, a grouping that is no longer regional in character; or on the level of all actors in the entire Communist movement with its many subnational units. Certainly the aftermath of the invasion cannot be studied adequately without taking into account its impact upon the Western European Communist Parties, or upon the North Atlantic Treaty Organization for that matter. This is what I mean by the *context* of analysis. Comparative analysis simply does not go far enough.

To turn to my opening question, what does the preceding discussion add up to? Certainly one can recognize among the contributors staunch supporters of an area approach who see very little utility in recent social science concepts and even less in social science methodology; area specialists who pay lip service to social science and express the hope that it might be potentially useful; area experts who believe in a pluralistic area *cum* social science approach; and other scholars who would emphasize social science and build their research around social science concepts and methodologies. So at this stage we have a diversified call for improvement and innovation in the study of foreign policies of the Communist states, preferably performed in a comparative way. This is not enough. And while this symposium might be the beginning of a stimulating exchange on the merits and demerits of the comparative method and the utility or non-utility of adding social scientific concepts and methodologies to the study of foreign policies and *foreign relations* of Communist states, the problem is not whether to accept or not, but to correct. What we really need is not so much the acceptance of existing social scientific concepts and methodologies for the study of Communist foreign policies and the Communist area field in general (and some contributors to this symposium have rightly doubted the utility or the priority of such a cross-fertilization), as the *globalization* of the social science theory formulation process, a process that must include area specialists. This requires at least two things:

First, that area specialists take time out from their preoccupations with parochial research to familiarize themselves with general theoretical propositions in their disciplines, and then take the trouble to point out, preferably in disciplinary journals, where Western culture-bound concepts and approaches are inapplicable or inadequate and why. This might force general theorists to take note of the non-Western world and to realize that one cannot generalize only on the basis of the Atlantic experience.[7] What would they make of the Chinese tributary system that rejected the notion of sovereign nation-states; or of Japanese decisionmaking, where policy formation moves from the middle levels of the bureaucracy upward by a long and tedious process of consensus-building (and where lack of precision in the Japanese language is a further problem); or, closer to our present discussion, of the ideology-jargon-laden esoteric communication practices of Communist parties, the special mode of relations among Communist states which uses party rather than state channels, and the like? Which leads to my second point, that the study of non-Western cultures be made an obligatory, integral part of our educational system (preferably, down to the high school level), and that in the future it will be impossible to rush through a Ph.D. program, acquiring only enough competence to manipulate statistically Congressional or United Nations voting records. (Alvin Rubinstein has nicely pointed out in this symposium what is being missed by a purely statistical approach in such an enterprise.) But to achieve the second, long-range goal, area specialists should, in addition to talking to themselves (which they have mostly done in the past), make an effort to reach out and start a dialogue with the generalists.

I realize, of course, that this symposium is being published in a specialized forum. But I hope not only that it will result in a lively exchange of opinion among area specialists, who make up the bulk of our readership, but that all of us will bring this symposium to the attention of our colleagues in our departments and schools and invite them to comment. We hope that this interdisciplinary journal can serve as a clearinghouse for ideas on both substantive and methodological issues between specialists and generalists, not only in the field of foreign policy and international relations, but in all areas of scholarship bearing upon what is surely one of the major historical developments of the twentieth century—the phenomenon of Communism.

P. B.

7. There are some "pure" social scientists unencumbered with area knowledge, except for a familiarity with the United States and Western Europe, who start from a social science position and dismiss most area expertise as exotica. This attitude extends beyond research. A colleague once seriously assured me that given a solid grounding in international relations theory, one can teach the international relations of any area: Latin America, Africa, East or Southeast Asia, the Middle East, and so on.

David D. Finley

Détente and Soviet-American Trade: An Approach to a Political Balance Sheet *

> The United States and the Soviet Union regard commercial and economic ties as an important and necessary element in the strengthening of their bilateral relations and thus will actively promote the growth of such ties. They will facilitate cooperation between the relevant organizations and enterprises of the two countries and the conclusion of appropriate agreements and contracts, including long-term ones.

This is the Seventh Principle in the " Basic Principles of Relations Between the United States of America and the Union of Soviet Socialist Republics," signed at the Moscow Summit in May 1972 by

* This is a revised version of a paper presented to the Central Slavic Conference, St. Louis, Mo., November 8, 1974. The first section was originally presented to a Conference on Détente and American Foreign Policy held by the Colorado Association for International Education, U.S. Air Force Academy, September 27, 1974. I am grateful for useful criticism and suggestions from fellow participants on both these occasions, as well as from Frank Bowman, Robert Lee, and Fred Sondermann of Colorado College. I want also to acknowledge with thanks the assistance of the Carnegie Endowment for International Peace, which helped support research from which this article is drawn. I remain solely responsible for the views expressed.

President Nixon and Secretary Brezhnev.[1] The subsequent agreements and contracts have been numerous, and the expansion of trade remarkable. Who stands to gain, and at what cost?

In this paper I look at the policy of expanded Soviet-U.S. economic relations, particularly trade, in the context of the larger political course of Soviet-U.S. relations now sailing under the uncertain banner of détente. I will try in what follows, first, to specify among the disparate popular conceptions of détente what I take to be a reasonable and realistic meaning, and to indicate some standards drawn from that analysis by which one might assess the pros and cons of trade policy, among others. Thus prepared, I will review the volume and recent composition of Soviet-U.S. trade and prospects for its future development. I will finish by weighing the expectable consequences for the course of Soviet-U.S. political relations of a projection of feasible trade relations.

Images of Détente

As usual, a dictionary definition of the term does not take us far,[2] for in détente we have a vague abstraction, useful in the traditional parlance of diplomacy, which has been infused with sometimes overlapping but distinct meanings in the rhetoric and grammar of different parties. The diversity stems from the differing premises, differing purposes, and differing expectations of the parties.

I find it helpful to classify the meanings of détente under three headings. First among them is *détente as a prelude to or way-station toward entente*. Seen thus, détente is a manifestation of a trend of history toward a meeting of interests and purposes between the United States and the U.S.S.R., prompted by similar imperatives created by the functional requisites of technological society or a rational extrapolation of interests in national survival. This is détente as a reincarnation of "convergence," although the latter concept is sometimes stripped of its more euphoric notions of probable structural congruence.

Several rationales under this heading have led to strange con-

1. As quoted in and discussed by Edward T. Wilson *et al.*, "U.S.-Soviet Commercial Relations," in U.S. Congress, Joint Economic Committee, *Soviet Economic Prospects for the Seventies* (Washington: Government Printing Office, 1973), p. 645. For details of subsequent agreements, see U.S. Department of Commerce, Bureau of East-West Trade, *U.S.-Soviet Commercial Agreements 1972: Texts, Summaries and Supporting Papers* (Washington: Government Printing Office, 1973).

2. "A slackening or relaxing . . . especially an easing or relaxing of strained relations and political tensions between nations," to quote *Webster's Third New International Dictionary*.

ceptual bedfellows. First, this meaning is compatible with the theories of political and economic modernization which culminate in pluralism, or at least find pluralist society and industrial society co-determined or the product of one another.[3] The events of the early 1960s encouraged many in the West to project the inevitable disintegration of domestic as well as international monolithism in the socialist camp, leading to the sort of interest-group factionalism which would bring consumer demand, both economic and political, to harness government, with the consequent disappearance of ideological monism and of expansionist drives. Soviet industrial advances, the "goulash Communism" thrust of the CPSU program, incipient economic reforms in the U.S.S.R., some relaxation of coerced cultural conformity, the post-missile-crisis Soviet interest in easing the balance of terror and removing probable sources of direct Soviet-American threat and counterthreat, a shift of rhetoric and style in which the Cold War is spoken of in the past tense with disapproval—all of this seemed to portend definitive changes in the relationship between the countries and to sustain logical extrapolations about the consequences of modernization for foreign relations.

The painfully evident reversal of some of these domestic policies in the U.S.S.R. in the later 1960s could still be understood as temporary phenomena, chargeable to regime insecurity, in what remained a socio-economically determined evolution. The Czechoslovak invasion could be identified as a divided decision, when too much change too fast frightened a conservative leadership group. Modern social democracy in the West, equally unimpressed by the long-range validity of free-enterprise capitalism and of Soviet state capitalism, reinforced this outlook and seemed to find confirmation of its expectations in the evolutionary steps, faltering as they might be, on both sides of the chasm. Policies undertaken upon this premise soon created a vested interest in its accuracy.[4]

In the late 1960s a new awareness of the finite limits of the earth's natural resources, and of the vulnerability of the human race to incremental as well as sudden self-destruction, quickened the sense of Soviet-American interdependence. The theme was reflected in appeals to reason from the scientific communities of either country,[5]

3. I am thinking particularly of Gabriel Almond and G. Bingham Powell, *Comparative Politics: A Developmental Approach* (Boston: Little, Brown, 1966).

4. For example, Willy Brandt's *Ostpolitik*, as described in his book, *A Peace Policy for Europe* (New York: Holt, Rinehart & Winston, 1969).

5. Note the wide popularity of the themes in Andrei D. Sakharov's dramatic "letter" of 1968, translated in *Progress, Coexistence and Intellectual Freedom*

and it underlay the U.N. Conference on the Environment at Stockholm in 1972.

The understanding of détente as a prelude to entente is also compatible with the traditional Peace Movement's less deterministic vision of world peace through world law, or of world peace through overarching regional or global political institutions.[6] With an assist from a revisionist school of Cold War history, most conflict between the U.S.S.R. and the United States could be understood as the result of multiple accretions of mutual misunderstanding and mutual fears.[7] The shadow of the Bomb or other cataclysms must impel people of reason to clarify their purposes, recognize their common interests, and crystallize the measure of their agreement into norms and institutions that could survive the occasional stress of irrational malice and provide adjudication to defuse, or manage, conflict. There is plenty of evidence that Soviet leaders appreciate the futility of an accelerating arms race and that they have been hard pressed by alternative domestic needs for the wealth absorbed by such a race. At a time when rigid ideological Marxism-Leninism and anti-Communism have both seemed to be eroding, hopes for the prevalence of reason codified into international law could grow.

(New York: Norton, 1968), which found resonance throughout the world. At one point he concludes:

> . . . the facts suggest that on any other course except ever-increasing coexistence and collaboration between the two systems and the two superpowers, with a smoothing of contradictions and with mutual assistance, on any other course annihilation awaits mankind. There is no other way out (p. 74).

Y. Izrael, chairman of the Soviet section, U.S.S.R.-U.S.A. Joint Committee on Cooperation in the Field of Environmental Protection, and B. Kuvshinnikov describe the public Soviet view of the potential of Soviet-American cooperation against common environmental challenges in "U.S.S.R.-U.S.A.: Cooperation in Protection of the Environment," *International Affairs* (Moscow), March 1975, pp. 30–37.

6. For a moderate view of this prospect, see Richard N. Gardner, "The Hard Road to World Order," *Foreign Affairs,* Vol. 52, No. 3 (April 1974), pp. 556–576. I quote a relevant paragraph:

> At some point in the years ahead the world will move beyond U.S.-Soviet agreement on strategic weapons, and NATO-Warsaw Pact agreement on some measure of force reduction, to a truly multilateral set of negotiations (comparable to the non-proliferation treaty) designed to limit *conventional weapons.* It seems inevitable that the United Nations and perhaps regional bodies will be given new responsibilities for the administration of these arms control and disarmament measures, including means of verification and enforcement (p. 562).

7. See Anatol Rapoport, *The Big Two* (New York: Pegasus, 1971).

Thus, although events in the U.S.S.R. made doubtful the claim of the socio-economic determinists in the late 1960s and early 1970s, other forces have kept alive the image of détente as a prelude to entente.

Détente as entente is not an image restricted to optimists. It is also current among apprehensive third parties, to whom an entente appears to be a potentially all-enveloping condominium of the world. Such third parties come in all ideological flavors:

On the one side are West Europeans who detect in Soviet-American cooperation incident to the 1973 Arab-Israeli War the fore-image of high-handed attempts to arrogate to the superpowers not only the policing of international affairs but also the control of scarce world energy supplies needed to fuel their ever hungrier industrial machines.[8]

China is similarly apprehensive, visualizing condominium in terms not so much of economic impulse as of the ideological decay of an erstwhile socialist state now captured by a self-serving bourgeois oligarchy—" social-imperialists " still naturally pitted against the old imperialists, but colluding as well as contending and making common cause against the world's proletariat, including the Chinese.[9] This outlook is only a step away from the fearful, plague-on-both-your-houses view expressed frequently in the Third World, which holds that détente between the U.S.S.R. and the United States implies twin imperialist threats mounted against the Third World countries, wrapped in professions of Communism and democracy but based on economic greed and aggravated by racialism. The suspicions that virtually scuttled the Bucharest Conference on World Population in 1974 were one manifestation of this outlook.[10]

8. See, for example, French Foreign Minister Jobert's publicized clash with Secretary Kissinger in December 1973: Flora Lewis, "U.S. French Clash Opens NATO Talks," *The New York Times,* December 11, 1973, p. 1.

9. For example, " World in Great Disorder: Excellent Situation," a New Year's survey in *Peking Review,* Vol. 17, No. 3 (January 18, 1974), pp. 7–11. For emphasis on the continuing " conspiracy " of the two superpowers to exploit cooperatively the world proletariat, see " First Round Victory Over Two Superpowers," *Peking Review,* Vol. 17, No. 27 (July 5, 1974), pp. 10–11. For emphasis on the alleged Soviet-American struggle, see " Soviet Revisionist ' Détente ' Smokescreen in Europe," *Peking Review,* Vol. 16, No. 51 (December 21, 1973), pp. 4–5; also " Soviet-U.S. Contention for Sea Power," *Peking Review,* Vol. 17, No. 29 (July 19, 1974), pp. 16–17.

10. See the " Lima Declaration " and proceedings of the Second General Conference of the United Nations Industrial Development Organization (UNIDO), March 12–26, 1975, as reported in the *U.N. Chronicle,* XII, 4 (April 1975), pp. 28–30. See also the Sixth Special Session and 29th Regular Session debates of the U.N. General Assembly, in which a welcome for détente

A second heading under which images of détente may be classified is that of a *stabilized interstate system* whose balanced configuration is the reference datum for the rest of international behavior. In this view, the pre-eminent interests of nation-state security and prosperity greatly outweigh the visions of a radically changed world political structure. The latter may play a symbolic role in domestic politics, even an important one, and occasionally may distort international discourse; but they tend to shrivel away as determinants of national behavior in concrete situations. Détente is simply a clear-headed recognition of the measure of interdependence which attends the possibility of maintaining a balance of security and domestic prosperity in the U.S.S.R. and the United States in contemporary circumstances.

Whatever structural-functional changes may be occurring in either country (or elsewhere) do so at a glacial pace compared with changes of leadership personalities and the rise and fall of economic issues and unforeseen crises among third parties, all of which demand immediate, conscious decisions reflecting short-term national interests. It is not to deny the structural-functional movement, but to relegate it to the background condition against which international relations take place and to emphasize the relatively decisive role of personal judgment in concrete situations. Détente, then, is the conscious appeal to mutual interests to act so as to avoid volatile and unpredictable and uncontrollable sequences of events that would threaten nation-state security and prosperity. Détente further means the gradual establishment of a body of precedent to confirm the mutual utility of such a relationship. Thus it includes concrete transactions calculated to build that sort of precedent. In this view, détente emphasizes the conservation of a satisfactory *modus vivendi* rather than radical change from a currently unsatisfactory relationship.

I have noted the departure of this image from détente-as-entente by way of downgrading the significance of technological determinism or other modernization processes. It also represents a departure in its skepticism over the power of rationally extrapolated threats to survival to impel men consciously to build a Utopian legal order wherein nation-state frontiers and the traditional instruments of diplomacy fall away. The conflict inherent in the nation-state system

between the superpowers is repeatedly linked by Third World representatives to the need for a new international economic order atuned to the interests of developing states to resist exploitation by those superpowers. *U.N. Monthly Chronicle*, XI, 5,9 (May and October 1974). With regard to population issues see "Too Many Children for Whom?" *Africa Report*, July–August 1974, pp. 33–41.

may thus be expected to remain. The task that also remains is to successfully manage and limit that conflict.

In the term *successfully* we encounter what seems to me the most important distinction between the parties best characterized by this image of détente as balance, Secretary Kissinger and Brezhnev. For the former, the relationship is a desirable and achievable accommodation to the basically unchanging pluralism of the international system. For Brezhnev, on the other hand, it is a configuration of indefinite duration which will eventually be modified significantly.

That is not to say that Brezhnev harbors real expectations about an orthodox socialist world order. Events of the past twenty-five years must make abundantly evident the fatuousness of that Utopia, other than as a rallying cry in party congresses. But whereas Kissinger's outlook disposes to conservation of the present balance of power between the United States and the U.S.S.R, and perhaps the three or four other powers that give the present international system its shape, Brezhnev is not content with the present balance. He sees both the desirability and the opportunity cautiously to enlarge the Soviet share of power and sphere of influence relative to those of the United States and the other major powers. Soviet military expenditures and research and development directions, Soviet behavior in the Middle East, Soviet political initiatives elsewhere, and clear Soviet professions—all unmistakably substantiate the Soviet leadership's commitment to *modifying* the balance, while adhering to the image of détente in which the parties are accepted as permanent elements and their actions are characteristically prudent and restrained.

I have thus far avoided lengthy quotation. Consider the following, however, as a justification for putting Kissinger and Brezhnev under the same heading, and also as an illustration of important differences between their outlooks:

First Kissinger, in the course of defending himself at the *Pacem in Terris III* Conference in Washington in 1973:

> We are at one of those rare moments where through a combination of fortuitous circumstances and design man seems in a position to shape his future. What we need is the confidence to discuss issues without bitter strife, the wisdom to define together the nature of our world, as well as the vision to chart together a more just future.
>
> Nothing demonstrates this need more urgently than our relationship with the Soviet Union.

This administration has never had any illusions about the Soviet system. We have always insisted that progress in technical fields, such as trade, had to follow—and reflect—progress toward more stable international relations. We have maintained a strong military balance and a flexible defense posture as a buttress to stability. We have insisted that disarmament had to be mutual. We have judged movement in our relations with the Soviet Union, not by atmospherics, but by how well concrete problems are resolved and by whether there is responsible international conduct.

Coexistence to us continues to have a very precise meaning:

> We will oppose the attempt by any country to achieve a position of predominance either globally or regionally.
>
> We will resist any attempt to exploit a policy of détente to weaken our alliances.
>
> We will react if relaxation of tensions is used as a cover to exacerbate conflicts in international trouble spots.

The Soviet Union cannot disregard these principles in any area of the world without imperiling its entire relationship with the United States.

On this basis we have succeeded in transforming U.S.-Soviet relations in many important ways. Our two countries have concluded an historic accord to limit strategic arms. We have substantially reduced the risk of direct U.S.-Soviet confrontation in crisis areas. The problem of Berlin has been resolved by negotiation. We and our allies have engaged the Soviet Union in negotiations on major issues of European security, including a reduction of military forces in Central Europe. We have reached a series of bilateral agreements on cooperation—health, environment, space, science and technology, as well as trade. These accords are designed to create a vested interest in cooperation and restraint. . . .

We are engaged in an intense debate on whether we should make changes in Soviet society a precondition for further progress. . . .

For half a century we have objected to Communist efforts to alter the domestic structures of other countries. For a generation of Cold War we sought to ease the risks produced by competing ideologies. Are we now to come full circle and *insist* on domestic compatibility as a condition of progress? . . .

Our policy with respect to détente is clear: We shall resist aggressive foreign policies. Détente cannot survive irresponsibility in any area, including the Middle East. As for the internal policies of closed systems, the United States will never forget that the antagonism between freedom and its enemies is part of the reality of the modern age. We are not neutral in that struggle. As long as we remain powerful we will use our influence to promote freedom, as we always have. But in the nuclear age we are obliged to recognize that the issue of war and peace also involves human lives and that the attainment of peace is a profound moral concern.[11]

Now Brezhnev, on June 7, 1969, in what I think time has ratified as one of his more important formulations, made before the International Conference of Communist and Workers' Parties:

> The Soviet state's relations with the countries of the capitalist world are based on the principle, established by V. I. Lenin, of the peaceful coexistence of states regardless of their social systems. This principle means that disputed questions that arise between states should be resolved not by force of arms, not through war, but by peaceful means. It has received wide international recognition.
>
> Peaceful coexistence does not extend to the struggle of ideologies, and this must be given the most decisive emphasis. At the same time, it does not come down simply to the absence of war between socialist and capitalist states. The observance of the principle of peaceful coexistence also opens up broader opportunities for the development of relations between these states. This involves the settling of international problems at the negotiation table, agreement on measures to reduce the danger of war and to ease international tensions, and also mutually advantageous economic, trade, scientific and technical and cultural ties. . . .
>
> For us, peaceful coexistence is not a temporary tactical device but an important principle of a consistently peace-loving socialist foreign policy. This policy creates the most favorable conditions for the construction of a new society in the socialist countries and for the development of the revolutionary and liberation movement.
>
> We know very well that the formulation of foreign policy in the major capitalist states is frequently influenced by extremely aggressive circles. In order to curb their activeness, what is necessary is firmness, exposure of their intrigues and provocations, and constant readiness to administer a resolute rebuff to such aggressive impulses. The CPSU and the Soviet Union are carrying on just such a foreign policy.
>
> We also recognize the existence of a more moderate wing in the capitalist camp. While remaining our class and ideological adversaries, the representatives of this group evaluate the present balance of forces in the world quite soberly and are inclined to seek mutually acceptable solutions to disputed international questions. Our state takes these tendencies into account in conducting its foreign policy.

11. Henry Kissinger, address to the Pacem in Terris III Conference, Washington, D.C., October 8, 1973, reprinted in the expanded edition of his *American Foreign Policy* (New York: Norton, 1974), pp. 261–265.

> Barring the road to the threat of war and not relaxing our vigilance with respect to the machinations of aggressive and revanchist circles, we shall continue to do everything in our power to eliminate hotbeds of the danger of war on our planet. . . .
>
> The Soviet Union is prepared now, as it has been in the past, to reach an agreement on general and complete disarmament and on measures for limiting and checking the arms race, above all in nuclear arms and missiles. Compelling the imperialists to curtail the arms race—this means shaking the positions of the instigators of a new war, transferring colossal resources to constructive purposes and strengthening peace the world over.[12]

Allowing for differences of style and for the traditional phrases, I think that these are fairly accurate statements of policy, both of which belong in the category of détente seen as balance.

The last of my three classifications pictures *détente as deception and self-deception.* Observers grouped under that heading view détente as a stratagem of subterfuge propagated by a determined adversary to gain an advantage in a continuing contest for hegemony or power.

In the West we find at least three important variations on the theme. First among them I would identify conservative adherents of the view that the Cold War has only undergone cosmetic surgery and remains essentially on the course it took after World War II. Premises underlying this outlook differ. For some analysts they are to be discovered in a religiously founded belief that the Marxist-Leninist worldview is so categorically dominant in Soviet motivation and so exclusive of contrary philosophies that compromise is definitively foreclosed as a logical possibility, that it is folly to pursue hopefully a policy aimed at compromise. By such self-delusion we can only disarm ourselves, as our adversary wishes.[13] Others are led to much the same conclusion by their reading of an historical record that seems to show a consistent Soviet effort to seize every offer of compromise as an indication of weakness and to maximize Soviet power by overt or covert means, thus continually reinforcing the conviction that unlimited success will reward sufficient Soviet

12. Leonid Brezhnev, speech to the International Conference of Communist and Workers' Parties, June 7, 1969. Text in *Current Digest of the Soviet Press,* XXI, 23 (July 2, 1969), pp. 16–17. See also the Basic Document, adopted by this Conference, *ibid.*, XXI, 28 (August 6, 1969), pp. 22–23; and Constantin Olgin, "The Brezhnev 'Peace' Offensive and World Revolution," *Radio Liberty Dispatch,* RL 251/74 (August 7, 1974).

13. Thus, for example, Anthony Bouscaren, *Is the Cold War Over? A New Look at Communist Imperialism* (Washington: Capitol Hill Press, 1974), in which the author contends that Communism is "pre-eminently a disease of the mind" (p. 5).

persistence and patience,[14] two qualities in which a totalitarian regime exceeds a democratic one. Finally, there is the premise of "safety first." In a thermonuclear world, with open-ended weapons research potential, foreign policy based on the competition between superpowers to surpass each other's military capacity entails an arms race and makes intensified Cold War a self-fulfilling prophecy. From such a position détente appears as a dangerous, unjustifiable policy based on a dubious calculation of intent rather than capacity.[15]

A second variation on the theme of détente as deception comes in the powerful statements of émigrés from the Soviet Union, and the vocal, dissenting intelligentsia within. These groups speak from personal experience to tell us "this is what the Soviet regime is like," and they contend that that regime can never be induced to modify voluntarily its inherent nature. Compromises only have the effect of disarming the forces within the U.S.S.R. which alone offer a prospect of forcing significant internal reform. Only after such reform can one expect the nature of Soviet foreign policy to change. Solzhenitsyn is perhaps the most eloquent and uncompromising in his viewpoint and the man who has documented his claim the best.[16]

14. For thoughtful recent developments of this view, see Kurt L. London (ed.), *The Soviet Impact on World Politics* (New York: Hawthorn, 1974); also, Robert Conquest *et al.*, "Détente: An Evaluation," *Survey*, Vol. 20, Nos. 2–3 (Spring–Summer 1974), pp. 1–27.

15. Thus we have the late Chief of Staff of the U.S. Army, General Creighton Abrams, reflecting the position of the U.S. Army:

> The major military challenge to our global interests is the Soviet Union. It is the only other truly global military power. And so we must gauge our ability as a nation to maintain freedom of action in terms of the Soviet Union, and in terms of the challenges that Soviet global interests and action pose for us. . . .
>
> The Soviet Union is not reducing its military power. On the contrary, every responsible estimate shows that they are building, increasing, and extending their power at an impressive rate. . . .
>
> We must be willing to meet these real challenges. . . .
>
> So we must be strong. We must have an Army of the proper size. . . . It must be equipped to respond effectively anywhere on the globe that our country's well-being is threatened.

Address to the Association of the U.S. Army, Colorado Springs, Colo., March 21, 1974, reprinted and circulated among military personnel.

The same theme is illustrated in "Sen. Jackson Warns on Détente Pitfalls," giving the text of Senator Jackson's speech opening debate on the Fiscal 1974 Defense Authorization Bill, reprinted in *Aviation Week and Space Technology*, Vol. 99, No. 15 (October 8, 1973), pp. 65–66; also in a recent pair of articles by Capt. George E. Dials and M/Sgt. Dick Larsen on "NATO: Two Views," *Army*, Vol. 25, No. 2 (February 1975), pp. 10–19.

16. See his Nobel lecture (*The New York Times*, September 30, 1972) and, of course, *The Gulag Archipelago, 1918–1956* (New York: Harper and Row, 1974).

Sakharov diverges somewhat,[17] and others, such as Roy Medvedev, diverge further;[18] but all treat the likelihood of rapid change in the Soviet regime with profound skepticism.

Allied in outlook with the latter position come the soul-brethren of oppressed groups within the U.S.S.R.—notably large portions of the American Jewish community. It is hard for them to justify détente when it appears to be simply a shelter under which political oppression is licensed to operate without challenge.[19]

Finally, in the West, I should call attention to some of the radical socialist organizations, for whom détente is a sign of weakness and corruption in a Soviet Union that has long since sold out the cause of socialism in the West and that makes cynical common cause with the capitalists, freeing the Soviet hand for state exploitation at home and freeing the U.S. hand to prolong the reign of monoply capitalism both domestically and abroad.[20]

Like the other two images of détente, the image of deception is confined neither to groups in non-Communist West nor to dissidents in the U.S.S.R. There is good evidence that the conservative Soviet adherent of a Cold-War-as-usual outlook may share the premises of his Western opposite number. Thus we have the orthodox Marxist-Leninist who excludes " coexistence " at the state level as a probable prologue to *de facto* " ideological coexistence," and who equates that with heresy. We also have the historically motivated conservative who correlates the Cold War with the most remarkable successes of

17. For a summary of Sakharov's views in his own words, see *The New York Times,* March 5, 1974, p. 8.

18. R. A. Medvedev, " The Problem of Democratization and the Problem of Détente," *Radio Liberty Dispatch,* November 19, 1973. Extensive excerpts of ths *samizdat* statement appear in *The New York Times,* November 17, 1973.

19. See Theodore Draper, " Détente," *Commentary,* Vol. 57, No. 6 (June 1974), pp. 25–47.

20. For example, Gus Horowitz, " Détente and World Revolution," *International Socialist Review,* Vol. 35, No. 8 (September 1974), pp. 12–19:

> The détente was brought on, to a large extent, by the Vietnam war and its consequences, which highlighted the exacerbated problems of United States imperialism. Washington had to turn to the counterrevolutionary Stalinist bureaucrats in Peking and Moscow for help in pressuring Hanoi to accept a setback. That is the way we characterize the situation, in contrast to other currents within the American radical movement who held illusions that the accords signified an advance (p. 13).

We should note that Gus Hall, representing the CPUSA, considers détente to be an advance, because he believes it reflects United States weakness and retreat.

Soviet national and international policy. He is thus skeptical of "revisionism" or perhaps wishful for the "good old days." At present he is likely to stress the danger of broad-gauge contamination of Soviet society, induced by more extensive economic and cultural contacts with the capitalists.[21] And lastly we have the Soviet "safety first" community, whose policies of military strength entail intensified Cold War as a by-product of an adequate effort to provide a military shield against all possible assaults.[22]

Enough of classification. Too much can be made of the distinctions in the abstract, but I believe that they may be analytically useful. That there are departures among the three images of détente, or that a common terminology is necessary to a productive discussion of the benefits to be expected from particular policies, I need no longer belabor. But is there overlap among the images? What is its content? And what about the relative validity of the images?

I suggest a simple diagram of three overlapping circles to help in thinking about the relation of these three images of détente.

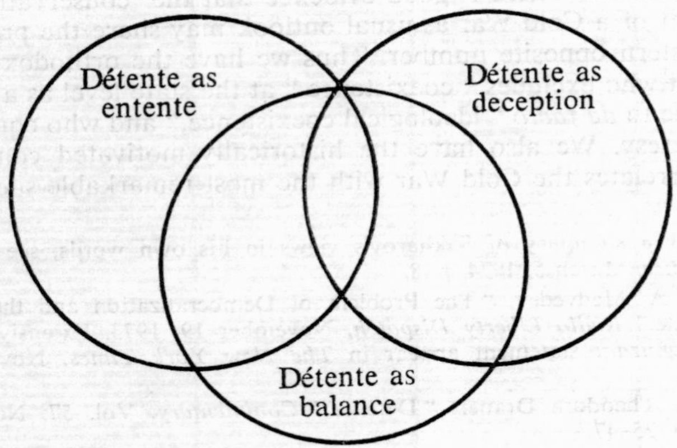

21. For a fascinating glimpse of the interplay among conservative Soviet viewpoints on détente, see the report of V. N. Iagodkin's speech to a symposium on "The Ideological Struggle in Historical Science," on June 14, 1973: *Radio Liberty Research Report,* RL 274/73 (September 5, 1973). Also, Constantin Olgin, "Arcady or Armageddon? Conflicting Views of Soviet Ideologists on the Future of East-West Relations," *Radio Liberty Dispatch,* RL 180/74 (June 14, 1974).

22. For recent analyses of the Soviet military views, see John Reppert, "Reaction of the Soviet Military Leadership to the Force Reduction Talks," *Radio Liberty Dispatch,* April 17, 1974; and Peter Kruzhin, "Grechko: 'The Danger of War Remains a Grim Reality,'" *Radio Liberty Dispatch,* RL 200/74 (July 8, 1974).

Common to all three is, first, an interest in avoiding general war between the two countries, an event that (to put it in the mildest way) is perceived as a net loss to everyone; second, a conviction that this is a rationally understandable relationship that will only be more dangerous if its real nature is obscure or misperceived by either party; third, a desire to reduce the exceedingly high material costs of the conflict relationship and employ some of the resources elsewhere; and, fourth, an interest in a stability that is threatened by some common exterior factors.

The diagram can also be used to illustrate my contention that the balance image has more in common with, or is less unacceptable to, the entente and deception images than either of these is to the other. Policies compatible with the balance image are less likely to isolate their advocates in a minority position than policies based on entente or deception images. Thus, if any change in the relationship is to be induced *through agreement*, policies based on the balance image are most likely to cause it. This image dominates in the current leadership groups of both countries; it is therefore the common ground on which the policies of each must build, if the parties are seriously concerned to maximize agreement.

I have gone to some length to portray the various premises for each image because it appears to me that each possesses a degree of validity, although I shall also argue that each is flawed.

The area of the figure which the balance image shares with the deception (but not with the entente) image is occupied chiefly by perceptions of limits to potential agreement and cooperation. If those limits do exist—born of historical momentum, of the residue of ideological commitment, and of inherent conflicts in the nation-state system—then they manifest the relative inadequacy of the first image, entente. I would argue that the " it need not be so " premise inherent in the entente image is sufficiently open to challenge that policies should not assume the answer. Policies should neither preclude the possibility of entente nor rely upon it.

Similarly, the area that the balance image shares with the entente (but not with the deception) image is occupied by perceptions of the possibility of constructive, non-zero-sum, cooperative interaction. Policies should strive to test and confirm this area. The measure of its confirmation is the measure of the flaw in the deception image.

In my view the balance image is also flawed. While it takes into account the inadequacies that both the entente and the deception images illuminate in each other, it fails to acknowledge the long-term inadequacy of trying to maintain the *status quo*. That is, it may be descriptively adequate but it falls short prescriptively.

The common threats which the U.S.S.R. and the United States confront in the projection of world and regional food, population, pollution, and energy curves mean that the constructive, non-zero-sum cooperation of the two countries is probably a requisite for survival. Cooperation must undertake the alleviation of these problems in the rest of the world, rather than at the expense of the rest of the world, if the stability that is the value most strongly served by the balance image is to be maintained. The *status quo ante* of the components of these contemporary material problems cannot be restored; thus it is impossible that the old political world can be restored, for it did not even contemplate these contemporary problems. In short, policy adequate to the longer term *must* enlarge the validity of the entente/balance overlap. It would be nice, but not nearly so critical, to reduce concurrently the validity of the deception/balance overlap.

It is within this framework of the reasonable and realistic meaning of détente that a political balance sheet of Soviet-U.S. trade should be constructed. I would summarize the conditions against which the wisdom of trade policy, as of other policies, should be assessed, in the following set of questions:

1. Does the policy avoid the increased vulnerability of either party to real or suspected threats posed by the other?
2. Does the policy imply a balance of concessions insofar as any concessions are inherent on either side?
3. Will the policy help to clarify areas of agreement and disagreement, rather than distort or obscure them?
4. Is the policy compatible with those interests that the parties manifest in common? That is, does it promise to confirm in practice areas of theoretical agreement?
5. Is there a reasonable probability of balanced, mutually perceived benefits—benefits that do not come at the expense of the other party?
6. Does the policy invite or foster entente-image attitudes and behavior?
7. Does the policy promise to reduce deception-image attitudes rather than to provoke them?
8. Insofar as it affects them, does the policy promise to alleviate rather than aggravate third-party problems that threaten international stability?

A proposal to which any of the answers to these questions is " no " should, it seems to me, be regarded with skepticism. The presumption is that it is incompatible with the realistic potential of détente

Soviet–U.S. Trade

What now can be said of Soviet-U.S. trade, its past and its future, against this background? The past can be reviewed in short order.

Table 1 underscores the familiar fact that until the past three years Soviet-U.S. trade has been negligible, regardless of the standard of assessment employed: total value, exports or imports as a percentage of total exports or imports of either side, composition relevant to the domestic needs of either side, and the like. Political circumstances account in large part for this record, of course, but an historically low level of economic complementarity between the two countries has been a contributing factor of great importance.

If we go back to the interwar period in Soviet-U.S. trade relations (Table 2), we find that while the Soviet role in United States exports and imports was insignificant, the United States role for the U.S.S.R. was at times substantial, especially as regards imports from the United States for the developing Soviet industrial economy. The disparity between Soviet exports to the United States and imports from the United States reflected then what is still true: the United States demand for Soviet export products falls far short of the Soviet demand for United States exports. If we take trade levels in the interwar years as one indicator of the potential Soviet demand for United States exports, the economic opportunity for greatly expanded United States sales to the U.S.S.R. in the future seems good. But the relationship must be a two-way street if it is to be effective and lasting. As Samuel Pisar puts it,

> The United States is not nearly as complementary a trade partner to the East as is Western Europe. On the basis of industrial capacity alone it could easily play the part of a major supplier of modern machinery to the region. What it lacks is the other basic prerequisite for an effective commercial partnership, a level of demand for the exports of East European countries sufficient to support a sizable flow of industrial imports.[23]

If we dismiss for the moment the politically inspired barriers of the postwar years (export restrictions on the sale of goods and technical data to Communist countries, Soviet restriction of the activity of United States businessmen, domestic pressure on United States companies not to "help the Communists"), the technical barriers (asymmetries of state-trading monopolies operating within a Plan

23. Samuel Pisar, *Coexistence and Commerce* (New York: McGraw-Hill, 1970), p. 75.

TABLE 1. SOME MEASURES OF RECENT SOVIET-UNITED STATES TRADE

Year	Soviet Exports to U.S. ($ million)	Soviet Exports to U.S. as % of Total Soviet Exports	Soviet Imports from U.S. ($ million)	Soviet Imports from U.S. as % of Total Soviet Imports	U.S. Exports to U.S.S.R. as % of Total U.S. Exports	U.S. Imports from U.S.S.R. as % of Total U.S. Imports
1958	26	0·6	3	0·06	0·01	0·2
1963	25	0·3	28	0·3	0·08	0·1
1964	21	0·3	163	2·1	0·6	0·1
1965	34	0·4	65	0·8	0·2	0·2
1966	47	0·5	63	0·8	0·1	0·2
1967	39	0·4	63	0·7	0·2	0·1
1968	43	0·4	57	0·6	0·2	0·1
1969	61	0·5	117	1·1	0·3	0·2
1970	64	0·5	115	1·0	0·3	0·2
1971	57	0·4	162	1·3	0·4	0·1
1972	95	0·6	542	3·7	1·1	0·2
1973	221	([a])	1,193	([a])	1·7	0·3
1974 (Jan.–Sept.)	264	([a])	417	([a])	0·5	0·3

[a] Unavailable.

Sources: *U.N. Yearbook of International Trade Statistics, 1970–71*, Table B; *U.N. Statistical Yearbook, 1973*, Table 144; United States Department of Commerce, Bureau of East-West Trade, *East-West Trade*, quarterly reports; John T. Farrell, "Soviet Payments Problems in Trade with the West," in United States Congress, Joint Economic Committee, *Soviet Economic Prospects for the Seventies* (1973), Appendix; Marshall I. Goldman, "Who Profits More from U.S.-Soviet Trade?", *Harvard Business Review*, November–December 1973, pp. 79–87. It should be noted that totals vary considerably among sources and therefore should be considered no more than crude approximations, sufficient to indicate order of magnitude. For a short discussion of why the statistics vary, see Goldman, *op. cit.*, p. 84.

TABLE 2. PRE-WORLD WAR II SOVIET-UNITED STATES TRADE
(Millions of rubles)

Year	Exports to U.S.	Total Exports	Exports to U.S. as % of Total Exports	Imports from U.S.	Total Imports	Imports from U.S. as % of Total Imports	Trade with U.S. as % of Total Trade
1918[a]	0·6	6·4	9·4	11·2	82·5	13·6	13·3
1920	0·0	1·1	–	0·8	22·5	3·6	3·4
1926/27	18·4	632·7	2·9	114·4	559·5	20·4	11·1
1927/28	21·9	620·7	3·5	147·2	741·4	19·9	12·4
1937	22·8	295·1	7·7	41·8	228·6	18·3	12·3
1940	19·2	239·7	8·0	76·1	245·5	31·0	19·7

[a] In 1913, Russian trade with North and South America is reported to have totaled 94·2 million rubles, or 3·3 percent of total Russian foreign trade.

Source: Roger Kanet, "International Transactions," in Ellen Mickiewicz, *Handbook of Soviet Social Science Data* (New York: Free Press, 1973), Tables A.1, A.2, A.3, A.4; pp. 199–201.

versus private United States companies, non-convertible currency, widely disparate marketing systems) still present a major drawback to rapid expansion. But most critical of all, the U.S.S.R. will have to sell more than vodka, furs, and specialty items in the United States if it is to get the foreign exchange necessary to purchase what it clearly needs from the United States.

One way around this obstacle might be long-term deliveries contracted in return for United States credits and United States technology (e.g., the oil and gas deals under study in both countries for the past two years). Another way might be the development of multilateral trade—which would seem to depend on substantial progress toward a convertible ruble, first among the socialist countries and ultimately with the non-socialist world.

There are serious difficulties with both of these avenues. A policy of United States underwriting of industrial development in the U.S.S.R., might lead to a " peaceful competition " that would threaten United States jobs with imports, and so cannot be expected to prosper in the environment of domestic United States politics during a time of economic hardships.[24]

The conditions for multilateralization imply Soviet acceptance of a cosmopolitan international economic system, abandonment of autarchy, and vulnerability to the international " crises of capitalism." A convertible ruble, when and if technically achievable, still runs strongly against ideological fundamentals of the Soviet outlook.

A full examination of factors that limit the prospects for expansion of U.S.-Soviet trade is beyond the scope of this analysis. It should nevertheless be clear from what has been said that limits do exist. It is evident from the experience of the past three years that within these limits substantial expansion is now taking place.

Through the 1960s—except for 1964, when the total was increased by the Soviet $110 million wheat purchase—United States exports to the Soviet Union averaged well below $100 million a year and less than half of 1 percent of United States exports. The percentage of United States exports is still below 2 percent per annum by current indications, but the absolute increase, especially since the May 1972 Summit, has been remarkable, outstripping even the more extravagant prior estimates. The 1972 total, which more than tripled that for 1971, doubled in 1973, to break the billion-dollar line for the first time and make the United States the largest non-Communist

24. See George Meany, president of the AFL-CIO, quoted in " Is U.S. Giving Away Too Much to Russia? ", *U.S. News & World Report,* September 23, 1974, pp. 68–70.

exporter to the U.S.S.R. Of course, the 1973 figure was swollen by the presumably non-recurrent Soviet grain purchase of the equivalent of one-fourth of the United States 1972 wheat crop. So far, the 1974 figures indicate a probable total trade for the year of about $1 billion.

Table 3 indicates the composition of recent United States exports

TABLE 3. COMPOSITION OF SOVIET-UNITED STATES TRADE
($ million)

SITC Category	U.S. Exports to U.S.S.R. 1971	1972	1973	1974 (Jan.–Sept.)	U.S. Imports from U.S.S.R. 1971	1972	1973	1974 (Jan.–Sept.)
Food and Live Animals	16	366	842	197	–	1	–	1
Beverages and Tobaccos	1	1	–	1	–	–	1	–
Crude Materials, excluding Fuels	27	71	78	15	16	18	12	14
Mineral Fuels	–	–	–	2	1	7	77	77
Animal and Vegetable Oils and Fats	–	2	6	–	–	–	–	–
Chemicals	38	21	17	20	1	1	2	9
Basic Manufactures	10	10	35	18	35	64	123	158
Machinery and Transport Equipment	63	62	204	151	–	–	–	1
Miscellaneous Manufactured Goods	7	9	9	10	3	3	4	3
Other	–	–	2	1	1	1	1	1
Total	162	542	1,193	417	57	95	221	264

Sources: United States Department of Commerce, Domestic and International Business Administration, *Overseas Business Reports* (January 1974), Appendix 1; United States Department of Commerce, Bureau of East-West Trade, *East-West Trade* (quarterly report for fourth quarter 1973), Appendix B, Table 4. U.S. Department of Commerce, Bureau of East-West Trade, *Export Administration Report* (quarterly report for fourth quarter, 1974), App. A, Table 5.

by SITC category. Soviet interest in United States exports focuses on agricultural products and high technology. The reasons for this are not obscure. First is the continuing uncertainty of Soviet agriculture and the likelihood of future shortfalls, which with varying degrees of urgency may be expected to prompt a demand for major food grain imports. Second is the Soviet inability, given present organization and human resources, to catch up in rapidly changing areas of high technology such as computers, complex electronic equipment, and chemicals. The present Ninth Five-Year Plan contemplates major growth and productivity increases in these fields; returns on domestic development as a consequence of various internal organizational reforms in the 1960s have been disappointing thus far.[25]

At the Washington Summit in June 1973, Nixon and Brezhnev projected a total trade over the next three years of two to three billion dollars. A general assessment from the United States Department of Commerce early in 1974 concluded:

> Long run trade projections indicate that the objective of a $2 to $3 billion U.S.-Soviet trade turnover (imports plus exports) for the next three years, expressed at the Washington Summit, is a feasible though challenging goal.[26]

Ray Cline, Director of the Bureau of Intelligence and Research of the United States Department of State, made some hypothetical projections based on the precedent of U.S.-Yugoslav trade development, in testimony before the Joint Economic Committee in July 1973. He suggested United States exports of $1·7 billion and imports of $2 billion, for a turnover of about $3·7 billion per year (3 to 3½ percent of United States foreign commerce) after "quite a few years."[27]

Apart from actual shipments, however, the roots of future expansion appear to be multiplying. Intermittent reports have indicated the possibility of a $125–300 million contract for sales of Boeing 747s to Aeroflot. New grain sales indicate a continuity of Soviet demand even in years of relatively satisfactory domestic production.

25. The Bureau of East-West Trade of the United States Department of Commerce identifies "the following categories in which the United States is competitive with other nations and which have a current import market in the U.S.S.R.:

- Machine tools for metalworking
- Aluminum hydroxide
- Lifting and loading machinery
- Electric furnaces and welding apparatus
- Products of polymerization
- Iron and steel tubes and pipes
- Textile machinery
- Excavating and leveling machinery
- Off-road tractors
- Statistical machines, including computers.

Department of Commerce, *Overseas Business Reports,* January 1974, pp. 3–4.

26. *Ibid.*, p. 8.

27. "Statement of Mr. Ray S. Cline Before the Joint Economic Committee, July 18, 1973," p. 18.

The basis for great growth of future sales to the U.S.S.R. clearly rests in the field of industrial cooperation, which the Soviet Union has been actively pressing. The furthest developed of such undertakings is the Kama River Truck Plant, whose assembly lines are scheduled to begin production in 1975. The most far-reaching in potential is the proposed collaborative exploitation of Siberian natural gas resources, drawing on United States capital and technology, with returns in kind projected over a period of twenty years or more.

The cost of the Kama River plant is estimated to reach \$3·5–4 billion, with participation by six West European countries and Japan as well as the Soviet Union and the United States. United States involvement alone amounts to more than \$300 million in long-term credits, about equally divided between the United States Government and United States private industry. Some four hundred Americans will be employed at the plant among a total of a thousand foreigners when it starts up. The projected output is 150,000 diesel trucks and buses a year, making it the largest such plant in the world.[28]

Lesser cooperative agreements now exist between Soviet ministries and enterprises and the following United States corporations, among others: Lockheed, Armco Steel, Monsanto, IT&T, and General Dynamics. Since 1972 a dozen other United States corporations have been authorized to set up offices in Moscow, including Chase Manhattan, Bank of America, First National City Bank, General Electric, International Harvester, Hewlett-Packard, and Pullman. Armand Hammer, chairman of Occidental Petroleum, whose association with the Soviet Union dates back to his personal authorization from Lenin to construct an asbestos mine in the 1920s, has signed an \$8-billion, 20-year contract to produce and trade fertilizer in the U.S.S.R. Moreover, Occidental, with two other firms, plans to develop the Yakutsk natural gas fields in eastern Siberia and to supply natural gas to the United States West Coast from there.[29]

Details on the present growth and future potential of United States exports to the Soviet Union and on Soviet-U.S. industrial cooperation are readily available and would serve no additional purpose in this paper. Let us turn to the other side of the equation: what the Soviet Union can provide that the United States needs, and what the prospects are for *two-way* growth in the flow of trade.

In 1973 the U.S.S.R.'s imports from the United States were valued

28. " Is U.S. Giving Away Too Much to Russia? ", p. 72; also *The New York Times,* January 16, 1975, p. 18.

29. Harvey D. Shapiro, " Alexei Kosygin Has a Friend at Chase Manhattan . . . ", *The New York Times Magazine,* February 24, 1974, p. 65.

at nearly $1·2 billion, while exports to the United States were valued at a little over $200 million, leaving an imbalance of more than $900 million. While this imbalance is allegedly shrinking in 1974, with larger Soviet sales and smaller purchases leading to a projected $200–300 million disparity in favor of the United States,[30] the figures still show a major obstacle to the indefinite expansion of the trade relationship.

United States imports from the U.S.S.R. have been concentrated in raw and semiprocessed materials, such as platinum and palladium (needed for catalysts in automobile air-pollution control devices), chrome ore, and diamonds. Perhaps most notable here is the very small role played by the more visible traditional Soviet exports in the consumer categories. Despite a tripling of the previous year's total, just $520,000 worth of Soviet vodka was imported to the United States in 1973; furs accounted for just over $3 million.[31] While there may be some sizable relative increases here, United States imports from the U.S.S.R. will never rest on consumer goods. The United States, rather, is newly aware of its projected shortages of raw and semiprocessed materials; the Department of Commerce has compiled a long list of such materials which the Soviet Union may have available for export.[32]

The difficulties that East European countries have encountered in their efforts to penetrate West European markets with consumer-oriented manufactured goods suggest that the growth of Soviet exports to the United States will remain confined to the raw and semiprocessed materials categories for the foreseeable future. But the U.S.S.R. has indicated an interest in exporting and may have

30. "U.S. Rates China No. 1 Red Buyer," *Denver Post,* October 25, 1974, p. 1. See Marshall I. Goldman, "Who Profits More from U.S.-Soviet Trade? ", *Harvard Business Review,* November–December 1973, pp. 79–87.

31. Department of Commerce, Bureau of East-West Trade, *East-West Trade* (quarterly report for fourth quarter 1973), Appendix B, Table 4.

32. Department of Commerce, *Overseas Business Reports,* January 1974. pp. 4–5, lists the following:

Manganese ore	Titanium sponge
Asbestos	Rhenium
Nickel	Germanium
Lead	Ferro-alloys
Steel	Rhodium
Pig iron	Chemical products
Zinc	Fiberboard
Cadmium	Sawn timber
Aluminum	Newsprint
Titanium alloys	

available specific manufactured items, such as gas-turbine hydrofoil boats, helicopters, specialized forging and pressing equipment, oil tankers and ore carriers, motorcycles, and bicycles.[33]

One key to major expansion in the first of these areas, and to Soviet competition in narrow consumer and manufactured goods areas, is probably Congressional approval of Most Favored Nation treatment for the U.S.S.R.[34] In the short term, the export of gold can be used as an expedient, but there are complex obstacles to that avenue as a more permanent solution to Soviet balance-of-payments deficits.

A Balance Sheet

The arguments in favor of and against the expansion of United States trade with the Soviet Union usually rest on one or more of the following premises and contentions.

In favor:

1. Trade increases the variety and volume of official and unofficial contacts between countries; hence, it tends to counteract or reduce suspicions, tensions, and frictions.
2. Trade must be based on agreement; therefore, it ratifies common interests, emphasizing areas of agreement rather than of disagreement.
3. Trade represents a penetration of the ideological frontiers erected by the Cold War. From the initial entry point of commercial exchange, it encourages ancillary penetration of ideas and values.
4. Trade relations, successfully developed, foster the recognition of prospects for cooperative action and even interdependence. They thus invite subsequent functional and political cooperation.
5. United States resistance to the expansion of Soviet trade would isolate the United States progressively from its West European allies and retard common approaches to international economic problems.
6. United States restraint toward Soviet Union trade expansion leaves these opportunities to other Western countries, who will willingly seize and profit from them.

33. *Ibid.*, p. 4. I am indebted to Mr. Osmond Jackson, international trade consultant, Denver, Colorado, for discussion and correspondence on the subject of commodity prospects for Soviet-U.S. trade. He is in no way responsible for views expressed in this paper, however.

34. See in this regard the statement of Mr. Ray Cline, referred to in fn. 27, *supra*, pp. 22–24.

7. Expanded U.S.-Soviet trade encourages the hand of the politically moderate "builders of socialism" among the Soviet leadership rather than protagonists of confrontation with the United States and the capitalist world.
8. Expanded U.S.-Soviet trade establishes a precedent for co-operative economic relations between socialist and capitalist countries, which makes the prospect for expanding these relations with other socialist countries difficult to resist. The promise of political correlates to such trade may be greater with Eastern Europe than with the U.S.S.R.
9. Expanded trade between the United States and the U.S.S.R. promises to encourage consumer appetites in the U.S.S.R., and subtly to shift the guns-vs.-butter pressures in the Soviet Union over the longer term. This may eventually nudge both the foreign and the domestic policy of the Soviet Union in more tolerant directions.
10. Expanded trade between the United States and the U.S.S.R. promises substantial economic advantage to the United States. Compatibility is limited, but where it is found it is significant —particularly in areas where the United States is short of raw materials and energy. Expanded trade would help to relieve United States balance-of-payments difficulties.

Against:

1. Expanded U.S.-Soviet trade, which would be of unbalanced advantage to the U.S.S.R., conflicts with the continuing objective to resist the expansion of Communist influence in the world. It is contradictory to both "feed and fight" Communism.
2. Expanded trade with the U.S.S.R. directly or indirectly increases Soviet strategic power, and there is no evidence that the U.S.S.R. will not use that power to enhance its policies of opportunistic diplomatic, political, and economic aggrandizement.
3. A more affluent U.S.S.R. is unlikely to make the Soviet leadership any less belligerent toward the non-socialist world. To the contrary, affluence would reinforce its domestic base and thus remove one effective restraint.
4. Intense economic interaction, including trade, does not necessarily lessen or preclude political and military conflict. History suggests no such relationship to be necessary.

5. Political trust will not be fostered by trade; the reverse is more likely. A relaxed political atmosphere, established by unambiguous diplomatic and military restraint on both sides, is the proper prelude for expanded economic cooperation.
6. Expanded U.S.-Soviet trade would bolster the hand of a flagrantly repressive regime in the U.S.S.R. domestically, encouraging and enabling it to withstand more resolutely the pressures for internal relaxation.
7. The illusion of substantially changed political relations and a retreat from the dangerous conflicts of the Cold War could be cultivated by expanded U.S.-Soviet trade. The domestic political consequences of that illusion would be an erosion of popular tolerance for a strong military face toward the U.S.S.R.
8. Subsequent disillusion about an artificially constructed era of false security could dangerously destabilize the real relationship between the United States and the U.S.S.R.
9. Real economic advantage to the United States from increased trade with the Soviet Union is doubtful. Reciprocity, such as payment for technology through long-term deliveries, could be unilaterally aborted by the U.S.S.R. by contriving another transformation of the international political climate.
10. Hope for political payoff from more United States economic interchange with other socialist countries is visionary. History shows that Soviet hegemony is firmly based in power differentials that will not be materially altered by minor shifts in economic relations.

Given the rough projections of a feasible growth of United States trade with the U.S.S.R., and given our view of the potential and the limitations of détente, how may we assess the relative weight of these opposing arguments? Let us take them up more or less in order.

First, it is indisputable that trade increases the volume of official contacts, and to a lesser extent that of unofficial contacts. The question is whether these contacts help to counteract or reduce suspicions and frictions. History shows they do not prevent wars. One need only look at the high volume of trade between Germany and England right up to the outbreak of war in 1914, or to U.S.-Japanese trade in 1941. The best we can say is that trade in all probability will not cause war either, and that the relative isolation of the two societies appears to have been one perpetuator, if not a cause, of misunderstanding and suspicion. As the United States has traditionally bet on the superiority of the open society to the closed, such intersocietal contact, or contamination, as may result from or be encouraged by expanded economic interchange is to be considered a social and political asset to the United States rather than to the Soviet Union. To the latter a positive payoff of these contacts lies in economically useful scientific and technical information.

Does trade promise to ratify areas of agreement rather than of conflict? Insofar as trade implies and demands cooperative behavior, it tends to establish common purposes, however limited. So long as we do not delude ourselves that it necessarily *expands* areas of agreement, or *eliminates* previously existing areas of disagreement, we can enter this characteristic on the positive side of the balance sheet for both countries.

Trade across the ideological frontier between Communism and capitalism, so far as it does increase contacts at many levels, probably encourages the ancillary penetration of ideas and values. But it would be a mistake to infer necessary political consequences. There is clear evidence that the Soviet leadership is currently taking steps to try to assure that there are none.[35]

Because trade, if it is truly perceived to be mutually advantageous economically, is self-reinforcing, and because it is facilitated or hindered by numerous social mechanisms, it encourages the regularization of processes of interaction that may apply beyond the strict economic transactions that prompted it.

It is disputable whether resistance to expanded East-West trade opportunity would place us progressively at odds with our traditional West European allies. The expansion of trade implies competition with our allies and thus some conflict too. But the history of our efforts to stimulate COCOM collaboration to prevent certain forms of economic association between these allies and the U.S.S.R. has not been conspicuously successful. It is unlikely that such a trend will reverse itself, judging from the more rapid growth of West European trade with the U.S.S.R. over the past decade. Recognition of reality seems the best policy. The Director of the Central Intelligence Agency, William Colby, has observed that the U.S.S.R. could probably get the technology that interests it in trade with the United States from Western Europe and Japan;[36] thus the argument that the United States would invite economic disadvantage

35. See Terry McNeill, "Ideological Trends and Portents: A Review of Some Recent Developments," *Radio Liberty Dispatch,* RL 322/74 (October 4, 1974).

36. Quoted from Congressional testimony in "Is U.S. Giving Away Too Much to Russia?", pp. 71–72.

without prospects for a compensating political return seems a strong one.

The assumption that trade expansion would strengthen the hand of one, presumably more attractive, Kremlin faction against another rests on the earlier assumption that such a policy would indeed divide the Soviet leadership. While there are doubtless Kremlin conservatives who would regard such interchange as a compromise of the successful policy of autarchy, there is no reason to suppose they compose a major or powerful voice today among Soviet decisionmakers, or that they are congruent with a faction that might advocate a more intolerant domestic or a more belligerent foreign policy than those who seek greater economic interchange with the West. Referring to the earlier discussion of images of détente, we might observe that proponents of dissident viewpoints have far less influence in the U.S.S.R. than in the United States.

When we turn to the prospective effect of expanded trade on United States relations with the other socialist countries, we may acknowledge the possibility that the economic precedent could be of use in the event that the U.S.S.R. were trying to foreclose such relations between its clients and the West. In most cases, however, the historical sequence has already run the other way, with Eastern Europe leading the way in commercial interchange with Western Europe. And in the case of Rumania, no appeal to consistency appears likely to relieve the Ceausescu regime of Soviet economic reprisals. We would exaggerate the direct connection between economics and politics to think so.

The technological determinist will be captivated by the encouragement of consumer pressures against traditional defense-industry claims which may be inherent in greater Soviet contact with the West as stimulated by trade. It is true that the logical connection is there, but it is rash indeed to suppose that the Ministry of Defense will be much shaken by a thirst for Pepsicola. The Soviet regime is experienced in manipulating and deflecting consumer demand, and the entrenchment of defense-industry priority is at present secure. It is not unreasonable to project long-term assistance to such pressures already at work in the now more affluent Soviet Union, where per capita national income exceeds $2300 a year; but it is dangerous or naïve to suggest that such tendencies currently have much force against the decisions of " high politics." They potentially affect the background conditions of policymaking, and their prospect for impact is indirect and long range.

Finally, the argument of potential United States economic advantage through expanded Soviet trade is two-edged; for every claim of economic advantage there is the counterargument of a measure of dependency accorded to an adversary demonstrably ready to seize an opportunity for leverage. We observe the low level of international economic involvement of both the United States and the U.S.S.R., as contrasted with that of most of the smaller nation-states of the world. Total United States foreign trade lags short of 10 percent of the gross national product, and Soviet foreign trade is closer to 5 percent. When a liberal speculation concerning the potential growth suggests that total Soviet-U.S. trade is unlikely to go beyond 3 to 3½ percent of total United States foreign exchange, it seems ridiculous to speak of the danger of any general economic dependency in either direction. When the "strategic goods" argument is raised, we may note that that argument can apply equally, despite its historically demonstrated weakness in practice, to any level of interchange. The only way to apply such a principle with certain effect is to embargo all trade whatsoever. The prospect of that was rejected even in the depths of the Cold War. It is unlikely to attract advocates in strength today in the United States, much less among alternative Western suppliers to the U.S.S.R. Then too, the strategic argument itself cuts two ways. Dependency in technology may provide a leverage as great as or greater than raw material dependency. In fact, neither side is likely to be restricted on either score.

Some of the arguments against expanding Soviet-U.S. trade have been raised above in the course of discussing their obverse sides. The importance of resisting the temptation to harbor illusions over the socio-political promise of economic cooperation has been recognized and affirmed, as it has for the vision of an Eastern Europe wrested away from Soviet hegemony through economic independence. Such illusions are inherent dangers, but we need not succumb.

The really insistent arguments against trade expansion are those that rest on (1) its presumed assistance to a repressive regime otherwise unable to maintain its iron control on expressions of dissent or liberalizing reform in the U.S.S.R., and (2) the claim of implied assistance to the growth of power in an obdurate international adversary that consistently refuses to disavow its ultimate commitment to supersede non-socialist societies.

It is unreasonable to dismiss either charge. If one is to prefer the expansion of Soviet-U.S. trade, it must be because of a claim that these negative consequences are overridden by compensating advantages. The latter, I would argue, is the case.

If the Soviet regime is to become less harsh in its domestic policy, it seems unlikely to me that such an eventuality will come about because of direct political pressures against it at home or abroad. (The latter pressures may have the opposite effect.) It will happen on a broad scale only when such measures no longer appear to an insecure leadership to be necessary to maintain its position. Even if this were not the case, it would seem presumptuous to suggest that beyond grudging, temporary, specific concessions, such as those implied in the repudiated bargain over the Jackson Amendment,[37] the United States may effectively use a trade weapon to coerce Soviet domestic change. Roy Medvedev, in his role of domestic dissident and victim of repression, has accurately pointed out that greater contact with the West, not Cold War isolation, promises the sort of environment conducive to the evolution of domestic Soviet institutions.[38]

Finally, to the question of assisting the growth of an international adversary's power, one can only argue that the marginal assistance is likely to be very small and is outweighed by the compensating advantages. It would be naïve to suggest that the sheer military power of the U.S.S.R. would be eroded were it not for United States trade and technology. History has not shown that deprivation to be a significant deterrent in the past to the growth of Soviet power. Might it not be better to pursue a balanced reduction of the mutual military threat by voluntary agreement, impelled by numerous rationally perceived factors on either side, than to continue a policy of superiority that has not worked in the past?

Looking back then to the criteria, suggested at the end of the first section of this paper, for judging the compatibility of policies with the realistic potential of détente, I think that we can summarize as follows:

Expansion of Soviet-U.S. trade need not imply an imbalance of concessions on either side; there are mutual advantages to be accrued which do not make trade a zero-sum game between the United States and the U.S.S.R. Trade negotiated thoroughly and formally may be expected to clarify rather than to obscure areas of agreement and disagreement, and need not give rise to dangerous illusions on either side. It is entirely possible that trade growth will have a self-reinforcing effect, for mutual benefits are promised, and the behavior reinforced should be of an inherently cooperative rather than conflictual nature. Because the problems faced in Soviet and United States society are not exclusive to each, or to these countries alone,

37. Joseph Albright, "The Pact of Two Henrys," *The New York Times Magazine,* January 5, 1975, pp. 16 ff.
38. Medvedev, *op. cit.*

the cooperative trade relationship *may* provide a useful precedent for pursuing further cooperative approaches to common problems not directly enmeshed in the remaining areas of conflict between them. It is to be emphasized, however, that the advantages of expanded trade do not include the direct modification of domestic structures or policies in either country, or of the very real conflict areas that continue to divide them internationally.

I can conclude that the economic prospect for substantial growth of Soviet-U.S. trade and other economic relations is good and works to the economic interest of the United States as well as of the U.S.S.R. But the extrapolation of this prospect to interdependence is visionary. There are limits in payments problems for the Soviet Union, lack of competitive Soviet goods for the United States market, and technical difficulties springing from the different economic systems. The Soviet side has a great deal to gain economically from the growth of trade with the United States, enough to make United States negotiators cautious against overly concessionary deals. The Soviet negotiators are informed and patient, but they are people who want to buy and who will eventually conclude mutually desirable contracts and abide by them.

Though the Soviet Union may achieve more immediate economic gains from expanded trade than the United States, there is little to indicate an increase in United States vulnerability to a Soviet military threat as a consequence of Soviet economic prosperity. Present military priorities in the U.S.S.R. have already discounted that prospect.[39]

When, as we must, we go beyond the economic *quid pro quo* in our balance sheet, we must conclude that trade is not going to transform dramatically or suddenly the area of severe and dangerous conflict in which the United States and the U.S.S.R. continue to be engaged. The realistically understood potential of détente stripped of illusions is sufficient to indicate that. It is equally important to recognize, however, that the consequences of trade and economic relations do " spill over " into political and social dimensions, and vice versa. We must recognize that that spill-over promises a net positive return for stable and improving Soviet-U.S. relations, but that that change will be in the background conditions against which

39. For a review of Soviet risk-taking and crisis behavior which concludes that the Soviet Union may be expected to eschew the manipulation of the " risks of war " in future efforts to shape the international milieu, see Hannes Adomeit, *Soviet Risk-Taking and Crisis Behavior: From Confrontation to Coexistence?* (London: International Institute of Strategic Studies, Adelphi Paper No. 101, 1973).

" high politics " operates. The latter determines the response to events, but the background indirectly establishes the matrix of purposes and pressures within which political decisionmakers frame and implement policy. It is thus important to try to change this background in an undramatic, evolutionary fashion. Expanded Soviet-U.S. trade can help to do this. It would be dangerous, as all illusions are dangerous, to expect more of trade expansion than this. Thus viewed, it is an asset to but no guarantee of détente.

Jeanne Kirk Laux

Intra-Alliance Politics and European Détente: The Case of Poland and Rumania*

For the first time since World War II, the Conference on Security and Cooperation in Europe (CSCE) brought the foreign ministers of every European state (except Albania) together in a single forum along with representatives from Canada and the United States. The assembled ministers in Geneva were expected, at the very least, to find ways and means to further pan-European cooperation in the economic, techincal-scientific, and cultural spheres in order to supplement bilateral arrangements and exclusive subregional groups (such as Comecon, the European Economic Community, and the Organization for Economic Cooperation and Development). If the parallel talks on Mutual and Balanced Force Reduction (MBFR) showed some success, certain observers in 1972 went so far as to foresee the creation of a Security Commission for Europe, linked to the U.N. Security Council, which might supplant NATO and the Warsaw Pact within a decade.[1]

* An earlier version of this article was prepared for delivery at the Annual Meeting of the American Political Science Association, New Orleans, September 4–8, 1973.

1. See, for example, the analyses and prescriptions of the Working Group on Security and Cooperation in Europe, "Some Institutional Suggestions for a System of Security and Cooperation in Europe," *Bulletin of Peace Proposals*, 1 (1972), pp. 73–88. For a list of major contributions to the debate over Europe's institutional future, see note 26 in Johan Galtung's article "Europe —Bipolar Bicentric or Cooperative?", *Journal of Peace Research*, 1 (1972).

Whatever significance historians will attribute to the CSCE, its convocation reflected critical changes in both European and Soviet-American relations since the mid-1960s. For many at the time, it also portended, despite the invasion of Czechoslovakia, new foreign policy opportunities for the smaller European states—especially the neutral and socialist states. Whether or not substantial changes actually result from the CSCE, I assumed that the mere possibility of such transformations and the legitimation of consultations outside the closed alliance structures should have provoked the East European policymakers to reassess the place of their state in its alliance system and in European international relations as well.

The principal question motivating this study was this: to what extent would significant changes in the external environment for policymaking be accompanied by corresponding re-evaluations in the official foreign policy doctrine articulated at home? Brodin has loosely defined official foreign policy doctrine as

> a system of normative and empirical beliefs about the international system and the role of one's own country in that system, as declared in public by the official decision-maker of that country.[2]

Did the top party leadership, in its communication about foreign affairs during the period of rapid change between Prague (1968) and the Helsinki preparatory talks for the CSCE (1972), choose to re-evaluate the capability of the state to pursue its interests or reinterpret its place in the socialist alliance system? I assumed that even in so-called closed political systems, if the new opportunities in European international relations generated by the conference proposal were regarded seriously by the leadership, these changes would be reflected in the authoritative overviews of official policy given to the political groups to which the Head of Party is deemed accountable. If so, can we differentiate between countries according to their articulated identification of the state and its international relations? Here I followed Kenneth Jowitt's suggestion that the documentation of identity references, which when taken together constitute the "political identity" of a regime, may best alert the student to qualitative policy changes within and between East European states.

2. Brodin: 1972. No assumption is made regarding the private views of speakers. To interpret the instrumental purposes of the words used, I rely only on manifest content.

What, he asks, are "the different ways in which they define the relative weight and character of the distinct but related settings within which they will operate: national, bloc, regime (inter-party), and European?"[3]

This article then represents an effort to describe systematically, by means of content analysis, the foreign affairs content of domestic speeches given by the Heads of Party and Government in two East European states—Poland and Rumania—in two time periods (1969 and 1971–1972), so as to identify any variations in the official views of the state, its place in the socialist alliance system and in European international relations. After briefly discussing the methods and procedures used and their rationale, specific expectations will be brought out and analysed in light of the findings. Generally, I expected to find strong differences between cases, given different national attributes and differences in past foreign policy behavior. I also expected to find variations in official interpretations over time, given positive developments in several sets of East–West negotiations related to German borders, Berlin, arms control, and the CSCE. But these are causal inferences and here I am able only to catalog, in descriptive fashion (but including some speculative insights), the comparative findings—over time, across nations, and between themes—on the foreign affairs content of top-leadership speeches to domestic audiences in Poland and Rumania.

Sources and Methods

From among the several sources of information about foreign affairs disseminated by the East European political elites, I have chosen to look at the general public appeals contained in top-leadership speeches made to strictly domestic audiences. By restricting attention to speeches made at home, I hoped to minimize the amount of rhetorical posturing so essential to bargaining behavior in international diplomacy. The public speech, rather than the more detailed interpretations in the press, seemed the best starting place for discovering gross variations in the official evaluation of the role of the state or the salience of alliance ties, precisely because of its ritualistic and general nature.

By domestic speeches I refer to speeches made within the borders of the state by the Head of Party or Government to an exclusively national audience. Obviously there is no such thing as an *exclusively*

3. Jowitt: 1972, p. 184.

national audience—thanks to the Foreign Broadcast Information Service monitors, if to no one else! But I have excluded all speeches (a) made outside the country, (b) made in the presence of a visiting foreign official (the many toasts, press conferences, and remarks made on provincial tours in the company of, say, a North Vietnamese official delegation) or (c) in which direct reference is made to invited foreigners (as in greetings to the attendant diplomatic corps on a ceremonial occasion).

The only controversial element here may be the decision to exclude speeches made to the Party Congresses (one Congress took place in each country during our time periods). The Party Congress, after all, is the most critical public accounting of past performance and future directions made by the party leadership to both its cadres and the mass public. But at the same time it is an accounting to the fraternal parties. The Heads of Party of many socialist states, usually including the Soviet Union, lead delegations to the Congress and are present throughout, contributing speeches on their appreciation of the host party's progress and summarizing their own party-state preoccupations. It is because of this function of international accountability that I chose to eliminate Congress speeches.

Daily media commentary is sensitive to the stimuli of recent events, while in the occasional speech leaders tend to sweep across the recent past to construct an acceptable interpretation of international politics —thus providing citizens with a safe framework in which to fit incoming events. To a degree uncommon in North America, not only diplomats but scholars and journalists cite the speeches of the Head of Party as evidence in their analyses of foreign affairs. The public speech is the most authoritative statement on foreign affairs—implicating as it does the persons of the Head of Party or Government. The norms of democratic centralism, specific to the Communist Party states, allow for discussion of policy alternatives *until* the top party organs arrive at a consensual decision. Expressions of that consensus in speeches by the Head of Party are no longer subject for debate.[4] In sum, compared with media reporting, the public speech is more inclusive, more ritualistic (i.e., stable), and more authoritative.

4. Skilling: 1968. Henry Kissinger (Kissinger: 1971, p. 30) sees the public speech as fulfilling a similar function in pluralist systems. Presidential speeches, he observed, play an "important role in laying down guidelines for the bureaucracy. The chief significance of a foreign policy speech by the President may thus be that it settles an internal debate in Washington (a public statement is more useful for this purpose than an administrative memorandum because it is harder to reverse)."

Choice of Cases

Two Warsaw Pact states, Poland and Rumania, were chosen because they differ along geopolitical, economic, and leadership lines. Briefly, Poland spent World War II under Nazi occupation, then was reformed within new and unratified borders after the war. Unassured of the basic prerequisite of sovereignty—borders—and vulnerable to West German claims for renunification, Poland was thought to appreciate the military benefits of alliance with the Soviet Union. Soviet troops are stationed on Polish territory.

Rumania, in contrast, spent much of the war as an ally of the Third Reich. Located in the southern tier of central Europe and removed from Cold War conflict centers, it no longer has Soviet troops on its territory. One may assume from the fact that Rumania was the first East European allied state to recognize the Federal Republic of Germany (FRG) in 1967, that the leadership sees little direct threat from Germany. Rumania's refusal to condone the Pact invasion of Czechoslovakia attests to the belief that its leaders see little military benefit to be gained from alliance participation.

Looking at domestic variables, we note that both Heads of Party in Poland—Gomulka and Gierek—came to power because of socio-economic unrest. A workers' rebellion in 1970 elevated Gierek into the top-leadership post. The Rumanian leader, Ceausescu, has been in power since 1965—arriving there through an orderly process of succession. Poland, more highly developed industrially than Rumania, and with a more articulate working class, is committed under Gierek to extensive social changes at home. Rumania remains very centralized with no apparent social instability.

Ceausescu has adopted a striking foreign policy posture of autonomy—taking unilateral stances on questions of Pact reform, the Israeli-Arab war, nuclear non-proliferation, German recognition, Czechoslovakia, and China. Poland has largely conformed to Soviet cues in foreign policy.

Time Frame

Two time periods were selected in order to take account of secular trends. The first time period opens with the Budapest Appeal by the Warsaw Pact in mid-March 1969, which reintroduced the security conference theme after the hiatus created by intra-alliance crises in 1968. This Appeal has been labeled by expert observers (Shulman, 1969) as a serious diplomatic proposal initiated by the Soviet Union. The period closes at the end of 1969 after the East European allies have had the opportunity to react to the proposal and formalize their positions during the Warsaw Pact meetings in October and December 1969.

The second time period (September 1971–November 1972) opens after all pre-conditions to the conference set by NATO have been met —most importantly the signature of a four-power agreement on Berlin in September 1971 and an expression of Soviet willingness to discuss MBFR. Also, bilateral negotiations between the U.S.S.R., Poland, German Democratic Republic (GDR), and the FRG settled many national security claims and thus removed immense legal political-psychological barriers to the conference. By September 1971, then, the conference proposal was no longer strictly a Soviet proposal but a generally accepted idea assumed to be realizable in the near future. The period continues through to the beginning of the multilateral preparatory talks in Helsinki in November 1972.

Choice of Source

Speeches were taken from the Foreign Broadcast Information Service's *Daily Bulletin*, a monitoring service report now published by the U.S. Department of Commerce. This choice was dictated by the fact that FBIS offers the most nearly complete coverage of media output for Eastern Europe. In contrast to, for example, Radio Free Europe reports, which digest and interpret most of their translations, or the BBC monitoring reports, which tend to collapse texts into summary reports, the *Daily Bulletin* gives the full text of the first published or broadcast report of the top-leadership speeches. Thus if the national or provincial press, the radio, or the television in Poland (or Rumania) *itself* gave the full text of a speech, it will be found in FBIS.

From FBIS I could also induce the apparent universe of speeches. Examining the table of contents of every FBIS issue, I recorded all references to all speeches made to domestic audiences—including those that could not be coded because they had been either summarized in the third-person singular or reduced to " extensive excerpts " by the East European media. We do, however, know the date, place, speaker, and occasion of every speech made by Heads of Party or Government during the two time periods.

The Sample

The universe of domestic speeches for the combined time periods (23 months) was 121. Every speech for which a full text was available was coded, giving a non-random sample of 88 speeches for the two states—48 for Rumania and 40 for Poland. Standard content analysis procedures were followed.[5] The non-random sample afforded a much more accurate impression of the foreign affairs messages communicated to the Rumanian public than of those communicated to the Polish public. Not only does the Rumanian sample represent 93·7 per cent of all speeches made during the two time periods, but there is much less division of labor (so to speak) in Rumania. Very few persons *besides* Ceausescu made any public speeches. The Foreign Minster virtually never spoke to domestic audiences, and the Prime Minister did so only once or twice in the entire 23 months covered. Only a very few celebratory occasions, such as Armed Forces Day, are reserved for the pertinent official—in this instance, the Minister of Defense.

In sharp contrast, in Poland, both under Gomulka (1969) and under Gierek (1971–1972), it is common in any given month to find as many as five party officials making public speeches that received at least a short summary in the press. For example, during one week in April 1969, five Politburo members addressed five separate audiences. The bulk of these speeches did not—judging by the summary—make reference to foreign policy issues. There is thus little risk of bias in my analyses of foreign policy content, although there is a risk of distortion in my discussion of the relative salience of audience types (see below, footnote 7). In order to approximate equivalence in the amount of content coded for the two countries, I included speeches made by both the Head of Party and the Head of Government in Poland—the non-random sample for Poland represents 54·8 percent of all their speeches.

Differences in leadership style contributed to make the foreign affairs content communicated orally to Polish audiences more elusive than that to Rumanian audiences. Especially under Gierek, numerous encounters with occupational or regional party groups were

5. A simple random sample of the 88 speeches (*n*-3) was coded both by myself and by a research assistant, and the two codings were then compared to ascertain the degree of intercoder reliability in terms of percentage agreement. Later a second reliability test was made to check for *intra*-coder reliability (consistency of a single coder over time). In all instances test results were satisfactory.

For details on reliability tests, coding procedures, and the text of the code sheet, see the earlier version of this study "Intra-Alliance Politics and the European Security Conference: The Case of Poland and Romania" delivered at the 1973 Annual Meeting of the A.P.S.A. in New Orleans. I would like to express thanks to Michael Kelly, M.A. candidate at the University of Ottawa, for his assistance with coding.

characterized by the party leader as working discussions and thus did not generate the fanfare of a formal speech or full media coverage. Characteristically, on his visit to the Kosciuszko Foundry in 1971, Gierek explained: " I did not come here to make speeches. I would like to see your working conditions and talk about your problems." We cannot know whether he actually offered his view on external politics as well. Equally characteristically, Ceausescu rarely made any public appearance without an accompanying speech, which was always relayed in full by the media to the nation. For example, after a 1969 visit to seven townships in thirty-six hours, the full text of all seven speeches (despite their essentially redundant message content) was preserved in the press as well as in his bound collected speeches.

Findings

The code sheet was designed to permit both descriptions of subject matter and summaries of statements of evaluation and identification in domestic speeches. Section I began with descriptive information such as time, date, speaker, location, audience, and occasion. Section II described the subject matter by measuring the column inches of FBIS text and the column inches of foreign affairs content—then calculating a percentage. In the remaining coding sections I sought to summarize the foreign affairs content according to categories that would allow me to determine (a) variations over time and between nations in the official evaluations of the international political situation; (b) the state's relationship to the Soviet Union and to the international socialist system; (c) linkages to extra-socialist states; and (d) the capability of the state to pursue its objectives (autonomously or only with outside support).

The Subject Matter—Foreign Affairs

Lacking hypotheses from the academic literature on the national dissemination of information about foreign affairs in Eastern Europe, I began my inquiry with three intuitive expectations:

Expectation 1: Rumania, pursuing a more flamboyant foreign policy than Poland, should communicate more about foreign affairs at home.

Expectation 2: Over time, Poland should reduce the amount of foreign affairs content given leadership change in response to domestic crisis.

Expectation 3: All speakers should communicate more, including more of foreign affairs content, to party organizations than to other audiences, since direct accountability is to the party.

Looking at the total sample over both time periods, I found Expectation 1 confirmed in that 93 percent of all Rumanian speeches coded actually contain some foreign affairs content, as compared with 70 percent of all Polish speeches. The only exception, in 1969, is in terms of the total column inches of foreign affairs content considered as a share of total column inches of text. Here the two states are equivalent, although in the second period Rumania ranks first for this measure as well. Generally, the Rumanian leadership treated more of its audiences to some analysis of foreign affairs and, as a proportion of each speech, to a more substantial analysis than did the Polish leadership.[6] Broken down into the two time periods, the summary figures (rounded) are shown in Table 1.

TABLE 1: COMPARATIVE FOREIGN AFFAIRS CONTENT OF TOP-LEADERSHIP DOMESTIC SPEECHES, POLAND AND RUMANIA

Item	*1969*		*1971–1972*		*Totals*	
	Poland	*Rumania*	*Poland*	*Rumania*	*Poland*	*Rumania*
Percentage Share of Speeches with Foreign Affairs Content	60%	100%	73%	89%	70%	93%
Number of Speeches with Foreign Affairs Content	N=10	N=16	N=30	N=27	N=40	N=43
Average Share of Foreign Affairs Content per Speech	14%	20%	16%	18%	13%	21%
Overall Share of Foreign Affairs Content	19%	19%	14%	18%	15.5%	18.4%
Number of Column Inches of Foreign Affairs Content	N=555	N=890	N=1618	N=2404	N=2173	N=3294

6. Because the sample of speeches used in this study is not random, significance tests are not appropriate. It can be pointed out, however, that for Rumania the *observed* number of speeches with foreign affairs content is higher than the *expected* number in both periods.

Looking at changes over time in the Polish case, we see that although the overall share of foreign affairs content diminished in 1971–1972, the Polish leadership referred to foreign affairs questions in more of its public speeches and offered a more substantial discussion than in 1969. Whether Expectation 2 is fulfilled depends on the proper definition of "more" for public communication—more numerous exposures? more substantial ones? If Gierek dealt publicly with a larger share of socio-economic issues, overall, than Gomulka did in 1969, it is nonetheless clear that within each speech, and in 73 percent of all speeches, the Polish leaders were drawing more attention to foreign policy questions, especially (from impressionistic readings) to their successful negotiations with West Germany.

In order to assemble data to explore Expectation 3—that leaders in both states would communicate more, including more of foreign affairs content, to party organizations than to other publics—we cross-tabulated categories on Audience Types and on Subject Matter. The summary figures can be found in Table 2, where any share larger than 20 percent has been italicized. For both states, in both time periods, party-related political organizations (Audience Types 3 and 4) are the preferred public—in terms of receiving the largest share of overall text communicated by the top leaders. The expectation that leaders in both states would likewise communicate the largest share of foreign affairs content to these audiences, to whom they are formally deemed to be accountable, is also confirmed if we look at the combined figures for the two time periods.

A closer examination of Table 2, however, suggests several interesting insights into the pattern of public communication about foreign affairs in Rumania and Poland. While in Poland the political organizations at the national level always received more than half the total of general and foreign affairs content, in Rumania the pattern is somewhat different.[7] In the first period, attention (in terms of overall share of text) is fairly evenly divided between National Political

7. Here we face a bias in the non-random sample. It is clear from my knowledge of the universe of speeches that the Polish media favor (tend to reprint in full) more speeches made in the capital than made in the rest of the country, and more speeches to party groups than to occupational groups. In 1971–1972 we are missing 14 of the 16 speeches to occupational groups, and 7 of the 11 speeches to regional party groups, made outside the capital. Obviously, had we been able to obtain the full texts of these speeches and thus to calculate their total column inches for inclusion in Table 2, the salience of occupational groups to the new Polish leadership in the second period would appear much greater. As mentioned in my earlier discussion of the sample used, however, the missing data are not presumed to affect seriously my analyses of foreign affairs content.

Organizations, Occupational Groups, and Town Meetings. Citizens at provincial town meetings received the largest share of all foreign affairs content communicated in 1969—a disproportionate 36 percent. This leads us to infer the influence of two factors. The upcoming Tenth Party Congress (August 1969) may explain the number of speeches made in the towns, but it is more likely that the exceptional share of foreign affairs content can be explained by leadership fears of Soviet invasion. Ceausescu had created armed peoples' militia late in 1968 as a dramatic response to the invasion of Czechoslovakia, and by spring was engaged in tense bargaining with the Soviet Union to resist pressures for joint Warsaw Pact maneuvers on Rumanian soil. By the second period, the two most salient audiences are National Political Organizations and Occupational Groups.

If the Rumanian leader devoted exceptional attention to foreign affairs when speaking to town meetings owing to the exceptional circumstances of 1968–1969, a more general pattern of "favoring" certain audiences with more than their expected share of foreign affairs content reveals itself in both states when the columns in Table 2 summarizing both time periods are compared. That is, the correspondence between the share of overall text received by an Audience Type (e.g., 14 percent for Mobilization Meetings in Poland) and its share of foreign affairs content (24 percent) is not perfect. Certain audiences receive more foreign affairs content than would have been predicted by their presumed overall salience.

In both Poland and Rumania, the top leaders favor the citizenry attending Traditional/Celebratory occasions, Mobilization Meetings, or, in Rumania, Town Meetings (a rare phenomenon in Poland) with an unexpectedly large share of messages about foreign affairs.[8] Conversely, those audiences most salient in the general distribution of political symbols—National Political Organizations or Occupational Groups—receive a disproportionately large share of messages relating to domestic issues. My observation that the general public, presumed not to play a direct role in elaborating the party's program, receives

8. Thus in speeches on traditional/celebratory occasions, the Polish leaders communicated 6 percent of their total public speech texts. *Ceteris paribus*, we might expect 6 percent of foreign affairs content to be communicated to that same type of audience. In fact, the observed figure is 7 percent or + .17 above our indifferent expectation. In Rumania, foreign affairs content communicated to the same audience type was + .50 above expectation (based on its share of overall speech content). At mobilization meetings in Poland, foreign affairs content is + .71 above expectation; in Rumania, + 3.50. Town meetings in Rumania received + .33 more than their expected share of foreign affairs content.

TABLE 2. COMMUNICATION OF FOREIGN AFFAIRS CONTENT IN POLAND AND RUMANIA, BY AUDIENCE
(All columns total 100%, allowing for rounding errors)

	Percent of Total Text[a]						*Percent of Foreign Affairs Content*[a]					
	Poland			*Rumania*			*Poland*			*Rumania*		
Audience Type	*1969*	*1971/2*	*Both*	*1969*	*1971/2*	*Both*	*1969*	*1971/2*	*Both*	*1969*	*1971/2*	*Both*
1. Traditional/Celebratory	11	4	6	12	1	4	6	8	7	14	3	6
2. Town Meetings	—	3	2	*22*	8	12	—	1	·05	*36*	9	16
3. Political Organizations: National	*63*	*66*	*65*	*31*	*49*	*44*	*53*	*56*	*55*	19	*44*	*37*
4. Political Organizations: Regional/Municipal	—	11	8	12	3	5	—	18	10	16	3	7
5. Occupational Groups	7	3	4	*24*	*39*	*35*	—	4	3	18	*29*	*25*
6. Mobilization Meetings	19	13	14	—	2	2	*41*	13	*24*	—	13	9

[a]Measured in column inches.

a disproportionate share of foreign affairs content suggests an interesting conclusion. This pattern of public speaking implies that the Communist party-state leaders use foreign affairs for legitimizing purposes—seeking to identify the party with the nation-state, or to use themes of nationalism or external threat for support-building functions among the general populace.

Evaluation of the International Political Situation

In rationalizing the choice of two time periods above, I emphasized the shift to detente from 1969 to 1971–1972. That is, given favorable progress in several sets of East-West negotiations, the international political situation was by 1971 propitious for conciliatory East-West interstate relations. Did the East European leadership choose to convey to domestic publics an appreciation of this changing international political situation? I looked for a general assessment of the state of the world—a self-conscious identification of threats, a positive-negative interpretation of the environment for policy. It was my expectation that the evaluation of the international political situation would become more positive for each state over time, although Rumania's evaluation would always be more positive than Poland's. The second portion of this expectation derives both from intuition that the less conformist alliance partner would minimize external dangers so as to deny the need for cohesion and from recognition of Poland's more sensitive strategic location.

In coding, I could infer from each speech a single evaluative assertion about the degree of relative threat or promise in the international situation. Each abstracted assertion was assigned a score based on a nine-point scale ranging from +4 (conditions are very positive) to −4 (danger persists, vigilance is needed). By combining the scores assigned to each speech we arrived at a composite score for each time period which expresses the extent of pessimism or optimism about the international political situation communicated in public by the Polish and Rumanian leaders. Evaluations of the international political situation were shown to be relatively more positive in the second period than in the first in both states. Our expectation over time was thus confirmed, but that between cases was not. When Rumanian scores were combined, they yielded a composite score of −5 in the first period; changing to a more optimistic +11 in the second period. The shift in Poland, however, was more dramatic—the score moving from a composite score of −8 in the first period to +18 in the second. Thus the Polish leadership during 1971–1972 presented to its people a highly optimistic view of the world, more so than in Rumania. Ceausescu constantly qualified his general evaluations of improving relations with a cautionary note—for example, warning that all dangers had not yet receded. Because his evaluations of international conditions were couched in very general terms, there is no way to confirm or disprove the intuition that the Rumanian leader's warnings of danger refer to fear of Soviet, rather than Western, intentions.

Generally, we found that both the Polish and the Rumanian leaders communicated their appreciation of an increasingly positive international situation to their domestic publics. What then has been the consequently of détente for leadership interpretations of the place of their state in the socialist alliance system?

Relationship to the International Socialist System

Almost without exception, Communist Party leaders ritually refer to their cooperation, collaboration, or developing relations with the socialist community. But which socialists?

Expectation 1: Based on observation of external behavior, Poland should refer to collaboration with the Soviet Union more often than Rumania in each time period.

Expectation 2: Poland should refer to the regional alliances, CMEA and the Warsaw Pact, more often than Rumania in each time period.

Expectation 3: Rumania should refer to developing relations with all socialist states and to all workers' parties more often than Poland.

In interparty relations among the Communist party-states, Rumania has acted as mediator between China and the U.S.S.R. and has consistently protested party meetings at which the Chinese interpretation of Marxism-Leninism was condemned. Thus in Expectation 3 I assumed that Rumania would opt for the most catholic expression of solidarity—thereby avoiding implied obligations to apply a prefabricated version of Marxism-Leninism in its own policymaking.

In Table 3, summarizing the results, I find my expectations largely confirmed. Polish leaders singled out the Soviet Union in 71 percent of all speeches, while Rumania did so in only two instances (or 5 percent) for the two time periods. Poland also referred to the regional economic and military alliances more regularly and added, in three instances, policy recommendations for further strengthening the Warsaw Pact. Only once did Rumania suggest strengthening relations among Pact nations. Of two other policy recommendations, one suggested revision for the purpose of perfecting relations (implying dissatisfaction) and the other advised dissolution of NATO and the Pact simultaneously. Rumanian disapproval of the Brezhnev doctrine of socialist state relations was expressed in the insistence that the Pact was intended to defend against " imperialist " threats (not counterrevolution within socialist states).

TABLE 3. RELATIONSHIP TO THE INTERNATIONAL SOCIALIST SYSTEM

Did the speaker refer to cooperation, collaboration, or developing relations with 1 or 2–6, or both? [a]

Item	Poland			Rumania		
	1969	*1971/72*	*Both*	*1969*	*1971/72*	*Both*
0. No Reference	—	14	11%	—	—	—
1. U.S.S.R.	83	68	71%	6	4	5%
2. Neighboring Socialist States	—	14	11%	13	13	13%
3. CMEA Member States	67	41	46%	44	29	35%
4. Warsaw Pact States	67	23	32%	19	—	8%
5. All Socialist Countries	50	45	46%	100	88	98%
6. All Communist/Workers' Parties	17	9	11%	50	54	53%
Total Speeches with Foreign Affairs Content	$N=6$	$N=22$	$N=28$	$N=16$	$N=24$	$N=40$

[a] Each item was coded once per speech, if present. Figures in the table thus refer to the percentage of all speeches wherein reference was made, e.g., to collaboration with the U.S.S.R.

For those familiar with Rumania's elaborate statements to external audiences in favor of revising the Pact, the paucity of references at home may be surprising. Two considerations come to mind. First, rarely are specific foreign policy issues elaborated in public appeals. Second, the nature of a ritualistic appeal should be remembered. Ritual is created through repetition, gaining power through reinforcement over time. The very absence of a theme from a ritualistic litany can be significant.

Expectation 3 was also fulfilled, since we see from Table 3 that references to *all* socialist states are present in nearly every Rumanian speech but in just over half of the Polish speeches. Looking at the Rumanian statements in context, we often found that an appeal for cooperation with, for example, CMEA would be somewhat downplayed by immediate reference to all-socialist cooperation. Ceausescu's speech to the citizens of Tirgoviste (July 22, 1969) will illustrate:

> We are also determined to develop relations of many-sided cooperation with CMEA member countries, yet at the same time we want to develop relations with all the socialist countries. . . .

The relative weight given to different characterizations of the socialist system does not alter significantly from the first period to the second. Variation across cases is clear; variation across time is largely absent. The changing European political context does not, in the 1969–1972 time span under study, appear to have provoked re-evaluations of intra-socialist relations by either Poland or Rumania. Rather it may be assumed that the sharply different characterizations reflect more permanent differences in national attributes, as suggested in the explanation of our choice of cases, above.

East-West Relations

In discussing intra-socialist relations, we saw that the state (Poland) referring most frequently to collaboration with the Soviet Union referred less frequently to collaboration with the wider socialist community, and vice versa. It is our broad assumption that the centrality of the Soviet Union and the Soviet alliances should also vary inversely with the amount of attention paid to non-socialist state actors. Two categories in the code sheet were intended to bring out leadership evaluations of relations with non-socialist states—one on East-West relations, in which we looked for one assertion per speech in which the development of extra-socialist relations was advocated, and another in which each approving or disapproving reference to a state *by name* was recorded to identify partner preferences from among the entire set of European states, socialist and non-socialist.

We look first at general advocacy of East-West relations:

Expectation 1: Advocacy of East-West Relations will be more frequent for Rumania than for Poland.

Expectation 2: Advocacy of East-West Relations should increase for both states over time.

The first expectation is strongly confirmed. In summary, the share of speeches promoting East-West relations (referred to in East European jargon as relations with " states regardless of social systems" or "with an order different from ours") for each state was:

	1969	*1971–1972*	*Combined*
Rumania	87%	83%	85%
Poland	66%	36%	43%

Expectation 2 is not fulfilled. If the drop in the Rumanian case is negligible, it is clear that in 1971–1972, even with the European security conference considered increasingly likely and negotiations with a Western state (Germany) having succeeded, the Polish leadership did not generalize these developments into advocacy of further East-West contacts in Europe.

Despite the unexpected finding that Polish leaders did not intensify their support for general East-West relations over time, I held to the original expectations outlined before actual coding began in order to assess the more specific references made to single East, West, or neutral states.[9]

Expectation 1: Rumania should refer with approval to more non-socialist states than Poland, but both states should increase references to non-socialist states over time.

Expectation 2: Poland should refer favorably to the U.S.S.R. and its socialist neighbours, Czechoslovakia and the GDR, more often than Rumania. (Note that the general ritual references to collaboration with the U.S.S.R., coded earlier, are not double-coded here.)

Expectation 3: Poland should refer more favorably to the Federal Republic of Germany in the second period (after engaging in bilateral negotiations) than in the first.

Expectation 1 was confirmed. Rumania paid more attention by name to non-socialist states in each time period. For the combined time periods 67 percent of all positive Rumanian references were to non-socialist states as compared with 22 percent of all such Polish

9. Poland, it appears, was more inclined to single out states for approval or disapproval by name (a total of 158 approving references in 382 column inches of foreign affairs text as compared with 51 references by Rumania in 607 column inches of foreign affairs content). This is the only coding category where the speech is not the context unit. Here I was interested in locating all positive references and then in calculating the relative share for the non-socialist actors.

references. Lest any reader jump to simple pro-Western conclusions regarding Rumanian official rhetoric, the results also demonstrate that 100 percent of the negative evaluations (22) chastized the United States either for the war in Vietnam or, on two occasions, for support given to the Greek junta. Over time, each state confirmed my expectation by increasing its positive references to non-socialist states —Poland from 13 to 24 percent of all positive references, Rumania from 57 to 70 percent.

In expressing bilateral partner preferences, rather than more general characterizations of the socialist alliance, it might be asked whether Poland singled out the iron-triangle states as do so many observers of East European international relations. Poland conforms to Expectation 2 in that the U.S.S.R., the GDR, and Czechoslovakia account for some 71 percent of all approving references in the two time periods, while for Rumania six references to these three states make up just 12 percent of the total favorable mentions by Ceausescu of all states.

How does the characterization of West Germany in official Polish rhetoric vary over time after the intervening twenty months during which border questions were negotiated with Bonn? Positive mention of the FRG government went up from 2 to 5—a decrease in percentage terms. Yet we see that negative evaluations of the FRG dropped from 12 in the first period (66 percent of all negative references) to none in 1971–1972. Expectation 3 is thus effectively fulfilled.

From 1969 to 1971–1972, then, successful bilateral East-West negotiations and a widening acceptance of pan-European negotiations did seem to be reflected in an increase in positive references to non-socialist European states made by the Heads of Party or Government, when speaking to home audiences about foreign affairs. My impression that the leadership was willing to convey to internal groups a positive view of cooperative relations outside ideological boundaries is reinforced by the introduction, in the second period, of positive references to two subregions—Scandinavia and the Balkans.

Rhetorical promotion of cooperation within a Scandinavian or Balkan (or, for Hungary, Danubian) framework had been used symbolically in elite writings and speeches in the period prior to the Czechoslovak crisis, but it was vigorously denounced as being anti-Soviet, along with all theories of small-state solidarity, by the official press in most Warsaw Pact countries in the period following the invasion. Now we find renewed references to these subregions, references that were not simply made in passing (in either case), but that were developed, as when First Secretary Gierek told the Szczecin Voivodship party conference:

> We also seek to promote economic and political cooperation with our Scandinavian neighbors. This is because constitutional differences should no longer be an obstacle to economic, cultural and scientific cooperation and to joint peace initiatives in Europe.

He continued to underscore the strategic importance of the Baltic Sea to Poland (November 17, 1971). The Baltic region seems to include, in Polish rhetoric, the U.S.S.R., the GDR, Poland, and the four largest Scandinavian states (not Iceland).

Similarly, Rumania's promotion of the Balkan subregion groups together Warsaw Pact, NATO, and non-aligned (militarily) states—Albania and Yugoslavia. On two occasions permanent institutions were recommended (a bit optimistic given the divergence of political systems represented and Albania's refusal even to take part in the security conference). Both the Balkan and the Baltic or Scandinavian references, in the fourteen months prior to the Multilateral Talks, expressed to domestic groups the acceptability of intensifying relations between members of opposing alliances, with a very important difference in degree between Poland and Rumania.

The Role of the State

Faced with the prospect of engaging in multinational bargaining on substantive questions in the CSCE, did the leadership attempt to give domestic groups a general assessment of national possibilities—explaining the need for socialist solidarity to protect acquired interests, or alternatively suggesting the importance of national interests? In other words, did the top party spokesmen emphasize dependence on others or the ability of the state to achieve its goals autonomously? In all speeches with foreign affairs content, some evaluation of the role of the state in international affairs was offered. In many instances, however, the speaker sought to strike a balance: although the strength of socialism lay in the efforts of his nation's working class, " at the same time " it should not be forgotten that the framework for national achievements had been created by ties to the fraternal socialist states! This ambivalence is indicated in Table 4 by the coding (0) Balanced Assertion. To code a speech either (1) National Sovereignty or (2) Proletarian International Solidarity, key words were mandatory—such words as "primarily" or "main guarantee"—indicating the preeminence of either self-determination or international solidarity in the speaker's assessments of the state's policymaking capabilities. Thus ritual references to cooperation, such as those already used to evaluate the relationship to the socialist system, did not suffice.[10]

It was my expectation that Rumania should express the National Sovereignty theme more frequently than Poland, but that both states should tend toward expressions of sovereignty over time. Summarizing the findings, we see in Table 4 that Rumania expressed the National Sovereignty theme more frequently—indeed Polish leaders *never* communicated an impression of self-reliant capabilities during either time period.

TABLE 4. SOVEREIGNTY AND/OR SOLIDARITY?
(All columns sum to 100%)

Item	*Poland* 1969	*Poland* 1971/72	*Poland* Both	*Rumania* 1969	*Rumania* 1971/72	*Rumania* Both
0. Balanced Assertion	16.7%	40.9%	35.7%	56.3%	41.7%	47.5%
1. National Sovereignty	—	—	0.00	31.3%	58.3%	47.5%
2. Proletarian Internationalism	83.3%	59.1%	64.3%	12.4%	—	5.0%
Total Speeches with Foreign Affairs Content	$N=6$	$N=22$	$N=28$	$N=16$	$N=24$	$N=40$

Ceausescu asserted sovereign capabilities for his country in 47.5 percent of all speeches, as for example on November 3, 1971: "International cooperation is of great significance . . . but the *essential, decisive* factor is the creative efforts of the working people in our country."

In both time periods, the Rumanian leader reinforced the impression of a national alternative in international affairs by including a litany of principles critical to policy:

> At the base of our foreign policy are the principles of the equality of rights for all states, respect for sovereignty and

10. Coders first skimmed the entire foreign affairs text, making marginal note of all sentences relevant to the theme, and then collapsed these into a single abstracted sentence that best summarized the evaluation for the speech as a whole. Later these abstracted sentences were coded (1) National Sovereignty, (2) Proletarian International Solidarity, or (0) Balanced Assertion.

> national independence, noninterference in internal affairs, and respect for the right of each people to decide freely on their economic and social development without outside interference. (July 13, 1969).

At times Ceausescu applied these normative principles to relations among the socialist states; at other times to East-West relations in order to assure listeners that Rumania would not be exploited in cooperation with unequal partners; and at still other times to relations with the Third World in order to insist that Rumania would not itself take advantage of other nations' weaknesses. For this reason, and because the principles are of a high level of generality, coders were instructed to note their presence but not to rely on the " List of Principles " to infer sovereignty. Yet, as evoked in 75 percent of all speeches in 1969 and 83·4 percent of all speeches in 1971–1972, the principles reinforce my impression that independent options in international relations were officially interpreted to domestic elites as being both proper and possible.

Polish emphasis is quite contrary altogether. Solidarity assertions were abstracted from more than half the speeches. Several examples of these assertions give the flavor of official Polish rhetoric:

> All our achievements, including our growing prestige in the world, are the results of our friendship and alliance with the Soviet Union. . . . (May 27, 1972)
>
> The foundation of our foreign policy is our friendship, alliance and unity of action with the Soviet Union and the other fraternal countries of the socialist community. This creates the possibilities for intensifying our development and gives us permanent guarantees for our security. . . . (February 27, 1972)

Looking for changes over time which fulfill the second part of the expectation, we see that the Rumanian leader increased the share of National Sovereignty assertions in 1971–1972 and dropped any references to the benefits of alliances which were not then qualified with equally strong national affirmations (and thus coded as (0)). For Poland, which never asserted unqualified national capabilities, my expectation should have been formulated more cautiously. Had I looked merely for a decline in assertions of solidarity, then I would have found support in the fact that there was a drop to 59·1 percent in the theme. Movement away from extreme protestations of impotence to a balanced characterization of capabilities in 40·9 percent of all 1971–1972 speeches seems significant in this case.

Summary of Findings and Implications

Let us return to the original assumption motivating this study—that the changing external environment for policymaking, especially the likelihood of multinational negotiations on substantive East-West issues (at the CSCE), should have particular impact on the small states belonging to the socialist alliance. Impact, as defined in this study, refers to changes in the official evaluation of national capabilities and intra-alliance relationships offered by Heads of Party or Government to domestic audiences. Having analyzed the content of all available speeches in two selected time periods for two states—Rumania and Poland—according to categories presumed to tap relationships among socialist states, extra-socialist linkages, and appreciations of the international political situation, can we conclude that there were variations either across cases, across time, or between themes?

Clearly, there are strong differences between cases. These differences not only are found in comparing results for individual categories, but are strengthened by the reinforcing linkages between themes in each case. Let us pull together some of the patterns found for each state.

We saw that, in their characterization of intra-socialist relationships, the Polish leaders gave predominant attention to the Soviet Union—singled out in 71 percent of all speeches. The centrality of the Soviet Union in ritual descriptions of collaboration with the socialist community was reinforced when we found that the Soviet Union accounted for more than half of all favorable references to individual states by name. And if we added favorable references to Poland's neighbors—the GDR and Czechoslovakia—the impression of a narrow conception of desirable relationships expressed to exclusively domestic audiences was strengthened. The centrality of the Soviet Union in the alliance correlated inversely with references (in bilateral preferences) to non-socialist states, as well as with general assertions advocating East–West relations in Europe. Finally, looking at official evaluations of national capability to achieve objectives, we observed that the predominance of the Soviet Union in bilateral and intra-alliance relationships correlated with depreciation of national capabilities (i.e., assertions of reliance on others for security) as well as domestic achievements in 64·3 percent of the 28 speeches coded for foreign affairs content.

The profile that emerges in the Rumanian case is markedly different when we put together the findings from different categories. In his official characterization of intra-socialist relations, Rumania's leader gave overwhelming priority to developing relations with all fourteen socialist states (in 98 percent of the speeches) and inattention to the Soviet Union (5 percent)—a catholic interpretation of alliance which coincided with a heavy emphasis on the need for East–West relations (in 85 percent of all speeches) and a special attentiveness to non-socialist European nations in favorable references. Finally, the Rumanian leadership, in 95 percent of all speeches, either offered a balanced assessment of national capabilities versus alliance dependencies or clearly asserted the right and ability to engage in an autonomous pursuit of national objectives. Thus, in both cases, internal consistency among themes builds up a contrasting summary description of official foreign policy doctrine communicated to domestic publics in the two states.

I have also posited the broad assumption that the different nature of the international environment in the two time periods (particularly the widening support in the second period for a pan-European conference) should lead to shifts in leadership interpretations of intra-alliance relations and the role of the state over time. Changes in content across time are indeed documented in this study, although confidence in any conclusion as to their real importance is mitigated because of the small share of total speeches available for coding in the Polish case.

Over time, we found that for both states the characterization of its relationship to the socialist system remained basically the same. To my surprise, general advocacy of East–West relations also declined somewhat in both cases. Yet, on three other items, both states changed dynamically in the same positive direction: both saw the conference as being more likely in the second period; both gave a much more positive assessment of the international political situation; and both increased the proportion of favorable references to non-socialist actors. Regarding extra-socialist linkages, we also saw the introduction of references to pluralist (socialist–non-socialist) regional groupings (Balkans and Scandinavia) by both states and, in Poland, the dramatic elimination of negative references to Germany in 1971–1972. The composite picture of shifts over time shows change most clearly in the realm of extra-socialist relations and in interpretations of a propitious international situation.

A study founded on descriptive content analysis is not intended to provide bases for causal inference.[11] The changes that we have

11. There is persistent disagreement in the methodological literature as to whether content analysis is a suitable technique for hypothesis testing. Clearly its *principal* utility is, as Bernard Berelson and others point out, as a summarizing procedure for unmanageable amounts of material and thus as a data generation technique. But Berelson also insists on the importance

documented in official interpretations of intra-alliance politics over time may well derive from internal leadership changes rather than from external changes. Strong differences noted between the two nations persisted in both time periods and doubtless take their origin in more permanent differences in national attributes.

But the data produced in this study allow us to affirm that the official foreign policy doctrines—the evaluations of the role of the state and its relationship to the alliance made by the top party leadership to groups at home—are clearly not identical in the two cases summarized here. This set of evaluative references (what role for the state; what relationship to the socialist community; what contacts outside the alliance) would seem to provide an operational definition for the concept of political identity promoted by Kenneth Jowitt as a means of classifying individual East European states and, over time, of sensitizing the student to subtle changes in political identities, so that he need not leap to conclusions of system-crisis at each instance of non-conformist behavior.[12]

of creating formal hypotheses, translating these into indicators that are used to create the content-analysis categories and that then constitute the test for the hypothesis. Alexander George, on the other hand, contends that content analysis is an inappropriate technique for hypothesis testing. R. E. Mitchell has given the most intelligent discussion of the circular methodology and consequently the deceptive results obtained when hypotheses are "tested" through content analysis. His key caveat should be recalled: Since the content-analysis is of materials that have not been produced in response to structured stimuli, the information available is typically incomplete with regard to the dimensions being measured.

12. Although content analysis is decidedly tedious, students of comparative foreign policy interested in Eastern Europe need data that are both sensitive to small changes and yet susceptible to systematic analysis. We know, for example, that despite shared dependence on the Soviet Union and shared Marxist-Leninist ideology among political elites, different national attributes and domestic factors have led to different appreciations of foreign policy needs on the part of Eastern European elites. (See Klaiber: 1970 or Laux: 1973 for efforts to identify national distinctions between Eastern European states in the European security issue area.) The indicators for foreign policy outputs used in aggregate studies—such as U.N. votes or events data—are insensitive to marginal differences as among smaller, dependent states. Content analysis, organized so as to summarize official foreign policy doctrines, can provide sensitive indicators that are comparable from case to case.

References

Angell, Robert C., " Content Analysis of Elite Media," *Journal of Conflict Resolution*, VIII, 4 (December 1964), pp. 330–385.

Berelson, Bernard, *Content Analysis in Communication Research* (Glencoe, Ill.: Free Press, 1952).

Brodin, Katarina, " Belief Systems, Doctrines, and Foreign Policy," *Cooperation and Conflict*, VII (1972), pp. 97–112.

Bromke, Adam, " Poland Under Gierek: A New Political Style," *Problems of Communism*, XXI, 5 (September–October 1972), pp. 13–28.

Ceausescu, Nicolae, *Romania on the Way To Building Up the Multilaterally Developed Socialist Society* (Collected Speeches), Volumes 4, 6 and 7 (Bucharest: Meridian, 1969, 1971, 1972).

Department of Commerce, Foreign Broadcast Information Service, *Daily Report Eastern Europe.*

George, Alexander L., *Propaganda Analysis: A Study of Inferences Made from Nazi Propaganda in World War II* (Evanston, Ill.: Row Peterson, 1959).

Holsti, Kalevi J., " National Role Conceptions in the Study of Foreign Policy," *International Studies Quarterly*, XIV, 3 (September 1970), pp. 233–309.

Holsti, Ole R., *Content Analysis for the Social Sciences and Humanities* (Reading, Mass.: Addison-Wesley, 1969).

Hopmann, P. Terry, " International Conflict and Cohesion in the Communist System," *International Studies Quarterly*, XI, 3 (September 1967), pp. 212–236.

Jowitt, Kenneth, " Comments," in S. Sinanian, I. Deak, and P. C. Ludz (eds.), *Europe in the 1970's* (New York: Praeger, 1972), pp. 180–184 (Special Studies in International Politics and Government).

Kissinger, Henry A., " Domestic Structure and Foreign Policy," in W. F. Hanreider, *Comparative Foreign Policy* (New York: McKay, 1971), pp. 22–50.

Klaiber, Wolfgang, " Security Priorities in Eastern Europe," *Problems of Communism*, XIX, 3 (May–June 1970), pp. 32–44.

Laux, Jean Kirk, " Divergeance ou coalition: la position des pays de l'Europe de l'Est à l'égard de la C.S.C.E.: 1965–1972," *Etudes internationales*, IV, 1–2 (mars-juin 1973), pp. 89–120.

Marer, Paul, " The Political Economy of Soviet Relations with Eastern Europe: 1945 to Present," paper presented to the International Studies Association meeting, New York, March 15–16, 1973.

Mitchell, R. E., " The Use of Content Analysis for Explanatory Studies," *Public Opinion Quarterly*, XXI, 2 (Summer 1967), pp. 230–241.

Rosenau, James N., " Foreign Policy as an Issue-Area," in James N. Rosenau, *The Scientific Study of Foreign Policy* (New York: Free Press, 1971), pp. 401–440.

Remington, Robin Alison, *Case Studies in Communist Conflict Resolution* (Cambridge, Mass.: MIT Press, 1971).

Shulman, Marshall, " A European Security Conference," *Survival*, XXI, 12 (December 1969), pp. 373–381.

Singer, J. David, " Soviet and American Foreign Policy Attitudes: Content Analysis of Elite Articulations," *Journal of Conflict Resolution*, VIII, 4 (December 1964), pp. 424–479.

Skilling, Gordon, " Background to the Study of Opposition in Communist Eastern Europe," *Government and Opposition*, III, 3 (Summer 1968), pp. 294–324.

SIMON SERFATY

An International Anomaly: The United States and the Communist Parties in France and Italy, 1945-1947*

"The Truman administration was not helpless, defensive, drifting, or ignorant in its Cold War diplomacy." [1] Among the postwar policymakers, there was an appreciation of power politics which latter-day Cold War revisionists have helped to rediscover. Like other great powers throughout history, and despite its rhetorical pretenses, the United States exploited opportunities where it found them and where it created them. There is no need to deplore such "realism"; America's resources, its ability to aid or refuse aid to other countries especially anxious to secure it, were used by policymakers in Washington as means of winning support in a political battle which, by the time the Korean conflict broke out, was understood to be worldwide. To argue now that America's interests were not well served by policies which too easily assumed superior Soviet strength—strength that in fact lacked both capabilities and intentions—is probably true, with the benefit of hindsight. But it is not surprising that such a case could not be made convincingly at the time: any historical record ought to be

* The first part of this paper was written under the auspices of the California Arms Control and Foreign Policy Seminar. The author gratefully acknowledges his indebtedness to Mr. James Finkle for his valuable research assistance on the second part.

1. Thomas G. Paterson, *Soviet-American Confrontation, Postwar Reconstruction and the Origins of the Cold War* (Baltimore, Md.: Johns Hopkins University Press, 1973), p. 13.

read in relation to the conditions prevailing when the events under investigation occurred.

The unfolding of U.S. influence can be seen especially well in France and in Italy, where the Truman administration, rightly or wrongly, clearly preferred a French or an Italian government from which the Communists would be excluded. This paper, however, will argue that America's policy alone was not *the* key factor which brought about the political changes that took place in these two countries in the spring of 1947. To be sure, America's command over capital cannot be underestimated; it helped win to America's cause rulers who were inclined to bargain, and it was so used. But this was not enough; neither the French nor the Italian government surrendered its sovereignty over domestic affairs. With respect to internal matters, neither country became an obedient satellite of America. Within the bipolar international system of the postwar period, tripartism was an anomaly that was resolved out of domestic choice as well as out of international necessity.

America, France, and the French Communist Party

It is not the least complication of French political life that there are several " lefts " in France. Thus an examination of the relationship between the U.S. government and the French left suffers from a problem of definition in a nation where one speaks of the loyal and disloyal left, the center left, or the extreme left, and where the left of the extreme left was occupied for a time by a political group known as the " Progressists."

In many ways the French Communist Party is regarded by the non-Communists as an outsider, an alien not only to the French left but also to France. Writing at different times and with different perspectives, such political analysts as André Siegfried and Jacques Fauvet found it equally difficult to locate the French Communist Party on the left or on the right of the political spectrum.[2] On either side of the spectrum, the presence of the Communist Party indeed appears to be somewhat " unnatural ": a foreign party among a chauvinistic people, a totalitarian party among an individualistic people, and a proletarian party in a rural and middle-class country.[3]

2. André Siegfried, *De la Troisième à la Quatrième République* (Paris: B. Grasset, 1958), pp. 208–209; Jacques Fauvet, *Histoire du Parti Communiste Français, II, Vingt-Cinq Ans de Drames, 1939–1965* (Paris: Fayard, 1965).

3. Mario Einaudi, Jean Marie Domenach, and Aldo Garosci, *Communism in Western Europe* (Ithaca: Cornell University Press, 1951), p. 62.

An " outsider " party, the Communists nevertheless enjoyed, in the aftermath of World War II, an appeal that might seem especially surprising in view of the Party's misfortunes during the first eighteen months of the war. Dissolved and forced to go underground in September 1939 after it had denounced the Anglo-French " fomenters of war " and had condoned Moscow's invasion of Eastern Poland, the Party was represented in the French government exactly five years later. In the first elections held after VE-Day, the Communists obtained nearly 30 percent of the vote. The following year, the presidential candidacy of the Party's secretary general, Maurice Thorez, failed by only a few votes and only after intricate parliamentary maneuvering.

Such electoral success cannot be understood without reference to the war years when, following Moscow's entry into the war against Nazi Germany, the Communist Party emerged rapidly as a stronghold of the French Resistance. In later years the Communists could make effective use of their claim that 75,000 members of the Party had been shot by the Germans during the Resistance.[4] Having thus established its national credentials, the Party—*le parti des fusillés*—moved all the more easily into the political vacuum caused by the collapse of the traditional forces of the Third Republic. A doctrine, a church, and an army all combined, the Party offered a program of action based, in appearance at least, on an irresistible faith in the future of France. Such faith was especially comforting in the face of an economic debacle that lent appeal to the Communist promises of rapid recovery and welfare for all.

Furthermore, the war also appeared to confirm the main Communist thesis: namely, that the bourgeoisie (most of which had rallied to the Vichy government) was condemned by history and was not qualified to reassume the leadership of a country that it had betrayed. The working class, faithful and organized, alone was capable of giving France a future.[5] Such a claim would be made even more acceptable by the mild quality of anti-Communism in France where everyone not Communist could be said to be " anti-Communist, but . . . ."[6]

4. This Communist claim of 75,000 casualties is itself very much in doubt. At the Nuremberg trials the *total* number of Frenchmen shot under the German occupation was reported by the French government to have been 29,660.

5. Einaudi et al., *op. cit.*, p. 137.

6. Alexander Werth, *France, 1940–1955* (London: Robert Hale, 1956). The role played by Communism in the French intellectual community is analyzed especially well in Raymond Aron, *The Opium of the Intellectuals* (New York: Doubleday, 1957).

The mildness of France's anti-Communism was not particular to the time; Marxist ideology had penetrated very early into even anti-Communist thinking in France. To the French people the Communist Party was (and is again today) a party like any other: the party of the industrial workers (in competition with the other Marxist party, the Socialist Party), just as there was a party of farmers and one of small shopkeepers. In France regular interaction with Communist personalities did not have the same pejorative connotation that it might have had in the United States at the time. Those individuals who joined the Party were not always fools and the Party itself was not always wrong. The " respectability " of the Party was enhanced further by French intellectuals' beliefs in the nation's revolutionary tradition and their latent guilt feelings regarding the working class—the so-called " leftist complex."

In fact, France's anti-Communism coexisted with a strong dose of anti-Americanism, with the latter perhaps more pronounced in the aftermath of World War II. Generally speaking, this anti-Americanism needs to be placed within the historic French tendency toward xenophobia. On the right, this tendency was intimately connected with other aspects of French nationalism, making suspect all that was not French (whether British, German, or American). On the left, America was an ideal target as the bulwark of capitalism.

France's anti-Americanism, however, went beyond ideological differences, since many American actions—before, during, and after the war—met with widespread French antipathy. Examples include the economic assistance provided by Washington to Germany during the interwar period; America's delayed entry into both world wars; the maintenance of diplomatic relations with the Vichy regime and the belated recognition of the de Gaulle government; America's postwar insistence on standing firm against Soviet pressure, at the risk of war, at a time when a large proportion of Frenchmen would have given up almost everything rather than go to war; and the pro-British and pro-German (as opposed to pro-French) outlook of the American government, as perceived by the French government and people. There was, in short, much mistrust of America's goals as well as of America's reliability. Thus, a public opinion poll held in January 1945 showed that only 24 percent of a cross section of Frenchmen thought that the United States would be the country that would most aid France's recovery after the war—as compared with 25 percent who said that Russia would be.[7] Embittered by the humiliation of her defeat, France

7. Arnold M. Rose, " Anti-Americanism in France," *Antioch Review, XII* (December 1952), p. 471.

opposed the " Americanization " process with a wall of stubborn suspicion and resistance, naturally most evident among the French *gauchisants*. Yet this mistrust was self-contained, and there was an " American complex " too. Many of the Frenchmen who disliked the United States and resisted its growing influence, at the same time loved and admired it; ultimately they ensured that this influence could grow according to French needs.

Despite the fact that anti-Communists were a majority of the French people, the Communist Party remained a part of the French government until May 1947. However mild French anti-Communism may have been, the Communist Party never again entered the French government *after* May 1947. However anti-American a majority of the French people were, America nonetheless played an important role, implicitly at least, in the postwar domestic affairs of France. But it will be argued here that although anti-Americanism may have been mild, America did not and probably could not play a major role in assuring the departure of the Communists from the Ramadier government.

De Gaulle, the Communists, and the United States

As already mentioned, the role of the French Communist Party during the war years was crucial; it is estimated that the Party and the men under its control furnished about half of the military, and a third of the civilian *résistants*.[8] The very nature of the Party—its organization in cells, the carefully preserved anonymity of its leadership and hierarchy, the unfaltering devotion of its cadres—made it especially effective during the underground war waged by the French Resistance after June 1940. From the start, de Gaulle was anxious to enroll their services. " I want them to serve," de Gaulle recalled in his *Memoirs*. " There were no forces that should not be employed to beat the enemy, and I reckoned that theirs had great weight in the kind of war imposed by the occupation." [9] But in seeking Communist support, de Gaulle faced the problem of maintaining his control over a party that remained, even in wartime, an army of liberation determined to gain from the war the prize they sought most: to establish their control throughout France. Clearly, the agreement reached between de Gaulle and the French Communists was a matter of convenience. With such an agreement knowingly limited in time to

8. Einaudi et al., *op cit.*, p. 75
9. Charles de Gaulle, *War Memoirs, I. The Call to Honour* (New York: Simon & Schuster, 1955), p. 271.

the duration of the conflict against Germany, each side attempted to secure with the assistance of the other what it might need most in the aftermath of Germany's defeat.

That the French Communists expected to seize power following Germany's defeat is hardly to be doubted. As the only sound political organization left in France, the Party would probably appear to a grateful and forgiving French people to be the only national organization capable of ensuring order in the midst of the anarchy that would follow the collapse of Germany and the dismemberment of the Vichy regime. Furthermore, confident of the active support of Russia, the greatest military power on the continent, the French Communists would also provide security against a potential revival of German militarism.

This is not to say that the Communists expected to seize power by force; they had neither the inclination nor the capability to do so. Instead, to attain its objective the Party attempted to reconstruct its national image. Its platform became that of a national mission. "We are a government party," proudly claimed Thorez in late 1945. "We must be conscious everywhere of the gravity of our responsibilities before the Party and before the nation." "Today," the Communist leader stated on another occasion (November 25, 1945), "we are all partisans of de Gaulle, since we have chosen to work with him, the President of the French Provisional Government."[10] Ultimately, the Party would seize power, to be sure, but it would do so legally, since its majority would be reached by promoting fronts and other groupings that it could easily dominate, thanks to its own cohesion. The potential *groupement de gauche* might go so far as the growing Christian-leftist *Mouvement Républicain Populaire* (MRP). Reflective of such a strategy were the Party's efforts to merge with the Socialists, or its attempts to merge the Communist-dominated union General Confederation of Labor (CGT) with the Catholic Trade Union Federation (CFTC).

The legalism of the Party was especially apparent as long as de Gaulle remained in power. Thus during this period not a single strike occurred (in effect, there was no strike in postwar France until April 1947). Maximum effort at work, and production at any cost, became the basic Communist *leitmotivs*, as they had been in 1936 during the days of the Popular Front.[11] Until de Gaulle's withdrawal in January

10. Einaudi et al., *op. cit.*, p. 77; J. B. Duroselle, "The Turning Point in French Politics: 1947," *Review of Politics*, XIII, (July 1951), p. 306. See also Jacques Duclos, *La France devant son Destin* (Paris: Editions du Mail, 1946), p. 31.

11. "I say it frankly," Thorez bluntly warned striking miners in July 1945, "it is impossible to approve the smallest strike." Alfred J. Rieber, *Stalin and the French Communist Party* (New York: Columbia University Press, 1962), p. 231.

1946, the Communists also carefully avoided any personal attack against the General.[12]

A major obstacle to a Communist takeover was naturally raised by de Gaulle's growing influence. Undoubtedly it was his presence, in July 1944, which deprived the Party of an opportunity to exploit a blatantly revolutionary situation.[13] Yet de Gaulle was not, as he liked to believe, the only obstacle to a Communist takeover in France; that the Communists chose to follow a legal route reflected their certainty that time was on their side. It also reflected a cautiousness dictated (to Thorez as well as to Stalin) by the presence of American troops in Europe.

By objecting to de Gaulle following the Liberation, Stalin played the Communist game well. But Roosevelt, who also objected to de Gaulle, played a game that was more difficult to understand, since alternatives to de Gaulle were few and generally unpleasant. The view in Washington was that neither de Gaulle and his followers nor the left-wing groups were strong enough to run the French government.[14] In 1945 there was in France a disturbing scarcity of qualified men. Painfully apparent during the war years, the lack was increased when the political reckoning that took place under the cover of postwar justice far exceeded de Gaulle's casual estimate of " twelve dozens of traitors, twelve hundred of cowards, and twelve thousands of idiots." [15] As the war progressed, the future of the old political parties appeared uncertain, and a return to the political instability of the Third Republic was clearly undesirable from the viewpoint of America's objectives. If a strong man was needed, the Giraud option was a weak choice. The " Kingpin," as Eisenhower was reported to call Giraud, had been

12. De Gaulle, *War Memoirs, III. Salvation* (New York: Simon & Schuster, 1960), pp. 236 and 102.

13. According to Robert Aron, for example, " De Gaulle and his men prevented a Communist insurrection." *France Reborn: The History of the Liberation* (New York: Scribner's, 1964), p. 416.

14. Robert Murphy, *Diplomat Among Warriors* (New York: Doubleday, 1964), pp. 158–160.

15. Quoted in Jacques Fauvet, *La Quatrième République* (Paris: Fayard, 1960), pp. 34–35. Some of the following figures illustrate the disagreements over the exact numbers. According to Fauvet, there were 2,071 death sentences (and twice as many handed down with the accused *in absentia*), 40,000 detentions (2,777 for life), and 48,273 condemnations for national indignities (Fauvet, *op. cit.*, pp. 32–38). Paul-Henry Teitgen, former Minister of Justice, at the National Assembly on August 6, 1946, reported 4,783 death sentences, 11,000 life sentences, and 19,000 time sentences (Joseph Barsalou, *La Mal-Aimée* [Paris: Plon, 1964], p. 41). Robert Aron refers to estimates ranging from 30,000 to 40,000 summary executions (Aron, *op. cit.*, p. 423).

strikingly unsuccessful in winning the allegiance of Frenchmen; accordingly, he himself tended to reduce his own ambitions and intentions even faster than those in Washington who continued to support him.[16] A third force headed by Giraud could not survive long without considerable support from the Allies, both during and after the war. Assuming that Washington was willing to provide such support, it still remained doubtful that the French people would acquiesce to American supervision of their postwar status, especially if such supervision were to imply the continued presence of an American " army of occupation."

In fact the triangle formed by de Gaulle, the French Communists, and the United States was an unstable one. In part de Gaulle's early alliance with the Soviet Union was aimed at strengthening Communist support at home.[17] To be sure, the Communist Party had already decided to stay and work within the government. But by going to Moscow de Gaulle was also attempting to blackmail Washington into giving him further support. Hence the following paradox: the more a policy of rapprochement with the Soviet Union succeeded in " forcing " Washington into additional assistance for de Gaulle, the more de Gaulle would be capable of releasing himself from the support of the Communists at home. Moscow's reading of the situation was, of course, different from de Gaulle's: the Paris-Moscow pact would strengthen the Communist position within France while reducing America's influence. The less fear Stalin created, the less Truman might appear to be needed. Germany was, of course, the key to this set of bilateral relations.[18] On the one hand, Germany was the point of reconciliation between Moscow and Paris, which were united in their common fear of a revival of Germany's militarism. On the other, Germany soon emerged as the point of contention between Paris and Washington, which disagreed about Germany's role in the face of a Soviet threat that was perceived differently in each capital.

De Gaulle (and his successors) used the Communist Party as a counterweight to the coolness shown by the United States and Great Britain. In so doing, the French premier was inaugurating a policy that would become quite common in later years. But de Gaulle also

16. Gabriel Kolko, *The Politics of War* (New York: Random House, 1968), p. 67; William McNeill, *America, Britain and Russia: Their Cooperation and Conflict, 1941–1946* (London: Oxford University Press, 1953), p. 258.

17. A. W. De Porte, *De Gaulle's Foreign Policy, 1944–1946* (Cambridge, Mass.: Harvard University Press, 1968), p. 74.

18. Needless to say, the German menace remained foremost among French preoccupations. Both the Franco-Russian treaty of December 1944 and the Anglo-French treaty of March 1947 were explicitly directed against Germany.

needed and sought an entente with the Communists, the largest single element of the Resistance, despite the risk that the Party might pose at a later stage. By communicating to the Communist leadership his willingness to incorporate them in a postwar government of national solidarity, de Gaulle was gaining a reprieve during which he might strengthen his leadership both from within and from without. Confident of their ability in the long run to displace de Gaulle and assume full control (thanks to the same characteristics that were now shaping their leading role in the Resistance), the Communists were willing to pay de Gaulle's price in the short run for fear of being isolated once again. Besides, any Communist action against de Gaulle, especially following the liberation of Paris, might cause an anti-Communist reaction from without; in 1945, as under the Fifth Republic, de Gaulle could indeed take America's protection for granted. This was Thorez's own reading of the situation. " With the Americans in France," he later explained, " the revolution would have been annihilated." [19]

Thus de Gaulle both needed the Communists (to counteract Soviet pressure, to promote national unity, and to avoid an Allied military government) and feared them (" the risks of adventure "). The Communists both needed de Gaulle (because of his foreign policy and for national respectability) and feared him (as the major obstacle to their exploitation of the obviously revolutionary situation). America both needed de Gaulle (as an alternative to left-wing governments and civil war) and feared him (because he was too unpredictable and because of the prevalent feeling that a civil war might very well erupt anyway among de Gaulle, the Communists, and the old Vichy forces).[20] Ultimately all lost during most of the Fourth Republic, as the non-Gaullist, non-Communist parties tenuously held power and gave France an instability that was clearly incompatible with American objectives in Europe.

From Cooperation to Showdown

The Communists still hoped in early 1947 to be part of the government despite their opposition to it on such crucial issues as wages and the colonies (primarily Indochina, but also Algeria and Madagascar). In January 1947, the domestic necessity of protecting the

19. Georgette Elgey, *La République des Illusions, I. 1945–1951* (Paris: Fayard, 1965), p. 23.

20. Until the very last moment, the Roosevelt Administration remained convinced that de Gaulle lacked public support, and it continued to make inquiries with representatives of the Vichy government. Cordell Hull, *Memoirs, II* (New York: Macmillan, 1948); Rieber, *op. cit.*, p. 197.

progressive reputation of the Party gave way to the international necessity of preventing a final breach between East and West, or, should the split between Washington and Moscow be final, at least of preventing France from falling into the American camp.

The Communist presence in the government, however, appeared more and more anomalous, and its surgical removal was sought by both foreign and domestic groups. In France, the fear was growing that continued Communist participation might result in diminished American assistance. The Soviet Union, it was pointed out, could not provide the credits needed for France's economic recovery. Nor would Moscow provide the military assistance that was needed to preserve the Empire. Washington, on the other hand, could and would do both. Interim economic assistance granted by Washington had proved indispensable, but it had remained less than what was hoped for. It was rumored that Secretary of the Treasury Fred Vinson had explicitly requested from visiting Leon Blum that "the Socialists join an anti-Communist coalition, and so oust the Communists now occupying important posts in the French cabinet." [21] Only then would American assistance reach the "billions of dollars" that had been expected.

Regarding the colonies, too, America's policy appeared to be constrained by the ambivalent orientation of a half-left, half-right French government. In Indochina, Washington on the whole resisted early intelligence appraisals and advice for recognition of Ho Chi Minh's government.[22] Thus, eager not to antagonize the French, Secretary of State James Byrnes had disclaimed any American opposition to a French return to Indochina.[23] Yet the United States still resisted urgent appeals for assistance, and demanded, for example, that American-produced propellers be removed from the British aircraft given by the London government to the French for military use in Indochina.[24]

The rearmament of the French army also illustrates Washington's ambivalence toward a nation where Communist influences were so obviously pronounced. With VE-Day approaching, there had been much eagerness in the de Gaulle government to reconstitute an army

21. Jean Davidson, ***Correspondant à Washington: ce que je n'ai jamais cablé*** (Paris: Editions du Seuil, 1954), pp. 15–16; Werth, *op. cit.*, p. 314.

22. "An awfully sweet guy," said an intelligence report of Ho Chi Minh in 1945, whose outstanding quality is "his gentleness." Bernard Fall, *The Two Vietnams* (New York: Praeger, 1964), p. 82.

23. Simon Serfaty, *The Elusive Enemy* (Boston: Little, Brown, 1972), p. 176.

24. John G. Stoessinger, *Nations in Darkness: China, Russia and America* (New York: Random House, 1971), p. 64.

that would play a major role in the liberation of France and the final defeat and subsequent occupation of Germany. On October 25, 1944, de Gaulle had claimed that it was only " a matter of a few months " before " France can make . . . an impressive army." [25] But to the Allies it appeared that the revolutionary potential present in the French army created risks of internal disruption far in excess of the military contributions that such a revived French force might make; a high proportion of FFI (Home Army) officers, for example, were known Communists. For this reason de Gaulle's repeated requests for military assistance were not met.[26] In early 1947 the situation was obviously not alleviated, since the Minister of Defense was a member of the Party, and the defense department was being swamped with crypto-Communists or Communist sympathizers.[27]

America's position also evolved as Washington's attitude toward Moscow became tougher. In 1946 Washington generally tolerated the French Communists. The Truman Administration merely hoped that the Communists would be sufficiently " grouped " by the other, non-Communist parties. It is this interpretation of Washington's wishes which prompted the MRP to form a coalition government with the two major parties of the left after de Gaulle's withdrawal.[28] Thus General Billotte, then the acting chief of the French Joint Chiefs of Staff, had warned against a *Front Populaire* type of government which would fall slowly under Communist domination. Relying upon his contacts with America's military, Billotte warned that such a situation was of great concern to the United States on the ground that it would signify the emergence of a hostile government behind American occupation troops, which also, of course, faced hostility in Germany. The retaliation that Billotte foresaw included no less than American seizure of French bases in Asia, withdrawal from continental Europe, and termination of economic assistance.[29]

25. Werth, *op. cit.*, p. 234. America's fears of Communist infiltration in the French army survived the Communists' departure from the government, as Washington kept questioning the reliability of a nation where about one-fifth of the population and a considerably greater proportion of the crucial male population in the factories and in the army sympathized with the opposing camp.

26. The Gaullist leaders, too, were suspicious of how the Communists were planning to use these arms. Rieber, *op. cit.*, p. 133. Nevertheless, they complained bitterly. Werth, *op. cit.*, p. 235.

27. Rieber, *op. cit.*, pp. 289–292.

28. Simon Serfaty, *France de Gaulle and Europe* (Baltimore: Johns Hopkins University Press, 1968), p. 30. " It is not to a socialist-communist government that the United States will consent to loan the money we need," warned Pierre-Henry Teitgen. See Jacques Fauvet, *La Quatrième Républic*, p. 75.

29. Elgey, *op. cit.*, p. 103.

The U.S. desire to see the Communists "grouped" was also regarded as a good bargaining point by French politicians. "The Communists are rendering us a great service," would say Pierre Mendes-France a little later. "Because we have a 'Communist danger,' the Americans are making a tremendous effort to help us. We must keep this indispensable Communist scare."[30] This line had been followed by Blum during his visit to Washington in the spring of 1946. The choice of Blum as the chief French negotiator was itself significant. A Marxist, Blum was nevertheless a staunch anti-Communist and an outspoken critic of the Soviet Union. As previously mentioned, press reports in both the United States and France indicated America's interest in the French domestic situation. But the Truman Administration kept such pressures informal; forcing Blum into concessions would probably prove self-defeating, since the Communist Party would gain the support that the Socialist party lost. Thus Blum could state, upon his return, that American assistance was being provided without imposing "explicitly or implicitly, directly or indirectly, any condition of any kind, civilian, military, political or diplomatic."[31]

In early 1947 however, the possibilities of domestic as well as international tripartism had diminished, if they had not disappeared altogether. With Greece and Turkey threatened, the Truman Administration saw with increased concern the leading position of the Communist parties not only in France but also in Belgium and Italy. If the Communists seized control of Greece, Turkey would soon fall, and then Iran. If they seized control of Turkey, Greece would soon fall, followed by Iran. If it were Italy or France that became the prey of Communist subversion, then the area threatened would extend to Greece and Turkey, as well as to the Middle East. In all cases, the Soviet objective was to gain control of the eastern Mediterranean and the Middle East, with these areas serving as springboards to South Asia and Africa. The situation was especially dangerous in France. "With four Communists in the Cabinet," warned Dean Acheson, "one

30. Werth, *op. cit.*, p. 351. Side by side with Communist actions there was therefore what Alfred Grosser has called the "passive influence" of the Party. Such passive influence could take several forms, only one of which is of the blackmail variety. In other situations the Communists would also force implicitly the position of the other parties (if "they" are for, "we" must be against; or if "they" are for, "we" must be for also, so that they do not acquire a monopoly of liberalism). See Grosser, *La Politique Extérieure de la Cinquième République* (Paris: Editions du Seuil, 1965).

31. Blum's statement has become a fixture of any account of his visit to Washington. It is quoted, for example, in Grosser, *op. cit.*, p. 217; Elgey, *op. cit.*, p. 140; and Werth, *op. cit.*, pp. 315–316.

of them Minister of Defense, with Communists controlling the largest trade union and infiltrating government offices, factories and the armed services, with nearly a third of the electorate voting Communist, and with economic conditions worsening, the Russians could pull the plug any time they chose." [32]

In France, meanwhile, the position of the Communists had become increasingly difficult. On March 22, when military appropriations were voted for Indochina, the Communists abstained. Only the Communist ministers voted for the appropriations in order to avoid a schism that they still did not want. From within, the Communists faced their own contradictions; the government was following policies that were increasingly incompatible with the Party line, and the " double game " that the Party had been playing since the Liberation was not coming to an end. In Raymond Aron's words, as a revolutionary party,

> it denounced colonialism, the war in Indochina, clerical reaction . . . and supported the demands of the workers. As a government party, it preached the gospel of work and the reconstruction effort, eliminated anti-militarist propaganda, endeavored to gain cadres by raising the salary scale, and obtained followers who were attracted by the promises of jobs and advantages.[33]

At first, the Party's support for the government might have reflected the overall objective of maintaining a symbolic measure of East-West cooperation. Now, it obviously aimed at containing and obstructing America's influence in France. If tripartism could not maintain East-West cooperation, at least it would prevent the " fall " of France into a U.S.-sponsored Western bloc. Yet the French Communists still regarded their position as moderately secure, and Thorez simply assumed that there could not be any government without Communist participation. In effect, of course, there could always be a coalition government, but the constant opposition of a substantial fraction of the National Assembly rendered any such coalition intrinsically fragile and greatly contributed to the political instability of the Fourth Republic.

Thus the untenability of the Communist position was intimately related to the conditions that prevailed not only abroad but also (and perhaps above all) within the Party itself and in France. Assuming, as did Thorez, that there could not be a viable government without

32. Joseph Jones, *The Fifteen Weeks* (New York: Viking Press, 1955), p. 140.
33. Raymond Aron, *Le Grand Schisme* (Paris: Gallimard, 1948), p. 190.

Communist participation, de Gaulle, now eager to return to power, asked for their expulsion. This would force a political crisis which, in the General's view, he alone could solve. A Gaullist party was in the making, and its growth was largely predicated on the existence of a Communist threat to the continuity of national institutions. But the Gaullist position in turn further convinced the French Prime Minister to deal with the Communist cancer, since the growth of de Gaulle's appeal would conceivably occur at the expense of the electoral support of the Radical party (and, of course, of the MRP). In May 1947, then, Communist participation in the French government had become everyone's target—within the Party itself (and also in Moscow), within the government, within the opposition, *and* in America, where Truman had just declared war on "the totalitarian way of life." Ramadier's decision to expel the Communists was but the implementation of this consensus. Although it met with America's support, the decision proper was made in Paris.

America, Italy, and the Italian Communist Party

As in France, the Italian Communist Party (PCI) appeared, in the midst of the moral and material ruins left by two decades of fascism and several years of war, as the only sound and coherent political organization in the country. Even more than in France, though, the quality of the PCI's leadership enhanced further the Party's ability to reach the people directly and continuously. Much more reluctant than its French counterpart to implement the wholesale wrecking plans that would be officially urged in 1947 by the Cominform, Palmiro Togliatti proved to be especially skilled in squeezing maximum tactical independence from the directives of Moscow.[34]

As in France too, the Party's record of active underground opposition to fascism, as well as the wartime performance of the Partisan movements, added to the Party's prestige, while its ideology fitted the national mood of rebirth and utopianism. Thus, it was widely estimated that approximately two-thirds of all the overt Partisans had been enrolled in the Garibaldi formations, and although all of these were not Communists, they had been nevertheless subjected to vigorous indoctrination by the Party's political commissars.[35]

34. Thomas H. Greene, "The Communist Party of Italy and France," *World Politics*, XVIII (October 1968), pp. 3–5, 25.

35. H. Stuart Hughes, *The U.S. and Italy* (Cambridge, Mass.: Harvard University Press, 1968), pp. 130ff. See also Murray Edelman, "Causes and Fluctuations in Popular Support for the Italian Communist Party," *Journal of Politics*, XXVII (August 1958), p. 540.

It follows that, as in France, the workers, especially in the North, were believed to have arms in their hands, and, in the aftermath of the Liberation, the Allied Command ordered the demobilization and disarming of Partisan units. Even though these orders were only partially carried out, and quantities of weapons may have indeed been hidden away, it remains that, as in France too, such fears of a Communist-sponsored armed insurrection were not justified, as the conquest of power by military means remained outside of the PCI's plans.

Finally, as in France, the PCI faced an early political dilemma with the emergence of a "strong man," Ferruccio Parri, whose prestige as an anti-fascist organizer led to the creation of a government of national unity. In dealing with Parri, the Party's position was somewhat similar to that of the French Communists toward de Gaulle: excessive success for the new Prime Minister might win him the allegiance of the masses whose sole guardian the PCI expected to remain. The Parri experiment, however, collapsed even faster than the de Gaulle experiment (November 24, 1945). Furthermore, during his few months in power, Parri, far more than de Gaulle, resisted extensive cooperation with the Communists. As 1945 was coming to an end, the period of wartime (anti-fascist) solidarity had already ended, and newly formed political groups on the right were denouncing the Resistance as a Communist conspiracy, while nostalgia for the old regime was already being unveiled through such slogans as "one was better off when one was worse off." [36]

De Gasperi, the Communists, and the United States

From the start, De Gasperi's second government and Italy's first experiment in tripartism lacked stability.[37] From within, deprived of the unifying effect of the fight against fascism, the major groups that were part of the government were little motivated to come to a lasting agreement on any one subject; positions reached privately in Cabinet meetings were soon discarded at the Council door, as individual ministers often took an opposing position in public for the sake of ideological and tactical gains.[38] From without, as UNRRA assistance

36. Hughes, *op. cit.*, pp. 135–140.

37. Giuseppe Mammarella, *Italy After Fascism, 1943–1965* (Notre Dame: University of Notre Dame Press, 1966), pp. 134ff.

38. Upon his return from his American trip, De Gasperi explicitly told his colleagues that if he were to form a new government, "he would not compromise in questions of real collaboration among parties in government since it was not possible to govern with parties whose representatives in the Council

was scheduled to end shortly, dispatches from Washington regarding future aid added to De Gasperi's bleak perception of Italy's potential for recovery. In sum, from within and from without, pressures were being exerted on the Prime Minister, himself probably in favor of tripartism, to dismantle his coalition at the earliest possible opportunity.[39]

For the domestic and international settings could not be dissociated. Since the end of the war, Italy had been facing three major problems: security, reconstruction, and acceptance. Reconstruction could not be achieved without a level of external assistance which was itself dependent on erosion of the suspicion aroused by Italy's wartime status. In seeking such reacceptance, Italy could depend on the very special relationship that linked the country to the United States, where a substantial Italo-American lobby was naturally more inclined toward temperance and was therefore able to exert a moderating influence on some of the harsher demands made by America's allies. Similarly, security was dependent on both Soviet and American good will, and neither side could be offended without risking a measure of retaliation from the other. Thus, from Washington, Ambassador Tarchiani repeatedly warned " in the most explicit manner possible so as to avoid equivocations or illusory expectations, that American aid is indissolubly linked to the development of legislation and practical democracy in Italy."[40] At the same time from Rome, the Communist newspaper *l'Unità*, was also " warning " De Gasperi that " the supreme aim of [Italy's] foreign policy has been the defense of [her] independence. May [De Gasperi] not yield to the temptation of selling [it] for a mess of pottage."[41]

Undoubtedly, it was in order to examine the conditions under which Italy might become a recipient *à part entière* of America's assistance that De Gasperi accepted an invitation from *Time* magazine to attend an international conference in Cleveland, in early January 1947. Although unofficial, De Gasperi's trip was reminiscent of Blum's; but even more than in the case of his French counterpart the previous

of Ministers approved official acts only to criticize them later in public." According to the *Messaggiero*, as reported on an incoming telegram from the American Embassy in Rome to the State Department, Number 176, dated January 23, 1947. Department of State files in the National Archives, Washington, D.C.

39. On De Gasperi's own position, see, for example, Norman Kogan, *A Political History of Postwar Italy* (New York: Praeger, 1966), p. 34.

40. Alberto Tarchiani, *America-Italia, Le Dieci Giornate di De Gasperi Negli Stati Uniti* (Milan: Rizzoli, 1947), p. 30.

41. *The New York Times*, January 4, 1947, p. 7.

spring, the Italian Prime Minister was undertaking a dialogue of unequals. Received in Washington almost as an afterthought—a thirty-minute meeting with Secretary of State James Byrnes, and a thirteen-minute meeting with President Truman[42]—De Gasperi relied heavily on the Communist threat as his main trump card. "The greatest political pressure," he pointedly told Secretary Byrnes, "was being brought at this time by the Communist Party to bring Italy within the orbit of Russian influence. Of course," the Prime Minister argued further, "his entire effort was to combat this movement as he was of an entirely different opinion." But for such an effort to be successful, help was required at once, as there were "no stocks and no reserves, and the delay of one ship arriving in Italy meant that they were faced with semi-revolutionary riots and disturbances in the country."[43] Reading from the record of the meeting, it is difficult to say who was using whom. The Italian Prime Minister was telling the American Secretary of State what the Italian Ambassador thought the Secretary wanted to hear. Yet, upon his return to Italy, De Gasperi insisted that "in America (where anti-Communism is widespread)" he had made great efforts not to permit himself to make declarations inspired by his surroundings. "I dodged," explained the Italian leader, "indiscreet questions and recalled the contributions with blood given by Communists to the struggle of liberation."[44] But in Washington the "surroundings" had been shaped so that the Prime Minister too was exposed to what he wanted to hear; the Senate's good will would be extended to, as Senator Taft put it, "meriting nations that are struggling strenuously for their rebirth," first and foremost Italy.[45] Asked about the future of Italy's government, De Gasperi would be reminded, in Senator Vandenberg's words, that the United States did "not want to waste [its] resources aiding tendencies that are contrary to [its] principles and [its] goal of internal and international democracy."[46]

42. "Papà, you act like you're going to take an examination!," exclaimed Maria De Gasperi to her father during the flight to Washington. For further reminiscences, see Maria Romana Catti De Gasperi, *De Gasperi, Uomo Solo* (Milan: Arnoldo Mondatori Editore, 1964), pp. 240 *et seq.* See also Tarchiani, *op cit.*, Ambassador Tarchiani notes De Gasperi's concern when he learned that neither Secretary Byrnes nor Under Secretary Acheson would be on hand to greet him at the airport. President Truman did not recall his meeting with De Gasperi in his own *Memoirs.* A brief account of the meeting can be found, however, in *The New York Times*, January 8, 1947, p. 8.

43. See the memorandum of the conversation, as prepared by Ambassador Dunn, Department of State Memorandum dated January 6, 1947.

44. As reported in the *Messaggiero.* Incoming telegram from the Embassy in Rome to the Department of State, No. 176, January 23, 1947.

45. Tarchiani, *op. cit.*, p. 68.

46. *Ibid.*, p. 46.

Thus, upon his return to Rome, with only a small loan and a few promises, De Gasperi announced his resignation, giving as reasons for his limited success in Washington America's lack of confidence in the stability of the Italian democratic system, and adding that without a clarification of Party relations such confidence could not be promoted further. "No political conditions have been set by the American government for its help," had said De Gasperi to the press.[47] Yet, clearly enough, America's implicit offer was tempting, and the Italian Prime Minister was tempted. At the same time, however, De Gasperi himself was implicitly making a tempting offer, and America too was tempted. Thus, the American Embassy in Rome was cabling hopefully:

> A prominent democratic Christian party member told us today that [the] Prime Minister has decided to submit his government's resignation in order to form [a] new government "with less pressure from the Communists." . . . De Gasperi will attempt to form a more broadly based government including some Liberals and Saragat Socialists. The relative strength of the Communists will probably then be reduced in the new government.[48]

Yet the possibility of actually expelling the Communists was not seriously entertained by the Prime Minister himself. Responding to a perceived interest in America, De Gasperi was also responding to the explicit interest shown by his political colleagues in a cabinet reshuffle—while he was still in the United States, the majority of the parliamentary group of his party had requested a break with the PCI, thus reasserting a position made clear the previous fall, a position which De Gasperi had then opposed, and which he continued to oppose at the time of the January crisis.[49]

From Cooperation to Showdown

From February to May 1947 the deterioration of the international setting, and Washington's perception of that deterioration (especially as it was being fed by the pessimistic appraisals presented by such visitors as Blum and De Gasperi) worsened steadily. "The new

47. *The New York Times*, January 9, 1947, p. 7.

48. Incoming telegram from the Embassy in Rome to the Department of State, No. 158, January 21, 1947.

49. Sari Gilbert, "From Armistice to Alliance: Goals and Methods in Italian Foreign Policy, 1943 to 1949," unpublished Ph.D. dissertation, Johns Hopkins University, Baltimore, 1969, p. 128.

Italian government is looked upon with greater favor than the last," wrote Ambassador Tarchiani in early February, " but there is fear of a counterattack by the extreme left and some electoral surprise." This was all the more damaging, he went on, as Italy's " economic conditions will obligate [her] to periodically turn to the United States as they are the only ones capable of aiding [her]." In short, the Ambassador concluded, Italy must " hold [the United States] in particular consideration." [50]

In the aftermath of the Truman Message to Congress on Greece and Turkey, the State Department was indeed growing increasingly concerned. On May 1, in a secret telegram to the American Embassy in Rome, Secretary Marshall expressed his misgivings to Ambassador Dunn and asked " what political and economic steps if any this government could take toward strengthening democratic, pro-U.S. forces." [51] The Ambassador's answer was much to the point, and deserves to be quoted at length:

> We are convinced that no improvement in conditions here can take place under [the] government as at present composed. [The] Communists who are represented in Cabinet by [a] second-string team are doing everything possible outside and within the government to bring about inflation and chaotic economic conditions. . . . The pity is that there exists all over Italy a real will to work and there could easily be a general confidence in the future if it were not for the political agitation of the Communists and I doubt if there can be any real effective measures taken to improve the situation as long as the Communists participate in the government. The Communist Party would, of course, fight hard against any effort to form a government without its participation but I do not believe it is too late for a government to be formed without their participation and there appears to be a growing realization that the Communist Party is not really trying to bring about the restoration of economic stability.

In short, Dunn concluded, " if [Italians] had any idea that adoption of Communism in Italy would cut them off from relations with the U.S., I feel sure the vast majority would reject Communist advances." [52] In the meanwhile, Dunn added a few days later, there

50. Tarchiani, *Dieci Anni Tra Roma e Washington* (Milan: Arnoldo Mondadori, ed. 1955), pp. 134–135.

51. Outgoing telegram from the Department of State to the Embassy in Rome, " personal for the Ambassador," Secret, No. 622, May 1, 1947.

52. Incoming telegram from the Embassy in Rome to the Department of State, " For the Secretary," Top Secret, No. 1031, May 3, 1947.

was little the United States could and should do beyond providing wheat "so as to maintain life and hope." [53] Here again, the American Embassy in Rome and the Italian Embassy in Washington were reporting along parallel lines, as Ambassador Tarchiani was warning the State Department that there was a "very real danger that [the PCI] will become the leading party after the October elections" and that it was "probable" that "the Communists and the Nenni Socialists will have an absolute majority of the Italian parliament." And in case his message was not being understood properly, Tarchiani concluded: "De Gasperi is considering reorganizing his government either through the exclusion of the Communists or through broadening its base, thus diluting Communist influence in the government." [54]

The Department's attitude was relayed to the Embassy by means of a Top Secret telegram that stated its support of any action De Gasperi might take to disengage himself from his Socialist-Communist ties. Support was also envisioned should the Prime Minister only reduce, rather than eliminate, leftist participation. The Department's policy now was that "every available source [of] economic assistance [to] Italy be utilized, including post-UNRRA relief. Congress is to be urged [to] pass promptly enabling legislation for return to Italy [of] assets in the United States, including seized ships; Eximbank to be urged [to] expedite [the] availability [of the] $100 million earmarked loan; [The] War Department [is] to be asked to expedite [the] final settlement [of] suspense account." But such aid was to be granted only after a new government was established.[55]

In Rome, De Gasperi's own views had also evolved. Increasingly convinced of Tarchiani's analysis, he had moved openly in his support of the U.S. position. Thus, on April 22, 1947, *The New York Times* described him as being in favor of "continued and increased American participation in European and Mediterranean affairs . . as the key to the solution of both international disputes and Italian internal problems." The newspaper added that De Gasperi, "spoke with full knowledge that the publication of his views might increase the difficulty of holding together his coalition government." [56]

A few days later De Gasperi took another significant step, as he

53. Incoming telegram from the Embassy in Rome to the Department of State, "For the Secretary," Secret, No. 1078, May 7, 1947.

54. Department of State, Memorandum of Conversation between Ambassador Tarchiani and Mr. Matthews, Director, Office of European Affairs, May 8, 1947.

55. Outgoing telegram from the Department of State to the Embassy in Rome, "For the Ambassador," Top Secret, No. 726, May 20, 1947.

56. *The New York Times*, April 22, 1947, p. 20.

denounced publicly " the disloyalty of the two other parties of the Government, the Socialists and the Communists, accusing them of refusing him ' solidarity within the state administration and in the legislation on public matters '." [57]

The actual crisis was precipitated by rumors, said to have originated in Washington. In a May 28 article written by Arnaldo Cortesi, *The New York Times* reported that " a crisis within the Italian Cabinet was precipitated today by unfavorable reports reaching Rome concerning the progress of the economic mission at present in the U.S. headed by Deputy Ivan Matteo Lombardo." The latter, it was further reported, " as a consequence . . . of attacks made by . . . Palmiro Togliatti . . . on the American people generally . . . [had] succeeded in seeing few American officials of importance, and even those that did receive him seemed hardly inclined to take him seriously. As a consequence," the *Times* concluded, " hopes that Italy had . . ., ranging from a settlement of all outstanding financial questions to the concession of a sizable loan, seemed to be receding into the distance." [58]

On that same day the Minister of the Treasury, Campilli, met, at his request, with Henry Tasca to discuss post-UNRRA aid for the remainder of 1947. The reply was clear: " Unless [a] totally new situation developed, [aid] beyond post-UNRRA year [was] unlikely."

The question remains as to what kind of " totally new situation " the Embassy and the State Department meant. Campilli seemed to interpret Tasca's statement as an introduction to a firm American commitment. He therefore spoke of the possibility of forming a government without the Communists. " Such [a] government," he observed, " would, of course, be very difficult to form and would have to have something spectacular to offer Italian people in order to make it a success." [59]

While Tasca could not, at that time, make any such commitment, once the crisis had been settled and a Christian Democrat " monocolore " (with the help of some independent technicians) had been established, the Ambassador directed the following Top Secret communiqué to Washington:

> Now that a government has been formed by the Christian Democrats . . . with outside experts but without Communists or their affiliates I recommend most strongly that our government

57. Mammarella, *op. cit.*, p. 145.
58. *The New York Times*, May 28, 1947, p. 5.
59. Incoming telegram from the Embassy in Rome to the Department of State, Secret, No. 1328, May 28, 1947.

> take whatever steps may be possible to demonstrate our support and readiness to aid in their efforts to save the lira and secure their economy.[60]

The expulsion was a daring act on De Gasperi's part.[61] But in the following weeks De Gasperi's new government received many indications of both moral and material support from the United States. Indeed, a " new situation " had in fact developed. And it was one that the United States not only preferred but actively sought to maintain.

In point of fact, the United States did not openly demand that Communists be excluded from the Italian Cabinet as a prerequisite to American economic aid. Rather, the Christian Democrats published an excessive list of such " demands." It was a shrewd maneuver, one designed to convince the Italian public that Communist exclusion was the only effective key to America's pocketbook.[62]

Did De Gasperi then exploit America's anti-Communism? This is likely, as the maneuvering of 1947 seems to prove. Was there an actual American demand for expulsion? The Tasca statement aside, there are no specific and direct statements of that nature by government officials. Was aid tied to a change in government? American communications between the Rome Embassy and Washington, and the timing of American aid, leave little doubt of it. Was the American stand crucial to the expulsion? Yes, to the extent that it moved De Gasperi to implement an objective that had become increasingly his own since January, and then provided him with the material bounty with which he could pacify the masses.

Secretary of State Marshall's statement of June 2, on the occasion of the formation of De Gasperi's new government, provided the legitimacy which both the American Embassy in Rome and the Italian Embassy in Washington had requested. It stressed the strong bonds between the American and Italian peoples and America's commitment to the reconstruction of the Italian economy. And, no less importantly, its reference to future aid was shaped so that it could be interpreted as a threat to cut off such assistance should the Socialist-Communists ever regain the ascendancy. Thus, the reading of the phrase, " We shall continue to give aid to the Italian people who have demonstrated their sincere and abiding faith in the democratic pro-

60. Incoming telegram from the Embassy in Rome to the Department of State, Top Secret, No. 1364, June 1, 1947.

61. Maria Romana Catti De Gasperi, *op. cit.*, p. 253.

62. See an account of the crisis in *Newsweek*, " Right Key to Washington," XXIX, June 9, 1947.

cesses for the preservation of their individual liberties and basic rights."[63] "The Italians have already overcome many of their most immediate postwar difficulties," continued Secretary Marshall. But, as the past twenty-seven years have shown, it was not all that simple; by 1975 Italians are still asking whether they were not better off when they were worse off.

Conclusion

By January 1947 the question of whether the United States would help in the reconstruction of Western Europe had been affirmatively settled. Once this was established, "most foreign policy debate centered on how much to spend, not whether to spend," and when American diplomats suggested that no decision could be made because the elusive American people would not stand for it, as they told Blum and De Gasperi, such statements stood far more as classic diplomatic ploys than as expressions of actual apprehension.[64] Interpreting Communism as a totalitarian force that bases its advances on continued poverty, and assuming therefore that prosperity would help curb it, the United States relied upon a certain level of dollar diplomacy to fulfill its objectives. As Herbert Feis put it in early 1947,

> We are using [our command over the dollar] regularly to do the work done during the war by the Lend Lease program. We are favoring the countries which we trust; using loans to prove our good will to rulers inclined to bargain; encouraging countries that are wavering in their allegiance to our purposes or our interests; denying those we fear.[65]

Without the early unifying personality of a de Gaulle, and without the French political traditions, Italy was naturally more sensitive to such pressures than France.

In the French case, Ramadier's expulsion of the Communists from his tripartite coalition was received with much approval in Washington, and was indeed rewarded with additional support. But by then the Communists were at marked variance with the government's policies on social and colonial questions, and their continued participation in the governmental coalition was no longer compatible with the Party's line. The Communist "forced" withdrawal therefore satisfied everyone, including the Communists themselves, the American lobby, the non-Communist parties, and the Gaullists.

63. *Department of State Bulletin*, Vol. XVI, No. 415, June 15, 1947, p. 1160.
64. Paterson, *op. cit.*, pp. 264–265.
65. Herbert Feis, "Diplomacy of the Dollar," *Atlantic Monthly*, Vol. 179, January 1947, p. 26.

In the Italian case, America's pressure was more significant. It aimed clearly at the expulsion of the Communists from the De Gasperi government, but it essentially took the form of the timing of relief and of innuendos, as opposed to open threats of aid cutoffs and other such retaliations. Overwhelmed by the burdens of leadership, personally motivated by the orientation of his political philosophy, sincerely angered by what he considered to be unacceptable leftist obstruction, and increasingly responsive to the reports cabled to Rome by his representative in Washington, De Gasperi moved closer and closer to the American position. At times he pressured the Americans to pressure him in order to give him cause to justify his own action while ensuring that he was in fact fulfilling U.S. goals and aspirations. At least until the Communists were officially out of government, it is often difficult to determine precisely who was using whom.

In both instances, France and Italy were admittedly dependent, in many key areas of security and reconstruction, upon Washington's good will; but Washington was nevertheless unable to dictate an overall domestic course of action. Both De Gasperi and Ramadier remained in control of their respective domestic scenes. They alone determined when the time for such a dramatic reshuffle of their governments had come. And the time had come, because in this period of tight international bipolarity, the tripartism of the French and Italian governments was an anomaly. In sum, in the spring of 1947, the regimes of the Resistance parties came to an abrupt end, casualties of an external confrontation that made their continuation impossible.

Jiri Valenta

Soviet Decisionmaking and the Czechoslovak Crisis of 1968*

The Soviet decision to crush the Czechoslovak reform program of 1968, perhaps more than any other foreign or domestic policy issue since Khrushchev's fall, generated serious conflicts within the Soviet power elite. Yet most Western foreign policy analysts have tended to approach this matter from a *unitary actor* perspective.[1] They have perceived the locus of Soviet decisionmaking, the Politburo, as being free of constraints of bureaucratic politics when formulating and exercising its policy options.[2]

*This is the third in a series of graduate student essays accepted for publication in this journal (Ed.)

I am indebted to Professor Herbert Dinerstein of the Johns Hopkins University, who guided me through the research, encouraged me to complete this work, and was a constant source of help and information. I wish to thank Professor Melvin Croan of the University of Wisconsin, Michel Tatu of *Le Monde* in Paris, Victor Zorza of the *Washington Post*, Terese Sulikowski and I. M. Destler of the Brookings Institution, and Bennett Ramberg of the Johns Hopkins University, for useful comments. I also wish to thank the Brookings Institution for lending me the facilities necessary to complete this paper. However, none of the above is in any way responsible for the content of this work; that responsibility is mine alone.

1. Allison refers to this methodological approach as the "rational policy model." Graham Allison, *Essence of Decision: Explaining the Cuban Missile Crisis* (Boston: Little, Brown, 1971), pp. 10–38.

2. To the best of my knowledge, most studies on this subject describe the Politburo as a united entity with slight differences of opinion but none of fundamental importance. Very few writers have tried to approach the Soviet foreign policy toward Czechoslovakia in 1968 differently. On the question of

This study uses the "bureaucratic-politics model" to explain the formulation of Soviet policy toward Czechoslovakia.[3] It assumes that Soviet foreign policy actions, like those of other states, result not from a unified concept of national security but from the interplay of many other factors, including bureaucratic interests and pressures. This model is based on the notion of decisionmaking as a process of interaction among *several actors*—not only the senior policymakers but also the bureaucratic elites and pressure groups outside the Politburo.[4] The bureaucracies, the pressure groups, and the decision-

divergent viewpoints within the Soviet Politburo toward Czechoslovakia, see Philip Windsor and Adam Roberts, *Czechoslovakia 1968* (New York: Columbia University Press, 1969), pp. 67–77; Thomas W. Wolfe, *Soviet Power and Europe 1945–1970* (Baltimore: Johns Hopkins University Press, 1970), pp. 368–390; Anatole Shub, *The New Russian Tragedy* (New York: Norton, 1969), pp. 95–112; T. H. Rigby, "The Soviet Leadership: Towards a Self-Stabilizing Oligarchy?" *Soviet Studies*, XXII, 2 (October 1970), pp. 167–191. David W. Paul's "Soviet Foreign Policy and the Invasion of Czechoslovakia," *International Studies Quarterly*, XV, 2 (June 1971), pp. 159–202, is based on data analysis of Soviet elite attitudes as reflected in the "selective reading of several newspapers." Paul discovered certain differences among various elite perceptions regarding the Czechoslovak crisis and sought to identify the views of one elite group's representative in the Politburo, Alexei Kosygin. However, Paul did not identify the views of other Soviet decisionmakers and elites, as these may be gleaned from speeches and pronouncements of Soviet leaders. Also, Paul's coding of the articles is questionable and ambiguous, as is his analysis of only a few selective time periods (skipping such important occasions as the two meetings of the Central Committee of the CPSU in April and July 1968).

3. The "bureaucratic-politics model" is developed in works by Allison and Halperin. See, besides the already cited work by Allison, Graham Allison and Morton Halperin, "Bureaucratic Politics: A Paradigm and Some Policy Implications," in *Theory and Policy in International Relations*, edited by Richard Ullman (Princeton: Princeton University Press, 1972), pp. 40–79. See also I. M. Destler *President, Bureaucrats, and Foreign Policy* (Princeton: Princeton University Press, 1972); and Alexander George, "The Case for Multiple Advocacy in Making Foreign Policy," *American Political Science Review*, LXVI, 3 (September 1972), pp. 751–785.

4. Allison and Halperin's model assumes that bureaucratic politics is the process primarily *inside* the top policymaking body. Analyzing American bureaucratic politics, Destler suggests that "concentrating on the bureaucracy can be misleading." He argues that it is important to keep in mind the influence of the other interest groups and elites in society. See Destler, *op. cit.*, pp. 64–67. The same is true for Soviet politics. The suggested bureaucratic model applied to the Soviet political context is derived primarily from studies of the Soviet decisionmaking process by authors who have used similar methodological approaches without labeling them "bureaucratic politics." See Vernon Aspaturian "Internal Politics and Foreign Policy in the Soviet System," in *Approaches to Comparative and International Politics*, edited by R. Barry Farrell (Evanston, Ill.: Northwestern University Press, 1966).

makers are treated together because all exercise political influence and rely on each other's support. The final decisionmaking at the top of the Soviet decisionmaking process is the Politburo's prerogative. Yet bureaucratic and pressure groups do have access to the top and are in a position to contribute to the final policy outcome. Some of these groups exercise their influence through their representatives at the level of the Central Committee of the CPSU and even in the Politburo. Others have direct access to the Politburo through the advisers and consultants of the various members of that body.

Political groupings are found not only within the formal bureaucratic structure, including the highly organized and stable bureaucratic elites,[5] but also across organizational lines, including less formal, "loose" pressure groups and lobbies.[6] The connection between the decisionmakers, the bureaucracies, and the pressure groups may be described primarily along the lines of their national security, domestic, and organizational interests.[7] In the present paper,

pp. 212–287; Isaac Deutscher, "Moscow: The Quiet Man/Constellations of Lobbies," *Nation,* Vol. 200, No. 14 (April 5, 1965), pp. 352–357; Jon D. Glassman, "Soviet Foreign Policy Decision-making," in *Columbia Essays in International Affairs,* III, The Dean's Papers, 1967 (New York: Columbia University Press, 1968), pp. 373–402; Roger Pethybridge, *A Key to Soviet Politics: The June Crisis 1957* (London: Allen & Unwin, 1962); Sidney I. Ploss, *Conflict and Decision-making in Soviet Russia; A Case Study of Agricultural Policy, 1953–1963* (Princeton: Princeton University Press, 1965); and Michel Tatu, *Power in the Kremlin* (New York: Viking, 1970), pp. 429–443.

5. Brzezinski and Huntington have identified these groups as "policy groups," in Zbigniew Brzezinski and Samuel P. Huntington, *Political Power U.S.A./U.S.S.R.* (New York; Viking, 1964), pp. 196–197. Skilling refers to them as "official and bureaucratic" groups that "occupy the key position in the power structure." See H. Gordon Skilling and Franklyn Griffiths (eds.), *Interest Groups in Soviet Politics* (Princeton: Princeton University Press, 1971), p. 24. For more on the discussion of the influence of Soviet interest groups on the decisionmaking process, see Michael Gehlen, "Group Theory and the Study of Soviet Politics," in Sidney I. Ploss, *The Soviet Political Process* (Waltham, Mass.: Ginn, 1971), pp. 35–54; Philip Stewart, "Soviet Interest Groups and the Policy Process," in *World Politics,* XXII, 1 (October 1969), pp. 29–50; Joel Schwartz and William Keech, "Group Influence and the Policy Process in the Soviet Union," *American Political Science Review,* LXII, 3 (September 1968), pp. 840–851.

6. Deutscher observes that "the spokesmen of the most powerful lobbies have direct access to the presidium (Politburo) whose sessions they often attend, if not as parties to conflicts, then as experts and consultants." Deutscher, *op. cit.,* p. 355.

7. Allison and Halperin have developed a very useful typology of the interests of the various actors, one that can be applied to Soviet as well as to American politics: (1) national security interests, (2) organizational

the main question is how their interests were affected by the developments in Czechoslovakia.

The first section of the paper identifies the senior policymakers, the advocates of economic reform, and the bureaucratic elites, including the trade union, the military, the security police, and the party apparatus. The second seeks to explain their participation in the decisionmaking process.

Policymakers and the Bureaucratic and Pressure Groups

Economic Pressure Group

Some economists, inspired by the proposals of Y. Liberman and A. Birman, formed a pressure group advocating reform of the Soviet economic system. After Khrushchev's fall, economic reform found support even among powerful members of the Soviet Politburo, notably Kosygin, Polianskii, and Shelepin.

The economic reforms in other Eastern European countries, mainly the Czechoslovak Ota Sik's reform proposals, served as catalysts in the struggle between the advocates and the opponents of Soviet economic reform. The advocates in the debate were a coalition of economists, managers, and economic planning officials—their opponents, primarily regional party officials. Soviet reformers considered the Czechoslovak experiment, especially the education of the *rukovoditeli* (managers), a good example for the Soviet Union.[8] They also submitted that, as in Czechoslovakia, reform required not just a reorganization, but a complete modification of the centralized bureaucratic system.[9]

In his February 1968 speech, Prime Minister Kosygin indicated the existence of debate in the Soviet Politburo on the issue of economic reform in typical Soviet "language of conflict" when he stressed several times that economic reform was "correct." His stand on this issue stemmed from his realistic understanding of the unsatisfactory conditions in the Soviet Union: "We still lag behind the U.S.A.

interests, (3) domestic interests, and (4) personal interests. Allison and Halperin, *op. cit.*, p. 43.

8. V. Lisitsyn and G. Popov, "On the Administration of Cadres," *Planovoe khoziaistvo*, XLIV, 5 (May 1968), p. 11.

9. Alexander Birman has described Soviet economic reform and its goals, which were similar in some respects to those of Czechoslovak reform. "Economic Reform Today," *Reporter* (Prague), May 22, 1968, p. 19. For a Soviet discussion of the modification of a centralized economic system, see G. Dzhavadov and E. Dunaev, "Industrial Unification under the Conditions of Economic Reform," *Voprosy ekonomiki*, No. 4 (April 1968), pp. 81–91.

in total volume of industrial output, volume of national income and, particularly, level of labor productivity." [10]

Kosygin also pointed out his personal disagreement with some of his critics on the matter of national security, particularly with regard to developments in Central Europe. Even though Kosygin mentioned the peril of West German " revanchism and militarism," he criticized the hard-liners by saying that " all this does not, of course, signify that a military situation is shaping up in Europe. *Such* [*a*] *situation* does not exist, but it is imperative to keep watch. . . ." Instead, Kosygin emphasized " the subversive and anti-Soviet activity of the Mao Tse-tung group " as a major threat.[11]

Trade Union Organization

Beginning in the summer of 1967, the trade unions' organization lent powerful assistance to the advocates of economic reform.[12] As a result of the power struggle within the Politburo, Shelepin, Brezhnev's most dangerous rival, was removed from the secretariat and transferred to the chairmanship of the All-Union Central Council of Trade Unions. Shelepin, a man with experience as chief of many bureaucracies (Komsomol, security police, and the party-state control committee), soon made known in a speech at the Trade Union Congress his intention to exploit his new position in the Politburo power struggle. Shelepin spoke on behalf of economic reform and went even further than Kosygin. Along with the economic theoreticians, he maintained that " Economic reform is inseparably connected with the further *democratization* of production management." [13] He tried to improve his popularity among his trade union constituents by advocating " citizens' labor rights " and the " improvement of working conditions." He also urged the trade unions to " stop the violation of the labor laws " and to prevent " illegal dismissal of workers." Such demands, made for the first time in Soviet history since the Workers' Opposition in the early 1920s, indicated Shelepin's intention of extending the role of the trade unions, and with it his personal political influence. The opponents of economic reform undoubtedly viewed this as a threat to their power. (The omission of these citations in *Sovetskaia Rossiia* very likely reflected this con-

10. *Sovetskaia Belorussiia,* February 15, 1968, pp. 1–2.
11. *Ibid.*; emphasis added.
12. For a brief discussion of the trade union organization as an important lobby and its role in Khrushchev's overthrow, see Deutscher, *op. cit.*, pp. 353–357.
13. *Trud,* February 28, 1968, pp. 2–5; emphasis added.

cern.) [14] Also remarkable was his praise of intellectuals and writers at a time when the Party " shaped the ideological struggle."

Shelepin declared the renaissance of the popular front in the trade unions' international policy one day before Suslov's appeal [15] for cooperation between Communist and social democratic parties. Shelepin urged cooperation with all trade unions " regardless of their orientation or affiliation with international organizations." [16] This represented a sharp break with the post-World War II policy of the Soviet trade unions. In the past they had generally refused to cooperate with " reformists." Shelepin emphasized that his offer represented a new consensus among some Politburo members on the international situation: " This is not a temporary tactical slogan but our *principled policy* dictated by concern for the common interest of the working class " (emphasis added). Shelepin went on to say that contacts had been established with several Western non-Communist trade unions, among others with the West German Association of German Trade Unions. (This part of his speech also was omitted in the *Sovetskaia Rossiia.*) [17]

The policy of " world trade union unity," however, excluded the Chinese and Albanian trade unions. Shelepin launched a vigorous attack on the Chinese leadership: " Mao Tse-tung's group, betraying the cause of the working class, has dealt a blow to the rights and interests of the working people of China and to their socialist gains." Actually, Shelepin's description of the international policy of the trade union organization was a reflection of his own perception of national security—the policy of rapprochement with the West (especially West Germany), on the one hand, and the isolation of China, on the other.

The Internationalists

Suslov and Ponomarev, the Soviet leaders mainly responsible for relations with foreign Communist parties, favored a foreign policy

14. *Sovetskaia Rossiia,* February 28, 1968, p. 2.
15. *Pravda,* February 29, 1968, p. 4.
16. *Trud,* February 28, 1968, pp. 2–5.
17. *Ibid.* Also see *Sovetskaia Rossiia,* February 28, 1968, p. 2. The trade union newspaper *Trud* was even more specific in showing the importance of cooperation with the non-Communist trade unions of West Germany by stating that they " can play a very serious role in the safeguarding of peace and security in Europe." This statement appeared in an article signed by Louis Saillant, Secretary General of the World Federation of Trade Unions (WFTU) the day before Shelepin spoke. *Trud,* February 27, 1968, p. 3.

that would take into account the interests of the Soviet Union as the leader of the " cohesive " socialist camp and the world Communist movement. These interests were threatened by the deepening of the Sino-Soviet dispute during the Great Proletarian Cultural Revolution and the struggle for supremacy within the world Communist movement. Suslov, the Soviet Politburo secretary responsible for liaison with the international Communist movement and an advocate of the hard-line China policy, realized that there was no possibility of restoring friendly relations with China. He and his associate, the head of the International Department (ID)—in charge of relations with non-ruling Communist parties—Politburo candidate Ponomarev, attached great importance to the convening of a world Communist conference in 1968. This conference, as pointed out by comments in the Chinese press, was intended to restore " unity " within the Communist movement on an anti-China platform.[18]

After several years of effort and difficulties, Suslov and Ponomarev finally succeeded in assembling a majority of Communist parties at the Budapest preparatory meeting in February 1968.[19] Suslov, in his speech at this meeting, stressed the impossibility of cooperation and unity with the Chinese Communists: " The Mao Tse-tung group once again demonstrably displayed its unwillingness to cooperate with Communist parties in solving the problems of our movement and against imperialism." [20] Senior Politburo member Suslov made some important concessions to other Communist parties in the interest of " unity." He pleased the Czechoslovaks (whose delegation included the liberal, Frantisek Kriegel) and the Rumanians by claiming, " We are for strict observance of the *autonomy, independence, and equality* of all parties." [21]

The offer of " united action " in a popular front was convincing evidence of Suslov's willingness to cooperate with Western social democrats, because he considered China a major challenge to the interests of the Soviet party and state.[22] The major goal of the

18. The Chinese press reflected an awareness of Suslov's anti-Chinese policy and called Suslov " chieftain of the Soviet revisionist clique." On this see " Closer Collusion," *Peking Review*, Vol. 11, No. 8 (February 23, 1968), p. 30.

19. On the preparation of the world Communist conference, see William Griffith, *Sino-Soviet Rift* (Cambridge, Mass.: M.I.T. Press, 1967), pp. 79–106; and John Gittings, *Survey of the Sino-Soviet Dispute* (London: Oxford University Press, 1968), pp. 229–232 and 274–275.

20. *Pravda*, February 29, 1968, p. 4.

21. *Ibid.*; emphasis added. This may have been a concession to the Yugoslav Communists (despite their non-participation in the preparatory meeting, apparently because of Suslov's hope for their participation in November).

22. The edition of *Kommunist* published in the month of the conference

" internationalist " policy met with success. At the Budapest preparatory meeting it was decided to hold the world Communist conference in November-December 1968 in Moscow.

It is now apparent that the Suslov-Ponomarev conception of national security was similar to Shelepin's and not far from Kosygin's policy of détente. There also seemed to be some degree of tacit agreement on domestic policy between the " internationalists " and the advocates of economic reform in the Politburo. Needless to say, the interests of the Soviet decisionmakers are not necessarily consistent, and may vary from issue to issue. Suslov, Ponomarev, and Shelepin seemed to put more emphasis on seeking rapprochement with West Germany, while Kosygin was primarily interested in détente with the United States. Suslov's public pronouncements during the crisis, as well as the tenor of articles in the ideological periodical *Kommunist*, indicate that—even though there is insufficient evidence to claim Suslov's support for economic reform—he may have given, for tactical reasons, his backing to the domestic policy of economic reform supported by the Kosygin-Shelepin coalition.[23] Later developments served to strengthen the cohesion and cooperation among the reformist Kosygin, ambitious trade union chairman Shelepin, and " internationalists " Suslov and Ponomarev. When the hard-liner Politburo coalition opened its campaign against Czechoslovakia, the framework of a coalition advocating reconciliation with Czechoslovakia was formed and given substance.

The Military

The battle over the new minister of defense after the death of Malinovskii in March 1967 indicated disagreement between the " civilians " and the military, as well as differences over the issue of resource allocation perhaps within the Politburo itself. It was reported that Secretariat member Ustinov was considered a possible candidate for this position. The nomination of Marshal Grechko as the new Minister of Defense suggested that the Soviet military, as a bureaucratic group, had successfully resisted an attempt by some

firmly supported Suslov's Budapest speech. See Ernst Henry, " Historical Perspectives of Social Democracy," *Kommunist,* No. 3 (February 1968), pp. 89–100.

23. For Suslov's statement, see *Pravda,* May 6, 1968, pp. 1–3; see also V. Fedinin, " Economic Reform and Ideological Upbringing," *Kommunist*, No. 11 (July 1968), pp. 33–44. Before 1968, Suslov was reported to show scant interest in economic reform. See Tatu, *op. cit.*, pp. 286, 456–458.

members of the Politburo to reassert civilian control over the military.[24]

Unfortunately, there is little evidence on the views of the military establishment during the Czechoslovak crisis. Even though in his February 1968 speech, Minister of Defense Grechko contradicted Kosygin in his evaluation of the strategic situation in Central Europe —" the danger of military conflict in Europe cannot but cause great concern "[25]—it seemed to be a rather typical alarmist statement demonstrating the military establishment's interest in continuing the high level of investment in defense. Nevertheless, there were signs that the army establishment—particularly some segments of the Warsaw Pact command, the ground forces, and the Main Political Administration—was concerned about political stability in Czechoslovakia. As early as April the head of the Main Political Administration of the Soviet Armed Forces, General Yepishev, reportedly expressed the willingness of the military to respond to an appeal by " loyal communists " in safeguarding socialism in Czechoslovakia.[26]

The Security Police

A significant change also occurred in 1967 in the Soviet security police. Semichastny, head of the security police and a friend of Brezhnev's rival, Shelepin, was purged. Secretariat member Andropov became the new head of the security police and was promoted to alternate member of the Politburo. Andropov's promotion was possibly the result of Brezhnev's decision to have in that post a trusted man with expertise in East European affairs. Andropov had advanced politically during the Hungarian Revolution of 1956 by his conduct as Soviet ambassador in Budapest. As head of the CPSU

24. On the military elite's participation in the decisionmaking process, see Roman Kolkowicz, " Strategic Elites and Politics of Superpowers," *Journal of International Affairs,* Vol. 26, No. 1 (1972), pp. 40–59; Malcolm Mackintosh, " The Soviet Military Influence on Foreign Policy," *Problems of Communism,* Vol. 22 (September-October 1973), pp. 1–12; and Roman Kolkowicz, " Interest Groups in Soviet Politics—The Case of the Military," *Comparative Politics,* Vol. 2, No. 3 (April 1970), pp. 445–472. See also Vernon Aspaturian, " The Soviet Military Industrial Complex—Does It Work?" *Journal of International Affairs,* Vol. 20, No. 1 (1972), pp. 1–28.

25. *Pravda,* February 24, 1968, p. 3.

26. This was first reported by Tatu in *Le Monde,* May 5, 1968. Yepishev denied this statement in his visit to Prague. However, Tatu told this writer that he had obtained the information about Yepishev's statement from " Czechoslovak sources close to Dubcek " who had " got the information from reliable Soviet sources." (Interview with Michel Tatu, August 7, 1973, Paris.)

Central Committee Secretariat Department for liaison with ruling Communist parties, he accompanied Brezhnev on "discipline trips" to the East European countries in 1966–1967. These trips were intended to prevent the establishment of diplomatic relations between West Germany and the countries of Eastern Europe. His promotion may also be interpreted as an upgrading of the political influence of the security police. For the first time since Beria's liquidation in 1953, the Soviet security apparatus was represented at the top in the decisionmaking process.[27]

Shortly after the first signs of the Czechoslovak crisis appeared in December 1967, Andropov depicted the "real danger" to the Soviet Union from Western imperialism. He also stressed the importance of Soviet security police activity in Eastern Europe, because "the threat to the security of the Soviet Union and other socialist countries has not disappeared."[28] Of the entire bureaucratic organization, the Soviet security police must have been the most frustrated by subsequent developments in Czechoslovakia. Many of the most trusted Soviet agents in the Czechoslovak intelligence service and many of their collaborators in the Czechoslovak Ministry of Interior were removed from their posts, thus depriving the KGB of the services of its informers in that fraternal socialist country.

The Party Apparatus

The Shelest-led advocates of a hard-line[29] policy toward Czechoslovakia were suspicious of Kosygin's policy of détente and Suslov's "flirting" with social democracy. These ideological heirs of Molotov argued that, in view of the continued hostility of the "capitalist" world, the situation called for high levels of political and military preparedness focusing on the defense of the Soviet Union's position in Central and Southeastern Europe. These Soviet Politburo members from the western part of the Soviet Union, where the population was more exposed to Czechoslovak reformist ideas, perceived them as

27. For more on the role of the Soviet security police in the decisionmaking process, see Frederick C. Barghoorn, "The Security Police," in Skilling and Griffiths, *Interest Groups,* pp. 93–129.

28. *Pravda,* December 21, 1967. As Barghoorn notes, the most interesting part of Andropov's speech was its "heavy emphasis on the ideological functions of the KGB." Andropov also interpreted détente as a form of class struggle. *Ibid.*, p. 109.

29. The terms "hard-liner" or "interventionist," and "moderate" or "anti-interventionist," signify the differences among Soviet policymakers' perceptions of the issues of national security and domestic interests in relation to events in Czechoslovakia.

guideless encouragement for national Communism in their own non-Russian republics—Shelest in the Ukraine, and Pelshe in Latvia.[30]

Members of this group were supported in their advocacy of a hard-line policy toward Czechoslovakia by the regional party officials and their representatives in the Soviet Central Committee. They feared that any kind of economic reform posed a threat to their monopoly of power, and that economic reform in the Soviet Union would have political consequences, as it did in Czechoslovakia.[31]

The forced resignation of Czechoslovak President Novotny was viewed with alarm by the conservative Soviet party officials and by their Eastern European colleagues. Both regarded this event as the beginning of a potentially irreversible process unless immediate action was taken. Therefore, it was quite logical that the Dresden meeting, held one day after Novotny's resignation, was devoted exclusively to the Czechoslovak issue.[32]

30. As early as February 1968, Shelest warned about "imperialist intrigues aimed to intensify the struggle against the Soviet Ukraine and to use the poison of nationalism to influence the émigrés and possibly some of our politically immature and ideologically vacillating people," *Pravda Ukrainy,* February 17, 1968. For more on Shelest's role in the Soviet decisionmaking process and in the formulation of policy toward Czechoslovakia, see Grey Hodnett and Peter J. Potichnyj, *The Ukraine and the Czechoslovak Crisis* (Canberra: Australian National University, 1970).

31. The strongest attack against the principles of economic reform was launched by economist Strumilin. He criticized Yevsey Liberman, the father of Soviet economic reform, and his "high-profit" proposals, labeling them "non-socialist ideas." Strumilin also lamented the fact that Liberman's ideas had found "followers." This hint, because of its timing (one day after Kosygin's liberal speech in Minsk), could be interpreted as a personal attack on Kosygin. *Komsomolskaia pravda,* February 16, 1968, p. 2.

32. Dubcek in his speech of September 1969 at the plenum of the Central Committee of the Czechoslovak Communist Party admitted that there had been discussion of a change of presidents at the meeting in Dresden. Pavel Tigrid, *Kvadratura Kruhu* (Paris: Edice Svedectvi, May 1970), p. 177.

The unusually direct attack against the prominent Czechoslovak leader Smrkovsky was initiated by *Neues Deutschland* (March 26, 1968), p. 4, only three days after the Dresden meeting and could certainly not have been published without the approval or support of the hard-line coalition in the Kremlin. Evidence of this support was indicated in *Sovetskaia Rossiia.* "The strong emphasis on national peculiarities, leading necessarily to the explanation of the specific road to socialism . . . is not Marxist." *Sovetskaia Rossiia,* April 4, 1968. See also *Literaturnaia gazeta,* April 2, 1968.

This newspaper became outspoken in its criticism of and attacks on the Dubcek leadership. Even though *Sovetskaia Rossiia* tended to reflect Brezhnev's views, it cannot be said that it acted as his "mouthpiece." Brezhnev was a chairman of the Bureau of the Central Committee for the RSFSR, under whose auspices this newspaper had been published since

Secretary General Brezhnev himself soon seized the opportunity to attack his opponents in the Politburo on the issue of domestic and foreign policy. While Kosygin spoke of the backwardness of the Soviet economy as compared with that of the United States, and joined Shelepin in urging the necessity of economic reform, Brezhnev presented himself as the defender of the planned, centralized system and the interests of the opponents of economic reform.

> In discussing scientific-technical progress, some workers obviously underestimate the achievements of scientific-technical progress in our country and other socialist countries. By the same token, these people overestimate the achievements of science and technology in the capitalist world. The facts are, however, that it is exactly socialism and *planned economic management* that ensure unparalleled opportunities for the flourishing of science and the use of scientific-technical progress in the interest of the whole society.[33]

Contrary to Shelepin, who called for the maintenance of " citizens' labor rights " and praised Soviet intellectuals and writers, Brezhnev stressed " discipline " and pointed out the presence of " ideological immaturity . . . among the individual representatives of the intellectuals." [34]

Clearly, Brezhnev's perceptions of national security interests appeared to be different from those of Suslov, Kosygin, and Shelepin. Brezhnev did not stress China as the major threat to Soviet security; in fact, he never brought up that issue. The most remarkable thing in the speech was his failure to refer to the Suslov-Ponomarev activity at the Budapest meeting for the preparation of the world Communist conference. Instead, he spoke of the Sofia and Dresden " discipline " meetings. Furthermore, he made his first indirect reference to Czechoslovak and Soviet reformers when he warned that " the various anti-Soviet organizations and services set up by the imperialists ferret out morally unstable, weak, and politically immature people," and he gave explicit notice to the Czechoslovak leaders: " The renegades cannot bank on going unpunished." [35]

November 1964. The Bureau, however, was abolished at the Twenty-third Party Congress in 1966. See M. Morosov, *Leonid Breschnew* (Stuttgart: Kohlhammer, 1973), pp. 204, 219. Tatu argues that some other Soviet leaders who worked for the Central Committee Bureau for the RSFSR in the early 1960's—such as Kirilenko and Voronov—were in control of *Sovetskaia Rossiia*. See Tatu, *op. cit.*, p. 333.

33. *Pravda,* March 30, 1968, pp. 1–2; emphasis added.

34. *Ibid.*

35. *Ibid.*

The Decisionmaking Process

The April Plenum

According to Czech sources, pressure from the Soviet hard-liners was registered at the April plenum of the Central Committee of the Communist Party of the Soviet Union on the same day that a liberal " Action Program " was published in Czechoslovakia.[36] The plenum's original agenda called for a discussion of economic matters, particularly as relating to agriculture.[37] It was, however, devoted almost exclusively to the issue of political and ideological discipline on the national and international levels, especially to the situation in Czechoslovakia.

Brezhnev had already indicated in March that he would adopt the hard-liners' demands for the restoration of intraparty order and discipline, and would integrate them into his new policy for use against his Politburo opponents. His speech at the April plenum has never been published, but on the same day he spoke, *Pravda* stated:

> As was emphasized by the Secretary-General of the CC of the CPSU, L. Brezhnev, at the XIX Moscow City Party Conference, " Our Party is a Party not only of those who think alike, but also who act alike. . . . The greater the tasks which the Party must resolve, the higher must be the discipline and order in its ranks: During the course of reviewing one or another problem, different points of view may collide and conflict with one another, but as soon as a decision is accepted . . . we act as one man." [38]

This was an explicit warning to members of the moderate coalition to cease discussing controversial issues. Of the other members of the Politburo, only Shelest spoke. He apparently stressed the impact of developments in Czechoslovakia upon national sentiment in the Ukraine.[39] The most striking fact was that no one member of the Soviet delegation to the important Budapest meeting presented a report or participated in discussions. Furthermore, no party ideologue spoke, despite the fact that the April plenum was concerned with ideological issues.[40] The unexpected nomination of an inexperienced

36. *Rude Pravo,* April 10, 1968, p. 3.
37. *Rude Pravo,* April 9, 1968, p. 7.
38. *Pravda,* Editorial, April 9, 1968.
39. On Shelest's activities during the Soviet-Czechoslovak crisis, see Hodnett and Potichnyj, *op. cit.*
40. Victor Zorza argues that in the context of the Soviet political process the silence of some Soviet policymakers on an important issue has to be

regional party official, F. Katushev, to the sensitive post of party secretary in charge of the Central Committee Secretariat department for relations with the ruling Communist parties, indicated that Brezhnev wanted to have this section under tight control by a personal political ally.

However, the final resolution adopted at the April plenum was a compromise between the Brezhnev " great power " approach and the Suslov " internationalist " approach to the international political situation. The resolution underscored the importance of the Dresden meeting and pointed out that " The CC plenary session *confirms the correctness* of the policy exposing revanchism and militarism in West Germany." (That the plenum had to confirm the correctness of this policy perhaps means that there was disunity.) It also emphasized the significance of the Budapest meeting—which Brezhnev ignored in his speech in March—and charged the Politburo with maintaining " close contacts with the fraternal parties . . . to make every effort for the success of the international conference." [41]

The May Crisis

The hard-liners' response to events in Czechoslovakia came in the form of political, economic, and psychological pressure applied on many fronts at the beginning of May. Czechoslovak leaders were unexpectedly ordered to a summit in Moscow, and under Soviet military pressure Czechoslovak Minister of Defense Dzur announced that " staff exercises " would be held later in the year.[42] Podgorny,[43] Chairman of the Supreme Soviet and Shelest's predecessor as head of the Ukrainian party bureaucracy, issued an official statement to the Czechoslovak ambassador, promising Soviet assistance to Czechoslovakia against " imperialist intrigues," [44] thereby suggesting that he as well had joined the hard-line coalition led by Shelest.

interpreted as their tacit disagreement with the view of their colleagues. Quoted in Ploss, *Conflict and Decision-Making*, pp. 17–18.

41. *Pravda,* April 11, 1968, p. 1; emphasis added. Interestingly, the resolution's publication coincided with Suslov's first public appearance after an absence of several weeks.

42. The announcement emphasized that the exercise would be held " late in the year 1968 and [would] be only staff maneuvers," unlike the Warsaw Pact Vltava maneuvers of 1966. *Rude Pravo,* May 4, 1968, p. 1.

43. Tatu characterized Podgorny as liberal-minded on the issues of economic reform and light industry, but as an opportunist both in his ideological convictions and in his personal loyalties. Tatu, *op. cit.,* pp. 423 and 499.

44. *Pravda,* May 7, 1968, p. 2.

The Czechoslovak leaders took pains not to reveal the full extent of their dispute with the Kremlin hard-liners.[45]

The celebration of the 150th anniversary of Karl Marx's birthday provided a good opportunity for the Soviet leaders to articulate their political differences regarding the international situation, especially Czechoslovakia. Pelshe, speaking in East Germany, and Suslov, speaking in Moscow, expressed opposing points of view. While Pelshe—former head of the Latvian party apparatus, and since 1966 the head of the Party Control Committee (responsible mainly for ideological supervision) and a member of the Politburo[46]—stressed "revisionism" and "dangerous nationalist tendencies"[47] in the Communist parties as a major threat to Marxism-Leninism, Suslov emphasized the danger of "*left revisionism* and Mao Tse-tung's *blatant manifestation of the left adventurist perversion of Marxism*,"[48] though he took care to attack the opposite deviation as well. Pelshe, however, did not mention the Mao Tse-tung group at all. Instead, he thoughtfully pointed out that the "left opportunists ignore the real situation at the various stages of the Communist workers' movements."[49]

While Pelshe spoke for discipline and obedience within the Communist movement—"All Communist parties are obliged to accept the Marxist-Leninist doctrine that the proletarian revolution follows certain laws of development"—Suslov placed emphasis on the "rights of sovereignty and autonomy" of Communist parties and pointed out that "the norms for relations between Communist parties are full democracy, equal rights, and mutual respect *for each other's views*." He reiterated his pledge about the right of Communist parties to maintain "*divergent views on certain questions*" owing to the existence of "diverse conditions of economic and social-political development in the countries where Communist parties operate."[50]

45. See the interview with Dubcek: "The Soviet comrades expressed their fears that the democratization process can be used against the socialism in our country." *Rude Pravo,* May 7, 1968, p. 1.

46. For more on Pelshe's background, see Tatu, *op. cit.,* p. 34; or *Der Spiegel,* Vol. 25, No. 49 (November 29, 1971), pp. 84–86.

47. *Neues Deutschland,* May 4, 1968, p. 9.

48. *Pravda,* May 6, 1968, pp. 1–3; emphasis added.

49. *Neues Deutschland,* May 4, 1968. *Pravda* "corrected" Pelshe's speech to emphasize Chinese policy as "the most brutal form" of violation of the principles of internationalism. The *Pravda* version also stressed the importance of the world Communist conference. *Pravda,* May 4, 1968, p. 4.

50. *Pravda,* May 6, 1968, p. 3; emphasis added. This might have been a reference not only to the French and Italian Communist parties but also to the Czechoslovak party. The Czechoslovak Communist Party was the only one in

The particulars of the May summit meeting of the Eastern European and Soviet leaders in Moscow are still unknown. There were reports in the Czechoslovak press indicating Kadar's disagreement with Ulbricht at this summit.[51] Also, during the meeting Czechoslovakia was placed under great psychological pressure when Soviet military divisions unexpectedly began to approach its borders.[52] However, the Moscow conference failed to take a clear stand on the Czechoslovak issue.[53] Apparently, a majority in the Soviet Politburo opposed military intervention at that time. Brezhnev probably sided with the moderates, either because he was convinced that caution was the better policy, or because he was unwilling to find himself in the minority. The divergent opinions held by Politburo members were reflected to some extent in the Soviet press.[54]

It is conceivable that one of the compromise solutions reached at this summit meeting called for an " on the site inspection " in the

Eastern European countries to come to power in an industrialized country with indigenous democratic traditions.

51. " Kadar had some reservations about this meeting, that took place at Ulbricht's initiative." *Rude Pravo,* May 12, 1968, p. 7.

52. Tigrid, *op. cit.,* p. 43.

53. " Contrary to previous conferences of this kind, the communiqué [on the results] of this meeting did not say anything about ' unanimity.' Therefore, foreign correspondents infer that the unity of all participants was not achieved." *Rude Pravo,* May 11, 1968, p. 3.

54. After the Moscow summit, *Pravda* again stressed the significance of " Budapest " and the " common desire for unity ": " In the Interests of Unity " (editorial), *Pravda,* May 11, 1968, p. 1. *Kommunist* continued its forceful anti-China campaign: " About the Character of the ' Cultural Revolution ' in China," *Kommunist,* No. 7 (May 1968), pp. 103–114. Shelepin's newspaper *Trud* reflected the official line by both criticizing and accepting some features of the developments in Czechoslovakia. Whereas other newspapers presented either one side or the other, *Trud* presented both. It mildly criticized an article in the Czechoslovak newspaper *Prace* which advocated the creation of a pluralist, parliamentary political system in Czechoslovakia. *Trud* asked, " Into whose hands does it play?"—which was not difficult to answer in the reality of May 1968: *Trud,* May 15, 1968, p. 3. On the same day, *Trud* also encouraged in a rather extraordinary way Czechoslovak-Soviet friendship in a front-page article entitled " A Good Trip " —two days before Kosygin unexpectedly left for Czechoslovakia: *Trud,* May 15, 1968, p. 1.

The pressure of the hard-liners toward Czechoslovakia during the May crisis was indicated in the pages of *Sovetskaia Rossiia.* Three days before Kosygin left for Czechoslovakia, *Sovetskaia Rossiia* (May 14, 1968, p. 3) pointedly attacked the founder of the Czechoslovak Republic, President Masaryk, following the lead of Czechoslovak conservative Indra a month earlier: " Good or Bad Masaryk?", *Reporter* (Prague), May 8, 1968, p. 9. The publication of such an article at a time of political tension and negotiation could only have had a provocative effect.

form of a visit by a Soviet military delegation in Czechoslovakia. Only a few hours after the arrival of the military delegation, Premier Kosygin unexpectedly turned up in Prague on an "unofficial visit." The Czechoslovak leaders barely had enough time to greet him. Kosygin's appearance in Czechoslovakia was probably aimed at maintaining the bureaucratic balance of pressure within the military delegation led by Minister of Defense Grechko and "interventionist" Yepishev.

However, Kosygin's carefully timed journey was only partially successful in eliminating the pressure of the hard-liners and reducing tensions between the two countries. The visit resulted in an agreement between Kosygin and the Czechoslovak leaders, providing for Warsaw Pact joint maneuvers on Czechoslovak territory in June, instead of the military's demand to station Warsaw Pact troops on the Czechoslovak–West German border.

The July Plenum

The advocates of the hard-line policy in the Soviet Politburo were mollified to some extent by the agreement between Kosygin and the Czechoslovak leaders, mainly because it guaranteed the presence of the Soviet Army on Czechoslovak territory.[55] The Soviet Army could now apply considerable pressure on the liberal leadership and, by virtue of its presence on Czechoslovak soil, enhance the prestige of the pro-Soviet elements in the Czechoslovak party.

The Fourteenth Congress of the Czechoslovak Communist Party was scheduled for the beginning of September. It was expected that this congress would expel most of the pro-Soviet Central Committee members and elect a new, pro-Dubcek slate. Thus, it must have been more than a coincidence that on May 29, the same day that the plenary session of the Central Committee of the Czechoslovak Communist Party met, the first Warsaw Pact troops under General Kazakov arrived in Czechoslovakia.[56] As indicated by the commander-in-chief of the Warsaw Pact, Marshal Yakubovskii,[57] the plan of the Moscow hard-liners was to keep the Warsaw Pact troops deployed

55. The first announcement that joint maneuvers would be held in June was published a day before Kosygin's departure for Moscow. *Rude Pravo,* May 14, 1968, p. 2, and May 25, 1968, p. 1; and Tigrid, *op. cit.,* p. 44.

56. *Reporter,* December 25, 1968 (supplement), p. 6.

57. Yakubovskii was reported to have announced at the meeting of the Soviet generals that Soviet troops would stay on Czechoslovak territory "at least until September 20"—when the party congress of the Czechoslovak Communist Party was supposed to close. Tigrid, *op. cit.,* p. 44. Tigrid based most of his reports on original sources from the Central Committee of the

as a pressure factor supporting the anti-Dubcek elements until after the Czechoslovak party congress convened in September.

Brezhnev's intentions, however, were still not very clear, and he vacillated between a hard line and a moderate position regarding Czechoslovakia. In discussion with the Czechoslovak parliamentary delegation, Brezhnev disclosed that he was " aware that there occurred some mistakes on the Soviet side " and even pledged the willingness of the Soviet Union to defend itself at " the International Court " in order to prove its readiness to work toward a peaceful solution with Czechoslovakia.[58]

The partial success of a policy of limited détente with the United States resulted in the July 2 conclusion of the Non-Proliferation Treaty on nuclear weapons, and in the possibility of a visit to Moscow by President Johnson. Kosygin hailed the treaty as a " major success for the cause of peace " and expressed his hope for the launching of the SALT talks with the United States. " *In the near future . . .* we will make it possible to achieve concrete results in the disarmament that all people of the world are waiting for." [59] This improvement in Soviet-American relations threatened to take the wind out of the hard-liners' sails.

The hard-liners apparently interpreted Kosygin's statement as a weakening of the pressure on Czechoslovakia. Also, Brezhnev may have considered Kosygin's image as a successful statesman for peace to be a personal threat to his own position and prestige in the Politburo. This, then, was probably the decisive point in the course of events culminating in the Czechoslovak crisis: Brezhnev took the lead in opposing Kosygin—just as Khrushchev had opposed Malenkov's policy of peaceful coexistence in 1954. Two days after Kosygin's announcement, Brezhnev delivered one of the most uncompromising foreign policy speeches of the post-Stalin period. Reflecting his disagreement with Kosygin's moderate policy of détente, Brezhnev—using Zhdanov's terms—described the United States as a " rotting and disintegrating society," adding, " Yes, monopolistic America is decaying, but it will inevitably be replaced by another America—an America of the working people." [60] Attacking Bonn's *Ostpolitik*, he announced a new hard-line policy, later referred to by Western observers as the so-called " Brezhnev Doctrine ": " *We*

Czechoslovak Communist Party, as well as on the oral reports of Czechoslovak witnesses to the meetings with Soviet leaders. Interview with Pavel Tigrid, August 5, 1973, Paris.

58. " Navsteva u Brezhneva " (Visit by Brezhnev), *Lidova Demokracie*, June 14, 1968, p. 1. 59. *Izvestiia*, July 2, 1968, p. 1; emphasis added.

60. *Pravda*, July 4, 1968, pp. 1–2.

cannot and never will be indifferent to the fate of socialist construction in other countries." [61] The same hard line was expressed in a menacing Soviet memorandum [62] to West Germany two days after Kosygin's speech. On July 11 *Pravda* published the well-known Alexandrov article—a semi-official analysis of the seriousness of the Czechoslovak situation—which implied that the Moscow hard-liners were alarmed by the incipient politic debacle of the pro-Soviet elements in Czechoslovakia.[63]

" Interventionists " Shelest and Podgorny, as well as Brezhnev and Katushev, flew to Warsaw to attend the summit of Eastern European leaders called to deal with the Czechoslovak situation. Meanwhile, Kosygin held a press conference in Sweden where he expressed his confidence in the Czechoslovak Communist Party. Kosygin stated that " *We are confident* that the Czechoslovak Communist Party will never yield its guiding role. The encroachment on Czechoslovakia's socialist foundations will be effectively rebuffed *by the Czechoslovak people and communists.*" [64] He joined the Warsaw meeting a day later—perhaps a sign of the unexpectedness of the meeting. Even though Kosygin put his hope in the Czechoslovak Communist Party, his remarks regarding the Alexandrov article [65] in *Pravda* reflected his sense of obligation to keep party discipline and also indicated the defensiveness of the anti-interventionist coalition. Kosygin's passive behavior at the Warsaw meeting bespoke his disapproval of the hard-liners' offensive. According to Erwin Weit, a former interpreter for Gomulka, Kosygin—contrary to Brezhnev—" gave the impression of a very worried man. The role of judge which he had adopted at this meeting did not seem to agree with him." [66]

Brezhnev, however, was reported to have taken a tough line, disregarding *all* reservations of the Hungarian delegation and all considerations regarding the Western Communist parties. One of his statements included the following: " It was the duty of communists and of leading statesmen to afford every assistance to the Czecho-

61. *Ibid.*; emphasis added.

62. G. Duckwitz, " Gewaltverzicht und Interventionsrecht," *Aussenpolitik*, Vol. 19, No. 9 (September 1968), pp. 519–536.

63. *Pravda*, July 11, 1968, p. 4.

64. *Pravda*, July 15, 1968, p. 4; emphasis added.

65. *Ibid.* " I would advise you to read the article published the other day in the newspaper, *Pravda.* It reflects our appraisal of the events now taking place in Czechoslovakia. . . ." Kosygin was referring to the Alexandrov article, *Pravda*, July 11, 1968, p. 4.

66. Erwin Weit, *At the Red Summit: Interpreter Behind the Iron Curtain* (New York: Macmillan, 1973), p. 211.

slovak working class and the whole Czechoslovak people." [67] Perhaps to balance this he conceded " the right of each party to take its own path." These apparent contradictions in Brezhnev's statements indicated that the final decision for military intervention had not yet been made in the Kremlin. Although Brezhnev seemed to have adopted a hard-line policy, he left his options open; in fact, he attempted to present the views of both Kremlin coalitions.

Following the Warsaw meeting the CPSU held another plenum of the Central Committee devoted exclusively to the situation in Czechoslovakia. As at the April plenum, Brezhnev and Shelest were the only Politburo members to speak.[68] The hard-liners in the Politburo used the Khrushchev ploy of permitting some non-members of the Central Committee to speak—for example, the Latvian party chief Voss and Ilnitskii, first secretary of the Transcarpathian Province Party Committee.[69] The presence of the latter could only be interpreted as a shrewd psychological attempt to highlight the urgency of the Czechoslovak threat to the western part of the Ukraine (Transcarpathia), which had been Czechoslovak territory before World War II.[70] The presence of non-members of the Central Committee might have aroused criticism from other Politburo members (especially Suslov) who did not have an opportunity to present their views.

The August Intervention

While the Central Committee of the Communist Party of the Soviet Union was in session, the Soviet hard-liners were preparing a

67. *Ibid.*

68. Shelest made a speech several days prior to the plenum which appeared in conflicting versions in various newspapers. Both official newspapers, *Pravda* and *Izvestiia,* published Shelest's attack on the Prague reformers. But the *Pravda* version was harder than that of *Izvestiia* and attacked not only the Czechoslovak leaders, but also the moderate members of the Soviet Politburo—their " yesmen." See *Pravda*, July 5, 1968, pp. 3–4; and *Izvestiia*, July 6, 1968, p. 3.

69. *Pravda,* July 18, 1968, p. 1. It is noteworthy that six of the speakers —more than half—were representatives of the party establishment in the Ukraine and the Baltic Republics (Shelest, Ilnitskii, Korotov, Degtiarev from the Ukraine; Voss from Latvia; and Snechkus from Lithuania). Apparently the Politburo hard-liners decided to mobilize some segments of the party establishment in the Western part of the Soviet Union in order to shift the balance in their favor.

70. As Hodnett and Potichnyj note (*op. cit.*, pp. 144–145), Ilnitskii's anti-Czechoslovak views were very easily detected in his articles, published before and after the invasion.

political, psychological, and military assault on Czechoslovakia. The announcement of the discovery of a secret cache of weapons on the Czechoslovak–West German border could have been used as a pretence to signal military action. In any case, it was an important psychological weapon used to condition the public to eventual intervention.[71] *Pravda*'s editorial after the July plenum described developments in Czechoslovakia as dangerous, and an attempt to " undermine the foundations of socialist statehood and liquidate the socialist system in Czechoslovakia," but added that:

> *Needless to say the forces of socialism in Czechoslovakia objectively mentioned are far greater than those now striking at the revolutionary gains of the Czechoslovak people.* The rightist elements, despite all their noise and attack, lack support among the broad masses of working people. But a determined, uncompromising and consistent struggle is necessary to defeat them.[72]

In other words *Pravda* stated, just as Kosygin had in Stockholm, that the danger in Czechoslovakia was not " mortal " and allowed that the Czechoslovak Communists were able to solve their own problems. Therefore, there was no necessity for a military solution to the crisis. Thus, as late as mid-July 1968 a substantial number of Politburo members still preferred a political solution and were exercising caution. However, at the same time the hard-line coalition was pressing for intervention. At a session of the Supreme Soviet of the Russian Republic, Podgorny again spoke of " blows at the foundations of socialist statehood,"[73] but his speech did not convey *Pravda*'s confidence in the " Czechoslovak forces of socialism." This naturally implied the assistance of " fraternal socialist " countries.

Since the absolute majority of the non-ruling Western European Communist parties, Yugoslavia, and Rumania supported the Czechoslovak Communist Party, and since the anti-interventionist coalition was still seeking a political solution, the Soviet Politburo agreed upon a common meeting of almost all members of the Soviet and Czechoslovak Politburos—an act unprecedented in the history of the Communist movement.

Perhaps the Soviet advocates of military intervention agreed to this

71. *Pravda*, July 19, 1968, p. 4. Interestingly, while *Pravda* spoke of only one discovered cache, *Krasnaia zvezda* (July 21, 1968, p. 3) spoke of several such discoveries.
72. *Pravda*, July 19, 1968, p. 1; emphasis added.
73. *Pravda*, July 20, 1968, p. 2.

meeting thinking that they could play the Czechoslovak leaders against each other, but later developments showed that the crucial element in the agreement to a joint meeting was a mutual distrust among the Politburo members and the fear that a small, select delegation would make a deal at the expense of the others. Therefore, in an attempt to achieve a balance, the delegation from the Soviet Politburo was made up of members of both coalitions. They included advocates of the intervention: Podgorny, Shelest, Pelshe; anti-interventionists Suslov, Shelepin, Kosygin, Ponomarev; and undecided Brezhnev, Demichev, Mazurov, Masherov, Katushev, and Voronov. Even during the meeting in Cierna the balance was maintained in Moscow by the two Politburo members left behind—moderate Polianskii and hard-liner Kirilenko.

This was the first opportunity for most members of the anti-interventionist coalition—especially Suslov, Shelepin, and Ponomarev—to negotiate with the Czechoslovak leaders. Despite Soviet pressure and anti-Semitic insults directed at Czechoslovak liberal Kriegel, the Cierna meeting was a partial victory for the Czechoslovak reformers. An agreement was reached primarily because of the presence and conciliatory attitude of the moderate members of the Soviet Politburo in general, and Suslov in particular. (The final stage of negotiation was conducted on the Soviet side by a team of four senior Politburo members—moderates Suslov, Kosygin; hard-liner Podgorny; and Brezhnev.) The agreement was also a personal success for Suslov, who again expressed his moderate and "internationalist" views by stating that he found "the Czechoslovak January policy a renaissance of Marxism in a certain sense" and stressed the need for a peaceful solution to the Soviet-Czechoslovak schism: "The Czechoslovak question must be settled by agreement if great harm is not to ensue for the international Communist movement and its unity."[74]

The Bratislava agreement seemed to be a compromise both between the Czechoslovak and Soviet leaderships, and between the Soviet moderate and conservative approaches to the Communist movement in Eastern Europe. Thus, the agreement spoke simultaneously of "law governing the development of a socialist society common to all socialist societies" and "national particularism."[75]

Some articles in the Soviet press praised the result of the Cierna

74. Tigrid, *op. cit.*, pp. 86–87. Tigrid here based his information on oral reports of Czechoslovak witnesses to the negotiations.

75. See "Statement of Communist and Workers' Parties of Socialist Countries," *Pravda*, August 4, 1968, p. 1.

and Bratislava meetings.[76] *Pravda*'s editorial reminded the hard-liners, and Brezhnev himself, why the meetings succeeded:

> The meetings in Cierna and Bratislava have reconfirmed the premise that *wise, calm, thoughtful and patient discussion* of complex questions on a principled basis and imbued with profound concern for the *vital interests* of world socialism and the international communist movement, is a norm that has justified itself in relations among the socialist countries and their Communist and workers' parties.[77]

Pravda also published a rather unusual statement praising the entire Politburo for the Cierna and Bratislava agreements.[78] Emphasizing the activity of the entire Politburo, the statement stressed " collective leadership " as the guiding principle of the Communist Party of the Soviet Union; consequently, it undermined the leading position of Secretary-General Brezhnev, who had presumed to be "first among equals."

The advocates of military intervention considered the Bratislava agreement of a kind of " unhealthy " compromise. They would have liked the agreement to be a clear directive for Czechoslovakia, and they stressed that " *all* Soviet Communists and people . . . express the full confidence that the collective working-out of decisions will be carried out. . . ." [79] However, the hard-liners soon realized that the Czechoslovak interpretation of the Bratislava agreement was far different from their own, and that the result reached in Cierna and Bratislava actually encouraged the Czechoslovak reformers.

The dissatisfaction of the *apparatchiki* from the non-Russian republics in the western part of the Soviet Union was depicted again, in the newspaper *Literaturnaia gazeta.* This paper began to reprint articles from the Ukrainian and Baltic press on the problems of nationalism. Only two days after the Bratislava agreement was reached, an article in its pages made an unusual comment on the

76. *Trud* called it a " new contribution in the strengthening of unity of the fraternal parties " (" Unity of the Fraternal Nations," *Trud*, Editorial, August 6, 1968). *Kommunist*'s editorial likewise applauded the Bratislava agreement. While again violently attacking " Chinese Marxism " as the most prominent threat to Soviet interests, it also stressed the importance of the convening world Communist conference and promised to take " all measures " for its successful preparation. *Kommunist*, Editorial, No. 12 (1968), pp. 24–30.

77. " Strength in Unity," *Pravda*, Editorial, August 5, 1968, p. 1; emphasis added.

78. *Pravda,* August 7, 1968, p. 1.

79. *Sovetskaia Rossiia*, Editorial, August 6, 1968; emphasis added.

potential danger of theories of *samostiinost* (Ukrainian term for self-determination) developed in the "anti-Communist centers created by the U.S. State Department" and aimed at "driving wedges between the fraternal peoples of the Soviet Union."[80] Such an article, in post-Bratislava reality, implied that Czechoslovakia's experiments with federalization were a catalyst to nationalist demands in the Soviet Union, especially in the Ukraine.[81] There is some evidence that one of the most outspoken advocates of the hard line toward Czechoslovakia—Ukrainian party leader Shelest—was in charge of party business after the Bratislava conference (August 5–15) when most of the Politburo members, including Brezhnev, left for a holiday.[82]

The military's dissatisfaction with the Bratislava agreement and its attendant pressure apparently brought about the nomination of General Shtemenko—one of the few Soviet officers with the requisite experience of handling a senior operational staff[83]—as the new chief of staff of the Warsaw Pact on August 7. Several days later the new Sky Shield maneuvers commenced, combined with other "signal corps" exercises around Czechoslovakia.

The official campaign started after publication of the new statutes of the Czechoslovak Communist Party. The statutes guaranteed for the first time in Communist history the rights of minority within the party. *Pravda* called this act a "legalization of factions," saying that it was but a "short way to total disintegration of the party."[84] The visits of Tito and Ceausescu to Prague further intensified political

80. V. Volny, "Before the Court of History," *Literaturnaia gazeta*, No. 32 (August 7, 1968), p. 2. The editor's note was very interesting: "We are opening a new column reprinting the most interesting materials from the literary newspapers of the Soviet Union. We present to our readers an article by the writer V. Volny that was published a few days ago in *Literaturna Ukraina*; the selection . . . dealing with the collection of articles, 'Socialist Reality and National Fabrication,' [was] published by the Ukrainian Republic's Political Publishing House."

81. M. George Zaninovich and D. A. Brown, "Political Integration in Czechoslovakia: The Implications of the Prague Spring and Social Intervention," *Journal of International Affairs*, Vol. 27, No. 1 (1973), pp. 66–79. Zaninovich and Brown concluded that "one of the few durable achievements of the Prague Spring was that a legal framework for federalization was drawn up just prior to the Soviet invasion in August 1968."

82. "The Unexpected Soviet Initiative—Thaw in Prague," *Le Monde*, June 17–18, 1973; and *Svedectvi*, XII, 46 (1973), pp. 184–185. The Soviet press (August 5–15) did not indicate whether Shelest was actually in Moscow during this period.

83. John Erickson, *Soviet Military Power* (London: Royal United Services Institute for Defence Studies, 1971), p. 21.

84. *Pravda*, August 9, 1968, pp. 3–4.

tension and led to increased polemics in the Kremlin because of fears of a new "Communist little entente" in Eastern Europe.

Eight days before the Slovak party congress was to begin, Shelest reportedly convened a meeting of the Soviet Politburo (August 15–16) at which he and some of the other hard-liners pressed for military intervention.[85] *Pravda*'s publication of another semi-official article signed by Alexandrov (as on July 11) indicated that the interventionist coalition may have pushed the Politburo to adopt a hard line.[86]

But it can be said with certainty only that there was still resistance within the Politburo to military intervention, especially on the part of Suslov and Shelepin, who were still attempting to seek a *modus vivendi* with the Czechoslovak leaders. They contended that "in spite of the undeniable upsurge of counter-revolutionary forces, it was still possible to settle the Czechoslovak affair by political means."[87]

There were other indications of uncertainty in the Politburo, such as Brezhnev's letter to Dubcek and Kosygin's to President Johnson. In his letter Kosygin informed President Johnson that the Politburo had agreed to start SALT talks with the United States.[88] A precise insight into the Politburo voting is of course not possible. But it is plausible to draw the conclusion that the decision to invade Czechoslovakia was made under the pressure of the Politburo hard-liners supported by some bureaucratic elites, particularly the regional party apparatus, the party establishment in the western part of the Soviet Union, the military, and the secret police, despite the resistance of the anti-interventionist coalition that in the final analysis found themselves—as one of them, Ponomarev put it—"unluckily in the minority."[89]

85. Additional information on the role of Shelest in the preparation of the invasion was revealed by Soviet diplomats in Prague and in some Western countries. According to these reports, published in the Western press, Shelest deceived the Politburo and Brezhnev himself by presenting the situation in Czechoslovakia as disastrous. "The Unexpected Soviet Initiative—Thaw in Prague," *Le Monde*, June 17–18, 1973; and *Svedectvi*, XII, 46 (1973).

86. Ivan Aleksandrov, "The Blatant Attacks of Reaction," *Pravda*, August 18, 1968, p. 4.

87. Tigrid, *op. cit.*, p. 96. Tigrid's source here was the official report of Czechoslovak Prime Minister Cernik.

88. John Newhouse, *Cold Dawn—The Story of SALT* (New York: Holt, Rinehart, and Winston, 1973), p. 13. See also William E. Griffith, "U.S. Policy and the Invasion of Czechoslovakia," in I. W. Zartman (ed.), *Czechoslovakia: Intervention and Impact* (New York: New York University Press, 1970), pp. 55–57.

89. See Ponomarev's statement in Pavel Tigrid: *Why Dubcek Fell* (London: Macdonald, 1971), p. 127.

Conclusion

The bureaucratic-politics model of the Soviet intervention in Czechoslovakia has improved upon the performance of the generally accepted unitary-actor model. During the crisis, particularly in the initial stages of policy formulation, the bureaucratic elites and pressure groups participated heavily in the decisionmaking process. These groups communicated their opinions on the issue of Czechoslovakia to Soviet policymakers, and later were mobilized by the decisionmakers for consensus-building and support. The decision to intervene was an outcome of the Soviet bureaucratic process, which included the building of coalitions and countercoalitions, and hard internal bargaining games among the decisionmakers and the various bureaucratic and pressure groups.

Even Secretary General Brezhnev was subsequently shown to have been hesitant before the final vote that resulted in the small margin within the Politburo for military intervention. But finally he decided to put domestic and national security interests, as perceived by some segments of the party apparatus, ahead of Kosygin's policy of détente and Suslov's policy of isolating China by strengthening the Soviet Union as the head of the international Communist movement. Apparently he decided to join the pro-interventionist coalition because the Bratislava agreement—a victory for the moderates—threatened to undermine his bureaucratic position of Secretary General, *primus inter pares* in the Politburo.[90]

This conclusion seems to be correct in the light of post-invasion developments. The immediate consequences of the intervention seemed to diminish the moderate coalition's leverage at the top of the decisionmaking process. The defeat of Sik's economic reforms in Czechoslovakia was paralleled by the rejection of the Kosygin-supported Liberman proposals in the Soviet Union. The subjugation of Czechoslovakia brought increasing consensus in the Politburo against economic reform. In foreign affairs it led to a temporary worsening of Soviet-American relations. President Johnson refused to begin SALT talks and cancelled his expected visit to Moscow. The intervention forced the postponement of the world Communist conference from November 1968 to July 1969.

But in the long run the proponents of the military invasion seemed to suffer a hard setback. Shelest, one of the most outspoken advocates of intervention and opponents of détente, was purged. One of

90. For more on Brezhnev's behavior during a different type of crisis, see Jiri Valenta, "Soviet Foreign Policy and the Moscow Summit of 1972." *SAIS Review*, Vol. 17, No. 2 (Winter 1973), p. 19.

the reasons for his purge was reported to be his role in the formation of the policy toward Czechoslovakia in 1968.[91] Brezhnev later shifted his foreign policy—as Khrushchev did in mid-1955 when he adopted Malenkov's policy of peaceful coexistence—to include his opponents' policies: Kosygin's policy of détente and Suslov-Ponomarev's policy of rapprochement with the West German social democrats.[92]

On the whole, an examination of the Czechoslovak case provides several generalizations of interest for the analysis of Soviet decision-making processes. In the event of an unresolved dispute among senior policymakers on questions of national security and domestic interest, bureaucratic politics can play an important role in decisionmaking. However, one should be aware of the limitations of such an approach. This study suggests that the bureaucratic-politics model probably can be best applied to Soviet politics when domestic interests play as important a role as national security interests, and when data on the individual interests of the actors are readily available from published sources. This approach seems appropriate for the study of "intra-bloc" relations where, because of the close interdependence of their politics, the Soviet Union is directly affected when in conflict with other socialist countries. It is probably less useful for explaining Soviet actions vis-à-vis non-socialist countries, where internal Soviet policy is not directly affected, and where national security dominates.[93]

91. The Politburo reportedly established a committee for the re-examination of the Soviet policy toward Czechoslovakia which concluded that the developments were dangerous but did not "necessarily require the military intervention." Basically, the conclusion followed Suslov's line of reasoning during the confrontation. Also, the Soviet ambassador to Czechoslovakia, Chervonenko, was forced to leave Prague (for a new assignment in Paris), and three hundred other Soviet officials left at about the same time. See *Le Monde*, June 17–18, 1973. Voronov was purged with Shelest in 1973. Unfortunately, the evidence is insufficient to establish whether his purge was connected with his stand on the Czechoslovak issue.

92. On Brezhnev's latest "metamorphosis" in foreign policy, see Valenta, *op. cit.*, pp. 15–20, and a forthcoming article in *Problems of Communism*.

93. During the Cuban missile crisis the Soviet foreign policy decisionmaking process was highly concentrated in the hands of a kind of "Soviet national security council" comprising only five or six Politburo members. See Glassman, *op. cit.*, pp. 296–297. Allison and Halperin suggest a generalization for application of their bureaucratic-politics model to American politics: "The bureaucratic rules of the game, where organizational and domestic interests predominate, or where one wishes to treat the details of action." Allison and Halperin, *op. cit.*, p. 58.

Dimitri K. Simes

The Soviet Invasion of Czechoslovakia and the Limits of Kremlinology

On August 21, 1968, troops of five Warsaw Pact nations crossed the borders of Czechoslovakia. Obviously, the governments of Bulgaria, East Germany, Hungary, and Poland—each in its own way—had a significant part in determining the tragic fate of the "Prague Spring." However, there is little doubt that, while the Soviet Union's East European allies could submit their advice and presumably exert political pressure, only the Soviet leadership had the authority to launch the invasion. It was up to the Kremlin to make the difficult decision between continuing the attempts to influence developments in Czechoslovakia by political means and using the Moscow-controlled Warsaw Pact military machine. The Soviets chose the latter. Why? Was the decision to intervene by force inevitable under the circumstances—as they were seen through the prism of officially interpreted Soviet national security interests?

Answers to these questions are of interest not only to historians but to political analysts and decisionmakers as well. After all, the Soviet decision to invade Czechoslovakia is a dramatic illustration of Soviet national security policy formulation in a crisis situation. A better appreciation of the channels and rules of this process is indeed of vital importance.

There are two major approaches to analyzing the Soviet decision-making process. The first focuses on general Soviet political, ideological, and strategic doctrines as well as on Soviet interests with regard to specific cases. This is the "black box" approach. The second focuses on Soviet bureaucratic politics, assuming that actions of the Soviet leadership are determined by a number of bureaucratic influences and pressures. Jiri Valenta has done an excellent job of applying the " bureaucratic-politics " model to his study of Soviet decisionmaking with regard to the crisis in Czechoslovakia. But precisely because of the high quality of his paper, some questions emerge about the limits inherent in the bureaucratic-politics approach to analyzing Soviet policy formulation.

Actually, the two approaches have much in common. Most adherents of the first agree that bureaucratic interests play an important role in Soviet decisionmaking. Yet it should be pointed out that, while routine cases in bureaucratic politics dominate Soviet policy formulation, in crisis situations all factions of the Soviet ruling elite demonstrate a significant ability to act in concert on the basis of interests vital to the regime. Thus the real difference lies in the relative emphasis placed on different elements of the Soviet decision-making process rather than in total rejection of the other school's logic.

The issue between Valenta and myself lies in the relative weights we attach to bureaucratic and national security considerations in Soviet decisionmaking concerning Czechoslovakia.

Pluralism and Control in the Soviet Decisionmaking Process

All efforts to construct a model of Soviet decisionmaking ought to strike a balance between latent bureaucratic pluralism and state controls, on the one hand, and pressures for political, ideological, and social conformity, on the other. Valenta had done an excellent job of identifying specific factions in the Soviet bureaucracy, their positions and their spokesmen. Especially interesting and rather convincing is his description of Suslov, chief Communist Party ideologue, who is usually considered a leader of the Soviet hard-liners. However, according to Valenta's persuasive analysis, in the case of Czechoslovakia, Suslov—longer than many of his Politburo colleagues—was among the skeptics of the wisdom of armed intervention.

The same is basically true with regard to another Politburo member, Shelepin. Shelepin, like Suslov, is often considered an extreme conservative. At the same time, those who know Shelepin personally point out that while he is certainly a very tough-minded individual, a kind of a Soviet strong man, he seems to be more of an opportunist than a firm supporter of any particular political orientation. Valenta provides good data to justify his suggestion that with regard to both Soviet economic reform and the invasion of Czechoslovakia, Shelepin tended to favor the moderate side.

Undoubtedly, there were substantial disagreements within the Soviet ruling elite over the formulation of an appropriate response to developments in Czechoslovakia. But what was the nature of these disagreements? How intense and deep were they? Finally, what role did these disagreements—whatever their nature and depth—play in Soviet decisionmaking on the Czechoslovak issue?

Valenta believes that the bureaucratic interests of the Soviet players determined their stands on the invasion of Czechoslovakia. According to him, even before the Soviet leadership was confronted with the Czechoslovak issue, two coalitions had emerged within the Politburo: the technocrat-reformers, allied in a certain way with foreign policy internationalists, and the hard-liners. Thus, the debate over Czechoslovakia intensified rather than produced the contradictions among the Soviet decisionmakers. The conflict became extremely intense. As a result of a political battle between the intervention Politburo coalition and the moderate coalition, the Politburo moderates were defeated and the decision to invade Czechoslovakia " was made under the pressure of the Politburo hard-liners supported by some bureaucratic elites " who in the final voting found themselves—as one of them put it—" unluckily in the minority " (p. 171).

Obviously, the institutional and bureaucratic affiliations of the Soviet decisionmakers had a significant influence on their perceptions of events in Czechoslovakia. And it is impossible to argue with Valenta when he points out that members of the party apparatus were, in principle, more concerned over Czechoslovakia than were economic managers or trade union officials, or that such Soviet leaders as Suslov and Ponomarev—because of their responsibility for relations with foreign Communist parties and for the organization of the international Communist conference, in particular—were less enthusiastic about the invasion than were the Soviet security police. However, interestingly, the coalitions that emerged in the process of the debate corresponded only to a small extent to institutional lines. Rather, they tended to reflect the functional responsibilities of their members. Representatives of the party apparatus, government agencies, and the military establishment were to be found in both camps. The composition of both coalitions was based on functional rather than institutional interests, and those who were " doves " with regard to Czechoslovakia could easily become " hawks " with regard to some other international crisis. Valenta shows his appreciation of this fact by emphasizing that the " interests of the Soviet decisionmakers are not necessarily consistent and may vary from issue to issue " (p. 154).

It seems that certain differences exist between functional and bureaucratic interests. Bureaucratic interests correspond not only with specific functional responsibilities, but also with loyalty to a specific bureaucratic constituency. In the Soviet political system such loyalties and bureaucratic affiliations, as a rule, play only a marginal role. The supreme loyalty of the Politburo members is to the Politburo itself. These Soviet officials usually consider themselves as Politburo representatives in their respective bureaucracies rather than as representatives of these bureaucracies in the Politburo. Those persons, such as Voronov and Shelest, who violate this unwritten rule pay by losing their jobs. Lenin's doctrine of " democratic centralism " still determines the rules of the Soviet decisionmaking process. It can be said that players in this process present their cases but very seldom insist on their own recommendations, and almost never go so far as to ignore or sabotage the implementation of an official policy.

There is no hard evidence to suggest that there were outright opponents to the intervention within the Soviet leadership. Rather, it seems that some officials were more hesitant to go along with it than others.

Advocates of military intervention were to be found in the Department of Liaison with Ruling Workers and Communist Parties of the CPSU Central Committee apparatus; in other departments charged with ideological indoctrination, administrative affairs, and party organizational work; in the main political administration of the armed forces; and among party leaders from the major cities and national republics—as well as in some government agencies responsible for political, economic, and trade relations among the Comecon countries. In addition, the Committee for State Security (KGB) and representatives of the conventional armed forces, especially those concerned with Warsaw Pact problems, were counted among advocates of armed intervention.

Among the skeptics on the issue of armed intervention were the International Department of the CPSU Central Committee apparatus, certain divisions of the Foreign Ministry, some government agencies charged with trade relations with non-Communist countries, and (to some extent) representatives of the Soviet General Staff, particularly those from the strategic armed forces.

One group of advocates argued that invasion was necessary to forestall serious damage to Soviet political, economic, and military interests in Eastern Europe. They included representatives from the

Department for Liaison with Ruling Workers and Communist Parties, the East European divisions of the Foreign Ministry and their counterparts in the Foreign Trade Ministry, the Commission of the Council of Ministers Presidium for Comecon Affairs, and the State Planning Committee, as well as military leaders charged with responsibility for Soviet forces stationed in Eastern Europe. Members of this school shared the fear that events in Czechoslovakia would jeopardize relations with both Comecon and the Warsaw Pact, encourage nationalist and anti-Soviet tendencies in other East European countries, and possibly even result in forcing Czechoslovakia, Rumania, and Yugoslavia closer to one another and away from Moscow's influence.

A second group of advocates was primarily concerned about the potential domestic impact of developments in Czechoslovakia. Composed of representatives from institutions charged with indoctrination and from the KGB, and party authorities from the major cities and national republics, they were united in their fear of intellectual dissent and nationalist movements as well as of prospective demands from industrial managers and other professionals for greater independence from the party.

While alarmed that events in Czechoslovakia could, to some extent, shift the " balance of forces " in favor of the West, skeptics of armed intervention, including powerful elements in the foreign policy establishment, warned that an invasion could jeopardize Soviet hopes of achieving some kind of accommodation with Western Europe and force independent-minded Europeans back into the arms of the United States. These skeptics pointed to the impact that such an action would have on world public opinion and the international Communist movement, and the suspicions that would inevitably arise about Soviet intentions in the Third World. From the standpoint of the stability of Europe, an invasion could be counterproductive; ostracism of the Soviet Union by the West could work to the advantage of China, while a simultaneous consolidation of NATO could bring to reality the traditional nightmare of a two-front threat. In addition, skeptics of armed intervention from the strategic armed forces warned that such a Soviet action would weaken American opponents of the MIRV and ABM systems and enhance the electoral prospects of the anti-Communist Presidential contender Richard Nixon.[1] It seems, then, that what was involved in Soviet decision-

1. A senior Soviet analyst of American foreign policy declared in a lecture at the Moscow Institute of World Economy and International Relations that the results of the American Presidential election would have been quite different had it not been for the invasion of Czechoslovakia.

making on the Czechoslovak issue had more to do with the conflict among different Soviet foreign and domestic policy interests—as voiced by the various bureaucracies—than with the conflict between bureaucracies *per se*. The balance of Soviet interests, rather than a correlation of forces among Soviet bureaucratic players, determined the outcome of the game. No member of the Politburo lost his position, no senior Soviet official was dismissed as a consequence of this debate. There was a four-year gap between the invasion of Czechoslovakia and the expulsion of Shelest from the Politburo and his dismissal from a top position in the Ukraine. There is very little relationship between these two events beyond providing, more or less as an afterthought, an additional article for Shelest's removal.

The fate of Czechoslovakia was determined to a larger extent in Prague than in Moscow. The most vital interests of the Soviet ruling elite were at stake. As the situation in Czechoslovakia developed further, less and less opposition to the invasion was found in Soviet official circles. It is still not quite clear whether anyone in the Politburo actually voted against the invasion. According to reliable sources within the Soviet bureaucracy, the vote of the CPSU Central Committee plenum was unanimous. In short, the internal debate over armed intervention in Czechoslovakia in no way substantially deviated from the standard operating procedure of the regime.

The Limits of Kremlinology

The Soviet decisionmaking process is a confusing subject. The closed nature of Soviet society prevents an adequate flow of information vital for analytical purposes. Students of Soviet policy formulation usually find themselves raising more questions, rather than providing real answers. Very often guesses are proffered on the basis of incomplete information, with predictably uncertain results. What can the Western analyst do about it? Some believe that Kremlinology with its special techniques can be a good answer.

A good Kremlinologist assumes that a careful examination of Soviet published material can provide sufficient information about hidden political developments in the Soviet Union. Certainly, despite severe official censorship, some leaks still exist and some slight disagreements are officially approved. It is also quite true that Soviet experts and journalists associated with different academic institutions and publications sometimes present conflicting points of view and even bitterly attack each other. Such debates among contending factions of Soviet academicians, regardless of individual motivations, are indicative of conflicting functional interests among the top party officials.

While all this evidence undoubtedly deserves careful analysis, it unfortunately portrays debates within the ruling group of decision-makers without necessarily mirroring them. The top officials are more restrained in their pronouncements than their academic clients, and usually avoid direct challenges to one another. The degree of consensus quite naturally is higher among the political leaders than among the academic experts. Moreover, while at the academic level ideological and political factors play some role, the conflict at the political level takes place among like-minded associates and is predicated almost exclusively on contradictory functional interests.

This presents a major problem for Kremlinologists, who tend to believe that differences in statements by Politburo members, Central Committee secretaries, and others reflect disagreements among them on policy issues. Sometimes this is indeed the case. But more often the top officials prefer to conceal rather than to reveal contradictions within the ruling elite, and differences in their speeches to a significant extent are determined simply by their functional responsibilities. It is natural for the trade union chairman to emphasize the role of trade unions in economic reform, and just as natural for a party official to emphasize the need for party control over economic management. The Minister of Foreign Affairs quite naturally stresses the Soviet "peaceful offensive," while the Defense Minister warns about intrigues sponsored by the foes of détente. And it can very easily be misleading to conclude—on the basis of these slight linguistic differences—that the Soviet leadership is involved in a major debate. Thus, contrary to Valenta's point of view, there was hardly any disagreement between such Soviet leaders as Brezhnev and Shelepin concerning a party approach to intellectuals. Both were dedicated supporters of a tough line. And if Brezhnev was attacking intellectuals more violently than Shelepin—who said simply that "The Soviet people do not greet all works of art with equal enthusiasm; some of these works of literature and art obviously do not meet their exacting demands"[2]—it is probably due more to Shelepin's better taste and (more important) lack of direct responsibility for the situation in the field of culture than to his sympathy with dissident intellectuals.

Valenta's article contributes significantly to a better understanding of the Soviet decisionmaking process. But it indicates also that Kremlinology—while useful—is still an imperfect instrument.

2. *Pravda*, February 28, 1968.

Rejoinder by Jiri Valenta

In his comment on my paper, Dimitri Simes provides extremely valuable, and, I must admit, very generous criticism, primarily focusing on some conceptual and factual problems. Many of his observations deserve careful examination and further research. Unfortunately, lack of space does not permit extensive analysis at this time. I would like, nevertheless, to make a few points.

The term " bureaucratic politics " has often been used in a rather ambiguous way. I used it as a very broad term, referring to the whole spectrum of Soviet politics. This obviously also includes the " functional interests " of Soviet senior decisionmakers. Hence there is really no need for a strict distinction between the bureaucratic and functional interests of Soviet decisionmakers. While agreeing with Simes' criticism of the superficial " Kremlinological approach," I should add that my paper was based not only on an examination of " Kremlinological leaks " but also on an analysis of all available information at the time of writing, including data provided by direct participants in and witnesses of the Soviet-Czechoslovak confrontation. Thus, there is less disagreement over facts between us than Simes seems to believe.

Simes has elsewhere argued that " There were people, especially in the International Department of the Central Committee, who opposed the invasion of Czechoslovakia. Even such powerful men as the Secretary of the Central Committee, now a candidate Politburo member in charge of International Affairs, Ponomarev, were against the invasion." [1] We both, therefore, agree that the Soviet decision to

1. See Dimitri N. Simes, " The Future of Detente," *Proceedings of a Symposium of the Coalition for Democratic Majority*, Washington D.C. 1973, p. 3.

invade Czechoslovakia was not an easy one and was taken despite the reluctance and tacit disagreement of some senior Soviet decision-makers, such as Ponomarev.

In short, the positions of some Soviet participants in the Czechoslovak crisis can best be comprehended and explained in terms of bureaucratic politics. Only further research of other events in Soviet foreign policy can validate the usefulness of the bureaucratic-politics approach in explaining Soviet foreign policy.

RESEARCH NOTE

Victor Baras

China and the Rise of Khrushchev

The Soviet succession struggle that began with Stalin's death in March 1953 may be divided into three phases: Khrushchev's battle with the Malenkov faction, which culminated in Malenkov's dismissal as Prime Minister in February 1955; the struggle against the Molotov faction, ending with Molotov's removal as Foreign Minister in June 1956; and Khrushchev's confrontation with the combined forces of Malenkov and Molotov, which led to the purge of the "anti-party" group in June 1957.

The contenders for power in the U.S.S.R. were eager for support from China. On March 10, 1953, *Pravda* published a photograph of Stalin, Mao Tse-tung, and Malenkov. The photo was taken, according to the caption, at the time of the signing of the Sino-Soviet Treaty on February 14, 1950. The original photograph, published in *Pravda* on February 15, 1950, told a different story. It showed Mao and Stalin watching the signing of the treaty, while many other observers, Malenkov among them, watched from the sidelines. The later photo represented a scissors-and-paste attempt to elevate Malenkov in political stature.

The Chinese were willing to express their views about succession struggles in other Communist countries, as they demonstrated in their attitude toward events in Eastern Europe in 1956. The Eighth Plenum of the Polish Central Committee, which began its deliberations on October 19, 1956, was given extensive coverage in the Chinese press from beginning to end. The New China News Agency reported on October 20 the first action of the Plenum, the reinstatement of "Gomulka and three others" in the Central Committee.[1] On October 25, after the crisis in Warsaw had begun to subside, NCNA issued a glowing report on the "great interest" with which the Polish people were following the events of the Plenum, at which one of the issues under discussion was Polish "national sovereignty." NCNA went so far as to praise those workers whose "great interest" had moved them to stage sit-ins at their factories. The article pointed out that the Poles were "concerned" about the visit of the CPSU delegation headed by Khrushchev.[2]

The NCNA coverage of similar developments in Hungary was markedly different. On October 16 NCNA issued an unenthusiastic report on the reinstatement of Nagy in the Hungarian Communist Party. The same brief report quoted from a Central Committee resolution recalling Nagy's previous mistakes.[3]

What was the position of the CCP in the Khrushchev-Malenkov contest? We should note first some general considerations—"circumstantial evidence"—which set the stage for our investigation. Malenkov was Stalin's heir-apparent and the leading candidate for supreme power after Stalin's death. Malenkov's support was centered in the government and economic bureaucracy, in opposition to Khrushchev's base in the Party apparatus. Malenkov thus emerged, probably unintentionally, as the defender of the "technocrats" against the "revolutionaries."

The major policy question dividing the Khrushchev and Malenkov factions was the problem of the relative priorities of light and heavy industry. Malenkov attempted, quite explicitly, to revise the dogma of the priority development of heavy industry; Khrushchev defended it.[4] The Chinese, in their own statements, repeatedly upheld the traditional

1. *SCMP* 1412, p. 42. The following abbreviations are used for periodical publications of the U.S. Consul General in Hong Kong: *SCMP Survey of the China Mainland Press; ECMM Extracts from China Mainland Magazines; CB Current Background.*

2. *SCMP* 1412, p. 43. The Chinese press not only continued to print articles favorable to the Poles, they honored Gomulka personally by publishing photos of him: Zbigniew Brzezinski, *The Soviet Bloc* (New York: Praeger, 1965), p. 277. The East German and Czechoslovak newspapers meanwhile were attacking the Poles, presumably at Soviet instigation: Brzezinski, p. 275; Donald Zagoria, *The Sino-Soviet Conflict* (New York: Atheneum, 1964), p. 58.

3. *SCMP* 1412, p. 41.

4. Howard Swearer, *The Politics of Succession in the U.S.S.R.* (Boston: Little, Brown, 1964), pp. 81–95.

view that heavy industry must be developed at a more rapid rate than light industry.[5]

Khrushchev and Malenkov also differed on the character of war in the thermonuclear age. Malenkov contended, with obvious implications for foreign policy, that world war had become unthinkable, since a future war would destroy all civilization. Khrushchev argued that if the imperialists were foolish enough to unleash another war, only the capitalist system would be destroyed.[6] The Chinese never accepted Malenkov's view.[7]

If the general circumstances surrounding the Khrushchev-Malenkov struggle suggest a Chinese preference for Khrushchev, the direct evidence from Chinese statements during that period is more ambiguous. For example, it was customary for the heads of non-Soviet parties to send telegrams of congratulation to Soviet leaders on November 7, the anniversary of the October Revolution. The Chinese telegram was addressed in 1953 to " Prime Minister Comrade Malenkov "; in 1954 to " President Voroshilov, Prime Minister Malenkov and Foreign Minister Molotov "; in 1955 to " President Voroshilov, Prime Minister Bulganin and Foreign Minister Molotov "; and in 1956 to " President Voroshilov, Prime Minister Bulganin and Foreign Minister Shepilov." The Poles, Czechs, Hungarians and Rumanians had addressed their greetings since 1953 to Khrushchev as First Secretary of the Party.[8]

In the period immediately following Stalin's death, the Chinese press treated Malenkov as the new ruler of the Soviet Union. The Chinese newspapers on March 8, 1953, published photographs of the members of the new Soviet Presidium. Malenkov was portrayed in a six-inch photo; the other leaders were given only four inches. The NCNA English-language dispatch explicitly called attention to the difference in size.[9] On April 4, 1953, a small item appeared in the

5. See, for example, *SCMP* 733, p. 7; SCMP 1496, p. 3; and *ECMM* 96, p. 1.

6. Swearer. *op. cit.* pp. 95–97.

7. Khrushchev, in his memoirs, gives this account of Mao's statement at the Moscow conference of more than eighty Communist parties in 1957: " Mao gave a speech, the gist of which was as follows: 'We shouldn't fear war. We shouldn't be afraid of atomic bombs and missiles. No matter what kind of war breaks out—conventional or thermonuclear—we'll win. As for China, if the imperialists unleash war on us, we may lose more than three hundred million people. So what? War is war. The years will pass, and we'll get to work producing more babies than ever before.' This last statement he put more crudely than I've related here." Strobe Talbott (ed.), *Khrushchev Remembers: The Last Testament* (Boston: Little, Brown, 1974), p. 255.

8. Klaus Mehnert. *Peking and Moscow* (New York: Mentor, 1964), p. 318.

9. *SCMP* 527, p. 11.

Chinese press informing the public of a growing demand for portraits of Malenkov in Peking bookstores.[10]

An NCNA article on March 14, 1953, referred to " the Communist Party of the Soviet Union and the Soviet Government led by Comrade Malenkov." [11] This formula was repeated on July 12 in the Chinese coverage of the purge of Beria.[12] Even more striking, it reappeared on December 3, after Khrushchev had been elected First Secretary of the Party. NCNA spoke of " the leaders of the Communist Party and the Government of the Soviet Union headed by Chairman G. M. Malenkov." [13] After December 3, 1953, this phrase was no longer used, although there was one occasion when it was invoked in modified form. Chu Teh, in a speech at the Soviet Embassy on November 7, 1954, concluded with a toast to " Malenkov and the leaders of the Soviet Government and the CPSU." [14]

The Chinese papers on July 12, 1953, gave extensive coverage to the purge of Beria. NCNA attributed the unmasking of Beria to " the Central Committee of the CPSU and the Government of the Soviet Union headed by Comrade G. Malenkov." [15] On December 27 NCNA released a follow-up article announcing the execution of Beria and his accomplices. The English-language dispatch called attention to the following passage in the Chinese text:

> " The Soviet people," the *Jen-min jih-pao* notes, " are now engaged in developing socialist agriculture and the production of consumer goods to endlessly enhance their own well-being." [16]

The absence of any reference to heavy industry, and the special emphasis given this sentence by NCNA, suggest at least a limited endorsement of Malenkov's consumer-oriented policies for the Soviet Union. This endorsement was not unqualified as Chu Teh indicated a month later in an editorial written for *Pravda*. The Chinese Five-Year Plan, he pointed out, emphasized the development of heavy industry.[17]

The Chinese press continued to give Malenkov top billing among Soviet leaders through the beginning of 1954. An editorial in *Kuang-ming jih-pao* on January 5 praised Malenkov's performance in an interview with a Western journalist.[18] On April 28 NCNA reported that all Peking papers had published the full text of Malenkov's

10. *SCMP* 545, p. 23.
11. *SCMP* 532, p. 6 .
12. *SCMP* 608, p. 1.
13. *SCMP* 701, pp. 1–2.
14. *SCMP* 924, p. 13.
15. *SCMP* 608, p. 1.
16. *SCMP* 715, p. 7.
17. *SCMP* 733, p. 10.
18. *SCMP* 722, p. 1.

speech to the Soviet of Nationalities.[19] No other Soviet leader was accorded such an honor during this phase of the succession struggle. From this point on, however, Malenkov began to decline in Chinese press coverage of Soviet affairs, while Khrushchev became increasingly prominent. It is difficult to know whether this indicated a change of preference in Peking or a recognition of the shifting power balance in Moscow.

On April 17, 1954, NCNA published congratulations on the sixtieth birthday of Nikita Sergeievich Khrushchev, First Secretary of the Central Committee of the CPSU and " the outstanding leader of the CPSU and the Soviet Union and the Soviet people."

During the next few months neither Malenkov nor Khrushchev got much recognition in the Chinese press. Then, on September 29, 1954, Khrushchev arrived in China at the head of a high-level Soviet delegation (which did not include Malenkov or Molotov). The Chinese newspapers reported in detail on every aspect of the visit. Every news article and every quoted speech (of which there were many) singled out Khrushchev by name or identified him as the head of the delegation.[20] At the end of the delegation's visit, the Soviet Union presented China with a gift consisting of the equipment for one state farm. Mao's letter of thanks for the gift seemed especially directed to Khrushchev. Mao wrote:

> [The state farm] will help China . . . learn the valuable experience of the Soviet Union in the opening of virgin soil and the reclamation of idle land.[21]

The " virgin lands " program was Khrushchev's pet project. Any praise of the virgin lands program was indirectly a praise of Khrushchev.[22]

On February 9, 1955, *Pravda* published Malenkov's request to the Supreme Soviet that he be released from his duties as Prime Minister. In this statement Malenkov confessed his lack of experience and incompetence for his position. *Pravda* gave no indication that Malenkov was to be removed definitively from the leadership but only that he would be demoted. The Chinese press, with typical caution, did not carry any news of Malenkov's " confession." Chinese

19. *SCMP* 797, p. 18.
20. *SCMP* 906, p. 1 and 907, p. 1.
21. *SCMP* 907. p. 1.
22. It was understood during 1954 that Malenkov opposed the virgin-lands plan; Swearer, *op. cit.*, pp. 75–81. After the " anti-Party " purge, Malenkov was attacked publicly for his opposition; *ibid.*, pp. 266–268.

readers learned of the change in the Kremlin from Chou En-lai's message of congratulation to the new Prime Minister, Bulganin. Chou wrote:

> You, under the leadership of the united and monolithic Central Committee of the Communist Party of the Soviet Union, will surely make great achievements. . .[23]

Chou's message recognized the new leadership situation in Moscow. Bulganin was not, like Malenkov before him, a power in his own right. He was a subordinate, carrying out the policy of the Central Committee. Formerly the Chinese press had referred to Prime Minister Malenkov as the head of the Soviet government. This formulation could not be used in describing Bulganin. Nor had the Chinese simply adopted a new format for letters of congratulation, for when Khrushchev became Prime Minister in 1958 no mention was made of his subordination to the Central Committee.[24]

In the Soviet Union during 1955 there emerged parallel " cults " of Khrushchev and Bulganin. The Chinese did not go along wholeheartedly with this development. They hedged by fostering only the Bulganin cult, thus giving only indirect support to the growing prestige of Khrushchev. The Chinese press did not refer to Khrushchev by name in 1955. His rival, Foreign Minister Molotov, was mentioned twice (in addition to the customary holiday greetings)—once in a February editorial on Taiwan and again in a June editorial on his speech at the United Nations.[25]

On June 10 the Chinese papers published two messages of congratulation to Bulganin on the occasion of his sixtieth birthday. One was signed by Chou En-lai, the other by the CCP. The CCP statement was the more profuse of the two, describing Bulganin as:

> one of the closest comrades in arms of J. V. Stalin—disciple of the great Lenin and successor to Lenin's cause—one of the outstanding leaders of the CPSU and the Soviet people and beloved friend of the Chinese people.[26]

This formula was noteworthy not only for the lavishness of its praise but because the CCP had apparently modeled its statement on Khrushchev's introduction of Bulganin to the Supreme Soviet for appointment as Prime Minister the previous February. On that occasion Khrushchev said:

23. *SCMP* 985, p. 12.
24. *SCMP* 1744, p. 38.
25. *SCMP* 987, p. 17 and 1079, p. 7.
26. *SCMP* 1067, p. 4.

> A worthy pupil of the great Lenin and one of the closest co-workers of J. V. Stalin, who continued Lenin's work, Comrade Bulganin is an outstanding Party and State administrator. . . .[27]

On the eve of the celebration in Peking of the anniversary of the October Revolution, NCNA pointed out that portraits of Mao and Bulganin were much in evidence.[28] No such observation had been made about portraits of Malenkov in previous years.

The great issue in Soviet politics in 1955 was the question of policy toward Yugoslavia. It was quite apparent that Khrushchev, with Bulganin's support, was the main proponent of *rapprochement*, while Molotov opposed it.[29] This problem was clearly of vital concern to the Chinese, since it touched on the entire question of Soviet policy toward Communist allies. Whatever misgivings the CCP may have had about Tito's method of building Communism, the Chinese seemed genuinely pleased at the improvement in Soviet-Yugoslav relations. The Chinese commented favorably on this development in editorials published in June and September 1955 and again in June 1956 (after Khrushchev's secret speech at the Twentieth Congress).[30] The Chinese attitude toward Tito began to harden only after October 1956, when he was slow in supporting the Soviet intervention in Hungary.

At the Twentieth Congress of the CPSU in February 1956, China was represented by Chu Teh. Chu's address to the Congress consisted primarily of a message from Chairman Mao, in which Mao referred to the "Central Committee of the CPSU headed by N. S. Khrushchev," an unusually strong description of Khrushchev's power. None of the First Secretary's Soviet supporters had yet gone so far as to refer to him as the "head" of the Central Committee.[31] Mao also gave implicit sanction to the removal of Malenkov by commending the CPSU for its "correct line" on the priority development of heavy industry. In addition, Mao relied exclusively on post-Malenkov examples to illustrate the "correct leadership" of the Soviet Party in foreign policy.[32]

27. Swearer, *op. cit.*. p. 116.
28. *SCMP* 1165, p. 23.
29. The Soviet delegation that went to Belgrade included Khrushchev and Bulganin but not Molotov; Swearer, *op. cit.*, p. 130. At the July 1955 Central Committee Plenum it was Khrushchev who delivered the report on relations with Yugoslavia; *ibid.*, p. 137.
30. *SCMP* 1062, p. 10.
31. Myron Rush, *The Rise of Khrushchev* (Washington: Public Affairs Press, 1958), p. 107, note 3.
32. *SCMP* 1231, p. 3.

The high point of the Twentieth Congress was Khrushchev's secret speech attacking Stalin. As is now well known, the Chinese had serious misgivings about the wisdom of this move. It would be a mistake, however, to assume that the Chinese immediately attached their hopes to Khrushchev's Stalinist rivals. The Chinese valued Stalin as an important link in the revolutionary tradition, but they were not anxious to see all his policies continued. They would have preferred, like many other Communists, to see a quiet modification of Stalin's policies without an all-out attack on the Stalin legend. They were concerned by the disarray into which Khrushchev's revelations had thrown the international Communist movement. The CCP statements of April 5 and December 29, 1956, therefore took the form of a "retrenching" on the Stalin question. In these statements the Chinese attempted to provide a theoretical framework within which constructive criticism of the past could be carried on.[33]

On June 2, 1956, *Pravda* announced the replacement of Molotov by Shepilov as Foreign Minister, a development that was not reported at the time in the Chinese newspapers. This contrasted with the situation in February 1955, when the Chinese press promptly published letters of congratulation to Bulganin on his appointment as Prime Minister and to Zhukov, Bulganin's replacement as Minister of Defense.[34]

Khrushchev's leadership was tested severely in October 1956 by the disturbances in Poland and the uprising in Hungary. The Chinese recognized the connection between the Secret Speech and the events in eastern Europe,[35] but they were aware that the developments in Poland, which China welcomed, were just as much a result of the Twentieth Congress as the uprising in Hungary, which they deplored. The CCP statement of December 29, 1956, seemed to attribute the unrest in the satellites to Stalin's errors rather than Khrushchev's; Stalin had followed an incorrect policy of "great nation chauvinism" in relations with other socialist states.[36]

During 1957 the Chinese press seemed to lose interest in following current developments within the Soviet Union. This may have been the first symptom of a gradual cooling of relations between the two powers. The big news in the Soviet Union at this time was

33. *CB* 383, p. 1 and 433, p. 1.

34. *SCMP* 985, p. 12 and 988, p. 12.

35. *CB* 433, p. 1.

36. *CB* 433, p. 1. The Chinese maintained in 1956, and they have continued to maintain, that intervention was necessary in Hungary but not in Poland. This is precisely the policy followed by the U.S.S.R. The Chinese have since

Khrushchev's proposal for a sweeping reorganization of the government bureaucracy, including virtual abolition of the central economic ministries. This controversial suggestion proved to be a major factor in precipitating the "anti-Party" affair. NCNA mentioned the proposal only once, in passing, in a report of an interview of Khrushchev by some Chinese journalists.[37]

The Chinese press also failed to pay much attention to the purge of the "anti-party" group. On July 5, 1957, the Central Committee of the CCP published the following message to the Central Committee of the CPSU: "Thank you for informing us through Comrade P. F. Yudin [Soviet ambassador to China] of the resolution passed at the Plenum of the Central Committee of the CPSU which met June 22–29 on the anti-Party group of Malenkov, Kaganovich and Molotov." The message went on to express the confidence that this action would further the unity and consolidation of the CPSU. Unlike the Beria affair in 1953, the "anti-Party" purge elicited no editorials in the Chinese papers denouncing the villains or praising the Party for its vigilance. This was also true of Chinese reporting during the period of Khrushchev's consolidation of power. The press took no notice of Zhukov's replacement by Malinovsky in November, although a letter of congratulation was published to Khrushchev on becoming Prime Minister when he replaced Bulganin in March 1958.[38]

In summary, the Chinese seem to have favored Khrushchev throughout much of the succession struggle. Their support was most vigorous in late 1955 and early 1956. During the rest of the time their attitude varied from unenthusiastic preference to near indifference. By the middle of 1957 the Chinese no longer cared to use their own public statements to boost Khrushchev's prestige.

claimed that certain Soviet leaders favored a policy of intervention in Poland and "capitulation" in Hungary, but the Chinese have not accused Khrushchev of belonging to this group; "The Origin and Development of the Differences Between the Leadership of the CPSU and Ourselves—Comment on the Open Letter of the Central Committee of the CPSU," by the Editorial Departments of *People's Daily* and *Red Flag*, September 6, 1963 (complete text), *Peking Review*, VI, 37 (September 13, 1963), pp. 6–23, cited in William E. Griffith, *The Sino-Soviet Rift* (Cambridge, Mass.: M.I.T. Press, 1964), p. 395. Khrushchev, in his unofficial autobiography, says: "We asked Mao Tse-tung to send a representative to consult with us about the events in Hungary. The Chinese responded quickly. A delegation led by Liu Shao-chi flew in." Khrushchev admits that the Soviet leadership decided at first not to intervene. He implies, however, that the Chinese supported this decision as well as the later decision to intervene: Strobe Talbott (ed.). *Khrushchev Remembers* (Boston; Little, Brown, 1970), pp. 418–419.

37. *SCMP* 1529, p. 32.

38. *SCMP* 1744, p. 38.

REVIEW ARTICLE

WILLIAM TAUBMAN

Political Power: USA/USSR Ten Years Later—Comparative Foreign Policy*

Let me begin by declaring my fealty to *Political Power: USA/USSR* ten years after it was first published in 1964. I have read it and re-read it, assigned it and re-assigned it to my students. That I shall be raising some critical questions in no way betokens a change in my judgment that what we are considering on its tenth anniversary is a pioneering and provocative work.

I shall confine my remarks to the book's treatment of comparative Soviet-American foreign policy, and particularly to its analysis of the American role in world affairs.[1] From the point of view of international relations, 1964 was a pivotal year—a year of American escalation in Vietnam, the year when Nikita Khrushchev was forced

* This review essay is based on remarks delivered by the author at the March 6, 1974, meeting of the Regional Faculty Seminar on Communist Studies at Yale University. The session was addressed to a critical reassessment of Zbigniew Brzezinski and Samuel P. Huntington, *Political Power: USA/USSR* (New York: Viking, 1964), a pioneering work in the field of comparative Communist studies.

1. For a brief introduction (with selected examples) to comparative foreign policy analysis, see Harold Karan Jacobson and William Zimmerman (eds.), *The Shaping of Foreign Policy* (New York: Atherton, 1969).

to give way to new Soviet leaders with a new slant in foreign affairs. That these important events of 1964 and their important consequences were not predicted by Brzezinski and Huntington constitutes no very serious shortcoming. One could contend that their book serves as a benchmark against which to measure developments occurring since 1964. Yet we must be more critical than that, I think, on at least two counts. For the problem is not so much that certain changes were not predicted, but that they do not fit very well into a comparative framework offered as valid not just in 1964 but for an extended period thereafter. And a further problem is that when one looks back at the time before 1964, which *Political Power* was explicitly designed to interpret, one finds patterns that seem to belie the book's comparative judgment.

There were times in preparing for this discussion when I was tempted to say (not alone for the sake of provoking controversy) that their comparison should be exactly reversed, with American foreign policy better understood in the terms they apply to Soviet behavior and vice versa. Instead I shall argue for the proposition that while there may be significant differences between Soviet and American foreign policies, there are also more important similarities than are recognized in *Political Power: USA/USSR*.[2]

Political Ideas and Politics

The major theoretical section of *Political Power*, entitled "The Political System," compares and contrasts American and Soviet systems under four headings, of which three bear directly on foreign policy—"Political Ideas and Politics," "Political Leadership," and "Power and Policy." Let me treat these in turn, beginning in each case by summarizing the Brzezinski-Huntington argument and then commenting on it.

Perhaps the central theme of the section on political ideas is that whereas Soviet thinking qualifies unquestionably as ideological, American just as surely does not. Given their definition of ideology (a "set of political ideas that are overt, systematic, dogmatic and embodied in a set of institutions"),[3] Brzezinski and Huntington are justified in affixing the label to one side and not to the other. Yet the specific contrasts they draw are so open to question as to raise doubts about the usefulness of their definition of ideology itself.

2. This article draws on a larger work currently in progress on Comparative Soviet-American Foreign Policy.
3. *Political Power*, p. 19.

The contrasts are made on several levels. As a general proposition it is said that whereas the Soviets are "obsessed with 'the unity of theory and practice,'" the "more amorphous American values and doctrines are seldom directly related to political action," are usually "thought to be inoperative in day-to-day political action."[4] And whereas Soviet Party doctrine is distinguished by its integrated treatment of a whole range of issues, "American political action is justified by an immediate consensus quite distinct from the consensuses which may be developed on other issues and from the overall agreement on the key elements of the American political beliefs."[5]

The contrast between Khrushchev and Kennedy is said to be a case in point. For all his earthy pragmatism, the late Soviet leader was a true believer. For all his intellectual curiosity, Kennedy was a political pragmatist in the tradition of most American chief executives. That is, "there was little indication as to where the world, in his [Kennedy's] view, is heading."[6] He was not "at home with the idea of permanent and inevitable conflict among nations" ("the struggle between USA and USSR was the result of certain specific causes, such as the expansionist motives of the present Soviet leadership, which are not inherent in the situation . . ."), nor did Kennedy base his views on any "self-evident historical or philosophical premise."[7]

According to Brzezinski and Huntington, "the closer a man is to power [in America] the less likely he is to think in ideological terms"[8] —the corollary to which is that "the principal habitat of the ideologue in American politics is the minor parties, ideologically oriented pressure groups such as Americans for Democratic Action or the Committee for Constitutional Government, the journals of opinion, and the universities."[9] One effect of this in foreign policy is that whereas the Soviets possess a keen Leninist sensitivity to the domestic roots of international relations, Americans suffer from a Wilsonian preoccupation with "the interplay of nation states" at the expense of any major concern for "internal socio-economic and political dynamics" as they affect international relations.[10]

There is, in short, a fundamental contrast between Soviet and American conceptions of the national interest. "Despite shifts and turns in Soviet foreign policy in the last several decades," Moscow persists in "the sense of historical obligation to encourage the spread of Communism throughout the world although preferably without

4. *Ibid.*, p. 22.
5. *Ibid.*, p. 23.
6. *Ibid.*, p.36.
7. *Ibid.*, pp. 36–38.
8. *Ibid.*, p. 43.
9. *Ibid.*, p. 44.
10. *Ibid.*, p. 58.

excessive Soviet sacrifices." And it is precisely "this universality of goal which makes Soviet foreign policy something altogether different from . . . the rather generalized American desire to see a 'free' but otherwise undefined world." To be sure, the Kremlin is concerned in the short run with various non-ideological goals—security, frontiers, power—yet "Soviet leaders' conception of their security is inherently offensive; as long as alternative political systems exist, there is continued need to be preoccupied with security issues." [11]

The trouble with the Brzezinski-Huntington conception of ideology is that it settles the comparative problem which it should be the purpose of analysis to investigate. For theirs is by no means the only possible definition. Andrew Hacker, for example, has attached the label to ideas of which "social scientists whether they acknowledge it or not, cannot help being bearers," ideas which may be "purportedly normative" but which may also be "purportedly scientific: an unintentionally distorted picture of social reality, the distortion arising because the observer sees what he wants to see." [12] Or one may prefer a stance somewhere between ideology as institutionalized dogma and ideology as unintended bias, the approach suggested by Willard Mullins, who points to a series of traits—historical consciousness, cognitive power, evaluative power, action-orientation—which characterize ideological thinking about man and his relation to society and the universe.[13]

The point, in any event, is not the precise definitional wording. The point is that at the heart of America's foreign policy since 1945 has been a combination of conceptions which Brzezinski and Huntington do not prepare us to recognize and understand, a combination of "idealism" and "realism" deserving the name ideology in that each component transcends the national interest narrowly defined on behalf of generalized assumptions about the nature of man and society.

By idealism, I mean the conviction, the roots of which run so deep in American experience that they have become part of our national style, that America stands for the freedom, self-determina-

11. *Ibid.*, p. 64. It should be noted that Brezezinski and Huntington do concede (in a brief parenthetical sentence) that: "There are, however, some striking parallels between the Soviet view and the traditional American image of America as the active symbol of certain universal norms."

12. Andrew Hacker, "Sociology and Ideology," in Max Black (ed.), *The Social Theories of Talcott Parsons* (Englewood Cliffs, N. J.: Prentice-Hall, 1961), p. 298.

13. Willard Mullins, "On the Concept of Ideology," *American Political Science Review*, LXVI, 2 (June 1972), pp. 498–510.

tion and well-being of other peoples, that, in the words of President Lyndon Johnson, " America's only interests in the world today are those we regard as inseparable from our moral duty to mankind." [14] What *Political Power* has to say about the Soviet Union applies to the United States with minor adaptation: Americans have persisted in the sense of historical obligation to *discourage* the spread of Communism throughout the world; what's more, they have done exactly that since 1945 with what some would view as too little but many would consider excessive sacrifice, not only or even mainly of American lives and treasure but of other peoples' as well.

Those who have followed the Vietnam-triggered debate about American foreign policy know that it was precisely against " anti-Communist crusading " that so-called " realist " critics have directed their sternest attacks. Hans Morgenthau and Stanley Hoffmann (and Henry Kissinger too) have not hesitated to describe American " globalism " as a species of ideology; Morgenthau, in particular, has urged as an antidote to ideological thinking that we raise high the more realistic standard of the " National Interest." [15] Yet in truth American idealism has been inextricably intertwined since the late 1940s with a militant sense of realism centered around the proposition that national survival depends on the preservation of a balance of power. In the words of Seyom Brown:

> Each of the four postwar Administrations have [sic] agreed on at least this much: if Communist success in a given conflict would critically undermine the power of the non-Communist world to dissuade the Communist world from further advances, then, presumably, the balance of power itself was at stake, and, since, by extension, this meant the survival of the United States, there was no question of where the national interest would lie. In such situations, peace would have to give way temporarily to the active containment of Communism, even if the temporary breakdown of peace would place the United States in danger of direct attack.[16]

14. Lyndon B. Johnson, " The Morality of Nations," *Department of State Bulletin*, June 28, 1965, p. 1026. On the concept of national style, and for a detailed analysis of American style in foreign affairs, see Stanley Hoffmann, *Gulliver's Troubles* (New York: McGraw-Hill, 1968), esp. pp. 87–213.

15. See Hans J. Morgenthau, *A New Foreign Policy for the United States* (New York: Praeger, 1969); Hoffmann, *Gulliver's Troubles*; and Henry Kissinger, *American Foreign Policy* (New York: Norton, 1969). For selections (with interpretive analysis) from those and other critics, see William Taubman (ed.), *Globalism and Its Critics* (Lexington, Mass.: Heath, 1973).

16. Seyom Brown, *The Faces of Power* (New York: Columbia University Press, 1968), p. 13.

Was the national survival really at stake in Indochina? Did the threat presented by Khrushchev's placing Soviet missiles in Cuba justify President Kennedy's incurring what he himself estimated as a "between one out of three and even" chance of nuclear war? Those who hesitate to answer a clear and unequivocal yes to such questions should be particularly interested to ask what assumptions lie at the root of American realism. The answer, I suggest, is a series of pessimistic beliefs about deep-seated Communist malevolence toward the West, about the indivisibility and hence fragility of peace, about the vulnerability of the American people—and indeed all people—to what Eugene V. Rostow has called "the kind of panic, the kind of atmosphere of rage which is the real cause of war," war that "comes when people feel that the moorings are slipping, when the situation is getting out of hand and there's a slide toward chaos which threatens their sense of safety."[17]

At the risk of further debasing the definitional currency, I suggest that American realism constitutes ideology in the guise of anti-ideology.[18] Somehow it manages to coexist with idealism, sometimes even in the same person—e.g., John Foster Dulles or W. W. Rostow.[19] Now if, as Huntington suggests, ideology is not ideology when it is "bifurcated," then American political ideas may indeed require a different label.[20] But why should "bifurcation" settle the matter? Granted, American ideas are less overt than Soviet ideology, less systematic, less dogmatic, and certainly not embodied in any institution like the Communist Party of the Soviet Union. But is American ideology any less influential for being different? Is it not in fact more influential as a guide to action because, in contrast to the Soviet case, it is not generally perceived as ideology, because it is less crude and therefore more widely credited, because in a democratic system it is

17. William Whitworth, *Naive Questions about War and Peace* (New York: Norton, 1970), p. 23.

18. Ideology in the sense that realist assumptions (1) transcend what Brzezinski and Huntington call non-ideological goals—security, frontiers, power—and (2) deal at root with, in Kenneth Waltz' phrase, "man, the state and war." "Anti-ideology" in the sense that realists claim to be non-ideological. See also Kenneth Waltz, *Man, the State and War* (New York: Columbia University Press, 1959).

19. On Dulles, see Townsend Hoopes, *The Devil and John Foster Dulles* (Boston: Atlantic Monthly Press, 1973), plus Coral Bell, *Negotiation from Strength* (London: Chatto and Windus, 1962). For a distillation of Rostow's dualism, see his definition of the national interest in his *The United States in the World Arena* (New York: Simon and Schuster, 1969), pp. 543–552.

20. Huntington commented to this effect during the Yale panel discussion at which this article was first presented.

" fed back " from masses to leaders in elections which the latter stand to lose as well as win?

These remarks are admittedly rather abstract. I am attempting to develop them elsewhere; here let me conclude with a series of propositions and questions framed in response to specific Brzezinski-Huntington assertions quoted above:

—American foreign policy values are *not* so amorphous. Furthermore, they *are* directly related to action in the world arena.

—American foreign policy during the cold war reflects not separate and isolated consensuses on particular issues, but rather a widely shared idealist/realist " cold war consensus " which with some modifications still holds sway in 1974.[21]

—If the principal habitat of ideologues in American parties is the minor parties, then what were Dulles and Rostow doing in the White House?

—American leaders have not been " preoccupied with the interplay of nation states " at the expense of any concern for " internal socio-economic and political dynamics " as they affect international relations. Woodrow Wilson himself proceeded from the assumption (however wrong it may have turned out) that democracy and self-determination within states are the prerequisite for peace among them.[22] Or consider Clark Clifford's now famous 1946 Memorandum analyzing the Soviet threat for President Truman. For Clifford (as for George Kennan in his 1947 article on " The Sources of Soviet Conduct ") the Soviet danger stemmed not so much from the expansionist motives of particular Soviet leaders as from the sinister internal dynamics of a totalitarian system that trumped up external threats to hold itself together.[23]

—Is the Soviet Union alone in concentrating on security issues as long as alternative political systems exist? Is it only Moscow's conception of security which is " inherently offensive "? How then to explain the way the United States has parlayed its search for security

21. For the argument that containment continues in the guise of détente, see Robert Osgood, " Introduction: The Nixon Doctrine and Strategy," in Osgood *et al.*, *Retreat from Empire*? (Baltimore: Johns Hopkins University Press, 1973), pp. 1–28.

22. See N. Gordon Levin, Jr., *Woodrow Wilson and World Politics* (New York: Oxford University Press, 1968).

23. Clifford's September 1946 Memorandum, " American Relations with the Soviet Union," is reprinted as Appendix A in Arthur Krock, *Memoirs* (New York: Funk and Wagnalls, 1968), pp. 417–482. Kennan's article is in his *American Diplomacy* (New York: Mentor, 1952), pp. 102–121.

into what even some of its defenders have come to admit is an American empire? [24]

—Finally a comment concerning the Soviet side of the ledger. Just because one finds " more ideology " on the American side than Brzezinski and Huntington admit does not mean there must be less on the Soviet. And yet I suspect the latter is also the case. In which connection, two comments: First, granting that Soviet ideas are overt, systematic, and the like, how vital are they in the minds of Soviet leaders as a guide to foreign policy action? This is of course an old and much-debated question, but no less important for being so. For if the most sacred commandment of Communist ideology is to transcend the Russian national interest in support of world Communism, then is it not clear that the Soviet leaders long ago betrayed their trust? And if, on the other hand, ideology is only the lens through which the national interest, narrowly defined, is itself understood and interpreted, then how different is the Soviet situation from the American? Second comment: Even granting that the goal of world Communism is alive and well in the Kremlin, even granting that experience with China has not forever removed the bloom from the rose, the truth is that the Soviets have not—until very recently—had the resources to indulge their ideology's most ambitious instructions. The point, in short, is that the kind of intervention which the United States mounted in Indochina (perhaps the limiting case of idealism/realism in action) has simply not been a viable option for the Soviets in Latin America, or even the Middle East.

Political Leadership

The argument in this section of *Political Power* contains a partial sociology of the political beliefs analyzed above. The book seeks to establish a connection between the origins of leaders and their intellectual stance and style.

In the American case the link is between " the upper-middle class origin of the top political and business elite " and their " moderation, restraint, and a belief in the superiority of compromise solutions." [25] On the Soviet side, the leaders' " relatively humble social origins " are said to account for their toughness, including an acceptance of the taking of life as " necessary and politically normal." Furthermore, " the Soviet leaders, to a much greater extent than their American

24. See, for example, George Liska, *Imperial America* (Baltimore: Johns Hopkins University Press, 1967).

25. *Political Power*, p. 139.

counterparts, display the characteristics, psychological and otherwise, of self-made men . . . expansive self-confidence tempered by gnawing insecurity and the driving ability to succeed combined with the burning desire to be accepted." [26] Finally, whereas Soviet leaders are said to be political professionals, Americans are amateurs or at best semi-pros. Soviet leaders are often engineers by training—which helps explain their " down-to-earth problem-solving approach without concern for legal niceties and with little tendency toward compromise solutions." The fact that so many American electoral politicians are lawyers reflects " the pervasiveness of law in politics." [27]

How to respond to such comparisons? With more questions and propositions.

—Many American leaders are indeed of middle-class origin, but how much " moderation and restraint " have they shown in foreign intervention, in the Indochina war, particularly, in which they all too easily came to see " the taking of life as necessary and politically normal? "

—Soviet leaders are indeed often engineers by training. But who, if not the American leaders described by David Halberstam and analyzed by Hannah Arendt, employed a cold-blooded, hard-eyed " problem-solving " approach—as if the end in Indochina was justified by the super-rationalist means? [28]

—Finally, who in the Politburo since Stalin has revealed more " expansive self-confidence tempered by gnawing insecurity, and the driving ability to succeed combined with the burning desire to be accepted " than Lyndon B. Johnson and Richard M. Nixon? Pending the appearance of a good psycho-historical biography of Khrushchev (the most likely Soviet competitor), readers are referred to psycho-political analysts James David Barber and Doris Kearns (on Lyndon Johnson), and Barber, Bruce Mazlish, and Gary Wills (on Richard Nixon).[29] But there is also a more general question which can form a bridge to the third area treated in *Political Power*. In which system, Soviet or American, does the personality of the top leader have more scope for impact on foreign policy? As long as

26. *Ibid.*, p. 140.

27. *Ibid.*, p. 146.

28. See David Halberstam, *The Best and the Brightest* (New York, Random House, 1969–1971); and Hannah Arendt, " Lying in Politics," *The New York Review of Books*, November 18, 1971, pp. 30–38.

29. See James David Barber, *The Presidential Character* (Englewood Cliffs, N.J.: Prentice-Hall, 1972); Bruce Mazlish, *In Search of Nixon* (New York: Basic Books, 1972); Gary Wills, *Nixon Agonistes* (Boston: Houghton-Mifflin, 1970). Doris Kearns is writing a biography of Lyndon Johnson.

Stalin was alive the answer was clear. But what of the era of Kremlin oligarchy, or even limited one-man rule, when the contrast is between, say, Brezhnev and Nixon?

Power and Policy

Very briefly, Brzezinski and Huntington's major contrast under this heading is between America's open political system and the closed politics of the U.S.S.R. In the former, the dominant mode is said to be bargaining; in the latter, control and manipulation. The "values and goals of participants in the American political system may differ widely," with "major bargainers . . . spread across a political spectrum from Ross Barnett and Barry Goldwater to Martin Luther King and Walter Reuther. In the Soviet system, on the other hand, the principal bargainers are very much alike."[30] And whereas in American politics "bargaining takes place in a fishbowl," in the Soviet system it goes on "behind the closed doors of the Kremlin."[31]

Open versus closed—in a general and very important sense this is a valid distinction. Even critics of American pluralism would not deny that the American "mass media, although definitely biased, present a significantly wider range of information and opinion," or that "freedoms of association, assembly and speech are comparatively well protected here . . . even after one has corrected for the gap between official rhetoric and established practice."[32] Yet under the "power and policy" rubric, too, qualifications and revisions are needed.

The Brzezinski and Huntington analysis of Presidential power, for example, reflects the prevailing wisdom of the early 1960s. They do not use Richard Neustadt's term, but theirs like his is the conception of a "President in sneakers," armed mainly with the power to persuade, having to struggle to cumulate the coalitions of diverse forces needed to get anything done.[33] Ten years later we have come to know a very different "Imperial Presidency," one that ultimately overreached itself in Vietnam and Watergate, but that along the way managed to dominate much of foreign-policymaking, especially in relations with Communist powers.[34] Accounts of the American

30. *Political Power*, p. 199.
31. *Ibid*., pp. 200–201.
32. William I. Connolly, "The Challenge to Pluralist Theory," in Connolly (ed.), *The Bias of Pluralism* (New York: Atherton, 1969), p. 13.
33. Richard E. Neustadt, *Presidential Power* (New York: Wiley, 1960).
34. Arthur M. Schlesinger, Jr., *The Imperial Presidency* (Boston: Houghton-Mifflin, 1972).

involvement in Vietnam differ, but who would deny the tremendous impact on the course we have followed of Presidents Johnson and Nixon, of their personalities as well as their premises?[35] Futhermore, even before 1964 there was ample evidence that Washington's foreign-policymaking process was sufficiently closed to sustain comparison with Moscow's. It is not my impression that the "values and goals of participants" in Cuban missile crisis decisionmaking differed so widely as, say, from Barry Goldwater to Martin Luther King. If they had, then surely more attention would have been paid to the extreme options, whether forcible or non-forcible. Nor is it fair to say that deliberations of Kennedy's famous ExCom took place in a proverbial "fishbowl."[36]

Again, let me be careful. It is true, of course, that even the Imperial Presidents are democratically elected (and impeached), while General Secretaries, constrained as they may be by fellow oligarchs plus bureaucratic groups, are not. And it is also true that whether the closed inner sanctum in American policymaking is Kennedy's ExCom or Johnson's war room, or Henry Kissinger and James Schlesinger meeting as a rump National Security Council during a Middle East crisis, these deliberations are surrounded by a wide arena of pluralist politics. Nonetheless, at crucial moments, when the fate of the country and even the world is at stake, the "open" American system has a way of closing down around the President and a small circle of advisers, few if any of whom can challenge their master politically. Think of Richard Nixon brooding alone prior to unleashing the invasion of Cambodia or the mining of Haiphong. Compare that with the whole Soviet Politburo's taking the train to Cierna to consult with the Czechoslovak leaders during the summer of 1968.

Conclusion

Among the most remarked-upon sections of *Political Power* is the discussion, at the beginning and end of the book, of the prospects for a convergence between Soviet and American political systems. Despite certain similarities, it was the conclusion of Brzezinski and Huntington that the "evolution of the two systems, but not their convergence seems to be the undramatic pattern for the future."[37]

35. See George Reedy, *The Twilight of the Presidency* (New York: World, 1970), p. 18.
36. See Graham T. Allison, *Essence of Decision* (Boston: Little, Brown, 1971).
37. *Political Power*, p. 436.

What I have tried to suggest, in short, is that in foreign affairs there has occurred a species of convergence, one that may reflect the imperatives of "super-powerhood" in what has been, and in important ways remains, a bipolar world, one that reveals as well the influence of internal forces like ideology (which while different in content in the United States and the U.S.S.R. has a similar messianic thrust in both) as forces like the military-industrial complex (which seems similar in substance as well as shape in the two countries).[38]

One final note. My comparison, like those offered by Brzezinski and Huntington, is subject to erosion with time. Some of the very elements I have emphasized in the American scene—ideology, the impact of Presidential personality—may be on the wane in the 1970s. Likewise, the Soviet political scene could change drastically in the decade ahead. It might not be a bad idea, therefore, to convene again on the twentieth anniversary of *Political Power*, a good year for taking up the visions of two other observers as well—Orwell and Amalrik.

38. See Vernon V. Aspaturian, "The Soviet Military-Industrial Complex—Does It Exist?", *Journal of International Affairs,* Vol. 26, No. 1 (1972), pp. 1–28. For an argument that comparative Soviet-American foreign policy studies should distinguish among various "issue areas" in which the policy process differs, see William Zimmerman, "Issue Area and Foreign-Policy Process: A Research Note in Search of a General Theory," *American Political Science Review*, LXVII, 4 (1973), pp. 1204–1212. Zimmerman concludes that "the traditional dichotomization of authoritarian and pluralist foreign-policy processes needs re-examination."

CONTRIBUTORS

VICTOR BARAS is Assistant Professor of Political Science at Wellesley College and an Associate of the Russian Research Center of Harvard University. His doctoral dissertation (Cornell University, 1973) was on "East Germany in Soviet Foreign Policy: The Objectives of the New Course and the Impact of the Uprising of June 17, 1953." His recent publications include "Contemporary Soviet Society" in *Current History* (October 1974) and "Beria's Fall and Ulbricht's Survival" in *Soviet Studies* (July 1975). He is also the author of a critical review of *Khrushchev Remembers,* forthcoming in the *American Political Science Review.* Professor Baras is currently doing research on the foreign policy of the German Democratic Republic.

DAVID D. FINLEY is Associate Professor of Political Science at Colorado College in Colorado Springs, where he teaches courses in comparative and international politics and maintains research interests focusing on the Soviet Union and Eastern Europe. Professor Finley's publications include *Soviet Foreign Policy* (1968) with Jan F. Triska, and articles in *Western Political Quarterly, Journal of Conflict Resolution,* and *Military Review.*

CHARLES GATI is Professor of Political Science at Union College and Visiting Professor of Political Science at Columbia University. He specializes in Soviet foreign policy and the international politics of East Central Europe. He edited and co-authored *Caging the Bear: Containment and the Cold War* (1974) and *The Politics of Modernization in Eastern Europe: Testing the Soviet Model* (1974). He contributed chapters to *The Behavioral Revolution and Communist Studies,* edited by Roger E. Kanet, and *The Conduct of Soviet Foreign Policy,* edited by E. P. Hoffmann and F. J. Fleron. Articles by Professor Gati have appeared in *World Politics, Foreign Policy, Slavic Review, Problems of Communism, Journal of International Affairs, East European Quarterly,* and other journals. At present, he is completing a study of the international politics of East Central Europe in the era of détente.

ARNOLD L. HORELICK is a senior staff member of the Social Science Department at The Rand Corporation, Santa Monica, California, and Lecturer in Political Science at the University of California, Los Angeles. He has held visiting appointments at the City University of New York, Columbia University, California Institute of Technology, and Cornell University. Horelick has written extensively on Soviet foreign and military policies and on international relations. He is co-author (with Myron Rush) of *Strategic Power and Soviet Foreign Policy* (1966) and contributor to a number of volumes, including *Comparative Defense Policy* (1974), *National Security and American Society* (1973), *Political Dynamics in the Middle East* (1972), *The Conduct of Soviet Foreign Policy* (1971), and *The Future of Communism in Europe* (1968).

ROGER E. KANET is Associate Professor of Political Science at the University of Illinois-Urbana. He has published primarily in the area of Soviet foreign policy and is at present working on a study of political aspects of economic integration within the Council for Mutual Economic Assistance. He has taught at the University of Kansas, and in 1972–1973 he was Joint Senior Fellow at the Research Institute on Communist Affairs and the Russian Institute of Columbia University. Professor Kanet is editor of and contributor to *The Behavioral Revolution and Communist Studies* (1971), *On the Road to Communism: Essays on Soviet Domestic and Foreign Politics* (1972), *The Soviet Union and the Developing Countries* (1974), and *Soviet and East European Foreign Policies: A Bibliography* (1974). His articles have appeared in a number of scholarly journals and books.

HENRY KRISCH is Assistant Professor of Political Science at the University of Connecticut. His international-relations research focuses on GDR-Soviet relations with emphasis on GDR foreign policy and nationalism. He is the author of *German Politics Under Soviet Occupation* (1974) and "Official Nationalism in the German Democratic Republic," in *The German Democratic Republic* (forthcoming), and is co-editor (with Ilpyong J. Kim) of *Comparing Communist Systems: North Korea and East Germany* (1975).

JEANNE KIRK LAUX is Assistant Professor of Political Science at the University of Ottawa. She holds degrees from Cornell University, Johns Hopkins (SAIS), and the London School of Economics, where she wrote her dissertation on the role of small states in East-West relations. Professor Laux is the author of articles on European security in *Etudes internationales, Journal of Peace Research,* and *Politique étrangère.* Currently she is doing research on the Rumanian political economy.

JAMES N. ROSENAU is Professor of International Relations and Political Science, as well as Director of the Institute for Transnational Studies, at the University of Southern California. He has taught at Rutgers University and Ohio State University, and is the author and editor of numerous books, including *Linkage Politics: Essays on the Convergence of National and International Systems* (1969), *The Analysis of International Politics* (1972), *International Politics and Foreign Policy* (1961, 1969), *The Scientific Study of Foreign Policy* (1971), *The Adaptation of National Societies: A Theory of Political Behavior and Its Transformations* (1970), *The Dramas of Politics: An Introduction to the Joys of Inquiry* (1973), *International Studies and the Social Sciences: Problems, Priorities and Prospects in the United States* (1973), and *Citizenship Between Elections: An Inquiry into the Mobilizable American* (1974).

ALVIN Z. RUBINSTEIN is Professor of Political Science at the University of Pennsylvania. He is the author of a number of works on Soviet and Communist affairs, including *The Foreign Policy of the Soviet Union* (3rd ed., 1972); *Yugoslavia and the Nonaligned World* (1970), and *The Soviets in International Organizations* (1964). In addition he has edited several books, including *Soviet and Chinese Influence in the Third World* (1975). During the 1974–1975 academic year Professor Rubinstein is a Visiting Fellow at Clare Hall, Cambridge University.

SIMON SERFATY is Director of the Johns Hopkins Center of Advanced International Studies in Bologna, Italy, and Associate Professor of Political Science at the School of Advanced International Studies, Washington, D.C. He is the author of *France, de Gaulle and Europe: The Policy of the Fourth and Fifth Republics Toward the Continent* (1968) and *The Elusive Enemy* (1972), and he has contributed a chapter on Europe to *Great Issues of International Politics,* edited by Morton A. Kaplan (1974). He has also published articles in such journals as *Foreign Policy* and *Orbis.*

DIMITRI K. SIMES is a Senior Research Fellow at the Center for Strategic and International Studies, Georgetown University. He was born in the Soviet Union and was educated at Moscow State University, serving for a period (1967–1972), first as a research assistant and later as a research associate, at the Institute of World Economy and International Relations in Moscow. Mr. Simes has published numerous articles in America, Western Europe, and the Soviet Union. In 1969 his paper on U.S. policy regarding the Czechoslovak crisis appeared in the Information Bulletin for top echelons of the Soviet bureaucracy. He is currently engaged in a study of Soviet arms control policy.

WILLIAM TAUBMAN is Associate Professor of Political Science at Amherst College. He is the author of *Governing Soviet Cities: Bureaucratic Politics and Urban Development in the USSR* (1973) and *The View from Lenin Hills: Soviet Youth in Ferment* (1967)—based on his experiences at Moscow State University—and the editor of *Globalism and Its Critics: The American Foreign Policy Debate of the 1960's* (1973). During 1970–1971 he served on the Planning and Coordination Staff of the U.S. Department of State as an International Affairs Fellow of the Council on Foreign Relations. During 1974–1975 he is a Research Fellow of the Russian Research Center at Harvard University, and a Visiting Associate Professor of Political Science at Yale University. He is currently working on a comparative study of Soviet and American foreign policies during the Cold War.

JAN F. TRISKA is Professor of Political Science, Associate Chairman of the Department, and Member of the Institute of Political Studies, Stanford University. He has written extensively on Soviet foreign policy and on East European politics. Professor Triska has recently edited a special issue of *Survey* devoted to Soviet foreign policy in the 1970s. His current research interests include political development, political change, and citizen participation in community decisions in Eastern Europe.

JIRI VALENTA, Brookings Research Fellow 1973–1974, was recently appointed as a Research Associate Professor at the Center for Advanced International Studies at the University of Miami. He was educated in Czechoslovakia, Switzerland, and the United States, and holds advanced degrees from the Prague School of Economics and from Johns Hopkins University. The article printed in this issue won second prize in the student competition of the Washington chapter of the International Studies Association. Dr. Valenta is a contributor to *Problems of Communism* and *SAIS Review*, and co-editor of the *Handbook on Finland* (1974). Currently he is engaged in a study of Soviet foreign policymaking and in revising a study of Soviet bureaucratic politics and intervention in Czechoslovakia.

LAWRENCE L. WHETTEN is Professor and Resident Director of the German Graduate Program of the School of International Relations, University of Southern California. He is the author of *Germany's Ostpolitik: Relations Between the Federal Republic and the Warsaw Pact Countries* (1971), *Contemporary American Foreign Policy: Minimal Diplomacy, Defensive Strategy and Detente Management* (1974), and *The Canal War: Four Power Conflict in the Middle East* (1974). He is co-author with Gerald Livingston of a forthcoming book entitled *Germany East and West*. Professor Whetten has published numerous articles in such journals as *Survey*, *Survival*, *The World Today* and *Orbis*.

TO PROSPECTIVE CONTRIBUTORS

The editors invite the submission of articles and other communications on all aspects of comparative Communism. Priority will be given to articles attempting comparative analyses of historical as well as current developments in the Communist world and problems of Marxist ideology. Studies may be comparative with respect to other Communist states (or parties) or to non-Communist societies. Special attention will be paid to analyses of the divided countries (East and West Germany, North and South Korea, North and South Vietnam, Communist and Nationalist China), as well as of Outer and Inner Mongolia and the various republics, regions, and nationalities. In view of the difficulty of comparative analysis and the paucity of scholars specializing in more than one country, the editors will attempt to provide comparative foci on a given subject (e.g., education in China) by inviting or soliciting comments of a comparative character from scholars specializing in the same subject matter but on different Communist countries (e.g., education in Yugoslavia, the U.S.S.R., etc.). Through multiple assignments, book reviews and review articles will also be utilized as vehicles for comparative analysis. Thus, a book on Rumanian agriculture may be reviewed by an economist specializing in Polish agriculture, a sociologist specializing on Rumania, and a general expert on agriculture who does not profess any particular knowledge of Communist affairs. The journal will attempt to extend coverage to underdeveloped disciplines such as education, geography, religion, aesthetics, etc. in addition to the traditional strongholds of history, political science, economics, and international relations. Authors are encouraged, wherever appropriate, to accompany their articles with a list of primary documents, some of which may be reproduced in the journal's documentary section.

Advanced graduate students in the social sciences are encouraged to submit manuscripts of article and research-note length to: Graduate Students Essays (a new section of the journal which will feature studies by young predoctoral scholars). Correspondence about graduate essays, review articles and research notes should be sent directly to the Associate Editor:

Professor Rudolf L. Tökés, Department of Political Science
University of Connecticut, Storrs, Connecticut 06268

Manuscripts should be double-spaced throughout, including footnotes, and submitted in triplicate. Since manuscripts are sent out anonymously for editorial evaluation, the author's name and affiliation should appear only on a separate covering page. No responsibility can be assumed for loss of or injury to unsolicited manuscripts.

SUBSCRIPTION INFORMATION

All mail (except as noted above), including correspondence about subscriptions, should be sent to the Editorial and Business Offices, VKC 330, School of International Relations, University of Southern California, University Park, Los Angeles, California 90007.

Subscriptions: Institutions $16.00 a year, individuals $10.00 a year, foreign and domestic postage included.

Printed in Great Britain by The Eastern Press, Ltd., London and Reading

50th Year

1924 — 1974

SCHOOL OF INTERNATIONAL RELATIONS

Studies in

COMPARATIVE COMMUNISM

An International Interdisciplinary Journal

Autumn
1975

Studies in Comparative Communism
is published quarterly by the
Von KleinSmid Institute of International Affairs
School of International Relations
University of Southern California

Editor
Peter Berton

Managing Editor
Malcolm Palmatier

Associate Editor
Rudolf L. Tökés
University of Connecticut

Consulting Editor
Hammond Rolph

Studies in Comparative Communism is indexed in the *Social Sciences Index; Public Affairs Information Service; ABC POL SCI; Social Science Citation Index;* and *Current Contents, Behavioral, Social & Management Sciences.* Articles are listed in the *American Historical Review* and abstracted in *Historical Abstracts* and *International Political Science Abstracts,* abstracted and indexed in the *Universal Reference System,* and analyzed in the computer-based *United States Political Science Information System.* US ISSN 0039-3592

Studies in

COMPARATIVE COMMUNISM

An International Interdisciplinary Journal

Vol. VIII, No. 3
Autumn 1975

CONTENTS

THE SCIENCE OF COMMUNIST POLITICS

POLITICAL SCIENCE TEXTBOOKS ON THE SOVIET UNION, CHINA, AND EASTERN EUROPE

Rudolf L. Tőkés
Special Issue Editor

Introduction: Comparative Communism: The Elusive Target
Rudolf L. Tőkés 211

The Soviet Union: Consensus or Debate?
Erik P. Hoffmann 230

Comment
Alexander Dallin 245

China: Four Explanations
Steven Goldstein 248

Comment
Thomas P. Bernstein 274

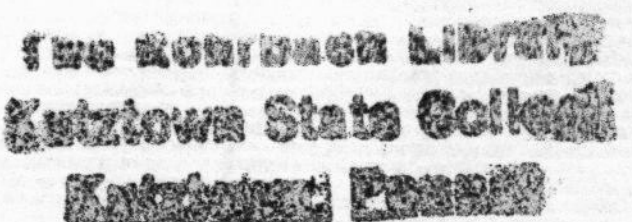

Eastern Europe: Toward a New Paradigm?
Barbara Jancar 278

Comment
Vernon V. Aspaturian 300

Monoliths or Plural Systems: Through Conceptual Lenses Darkly
Joseph LaPalombara 305

CONTRIBUTORS 335

Comparative Communism: The Elusive Target

RUDOLF L. TŐKÉS

The contributors to, and the editor of, this special issue of *Studies in Comparative Communism* on the subject of political science textbooks on the U.S.S.R., the People's Republic of China, and Eastern Europe have sought to accomplish three objectives. The first was to inform readers of the journal, most of whom are teachers or advanced students of Communist history, politics, economics, philosophy, and international relations, about the scholarly merits and general usefulness of available texts for the teaching of Soviet, Chinese, and East European politics at the university level. As an outgrowth of this "academic consumers' report," the second objective was to provide a set of critical analyses of the state of the art of the study of Communist politics, with particular attention to the way in which methodological and conceptual innovations of the "behavioral revolution" in the social sciences have become incorporated into the language and substance of Western political science scholarship on Communist political phenomena.

The third objective—originally the editor's afterthought, which as the issue began to take final form became a compelling concern—has to do with the present status of the field of comparative Communism, a subject of obvious interest to those involved in further development of the field. Specifically, through a brief review of the history and accomplishments of this area of scholarly endeavor, I have sought to prepare a tentative status report to see whether

" comparative Communism " as an offshoot of comparative politics and as a way of looking at Communist politics, ideologies, institutions, and processes in diverse developmental settings has become an established academic subdiscipline (complete with distinct problem-solving techniques, clear-cut conceptual boundaries, and indigenous semantic tools), or whether it remains as elusive a target as it was ten years ago when research strategies of this kind were first advanced by leading students of Communist politics.[1]

Textbooks as Scholarly Works

Before proceeding to a more substantive discussion of the points above, I shall comment briefly on the nature of textbooks as original scholarly works. As the authors of the following essays and discussions are careful to point out, the intellectual worth and academic usefulness of textbooks are subject to limitations that one should keep in mind when forming judgments about literature of this kind. Textbooks are—or should be—primarily *teaching* devices with which an instructor seeks to inform a group of students about the salient aspects of a subject matter within the temporal confines of one, occasionally two, academic semesters. Thus, constraints of time, the psychological drawbacks of a formal classroom learning environment, and the non-specialist nature of the audience tend to impose both parsimony and simplified explanations of often vastly complex issues. From this it would seem to follow that textbooks have little to offer to the specialist reader. However, as the essays of Professors Hoffmann, Goldstein, and Jancar make quite clear, there is, despite the similar or even identical data base on which all textbooks are built, a remarkable diversity of interpretation and emphasis which makes each such work a unique scholarly effort well worth the specialist's time and attention.

To what extent are textbooks representative of the " state of the art " in a given field? Unlike textbooks in some other social science disciplines such as economics, sociology, and modern history where periodic updating and partial revisions keep matters nicely *au courant*, textbooks on Communist politics are, with rare exceptions, one-shot affairs that are used in the original, or in a superficially revised, version until something more recent, if not necessarily better, comes along. As a rule, books of this kind, while useful guideposts for future historians of the profession, tend to become rapidly outdated by

1. For a representative statement see Robert C. Tucker " On the Comparative Study of Communism," *World Politics,* XIX, 2 (January 1967), pp. 242–257.

reason of their (unavoidable) failure to account for developments of the very recent past. Thus, it may be argued that by the nature of the enterprise most textbooks represent a combination of two things: an attempted synthesis of the most important findings of the currently available monographic literature and insights derived from the author's original research, presented in a manner suitable for classroom consumption. Concerning the former, the element of time is of essence. To begin with, many specialized monographs—especially those based on new data or dealing with previously unexamined aspects of Soviet, Chinese, or East European politics—originate with a doctoral dissertation. With few exceptions, academic treatises of this kind require much additional work before submission to an academic publisher or scholarly journal. The publication of such manuscripts often takes years, as does the appearance of knowledgeable critical reviews in learned journals. Since it is the latter that usually alerts the scholarly community to the appearance of a new work, the total time-lag between the birth of a new idea, a new or reformulated paradigm, or a new body of carefully presented evidence and its incorporation into a textbook could be as much as 8–10 years. Thus textbooks can at best convey outdated information interpreted according to methodologies of the previous 5–10 years.

It is worth recalling that such important events as the Sino-Soviet schism, the emergence of polycentric Communism, new patterns of political mobilization and participation, and the appreciable changes in the political life of several Communist states have taken years to find their way into textbooks—while other significant matters such as novel scenarios of political succession, debates about the implications of the scientific-technical revolution, the impact of new educational and welfare measures, the role of women in Communist societies, political, religious, cultural, and nationality dissent, and the rebirth of traditional political and religious philosophies have yet to become integral parts of a new academic consensus on Communist societies and politics in the 1970s.

If textbooks are methodologically outdated, fail to consider important recent developments, and present their findings in an oversimplified fashion, then why waste the time and effort to discuss them at all? A partial and perhaps not entirely persuasive answer to this question might be formulated as follows. The best social science textbooks can be viewed as efforts to reflect on and seek to resolve within the confines of a discipline or specialized subdiscipline some of the important philosophical and existential dilemmas of our age. In the realm of Communist politics the effort involves the making of choices and judgments about the fundamental dichotomies of the postwar era: democracy and Communism, freedom and oppression, political legitimacy and illegitimacy, individual and community rights, as well as a whole gamut of related issues that confront us as scholars and citizens. These dilemmas, when resolved, say, by an author of a textbook on Chinese politics, are articulated as implicit or explicit value judgments in the form of broadly conceived explanatory devices and are spelled out as models, paradigms, or a set of hypotheses. Textbooks, or scholarly analyses of current issues for that matter, thus are not merely vehicles for the articulation of the authors' personal ethics and political *Weltanschauung* but are tools of citizenship training as well. For most of us it *does* matter whether our students, as members of the next generation's educated elite, are given the best possible evaluation of the bewildering political complexities of the world that they are going to inherit. For this reason, this symposium, originally conceived as a " consumers' report " is also something of a sketchy diagnosis of the ideologies, temper, and sincerity of those of us who are professionally concerned with the study of Communist politics.

The Constipated Dialectic and Its Remedies

It is generally agreed that two factors have been mainly responsible for the origins of a movement to develop a comparative approach to Communist studies. The first was the emergence of polycentric Communism, which rendered obsolete the traditional image of an organizationally and ideologically monolithic international system. The Communist world could no longer be described either as homogeneous or, as events unfolded after Stalin's death, as one fully corresponding with the particulars of the totalitarian model. The surfacing of these new realities coincided with a growing acceptance of the behavioral approach to comparative politics. The behavioral approach offered themes of inquiry and research strategies that promised new insights and more accurate and verifiable explanations than those produced by the literature of the traditional or " area " approach to Communist studies. The latter came under vigorous, perhaps too vigorous, attack by proponents of the behavioral method who undertook to transform political science, including Communist studies, into a more " scientific " discipline.

The behavioralist–area studies confrontation—a subject, in terms of style and tone of argument, perhaps more suitable for students of academic psychoneuroses than for historians of ideas—has set into motion an interesting and, in its long-term implications, important trend in Communist studies. Although Robert Ward, in a brilliant presidential address to the 1973 meeting of the American Political Science Association, chose to label the results of this debate as evidence of the "constipated dialectic" of comparative politics, the actual record warrants a somewhat more generous evaluation.[2]

The area approach, we might recall, was characterized by importance attached to the study of one, preferably more than one, language of a foreign area; by "unusual sensitivity to the impact of culture on politics"; and by "a high regard for the importance and relevance of history as a determinant of political outcomes."[3] Viewed from this vantage point it is quite understandable that, at least initially, most traditionally trained Communist area specialists regarded the behavioral method not as a revolutionary alternative but merely as another, still untested research tool for the study of foreign political systems. In any case, the scarcity of (indeed, the downright impossibility of conducting) unhindered field work such as survey research and other forms of on-the-spot attitudinal measurements in any Communist country save Yugoslavia and Czechoslovakia during the short-lived reform period discouraged many potential converts to the behavioral method. Thus, apart from interesting and conceptually limited excursions into the realm of systematic quantification such as Milton Lodge's content analysis of Soviet elite attitudes between 1952 and 1965,[4] most area specialists soon gave up trying to embrace the new creed and returned to their traditional pursuits. Others—and this group included most leading scholars as well as many newcomers into comparative politics—began an earnest search for ways to take up the behavioralist challenge.

With some oversimplification of the record it may be argued that scholarly responses to demands for the "scientific" transformation of Communist studies took two forms. The first may be called flights from the scarcity of empirical data into grand theorizing—an exercise not unlike building a house by skipping the foundations (or taking their existence for granted) and concentrating on the structure and (pardon the expression) function of the roof. Others, while generally accurately diagnosing the shortcomings and inherently limited explanatory potential of the traditional area method, developed ambitious

2. Robert E. Ward, "Culture and the Comparative Study of Politics, or the Constipated Dialectic," *American Political Science Review*, LXVIII, 1 (March 1974), pp. 190–201. (Hereinafter cited as *APSR*.)

3. *Ibid.*, p. 193.

4. Milton Lodge, "'Groupism' in the Post-Stalin Period," *Midwest Journal of Political Science*, XII, 3 (August 1968), pp. 330–351.

research agendas and exhorted their professional brethren to fall in step and start building the edifice of comparative Communism.

Thus, over the years we have been urged to engage in "aggregative," "empirical," "generalizing," "cross-systemic," "vertical," "horizontal," or "diagonal" comparisons within the framework of one or another intellectual fad of the comparative field. These, during the past ten years, have included wholesale, and too often indiscriminate, borrowing and more or less successful application of models and theories from sociology (conflict theory), the philosophy of science (Kuhn's paradigms), the Almond-Coleman developmental theory, economic history ("stages of growth" and variations thereof), and applied metahistory ("convergence," "development and decay," "modernization" theses), followed by structure-functionalism, "mobilization system," "the change to change," "personality and politics," and most recently a renewed interest in political culture and *horribile dictu* in "culture" as such.

The "undiminished ardor", to quote Ward, "with which [the discipline] embrace[d] new causes and panaceas" was particularly evident among Communist specialists. As certified non-scientists they—at least the prominent leaders of the field—had nothing to lose and much to gain by boldly experimenting with new approaches. After many false starts two distinct trends emerged. The first, initiated by the formation of the ACLS Planning Group on Comparative Communist Studies, was a systematic and coordinated effort to consider several, hitherto insufficiently studied aspects of Communist politics: to wit, the dynamics of political change in Communist systems, political terror in Communist systems, Communist politics in Asia and Western Europe, the modernization of Communist societies, the implications of the scientific-technological revolution in Communist states, and the [political?] culture of communism.[5]

5. By saying "systematic" I am probably overstating the case, because to the best of my knowledge the Planning Group as such never issued a comprehensive research design or identified the philosophical concerns, if any, justifying its research and publication priorities. Perhaps Robert Tucker's essay cited in footnote 1 comes closest to a statement of this kind. For the published results, see Chalmers Johnson (ed.), *Change in Communist Systems* (Stanford: Stanford University Press, 1970); Alexander Dallin and George W. Breslauer, *Political Terror in Communist Systems* (Stanford: Stanford University Press, 1970); John Wilson Lewis (ed.), *Peasant Rebellion and Communist Revolution in Asia* (Stanford: Stanford University Press, 1974); Donald L. M. Blackmer and Sidney Tarrow (eds.), *Communism in Italy and France* (Princeton: Princeton University Press, 1975); Mark G. Field (ed.), *Social Consequences of Modernization in Communist Countries* (Baltimore: Johns Hopkins Univer-

The second trend, although somewhat heterogeneous, essentially consisted of various individual and (in at least two cases) collective efforts to study Communist politics in a comparative fashion. One of these collective undertakings was led by Professor Jan Triska; its results are analyzed in some detail in Professor Jancar's essay in this issue. The other, coordinated by Professor Ghita Ionescu, had as participants a group of leading British specialists in Soviet and East European affairs. This group focused on the general subject of "Political and Social Processes in Eastern Europe," dealing specifically with Poland, Czechoslovakia, and Yugoslavia. Unlike the Planning Group study with its seemingly eclectic choice of research topics, the British "interuniversity, interdisciplinary" study addressed three related subjects: (a) the changing role of representative institutions, (b) the changing role of the party, and (c) the changing role of the groups in the interplay between the government and the economy.[6] While it would be hazardous and indeed imprudent to compare the results of the Planning Group and the British project (for one thing, only about one-half of the planned studies of either group are available in print), some tentative observations, especially about the less well-known Ionescu project, may be advanced at this point.

The philosophy and the research strategy of the British approach to comparative Communist studies are spelled out in monographs

sity Press, 1976); and the forthcoming Frederic J. Fleron, Jr. (ed.), *Technology and Communist Culture* (tentative title), and Robert C. Tucker (ed.), *Communism and Culture*. I am indebted to Professor R. V. Burks for providing me with a copy of his "The Planning Group on Comparative Communist Studies: A Report to the Profession" (remarks made at the annual luncheon of the Conference on Communist Studies, American Political Science Association, San Francisco, September 3, 1975) for use in this essay.

6. The published works are David Lane and George Kolankiewicz (eds.), *Social Groups in Polish Society* (London: Macmillan, and New York: Columbia University Press, 1972); Jaroslav Krejci, *Social Change and Stratification in Postwar Czechoslovakia* (London: Macmillan, and New York: Columbia University Press, 1972); Vladimir V. Kusin, *Political Grouping in the Czechoslovak Reform Movement* (London: Macmillan, and New York: Columbia University Press, 1972), and volumes not yet published or still in progress, including Ghita Ionescu, *The Evolution of the Socialist State*; Jane Cave *et al., Politics and the Polish Economy*; A. H. Brown and G. Wightman, *The Communist Party of Czechoslovakia*; J. F. N. Bradley, *Czechoslovak Politics 1948–68;* Phyllis Auty, *The Changing Role of the Yugoslav Communist Party*; R. K. Kindersley, *The Yugoslav Federal Assembly: Relations Between Executive and Legislature*; F. Singleton, *The Yugoslav Social Groups and Institutions*; and D. Matko and D. J. R. Scott, *Career Patterns of Yugoslav Decision-Makers.*

by A. H. Brown and by Ionescu.[7] Brown's study offers an exceptionally thorough and elegantly argued critique and appraisal of the American behavioral literature on Soviet politics. Brown begins by distinguishing among approaches, models and ideal types, techniques of analysis, and areas of concentration in Soviet studies. He proceeds by systematically examining and thoughtfully deflating some of the unwarranted claims of the behavioral camp, concluding with this useful reminder: " Methodological exclusiveness and one-upmanship have no place in serious scholarship, and to the extent to which they have arisen in the study of Soviet politics, they should be resisted." [8]

Complementary to Brown's survey is Ionescu's *Comparative Communist Politics*. Ionescu, unlike most critics of behavioralism before him, quickly dispenses, in an extended review of Frederic J. Fleron's *Communist Studies and the Social Sciences*,[9] with the obvious shortcomings and the conceptual fallacies of what he calls " esotericism " in Communist studies. He submits that it is the Communist *state*, its institutions and laws—a subject that had fallen into disrepute as being of interest only to area-specialists—which should be the focus of comparative Communist studies. Citing E. H. Carr, Ionescu insists that as a direct consequence of the post-totalitarian evolution of Communist politics the state " the supreme, and universally comparable institution " assumes growing and, one might speculate, predominant importance.[10] From this position Ionescu convincingly argues that Communist political institutions constitute not only the most important but at the same time the most easily researchable sector of a Communist polity.

In sum, Ionescu's emphasis on the state and the Brown's recommendation that policymaking processes be studied more diligently seem to coincide with Joseph LaPalombara's counsel that the " black box " aspect of Communist politics be the focus of our attention,[11] as well as with the thrust of John Kautsky's arguments about the complete comparability—irrespective of ideological differences—of Communist and non-Communist political institutions and processes.[12] Thus what these leading comparativists—and in recent years a growing number

7. A. H. Brown, *Soviet Politics and Political Science* (London: Macmillan, 1974), and Ghita Ionescu, *Comparative Communist Politics* (London: Macmillan, 1972).

8. Brown, *op. cit.*, p. 104.

9. Chicago: Rand McNally, 1969.

10. Ionescu, *op cit.*, p. 11.

11. See p. 315 *et seq.* of this issue.

12. John H. Kautsky, " Comparative Communism Versus Comparative Politics," *Studies in Comparative Communism*, VI, 1 & 2 (Spring/Summer 1973), pp. 135–170.

of their colleagues—are saying is that we must bring back *politics* into comparative studies by restoring it to its proper place as the central subject of Communist studies.

As suggested above, individual studies make up the other component of scholarly contributions to comparative Communist studies. Because even a cursory listing of such works could add up to a substantial bibliography and because a list of this sort would inevitably duplicate works discussed in the following essays and comments, the following observations will be confined to four edited volumes and one original work that have been widely used as textbooks or textbook-substitutes for university courses on Communist politics.[13]

Comparative Communism: The Sum and Its Parts

Let us first consider the edited volumes. One might begin by distinguishing among different research strategies, disciplinary preferences, thematic foci, and editorial philosophies that the reader might regard as a frame of analysis for a given volume. On closer scrutiny of the actual contents of the volumes edited by Jan Triska, Frederic Fleron, Roger Kanet, and Lenard J. Cohen and Jane P. Shapiro, it becomes apparent that only the first volume is suitable for critical analysis according to the above criteria. The others, with due allowance to introductory editorial statements of intentions, are essentially collections, labeled "comparative," of previously published studies on one or another aspect of Communist politics. The contents of the Triska volume were conceived, written, and critiqued under close editorial control and were designed to provide a coherent statement from a specific methodological point of view. The three other texts, on the other hand, offer only nine essays out of a total of 64 which may be characterized as originally written for inclusion in the volume where they are found.

Apart from the melancholy fact that only a handful—the Triska book again excepted—of the 64 chapters in the other three edited books actually *compare* two or more Communist polities, societies, or economic systems with one another, a remarkable number of the other studies are, in fact, straightforward descriptive accounts whose authors display little or no inclination to heed the editors' advice and employ behavioral techniques of analysis. And this is why, para-

13. Jan F. Triska (ed.), *Communist Party-States* (Indianapolis-New York: Bobbs-Merrill, 1966); Fleron, *op. cit.*; Roger E. Kanet (ed.), *The Behavioral Revolution and Communist Studies* (New York: Free Press, 1973); and Lenard J. Cohen and Jane P. Shapiro (eds.), *Communist Systems in Comparative Perspective* (Garden City: Anchor Books, 1974).

doxically, most individual contributions to these volumes make fine teaching aids for university courses on Communist politics, notwithstanding introductory editorial statements heralding the coming of the behavioral revolution. One may or may not agree with Triska's and Robert North's choice of "political integration," which, both as a theme and as an intellectual organizing device, is perhaps better suited for the study of Communist international relations than for the comparative analysis of Communist political institutions and behavior. Nevertheless, the fact remains that this volume offers to the reader a set of well-articulated, substantive hypotheses about several carefully selected, comparable aspects of Communist politics.

All this, most emphatically, is not to say that many of the 77 individual essays that make up these four volumes are anything less than original, painstakingly researched, and occasionally brilliant contributions to Communist studies. Indeed, there is no doubt in my mind that the editors picked the best from the *available* literature. Rather, it is to argue that a collective enterprise where the whole is not more than the sum of its parts can accomplish little beyond putting scattered scholarly writing between two covers. As teachers we must be grateful for the effort, but as scholars we are well within our rights when we demand more than the saving our students a few trips to the library periodicals room.

Richard Gripp's *The Political System of Communism* is the first genuinely comparative textbook on Communist politics that covers all fourteen party-states.[14] Whatever we may think of this work, we must admit that it took a great deal of courage to undertake this project. Therefore, a pioneering effort of even marginally acceptable quality deserves both careful and generous criticism. Gripp's approach may be characterized as a search for, and perhaps an emphasis on, common denominators in Communist systems. He does not dwell at length on the philosophical, structural, and operational peculiarities of and differences between, say, China and Cuba, but provides succinct summaries of the way in which the Communist Party, the government, public institutions, economic planning, and the like actually work. In doing so he sensitizes the reader to, more than adequately informs the reader of, the extreme complexity of the workings of the various kinds of Communisms that exist in the 1970s. The only substantive attempt at theory-building comes in the concluding part of the book entitled "Success of Communist Political Systems."[15] Here Gripp submits that under the present international

14. New York-Toronto: Dodd, Mead & Co., 1973.
15. *Ibid.*, pp. 178–196.

balance of power Communism must be regarded not as an aberration but as a viable method of development in certain kinds of societies. Such liabilities as certain structural flaws, periodic crises, and the Communist movement's burdensome philosophical heritage should not blind us to the system's existence and to its future evolutionary potential for development and change. Gripp very sensibly reconstructs an all-purpose " Marxist-Leninist model " and explores it in the form of five linked hypotheses that identify and briefly analyze the dichotomies between the ideological postulates and the empirically observable record of polities built on this model. Although neither this nor the author's own " political-economic development " model is particularly original, let alone sufficiently documented, it is nevertheless a useful (and the only) comprehensive pretheoretical introduction to the subject.

Experience suggests that comparative Communism cannot be taught on the undergraduate level from texts devoted to esoteric excursions into game theory, sophisticated computer analysis, or quantitative psycholinguistics, and that Communist ideology cannot be explained from complex flow charts with " general classes of variables " that are said to " influence political behavior." This surely will not do. A way must be found to convey the essential elements of the perplexing but intellectually challenging realities of contemporary Communist politics without compromising the level of analysis or sacrificing the breadth and detail of evidence that one must provide to a satisfactory explanation of the phenomenon.

Needless to say, none of this should be construed as unqualified praise of simplicity or unfair criticism of interdisciplinary and experimental research. My point is that on the tenth anniversary of the " behavioral revolution " in Communist studies,[16] one still cannot compile from the currently available literature, even under the most liberal definition of comparative Communism, a volume featuring ten to twelve studies of equal sophistication and comparative scope on as many fundamental aspects of Communist politics. Apart from the imponderables involved in the choice of suitable themes, the real problem is to find scholars equally conversant with the latest (and applicable) research tools and with the rich complexities of each of the " areas " that constitute the Communist world.[17] As things stand

16. The launching of the Planning Group on Comparative Communist Studies in 1965 seems like an appropriate date to mark the beginning of this movement.

17. As one personally involved, along with an East Asian and an East European specialist, in an abortive attempt to undertake such a study in 1969, I can vouch from experience for the accuracy of this statement.

now, only a small team with a mastery of most of the languages of Communist nations, with a comparably high level of social science training, and preferably with a shared philosophical outlook could undertake the writing of a genuinely comprehensive textbook on comparative Communist politics with a hope of success. Since this is not likely to happen in the foreseeable future, we might next inquire into the general symptoms and underlying causes of the malaise that is responsible for the present, not very encouraging, state of affairs.

Political Science: Basic and Applied, Relevant and Irrelevant

According to the authoritative Lambert study on the state of area studies in the United States, the overwhelming majority of the so-called "area specialists" in Communist politics also happen to be deeply involved in the teaching of, and to a lesser extent in research on, the general subject of political science.[18] From this it follows that as practicing *political scientists* Communist specialists not only are aware of the main intellectual trends of their discipline, but for better or worse are influenced in their teaching, research, and writing by current intellectual, methodological, and philosophical dilemmas of their professional discipline.

To investigate the implications of this proposition, I turned to the texts of the annual presidential addresses of the American Political Science Association for the years 1964–1973.[19] The reading of these statements, from Herman Pritchett's "Equal Protection and the Urban Majority" (1964) to Robert Ward's address cited above, has been an enlightening and in some ways a traumatic experience.

APSA presidential addresses usually make an effort to take stock of the discipline's current dilemmas, to introduce and share with the audience the speaker's philosophical concerns, and to prognosticate

18. See Richard D. Lambert, *Language and Area Studies Review* (Philadelphia: American Academy of Political and Social Science, 1973).

19. C. Herman Pritchett, "Equal Protection and the Urban Majority," *APSR*, LVIII, 4 (December 1974), pp. 869–875; David B. Truman, "Disillusion and Regeneration: The Quest for a Discipline," *APSR*, LIX, 4 (December 1965), pp. 865–873; Gabriel A. Almond, "Political Theory and Political Science," *APSR*, LX, 4 (December 1966), pp. 869–879; Robert A. Dahl, "The City in the Future of Democracy," *APSR*, LXI, 4 (December 1967), pp. 953–970; Merle Fainsod, "Some Reflections on Soviet-American Relations," *APSR*, LXII, 4 (December 1968), pp. 1093–1103; David Easton, "The New Revolution in Political Science," *APSR*, LXIII, 4 (December 1969), pp. 1051–1061; Robert E. Lane, "To Nurture a Discipline," *APSR*, LXVI, 1 (March 1972) pp. 164–182; Heinz Eulau, "Skill Revolution and Consultative Commonwealth," *APSR*, LXVII, 1 (March 1973), pp. 168–191; Ward, *op. cit.*

the profession's future prospects. These statements constitute a rich source of ideas that may be read and interpreted in many ways. For example, from the Communist specialist's viewpoint one may ponder and very likely disagree with statements like "I would argue that the problems of political science are, if only because of the numbers of practitioners involved, chiefly problems of American political science," or with such profundities as "'Kremlinology' as an alternative to theory is in part traceable, I suspect, to scarcity of data," which one encounters in David Truman's 1965 presidential address.[20]

As a constructive alternative to speculation of this sort we can turn to presidential addresses of those who were specifically concerned with the philosophical issues that confronted the entire community of political scientists as scholars, teachers, and thoughtful citizens. Of the four (Gabriel Almond, David Easton, Karl Deutsch and Robert Ward) that I enjoyed most, I would like to discuss briefly David Easton's brilliant and insightful "The New Revolution in Political Science."

Easton's remarks were concerned with the confrontation of the "old" and the "new," or "behavioral orthodoxy" and "post-behavioral revolution" in the discipline. The latter, he suggested, was the result of the challenge issued in the name of "relevance" by today's "rebels," made up of politically concerned (not necessarily radical) members of the profession, to the former "rebels" against traditional political science, who have since become well-entrenched members of an orthodox Establishment. Easton's summary of the "post-behavioralist" platform that he calls the "Creed of Relevance" offers several challenging propositions, of which five excerpts are worth citing here.[21]

(1) "Substance must precede technique . . . it is better to be vague than non-relevantly precise."

(2) "Behavioral science conceals an ideology of empirical conservatism. To confine oneself exclusively to the description and analysis of facts is to hamper the understanding of these same facts in their broadest context. As a result empirical political science must lend its support to the maintenance of the very factual conditions it explores. . . ."

(3) "Behavioral research must lose touch with reality. The heart of behavioral inquiry is abstraction and analysis and it serves to conceal the brute realities of politics. . . ."

20. Truman, *op. cit.*, pp. 865, 870.

21. Easton, *op. cit.*, p. 1052.

(4) "Research about and constructive development of values are inextinguishable parts of the study of politics. Science cannot be and never has been evaluatively neutral despite protestations to the contrary. . . ."

(5) "Members of a learned discipline bear the responsibility of all intellectuals. The intellectuals' historical role has been and must be to protect the humane values of civilization. This is their unique task and obligation. Without this they become mere technicians, mechanics for tinkering with society. . . ."

It may be argued that views attributed by Easton to the post-behavioralists may be utilized in an *advocatus diaboli* fashion for a critical discussion of the present state of comparative Communist studies. First, however, let us place matters in a correct time perspective. The behavioral trend in Communist studies was perhaps the last ripple of a major wave of a "successful protest movement" whose end was foreseen as early as 1961.[22] It was only in the mid-1960s that a similar "intellectual movement" (in Robert Tucker's phrase) began in Communist studies.[23] During the next ten years this movement has refought every battle of the 1940s and 1950s, by 1975 [24] arriving at about the same point as had the "mother discipline" ten years ago. Although there have been stirrings of criticism against the new orthodoxies in Communist studies, these have not yet been presented in the form of a countertheory or a comprehensive alternative model. In lieu of a critique of either kind, we might consider the applicability of Easton's checklist as a diagnostic tool to our more immediate concerns.

Being "non-relevantly precise" in Communist studies, we might surmise, means being preoccupied with one or another aspect or partial process of a Communist state without reference to systemic—historical, cultural, philosophical—parameters of the observed phenomenon. This may include (and certainly has included) discussions of recent Chinese politics without reference to Mao's cult of personality, and analyses of the domestic policy processes of an independent-minded Communist state without consideration of its politically, ideologically, and militarily dependent status on the U.S.S.R., treatises on Communist nation-building scenarios that fail to mention the human (and economic) cost of forced collectivization

22. Robert Dahl, "The Behavioural Approach in Political Science: Epitaph for a Monument to a Successful Protest," *APSR*, LV, 4 (December 1961), pp. 763–779.

23. Tucker, *op. cit.*

24. In scholarly articles, at annual meetings of learned societies, and in the dark alleys of review and correspondence columns of professional journals.

and massive police terror, and ostensibly thorough statistical analyses of real wages and living standards (say, in today's Czechoslovakia) without accounting for the psychic costs and massive deterioration of the quality of life since the Soviet invasion of 1968.

Empirical conservatism may take many forms in Communist studies. Most often it begins with a search for the most easily and plausibly quantifiable elements of Communist politics, elements that with the help of judiciously manipulated models and paradigms borrowed from other social science disciplines (or from American field situations) can be analyzed and dispensed with according to the currently dominant methodology. The *choice* of elites rather than of the cumbersome masses of people living under Communism (who can understand them anyway?), of isolated (and perhaps non-representative) case studies rather than complex political or social processes, of published (and censored) newspapers, journals, and books rather than self-published (often confusing and incoherent but uncensored) materials in search for data on public opinion seem to fall in this category.

It may be said that the much-maligned totalitarian model was derived from the "brute realities" of Stalinist politics and was, certainly in the 1960s and thereafter, no longer useful as a realistic explanatory device. Critics of this model, while accurately diagnosing the shortcomings of (to borrow Robert Burrowes' phrase) both the "standard" and the "revised" versions,[25] often fell into the trap of ignoring such unpleasant realities of Communist politics as the lasting influence of totalitarian personalities, decisionmaking habits, institutions, unrepealed laws, and unrepentant ideologues which have effectively retarded or blocked liberalization and reform processes aiming at achieving a post-totalitarian political equilibrium. We all suspect or would like to believe that polycentric Communism and the classical totalitarian model are theoretically incompatible, but no one—behavioralist or traditionalist—has managed to do better than criticize the old model without making the effort to produce a better one adequately reflecting the brute realities of contemporary Communist politics.

Closely related to the matter of models is the philosophy, as well as the moral and ethical judgments, that the affirmation or the negation of a model entails. Many of those seeking to divorce themselves from the scurrilous label of "cold warrior" for being (often reluctant) adherents of the totalitarian model have found refuge in leaping to the other extreme, either by denying the continued influence

25. Robert Burrowes, "Totalitarianism: The Revised Standard Version," *World Politics*, XXI, 2 (January 1969), pp. 272–294.

of totalitarian ideologies in Communist polities or by labeling them philosophies of a new scientific-technical revolution that, in a kind of self-fulfilling prophecy, would ultimately converge with those of the comparably elitist technocratic brethren in non-Communist lands. To this, on a personal note, I might add that the conspicuous reluctance of most scientific and "traditionalist" political scientists to recognize the existence, ponder the implications, and incorporate into a new synthesis of contemporary Soviet politics the record of the post-Khrushchev dissident movement (made up of amorphous, non-elite, often uneducated and inarticulate groups of people), or to consider the ideas of the politically powerless in Communist countries, can be viewed as a new form of escapism from realities into a value-free "apolitical politics" kind of analysis.[26] Surely, one need not be a cold warrior to take Sakharov, Solzhenitsyn, and the thousands of their less well-known compatriots seriously, or even to regard them as harbingers of potentially significant changes in the U.S.S.R.

And finally, it behooves us to remember that George Orwell, Albert Camus, and the great generation of their liberal and radical fellow intellectuals were "Communist experts" too. As responsible intellectuals they dared to confront the agonizing moral dilemmas of their age and had the courage to affirm their personal beliefs by pronouncing moral judgments about fascism and Communism, and indeed about democracy, whenever any of these ideologies seemed to pose a threat to humane values and the dignity of man. This legacy of nonconformism, even in an age that seems to reward mechanics and tinkerers in the social sciences, is a compelling one that ought to be kept in mind when considering the intellectual priorities of professional students of Communist politics.

Whether we view, as Easton does, the post-behavioral challenge as an "opportunity for necessary change" or regard it as irrelevant for Communist studies, the record is such that it invites self-examination and raises questions as to where we are and where we are heading as a specialized branch of comparative political studies.

Conclusions

It should be clear from the preceding discussion that comparative Communism, contrary to the high hopes of prominent specialists, has, at least until now, failed to become an established subdiscipline.

26. For a more detailed discussion, see Rudolf L. Tőkés (ed.), *Dissent in the USSR: Politics, Ideologies and People* (Baltimore-London: Johns Hopkins University Press, 1975), pp. 16–22.

If this is in fact the case, then we may conclude that we have no business publishing books and journals and teaching university-level courses on a subject that has not yet come into being. If, on the other hand, we take another set of recent developments into consideration, we might—indeed, we should—arrive at a somewhat different and certainly more optimistic conclusion.

It should be stated at the outset that the overall quality of recently published scholarly monographs on Soviet, Chinese, and East European politics, history, economics, and society has been very high. There is every indication that their authors have benefited from the substantive and methodological debates of the past ten years. Perusal of outstanding (a) Soviet studies by John Armstrong, Stephen Cohen, Robert C. Tucker, Paul Hollander, David Lane, Zvi Y. Gitelman, and Roger Pethybridge, (b) Chinese and East Asian studies by Alexander Eckstein, Roderick MacFarquhar, Robert A. Scalapino and Chong-Sik Lee, Richard Solomon, and A. Doak Barnett, and (c) East European studies by Peter C. Ludz, Galia Golan, Thomas A. Baylis, Joseph Fiszman, and Kenneth Jowitt would prove, if such proof were needed, that when the dust settles after methodological debates it is still the individual scholar and his individual effort that makes the difference between stagnation and continued intellectual development of any field of academic endeavor.[27]

27. The following list includes only those books published after 1970 that I read with particular care *and* profited from in teaching Soviet, East European, and comparative Communist politics. John Armstrong, *European Administrative Elites* (Princeton: Princeton University Press, 1973); Stephen F. Cohen, *Bukharin and the Bolshevik Revolution* (New York: Knopf, 1973); Robert C. Tucker, *Stalin as Revolutionary 1879–1929* (New York: Norton, 1973); Paul Hollander, *Soviet and American Society* (New York: Oxford University Press, 1973); David Lane, *The Roots of Russian Communism* (University Park, Pa.: Pennsylvania State University Press, 1974); Roger Pethybridge, *The Social Prelude to Stalinism* (New York: St. Martin's Press, 1974); Zvi Y. Gitelman, *Jewish Nationality and Soviet Politics* (Princeton: Princeton University Press, 1972); Alexander Eckstein, *China's Economic Development* (Ann Arbor: University of Michigan Press, 1975); Roderick MacFarquhar, *The Origins of the Cultural Revolution, Vol. 1: Contradictions Among the People 1956–1957* (New York: Columbia University Press, 1974); Robert A. Scalapino and Chong-Sik Lee, *Communism in Korea*, 2 vols. (Berkeley and Los Angeles: University of California Press, 1972); Richard Solomon, *Mao's Revolution and the Chinese Political Culture* (Berkeley and Los Angeles: University of California Press, 1971); and A. Doak Barnett, *Uncertain Passage: China's Transition to the Post-Mao Era* (Washington, D.C.: Brookings Institution, 1974); Peter C. Ludz, *The Changing Party Elite in East Germany* (Cambridge, Mass.: M.I.T. Press, 1972); Galia Golan, *The Czechoslovak Reform Movement* and *Reform Rule in Czechoslovakia* (London: Cambridge University Press, 1971, 1973); Thomas A. Baylis, *The Technical Intelligentsia and the*

The appearance in the past two years of important and still not sufficiently reviewed and analyzed comparative monographs and symposia represents another sign of continued interest in the comparative approach to Communist politics. Volumes written or edited by Carl Beck and associates, Myron Rush, Robert King, Michael Waller, Charles Gati, Thomas Hammond, Thomas Robinson, Stuart Schram, Michel Oksenberg, and the late John Lindbeck suggest that, thanks to the continued efforts of the profession, many, though not all, of the " infantile afflictions " of the comparative method are being overcome.[28]

Complementary to these positive developments is the emergence of a body of new literature specifically focusing on the methodological and epistemological issues of the comparative Communist approach. Some of these writings have appeared or are scheduled to appear in this journal, while others have been published in the now defunct *Newsletter on Comparative Communist Studies*, specialized " area " periodicals (e.g., *Asian Survey*, *Soviet Studies*), and major disciplinary journals such as *World Politics* and the *American Political Science Review*. Perhaps more to the point is the fact that critical studies of this kind tend to draw heavily on the most recent methodological contributions of leading comparativists such as Gabriel Almond, Joseph LaPalombara, Harry Eckstein, Samuel P. Huntington, Dankwart Rustow, and David Apter, and in doing so, achieve a much-needed linkup with ongoing theorizing about the comparative approach to politics.

East German Elite (Berkeley and Los Angeles: University of California Press, 1974); Joseph R. Fiszman, *Revolution and Tradition in People's Poland* (Princeton: Princeton University Press, 1972); and Kenneth Jowitt, *Revolutionary Breakthroughs and National Development* (Berkeley: University of California Press, 1971).

28. Carl Beck *et al.*, *Comparative Communist Political Leadership* (New York: David McKay, 1973); Myron Rush, *How Communist States Change Their Rulers* (Ithaca and London: Cornell University Press, 1974); Robert R. King, *Minorities Under Communism* (Cambridge, Mass.: Harvard University Press, 1973); Michael Waller, *The Language of Communism* (London: Bodley Head, 1972); Charles Gati (ed.), *The Politics of Modernization in Eastern Europe* (New York: Praeger, 1974); Thomas T. Hammond (ed.), *The Anatomy of Communist Takeovers* (New Haven and London: Yale University Press, 1975); Thomas Robinson (ed.), *The Cultural Revolution in China* (Berkeley and Los Angeles: University of California Press, 1971); Stuart Schram (ed.), *Authority, Participation and Cultural Change in China* (Cambridge: Cambridge University Press, 1973); Michel Oksenberg (ed.), *China's Developmental Experience* (New York: Praeger, 1973); John M. H. Lindbeck (ed.), *China: Management of a Revolutionary Society* (Seattle: University of Washington Press, 1971).

With the completion of this special issue my three-year term as the Associate Editor of this journal has come to an end. Just as the authors of the following essays and comments enjoyed full freedom, apart from occasional stylistic editorial interference, to develop their respective cases, I too have sought to discuss the state of the art as I saw it—sometimes an exercise in excessive candor that may not be the best way to make new friends or keep old ones, especially if their works came under more criticism than praise. However, the sole motive behind this collective undertaking has been an earnest wish, fully shared by colleagues whom I have been fortunate to enlist for this purpose, to take stock of our achievements, to profit from our mistakes, and to initiate a new round of thoughtful discussion about our common concerns in the field of comparative Communist politics. We hope that the contents of this issue will be received in the same spirit.

Erik P. Hoffmann

The Soviet Union: Consensus or Debate?

I

By what criteria should one evaluate the newest textbooks on Soviet politics written by Western scholars? Is it fair to expect much original research and up-to-date information on the contemporary Brezhnev period? Should general studies be expected to offer imaginative theoretical and conceptual approaches to their subject, to raise new issues and questions, to provide new explanations, interpretations, and insights? Should they seek to refine or refute commonly accepted generalizations and assumptions about different types of Soviet political behavior? Should they stimulate and help readers to do likewise? Should they experiment with novel methodologies or techniques of analysis that might add to our understanding of Soviet political activity? Finally, how much credit should be given for skillful description, synthesis, stock-taking, replication, and comparison of behavior and institutions over time; for careful selection of significant themes, problems, issues and topics; for comprehensiveness; for clarity of presentation?

My own highly subjective view is that it is *desirable* to do all of these things and to do them well, but that it is not *reasonable* to expect that every general study should attempt to do all of them, or succeed in making contributions in each of these areas. Book size and cost considerations alone force hard decisions concerning scope and depth. Also, there are now so many texts on Soviet politics that it is increasingly difficult to offer novel interpretations. Hence, a book that performs a few of these functions may well make a very worthwhile contribution—either to the way social scientists look at the Soviet system and to the depth of our knowledge about it, or to our ability to disseminate existing information, interpretations, and disagreements to a wider audience, particularly in the universities, in the business and government communities, and among the general public.

I personally place an especially high value on studies that present and defend significant themes, ideas, and arguments, and thereby foster critical and original thinking, and enhance one's ability to understand and explain important dimensions of Soviet politics. I also have a special substantive interest in the processes by which public policies are shaped and reshaped. Essential to an understanding of these processes, I believe, are thorough descriptions of key institutions and personnel, analyses of the content of policies in different issue-areas, and attempts to assess the impact of policies on various organizations, groups, and individuals in Soviet society.

These, then, are a few of the considerations that have influenced my judgments in this " consumers' guide " to recent Western texts on the Soviet political system.

II

Before turning to the most recent literature, it is worth recalling that two of the earliest post-World War II studies of the Soviet system meet virtually all of our initial criteria and set very high standards for comparison. I have in mind Barrington Moore, Jr.'s *Soviet Politics —The Dilemma of Power* and Merle Fainsod's *How Russia Is Ruled*.[1]

Moore's work has a significant central theme—the impact of ideas on social change, and vice versa. Implicit is the approach of a social scientist who alternatively views both of these sets of factors as independent and dependent variables. Moore's study is particularly forceful because he carefully analyzes the reciprocal influences of the ideas and actions of Soviet leaders in different contexts. He also judiciously emphasizes the situational constraints on Soviet policymakers, their adaptability and responsiveness to rapidly changing events and conditions, and the changing functions performed by the values and beliefs of important Party figures. For example, Moore repeatedly affirms

1. Barrington Moore, Jr., *Soviet Politics—The Dilemma of Power* (New York: Harper & Row, 2nd ed., 1965); Merle Fainsod, *How Russia Is Ruled* (Cambridge, Mass.: Harvard University Press, 2nd ed., 1965). See also Julian Towster, *Political Power in the USSR, 1917-1947* (New York: Oxford University Press, 1948).

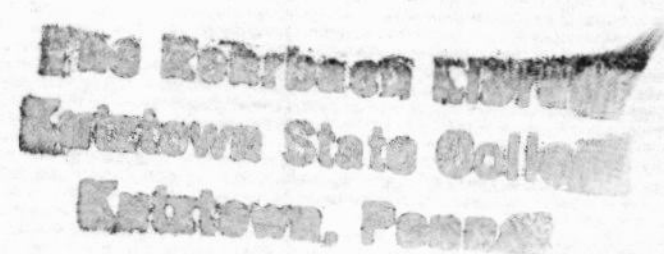

that the Bolshevik " ideology of means," exemplified in the words and actions of Lenin and in the Russian revolutionary tradition, has exerted a tremendous influence on the evolution of the Soviet political system. This instrumental ideology, according to Moore, has had a vastly greater impact on the behavior of Communist Party officials than has the much less authoritarian and less clearly thought-out goals and ideals of classical Marxism and Russian Marxism.

Fainsod, too, presents a distinctive and prodigiously documented theoretical analysis and interpretation of the Soviet system. His emphasis on the concept of " totalitarianism " helps to produce an even more macrotheoretical study than Moore's—perhaps more macrotheoretical than Fainsod himself intended—and one that profoundly influenced the questions posed by a generation of Western scholars. Rereading Fainsod, one is likely to evaluate even more highly than before his abilities as a social scientist and a " middle-range " social theorist, especially in the areas of mobilization, conflict, and communication theories. Fainsod is not usually thought of as a " conflict " theorist because of his stress on the dictatorial nature of Soviet policymaking, but he is acutely aware of the importance of inter- and intraorganizational conflict in the implementation of policies, and in the center's efforts to avoid " the pluralization of authority."

To be sure, the Moore and Fainsod books have some shortcomings —for example, Moore's insufficient treatment of Stalinist coercion, which he subsequently analyzed in *Terror and Progress—USSR*.[2] Also, Fainsod deemphasizes organizational inputs into the policymaking process, and he tends (in the second edition) to overstress the similarities between the purposes and powers of Khrushchev and Stalin. Nonetheless, the sophistication and scholarship of these two early general studies are of a very high order indeed.

III

Of the " second generation " postwar studies of the Soviet system (it is difficult, because of multiple editions, to provide precise dates), the works of John Hazard, Zbigniew Brzezinski, and Alfred Meyer deserve special mention. All offer fresh approaches to their subject and some new answers to new questions.

Hazard, in *The Soviet System of Government*,[3] stresses the explanatory, comparative, and normative advantages of viewing the Soviet

2. Barrington Moore, Jr., *Terror and Progress—USSR* (New York: Harper & Row, 2nd ed., 1966).

3. John N. Hazard, *The Soviet System of Government* (Chicago: University of Chicago Press, 4th ed. 1968).

polity as one in which " democratic forms " are subject to " counterweights " at key " peril-points." Developing the theory of totalitarianism, Hazard identifies the crucial characteristics of the Soviet system that inhibit " the democratic functioning of democratic forms " (e.g., a judiciary that is subject to Party domination in political cases, controls preventing the emergence of potentially independent institutional and associational pressure groups). Hazard's study is informed by his deep knowledge of legal sources and of the practical problems involved in translating general Party policies into specific legislation that can and will be implemented. Hazard is keenly aware of important post-Stalin developments—increasing recruitment of technical specialists into the Party, broader participation in policy formulation through the standing committees of the U.S.S.R. Supreme Soviet, for example—but he insists that if there is to be substantial change in the system as a whole, it must come in a few vital areas (i.e., at specific " peril-points "). Significantly, Hazard does not seem to consider " an expansion of the circle of the ruling elite " to be one of these areas, and he does not foresee changes in the " essentials " of the system.

Brzezinski's coauthored study, *Political Power: USA/USSR,*[4] is well known for its systematic comparisons of the Soviet and American polities, and for its rejection of " convergence " theories. In so doing, Brzezinski and Huntington offer a comparative analysis of the political consequences of modernization, particularly industrialization and urbanization. Stressing that " a multiplicity of expertises . . . is not the same thing as socio-political pluralism based on group autonomy," the writers forcefully argue that the nature of economic-political relationships depends heavily on specific characteristics of the existing political system. In the Soviet case, key variables are thought to be the political vision and skills of professional Party officials, and their capacity " to combine economic rationalization . . . with ideological revitalization " (pp. 424 *et seq.*).

With over ten years' hindsight, one is inclined to conclude that an even more significant contribution of the Brzezinski volume is its theoretical focus on the policymaking process. Of particular importance is its emphasis on policy initiation, consensus-building, and decisionmaking in different issue-areas, and on the vital role of Soviet leaders' goals, beliefs, perceptions, calculations, career experience, and formal and informal relations with one another. Fainsod, for example, had relatively little to say about the interrelationships of power,

4. Zbigniew Brzezinski and Samuel P. Huntington, *Political Power: USA/USSR* (New York: Viking Press, 1964). Also Zbigniew Brzezinski, *Ideology and Power in Soviet Politics* (New York: Praeger, 2nd ed. 1967).

ideology, and issues as inputs into policymaking in different periods of Soviet history. Brzezinski, in contrast, views Soviet politics as a " bargaining " process, and he analyzes the nature, stakes, and outcomes of this process in light of the " political resources " available to various participants and would-be participants (groups and individuals) at different stages in the formulation, execution, and reformulation of public policies in the post-Stalin era.

Meyer's *The Soviet Political System*[5] is best known for viewing the U.S.S.R. as " bureaucracy writ large," and for its striking comparison of the Soviet Union to a modern Western business corporation dominating a " company town." Meyer considers the CPSU to be the directing nucleus (" The Board of Directors " and " stockholders ") of a giant, highly complex, and differentiated bureaucracy. By conceptualizing the Soviet system as a *single* huge unit, Meyer focuses attention on what he considers to be the essentially *intra*organizational, rather than *inter*organizational, nature of Soviet politics. In particular, he stresses the capacity of CPSU leaders to make frequent changes in the structure and personnel of all of the major bureaucracies, and to adjust policy to new domestic and foreign opportunities, problems, and power relationships. What distinguishes Meyer's approach from the " totalitarian model " is his emphasis on the contradictory, unclear, and unattainable characteristics of the Soviet polity's central commands, and on the formidable bureaucratic obstacles to transforming national Party goals into workable policies and laws that lower-level officials can and will carry out. Industrialization and urbanization make these factors even more important, he believes, and place qualitatively new demands on the policymaking system. In short, Meyer is keenly sensitive to the importance of policymaking and administrative procedures, and to the reciprocal influences of decision-making practices and substantive decisions. He contends, for example, that " open debate has begun in the U.S.S.R. on many issues of public policy . . . covering matters of vital importance," and that " ever more frequent and open disputes are taking place among the various elites " and institutional " interest groups " (pp. 188, 231, 470ff.).

Elsewhere, Meyer deliberately jostles our thinking by suggesting that " there is no such thing as The Soviet Political System," but only " a succession of systems sharply differing from each other in purpose, structure, and functioning."[6] One must bear in mind, then,

5. Alfred Meyer, *The Soviet Political System* (New York: Random House, 1965).

6. Alfred Meyer, " The Soviet Political System," in Samuel Hendel and Randolph Braham (eds.), *The U.S.S.R. After 50 Years* (New York: Knopf, 1967), pp. 41 ff.

that Meyer places considerable emphasis on the Soviet system's capacity and propensity for change—political, economic, and social. Significantly, Meyer argues (sometimes implicitly) that Khrushchev's encouragement of freer discussion and greater decentralization of authority within "U.S.S.R., Incorporated" were essentially skillful management techniques. These maneuverings allegedly were intended to enhance, and to some extent did enhance, the power of the First Secretary and of the Central Committee apparatus. Khrushchev reportedly sought to increase the capability of central Party *apparatchiki* to direct and control the bureaucracies and society in accordance with "basic aims" which were fought over and determined by only some of the very highest leaders. Meyer might or might not wish to extend this interpretation to the Brezhnev administration, but in either case he would do so on empirical, not *à priori*, grounds.

IV

Of the general studies on Soviet politics written or revised in the 1970s, I have chosen to focus on the works of six authors: John Armstrong, Frederick Barghoorn, Darrell Hammer, David Lane, Robert Osborn, and John Reshetar, Jr.[7] My generalizations and observations about the "recent" literature will be based chiefly on these books.

What strikes one immediately is the impressive scope of these six studies. The authors write with ease about a wide variety of topics that cover a broad time span—usually the entire Soviet era, and in some instances earlier centuries of Russian political and social history. Numerous important aspects of the post-Stalin years are discussed, although different subjects receive different emphases; political institutions, the economy, "ideological work," social relations, law, ethnic and religious diversity, dissent, foreign policy, and other topics are included. For comprehensiveness, and for clarity of presentation too, these books are all commendable. A wealth of pertinent and accurate information, which reflects both the accomplishments and the

7. John A. Armstrong, *Ideology, Politics, and Government in the Soviet Union* (New York: Praeger, 3rd ed. 1974); Frederick Barghoorn, *Politics in the USSR* (Boston: Little, Brown, 2nd ed. 1972); Darrell Hammer, *USSR: The Politics of Oligarchy* (Hinsdale, Ill.: Dryden Press, 1974); David S. Lane, *Politics and Society in the USSR* (New York: Random House, 1971); Robert J. Osborn, *The Evolution of Soviet Politics* (Homewood, Ill.: Dorsey Press, 1974); John Reshetar, Jr., *The Soviet Polity: Government and Politics in the U.S.S.R.* (New York: Dodd and Mead, 1971). See also Roy D. Laird, *The Soviet Paradigm: An Experiment in Creating a Monohierarchical Society* (New York: Free Press, 1970); Robert Wesson, *The Soviet Russian State* (New York: Wiley, 1972).

shortcomings of Western scholarship on Soviet Russia, is now easily accessible to the general reader.

This is not to say, however, that all six books devote equal attention to the present Brezhnev-Podgorny-Kosygin period. Armstrong, for example, focuses on contemporary Soviet politics, whereas Reshetar concentrates on what he considers to be the fundamental and enduring characteristics of the Soviet system and their historical antecedents. Reshetar's book may be less easily dated, but Armstrong's is much more useful in describing and interpreting current developments. Reshetar's study strongly suggests that major changes in the Soviet system are not likely, whereas Armstrong examines key recent events and analyzes in a more inductive manner which developments do or do not seem to constitute breaks from past trends and traditions.

Collectively, these six texts do not present a substantial amount of information about the post-Khrushchev years. I would have liked to see these books add considerably more to our knowledge of the Brezhnev period—for example, the politics of the 1970s, which seem to differ in several important respects from the years 1964 to 1970. Also, I would have preferred more systematic comparison of the policies, policymaking procedures, and policy outcomes of the current " collective leadership " with those of previous regimes. Through more intensive comparison—particularly of the Khrushchev and Brezhnev, and of the Stalin and post-Stalin, administrations—one might have formulated more clearly some basic issues concerning continuity and change, and one might have presented more empirically grounded answers to questions regarding the direction, extent, and rate of change in different areas of present-day Soviet politics.

This relative lack of emphasis on the most recent period, while regrettable, is not difficult to explain. Here, especially, the recent textbooks reflect the current state of Western literature—that is, the paucity of monographic studies and, for that matter, of empirical research of almost any kind on many important aspects of contemporary Soviet politics (the subject of dissent is a notable exception). Furthermore, it may be premature to expect up-to-date studies in certain fields, and the authors of these texts seem to have conducted original research only or primarily in their special areas of competence.[8]

8. Armstrong's special interests include bureaucracy and the nationalities question; Barghoorn's, political culture and socialization and dissent; Hammer's, political elites and law; Lane's, Russian revolutionary history and political sociology; Osborn's, social policies and urban politics; and Reshetar's, the CPSU and the nationalities issue.

What strikes one next about these six studies is the *absence* of new theoretical or conceptual approaches to their subject. The works of Barghoorn and Lane, which are influenced by the structural-functionalism and systems analysis of Western social and comparative theorists, are surely the most innovative conceptually.[9] Both make serious attempts to use selected Western social science concepts (e.g., " political culture," " political socialization," " interest articulation," " interest aggregation ") to describe and explain Soviet political behavior. But Barghoorn's " analytic framework," I think, has a greater impact on his organization of material and manner of presentation than on his theoretical analysis and interpretations. It is not altogether clear that Barghoorn's functionalist conceptual vocabulary greatly influenced the questions he asked or the conclusions he reached, and perhaps not even the topics he chose to discuss or the relative weight he gave to each (e.g., his emphasis on political culture and political socialization). However, these may well be blessings in disguise, since structural-functional analysis—especially of whole political systems—seems to be of limited value in furthering our understanding of Soviet politics.

The same comments apply to Lane, but to a lesser extent. Lane, primarily in his two key chapters on policymaking (7 and 8), presents an innovative attempt to " adapt " a simplified " systems " model to Soviet politics. He also seems to be more optimistic than the other authors about the benefits of employing " the terms used in modern political science " to analyze the Soviet political systems, past and present (pp. 203 *et seq.*). Furthermore, Lane's important substantive disagreement with the other writers (to be discussed below) might possibly stem from, and is probably reinforced by, his borrowed theoretical orientation.

A less macrotheoretical approach is Osborn's focus on policymaking. Osborn, by analyzing the causes and consequences of " major political decisions," seeks to elucidate aspects of change and stability in the U.S.S.R. Osborn emphasizes the political, economic, and social contexts of important Soviet policies, and he has a particular interest in exploring the alternatives " open " to CPSU leaders, " the regime's capacity for making well-considered choices," and " the changing character of decisions " (pp. vii–viii, 122–124 *et seq.*). These topics are very important and promising, and the last especially has received insufficient treatment in the literature. But Osborn's significant topics and initial questions are discussed in a somewhat sporadic and un-

9. See also Richard Gripp, *Patterns of Soviet Politics* (Homewood, Ill.: Dorsey Press, 2nd ed. 1967).

systematic manner in the body of the text, with the result that he offers much valuable description and some persuasive explanations, but less, and less distinctive, analysis than one would have hoped. Moreover, in formulating and developing his themes, questions, and conclusions, the author makes virtually no use of the burgeoning Western literature on public policymaking in industrialized and industrializing societies. Thus, he only sketchily relates Soviet experience to many of the larger issues raised in this literature. I personally think that these are missed opportunities—especially if one chooses to focus on national policymaking—but I am well aware of the limitations of much of the recent " public policy " literature. In any case, Osborn's book is of conventional genre, and is much less innovative than one might expect from the author's statements of purpose and some of his chapter subtitles.[10]

Hammer deliberately eschews " current trends in comparative politics," focusing instead on the elite institutions and personnel of the Soviet system and on the organizational context in which the processes of decisionmaking, recruitment, and political socialization take place (p. vi). This traditional blend of formal, legal, and institutional analysis is reminiscent of the work of Leonard Schapiro and Derek Scott.[11] Hammer, more than Schapiro and Scott, describes the career patterns and experience of leading Party, state, and economic officials. Hammer does not present very different information about the operations of central and regional Party bodies from, say, that of Armstrong or Lane; but he does tell us more about the men and women who staff these bureaucratic units. Thus, instead of merely repeating that we just do not know what goes on in the Politburo, Secretariat, and departments of the Central Committee and provincial Party apparatuses, Hammer offers some additional potentially relevant information, from which he draws, and the reader can draw, some very cautious inferences about the political behavior of Soviet officials.

Another general characteristic of these six books is the absence of new techniques of data-gathering and analysis. Again, the reliance on established methods of research may be a strength, not a weakness; but it is noteworthy. Quantitative content analysis, extensive interviewing of recent émigrés or Western government and business officials who have dealt with their Russian counterparts—these and other unconventional data-collecting techniques and sources of difficult-to-

10. I use the word " conventional " in a descriptive, not a pejorative, sense.

11. Leonard Schapiro, *The Government and Politics of the Soviet Union* (New York: Random House, 1965); Derek Scott, *Russian Political Institutions* (London: George Allen & Unwin, 4th ed. 1969).

obtain information have, understandably, rarely been utilized. Some, although not many, interviews with Soviet officials are reported, and thus the preponderant data base of these studies is published materials from the Party, state, and specialized presses.

What strikes me, lastly, about these recent general studies is the *similarity* of their interpretations of the Soviet system and the role of the Communist Party within it in different historical periods. This is my most important and no doubt my most controversial observation. It is a somewhat difficult one to make, too—in part, because it is not easy to pick out the central themes, arguments, and assumptions of largely descriptive works that move from one topic or time period to the next, rather than from one idea or problem to another. Analyzing the Khrushchev years, for example, all six authors use many of the same primary sources and rely heavily on the same secondary works; so it is not surprising that there is broad agreement about the nature of Khrushchev's " grand design " and the reasons why he was unable to carry it out. The Western debate of the early 1960s about the nature and extent of the First Secretary's power would appear to be over. Explanations of key events and even of Khrushchev's downfall are quite similar.

In the interpretations of the Brezhnev administration, there is again a surprising degree of consensus. " Polar " positions are not expounded. No one depicts a political process that is compatible with the classic " totalitarian model," no one predicts the takeover of power by " technocrats," and no one embraces a theory of interest groups which rests on analogies with associational groups in the West. Indeed, Hammer's use of the term " bureaucratic pluralism " is a little misleading; for he, like all but one of the authors, emphasizes that top Party organs are in full command of the policymaking process, *and* are increasing institutional participation and consultation in decision-making at the national, regional, and local levels on various policy issues. Osborn insightfully adds that " far from being a threat to the Party's dominance of the policy process, the involvement of many outside groups and points of view may actually be an advantage " (p. 204).

Only Lane dissents from one or another version of this predominant " rationalization of Party control " thesis. Lane goes so far as to suggest that the CPSU should *not* be viewed as a " ruling Party," for to do so reduces one's awareness of the actual influence of outside institutions and of social forces on Soviet policy. In Lane's judgment

> the Communist Party articulates an ideology to which social and economic life should conform, it shapes the structure of

> the political system, and the form in which inputs should be made. But the Party's incapacity both to aggregate inputs and to perform specialist output functions has . . . led to its decline as a political power, and has increased the power of other institutions, the strongest of which is the state ministerial system (pp. 224–225, 230, 233 *et seq.*).

These differences between Lane and the other authors may be a matter of degree, not of kind; but, to this reader, they constitute *the* major—and perhaps the only major—substantive disagreement among the six writers.

One might reasonably expect to find significant differences among the six authors on such important questions as the relative influence of Lenin and Stalin on Soviet political development, continuity and change in the Soviet polity since 1953, the degree of " Russianness " of the Soviet system, the role of ideology, the utility of the totalitarian model, the nature of " group " politics, the rationality and effectiveness of Soviet policies, the adaptive capacities of the CPSU, the skills of top leaders and recruitment practices, the persistence of coercion and controls, the significance of dissent, the meaning of " détente " and the likelihood of " convergence ", and others.

To be sure, the six authors do take somewhat different positions on these issues and occasionally present alternative views for the reader to choose among. The disagreement between Lane and the other writers raises some very significant questions, and the authors' thoughtful concluding chapters suggest some others. Reshetar's final chapter also reminds us that the analyst can vary his theoretical orientation to a certain extent, and that the " models " one employs may have a decisive impact on the issues one raises and the conclusions one reaches. But these six authors do not seem to have any serious disagreements about what the major issues in Soviet studies *are*; their interpretations differ chiefly in emphasis, richness of detail, or nuance. Personally, I have an uneasy feeling that the textbooks in our field are of a somewhat homogeneous nature, and I would welcome more controversy over substantive issues, themes, and problems.

I am not suggesting that there are *no* differences on important issues among Western students of the Soviet political system.[12] I think, however, that one can find a broader range of interpretations and disagreements about Soviet politics in the Western periodical and spec-

12. An essay that emphasizes some of these differences is Roger Kanet, " The Communist Party of the Soviet Union and Soviet Politics: Recent Western Interpretations," paper delivered at the 1974 annual meeting of the American Political Science Association, Chicago, September 1, 1974.

ialized literature than in these most recent general studies. To be sure, the undergraduate student needs the basic factual information contained in these texts to understand more fully the issues debated elsewhere. But key ideas and arguments concerning change in the post-Stalin period, for example, can be presented most clearly, comprehensively, and succinctly by juxtaposing and comparing selected writings by Jerry Hough, H. Gordon Skilling, Franklyn Griffiths, Zbigniew Brzezinski, Sidney Ploss, Tibor Szamuely, and others.[13] For a deeper understanding of many issues, such as the relative impact of Lenin and Stalin on the Soviet polity and society, the dissent literature (cf. Solzhenitsyn, Roy Medvedev, Sakharov, Amalrik, Dzyuba, *et al.*) is particularly illuminating.

V

My undramatic conclusion is that all of the six new textbooks under review are very good, and that they are surprisingly similar. They are not interchangeable, however, and none is indispensable for the college student or the general reader.[14] Some of the first- and second-generation postwar studies of the Soviet political system *were* indispensable, not only because of their lack of competitors and our poorer knowledge of the subject at the time, but because they presented a substantial amount of new information and did so in an innovative, thought-provoking manner. The latest textbooks perform both of these functions to some extent. However, the chief impact of the " behavioral revolution " in political science, as reflected in these texts, apparently lies in increased *conceptual clarity,* not in creative macro- and middle-range theorizing, or experimentation with new research methodologies and data-gathering techniques. Greater care in the formation and use

13. Jerry Hough, " The Soviet System: Petrification or Pluralism? " *Problems of Communism*, XXI, 2 (March–April 1972), pp. 25–45; H. Gordon Skilling, " Interest Groups in Communist Politics," " Groups in Soviet Politics," " Group Conflict in Soviet Politics," in H. Gordon Skilling and Franklyn Griffiths (eds.), *Interest Groups in Soviet Politics* (Princeton: Princeton University Press, 1971), pp. 3–45, 379–416; Franklyn Griffiths, in *ibid.*, pp. 335–377; Zbigniew Brzezinski, *Between Two Ages* (New York: Viking Press, 1971), pp. 123–193; Sidney Ploss, " New Politics in Russia? " *Survey*, No. 89 (Autumn 1973), pp. 23–35; Tibor Szamuely, " The USSR Since Khrushchev," *Survey*, No. 72 (Summer 1969), pp. 51–59. This list could, of course, be supplemented by official Soviet sources.

14. In the field of Soviet foreign policy, for example, it is difficult to conceive of teaching an undergraduate or graduate course without Adam Ulam's *Expansion and Coexistence: Soviet Foreign Policy, 1917–73* (New York: Praeger, 2nd ed. 1974); or a graduate course without Vernon Aspaturian's *Power and Process in Soviet Foreign Policy* (Boston: Little, Brown, 1971).

of concepts is surely worthwhile, if for no other reason than that it makes it easier to understand and evaluate propositions and arguments employing these concepts. But, ironically, not very many new ideas, interpretations, and unconventional approaches are presented and developed in the most recent Western texts on the Soviet system.[15] Few authors pursue central themes, and only two or three, such as Armstrong and Reshetar, take a rather personal—and occasionally polemical—approach to their subject. Some of the authors present different theories and interpretations in hopes of stimulating critical thought. And all communicate accurate, but often quite familiar and repetitive, information about Soviet politics, to which the reader may or may not be able to attribute meaning and significance.[16]

When I observe that the six new Western textbooks are not interchangeable, I simply mean that one must give careful thought to one's teaching purposes before choosing among them. Reshetar's work is particularly strong on Russian political and social history, and their influences on the Soviet period. Barghoorn is especially insightful on Soviet political culture, and on the Party's efforts to reshape various subcultures through child and adult political socialization. Hammer's study focuses primarily on the Communist Party and its personnel; his forte should be of most interest to students of political science. Armstrong's analysis is particularly sensitive to the interrelationships of domestic and foreign policy in the contemporary period, and, like most of the other studies, to the nationalities question. Osborn's work breaks away somewhat from the focus on political institutions, assessing instead policy choices and outcomes, especially in the fields of economics and social relations. And Lane, a political sociologist, devotes even more attention to such topics as social differentiation and stratification, the family, and the educational system. What this all comes down to is the unsurprising conclusion that these six books are strongest in the substantive areas of their authors' special fields of competence.

Thus, if one wished, in teaching a university course, to stress the nature of political power and the composition of leading CPSU bodies,

15. Cf. L. G. Churchward, *Contemporary Soviet Government* (New York: American Elsevier, 1968); Frederick Schuman, *Government in the Soviet Union* (New York: Crowell, 2nd ed. 1967).

16. These comments give some indication of why I think that the most informative and insightful recent general study of contemporary Soviet politics may well be Roy A. Medvedev's *On Socialist Democracy* (New York: Knopf, 1975). Translated and edited by Ellen de Kadt. This book is *engagé*, intellectually stimulating, and replete with fresh evidence to support its arguments In short, it meets almost all of the criteria listed at the outset of this essay.

one would probably select Barghoorn or Hammer. If one wanted to highlight policy choices and the Party's policymaking procedures, one would perhaps be best advised to adopt Armstrong, Osborn, or Reshetar. If one chose to emphasize the substance of economic and social policies and their impact on Soviet society, one would probably be wise to pick Lane or Osborn. If one wanted to stress political culture and socialization, it would be best to select Barghoorn or perhaps Reshetar. If one wished to include Soviet foreign policy, Osborn should be avoided. If one considered it useful to present excerpts from primary source materials, Lane should be chosen. If one wanted a book that stresses contemporary Soviet politics, it would be better to use Armstrong than Reshetar (as noted); for succinct historical background, Lane or Reshetar rather than Armstrong. And so on.

I have found the revised edition of Barghoorn's book to be most suited to my own undergraduate course on Soviet domestic politics; but I have experimented with other texts and I shall continue to experiment with the newest and older works (I am using Armstrong and Hammer in different courses this year). Yet Barghoorn's book has succeeded in stimulating lively debate and critical thought among my students, and in communicating considerable factual information (e.g., the excellent charts in the back of Barghoorn's study).[17] It must be stressed, however, that this selection rests heavily on my choice of other readings in the course, and on my view that Soviet politics can best be introduced from the perspective of the Party leadership. Ironically, the weakest aspect of the Barghoorn book may be its discussion of policy issues in the U.S.S.R. (e.g., the *uses* of power, as distinguished from the struggle to obtain it); nonetheless, Barghoorn's study complements well the excellent works of Alfred Meyer, Leonard Schapiro, Robert C. Tucker, and Carl Linden.[18] For an alternative book in this sequence, one would probably choose Armstrong or Hammer; for a broader perspective, or in lieu of some of the above books, one would be likely to select Lane, Osborn, or Reshetar.

17. For a critical analysis of current textbooks in the field of comparative politics which places heavy emphasis on the criteria of "data provision," "provision for critical thought," and "provision for imaginative thought," see Norman Furniss, "Comparative Government Texts: Problems and Performance," *International Studies Quarterly*, Vol. 18, No. 1 (March 1974), pp. 105–127.

18. Alfred Meyer, *Leninism* (New York: Praeger, 1962); Leonard Schapiro, *The Communist Party of the Soviet Union* (New York: Vintage Books, 2nd ed. 1971); Robert C. Tucker, *The Soviet Political Mind* (New York: Norton, 2nd ed. 1971); Carl Linden, *Khrushchev and the Soviet Leadership, 1957–1964* (Baltimore: Johns Hopkins University Press, 1966).

In sum, the latest Western surveys of the Soviet political system reflect many of the strengths and weaknesses of the discipline of political science and of Soviet and Russian area studies. Collectively, the six new textbooks evaluated here suggest that there is considerably more consensus than debate in present-day Sovietology in the West, and they may leave one with the impression that the degree of consensus is much greater than it actually is. Most of the texts rely on similar concepts. All stress the importance of the same key events and trends. All acknowledge the same lacunae in our knowledge. All generally agree on what the major issues are. All pose essentially the same kinds of questions. All—with the probable exception of Lane—come to quite similar conclusions. And all of the authors avoid the main " biases and blunders " of the past, such as Cold War preconceptions and disproportionate emphasis on certain types of data.[19] Whether these developments are good, bad, inevitable, or changeable, the reader must decide for himself. Whether divergent opinions can be well presented within a textbook, or are best evaluated by comparing books, is another moot point. In any case, I believe that beginning students of Soviet politics should be exposed to a greater diversity of ideas, approaches, and interpretations, in the hope of encouraging them to think critically, judiciously, and imaginatively about the subject, to comprehend better its complexities, and to appreciate more fully the fascination and frustrations of study in this field.

19. Alexander Dallin, " Biases and Blunders in American Studies on the USSR," *Slavic Review,* Vol. 32, No. 3 (September 1973), pp. 560–576; and the reply by John Armstrong, in *ibid.*, pp. 577–587. For a sharply dissenting view, see Lev Navrozov, " Stalin Under Western Eyes," *Commentary,* Vol. 56, No. 5 (April 1974), pp. 66–70.

Comment by Alexander Dallin

Erik Hoffmann has provided a judicious, informed, and thoughtful review of recent books on Soviet politics. If despite his praise for the competence of his sample of textbooks, his consumers' guide fails to provide any striking product differentiation, he is probably well justified not to single out any one of the books for special endorsement. However, I do not share his perception that these books are substantially similar in their interpretation of the Soviet system.

How far do such similarities go? One would hope after all for similarity in regard to the factual material, the *dramatis personae,* and the chronology of events. We all suffer from the same limitations regarding access to sources. And it is only to be expected that a typical text would follow a fairly conventional organization—chronological or topical, or both, with emphasis on system and process. Professor Hoffmann is entirely correct, I believe, in saying that the most innovative contributions (in substance, concept, or methodology) are far more likely to appear in journal articles or monographs than in textbooks, whose publishers seek safety (and profit) in the numbers of purchasers. And yet. . . .

And yet it is my feeling (which I can no more prove or quantify than Hoffmann can his assessment) that there are fundamental differences in approach and assumptions, both among the authors he examines and within the profession at large. In fact, a number of the authors themselves present, at least in cursory form, alternative interpretations. Reshetar's final chapter examines six different models. Lane's Chapter 6 discusses "Critical Theories of Soviet Society." Osborn, both in his Introduction and in his Conclusion, surveys a number of alternative theories and interpretations. Assuredly, our authors do not wind up endorsing the same ones.

Take the eternal issue of the role of ideology in Soviet motivation and decisionmaking. Armstrong and Meyer, Reshetar and Lane, could hardly be farther apart. And this is after all not a trivial matter. While the question, "How Communist is Russia?" can be a naïve pitfall, one's assessment of the operational role of Communist beliefs and perceptions goes to the heart of the search for the essential characteristics of the Soviet system.

There is a similar variety of views in the interminable tug-of-war over "continuity and change." While to some of our authors Byzantium, the Tatars, and Muscovy are all essential forebears of the Leninists, others are content to accept the more parsimonious explanation based on a developmental model and the concept of mobilization (seeing greater utility than Hoffmann does in the application of structural-functional hypotheses); and still others manage to combine elements of both approaches.

The complementary problem of continuity and change within the Soviet era likewise divides the Western observers fundamentally, I believe. Some still insist that the post-Stalin era marked no fundamentally new departure—in substance, what William Zimmerman has called the " essentialist " argument—while others stress the importance of the changes that produced at least the rudiments of political pluralism and bargaining over an increasing range of available options.

Recently there has also been a welcome revival of interest in the 1920s—not only because the historian finds more sources on the New Economic Policy era than on more recent years, but primarily, it seems, because the 1920s can help provide the political scientist with important answers. What were the roots of Stalinism? What was crucial here—situational factors, one man's personality, the political system, Russian political culture, or " superstructural " accidents? Was Stalin a legitimate heir of Lenin, or was Stalinism an aberration or betrayal of the faith? Were there within the Bolshevik universe alternatives to Stalinism—i.e., was the Bolshevik elite " pluralistic " in the years up to Stalin's consolidation of power? These are not matters of idle academic speculation, nor only concerns of sectarian talmudism: the answers are crucial to one's assessment of the Soviet experience. And the answers that the authors give or imply—from Schapiro to Barghoorn, from Tucker to Moore, from Meyer to Armstrong—range all over the map.

We could find comparable differences on a large number of other issues, I believe—on specific problems, such as political participation, as well as on vague assessments of prospects for the future, where " developmental " optimism, stressing role differentiation and generational change, confronts (or should confront) the pessimism born of the persistence of coercion and controls, or else of the dead weight of bureaucracy and post-revolutionary conservatism. Even the old issue of totalitarianism remains, of course, unresolved. Whereas some recent writers have preferred to avoid the loaded connotations, the political primitivism, and the definitional gymnastics associated with its use, others continue to speak of " totalitarianism " without apologies (though Hoffman correctly observes that even the most hostile accounts describe the political process in the Brezhnev era in terms that could scarcely be called " totalitarian "). The whole problem of pluralism in Soviet politics and society very understandably continues to divide the academic community.

One other point. Hoffmann politely suggests that none of the texts are precisely thrillers, however worthy their quality in other regards. This is quite understandable and may be rooted in the nature of Soviet politics. There is indeed little excitement in detailing the relations of Party and State organs or memorizing the functions of a *raikom.* Pedagogically, the scene comes to life when we move from institutions and statutes to people and policies, be it the purges, the leaders, or the confrontations of "Red" and "Expert," Stalin and Trotsky, Khrushchev and his opponents, or Moscow and Peking. Virtually all the texts have, very sensibly and understandably, dealt with the Soviet political system from the top down: this is indeed where the first and major effort had to lie. But I suspect that the time has come to explore what the whole exercise has meant, what it has done—and what it means today—to the Soviet citizen. There may be plenty of excitement and innovation ahead once we turn to social history, political sociology, and social psychology in a further search for an understanding of Soviet reality.

Steven Goldstein

China: Four Explanations*

I

The invitation to review four new texts on Chinese politics presents an opportunity not only to evaluate the work of our colleagues, but also to examine the state of the field. As one reviewer of a text to be considered in this essay put it, " the book is both an epitome of American scholarship and one man's China."[1] A similar comment could be made regarding the other books. Each author's work reflects, in differing degrees, the academic achievements, controversies, and uncertainties that characterize the China field today. However, each presents a distinctive approach to the problem of conceptualizing the political process in China.

It should be stated at the outset that none of these books resembles a stereotypical textbook—a merely descriptive discussion of the bare-boned, institutional essentials of a political system combined with some very basic, often superficial, analysis. All are attempts to present both the essentials of the Chinese political system and original, thought-provoking interpretations. Because they are a cut above the

* Harold C. Hinton, *An Introduction to Chinese Politics* (New York: Praeger, 1973); Lucian W. Pye, *China: An Introduction* (Boston: Little, Brown, 1972); John Bryan Starr, *Ideology and Culture: An Introduction to the Dialectic of Contemporary Chinese Politics* (New York: Harper and Row, 1973); James R. Townsend, *Politics in China* (Boston: Little, Brown, 1974). This article has benefited from careful and critical readings by Zvi Y. Gitelman, Philip Green, David M. Lampton, and Stanley Rothman.

1. Arthur Huck reviewing Pye's *China: An Introduction*, in *Pacific Affairs*, Vol. 46, No. 1 (Spring 1973), p. 118.

average texts, they should be reviewed as interpretive works on China in their own right. Thus, in most cases their shortcomings are not the result of their being " only texts." Rather, they derive, to some degree, from the state of previous research as well as from the nature of the author's analytical framework—itself more or less indicative of broader trends in the field. For these reasons, it should be possible to consider these books as barometers indicating the state of the art in the study of Chinese politics and to derive from a review of them some general conclusions regarding the condition of contemporary studies of Chinese politics.

II

In the discussion that follows, I shall comment on the various demands for change that affected the study of Chinese politics during the late 1960s and early 1970s. Two that seemed most prominent are discussed either implicitly or explicitly in the books reviewed below. The first advocated an end to the field's isolation from the broader concerns of the social sciences. This was to be accomplished by the application of concepts and methodologies borrowed from comparative politics. The second raised the question of values and biases. For some, post-1949 China was an innovative social laboratory in which creative responses to the problems of the industrial era were being formulated. These innovations, it was charged, were being slighted by scholars hostile to radical or revolutionary change.

In *An Introduction to Chinese Politics,* Harold Hinton notes both of these currents. He cites the methodological debates in the field, and opts for what he terms " ' classical ' political analysis, based largely on historical method, primarily qualitative judgments, and (to the extent necessary) intuition." Before discussing the impact of this approach on Hinton's analysis, however, we should note his reaction to those who argue for the relevance of the Chinese experience.

In both the introduction and the first chapter, the author mentions the current propensity—particularly on the part of " intellectuals "—to " admire " China, and traces its historical roots back to eighteenth-century Jesuits. However, rather than dispassionately exploring the dangers of such an approach, he takes up the cudgels against other Americans over issues that can only be understood in the polarized academic milieu of the Vietnam War period. Consider the following:

> There is a tendency to feel that if Communism, in China or elsewhere, is making impressive progress in important respects, this must be because of a superior ideology and program; the crucial importance of organization and coercion (often veiled), as well as

> innate Chinese qualities, are all too easily overlooked. Or if the coercion is recognized, it is often excused on the ground, implicit or perhaps subconscious, that violence is thoroughly bad only when it is employed by the right; this attitude seems to be one of the many unfortunate legacies of the career of Adolf Hitler. American China policy, until 1969 at any rate, and Vietnam policy as its major extension, have been widely regarded in the West as a vast wrong-headed rain dance on the part of the American Establishment, and opposition to them as a necessary concomitant to support for civil rights and social justice at home.[2]

There can be no question but that the idealization of Chinese realities to serve one's political preferences does little to advance our understanding of the Chinese political process. However, the issue of how to evaluate China is one that deserves serious consideration, not this type of polemical approach equally reflective of an extraneous political atmosphere.[3]

But if Hinton seems to be fighting the academic battles of the 1960s on the issue of how to approach the Chinese political experience, his study of Chinese politics at the same time draws on much of the methodology of that period. This, more than the distracting barbs he casts at " intellectuals," shapes much of his approach to the subject matter—and creates problems in his analysis.

He adopts the " constant conflict " approach. This mode of analysis arose during the Khrushchev period as a partial adjustment of the totalitarian framework.[4] Refuting those who saw the new Soviet leader as the inheritor of Stalin's mantle as dictator, scholars subscribing to this view depicted Khrushchev's position as more tenuous. Policy was no longer seen merely as the embodiment of the dictator's preferences. This approach focused on the upper echelons of the political hierarchy and saw policies as the result of bargaining and accommodation among important political figures.

The limiting effects of this approach are obvious. The focus on elite personalities is achieved at the expense of an appreciation of political institutions and political processes at anything but the very

2. Hinton, *An Introduction*, p. 5.

3. One attempt to evaluate the Chinese experience in a somewhat more dispassionate manner is Michel C. Oksenberg (ed.), *China's Developmental Experience* (New York: Praeger, 1973).

4. For an extensive discussion of this approach see *Problems of Communism*, XII, 5 (September–October 1963), pp. 27–46 and *ibid.*, XII, 6 (November–December 1963), pp. 56–65. In the China field, Richard C. Thornton has reconstructed the policy conflicts of the 1950s by use of this method. See his " The Structure of Communist Politics," *World Politics*, XXIV, 4 (July 1972), pp. 498–517.

highest levels. "The Party," "the Army," and so on are all considered only in so far as they represent the political base for one of the contending political giants. Mass inputs into or local participation in the system is seen as unimportant or simply the result of enforced ritualized behavior.

Hinton's study, unfortunately, exhibits many of these limitations. The early parts of the book (which are extremely weak on pre-1949 historical background) do provide a brief historical overview of the years after the Communist victory and stress differences among the Chinese leaders over the political choices facing them. However, the focus on the political elite continues to dominate the remainder of the book. There is a large section on leadership, with the more structurally oriented chapters (e.g., those concerned with the Party, the army, and state institutions) primarily concerned with describing conflict among leaders over the nature of these bodies.

Of course, students of Chinese politics are sensitive to the fact that questions of structural reorganization and zoning of authority are highly political issues.[5] However, the one-sided emphasis on institutional arrangements as a source of political conflict—a hazard inherent in the constant conflict approach—is achieved at the expense of any real understanding of how institutions actually operate, what their role in society is, and how they structure political conflict.[6]

Moreover, to picture top leaders as struggling over the distribution of power within and among political institutions implies a relationship between the men at the top and the bureaucracies that manage society. The nature of this linkage, however, must be made explicit and precise. In particular, a balance should be struck between, on the one hand, a strongly personalistic view in which leaders are seen as simply using for their own ends the influence of the institutions they oversee and, on the other, a view that presents top leaders as mere conduits for impersonal organizational demands.[7]

5. This view is ably presented by Franz Schurmann in his "Politics and Economics in Russia and China," in Donald W. Treadgold (ed.), *Soviet and Chinese Communism* (Seattle: University of Washington Press, 1967), pp. 297–326.

6. A partial exception to this is his section on the army where Hinton presents William Whitson's hypotheses on how army structure causes cleavages. On this, see *An Introduction,* pp. 184–187. However, in the Party chapter, for example, there is much on organization and Leninist theory and little on what the Party actually does.

7. David Lampton argues that the interest-group approach assumes the latter view when it "portrays leaders as relatively passive responders who assess opinion within *and* outside the bureaucracy, modifying their stands in order to

Hinton seems sensitive to the question. He speaks of "four main functional constituencies within the Party leadership." These were, in the period before the Cultural Revolution, "Mao Tse-tung's ideologists and propagandists (for example, Ch'en Po-ta, Lu Ting-i), Liu Shao-ch'i and his Party apparatus men (for example, Teng Hsiao-p'ing, P'eng Chen), Chou En-lai and his government administrators (for example, Li Hsien-nien, Po I-po), and the military (for example, P'eng Teh-huai, Lin Piao) . . ."[8]

These are very broad categories, and the fact that both Ch'en Po-ta and Lu Ting-i would have been considered a part of the same grouping before the Cultural Revolution raises some serious questions about the usefulness of these divisions. The author, realizing this, provides other—not mutually exclusive—ways of categorizing leadership groups.[9] Still, he makes no attempt to build any meaningful hypothesis regarding policymaking on the basis of these very general guidelines. The linkages connecting elite contenders, organizational interests, and intermediate bureaucratic actors remain vague.[10]

Hinton's analysis is quite superficial concerning the impact of politics at lower levels. There is little discussion of the operation of the political system at the levels affecting the Chinese masses, and only a slight sense of how policies might be modified in the course of implementation. There is only a short description of basic level organizations, with such questions as participation, mobilization, and mass organizations dwarfed by the emphasis on elite politics. Hinton's concern with politics at the top thus presents a very partial view of the political process in China.

In his *China: An Introduction* Lucian Pye seeks to explain contemporary China through an understanding of the interrelationships between "three political systems": the traditional, "the republican or

build the largest possible coalition." "Policy Arenas and the Study of Chinese Politics," *Studies in Comparative Communism,* VII, 4 (Winter 1974), p. 410.

An interesting discussion regarding some of the problems involved in this type of view of the individual leader as spokesmen of interests can be found in Lenard J. Cohen and Jane P. Shapiro (eds.), *Communist Systems in Comparative Perspective* (Garden City, N.Y.: Anchor, Doubleday 1974), pp. xxxiv–xxxvii.

8. Hinton, *An Introduction,* p. 116.

9. *Ibid.,* pp. 120–122.

10. This imprecision is, in part, a factor of the little attention given this question by students of Chinese politics. However, it seems also to be the product of the author's approach to the Chinese political process. To him, politics "is an intensely personal process." Thus, personalities and preferences of individual leaders weigh heavily in his analysis.

early modernizing," and the Communist.[11] This historically oriented approach is quite different from that of Harold Hinton. However, in their discussions of post-1949 China—both in substance and approach—these authors share much common ground.

For Pye, as for Hinton, elite conflict is a major force generating political change in China. Consequently, he devotes the bulk of his analysis to the nature, views, and personalities of China's leadership. In contrast to Hinton, however, Pye speaks more explicitly of " constituencies " and coalition partners, while presenting in a slightly more systematic manner (with the aid of a chart) the views of the various leaders on policy questions.

Still, while he does not explicitly acknowledge using the constant conflict approach, Pye's depiction leaves him open to many of the criticisms levelled at it. Personality differences tend to overshadow any rigorous discussion of the nature of political institutions (a bare and inadequate fifteen pages) or of the impact of " constituencies " on policymaking. Unfortunately the reader is left with hardly any sense of how the most populous—and probably most directed—country in the world is administered.

However, Pye cannot be charged with having failed to discuss the views of non-elites in his analysis. Pursuing his earlier speculations, he makes a series of general assessments concerning the political expectations of " the Chinese." These generalizations are unsupported by data and are therefore sure to spark debate. However, there is the still more basic question: How can one view politics from two ends of a spectrum—elites conflicting on broad policy questions and masses holding general expectations of the system—yet barely treat the political structures that link the two or the manner in which they interact to create politics?

At the level of the Politburo, the injection of individual views into the decision process is something that the analyst can take for granted. But the accuracy and comprehensiveness with which they are presented are still open to question. This is particularly true with respect to Pye's extended discussion of Maoist ideology. Here also controversy is bound to arise. In contrast to discussions of the views of the Chinese masses, however, the evidence permits a more concrete and meaningful analysis.

The author clearly allocates to Mao an important role in shaping the course of China's domestic politics since 1949. Pye very strongly suggests that the Chinese leader's policy preferences inhibit, rather than promote, " modernization and national power," which, as the goal of

11. Pye, *China,* p. 4.

" all recent Chinese leaders," is considered by Pye to be an appropriate standard against which to judge the success of the Communist regime.[12] Mao is seen as apparently troubled by " pragmatic and technically sound policies," as a man who rejects " the benefits of technological specialization " lest a division of authority compromise his political power, as holding the " sciences of the economist and the engineer . . . [to be] bourgeois," [13] and as pursuing a " reckless course " by " turning his back on the advantages of modern technology and rejecting material incentives and the pragmatic considerations that have always been important to the Chinese and have influenced much of their behavior. . . ." [14]

The view of Mao as an ideological foe of what are considered to be the imperatives of modernization and as the friend of ideological purity was a picture quite frequently drawn by his admirers and critics alike during the Cultural Revolution. The presentation of a more balanced view of the Maoist developmental strategy for China is beyond the scope of this essay. However, the picture is not quite so clear as Pye would have it. Mao is addressing many real and difficult problems of development, and his views are not totally antithetical to " pragmatic considerations." It is true that his concepts seem to fly in the face of some assumptions held by Western social scientists regarding the process of development. However, recent studies have suggested that much of the Chinese leader's approach to the transformation of China reflects neither pure revolutionary romanticism nor total rejection of certain concerns expressed by Western social scientists.[15] In short, Pye's presentation of this problem simply does not capture—or even come to grips with—enough facets of the extremely complex Maoist perspective on the developmental process in China.

The author's view of Mao is more complex, however, when he discusses the sources of Mao's ideology. Aside from speculation concerning the role of personality factors, Pye makes a more concrete effort to tie Mao's views to historical elements. Thus, Mao's distrust of technical specialization is linked to a traditional Chinese antipathy to expertise and to a clash between " values " and " knowledge " that became " a central ingredient in the development of Chinese nationalism." His

12. *Ibid.*, p. 241.
13. *Ibid.*, pp. 207, 356, and 281.
14. *Ibid.*, p. 357.
15. See, for example, Martin King Whyte, " Bureaucracy and Modernization in China: The Maoist Critique," *American Sociological Review*, Vol. 38, No. 3 (April 1973), pp. 149–163, and Harry Harding, *Modernization and Mao: The Logic of the Cultural Revolution and the 1970's* (Santa Monica: Calif.: The Rand Corporation, 1970). P–4442.

faith in the power of right thinking is similarly traced to "the historical propensity of the Chinese to attach prime importance to intellectual and ethical considerations." Here we come to the central theme —and real strength—of the book: the strong emphasis upon lines of continuity between the Communist movement and the traditional and republican periods in Chinese history. Once again much of the author's interpretation will be considered open to question. But there should be no question about how important it is for students of contemporary China to understand the intellectual and political milieu of traditional and post-1911 China.

Pye's sensitivity to the impact of cultural and historical variables on the modernization process in China reflects a comparatively recent and salutary revision of theories of development. This was the result of an increasing awareness of the dangers of extracting universal laws of development from the Western experience. Yet, in the book's concluding paragraph, Pye suggests that the cultural variable operates within limits set by certain "processes" that "govern" modernization:

> Chinese culture will persist and steadily change in accordance with the historical processes that govern the modernization of traditional societies. Even as China modernizes the Chinese will continue to reflect much of their heritage, as have all societies that have advanced into the industrial era.[16]

What are the "historical processes that govern the modernization of traditional societies"? Are they inevitable and impersonal laws? What guidelines are there to evaluate the extent of a nation's reflection of its traditional "heritage" during "modernization"?[17]

There is no systematic discussion of these questions at any earlier point in the book. However, one suspects that Pye's overall evaluation of Mao is strongly conditioned by assumptions regarding the nature of specialization and differentiation required for "modernization." At least one author has suggested that care be taken in applying these elements as a measure of political development in China. Pye's discussion of these questions in relation to China is both ill-defined and abstract. Similarly, the application of certain of Pye's familiar categories of analysis for the process of nation-building (personality and politics, mass attitudes toward politics, and so on) seems inappropriate,

16. Pye, *China,* p. 358.

17. For a discussion of the controversies taking place among students of political development, see Samuel P. Huntington, "The Change to Change: Modernization, Development and Politics," *Comparative Politics,* III, 3 (April 1971), pp. 283–322.

because our knowledge of Chinese politics is still too deficient to warrant discussion on such a high level of generality. This can be seen by contrasting this work (or earlier ones by Pye on China) with his very careful and incisive study of nation-building in Burma.

Instead of theorizing broadly, Pye might have narrowed his focus. For example, one would expect that the author of a classic article on the role of the military in developing states would provide more than this book's very superficial comparison of the role of the People's Liberation Army and that of armies in other developing nations.[18] It might have been more productive to apply comparative theory to the role of the military, on which the Chinese data are relatively plentiful and the theoretical literature provocative, than to offer a series of generalizations about popular attitudes in China or the historical processes of modernization. Unfortunately, as the next book under consideration demonstrates, general conceptions can yield only general results.

The rather cumbersome title of John Bryan Starr's book—*Ideology and Culture: An Introduction to the Dialectic of Contemporary Chinese Politics*—expresses the essence of the author's approach to the study of Chinese politics. Following Franz Schurman's lead, Starr suggests " that it is possible to conceive of the political process in a post-revolutionary society as involving a dialectic between the revolutionary ideology and the traditional culture."[19] Thus, he posits that out of the dialectical relationship between ideology (" the purposes and goals of the Chinese leaders ")[20] and culture (" a set of orientations " held by members of society which stem from the " pre-revolutionary " period) will come a synthesis " which coincides with neither but contains elements of both."[21]

18. Pye, *China,* pp. 294 and 314.
19. Starr, *Ideology and Culture,* p. 20.
20. *Ibid.,* p. 144.
21. *Ibid.,* p. 11. Actually, Starr is quite elusive on the attribution of culture and ideology. " Ideology " is clearly the views of the leaders; that " culture " consists of the orientations of everybody else is unclear. The passages cited above suggest this view. However, later he writes:

> As the dialectical interaction of ideology and culture progresses, the ideology comes gradually to coincide with the orientations of the members of that system. It then begins to guide the political actions of the members of the system as well as the leaders, and thereby becomes a datum within the system as well as a rationale governing the system. In order to investigate this datum—the political orientations of the Chinese people—we must leave the realm of ideas divorced from practice and consider how political life is lived at the basic level in the Chinese political system (pp. 44–45).

The dialectic has a final use. Starr suggests that through the interaction between the understanding of the Chinese political process derived from the above approach and existing notions of comparative politics it is possible " to reach a synthesis of Chinese and non-Chinese categories that will provide a framework by means of which we can grasp, compare, and thereby comprehend our own political life and that of the Chinese." [22]

Thus, the achievement of the author's goal of conceptualizing Chinese politics and relating it to the study of other political systems rests upon his success in presenting the " culture " of society and the " ideology " of the elites, and in persuading us that the results of the interaction between them can enrich our understanding of other political systems.

How can one discern the attitudes of the masses of the Chinese people—the essence of the " cultural " half of the dialectic? [23] Starr finds Pye's " intuitive leaps to conclusions about political behavior and political culture " to be " unsatisfactory," [24] and laments that the only suitable method, survey research, is impossible. In the absence of data on the political views of the masses, he maintains that the best one can do is to describe the " local setting " in which " orientations are formed and actions take place." He provides concise and well-drawn descriptions of post-1949 policies in the rural, urban, and educational sectors. However, while this discussion deals with temporal changes, it lacks any real sense of the impact of institutions on the political process. At times the author speaks of local organizations as " channeling public opinion upward into the political system " and representing the individual " in the political structure of the city and the nation." [25] However, although he seems to favor a more " behavioral " and less institutional approach, Starr gives little sense of these institutions as

This suggests that the views of the masses are not the cultural part of the dialectic, nor are they representative of prerevolutionary values.

However, still later he indeed suggests that culture is the views of the masses of the people. He speaks of the " dialectical interaction of ideology—the purposes and goals of the Chinese leaders—and the Chinese culture—the orientations of the participants in the Chinese political system " (p. 144). Since this final view seems more consistent with the thrust of the book, I assume it for the purposes of analysis.

22. *Ibid.*, pp. 117–118.

23. Again I am assuming that " culture " is not simply an abstraction of traditional orientations but rather views held, for the most part, by the masses of the people.

24. *Ibid.*, p. 54.

25. *Ibid.*, pp. 93 and 99.

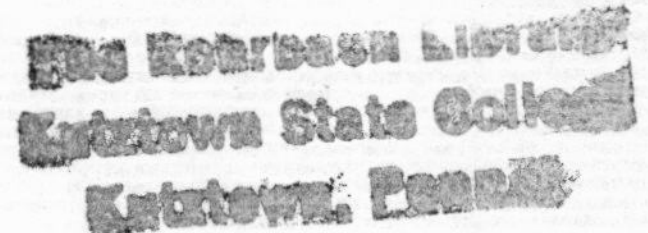

functioning political bodies or as influences on popular attitudes. In the end, Starr seems to make generalizations as broad as those he criticizes, and we are told that the Cultural Revolution may have disillusioned large segments of Chinese youth and accustomed urban residents to a " considerably more genuine form of political participation." [26] More essential, given his overall framework, is the fact that minimal discussion of prerevolutionary orientations and contemporary mass attitudes leaves the content of " culture " poorly defined.

The sections on the other half of the dialectic—elite ideology—are equally limited. In the first place, there is only a very inadequate discussion of the sources (in traditional China and the Party's revolutionary history) of the content of " revolutionary ideology." More fundamentally, Chinese political history during the past two decades has been the story of the erosion of a shared ideology. According to Starr's analysis, in the field of ideology Mao seems to be very much in command. Although we are cautioned at the beginning of the book regarding the need to be sensitive to the existence of a " fragmented " political culture, the author avoids all but the vaguest suggestions that the ideology component of the Chinese dialectic might be represented by anything but orthodox Maoist thought. Thus, the reader is inadequately prepared when toward the end of the book, Starr speaks of Party members who favored a routinized, bureaucratized Party with an emphasis on " technical and managerial proficiency rather than ideological fervor." [27]

Finally, there is his discussion of political institutions. In Starr's framework of analysis they are considered to be " the structures within which occurs the dialectic of Chinese politics." [28] In other words, one would expect his discussion of Party, state, and army organizations to concretize the dialectic of ideas introduced earlier. Yet these chapters fail to provide what the author implies they should. Although there is a suggestion that bureaucracies might be seen as interest groups and that functional systems in the Party and state might compete for resources, no attempt is made to illustrate the interaction of culture and ideology through the study of decisions made on specific issues related to the dialectic. In the absence of such a discussion, the dialectical

26. *Ibid.*, pp. 101 and 110.

27. *Ibid.*, p. 193. For example, while he feels that the Cultural Revolution was a " tripartite movement "—a power struggle, a revolution in culture, and a learning experience for its participants—the author does not really elaborate on the possibility that it might have involved differing views over the revolutionary ideology appropriate for China.

Some vague references to elite differences appear on pp. 160 and 166.

28. *Ibid.*, p. 167.

approach becomes a device to produce abstractions rather than testable propositions about very concrete political processes in China.

The failure to descend from high levels of generalization ultimately affects the author's attainment of his second goal, which is the creation of a dialectical synthesis of Western concepts of politics with Chinese practice. Starr is very critical of Western approaches that concentrate on elites, see stability as the norm, and emphasize familiar government functions and structures such as legislation, administration, and political parties.[29] He suggests that the dominance of such an outlook limits our understanding of the Chinese political process and inhibits the reconciliation of Mao's goals with those " that underlie the prevailing theories of political development in the West." [30]

Yet, in the end, the book remains keyed to such a high level of generality that the author is not able to reach his goal of synthesis. Unlike Franz Schurmann, who was careful to discuss both ideas *and* institutions, Starr places too much emphasis on the former. The concepts " ideology " and " culture " are too broad, and his identification of the attributes of each remains incomplete. Predictably enough, the author concludes that the Chinese emphasis on conflict and change should enrich our understanding of the political system through its focus on " the study of process " and " conflict and conflict resolution." [31] His broad analytic categories have generated rather familiar enrichments.

Yet one must not judge this study too harshly. While Starr fails to achieve the synthesis that he desires, he has written an innovative text that raises some very essential and difficult questions about the way we look at Chinese politics. Starr's emphasis on local systems, his impatience with the elite conflict model, and his desire to integrate the Chinese experience into the study of comparative politics are all helpful correctives to many of the shortcomings identified in the works of Pye and Hinton. He is beginning to explore new areas in the study of Chinese politics; thus the book may be regarded as a bridge between the previous two texts and James Townsend's *Politics in China*. This book is more successful in realizing some of the objectives set forth in *Ideology and Culture*.

Townsend's text is likely to be the standard introductory textbook in Chinese politics courses for some years to come. It appears in the Little, Brown series in comparative politics, which began with Gabriel Almond and G. Bingham Powell's functionalist study of the political

29. *Ibid.*, Ch. 5.
30. *Ibid.*, p. 7.
31. *Ibid.*, pp. 137–139.

process.[32] Townsend organizes his study roughly after the Almond-Powell model. He has, however, maintained a distinctive approach to Chinese politics. Rather than becoming captive to the classificatory schemes of Almond and Powell, he approaches them with a healthy skepticism. Moreover, to a greater extent than any of the other authors in the series, Townsend seeks to synthesize much of the previous work done in the area of Chinese politics. In this regard alone, the book is a *tour de force*.

The framework devised by Almond and Powell consists, essentially, of two interrelated parts. The first is a set of categories for the analysis of the political process. This consists of a combination of input-output analysis with such functionally oriented concepts as interest articulation and aggregation, political socialization, rule making, and the like. The second part of the framework presents a manner of classifying the relative development of various political systems. This is done in relation to the way in which the structures performing the various functions are organized (degree of differentiation of political structures and subsystem autonomy) and the nature of the political culture.

On the second, broader question—the classification of the Chinese political system—Townsend is critical of the designation of China as a "radical totalitarian system." Two difficulties are identified as obstacles to the application of such a definition to the Chinese system. In the first place, Townsend raises the question—one that concerned Starr as well—of the appropriateness of applying some generally accepted concepts of political development to certain distinctively Maoist elements in the Chinese political system. Although he does not pursue the point at great length, the author suggests that the Chinese experience raises doubts concerning the precision of certain of the underlying assumptions of Almond and Powell's classificatory scheme.

> In summary, the CCP has encouraged the development of both differentiation and secularization within limits while remaining on guard against some of their consequences and implications. Political development has not been dependent on an unequivocal commitment to increasing differentiation and secularization, but neither has it taken place in their absence. What the Chinese case appears to show is that ever-increasing structural differentiation and specialization is not always necessary for development and that an ideological political culture is not always incompatible with secularization.[33]

32. Gabriel Almond and G. Bingham Powell, Jr., *Comparative Politics: A Developmental Approach* (Boston: Little, Brown, 1966).

33. Townsend, *Politics in China,* p. 338.

Townsend's second reservation is empirical rather than theoretical: Has the Chinese regime displayed the attributes of the " radical-totalitarian " system? Here the author is skeptical. The " central theme " of his book is that the " Communist political system has been fluid and unstable " in its organizational characteristics, and so it is difficult to place any single label on the regime as it has evolved during the years after 1949. He feels that the only time when it did approximate the " radical-totalitarian " paradigm was during the 1950s.[34]

The reason for the changing character of political institutions is said to be tension among the leadership with regard to the choice between two variants of Communist ideology—the " Maoist " and the " bureaucratic." The latter favors the institutionalization characteristic of the radical totalitarian regime, and Mao has resisted it. Thus, unlike Starr's analysis, Townsend's depiction of the Chinese political process assumes that " since 1957 " conflicting elite values have been of " greater salience than the more generalized clash between CCP values and those of the bulk of the population." [35] This assumption, in contrast with Starr's account, leads to a more detailed discussion of the differing strategies of each approach and a much greater sensitivity to the importance of ideology as a divisive force among the elite.

Thus, here again elite differences are viewed as central to the Chinese political process. However, unlike Hinton, Townsend does not suggest that such conflicts dominate all other aspects of the political process. Chinese politics, in his analysis, becomes much more than the battles of political giants. This sensitivity to the totality of the Chinese political system seems to be the result of Townsend's careful use of the structural-functional approach, which highlights processes such as communication and socialization, and of his previous work on political participation in that country.

Townsend also discusses Chinese theories of administration and describes the workings of political institutions. He presents the most comprehensive attempt of any of the authors reviewed at conceptualizing the decisionmaking process within these structures. At the center of his process is the Party.

> In general ... the definition and resolution of major political issues is the responsibility of Party officials, whose conflicts are fought inside the bureaucracies in which they serve and are seldom expressed fully to public view. The process is political, but it does not lend itself to easy distinctions between articulation and aggregation, between decision-making and administration.[36]

34. *Ibid.*, p. 162.
35. *Ibid.*, p. 178.
36. *Ibid.*, p. 273.

Where do the conflicting viewpoints originate? In his listing of their sources, Townsend goes well beyond Hinton's vague categories and Pye's improved, but still inadequate, presentation. Townsend suggests that more than the basic ideological division between the Maoist and bureaucratic approaches is reflected in policy deliberations at the Politburo level. In addition, institutional interests are articulated by " elites who themselves head bureaucratic structures, replete with their own conflicts and interests." [37] Finally, there is an input from the masses. Proceeding from his earlier studies, the author argues that political participation can influence local, but not national, decisions. Grassroots interests are taken into account to the extent that these are " championed " in the policymaking process by those who count—the higher bureaucratic elites.[38] How are such interests injected into the policymaking process? Townsend suggests that elite recruitment is a crucial means, in that the Party " absorbed the basic contradictions of Chinese society, and its organization became an arena for conflict between the demands of different strata, regions, generations and institutions." [39] This is a suggestive yet imprecise statement. The reference to " strata " and " generation " suggests that background before entering the elite constitutes a major determinant of members' views. This has been an assumption of Frederic Fleron's studies of the Soviet elite.[40] Yet it is questionable. Other studies have shown that an individual tends to represent the " institutions " of which he or she is currently a part.[41] If that is so, then recruitment would be a very poor way of injecting broader societal demands into the political system.

The questions of how mass demands become a nationally significant political input and of the effect of various social background factors on political performance are two of the many decisionmaking issues raised in Townsend's book. Unfortunately, he presents these elements, as well as others that influence the policy process—the role of Mao, institutional arrangements, administrative and decisionmaking approaches subscribed to by the elite, for example—largely in the form of a series

37. *Ibid.*, p. 297.
38. *Ibid.*, pp. 241–242.
39. *Ibid.*, p. 272.
40. Frederic J. Fleron, Jr., " Towards a Reconceptualization of Political Change in the Soviet Union: The Political Leadership System," in Fleron (ed.), *Communist Studies and the Social Sciences* (Chicago: Rand McNally, 1969), pp. 222–243; and " Co-optation as a Mechanism of Adaptation to Change " in Roger E. Kanet (ed.), *The Behavioral Revolution and Communist Studies* (New York: Free Press, 1971), pp. 125–149.
41. William A. Welsh, " The Comparative Study of Political Leadership in Communist Systems," in Carl Beck et al., *Comparative Communist Political Leadership* (New York: McKay, 1973).

of variables to be considered. In part, this presentation appears to reflect the author's belief that the fluidity of Chinese political institutions makes difficult easy generalizations regarding the nature of the political process. Still, it is largely left to the reader to synthesize the elements identified into an integrated view of the decision process in China.

Townsend is more explicit in his synthesis of the historical influences that shaped the Communist movement. These discussions are most welcome from a pedagogical and methodological perspective. In particular, in addition to discussing the impact on contemporary Chinese politics of traditional political culture and the historical experience of the CCP, he wisely ties the development of Communism in China to the " ongoing revolution " that accompanied the decline of the Ch'ing dynasty. In this way, the Communist leadership is seen as unable to " define the issues wholly as they chose "; rather they were compelled to orient themselves to the " major problems of the times "—national independence, national unification, and socio-economic change.

In sum, of all the texts considered in this review—and for that matter published to date—Townsend's has the depth and balance that should assure it a warm reception by teachers of Chinese politics. While set in the Almond and Powell framework, it both questions some of the assumptions and avoids many of the pitfalls of the structural-functional view. The book is thoroughly reflective of the state of current scholarship on China. Its strengths and shortcomings, as well as those of the other texts reviewed here, provide insights into the state of the field and suggest future research priorities.

III

If you don't know where you are going,
any road will take you there—*The Talmud* [42]

Inevitably our approaches to the study of Chinese politics will be most decisively affected by the intellectual trends in the area of Communist studies and the broader discipline of which both are a part—comparative politics. However, as has been frequently noted, the study of Chinese politics is a " late developer " with regard to the application of conceptual frameworks from this latter area—even more so than is

42. Quoted by Daniel Bell in " Ten Theories in Search of Reality," in Bell, *The End of Ideology*, rev. ed. (New York: Free Press, 1962), p. 346.

the case with the Soviet and East European fields.[43] This situation should not be considered totally disadvantageous. Backwardness can be used to advantage to avoid the *culs de sac* in which those scholars seeking to develop concepts relevant to the study of political systems in general, or Communist systems in particular, have found themselves.[44]

The totalitarian framework once provided an all-encompassing view of the nature of society. In part because of its seeming inappropriateness—and also because of feelings of professional isolation from their colleagues—scholars involved in the study of comparative Communist systems began to abandon the concept during the mid-1960s.[45] Apparently uncomfortable without a similarly comprehensive concept to take its place, many turned to developmental theory.[46] Communist countries became "developing regimes," and work tended to focus on large questions of an evolutionary nature. Generalizations concerning mobilization politics and post-mobilization systems dominated the frontiers of the field, while speculation centered upon the possible evolutionary courses of Soviet and East European regimes. In addition, interest-group theory, complex organization theory, and, later, political culture became areas of inquiry for those seeking integration with the social sciences.[47] Finally, there was a rapid proliferation of elite studies. Works of this nature—easily quantifiable and instantly identifiable with the scientific approach—seemed a promising area for the marriage of Communist and comparative studies.

In retrospect, it seems clear that students of Communist political systems were naïve in assuming that they had entered a settled field. Many specialists, unaware that they would be "forced to resolve

43. Almond uses this term. See his "Some Thoughts on Chinese Political Studies" in John M. H. Lindbeck (ed.), *China: Management of a Revolutionary Society* (Seattle: University of Washington Press, 1971), p. 378.

44. Dankwart A. Rustow makes this point in regard to comparative Communist studies in his "Communism and Change," in Chalmers Johnson (ed.), *Change in Communist Systems* (Stanford: Stanford University Press, 1970), p. 346. See also Almond, "Some Thoughts."

45. For a good summary history of the evolution of this mood, see Cohen and Shapiro (eds.), *Communist Systems*, pp. xix–xliv.

46. Much of the discussion below draws from a study by William Taubman and from our experiences in teaching a course in comparative Communism together. Taubman, "The Change to Change in Communist Systems: Modernization, Postmodernization and Soviet Politics," in Henry W. Morton and Rudolf L. Tőkés (ed.), *Soviet Politics and Society in the 1970's* (New York: Free Press, 1974), pp. 369–391.

47. See Cohen and Shapiro (eds.), *Communist Systems*.

controversies inherent in the method before applying it,"[48] blithely set off on well-worn paths which were gradually being questioned by those concerned with the study of comparative political development. Thus, while comparativists were becoming sensitive to the Western-oriented quality of developmental theory, students of Communism were presenting evolutionary schemes that suggested the convergence of Western and Communist systems.[49] Cautionary statements from comparativists regarding the tendency of structural-functionalism to treat the political system as a dependent variable went unheeded by one scholar who depicted the "economic and social basis" of Communist countries as "beginning to transform the political superstructure in the familiar manner described by the Marxist interpretation of history."[50] Finally, while some comparativists complained that exponents of the behavioral revolution had erred by seeking to build "general theories" and then being "mesmerized" by them, students of Communist systems, with less empirical evidence than most, continued their broad theorizing.[51]

It is not surprising then that the grand breakthrough envisioned by

48. D. Richard Little, "Communist Studies in Comparative Perspective: Some Unorthodox Proposals," in Fleron (ed.), *Communist Studies,* p. 96.

49. This is a central theme of Taubman's study.

50. Roy C. Macridis discusses the tendency to see the state as a dependent variable in his "Comparative Politics and the Study of Government," *Comparative Politics,* I, 1 (October 1968), p. 85.

The quotation is from Richard Lowenthal, "Development vs. Utopia in Communist Policy," in Johnson (ed.), *Change in Communist Systems,* p. 112. For a similar approach see Dennis Pirages, "Modernization: New Decisional Models in Socialist Society," in R. Barry Farrell (ed.), *Political Leadership in Eastern Europe and the Soviet Union* (Chicago: Aldine, 1970), pp. 249–275.

Jeremy Azrael points to the tendency of those who use the mobilization approach to see the political system as excessively vulnerable to social and economic change. See his "Varieties of De-Stalinization," in Johnson (ed.), *Change in Communist Systems.*

51. Some critiques of grand-theorizing are Macridis, "Comparative Politics," Joseph LaPalombara, "Macrotheories and Microapplications in Comparative Politics: A Widening Chasm," *Comparative Politics,* I, 1 (October 1968), pp. 52–78, and Ralph Braibanti, "Comparative Political Analytics Reconsidered," *Journal of Politics,* XXX, 1 (February 1968), pp. 25–65.

Examples of broad conceptualizing regarding the future of Communist systems would include George Fischer, *The Soviet System and Modern Society* (New York: Atherton, 1968), Fleron, "Co-optation as a Mechanism," Zvi Y. Gitelman, "Beyond Leninism: Political Change in Eastern Europe," *Newsletter on Comparative Studies of Communism,* V, 3 (May 1972), pp. 18–43, and the grand debate occasioned by Zbigniew Brzezinski's provocative article on the future of the Soviet system. The original article and the responses to it are collected in Zbigniew Brzezinski (ed.), *Dilemmas of Change in Soviet Politics* (New York: Columbia University Press, 1969).

some optimists did not occur. While it would be too harsh to repeat Walter Z. Laqueur's judgment of 1964 " that the contribution to the field of Soviet studies of the more modern trends in sociology and political science has been on the whole negligible," [52] students of Communist systems have become more realistic today and more modest in their expectations. At present the mood seems to be one of retrenchment conditioned by a sensitivity to the importance of " head-[ing] off the mere mechanical borrowing of theories, paradigms and concepts which has rapidly increased in the past few years as a result of explicit efforts to integrate Communist studies into the mainstream of contemporary social science research." [53]

The study of Chinese politics has not been isolated from these trends. Scholars from this area have attended many of the conferences seeking new approaches to the study of Communist politics. Moreover, studies such as those of Robert Scalapino and Derek Waller on elites and works of Richard Solomon on political culture, Schurmann on ideology and organization, Pye on authority, Townsend on participation, and Alan Liu on communication have been explicit attempts to bring the " more modern trends " to the study of Chinese politics.

The present orientation of American scholarship on China suggests that works of this nature will increase in the years ahead. It would seem that appeals to integrate the study of the Chinese political process with the broader concerns of the social sciences, perhaps appropriate a decade ago, would now be unnecessary at best and mere cant at worst. However, it might be appropriate to consider fruitful points at which such an integration might be effected. The analytic frameworks and approaches that have emerged out of the " behavioral revolution " are numerous and variegated, and the often careless conceptualization or " mechanical borrowing " apparent in the field of comparative Communism should sensitize us to the dangers of facile adaptation. There are neither self-evident research priorities nor obvious frameworks of analysis with which to conceptualize the data of Chinese politics. In the study of China, where the gaps in our knowledge are surely as numerous as the alternative approaches, choices will have to be made.

While there are " many roads " by which to reach a meaningful integration, one orientation might prove particularly fruitful. The following discussion will consider some of the characteristics of cur-

52. Quoted in Fleron, " Introduction," in Fleron (ed.), *Communist Studies,* p. 2.

53. Fleron, " From the Editor," *Newsletter on Comparative Studies of Communism,* V, 4 (August 1972), p. 2.

rent approaches to the study of Chinese politics as they have been reflected in the books reviewed, those aspects of the political process in China most in need of illumination, and, most importantly, the hindsight provided to a "late developer." Moreover, the discussion is based on one central assumption regarding the terms of integration with the concerns and methods of the social sciences. In seeking this desirable goal, it would be unwise (for reasons to be discussed below) to abandon prematurely our area orientation.

Although the study of Chinese politics has not been so dominated by grand evolutionary speculations as the Soviet field has been, the work of some Sinologists has been equally as abstract and detached from reality. One example of this was mentioned above. During the Cultural Revolution students of Chinese politics were involved in a spirited debate over the nature of Maoist ideology—and, ultimately, over the nature of "modernization." Yet it often seemed as if issues were being debated in an empirical and theoretical vacuum.

This can be illustrated by the discussion of Mao's view of organization. The idea that Mao sought "to create organization without bureaucracy" was to his admirers evidence of his revolutionary genius; to his detractors such a view seemed inappropriate to China's needs.[54] Still, there was little rigorous analysis to see if this was in fact the case, or speculation as to what type of administrative structure might be appropriate for China.

Recently there have been some initial steps toward a more concrete and dispassionate analysis. For instance, Martin K. Whyte's study of Mao's views of organization suggests that they are neither incompatible with certain aspects of the familiar Weberian model nor totally detrimental to the successful administration of the Chinese state.[55] Moreover, Townsend's tentative remarks about specialization, differentiation, and development suggest that Mao's views not only were misapprehended but were judged against uncertain standards.

54. For example, compare Stephen Andors, "Revolution and Modernization: Man and Machine in Industrializing Societies," in Edward Friedman and Mark Selden (eds.), *America's Asia* (New York: Pantheon, 1971), pp. 393–444, with John W. Lewis, "Leader, Commissar, and Bureaucrat: The Chinese Political System in the Last Days of the Revolution," in Ho P'ing-ti and Tang Tsou (eds.), *China in Crisis* (Chicago: University of Chicago Press, 1968), pp. 449–481.

55. Whyte, "Bureaucracy and Modernization," and Harding, *Modernization and Mao*. See also Stuart Schram, "Introduction: The Cultural Revolution in Historical Perspective," in Stuart R. Schram (ed.), *Authority, Participation and Cultural Change in China* (Cambridge: Cambridge University Press, 1973), pp. 1–108.

While this debate is an underlying theme in some of the texts reviewed here, these books show the tendency towards abstraction in additional ways. Two authors—Pye and Starr—emphasize the centrality of the interaction between views of the elites and those of the masses in the Chinese political process. Starr speaks of culture altering ideology, while Pye depicts much of Mao's program as inappropriate to the special character and needs of the Chinese people. All of this may be true. But hypotheses of this kind must be demonstrated through the study of the making, implementation, and impact of public policy. It is within political structures that decisions are made; it is through these structures that they are carried out; and it is by means of these structures that information regarding their impact on the populace is received.[56] Yet both authors slight these questions. In their hands, politics in China becomes an elusive and ethereal process.

Indeed, in reading these books one is struck by the lack of attention to concrete instances or institutions of decisionmaking. Quite often, presentations of the division of labor between state and Party organizations remain unclear. Starr rather vaguely cautions that it would be a mistake to see the two hierarchies as either the same or totally competitive. But he gives little real evidence by way of elaboration. Pye takes the conventional view that the Party makes policy and the State administers it, while Townsend, consistent with his depiction of political institutions, warns that such clear differences are hard to prove in the Chinese case. Other examples could be cited. But the point is simply that we know very little about the actual structure and operation of political organizations in China. In the absence of such knowledge, much speculation is, at best, abstract and, at worse, ill-founded. How can we speak of a lack of differentiation or specialization when institutional studies do not provide the data for such assertions? Or, as Townsend's work suggests, how can we make assumptions regarding the limiting effect of ideology on decision-making when we have so few case studies of policy formulation? And finally, until we know more about organizational influences, can we really accept Pye's and Hinton's strong assertions regarding the role of personal idiosyncrasies and preferences?

These examples are related in that they show how the Cultural Revolution pointed up some of the inadequacies or areas of over-generalization in the study of Chinese politics. The events of these years not only challenged many political scientists to clarify previously

56. Although this type of view might seem quite basic, as Macridis demonstrates, analyses of political systems often lose sight of such essentials. Macridis, " Comparative Politics."

held assumptions regarding the nature of "modernity," they also demonstrated the potentially distorting effects that an emphasis on such questions would have for an understanding of the Chinese political process. Specifically, Red Guard newspapers dramatically revealed the intense debate that had taken place since 1949 over fundamental issues. China's domestic policies had not simply been a series of responses to objective socio-economic pressures—the challenge of "modernity," for example. They were revealed as highly *political* decisions made by a divided leadership within a complex institutional environment. In these circumstances, the inadequacy of approaches that slight or simplify the policy alternatives, institutional environment, and political strategies of those who make consequential decisions in favor of an emphasis on socio-economic imperatives and the description of policy outputs became particularly obvious.

Writing in 1968, Roy Macridis and Joseph LaPalombara expressed a concern that certain similar emphases in research were having a deleterious effect on the formulation of approaches to comparative political analysis. Macridis argued that the behavioral revolution had gone "wrong" by its emphasis at two extremes: broad, theoretical generalizations about whole "systems" and their evolution, on the one hand, and studies of behavior only marginally related to politics (child-rearing, school curriculum, and so forth), on the other.[57] The corrective that he and LaPalombara proposed was a renewed emphasis on the study of decisionmaking within governmental institutions—"institutions and institutional processes that are clearly, directly, intimately involved in the political process."[58] LaPalombara asserted that this kind of research not only would provide much needed empirical data about these political institutions, but would also create a firmer and empirically sounder basis for comparative theory.[59]

Of course, if it is wrong to "mechanically" borrow paradigms from comparative politics, it is equally wrong to borrow remedies for nonexistent shortcomings. Yet, judging from the books discussed here and the more general orientation of research concerns they represent, this would seem not to be a danger. Written after the Cultural Revolution, they reflect, to differing degrees, the impact that the events of these years had on assumptions about Chinese politics. Yet the general absence in most of them of any systematic discussion of the institutional settings and processes of decisionmaking seems to reflect both the generally poor integration of such concerns with our thinking about

57. *Ibid.*, p. 81.
58. LaPalombara, "Macrotheories and Microapplications," p. 62.
59. *Ibid.*

Chinese politics and the neglect of such topics in earlier research. This situation is an important reason why our understanding of Chinese politics is excessively abstract and often remote from important questions of the Chinese political process.

To ameliorate this situation, I propose that we return to basics. It may be that structural views, as John Lewis argues, "distort the analysis of leadership and power by making formal organizational patterns seem more important than they are." [60] But this can only be known when there are many comprehensive and sophisticated organizational studies. Such prosaic issues as zoning of authority, organization, communications, personnel policies, and the like should be examined.[61] A. Doak Barnett's study, now perhaps dated, was an excellent beginning.[62] Recent opportunities to visit China (at least in my experience) can be used to some advantage in collecting certain data on institutional arrangements. Officials seemed more willing to discuss these questions than broader political ones.

Studies of organization form the basis of, and are integrally related to, studies of decisionmaking. If, as has been argued, the nature of policies is shaped by the organizations from which they emerge, thus causing different actors to attempt to channel decisions into bodies favorable to them, we should know more about the structure and constitution of different organizations.[63] Moreover, questions regarding the zoning of authority and methods of bureaucratic communication become political issues in themselves that require resolution.[64] Finally, one author has suggested that changes in the pattern of bureaucratic communication made before the Great Leap Forward inhibited policymaking during that movement by thwarting accurate

60. Quoted in Andrew J. Nathan, "Models of Conflict in Chinese Politics," *Problems of Communism,* XXI, 3 (May–June 1972), p. 83.

61. Michel Oksenberg enumerates some of these points in his *A Bibliography of Secondary English Language Literature on Contemporary Chinese Politics* (New York: East Asian Institute, Columbia University, n.d.), pp. iii–xxxv.

62. A. Doak Barnett, *Cadres, Bureaucracy, and Political Power in Communist China* (New York: Columbia University Press, 1967). See also Donald W. Klein's excellent study of the foreign ministry in China, "The Chinese Foreign Ministry" (Ph.D. Diss., Columbia University, 1974).

63. Michel C. Oksenberg, "Politics and the Public Health Issue," in John Z. Bowers (ed.), *Medicine and Society in China* (New York: Josiah Macy Foundation, 1974), pp. 128–160.

64. Schurmann presents the problem of decentralization in this light in his *Ideology and Organization in Communist China,* 2nd ed. (Berkeley and Los Angeles: University of California Press, 1968).

On the conflict over methods of bureaucratic communication, see Michel C. Oksenberg, "Methods of Communication within the Chinese Bureaucracy," *China Quarterly,* No. 57 (January–March 1974), pp. 1–39.

policy feedback.[65] In such ways, as well as others, an understanding of structural patterns is related to any conceptualization of the decisionmaking process.

The assumptions of the totalitarian approach, and of the alleged paucity of data, may be partly responsible for the tendency to slight the impact of institutions and highlight the ability of the leader to make policy with little mind to institutional or societal influences and constraints. However, as we have learned, the picture of an Olympian Mao moving men and bureaucracies is illusory. Even a view that recognizes policy as being the result of cleavages among the elite is not enough. For leaders are often under organizational pressures, and the policies they adopt can be similarly subject to organizational and societal constraints.[66]

Townsend lists a number of variables—mass opinion, bureaucratic interests, economic constraints, the role of Mao, ideological divisions, and others—as potential influences on policymaking. For example, studies of elite ideology can be used if made more specific so as to provide information regarding decisionmaking style, perception of problem areas in society, and interpretation of feedback from policy outputs.[67] Studies of the economy can provide us with some sense of the resources available to decisionmakers.[68] Paul Harper's assertions concerning Li Li-san's attempt to build a political base in the trade union organization should inspire other attempts to find similar linkages.[69] Moreover, Harper's statement that the trade union organization "began to identify with and advocate the interests of the workers" indicates one way in which mass interests enter into the policy pro-

65. Oksenberg, "Methods of Communication," p. 34.

66. For a discussion of these points, see Lampton, "Policy Arenas."

67. A most interesting study along these lines is Harry Harding, "Maoist Theories of Policy-Making and Organization," in Thomas W. Robinson (ed.), *The Cultural Revolution in China* (Berkeley and Los Angeles: University of California Press, 1971), pp. 113–164.

For an exploratory attempt to discuss the manner in which Chinese leaders have perceived policy alternatives, see Michel C. Oksenberg and Steven Goldstein, "The Chinese Political Spectrum," *Problems of Communism*, XXIII, 2 (March–April 1974), pp. 1–13, and the comments stimulated by this article as well as a response by the authors: "Some Perspectives on Chinese Politics," *ibid.*, XXIV, 1 (January–February 1975), pp. 72–77.

68. The linkages between the economic environment and policymaking are suggested, for example, by Alexander Eckstein in his "Economic Fluctuations in Communist China's Domestic Development," in Ho and Tsou (eds.), *China in Crisis*, pp. 691–729.

69. Paul Harper, "The Party and the Unions in Communist China," cited in Lampton, "Policy Arenas."

cess.[70] The list could go on. But it is apparent that we have much of the basis for work in the areas I have suggested. What is needed is to draw all of it together into studies of specific decisions, series of decisions, or issue areas. David Lampton and Michel Oksenberg have begun to explore such possibilities, but there is more work to be done.[71]

While what I have suggested is apparently modest in its focus on institutions and decisionmaking, I would not be so ingenuous as to argue that with such an approach research opportunities and methods would be sharply defined.[72] From an empirical perspective there will, of course, be data problems. Moreover, we shall have to choose from among the numerous issue areas and institutions those that show the greatest promise of providing important insights into the political process. Similarly, the investigator will have several approaches from which to choose. Complex organization theory, the group approach, and models of factionalism have all been suggested as appropriate for such studies.[73] Thus, this type of orientation would not constitute a retreat to the parochialism and atheoretical nature of Chinese studies criticized in the past. It is most likely that researchers will adopt one or a combination of the approaches suggested above. If they do so critically, with sensitivity to the Chinese element in their study, such a focus could lead to deeper enrichments of these perspectives than Starr's suggestion that we study political conflict.

That students of Chinese politics will almost certainly apply approaches from various disciplines gives force to Robert E. Ward's contention that the distance between area studies and the political science discipline is diminishing. However, in light of the discussion above, of greater import is his advice concerning the necessity of main-

70. Paul Harper, "The Party and the Unions in Communist China," *China Quarterly*, No. 37 (January–March 1969), p. 92.

71. David Lampton, *Health, Conflict and the Chinese Political System* (Ann Arbor: Michigan Papers in Chinese Studies, University of Michigan, 1974), and "Policy Arenas," pp. 409–413.

For Oksenberg's views see "Policy Making Under Mao, 1949–1968: An Overview" in Lindbeck, *op. cit.*, pp. 79–115; "Methods of Communication," and "Policy Formulation in Communist China: The Case of the 1957–1958 Mass Irrigation Campaign" (Ph.D. Diss., Columbia University, 1969).

72. Joseph LaPalombara describes the many choices that must be made when using this putatively narrow focus in his "Macrotheories and Microapplications," p. 62.

73. See Andrew J. Nathan, "A Factionalism Model for CCP Politics," *China Quarterly*, No. 53 (January–March 1973), pp. 34–66, and his "Models of Conflict."

taining some area orientation in our research.[74] It would be unwise to abandon this view at a time when the ethnocentric roots of more generalized models are being questioned, the consideration of cultural idiosyncrasies is again being encouraged, and the role of historical factors in shaping subsequent patterns of development is becoming an important factor in approaches to modernization.[75] An area perspective provides two elements essential to the type of research advocated above. First, it emphasizes the "distinctiveness" of China, and, second, it attaches, as a matter of tradition, high value to the generation of basic data.[76] Such commitments are essential if our work on China is not to be overwhelmed by broad theorizing. But they also assure that enrichments of comparative concepts will be based on a sound understanding of the Chinese experience.

Many of the above recommendations regarding decisionmaking and institutions obviously constitute the substance of a case study approach. Moreover, this perspective is totally compatible with the requirements that I have suggested should be considered in pursuing research on this subject. As Helen Desfosses Cohn argued:

> The case study method—within an implicit or explicit conceptual framework—could increase our knowledge of specific systems without sacrificing the comparative perspective . . . Familiarity with the comparative method would help scholars to make significant contributions to our knowledge of specific areas and to ongoing efforts to improve the generalizations of comparative theory.[77]

74. Robert E. Ward, "APSA Presidential Address: Culture and the Comparative Study of Politics," *American Political Science Review*, LXVIII, 1 (March 1974), pp. 190–201.

After this review was completed, Chalmers Johnson published a discussion of the value of a case study approach within an area studies orientation. I was not able to integrate his argument into the body of this article. See his "Political Science and East Asian Area Studies," *World Politics*, XXVI, 4 (July 1974), pp. 560–575.

75. *Ibid*. For a brief summary of the emergence of an appreciation of the importance of historical factors in modernization, see Huntington's "The Change to Change."

76. G. William Skinner has argued that a more careful investigation of the distinctive elements of the Chinese experience can make important contributions to the social sciences. "What the Study of China Can Do for Social Science," *Journal of Asian Studies*, XXIII, 4 (August 1964), pp. 523–530.

77. Helen Desfosses Cohn, "Comparative Communism and Comparative Studies: A Note on Shared Concerns," *Newsletter on Comparative Studies of Communism*, VI, 4 (August 1973), p. 5. See also C. Johnson, "Political Science."

One work in the Soviet field which approximates this conception is Jerry Hough's study of Soviet prefects. This is an attempt both to illuminate an important aspect of the Soviet political system and to make some more generalized statements about the nature of administrative theory in light of the Soviet experience.[78] Similar case studies of institutions and decisionmaking in China can achieve much of the benefit derived from integration with the social sciences, while avoiding many of the pitfalls suggested above. While a lack of data might, at present, preclude studies as comprehensive as that of Hough, a *commitment* to such a concrete research orientation might provide some assurance that theorizing will promote and not impede the generation of much needed basic information regarding the nature of the Chinese political system. A case study approach to institutions and decisionmaking in China might go some way toward achieving what John K. Fairbank has whimsically referred to as "integrating the thought of Chairman Mao not only with that of Dr. Amitai Etzioni but also with that of the K'ang-hsi emperor."[79]

Comment by Thomas P. Bernstein

Professor Steven Goldstein's review essay is a penetrating piece of analysis. It is also a tribute to the writers of the four textbooks that their works can generate so much thinking about the state of the study of Chinese politics and where it should be heading. A central theme runs through Goldstein's critical comments on the four authors:

78. Jerry Hough, *The Soviet Prefects* (Cambridge, Mass.: Harvard University Press, 1969). In addition, a review of this book by Erik P. Hoffmann makes some useful points regarding the manner in which its value as a case study might have been increased. "Social Science and Soviet Administrative Behavior," *World Politics*, XXIV, 3 (April 1972), pp. 444–471.

79. John K. Fairbank, "The State That Mao Built," *World Politics*, XIX, 4 (July 1967), p. 675.

to differing degrees, none has paid enough attention to Chinese political institutions, especially to the question of how they actually work and what influences they exert on policy formulation. Hinton is criticized for failing to make "explicit and precise" the linkage between the men at the top and the bureaucracies that manage society. Goldstein notes that in Pye's book "personality differences tend to overshadow any rigorous discussion of the nature of political institutions . . . or the impact of 'constituencies' on policymaking." He points out that from Starr's book the reader cannot derive "any real sense of the impact of institutions on the political process." While Townsend, in comparison with the other three authors, is seen as more sensitive to Goldstein's concern with linking decisionmaking processes to institutional structures, he only lists various influences on the policy process, including the role of Mao and institutional arrangements, and fails to provide an "integrated view of the decisional process in China." Goldstein concludes that the reason why all four fail to provide an adequate view of policymaking is that ". . . we know very little about the actual structure and operation of political organizations in China." He calls not only for descriptive analysis of institutions and institutional relationships—e.g., we do not know as much as we should about the relationship between Party and government—but above all for answers to such questions as how organizations shape policies and constrain leaders.

Goldstein's thesis is likely to be of considerable interest to students of comparative Communism, because the prevailing assumption in the literature is that if one of the fourteen Marxist-Leninist systems exemplifies the mobilization model, it is China.[1] Yet what Goldstein seems to be saying is that the best way to understand China is in terms not of the mobilization model but of some model of bureaucratic or organizational politics. In his mind, policy seems to be the outcome of a complex and intricate interplay of various bureaucratic as well as societal and group interests. This image of the nature of Chinese politics strikes a familiar chord: It is the image that students of comparative Communism have of the post-mobilization stage, which is characteristic of the Soviet Union and Eastern Europe in recent years. It is noteworthy that the author is not saying that China has recently changed from a mobilization to a bureaucratic system (e.g., after the Cultural Revolution). Nor is he suggesting in line with the oft-noted cyclical fluctuations in Chinese politics that bureaucratic and

1. Carmelo Mesa-Lago, "A Continuum Model To Compare Socialist Systems Globally," *Economic Development and Cultural Change*, Vol. 21, No. 4, Part 1 (July 1973), pp. 573–590.

mobilization patterns alternate; even the Great Leap Forward can evidently be understood better from a bureaucratic politics perspective.[2]

The author thus raises some basic questions about how best to understand the Chinese political system. On the face of it, it would seem that the mobilization model is quite at odds with the bureaucratic politics model. The mobilization model stresses system transformation, the organization of rulers and ruled for the achievement of overriding goals and purposes, and the confrontation between old and new values. It is difficult to see how the revolutionary transformation of society can be tackled if central leaders find it difficult or impossible to impose a unifying conception on all political actors and if policies are indeed the outcome of incremental bargaining among more or less autonomous organizational interests. If in bureaucratic politics elite conflict reflects the clash of institutional rivalries and departmental perspectives, the mobilization approach tends to see elite conflict as centering around issues of left versus right—i.e., should the pace of change be fast or slow—and around issues of development and developmental rationality. The mobilization perspective assumes the capacity of leaders to override parochial interests and to use organizations as transmission belts; in the bureaucratic perspective leaders are more or less the captives of organizations. Only empirical analysis can reveal whether the two models are in fact incompatible with one another or whether and to what degree elements from both are present in Chinese politics, as indeed is implied in the "more or less" language used in the preceding sentences. The point is that Goldstein has usefully called attention to an approach that is gaining ground among students of Chinese politics. It is one, furthermore, that opens up possibilities for comparison of the Chinese with other Communist systems commonly identified as bureaucratic.

If the validity of the bureaucratic politics approach can only be tested in empirical research, the question of data arises. It seems to me that the author underestimates the data problem. In a political system whose spokesmen regularly use such obfuscating prose as "Party Central" (*tang chung-yang*) or "departments concerned" (*yu-kuan pu-men*) to avoid specificity in identifying organizations, it is not easy to establish, as he suggests, "...linkages between elite contenders, organizational interests, and intermediate bureaucratic actors." This is not to say that some important work has not already been done or

2. See David M. Lampton, *Health, Conflict and the Chinese Political System*, Ch. II, "The Great Leap Forward Reconsidered: Health Policymaking Arenas and Policy Diversity."

that future work cannot be done, especially if more data windfalls such as Red Guard publications appear. But until more data become available, excessive concentration on bureaucratic politics may be counterproductive.[3] Hasty application of such models without good data to test them may lead to the very same abstract speculations that Goldstein deplores in some of the currently available writings on the People's Republic of China.

3. In contrast to the author's remarks on visitors, I do not have the impression that visitors have succeeded in obtaining data on bargaining processes among organizations or on such questions as elite linkages with organizations or processes of resource allocation. Visitors have obtained useful material on the structure of organizations, as well as on some processes such as planning, but the information has not been sufficiently detailed to shed significant light on bureaucratic or organizational politics.

BARBARA JANCAR

Eastern Europe: Toward a New Paradigm?

It says something for the status of East European studies that sixteen years after its publication Zbigniew Brzezinski's *The Soviet Bloc* remains the arbiter and standard work on the area both for its conceptual approach and for the sweep and accuracy of its data. The 1960s and 1970s have witnessed the creation of many new texts on the subject. In view of the increasing input from behavioralism and systems analysis studies, it is useful and timely to review the contributions that the new texts have made in advancing or restructuring our knowledge of the field.

Because of their number, I shall not attempt to discuss every text on Eastern Europe published since 1960. Rather, I have exercised a certain selectivity based on methodology and material covered, with the aim of presenting a spectrum of the texts available.[1]

1. The eight texts chosen are H. Gordon Skilling, *The Governments of Communist East Europe* (New York: Crowell, 1966); Adam Bromke (ed.), *The Communist States at the Crossroads Between Moscow and Peking* (New York: Praeger, 1965); J. F. Brown, *The New Eastern Europe: The Khrushchev Era and After* (New York: Praeger, 1966); Stephen Fischer-Galati (ed.), *Eastern Europe in the Sixties* (New York: Praeger, 1963); Ghita Ionescu, *The Politics of the European Communist States* (New York: Praeger, 1967); Peter A. Toma (ed.), *The Changing Face of Communism in Eastern Europe* (Tucson: University of Arizona Press, 1970); François Fejto, *A History of the People's Democracies* (New York: Praeger, 1971); and Jan F. Triska (ed), *Integration and Community Building in Eastern Europe* (Baltimore: Johns Hopkins University Press, 1973). Triska's *Communist Party States* (Stanford: The Hoover Institution, 1968) was omitted, as was L. J. Cohen and J. P. Shapiro

At the outset, a few general comments are in order. Four of the texts were written by single authors, and four are compilations of contributions by well-known specialists in the field. The Triska series comprises eight individual books covering each of the countries of Eastern Europe, written by such familiar figures as Stephen Fischer-Galati (Romania), Arthur M. Hanhardt, Jr. (German Democratic Republic), and Zdenek Suda (Czechoslovakia). The failure to give unity to a multi-authored effort is a major drawback of the four edited volumes. It should be noted that five of the eight texts were written in the 1960s, raising the difficulty of outdatedness when addressed in 1975. As might be expected, the textbooks of the 1960s reflect the concerns and outlook of a period that was moving toward a less rigid view of Soviet behavior but that was yet to experience the possibility of détente.

Among the various reasons students have given me for enrolling in a course on Eastern Europe, three seem worth mentioning here: (1) They have a personal interest in the area either because of ethnic background or, less frequently, through simple curiosity. (2) They have studied the politics of the Soviet Union and believe their study to be incomplete without knowledge of the Soviet "satellites." And (3) they are students of comparative politics and consider Eastern Europe a proper subject of their concern. East European politics has been a relatively infrequent course-offering on the smaller college campuses, and although East European studies enjoyed a certain popularity in the 1950s at the height of the Cold War,[2] recent years have seen a decline in student interest in Soviet studies and hence in the East European area.[3]

Students thus tend to come to a course on East European politics with little preparation or background in the field. They also come with a set of ideas about how a Communist system functions, which exaggerates either the positive or the negative aspects. The task of the textbook on the area, therefore, becomes one of providing objective information relating a normative concept of the system to the widely differing political cultures in which it operates. As textbooks generally

Communist Systems in Comparative Perspective (Garden City, N.Y.: Doubleday/Anchor, 1974), because the scope of both, as their titles suggest, extended beyond Eastern Europe, covering China and the Asian Communist countries.

2. The author herself was a product of this popularity. In the atmosphere of student absorption with the United States characteristic of the 1970s, I might well have chosen another area.

3. Staffing practices of several political science departments may have also contributed to this trend. The replacement in recent years of a Soviet or East European specialist with "non-area" personnel in several institutions seems to support this contention.

constitute a digest of conceptual approaches and data gleaned from secondary sources, a review of them can tell us a good deal about the present state of political science research in a given domain. In the the case of East European studies, I regret to say, the prognosis is not good.

Methodology

The relating of system to population is a basic problem in methodology: it is in this area that the texts under consideration are weakest. The difficulty seems to be twofold. On the one hand, the books appear to reflect the conservative tendency on the part of many American scholars in the East European field to view Eastern Europe as what may be described as a subset of the Soviet Union, with the exception of Yugoslavia and possibly Albania. Brzezinski's *The Soviet Bloc* gave the impetus to the study of comparative Communism. Yet only three of the later texts—those by Skilling, Ionescu, and Fischer-Galati—attempt to formulate any areawide comparative criteria. Fischer-Galati indeed prefaces his volume with the assertion that his is a "pioneer effort," the first collaborative attempt to interpret the principal problems and developments in contemporary Eastern Europe on an "area" basis.[4] The other five texts contain country-by-country descriptive studies based mainly on each country's reaction to or interaction with Soviet developments.

In part, this approach stems from the reality of Soviet power in Eastern Europe, which was determined, particularly in the 1950s, to ensure that the social and political institutions of the "satellite" nations conformed to the Soviet model. The textbooks published in the 1960s suggest that their authors and editors are still very much under the influence of what may be called the "satellite mentality." And such an attitude was understandable given the drama of the Polish and Hungarian revolutions. The very real question in the 1960s was to what extent political forms deviating from the Soviet Stalinist norm would be permitted in Eastern Europe in the aftermath of de-Stalinization—hence the preoccupation with the degree of deviance rather than with the origin and content of the changes as new political expressions in their own right. Scholarship in the 1960s was absorbed in characterizing the loosening of totalitarian Soviet control over the area.

Toma's *The Changing Face of Communism in Eastern Europe* and

4. Stephen Fischer-Galati (ed.), *Eastern Europe in the Sixties* (New York: Praeger, 1963), p. v.

the Triska series are later products. As such, they might be expected to delve more deeply into the sources of the diversity of institutions that appeared in Eastern Europe during the Khrushchev era. In view of the fact that not one East European state conforms in its entirety either to the current Soviet model or to the political structure of any of its socialist neighbors, it is not enough to describe the differentiation that has taken place.

Nor is it enough to say, as Toma suggests, that the change in leadership in the Soviet Union was the necessary and sufficient cause for the awakening of latent nationalism, stimulating a new social mobilization, the result of which was "the legitimization of post-Stalinist national Communism as a direct reaction to the disintegrating Stalinist dictatorship."[5] Such generalities do not answer the fundamental question of what economic, social, and political forces were at work in each country to bring this "latent nationalism" to the surface and give it institutional form.

Regrettably, none of the texts explores the variables in the socio-economic and political cultures of the East European countries which may have contributed to the diverse manifestations of "national Communism" in the 1960s. Indeed, only the Triska series and Skilling's text provide any historical background. Skilling devotes his first three chapters to a discussion of the geography, demography, and political history of the area, a total of 31 pages out of a possible 234. Each of the books in the Triska series opens with a brief introductory historical sketch of the pre-Communist period; but the information is generally presented in descriptive form and is unrelated to the material on the Communist era introduced in the succeeding chapters. The other texts focus entirely on the changes that occurred after 1956, with no attempt to relate them to the past history of the countries concerned.

In short, the textbooks under review do not consider Eastern Europe as an area of study in its own right with its own indigenous problems, but always as an appendage of the Soviet Union, an extension of that country's domestic or foreign policy. In fact, the dominance of Russian influence in the area is a very recent occurrence, an imposition upon earlier layers of political culture. The oversimplified approach in the eight books leads the student to the erroneous conclusion that the change of leadership in the Soviet Union was the sole cause, rather than the catalyst, of the post-Stalinist political change in Eastern Europe.

5. Peter A. Toma (ed.), *The Changing Face of Communism in Eastern Europe* (Tucson: University of Arizona Press, 1970), p. 340.

A second failing of the methodology relates to the more general problem of integrating Communist studies within the comparative-politics framework. Since Steven Goldstein raises the question in his comments on China, there is little need to go into detail here. However, certain aspects of the problem need to be stressed. The identification by Friedrich and Brzezinski [6] of totalitarianism with the systematic application of terror made it useless as a conceptual model when terror ceased to play a prominent role in Soviet and Eastern European society after Stalin's death. The 1960s saw an attempt to apply the methodologies and research of behavioralism to Soviet politics with some success. At the macro-level, *Communist Studies and the Social Sciences,* edited by Frederic J. Fleron, Jr., presented a comprehensive overview of the methodological and conceptual problems involved in Communist studies and suggested some relevant social science theory.[7] Among the contributors are the better-known political scientists in the field, who have long been concerned with the problem of theory-building in the Communist area, as well as many younger researchers. Significantly, analysis focusing on Eastern Europe is minimal. Two later volumes, *Comparative Communist Political Leadership* by Carl Beck et al. and *The Behavioral Revolution and Communist Studies* edited by Roger Kanet, devote perhaps a little more space to Eastern Europe, but the input from the area is still not very significant. In the former book, two out of seven chapters relate to the East European countries; in the latter, only one out of thirteen![8] A lone pioneering attempt to put political development theory to work in East European studies is Jack Fischer's *Yugoslavia: A Multi-National State.*

Research at the micro-level of Soviet politics was well under way in the 1950s with Fainsod's *Smolensk under Soviet Rule,* Berliner's

6. For a definition of totalitarianism, see Carl J. Friedrich (ed.), *Totalitarianism* (Cambridge, Mass.: Harvard University Press, 1954), and Zbigniew K. Brzezinski, *The Permanent Purge* (Cambridge, Mass.: Harvard University Press, 1956).

7. One of the most intriguing chapters in the book is William A. Welsh, "A Game-Theoretic Conceptualization of the Hungarian revolt: Toward an Inductive Theory of Games." Welsh concludes his presentation of the revolt in game-theoretical terms by cautioning that game theory is at most descriptive rather than prescriptive theory. But he does provide a heuristic model by which the reader can explore the various options open to all parties in seeking equilibrium points. Frederic J. Fleron, Jr. (ed.), *Communist Studies and the Social Sciences* (Chicago: Rand McNally, 1969), pp. 420–459.

8. Carl Beck et al., *Comparative Communist Political Leadership* (New York: McKay, 1973), Chaps. 3 and 7. Roger Kanet (ed.), *The Behavioral Revolution and Communist Studies* (New York: Free Press, 1971), Chap. 7.

Factory and Manager in the USSR, and Bauer's *Nine Soviet Portraits*. The 1960s saw the publication of such works as Granick's *The Red Executive* (1960), Hazard's legal studies of the Soviet Union, Armstrong's work on the Soviet administration, Skilling's *Interest Groups in Soviet Society*, and Jerry Hough's *The Soviet Prefects*. These books represented substantial progress in the systemization of data collection and concept formation. More important, they contributed greatly to our knowledge of how the Soviet system functions. By comparison, the East European field saw little advance in documenting and quantifying the behavior of groups and institutions at the micro-level, the one exception being Jiri Kolaja's study, *A Polish Factory*.[9]

The difficulties with the behavioral approach can be generally located in two areas: (1) the availability of reliable data; and (2) the tendency on the part of students of Communism to deal with the whole social matrix in which the political system functions, on the assumption that Communism involves sets of problems which have no real counterpart in non-Communist phenomena.[10] The basic question here is whether Communist and non-Communist societies are really comparable, given the Western democratic status quo orientation of behavioralism.[11] The challenge of Marxism has been its ability through the dialectic to provide a dynamic model of change which appears to be operative in all societies. This challenge, in my opinion, has yet to be answered satisfactorily by either political development theory or any of the other contemporary behavioralist approaches, as these are essentially static, not dynamic. Moreover, granted that ideology and terror have been downgraded in the past decade in the Communist system, we still have little indication that any meaningful secularization of Communist society, in the sense of a separation of Party and state, is taking place or is about to take place. Despite the apparent atrophy of Marxism-Leninism into ritual and

9. Jiri Kolaja, *A Polish Factory* (Lexington: University of Kentucky Press, 1960).

10. For a discussion of these problems, see D. Richard Little, "Communist Studies in a Comparative Framework: Some Unorthodox Proposals," in Fleron, *op. cit.*, pp. 94–115, and Robert S. Sharlet, "Systematic Political Science and Communist Systems," in *ibid.*, pp. 207–211.

11. Robert Dahl's *Polyarchy* (New Haven, Conn.: Yale University Press, 1971) is a case in point, as is Karl Deutsch's cybernetic model of a political system described in *The Nerves of Government* (New York: Free Press, 1963). The Parsonian functionalist paradigm rests on the same assumption that a social system seeks equilibrium; while Parsons does try to provide some mechanism whereby change can occur, it is not entirely satisfactory (Talcott Parsons, *Societies, Evolutionary and Comparative Perspectives* [Englewood Cliffs, N. J.: Prentice-Hall, 1966], pp. 28–29).

dogma, ideology appears to remain essential to the Communist system as the chief inhibitor to the transformation of the Party into a pragmatic instrument, forced into policies of compromise and interest-group coalition behavior analogous to that in Western societies.[12]

The formulation of a coherent methodology that would lead to theory building in comparative Communist studies has been the subject of much thought in this country on the part of both groups and individual observers.[13] The prevailing view has been to set the Communist systems within the political development model.[14] The many problems inherent in such an approach will be discussed later. Suffice it to say here that while political development theory appears to enjoy a period of prosperity in Communist studies, others have argued for the constant-conflict model,[15] or for a general concept of pluralism based on bureaucratic behavior, not necessarily related to degree of modernization.[16] As can be seen from the works cited, a large part of the attempt at theory building has been undertaken primarily with the Soviet system in mind; until recently it had little visible impact on the East European field.[17]

12. See Brzezinski's comment on this point in Zbigniew Brzezinski, *Dilemmas of Change in Soviet Politics* (New York: Columbia University Press, 1969), pp. 25 ff.

13. In 1968, the ACLS held a Summer Workshop on the Comparative Study of Communism which was published in the *Newsletter on Comparative Studies of Communism,* II, 2 (June 1969). Among the individual pieces of research that could be mentioned are George Fischer, *The Soviet System and Modern Society* (New York: Atherton Press, 1968); C. J. Friedrich et al., *Totalitarianism in Perspective: Three Views* (New York: Praeger, 1969); Brzezinski, *Dilemmas of Change*; Chalmers Johnson (ed.), *Change in Communist Systems* (Stanford: Stanford University Press, 1970).

14. The publication of Samuel P. Huntington, " Political Development and Political Decay," *World Politics,* XVIII, 3 (April 1965), pp. 386–430, opened up the whole new possibility of the reversal of political development and bolstered Brzezinski's argument that some change toward the institutionalization of power and social participation in politics had to take place in Communist societies in their industrialized phase if political decay were not to occur (Brzezinski, *Dilemmas of Change,* pp. 32–35).

15. R. C. Thornton, " The Structure of Communist Politics," *World Politics,* XXIV, 4 (July 1971), pp. 498–517.

16. William Taubman, " The Change to Change in Communist Systems: Modernization, Postmodernization and Soviet Politics," in Henry W. Morton and Rudolf L. Tökés (eds.), *Soviet Politics and Society in the 1970s* (New York: Free Press, 1974), pp. 369–390. Taubman raises some questions about the prevailing enthusiasm for the political development model and concludes that whether the degree of pluralism in Soviet society correlates with " the amount of modernity " is " another question."

17. A recent excellent example is Allen Barton, Bogdan Denitch, and Charles Kadushin, *Opinion Making Elites in Yugoslavia* (New York: Praeger, 1972).

The textbooks on Eastern Europe reflect none of the controversy that has accompanied the ongoing study of Soviet politics and the newer subject of comparative Communism. On the contrary, the impact of modern political theory has been minimal as far as these books are concerned. Some excuse might be made for the early 1960s publications, but certainly the later volumes should reflect some of the current methodological discussions. Yet only four of the texts contain an identifiable unified conceptual approach. Fejto's and Skilling's books are essentially traditional. Fejto's study is in the English tradition of historiography, which provides exhaustive documentation without benefit of system. The student is thus constrained to read a book loaded with facts that are difficult if not impossible to organize. Skilling makes some effort to free his text from the totalitarian conceptual scheme, but he remains essentially within the institutional descriptive framework of an older generation of political scientists with some excursions into interest-group and public opinion formation.[18] In all fairness to his book, however, it has the decided merit of being truly comparative, which the other texts are not, except for Ionescu's.

The Triska series is the only text that attempts any systematic application of current political science paradigms. As stated in his foreword, Triska designed his eight-volume text around an international system's model of conflict and integration with the goal of "making a collective, systematic intellectual effort to assess empirically the scope, rate and direction of integration among the states ruled by Communist parties."[19]

The series is an outgrowth of Triska's *Communist Party States*, which sets itself the deliberate task of examining contemporary theory and its relationship to Communist studies. More sophisticated than either Fleron's or Kanet's volume, the contributions in *Communist Party States* offer a truly eclectic challenge to the reader with a background in political theory building, but the book is unsuitable for the general undergraduate. The East European series selects the conflict and integration model from this study and aims to apply it to the eight East European countries. Unfortunately, eight different scholars were asked to contribute to a single volume. The problems inherent in such a game plan are obvious. If the conflict and integration model is to be effectively used, the parameters of both conflict and integration must be operationally defined and standardized—if not to the general

18. H. Gordon Skilling, *The Governments of Communist Eastern Europe* (New York: Crowell, 1966), pp. xiii–xv.

19. As cited in Stephen Fischer-Galati, *The Socialist Republic of Romania* (Baltimore: Johns Hopkins University Press, 1969), p. v.

literature on the subject, then at least across the eight volumes. What, for example, does integration mean in terms of the interrelationship between the Soviet Union and the East European nations? Is this a goal or a process; is it sought by all states concerned or mainly by one? What are the boundaries and taxonomy of the conflict? Does conflict have a directional flow from one state to another, or is it a random process? These and other questions are never posed. The terms employed are not made precise but are determined at the discretion of each author. The result is that Triska's grand design is lost in the individual writers' idiosyncrasies. The final product becomes a reworking of well-worn facts essentially from the historical perspective.

It is a pity that the series does not carry out the editor's plan. Deutsch's application of communication theory might have been useful in examining the relations between the Communist states in terms of network transactions.[20] Herbert Simon's sociological conflict model would have adequately handled such problems as the identification of the intensity of interaction among members of the Communist bloc, the level of friendliness among members, the amount of activity carried on by the individual members, and the amount of activity imposed by the external environment (i.e., the international system as a whole).[21] Ernst B. Haas in his work on regionalism has come a long way toward a definition of regional integration,[22] which also might have been helpful to the Triska series. Numerous other studies on international relations behavior exist which the editor could have used with innovative results, instead of the present digest of *déjà vu*.

The Politics of the East European Communist States is a conceptually more integrated study. In his opening chapter, Ionescu deliberately attempts to isolate what he sees to be the distinctive characteristics of a Communist system. The sum of these elements he calls " the apparat-state." The term refers to what the author identifies as a network of eight organizational apparats governed by a monopolistic party, the power of whose leaders is held in check by (1) interactions among the various apparats, (2) conflicting demands emanating from socio-economic groups, and (3) dissent stemming from both intra-apparat factionalism and extra-apparat dissidence. Ionescu's concept borrows from the totalitarian and administrative models of

20. Deutsch, *op. cit.*

21. Herbert A. Simon, " A Formal Theory of Interaction in Social Groups," *American Sociological Review*, XVII, 2 (April 1952), pp. 202–211.

22. See Ernst B. Haas, " The Challenge of Regionalism," in Stanley H. Hoffmann (ed.), *Contemporary Theory in International Relations* (Englewood Cliffs, N. J.: Prentice-Hall, 1960), pp. 223–239.

Communist states and suggests an effort to forge a compromise between outright rejection of the totalitarian model and insistence on the uniqueness of the Communist political form. In this sense, his framework is essentially conservative.[23]

Given the conservative bias, it is surprising that virtually no mention is made of ideology either as a conflict-generating or an integrating-mobilizing factor in East European society. The author seems to suggest through this omission that ideology has played no substantial role in the politics of Eastern Europe, except tangentially as it interfered with expressions of nationalism and independence.[24] The absence of any developed discussion of the relation of ideology to the apparat-state seems to me a serious methodological flaw in Ionescu's model building.

Another flaw is the level of abstraction. The book never gets down to cases, to an examination of the actual functioning of the author's model. Examples are drawn from the history of Eastern Europe since World War II to support the apparat-state concept, but these are never truly comparative. The model itself remains the frame of reference for testing its validity. If such a state exists in real life, then we would like to see a comparison between individual cases and the model to determine whether isomorphism exists and under what conditions. What, for example, are the boundary criteria that permit diversity of institutions among the Communist states having the generic designation apparat-state? In other words, at what points on his continuum of plural checks can Ionescu's state revert to a bureaucratic state or even a democratic state? Has either of these alternatives occurred or threatened to occur in Eastern Europe, and if so in what way?

On the positive side, Ionescu uses his model well to integrate facts and events drawn from the East European experience. More important, *The Politics of the East European Communist States* is unique among the texts under review in offering some kind of systematic explanation as to how the Communist system might function in the area. Such an explanation is invaluable for students searching for a general conceptual framework within which to order individual facts.

The other books suffer markedly from the virtual absence of theory. Brown's study is little more than a sophisticated piece of journalism, recounting the author's view of the most important political, economic and cultural developments in the Soviet-dominated East European countries during 1956–1965. His discussion of political events adopts

23. Ghita Ionescu, *The Politics of the East European Communist States* (New York: Praeger, 1967), pp. 20ff.

24. See in particular Part III: "The Manifestation of Dissent," *ibid.*

the methods of "Kremlinology," tending to interpret the changes that occurred in the classic terms of a power struggle. His coverage of economic and cultural developments also depends heavily on descriptions of leading personalities, rather than on trends. Generally speaking, the text reads more like a solid piece of newspaper reporting than political science.

The three books edited by Bromke, Fischer-Galati, and Toma, respectively, suffer from the same problems as the Triska series: the difficulty of developing a coherent methodology in a book by several contributors. The method adopted by Toma and Bromke is the country-by-country analysis, accompanied by no visible comparative framework. Bromke attempts to set his analysis in perspective by focusing on developing Sino-Soviet relations, but it is hard to find any organizing principle for the Toma volume. While many of the authors refer frequently to political development and problems of modernization, the theory is regrettably given no systematic presentation. This is not to say that certain contributions are not very well written, notably Aspaturian's evaluation of the transformation of East European–Soviet relations after 1968,[25] but in general the book is another dreary repetition of well-worn facts without benefit of critical insight or conceptual innovation.

As noted earlier, the Fischer-Galati text claims an area-based orientation as a new approach to East Europe. However, the categories used are essentially descriptive rather than analytic: "the new social order," "the planned economy," "the politics of peaceful coexistence."[26] Once more, the result is competent journalism, not political science.

It is significant that the authors of the texts under review are known experts in the field; yet no text, with the possible exception of Ionescu's, provides a theoretical framework within which to view the problems and development of Eastern Europe. The absence of theory indicates that East European studies have yet to find a suitable mode of analysis which will at once distinguish it from Soviet research and place it within the context of comparative politics. It is apparent that the methods and techniques standard to behavioralism are a long way from becoming accepted tools of the field. The historical orientation

25. Vernon Aspaturian, "East European Relations with the USSR" in Toma, *op. cit.*, pp. 283–309. Aspaturian's central theme is that the Soviet invasion of Czechoslovakia marked a final "perversion" of "proletarian internationalism," linking Communism irrevocably with Soviet Communism. In the author's opinion, the 1970s will see the increasing "Europeanization" of Eastern Europe in the wake of steady ideological erosion.

26. Fischer-Galati, *Eastern Europe in the Sixties*, p. vii.

of the texts is all the more surprising in view of the rise of sociology as a discipline in its own right in East Europe and the increasing use of opinion surveys and attitudinal polls in the area.[27] While survey methods can still be used only with much discretion by Western researchers, countries like Yugoslavia have permitted survey projects in cooperation with Western specialists.[28] And the application of the techniques acquired in "Kremlinology" has become standard in leadership studies of the area.[29] It is as if the textbooks under consideration had been written in a vacuum, apart from the mainstream of thought which characterized Communist studies in the 1960s. Why this should be so is anyone's guess. The fact that concept formation in political theory has generally been Western-oriented, while the trainee in East European studies must needs spend most of his time acquiring language skills and historical background? The establishment of separate institutes for East European studies? The effects of the Cold War? At all events, the undergraduate coming to the East European field for the first time can only suffer from the lack of methodological precision which currently prevails in textbook writing on the area.

Presentation of Material

The data contained in all the books are discouragingly similar and similarly presented, relying mostly on the repetition of facts from other secondary sources and journals. The period covered is generally from 1945 to the mid-1960s, although Bromke, Brown, and Fischer-Galati concentrate on the Khrushchev era and its immediate aftermath. The technique of presentation is essentially historical-descriptive. There is a remarkable absence of statistical tables and no attempt at statistical analysis. When statistics are used, as in the Triska series and in Toma,

27. Czechoslovakia has been notably more backward in this area because of Novotny's conservative leanings. The first significant polls surveying public political opinion came out in 1968 and now have been published in Jaroslav A. Piekalkiewicz, *Public Opinion Polling in Czechoslovakia, 1968–1969; Results and Analysis of Surveys Conducted During the Dubcek Era* (New York: Praeger, 1972).

28. See, for example, Barton, Denitch, and Kadushin's excellent *Opinion Making Elites in Yugoslavia.*

29. See Daniel Kubat, "Patterns of Leadership in a Communist State: Czechoslovakia 1945–1958," *Journal of Central European Affairs,* XXI, 3 (October 1961), pp. 305–318, as well as the leadership studies appearing in Kanet, *op. cit.*, and Beck, *op. cit.* See also my study of the Czechoslovak 1968 leadership in Barbara Jancar, *Czechoslovakia and the Absolute Monopoly of Power* (New York: Praeger, 1971), Chaps. 5 and 6.

they are generally of the most basic kind—data on size of country, population, age, trade patterns. What is more, the information is not standardized for every country, but each contributor gives the data he believes to be important. There is no consensus on format. Skilling presents a breakdown of Party leadership on Czechoslovakia as well as a table of comparative Party membership in all the East European countries,[30] but the other texts contain no comparative statistics at all, except for Fischer-Galati's tables on East European trade.[31] The most valuable data in Brown are found in the appendix, which contains a list of Party leaders in Eastern Europe as of 1965 together with autobiographical sketches of the most important officials. But again this information is not systematized for easy assimilation by students.[32]

Avoidance of the historical-descriptive method of data presentation depends in large part on choice of analytic focus. In his investigation of Eastern Europe the scholar has many options, but the number diminishes if he chooses to develop a comparative framework. For example, he can consider the entire area as an international system in conjunction with the Soviet Union. The result will be an emphasis on comparative interstate foreign relations. He can attempt, like Ionescu, to focus on the Communist system and assemble supportive cross-national data. Or he can orient his analysis toward population subsets: the elites, the interest groups, the bureaucracies, the nationalities. To a limited extent, Skilling employs the last approach—the source, in my opinion, of his success at producing a comparative study. The use of categories such as the economy, culture, and political changes, which Bromke employs, tends to reinforce the descriptive presentation of data and, I believe, hampers the possibility of systematic analysis. The choice of a country as the unit of analysis also serves to impede the development of a comparative framework, as we have seen in Brown, Bromke, Toma, and Triska—unless this is set up carefully as a model at the beginning of the text.

Brzezinski clearly focused his analysis on the international system, as his title *The Soviet Bloc* suggests. The core of his study was the sources of agreement and disagreement of the East European countries with the Soviet Union. Triska's conflict and integration theme, like Bromke's and Toma's stress on the centripetal forces of nationalism, would seem to follow Brzezinski's emphasis, but in fact this is not the case. A close reading of the three textbooks reveals that their true focus is on the individual East European country. Brzezinski succeeds

30. Skilling, *op. cit.*, pp. 105–106, 108.
31. Fischer-Galati, *Eastern Europe in the Sixties*, pp. 126ff.
32. Brown, *op. cit.*

in his "unity and conflict" design because he is careful to lay out his framework at the beginning and then subordinate his data on individual countries. By contrast, the three texts' choice of a country-by-country analysis makes it impossible to develop comparative data within the concept of an international system, and the reader is left to digest historical factual description.

The selection of analytic focus is not an academic point. It vitally affects the type of data one chooses to present as well as the manner of presentation. Stress on a country's degree of divergence or convergence with the Soviet Union, as in Brown's and Bromke's books, means focusing on bloc rather than intrastate developments—i.e., on relations between the population and the leadership. In the 1950s a minimal amount of agreement was assumed to exist between the populations of Eastern Europe and the aims of its rulers. Communism, as has so often been pointed out, came to the area behind the barrels of Soviet guns and was maintained by the presence of the Soviet army.[33] Until the Khrushchev era, the East European countries' satellite position was taken for granted, with the sole exception of Yugoslavia. This meant that domestic leaders ruled over an essentially hostile population and were maintained in power by the support of the Soviet Union. Events in 1956 challenged that assumption. From then on, the evidence seemed to indicate that within certain parameters, whose outer bounds were eventually to be set by the Brezhnev "doctrine," national initiative could be shown. If such was the case, then the rule of the domestic leaders could no longer be assumed to rest solely on Soviet might but had to find anchors in the local population. The result was, on the one hand, a leadership still oriented toward Moscow but needing domestic support, and, on the other, the mobilization of an attentive public prepared to report its needs to a regime now ready in some degree to listen to them.

Two aspects of this support are especially worth consideration in a textbook on the area: (1) the "revisionist" ideas that challenged orthodox Communist concepts of leadership and economic rule; and (2) the proliferation of various groups as the source or disseminators of those ideas. As regards the pluralization of interests, it is remarkable that only Skilling and Ionescu pay any systematic attention to interest groups or bureaucratic factions and to the conflicting ideas and values they have represented in East European politics since 1956. Ionescu places chief emphasis on what he describes as the "plural checks" on the central core of his apparat-state. Two-thirds of his

33. The classic presentation of the evidence is Hugh Seton-Watson, *The East European Revolution* (New York: Praeger, 1951).

book is devoted to a discussion of how these forces operate, and how each represents a check on the central leadership and the other apparats. Borrowing on early taxonomies by Brzezinski, Huntington, and Rigby,[34] the author identifies three types of checks: checks by other apparats; social checks exercised by the interrelationship of the Party and the workers, peasants, and intelligentsia; and dissent. Skilling gives much less space (10 pages) to his analysis of interest-group activity and its relation to the apparatchiki in the formation and implementing of decisions. However, he does include a short discussion of checks on the bureaucracy in his chapter on bureaucratic behavior.[35] It is curious that the author does not place more emphasis on interest groups, in view of his own pioneering research on the application of interest-group theory to Communist studies.[36]

In view of the fact that East European scholars have themselves noted the growth of behavior akin to interest-group activity in their countries since 1956, one may well ask why such a vital factor in the "change to change" of the Communist system in Eastern Europe was given so little prominence in the other texts. A detailed discussion of interest groups might have provided students with indicators as to the relationship between pluralism and modernization in the area. George Fischer, for example, has argued that a highly industrialized monist society may be possible.[37] Dahl suggests, on the contrary, that there seems to be a high correspondence between what he terms hegemonies and low economic development, and a similar level of correspondence between competitive political regimes and high economic development.[38] Elsewhere I have argued that dissent may have become a permanent phenomenon in Communist society precisely because modernization appears to entail the broadening of political skills, the extension of the social benefits of technology, which cannot totally be controlled by the leadership, and the increasing interaction

34. T. H. Rigby, *Problems of Communism*, XII, 5 (September–October 1963), and Zbigniew Brzezinski and Samuel P. Huntington, *Political Power: USA/USSR* (New York: Viking Press, 1964).

35. Skilling, *op. cit.*, pp. 149–150.

36. Skilling, "Interest Groups and Communist Politics," *World Politics*, XVIII, 3 (April 1966), pp. 435–451. Of course, one of the first such studies was made some years earlier by J. Djordjevic: "Interest Groups and the Political System of Yugoslavia," in Henry W. Ehrmann (ed.), *Interest Groups on Four Continents* (Pittsburgh: University of Pittsburgh Press, 1958), pp. 197–228. For a comparative study, see Barbara Jancar, "The Case for a Loyal Opposition Under Communism, Czechoslovakia and Yugoslavia," *Orbis*, XII, 2 (Summer 1968), pp. 415–440.

37. George Fischer, *The Soviet System and Modern Society* (New York: Atherton, 1968), pp. 148–153.

38. Dahl, *op. cit.*, pp. 65–67.

of a growing number of social and economic interests.[39] Theorizing aside, it seems probable that as long as the Soviet and East European Communist systems follow the American pattern of industrialization, as opposed to the Chinese experiment,[40] the process of economic and social differentiation is going to continue. The analysis of this process and the ways in which it is institutionalized, either formally or informally, in Eastern Europe can give the student clues to the options for future political development open to Communist states, particularly those in East Europe.

The second aspect of the relationship between the leadership and the population, that of conflicting ideas, is equally important to an understanding of the political process in Communist states. Beginning with the Yugoslav " revisionists " of 1948 and continuing down through the Polish and Hungarian revolts and the Albanian rift to the " Prague Spring," there is ample evidence that these ideas are not uniform either across countries or within countries. In addition, as Solzhenitsyn's letter to the Soviet leadership so dramatically demonstrated, we cannot assume that every idea that conflicts with the prevailing Party line at a given moment is upholding a democratic-liberal position. Ideational conflict runs the political spectrum from the conservative orthodox right, which looks upon Stalinism with nostalgia, to traditional conservatives concerned with historic nationality and religious conflict, to those espousing Marxist humanism like Djilas, Kolakowski, or the proponents of " socialism with a human face " in Czechoslovakia.[41] The existence of such a broad diversity of opinion underscores the scope of the conflict between the Communist parties of the various countries, between Communists and non-Communists, and among the economic and social interests competing for their share of the national income. The whole complexity of the relationship between political culture, modernization, and Communism

39. Barbara Jancar, " Modernity and Dissent in Communist Systems," in C. Gati (ed.), *The Politics of Modernization in Eastern Europe* (New York: Praeger, 1974), pp. 338–357.

40. At a talk last spring to Union College students after a recent visit to China, Aspaturian located the main difference between the American and what he termed the Chinese model of industrialization, in that the former called for large-scale urbanization—bringing the countryside to the towns—while the latter sought to reverse the process by bringing the city to the countryside.

41. See Leszek Kolakowski, *Towards a Marxist Humanism: Essays on the Left Today*, translated by Jane Zielonko Peel (New York: Grove Press, 1968), or his later " The Fate of Marxism in Eastern Europe," *Slavic Review*, XXIX, 2 (June 1970), pp. 175–181. A thorough review of the ideas, aims, and tragedy of the Prague Spring is given in Ivan Svitak, *The Czechoslovak Experiment, 1968–1969* (New York: Columbia University Press, 1971).

in Eastern Europe can be discovered in the various multi-faceted domestic expressions of "revisionism."

The study of revisionist ideas acquires further significance as a source of future change in the Communist system. The reform movement in Eastern Europe has been an attempt not to return to "bourgeois democracy," but to find a "true" path to socialism and to define what socialism means in the context of the technological society. Yugoslavia, in its search for its own road to Communism, has certainly taken Marxism seriously, as did the Polish and Hungarian intellectuals of 1956. To analyze the "Prague Spring" solely in terms of nationalism and democracy is to mistake its direction and purpose: the development of a state whose values would not dehumanize man but would return him to the center of modern society.

Given the evident importance of the conflict of ideas in East European history in the past twenty years, it is un-understandable how the whole question of ideological rigidity and the revisionist response should have been overlooked by every one of the texts under review. How can the student obtain an insight into the undercurrents of post-Stalinist political development in Eastern Europe if the ideas that helped produce it are not systematically discussed? The failure of the texts in this respect, as in the case of interest-group activity, lies in their general tendency to see the East European states in the role of passive reactors to Soviet events, rather than as agents actively trying to assimilate the demands of Soviet power to their economic needs and political culture. The unhappy result is that, with the possible exception of Ionescu, none of the textbooks enables the student to grasp the nature of the increasingly interactional relationship between the East European political leaderships, the articulated socio-economic interests, and the populations-at-large.

In Search of a Theoretical Construct

If one judges from the present textbooks, there is need for new thinking on Eastern Europe to carry on where Brzezinski left off. The erosion of Stalinism forced a change of emphasis from the totalitarian paradigm to a search for a theory offering a better explanation of the present political reality. But so far there is no consensus as to the nature of this reality, on the part of either Soviet or East European specialists.

The search for a theoretical construct must still be predicated on an answer to the fundamental question of whether the Communist system is an entity unique unto itself or whether it can indeed be integrated into the broader field of comparative politics. The problems presented by the latter position are manifold, particularly in the realm of concept formation. There is some doubt whether the bureaucratic factions and Party divisions can or should be considered interest groups in the Western understanding of the term. Certainly, the organization and functioning of, say, the oil interests in the United States are of a much different nature from those of the Soviet Union. In the last analysis, it may be more of a hindrance than a help to talk of interest-group behavior or political participation in the Communist states. Nevertheless, however great the difficulties, research in these areas has been growing, as mentioned earlier. In addition, "Kremlinology" has provided Communist studies with their own tool with which to get a handle on "elite" behavior in Communist societies.

Communist model-building within the comparative politics framework is as problematical as concept formation. One possible model is, of course, the international system model, which Triska attempted. The difficulty with it is its tendency to focus on behavior between members of the system rather than on the domestic behavior of the individual member states. The identification of patterns of between-members behavior common to all international systems may obscure the specific characteristics of Communist interaction. In other words, use of an international system model might give us insight into the foreign affairs action-response patterns that the Communist states share with other countries, without telling us anything about the actual functioning of the Communist system per se.

The most widely accepted model and one which might lend itself readily to East European studies is that of political development. The main difficulty here is the meaning of the term, and whether it should be viewed as a dependent or an independent variable: the product or the cause of modernization.[42] If one considers political development to be a dependent variable, as a function of the level of economic development, time would seem to be a factor for Eastern Europe. Three of the states had already been industrialized before the Communist takeover. Parts of Yugoslavia were industrial, parts were not. Three countries were in the take-off stage. Yet every country exhibited a political structure based on the West European example. Were the Communist governments that followed more politically developed than their predecessors because of the progress of industrialization?

42. For a discussion of the meanings of political development as a dependent and independent variable, see Robert A. Packenham, "Political Development Research," in Michael Haas and Henry W. Kariel (eds.), *Approaches to the Study of Political Science* (Scranton, Pa.: Chandler Publishers, 1970), pp. 169–187.

If one considers political development to be a function of the legal-formal apparatus, such as the growth of the rule of law, here again there is a question of the advance of the Communist state upon the earlier political form. Other meanings of political development as an end product raise analogous questions when applied to the area: the rationalization of the administration, the promotion of a secularized social system, the emergence of a political culture enabling citizens to bear the responsibilities of a modern political process. Many of these definitions are circular. One wonders, for example, whether the rationalization of the administration should not in fact produce rather than be defined as political development. Furthermore, it is quite possible under these definitions to have an economically less developed state which is highly developed politically, and vice versa. What is lacking in the concept of political development as the dependent variable is the normative criteria of what a politically developed society should be, and how these criteria relate to the social and economic fabric.

Another way of looking at political development is as an independent or intervening variable that contributes to modernization. In the field of Communist studies, the seminal article using this concept is Samuel P. Huntington's "Political Development and Political Decay."[43] Huntington defines political development as "the institutionalization of political organizations and procedures." The definition frees the term from dependence on economic modernization while avoiding the problem of unidirection caused by viewing political development as an end product, by positing that institutions can decay as well as develop. His model of "reciprocal interaction" between the social and economic dimensions of industrialization and political development has been used by Brzezinski and others.[44]

Two problems are connected with this interpretation of political development, as I see it. The first is the danger of falling into the position that if political development does not keep pace with economic modernization, political decay necessarily sets in. There is a tendency on the part of Sovietologists to assume that the consequences of maintaining the present Soviet political system substantially as it is will be fatal to the economic development of the country. Change must occur, or else. The second problem is related to the first; it is the imprecision of the definition. Institutionalization, as Huntington

43. Huntington, "Political Development and Political Decay." See n. 14.

44. Brzezinski, *Dilemmas of Change*, pp. 30–34; see also Otto Ulć in Gati, *op. cit.*, where he argues that political decay was a major cause of the Prague Spring.

defines it, refers to "adaptability, complexity, autonomy and coherence of organizations and procedures." What it means, at any given time, to adapt is problematical. We only know that an organism has adapted if it survives, but the concept of adaptability requires criteria framed in terms of some norm identified as political maturity. Here such definitions as Harold Lasswell's "widespread participation in all preferred values,"[45] or Christian Bay's linking of psychological and social freedom as the end term of society,[46] may be at variance with the Soviet concept of Communism as "from each according to his ability, to each according to his needs."

What I am saying is that the use of the political development model whether as dependent or as independent variable runs aground on our own ignorance of what such development is, or whether it is indeed a meaningful concept, and hence runs the risk of being culture-bound, primarily associated with Western patterns of modernization. As an earlier agricultural era saw a variety of political forms at work in similar economic settings, so we cannot assume that modernization will bring all men to develop identical political institutions, or that the same mode of political development will characterize all countries seeking to modernize. The ideology and institutions rooted in the East European states must be an integral part of any model we choose to develop, in order to distinguish Communist developing states from non-Communist developing states. Otherwise the term "Communist" has little relevance.

The alternative to borrowing behavioralist theory and applying it to the Communist system is to concentrate on the formulation of generalizing hypotheses about the nature of the Communist system which permit cross-national empirical comparison with the eventual objective of developing an operational model of the Communist state. Robert Sharlet's six definitional characteristics of a Communist political system might be an appropriate starting point:

(1) A Communist political system is set within a "closed society," a society relatively inaccessible to the Western social scientist.
(2) A Communist system has no autonomous subsystems.

45. Harold Lasswell, "Toward a General Theory of Directed Value Accumulation and Institutional Development," in *Comparative Theories of Social Change* (Ann Arbor, Mich.: Foundation for Research on Human Behavior, 1966), pp. 12–58.

46. Christian Bay, *The Structure of Freedom* (New York: Atheneum, 1965). Bay observes that Lasswell, Easton, and others have left freedom off their list of fundamental societal values and argues a powerful case for the social primacy of maximum individual freedom in terms of the guarantee of basic human rights.

(3) The major political resources, that is, strategic political positions, are concentrated in the hands of a narrow elite stratum that enjoys hegemony over the policy-making process.
(4) The policy-making process is not directly observable or accessible to reliable methods of investigation.
(5) The structures, functions, and roles in a Communist system tend to be relatively undifferentiated.
(6) Boundaries between a Communist political system and social system tend to be weak or non-existent.[47]

I would add a seventh definition, " Communist political systems are not static but subject to change within certain parameters defined by ideology." I would stress the ideological dimension, as it is precisely Marxism-Leninism's theory of the relationship between political, economic, and social development which imparts legitimacy to the ruling elite and generates the tension between the ruling elite and the economic and social interests of a Communist society.[48] The Communist frame of reference claims that the " socialist " system supplants the capitalist system, as proletarian rule replaces bourgeois rule, because development is unidirectional and socialism is the historically determined advance over capitalism. As such, socialism is better able to satisfy the needs of society, whatever these may be identified to be. Communist rule is rooted in this claim of unique possession of the laws by which society can be led to its ultimate utopian end. Tension has arisen where Communist leaderships have been unable to support this claim, particularly in the economic field. It should be noted that the official Soviet Communist position does not view the Communist system as a model of modernization for developing countries, as may indeed be the case.[49] Rather, the Third World (in this view) is in a lower stage of development and has yet to reach a level where the transition to socialism can appropriately take place. The essence of the reform movement in Eastern Europe was not the abolition of

47. Sharlet, " Systematic Political Science and Communist Systems," in Fleron, *op. cit.*, p. 208.

48. Robert Putnam, in a recent article, censures American literature on ideology and politics for not contributing to an understanding of the practical and moral problems involved in different ways of thinking and acting politically. He observes that " as long as we consider those who conduct politics from the standpoint of a coherent, comprehensive set of beliefs to be psychopaths, we will be unable to objectively evaluate differing political styles." Robert Putnam, " Studying Elite Political Cultures: The Case of Ideology," *The American Political Science Review,* LXV, 3 (September 1971), p. 681.

49. See David E. Albright, " The Soviet Model: A Development Alternative for the Third World," in Morton and Tőkés, *op. cit.*, pp. 299–339.

socialism (this would have been a regressive step), but the transformation of the discredited Stalinist political model into a truly socialist state.

Of the two approaches suggested here—borrowing from behavioralist theory or generating a system-specific Communist model—my preference, as far as textbook writing on East Europe is concerned, is for the latter. Ionescu's text, in my opinion, is the most constructive of those under review because it attempts to define the elements of a Communist system, even though it lacks ideological perspective. The system-specific approach has several advantages over attempts to borrow from behavioralism. First, it avoids the problems of concept formation and theory-building, which run the risk of finding identities where in fact there may be none, or postulating a necessary political " decay " based on some poorly defined criteria of economic development. Second, the approach admits of truly cross-national comparative study both of an empirical and of a generalizing nature, while at the same time permitting the demonstration of institutional and cultural differences within a generic framework. Third, the system-specific model is capable of including modernization as a causal factor of change in Communist societies, but it is not tied to the necessity to prove any hypotheses relating political development to a particular variant of the Communist state, or demonstrating that the Soviet hegemonic structure must perforce change to meet the demands of a modern industrial society. Fourth, the model is capable of demonstrating comparisons between Communist and non-Communist states. As such, it views the Communist system as one among several " ideal types " of state in the contemporary world. Comparative aggregate data on elites, interest-group representation, or political participation can be presented to analyze the behavior of different population subsets within the Communist bloc, and to compare that with the behavior of analogous population subsets outside the bloc, thereby bringing out rather than suppressing differences between the two sets.

Fifth, a comparison of the variations of this model as institutionalized in Eastern Europe would give the student an appreciation of the specific problems presented by ideology when it deteriorates into dogma, as well as of the more general interrelationships between ideology and political structure. Finally, a text using the system-specific model would direct attention to the ability of Communism to provide solutions to the economic, social, and political problems confronting modern society as evidenced by the East European experience.

There are those who might argue that an eclectic approach is more suitable. Why not borrow from interest-group theory, organization theory, or political development theory, if these help to explain particular sets of data? In my opinion, eclecticism has its place in the continued pursuit of research. But even research must ultimately aim at theory construction, if the comparative Communist researcher wants to lay claim to being scientific. In the realm of textbook writing, the system-specific model would seem essential to a theoretical grasp of the nature of the states under study. Whether one accepts or rejects the development of such a model, it provides after all a fresh look at Eastern Europe which gets away from the older paradigms of totalitarianism or the U.S.S.R.-satellite approach, and it attempts to present a comparative framework within which the eight countries can be viewed as Communist states in their own right, not as appendages of the Soviet Union. It is clear that there are enough of the "appendage" accounts on the market. The real need is for the injection of new life into East European studies.

Comment by Vernon V. Aspaturian

Eastern Europe has long been the stepchild of comparative politics, and even of comparative Communist political systems. Among the number of reasons for this unfortunate state of affairs, two are the most important. First, the area is divided into several small or medium-sized states embracing an even larger number of small nationalities, each with its own distinctive language, history, and political culture. Mastering the necessary linguistic skills of a small nation is no less difficult and involved than mastering those of a nation with millions of speakers, but the professional and even intellectual yield is not sufficiently rewarding in proportion to the time and effort invested. Unless, as a young scholar, one already has a head start by being a native speaker of one or more Eastern European languages, there is understandable hesitation in investing one's professional future as an Albanian or Hungarian specialist, as compared with becoming a Soviet specialist. And the effort and investment involved in mastering the linguistic skills and country specialization of several East European nations, in order to go beyond being a mere country specialist to become an authentic East European regional/area specialist, would inordinately extend the period of professional training.

The second major reason for the underdevelopment of Eastern Europe as a distinct field of concentration has been the long shadow which the Soviet Union has cast westward to effectively blot out the separate visibility of the individual countries of the region. For many years, the area was homogenized into an amorphous conglomerate collectively referred to as "Eastern Europe." So long as the countries of Eastern Europe appeared to be mere inert appendages of the Soviet Union, they were intellectually unchallenging for scholars and uninteresting for undergraduates.

Ironically, just as scholarly and specialist interest in East European Communist political systems appears to have been enhanced, the general academic climate has not been conducive to the introduction and proliferation of courses on Eastern Europe. The lessening of the Cold War has had as one of its side-effects a diminished general interest in Soviet and Communist affairs, just at the moment when interest in Eastern Europe as a separate area of study was on the upswing. Hence, the anomaly of heightened scholarly interest combined with diminished—or, more appropriately, retarded—general interest for undergraduate students. It is no secret that institutions that have introduced separate courses on Eastern Europe are experiencing difficulty in attracting enrollment.

The state of scholarly research and publication on Eastern Europe reflects to a great extent this asymmetrical relationship between enhanced specialist interest and lessened general interest. This condition must be appreciated to evaluate properly the utility of scholarly books on Eastern Europe as textbooks in courses on Eastern Europe and related areas. It is especially incumbent upon the reviewer of these books to discriminate carefully between those books specifically designed as textbooks and those inspired by different purposes but nevertheless mustered in use as textbooks, rather than to proceed as if such distinctions were non-existent or immaterial.

Most of the books reviewed by Barbara Jancar were not designed specifically as textbooks, but are the products of conferences, symposia, or responses by individual authors to subjects or issues that challenged or interested them. It is, therefore, one thing to review books in terms of the author's original purpose and quite another to review them in terms of the uses to which they have been put. The reviewer must, to a certain extent, judge the books in terms of their original intent, which can be varied, rather than simply in terms of their common use. If books not written to be used as textbooks *are* used as such, the author can hardly be faulted for producing works that are deficient as undergraduate textbooks.

Furthermore, a review of books used as texts in terms of their usefulness in the classroom should be distinguished from the reviewer's notion of how the books should have been written or the classes taught. In my view, Jancar goes too far in attempting to impose both her methodological views concerning writers of books that may be used as textbooks and her pedagogical notions of how courses on Eastern European political systems should be taught. Readers may or may not share the reviewer's views on methodology and pedagogy. If they do not share the reviewer's preferences, the review is of little value to them.

Most of the books currently published on Eastern Europe are specialized works reflecting the varied research interests of the authors. Jancar's review, while deploring the usefulness of existing books as undergraduate textbooks, inadvertently reflects the same intellectual predisposition. Her emphasis on the need for more conceptualization and reconceptualization in undergraduate texts appears to reflect her personal scholarly interests rather than the pedagogical interests of undergraduates. Students in undergraduate courses are in need of "dreary facts" and routine descriptive information that may bore more advanced specialists. Already we have too many students (graduates and undergraduates) and professors continually conceptualizing and reconceptualizing in a vacuum. What the field needs in the textbook area is more data and information, not new theories and models, which can be better served at the graduate level.

There is, of course, always a certain amount of tension between pedagogically effective textbooks and material that intellectually challenges the specialist. This, in turn, results in books that may well make a contribution to knowledge without making a direct contribution to effective pedagogy. The intellectual interest and challenge perceived by the scholar, not textbook effectiveness, guides his or her research. Many scholars have conveniently forgotten that what may be intellectually challenging for them may bore the undergraduate who needs and can be challenged by basic information about institutions, processes, and behavior, rather than by speculative hypothesis, elaborate models, or innovative approaches that, of course, may sometimes reflect the instructor's own lack of basic information.

The comparative approach, in particular, must be designed very carefully for undergraduate students, lest the student be supplied with abstractions and schemata bereft of basic data and information to compare. Furthermore, at a time when general comparativists are re-examining the validity of their own " universal scientific " concepts, the exhortation to march in step with " contemporary social science " is a sign of cultural lag. " Scientific comparative politics " turns out to have been little more than generalizations and concepts based upon Western political institutions and processes, which were reduced to a shambles when applied to the underdeveloped countries and thus turned out to be simply " Western Area Studies " rather than universal comparative politics. To be sure, Eastern European specialists can learn a great deal from this experience, but the only lesson is not to emulate it or use these patterns as universal models and theories. Jancar, I detect, is ambivalent on this point, seeing both the benefits and the pitfalls of routinely co-opting models and theories of general comparative politics; but she appears not to appreciate the basis of her own ambivalence. It would have been useful if she had further clarified the reasons for her ambivalence.

Finally, while it would be great to have writers produce genuinely comparative works on Eastern Europe and while the task would certainly be simpler if there was a single grand paradigm, in my view no scholar at the moment has the necessary methodological and linguistic skills for such a monumental task, and not enough basic research has been done on individual countries to enable a great synthesizer to do the job. That is why most books in this area tend to be a symposium, or generalized descriptive treatments by a single author. The Eastern European picture is much too rich and complex now in terms of its varied evolution to allow the type of " tour de force " exemplified in Brzezinski's *The Soviet Bloc*. There are too many scholars who know a great deal about individual countries, and not enough who know a great deal about all of the countries simultaneously. So symposia, individual-country treatments, and inadequate general descriptive books are apt to be the rule for some time to come.

Hence, for the foreseeable future, we will continue to have three kinds of works in this area:

a. Functional comparative treatments in great breadth and depth, but restricted to isolated issues or institutions common to all Eastern European states—i.e., books dealing with " modernization," " nationality problems," " party organizations," "socialization," "participation," etc. These will be both multi-authored symposia and single-authored works.

b. General descriptive works, attempting to cover all themes in all countries, characterized by greater breadth but little depth.

c. Individual country treatments, which will cover the country in great depth in all its dimensions, but will have little comparative value taken alone.

Books in each category should be judged in terms of how well they perform in each dimension rather than establishing artificial and unrealistic criteria that cannot be met for many years to come.

Of course, poor books will continue to be written, whether for undergraduate or for specialist consumption; but a "poor" book should not be confused with one that *appears* deficient when put to uses not intended.

JOSEPH LAPALOMBARA

Monoliths or Plural Systems: Through Conceptual Lenses Darkly *

Introduction

My rashness in offering some observations on the papers and commentaries that precede this essay is impelled by two considerations. First, I have recently published a volume [1] that tries to overcome the tendency of Western " comparativists " to treat Communist systems as historical and developmental aberrations. That effort required an examination of the work of many scholars, some of whom are reviewed by the area experts whose evaluations appear in this issue. Second, I claim some mild qualification to assess the endeavors of recent years to bring Soviet, Chinese, and East European studies closer to the mainstream of comparative politics where I have tried to find intellectual footing.

These endeavors, on the whole quite salutary, represent a mixed blessing, as well as serious intellectual pitfalls. On the *salutary* side the conceptual and geographic outreach cuts against two shortcomings of area studies. Narrowly focused, area-centered scholarship by and large does not enrich the broader concerns of comparative politics. Nor does it often offer understanding and explanation that are better

* Leon Lipson and Rudolf L. Tőkés kindly offered me opportunities to improve and correct this manuscript. Its imperfections remain my personal responsibility.

1. Joseph LaPalombara, *Politics Within Nations* (Englewood Cliffs, N.J.: Prentice-Hall, 1974).

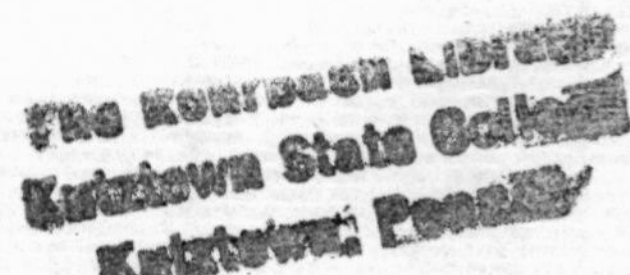

than the historian's tendency to discover what is unique in time and space.

Where area studies involve Communist systems, the outreach seems overwhelmingly necessary. It no longer surprises us that such studies are often marred by rigid ideological preconceptions, by an unfortunate tendency of scholarship to reflect popular moods and official postures in Western capitals, or by an American tendency to relate and react to Communist nations in a paranoid way.[2]

In a judicious appraisal of these problems, Alexander Dallin underscores the various sources of blunders committed by some of those who write about Soviet (and we may infer other Communist systems') political institutions, leadership, and behavior. Beyond the lack of information and the " disinformation " that area experts must wrestle with, Dallin notes that ". . . there remains the troubling circumstance that one finds an empirically observable congruence between the political temper of the times and the general thrust of dominant interpretations by specialists of the U.S.S.R." Although Dallin appropriately warns that a greater concern with methodology, with broader " models " and conceptual schemes, is no certain protection against such biases, we are safe in inferring that the outreach should at least raise the level of consciousness about such problems.[3]

But the *pitfalls* are there too. One of them has been underscored by several of the authors in this issue. The concepts, approaches, and so-called contemporary theories of comparative politics may be inappropriate when applied to Communist systems, particularly those in Asia that do indeed manifest radically different cultures, systems of values, ideologies, and even epistemologies. A second danger is that those who do comparative politics, and particularly those who use high-flown structure-functional and related *descriptive* (masquerading as analytical!) schemes, may be lulled into believing that meaningful generalizations hold for a very wide variety of highly dissimilar political systems.[4] In our understandable search for a unified theory

2. See David B. Davis (ed.), *The Fear of Conspiracy* (Ithaca, N.Y.: Cornell University Press, 1971).

3. Alexander Dallin, " Biases and Blunders in American Studies on the U.S.S.R.," *Slavic Review,* Vol. 32, No. 3 (September 1973), pp. 560–576. The quoted passage is at p. 565. In brief compass Dallin seems to me to provide an excellent roll-call of what it is about the systems observed, the observers themselves, and the methods they use that has led to highly questionable (and, alas, not often challenged) scholarly " findings."

4. In the symposium on the use of broader schemes published in *Studies in Comparative Communism,* Vol. 4, No. 2 (April 1971), pp. 30–70, Jan Triska rightly notes that the format provided by Gabriel Almond and G. Bingham Powell is useful as a way of gathering and ordering data about political

of political systems and processes, the tendency to deal with intractable dissimilarities by lumping them into a residual category is often overwhelming. Alternatively, we speak of functions, characteristics, or processes of government or politics at such a cosmic, all-embracing level of abstraction that much is described, almost nothing is explained, and what is explained is trivial or self-evident. This habit persists even as we experience some malaise about its logic or its scientific wisdom.[5]

systems. However, such schemes (see p. 32) may not have much analytical, as opposed to descriptive, power. And, as contributors like L. K. D. Kristof, P. A. Toma, and O. Ulc note, the schemes may be entirely too self-assured; they may claim more knowledge of Communist systems than we actually have; they may ignore critical variables (like national dependency on foreign countries); and they may therefore lead to sweeping, unwarranted, and inaccurate generalizations. See *ibid.,* pp. 36, 38, 41, 44, 57 *passim.*

G. A. Almond, " Toward a Comparative Politics of Eastern Europe," *ibid.,* pp. 71–78, seems to me to concede some of what the area experts assert and to recall that his scheme is " pre-theoretic." He is entirely correct in underscoring that schemes necessarily encounter difficulties and require modification in the light of countervailing facts. I am not reassured or persuaded, however, by his assertion (p. 71) that in scientific journeys a " poor map . . . [is better than] no map at all." Unless we have fairly good knowledge of what the map is, on what basic assumptions or considerations it is constructed, where it is supposed to lead, how we will presumably get there, and how we can tell when we have strayed or are lost, indeed, whether what we have (poor or otherwise) is a map at all (as opposed to an inventory check-list), we can wander endlessly in an intellectual wilderness.

Charles A. Powell, " Structure-Functionalism and the Study of Comparative Communist Systems," *Studies in Comparative Communism,* Vol. 4, Nos. 3 & 4 (July/October 1971), pp. 58–67, provides a biting, not always fair, often intemperate, but nevertheless important critique of the use of functional schemes like Almond's. I like in particular his warning that " it would be ironic if a substantive specialty were to accept a body of scientific belief just at the point that it became discredited in its original context " (p. 59). As for " maps," Powell is telling in his assertion that it is essential to discover what is the logical core of the map, or the categories, or whether the core itself meets simple canons of logic (p. 62). I would go further to insist that it is essential to explore the difference between *descriptive* and *analytical* categories, irrespective of how logical or free from culture-bias a particular scheme may be. Cf. R. E. Douse's review of Almond's collected essays in *American Political Science Review,* Vol. 65, No. 2 (June 1971), pp. 529–531, from which Powell quotes extensively.

5. This is merely a special case of a problem that deeply characterizes Western, but particularly American, social science. Anglo-American positivism, a massive misunderstanding of Max Weber, normative orientations built into dominant theories and methods of the social sciences, and (until recently) widespread self-congratulation about how well we were doing in social scientific development add up to a formidable obstacle to our efforts to create an intellectually viable *comparative* political science. I have touched on only a few aspects of this problem in the following places: *Politics Within Nations,*

Consensus and Dissensus

It is instructive that Alex Dallin mildly chides Erik Hoffmann for finding more agreement among writers of textbooks on the Soviet Union than is actually the case. This is also my reading. My certain knowledge is that several of these textbook authors—however much they may value or appreciate each other's scholarship—would prefer not to be portrayed on an undifferentiated intellectual canvas. Some of them, in writing about the Soviet Union, have pursued the *plus ça change* . . . theme to almost embarrassing extremes; some have taken to depicting Soviet politics as an inevitable extension of the Kafkaesque bureaucratic world that has come to characterize industrial societies wherever they are found; others have found in the slippery concept of " pluralism " a perhaps inevitable antidote for a somewhat poisoned view of the U.S.S.R. generated in the years of the Cold War; a few remain essentially unreconstructed Cold Warriors. These are important nuances, and they are evident in the textbooks reviewed.

Inevitably, as Hoffmann claims, writers of textbooks on the U.S.S.R. must rely on similar and not profusely available source materials.[6] Inevitably, too, the lack of attention to the 1970s reflects

Ch. 1 and pp. 58–66; " Political Science and the Engineering of National Development," in M. Palmer and L. Stern (eds.), *Political Development in Changing Societies* (Lexington, Mass.: Heath, 1972), pp. 27–65; " Parsimony and Empiricism in Comparative Politics: An Anti-Scholastic View," in R. Holt and J. Turner (eds.), *Methodology of Comparative Research* (New York: Wiley, 1970), pp. 123–150; " The Comparative Role of Groups in Political Systems," *SSRC Items,* Vol. 15 (June 1961), pp. 18–21; " The Utility and Limitations of Interest Group Theory in Non-American Field Situations," *Journal of Politics,* Vol. 22, No. 1 (February 1960), pp. 29–49.

Many political scientists, in the pursuit of greater semantic and conceptual precision, have succumbed to the temptation of selective and uncritical borrowing from sociology. However, as two perceptive critics of *that* discipline have pointed out, sociology too has had its share of conceptual difficulties of which political scientists should take notice before (or instead of) raiding that discipline for new conceptual tools. See A. Gouldner, *The Coming Crisis of Western Sociology* (New York: Basic Books, 1970); and C. Wright Mills, *The Sociological Imagination* (New York: Oxford University Press, 1969).

It seems to me a necessary precaution that area specialists venturing into the broader field of comparative politics give careful attention to the growing malaise, particularly among many younger scholars, regarding the conceptual, theoretical, methodological, and normative deficiencies of the discipline of political science as a whole.

6. Helen Desfosses Cohn, " Comparative Communism and Comparative Studies: A Note on Shared Concerns," *Newsletter on Comparative Studies of Communism,* VI, 4 (August 1973), pp. 3–5, is somewhat leery about arguments that turn on the lack of data about Communist countries. She cites Chalmers Johnson, " The Role of Social Science in China Scholarship," *World Politics,* XII, 2 (January 1965), pp. 256–272, for the stricture that it

the dearth of scholarly materials on Brezhnev's U.S.S.R. Additionally, it was predictable that sooner or later the overstated, emotional, ideologically dictated, and empirically (as well as theoretically) questionable model of " totalitarianism " would have to give way to many of the modifications and guarded restatements that now abound.

But it is precisely in the particular emphases that the textbook writers select, and in the particular aspects of polity and government that form the central focus of these textbooks, that the more or less subtle distinctions Dallin refers to emerge. It is one thing to acknowledge that an earlier " totalitarian " model of the Soviet system is now universally attenuated. It is quite something else to focus on descriptions of the policy process; to delineate what role is assigned to the Party, the bureaucracy, the army, or industrial managers; or to engage in sweeping generalizations about the persistent impact of Russian history or culture on the behavior of Soviet elites, masses, or political institutions.

Hoffmann correctly notes that the newer techniques of the social sciences are largely absent from the books he reviews, a lack that Vernon Aspaturian underscores for East European textbooks as well.[7]

is never too early to develop theoretical constructs. Although this view is instinctively appealing, one must nevertheless note at least the following caveats: (1) Theoretical constructs (of which we already have too many) cast at the highest level of abstraction are almost always immune to the threat of discomfirmation or demonstrated invalidity, no matter how many data may be available; (2) the relative lack of data on Communist systems makes highly problematical the discomfirmation of generalizations about Communist systems, irrespective of the level of generality on which such statements are focused; (3) it is an arresting fact that in the social sciences, and particularly among political scientists, *generalizations are most often made regarding political systems for which, relatively speaking, we have the least amount of verifiable information.*

7. It is worth remarking that the outreach of Communist systems specialists does involve some notable efforts to improve our data supply and to proceed with data gathering on the basis of the somewhat more rigorous methods of contemporary social science. Evidence of this is found, for example, in the important symposium volume edited by Roger E. Kanet, *The Behavioral Revolution and Communist Studies* (New York: Free Press, 1971). Kanet, in his introduction, recites the problems of gathering reliable, quantifiable data. Paul Shoup (pp. 15–47) shows how problems of data *and* of conceptual schemes still leave the foundations for the comparative study of Communist systems insecure. But he also shows a growing amount of data on Communist elites. The volume contains interesting efforts at innovative data analysis by Milton Lodge (pp. 79–101), Michael Gehlen and Michael McBride (pp. 103–124), and Carl Beck, G. A. Johnson, and J. T. McKechnie (pp. 187–203). There are also quite interesting conceptual articles by Rita Mae Kelly, Frederic Fleron, Jr., Erik Hoffmann, and Robert Sharlet.

Several of the authors reviewed in the present issue of *Studies in Comparative*

But as I read Alfred Meyer or John Reshetar, John Hazard or David Lane, and others, I have no difficulty at all in detecting that the persistent differences in conception and analytic approach which characterize political science as a whole are also present among these authors. It would be remarkable and astonishing if it were otherwise.

The Unique and the Universal

Barbara Jancar asks whether Communist systems are unique.[8] An immediate answer, and one she is aware of, is "yes," or "no," or

Communism are involved in these innovations. Steven Goldstein correctly numbers Lucian Pye, John Bryan Starr, and James Townsend among these. Townsend's textbook is in part an application of his interesting monograph, *Political Participation in Communist China* (Berkeley and Los Angeles: University of California Press, 1968). The China field, indeed, now counts a number of younger scholars (Steven Goldstein, Michel Oksenberg, Kenneth Lieberthal, Edwin Winckler, Harry Harding, Thomas Bernstein, and Steven Levine, to name but a few) who seem to me to be revolutionizing the study of Chinese politics and establishing it on a firm empirical and (it is hoped) theoretical basis. In any event, Steven Goldstein's excellent paper in this issue provides a solid description and evaluation of these developments.

This does not detract from Hoffmann's lament about the textbooks. The lament is even more justified in the case of books on Eastern Europe, for, as Aspaturian shows, these are largely *not* written as textbooks and one would therefore expect to find more methodological and conceptual innovation there. The prospects for this seem to me to be less discouraging than Aspaturian suggests. Comparative political science, for any area, will necessarily be the product of broad scholarly collaboration and not the work of a single scholar of Eastern Europe.

8. Readers of this journal will recall that opinions remain somewhat mixed on this issue. Basically the question would be whether countries with ruling Communist parties represent a sufficiently coherent subset to warrant the development of something like "comparative Communist studies." An extremely illuminating, if not definitive, treatment of the matter is John Kautsky, "Comparative Communism Versus Comparative Politics," *Studies in Comparative Communism*, VI, 1 & 2 (Spring/Summer 1973), pp. 135–170. Kautsky's essay is something of a *tour de force*. He has extremely perceptive things to say about what is or is not distinctive about Communist systems, but the essay seems to me to contain two major flaws. First, it is surely not a fair criticism of studies in comparative Communism to say that they "fall short of producing theory" (p. 170). This is true of political science writing pretty much across the board. Second, Kautsky has adduced no reason for the assertion (p. 170) that we will learn more if we compare Communist systems with non-Communist systems. That depends on *what* is being compared and for what reasons.

Robert C. Tucker, "On the Comparative Study of Communism," *World Politics,* Vol. XIX, 2 (January 1967), pp. 242–257, also argues that stress on the uniqueness of Communist systems impeded their being compared with other systems. This is only partly true, in the sense of inhibiting comparisons by Communist system specialists.

"it depends." It depends on such diverse considerations as level of generality; dimensions along which description or analysis is to proceed; whether one wishes to "control" for similarities or differences in comparative analysis; how "clean" the subject or typology *must* be to disconfirm some theory. In short, it depends on what those who might worry about this question really have in mind.

This simple but often finessed observation relates to a major shortcoming of the structural-functional mode of analyzing and comparing political systems and processes. All political systems involve both conflict and cooperation; all of them have leaders and followers; all of them manifest a variety of interests in a state of tension and competition; all of them have formal institutions that are remarkably similar and produce policies and behaviors that are equally remarkable in their similarities. All such systems, too, *must* have input and output characteristics (i.e., functions), and the relationship between inputs and outputs is widely acknowledged to involve processes located in the "black box" of government.

Little is known, however, about the relationship between and among "functions." Even less is known, for any country, about the "black box" itself. So much has the latter been ignored by political scientists, and for so long, that instantaneous academic stardom can be reached by persons who discover that public policies (foreign or domestic) do not spring full-blown and Jovelike from the brows of dictators, presidents, secretaries of state, or even a handful of party oligarchs. We are now treated to a growing avalanche of writing depicting a variety of "bureaucratic models" of policymaking, most of them adding up to the rediscovery of what an earlier generation of political scientists, however hobbled by legalism and formalism, learned in knee-pants. It is no wonder that, as attention is focused on bureaucratic structures (in party, industrial organization, civil or military administrative units), the temptation is strong to apply "interest-group theory" or "conflict theory" or "mutual adjustment theory" or "incremental satisficing theory" to political and governmental processes.

Scholars who are now dedicated to showing that Communist systems are *not* unique seem to me to partake of one or more of the following characteristics or impulses.

1. They are reacting (and sometimes overreacting) to the oversimplifications of the "totalitarian model" and to a Western ideological and propagandistic view of Communist systems which some of them no doubt helped to propagate.

2. They are increasingly aware not merely of how *different* along many dimensions Communist systems are when compared with each

other, but also of how *similar* they are to other systems not found in the Communist subset.

3. They have been exposed to, have perhaps helped to create, and, in any case, have accepted (however tentatively) some grand scheme (e.g., structural-functionalism, stages of development, politics as conflict-management by elites) for classifying and comparing polities, which makes it seem silly, illogical, even perverse to insist on a subset of systems labelled "Communist."

4. They assume that comparative political science will be hobbled in its theoretical development if typologies are created, or subsets of polities are identified, for which the labels or identifying tags used are purely nominal, on the one hand, or not empirically verifiable as distinguishing Communist from non-Communist systems, on the other.[9]

I find the question of uniqueness ill-put and essentially unnecessary; it also tends to perpetuate or to create more polemical heat than conceptual or theoretical light. For some purposes, it may be better to place the U.S.S.R. and, say, Czechoslovakia among Western industrial nations; for others, such a placement might make little sense. If one is thinking of one-party, or one-party-dominant polities, all Communist polities would be placed there and (by comparison with all other systems) might well constitute a coherent subset. Presumably Communist systems do have a fairly common (*almost* unique!) association with particular political philosophers and their ideas; they share basic views about the nature of property and the mode of production, social class, mobility, and inequality; they have essentially common commitments to centralized planning and command economies; they take a highly elitist and instrumental posture toward modes of mass political participation; they have an essential common orientation to political opposition, to certain individually centered rights and freedoms; and so on.[10]

9. Kautsky, "Comparative Communism," well represents the last three of these characteristics, and his article is a relentless effort to show that Communist systems are indeed dissimilar and that the most useful dimension along which to place all political systems is developmental. Thus, he prefers the "mobilization" and "post-mobilization" categories as heuristically more attractive in comparative analysis. See, also, John H. Kautsky, *Communism and the Politics of Development* (New York: Wiley, 1968); and his introductory essay in J. H. Kautsky (ed.), *Political Change in Underdeveloped Countries: Nationalism and Communism* (New York: Wiley, 1962), pp. 3–119.

10. Robert S. Sharlet, "Systematic Political Science and Communist Systems," in F. J. Fleron, Jr. (ed.), *Communist Study and the Social Sciences* (Chicago: Rand McNally, 1969), pp. 207–212, tries his hand at providing a set of defining characteristics of Communist political systems. Sharlet has

It is in no way fatal to such clustering or grouping of Communist nations to show that they are not *exactly* alike regarding these and other characteristics, that they are extremely dissimilar regarding some others, or that, in some characteristics, any single Communist nation may have more in common with non-Communist nations than it does with another Communist state. To demand that allegation of " uniqueness " of Communist systems be based on taxonomic purity would by implication quickly demolish any effort to constitute a subset of political systems. We must not react to simplistic claims of uniqueness by equally simplistic demonstrations that in many ways the systems involved are not unique at all.

Jancar rightly implies that similarities between Communist and other systems must not obscure important differences. While she worries about the lack of analysis that consciously compares East European countries with each other, as well as with countries outside the area, she also alerts us to the dangers of placing East European systems somewhere inside the " political development " model. If Marxism is not the best model for understanding change in such societies, she says one might perhaps better turn to " conflict " or " bureaucratic " models that center on the role of elites. I would add to this the caveat that, for political scientists at least, generalizations, propositions, and hypotheses should refer to specific political institutions and processes and should be susceptible to disconfirmation if we succeed in obtaining the relevant information. Far from being pretheoretic or atheoretical, such a focus on " partial systems," on specific political institutions and processes, seems to me to be the only way we will induce an empirically grounded comparative political science.[11]

been criticized (unfairly in my view) for not having come up with indicators that *do* make such systems unique in the strict sense. Barbara Jancar adds to Sharlet's list an intriguing seventh characteristic: namely, that such systems are not static (as simplistic believers in the totalitarian model might have argued) but that change occurs in these systems within limits set by ideology. It would be intriguing to have her spell this out.

11. It is of course regrettable that the funding of research on certain geographic areas should diminish just as enthusiasm for more venturesome comparative analysis reaches a peak. Funding agencies, in government and the foundation world, both set and follow academic fads. But this rarely includes a commitment to encouraging a vigorous comparative political science, as opposed to furthering academic attention to possible trouble spots in international affairs. In any event, a shrinkage of research funds would tend to delay even longer Jancar's call for the *comparative* treatment of Eastern Europe as a separate area, and the analysis of nations there free from the long shadow cast by the U.S.S.R. In this regard, it is essential to underscore the importance

Grand Theories, Institutional Processes, Other Foci

It is instructive, I believe, that so few of the textbooks on the Soviet Union or Eastern Europe are self-consciously theoretical or represent even modest efforts at theoretical innovation. The second generation of Soviet textbook writers, as Hoffmann notes, has produced no one of Merle Fainsod's or Barrington Moore's theoretical venturesomeness. Zbigniew Brzezinski and Samuel Huntington, as well as Meyer, have excellent control of middle-range theory and put it to strikingly effective use in their respective texts. No one, perhaps, has been more assiduous, and appropriately cautious, than Frederick Barghoorn in applying to the Soviet Union a number of concepts and descriptive categories deriving from recent developments in the field of comparative politics.[12] On the whole, however, Soviet and East European textbooks do not advance our theoretical understanding very far. Moreover, they are obviously time-lagged in the sense of not reflecting some of the methodologically and conceptually richer work on these political systems which has emerged in recent years. It would be a happier situation if basic teaching materials could tap these research findings more expeditiously.[13]

What about China? In one sense, Steven Goldstein's assessment is premature. What he wants from textbook authors could scarcely have emerged in an era when both U.S. and Chinese policies made close-range inspection of Chinese political institutions an unlikely intellectual enterprise. Establishing the linkage between institutional structures

of the efforts of Gordon Skilling and Ghita Ionescu in the books reviewed. Some of my reservations regarding these books will be found in my *Politics Within Nations,* pp. 335–350.

12. The word "ambivalent" may be more accurate in Barghoorn's case. See, for example, his "Analytic Framework: Soviet Politics in Comparative and Historical Perspective," *Studies in Comparative Communism,* Vol. 4, Nos. 3 & 4 (July/October 1971), pp. 42–57. Cf. F. Barghoorn, *Politics in the U.S.S.R.,* 2nd ed. (Boston: Little, Brown, 1972), pp. 57, 206 et seq.

13. See the essays designated in Kanet, *The Behavioral Revolution.* Cf. Rudolf L. Tőkés, "East European Studies in the United States: The State of the Arts and Future Research Strategies," *East European Quarterly,* VIII, 3 (September 1974), 337–352. Tőkés appropriately cites recent works by Joseph Fiszman, *Revolution and Tradition in People's Poland: Education and Socialization* (Princeton, N. J.: Princeton University Press, 1972); Peter C. Ludz, *The Changing Party Elite in East Germany* (Cambridge, Mass.: MIT Press, 1972); Kenneth Jowitt, *Revolutionary Breakthrough and National Development: The case of Romania, 1944–1965* (Berkeley and Los Angeles: University of California Press, 1971), and others as examples of an intellectually exciting development in the field of East European studies. Tőkés also provides an interesting roll-call of research endeavors that can and must be pursued in the years ahead.

and public policies, or between men at the top and the dynamics of institutions, is a tall enough research order in open societies. Even in the latter, access to data is problematical; the bureaucrat's penchant for secrecy is a universal phenomenon, underscored early on by Max Weber, and more recently attested to by Michel Crozier in France and "Nader's Raiders" in the United States.[14]

We can certainly agree with Thomas Bernstein that in China, too, policies emerge from a complex interaction between bureaucratic structures and the interests—inside and outside the bureaucracy—that impinge on decisions day-by-day. We can add, with Stanley Hoffmann, that there exist "high" and "low" policies in all political systems and that the former not only are more important and more "visible" but also bring into play the highest-level elites on the political (as opposed to the bureaucratic) side. The crying need in comparative political science is to illuminate exactly this sector (i.e., the "black box"), which a generation of political scientists, in concentrating their attention on "inputs" and "outputs," has left to intuition, speculation, or just plain guesswork. Where China is concerned, Bernstein is right to remind us about data availability as a necessary condition for the research attention and achievement that Goldstein sets as a high-priority goal.

Given the impediments to careful field work, it is little wonder that students of China followed in the footsteps of Kremlinologists who preceded them, or that others have used sweeping historical or psycho-cultural generalizations to "explain" what has happened there since 1949. It is inherent in historical explanatory generalizations, or in broad, long-distance psycho-cultural propositions, that they cannot be falsified, except by counter- (and often polemical) generalizations. Personality theory in particular is a murky, unstable basis for rigorous analysis when it applies to a nation's top elite. When applied to masses of Chinese, Russians, Poles, or what-have-you, it is often the older notion of national character masquerading under newer psychological labels. Personality theory or psycho-cultural explanation is not a better analytical tool when either represents labels pasted on old bottles. At best, historical and psycho-

14. See Michel Crozier, *The Bureaucratic Phenomenon* (Chicago: University of Chicago Press, 1964). Crozier's provocative depiction of French bureaucrats has been questioned, extended, and refined in the excellent and prodigious study by Ezra N. Suleiman, *Politics, Power and Bureaucracy in France* (Princeton: Princeton University Press, 1974). Both books involve access to persons and data that must surely be the envy of scholars who are interested in looking empirically and systematically at bureaucratic elites and institutions of Communist countries.

cultural discussions form an interesting backdrop against which some of the more proximate ideas regarding the interaction among leaders, institutions, and processes can be tested. And this would bring us back to exactly the kind of research focus which Goldstein wants and which Bernstein rightly tells us is extremely hard to come by. Nevertheless, it is quite apparent and remarkable that the younger generation of China scholars is now producing increasingly sophisticated and illuminating monographic work, superior, on the whole, to work on the Soviet Union produced by a comparable age cohort.

This leads me to differ somewhat with Goldstein in his enthusiastic evaluation of James Townsend's *Politics in China.* Unlike Barghoorn on the Soviet Union or Henry Erhmann on France,[15] my impression is that Townsend is something of a prisoner of the classification scheme devised by Gabriel Almond and Bingham Powell. It could hardly be otherwise where a country like China is concerned. The Almond-Powell scheme is at such a high level of abstraction that only knowledge in depth about *particular* institutions and processes permits one to show how inadequate may be their generalizations for a *particular* political system. Notwithstanding this, Townsend is concerned to " test " whether Mao's China does or does not conform to that category of political systems that Almond and Powell denominate " radical totalitarian." Even so, Townsend is uncomfortable (as well he might be) in discovering that " development " and " modernization " are simply not so neatly tied to structural differentiation and secularization as the Almond-Powell formulation suggests. Indeed, we will no doubt eventually discover that development, when it means economic modernity, can proceed rather well without any of the requisites suggested by highly abstract structural-functional schemes. We will perhaps finally understand as well that the so-called requisites of secularization, subsystem autonomy, and the like may have to do with the political freedoms associated with some pluralistic democracies, but with little else. Over and over again Townsend adduces enough information about China to lead the reader to wonder if his attempt to assess whether China fits the Almond typology of political systems was really worth the effort.

Townsend's book seems to me to depict the tension that occurs when a political system like China's is assessed against a " developmental " or "structural-functional-requisite " framework that not only emerges from a Western democratic " model," but also contains pro-

15. Barghoorn, *Politics in the U.S.S.R.,* and Henry Ehrmann, *Politics in France,* 2nd ed. (1971), are, like the Townsend volume, in the Little, Brown comparative politics series of country studies.

found (and sometimes hidden) *normative* orientations. Nothing in nature, or in inexorable processes of " development," decrees that the so-called functions of interest articulation and interest aggregation (whatever the latter is) should or can be neatly separated; nothing in the history of politics tells us that policy and administration ever have been effectively separated by something called structural differentiation; never in history—not even in the heyday of absolute monarchies or the so-called totalitarianisms of Hitler or Stalin—were public policies made except on the basis of complicated, often Byzantine conflicts among administrative and bureaucratic elites.

The critical consideration regarding China, the U.S.S.R., and other Communist systems may well be that raised by Samuel Huntington: namely, whether the Party and its apparat have become so " established " or institutionalized that political allocations take place within the Party framework, or within a context in which the single Party exercises hegemony. The striking thing about *some* Communist one-party systems is that they are successful in this regard; given this, there is every reason to call these systems " developed " and to predict that they will be able to " modernize " at least as well as countries that have competitive party systems, grant a variety of political freedoms, permit a certain amount of autonomous interest-group organization and activity, and so on.[16] Why should we be surprised that Chinese leaders can make rational decisions, solve monumental problems, and achieve remarkable goals of economic development even if certain " functional " or " structural " requisites of " political modernity " are not present in China?

Totalitarian, Bureaucratic, Mobilization Politics

It is now well understood that unhappiness with the " totalitarian model " led many students of Communist systems in search of better models. Scholars like Alex Inkeles, Alfred Meyer, and Robert Tucker led the way, but the discovery that Communist systems could change and that the systems themselves were notably quite diverse in some respects triggered what turned out to be an extensive reexamination of concepts and approaches.[17] Evidence that the debate is far from

16. See S. P. Huntington, " Social and Institutional Dynamics of One Party Systems," in S. P. Huntington and C. H. Moore (eds.), *Authoritarian Politics in Modern Society* (New York: Basic Books, 1970), pp. 3–47.

17. The first collection of articles on this topic appears in Fleron, *Communist Study*.

settled is found in more recent publications,[18] in the essays and commentaries that precede mine in this journal, and in very recent literature that has not yet been anthologized.[19]

Some scholars preferred to reconceptualize what Communist systems were " really " all about; others engaged in efforts to redress the totalitarian model to fit more recent developments; still others ventured into the broader area of comparative politics to see what might be available there that seemed promising. Scholars working on Communist countries began to try on for size such seemingly diverse conceptual garb as " constant conflict," " stages of development," " modernizing oligarchies," " movement regimes," " one-party systems," " mobilization systems," and so on. Others went the route of historical parallels looking for periods in the past with which later Soviet developments might be fruitfully compared. We even began to read about some Communist systems as " participatory " and " pluralistic," and I will return to these latter labels in the next section.

The concept of " mobilization regime " (or " system ") has attracted so much attention and seems to me to be fraught with so many difficulties that it is worth a few paragraphs of attention. John Kautsky, for example, is very much taken with David Apter's formulation of a " mobilization system." Although Kautsky considers the symposium edited by Chalmers Johnson [20] a " milestone " in Communist studies, he laments that the authors did not seize the opportunity to treat Communist countries as mobilization systems. Moreover, he voices objection to Johnson's suggestion that mobilization systems might also be totalitarian.[21]

James Townsend and Harold Hinton also seem to prefer the " mobilization model " as appropriate for China. Hinton stresses that the developmental objectives of the Chinese elite require that people be mobilized in supportive participation. Townsend seems to say that whereas a mobilization system is similar to a totalitarian one,

18. See L. J. Cohen and J. P. Shapiro (eds.), *Communist Systems in Comparative Perspective* (Garden City, N.Y.: Doubleday/Anchor, 1974).

19. In a recent article, Robert C. Tucker seems to be adopting a " naturalistic cultural " approach to the comparative study of national Communist systems that was advocated two years earlier by Alfred Meyer. See R. C. Tucker, " Communist Revolutions, National Cultures and the Divided Nations," *Studies in Comparative Communism,* VII, 3 (Autumn 1974), pp. 235–245; and Alfred G. Meyer, " Communist Revolutions and Cultural Change," *Studies in Comparative Communism,* V, 4 (Winter 1972), pp. 345–370.

20. Chalmers Johnson (ed.), *Change in Communist Systems* (Stanford: Stanford University Press, 1970).

21. Kautsky, " Comparative Communism," pp. 142–144.

the role of the Party differs in the former and such a system is more " fluid " and less " bureaucratic."[22]

There is clearly confusion as to what may be the referent for the concept " mobilization system," and not all of it results from Apter's formulation. Nevertheless, it is noteworthy that Apter sometimes defines the concept in terms of broad systemic characteristics, sometimes in other terms.[23] At the systemic level, the mobilization system would evince such broad characteristics as hierarchical authority, sacrosanct goals of the state, a confounding of instrumental and consummatory values, emphasis on thrift and the postponement of personal gratifications, and a future orientation on the part of society's leaders.

Apter also refers to mobilization as an " atmosphere . . . of crisis and attack." In such an atmosphere, privacy, individual or other particularistic values and preferences, even passivity are not tolerated, and all of social life is politicized. Apter goes on to specify several structural characteristics that are in the political sphere. These would include a mass elite " party of solidarity," replete with controlled auxiliary organizations, which monopolizes power; charismatic leadership for a while; a state bureaucracy controlled and instrumentally used by the Party; a Party network that is the core structure as well as the prime mobility channel in these societies; and a " political religion " (read ideology).

Now, taken all together *in systemic terms*, Apter's mobilization system is remarkably similar to what writers like Carl Friedrich and Brzezinski intended by the now-classic six characteristics of totalitarian systems. To be sure, Apter does not stress terror or one-man rule, but neither does he explicitly exclude them. Although he claims that mobilization systems " differ from other forms of hierarchical authority both in kind and degree," his empirical demonstration of this is at best very weak.[24] In fact, whereas he says at one point that these systems differ from modernizing autocracies and military oligarchies, at another point he allows that authority in such systems may derive from the Party or the army. He goes on to say that such systems " can move toward greater totalitarianism," which suggests that mobilization systems are already totalitarian to some degree.[25]

22. H. C. Hinton, *An Introduction to Chinese Politics* (New York: Praeger, 1973), pp. 233–234; James Townsend, *Politics in China* (Boston: Little, Brown, 1974), pp. 19–20.

23. D. E. Apter, *The Politics of Modernization* (Chicago: University of Chicago Press, 1965), Ch. 10. For the next few paragraphs, see pp. 359–365.

24. *Ibid.*, p. 360.

25. *Ibid.*, pp. 360, 379, 388.

Is it not true that the matter of degree is implicit in the totalitarian model? It is not a fatal objection to that model that some scholars who used it believed it to imply invariant one-man rule, unmitigated and steady-state use of terror, and the absolute incapacity of such systems to change or to resolve developmental problems. Concepts and models after all do not have lives and meanings of their own; they turn out to be as useful (and as fruitfully mirroring of reality) as the genius of those who invent or use them permits.

It is worth adding that just as Apter's concept of a mobilization system is not meant to be restricted to a given group of nominally identified countries, neither was the totalitarian model meant to be restricted to countries denominated Communist. The point is that when we are dealing with the complicated (and not always necessary or useful) task of creating typologies of whole systems, we do not solve very much by inventing new labels to describe essentially the same things.[26]

There are further complications. As I read the literature on Communist systems, it appears that the mobilization label does not refer to the system as a whole but rather to certain styles and patterns of administering (and perhaps making) public policies. This is surely the level at which Townsend, for example, distinguishes "bureaucratic" from "mobilization" politics in the Chinese People's Republic. The differences he underscores are important, but they strike me as false and misleading if they are intended to stand for distinctive or alternative *types of systems*.

Hierarchical administrative organization—more or less of the Weberian bureaucratic genre—characterizes all Communist systems, including that of China. This organization performs a number of activities, among which processing policy-relevant information and eliciting compliant behavior from the objects of public policy are paramount. To be sure, there are important nuances pertaining to such administrative hierarchies. One thinks of degrees of centralization and differentiation; geographic devolution of authority; the involvement of mass publics in certain administrative functions; patterns of recruitment to bureaucratic roles and the allocation of authority and responsibility to such roles; the distribution of authority among representative, political party, and administrative units in the

26. I am aware that both Apter and Kautsky are concerned with the processes of economic development and "modernity," and that the mobilization regime is associated with particular levels or phases of modernity. Nevertheless, it is unacceptable to confound politics and economics and to assume that, *politically speaking*, post-mobilization regimes will "converge."

public or private sectors. There will also be times when political leaders and others in society may want to limit the role of public administrative organizations. It is, however, inconceivable that large-scale nations can function without them.

Thus, when I read about what mobilization means in China, or other Communist societies, I understand it to be a particular, narrowly limited *technique*, a *method* or an *instrument* that is used *from time to time*, within a *general, hierarchical bureaucratic framework*, to produce certain kinds of compliant behavior. The behavior may be substantive in the sense of being directly related to the production of goods and services; it may be symbolic in the sense of providing manifestations of support for the regime and its leaders. " Plebiscitarian Democracy " is distinguished by the frequent use of the latter kinds of mobilization activities.

Where mobilization techniques come to predominate over the more normal administrative routines, situations are volatile and unpredictable; if stable patterns are to obtain, there must be exactly that turning back to bureaucratic apparatus which China has experienced since the Cultural Revolution. Nothing impedes, in China or elsewhere, the chances that mobilization techniques will be used again.[27] For as long as we have had nation-states, elites who have felt the need to overcome bureaucracy's dead hand have turned to such techniques. One thinks of leaders like De Gaulle and John F. Kennedy, Churchill and Lenin, the Great Elector and the later Hohenzollerns, Nehru, and of course Mao.

To think about mobilization as a type of system opposite to a bureaucratic system, or different from a totalitarian system, is to confuse technique with system. There is little conceptual clarity or profit in that.

To be sure, Chairman Mao, like Lenin, Max Weber, and Louis Brandeis, passionately recognizes the pathological aspects of bureaucratic organization. Mao is a knowledgeable and thus far astute practitioner of Michel Crozier's formula for minimizing bureaucratic pathology: Maintain a high level of uncertainty. Hand in hand with this prescription goes another: Too much differentiation of structure

27. Rudolf L. Tőkés, in a personal communication, takes exception to this statement, noting that for some years examples of " large-scale " mobilization have been rare in the U.S.S.R. and Eastern Europe. He adds that mobilization techniques, because they are volatile, may now be a luxury for such systems. This may be so on the scale of the Cultural Revolution. My conception of mobilization, however, encompasses many techniques of eliciting compliant behavior that are sometimes confused with freer or more voluntary modes of political participation in democratic societies.

and function can impede development. The arresting aspect of Fainsod's and more recently Jerry Hough's work on the Soviet bureaucracy is that at the lower, operating levels of policymaking and implementation the willingness and ability of the Party to intervene may be a necessary condition for successful political leadership. From time to time that intervention may require a return to mobilization techniques, but always with the expectation that mobilization does not get out of hand—a risk that Lenin himself, for all of his antagonistic feelings about bureaucracy, clearly understood.

Western democracies that have carried the concept of an independent bureaucracy to astonishing extremes, and that now experience paralysis in their efforts to cope with poverty, decaying cities, and other major economic and social dislocations, may well have to take some political interference and mobilization lessons from China, the Soviet Union, and similar systems. Far from signaling systemic transformation, such steps would simply involve greater use of certain patterns of administration already present in these societies. The underlying proposition seems to be this: The techniques of policy implementation by mobilization will come increasingly to characterize large-scale nations where the scope of public and governmental authority and activity is very great. We might add that single-party systems can more readily use such techniques precisely because these systems can keep them within bounds, turning them off when they threaten to get out of hand.

Pluralism, Participation, and Conceptual Spuriousness

The last observations I wish to make about recent literature on Communist studies involve what I judge to be a serious and unfortunate loss of precision regarding the meaning attached to the concepts of "pluralism" and "political participation." The intellectual steps —or leaps—that lead up to the present state are fairly well known, as is the debate among students of Communist systems.[28] In summary form, and at the risk of oversimplification, the steps seem to be these:

1. Communist systems are "discovered" not to be adequately described by the classical model of totalitarianism. The death of Stalin, the succession struggles thereafter, polycentrism, experiments with collegial leadership, attempted reforms within some Communist systems, evidence of intra-systemic struggles over public policies

28. I have treated the causes and flow of the revisionistic tendencies in the study of Communist systems in *Politics Within Nations,* pp. 338–349.

(including the advisability of command economies)—these and other factors [29] led to certain malaise among scholars regarding the rigid application of the totalitarian model.

2. Although state bureaucracies in Communist countries are found not to adhere in a strict sense to Weberian criteria, evidence of conflict among major sectoral divisions of public administration, between some of these sectors and the Party apparat, and between central and regional or local organizations suggested a much richer, more variegated structure of political decisionmaking than strict application of the totalitarian model would suggest. The diminution of terror as an instrument of control and the growing knowledge of the "brokerage" role of Communist parties, and of these parties' failure to exercise an absolute monopoly of political power, led scholars to recast basic conceptions of how these systems work in fact.

3. Attention is then turned to the literature on interest groups, political development, and modernization, and to very broad general schemes pertaining to whole societies and polities. These concepts and schemes are then applied to Communist systems, and some writers argue that they can be used—in pure or adapted form—in the comparative analysis of Communist countries.

4. Problems of unilinearity, of determinism, of the possibly history- and culture-bound nature of these borrowed concepts and schemes are ill-attended or finessed.

5. Efforts by Communist elites to involve members of the general public in certain forms of administration, to use survey research to get better information on public attitudes toward policies, to mobilize popular support for developmental programs, and to correct for serious errors in goal-setting and planning formats are viewed as evidence of "convergence." One extreme formulation suggests that economic modernity *requires* greater "differentiation" and "secularization," greater emphasis on "rationality," and greater political participation than ideologically dictated policies presumably allow.[30]

29. Among these other factors, I would underscore certain institutional changes, such as transformations of the national legislatures, in countries like Poland and the Soviet Union. See, for example, the fascinating discussion in David Lane, *Politics and Society in the U.S.S.R.* (London: Weidenfield and Nicholson, 1970), pp. 151–157.

30. The most impelling argument that social and economic transformations in Communist countries require more effective political participation, more differentiation, more "pluralism," and more interest-group politics is found in Zvi Y. Gitelman, "Beyond Leninism: Political Development in Eastern Europe," *Newsletter on Comparative Studies of Communism*, V, 3 (May

6. New labels—like mobilization—are attached to such systems, and they are then represented as "pluralistic" or "participatory," with or without qualifying adjectives.

It should be clear by now that my objections to broad classificatory schemes is in part that they tend to encourage a lack of precision in the formulation and application of concepts. Far from giving us keener vision as to how particular groups of systems work, they tend to create an overall blur.[31] Little wonder, then, that Alfred Meyer can say regarding the use of the "political culture" approach, "one gasps at the boldness with which, for instance, the entire universe of political systems is divided into four cultures . . . and at the simplicity, not to say simplemindedness, of the manner in which the several cultures are described."[32]

Beyond this, however, is our knowledge that pluralism, as used in political science, has been until recently a concept with quite specific denotation and empirical referents. A recent semi-authoritative definition tells us that "pluralism refers to specific institutional arrangements for distributing and sharing governmental power, to the doctrinal defense of these arrangements, and to an approach for gaining understanding of political behavior."[33] The historical, normative, and analytical aspects of this concept are intertwined. Historically, the concept is associated with liberal political philosophy, and especially with English political philosophers like Austin, Maitland, Figgis, and Laski, who sought to find a middle ground between unmitigated individualism, on the one hand, and the collective, centralized authority associated with statism, on the other. As Henry Kariel notes, the assumptions of the pluralists include at least the

1972), pp. 18–43. I believe Gitelman's argument is unsupported by the empirical evidence, some of which is now available in the books reviewed by authors in this issue of *Studies in Comparative Communism*.

31. William A. Welsh, "The Usefulness of Social Stratification, Input-Output and Issue-Processing Models in the Study of Communist Systems in Eastern Europe," *Newsletter on Comparative Studies of Communism,* V, 4 (August 1972), pp. 3–20, makes several wise and telling remarks on this score. It is interesting that he finds the comparative posture delineated by H. J. Spiro more useful than the approaches suggested by David Apter or David Easton. See H. J. Spiro, "Comparative Politics: A Comprehensive Approach," *American Political Science Review,* LVI, 3 (September 1962), pp. 577–595.

32. Meyer, "Communist Revolutions," pp. 353–354.

33. Henry S. Kariel, "Pluralism," *International Encyclopedia of the Social Sciences* (New York: Macmillan, 1968), Vol. 12, pp. 164–168. Cf. F. W. Coker, "Pluralism," *Encyclopedia of the Social Sciences* (New York: Macmillan, 1933), Vol. 11, pp. 170–174. Cf. R. A. Dahl, *Polyarchy: Participation and Opposition* (New Haven: Yale University Press, 1971).

following: (1) the state may not claim exclusive and overriding allegiance from the individual; (2) the individual can best find fulfilment in a context of small governmental units and voluntary membership in religious, cultural, economic, educational, and professional groups; (3) such groups must be reasonably independent of government and can rightly be interposed as units to which the individual gives his allegiance, even against the state under some circumstances; and (4) the role of government is to maintain equilibrium among these groups, such that binding public policies will be those that emerge from a free interaction among them.[34]

The right of free association is critical to this definition. This being so, it is essential that pluralism, in the political sense, not be confused with what other social scientists may describe as societies that are diverse (i.e., " pluralistic ") in cultural, ethnic, or economic terms.[35] It is the competitive and cooperative interaction among such voluntary associations, the acceptance of the legitimacy of such a pattern, and the openness of such associations to individual membership and participation that constitute the basic requirements of political pluralism.

Whatever else may be going on in Communist systems, it seems fair to say that pluralism is not included. Pluralism as doctrine, normative orientation, or basis for making political allocations is simply and clearly not acceptable to the elites of such systems. Indeed, the notion of an *individually* centered political order, of the *freedom and autonomy of group organization and association,* of *competing allegiances* that may be manifested in *organized political opposition* is anathema to these elites. This is true whether the system involved is closer to the Soviet, or the Yugoslav, or the Chinese versions of Marxism-Leninism.[36]

34. Kariel, " Pluralism." Compare the list of imperatives to the public that Hinton, *An Introduction*, pp. 233–234, outlines for China: (1) Do your economic job adequately! (2) Submit to propaganda cheerfully! (3) Be an active member of one or more organizations approved by the CPC! (4) Study in order to raise your ideological consciousness along lines approved by the Party! (5) If you are a white-collar worker, engage in some manual work! (6) Vote for officially approved and designated candidates! (7) Participate, when asked, in mass campaigns designated by the regime !

35. For a useful discussion of this point, see Bohdan Harasimiw, " Application of the Concept of Pluralism to the Soviet Political System," *Newsletter on Comparative Studies of Communism*, V, 1 (November 1971), pp. 40–54.

36. See A. J. Janos, " Group Politics in Communist Society: A Second Look at the Pluralistic Model," in Huntington and Moore, *Authoritarian Politics*, pp. 437–450. Cf. A. Rabushka and K. A. Shepsle, *Politics in Plural Societies: A Theory of Democratic Instability* (Columbus, Ohio: Merrill, 1972).

It is not helpful in the least, therefore, to take the data of political behavior in such systems and to force them to fit a procrustean bed of interest-group theory, voluntarism, associational group life, polyarchical decisionmaking, and other frameworks and formulations intimately associated with a concept that derives from very specific Western historical evolution and the political philosophies associated with it.

Something similar may be said about "political participation." Just as interest-centered conflict is true of all political systems, so may we say that the political process itself is unthinkable without some form of participation on the part of the members of the polity. Webster's dictionary tells us that "to participate" may mean to take part in, or to be a part of, the larger whole. In the first sense, a person hanged takes part in a lynching; in the second sense, the mere physical presence of a person in any political system is a form of participation. Webster's also goes on to specify that, in a *political* sense, the concept implies opportunities for *individual* participation. The emphasis on the individual is in exactly the same key that political liberalism intends; it is not by chance that Webster's associates this meaning of participation with democracy.

I do not wish to discuss here whether pluralism is "natural" to man, whether values such as participation associated with liberalism are the only, or even the most important, values worth pursuing.[37] Nor do I wish to debate whether so-called pluralist democracies, or polyarchies, work as theory would suggest, for very obviously they often do not—and that's another problem. I wish only to insist that placing qualifying adjectives before pluralism (*e.g.*, *corporative* pluralism, *institutional* pluralism, *quasi*-pluralism, *elite* pluralism),[38] restricting the idea of interest group to those leaders who are inside the system more or less controlled by the Party, or coining expressions like "informal groups" or "interest groupings"[39] does not

37. Kariel, "Pluralism," pp. 167–168, in his critique of pluralism, raises some of the basic objections to such a posture.

38. See, for example, J. F. Hough, "The Soviet System: Petrification or Pluralism?," *Problems of Communism*, XXI, 2 (March/April 1972), pp. 25–45. Hough's basic point is that the relationship between Party leaders and leaders in key institutional sectors has changed (pp. 32–38), that the U.S.S.R. is neither the "directed society" nor the "petrified oligarchy" described by others. This may be true, but why call the U.S.S.R. a pluralist system or fudge the issue by writing of "pluralistic tendencies"? Cf. Andrzej Korbonski, "Bureaucracy and Interest Groups in Communist Societies: The Case of Czechoslovakia," *Studies in Comparative Communism*, Vol. 4, No. 1 (January 1971), pp. 57–79, who argues that the interest-group model "works" for Czechoslovakia and concludes that the system, when he looked at it, was quasi-pluralistic (pp. 69–70). Further elaboration of Hough's view is found

advance our theoretical knowledge very far. It may seriously impede our understanding of how Communist systems work. These tendencies, as Meyer points out, may even lead us backward in the sense of impeding our *ever* learning what these systems really are.[40]

In short, we risk falling into the entrapment of contemporary scholasticism. Moreover, if, as Bohdan Harasymiw says, the " pluralism " that is likely to evolve in Communist systems will be neither individualistic nor democratic,[41] we will have added one more of those concepts that are meaningless because they have no opposites, are all-encompassing, and therefore illuminate or explain little or nothing.[42]

It is somewhat reassuring that specialists in Communist systems have themselves tried to stem the headlong plunges I have been discussing. Typologies such as those provided by David Lane cannot obscure what he himself acknowledges: namely, that the " groups " he discusses are far from meeting the requirements of pluralism. Patrick O'Brien is right on target in stressing that in Communist countries a narrow elite, however much its members may bicker among themselves, still monopolizes power. He adds that the key questions to ask about governments would center on their attitudes toward opposition, on the internal and external diffusion of information, on the techniques used to limit or nullify the impact of opponents, and on how elites react to those considered a threat to the dominant system of power and ideology.[43]

O'Brien warns us of the dangers of applying to Communist systems models that are inextricably tied to Western, democratic, and capitalist societies. In another view, Kenneth Jowitt objects to those who assume that oligarchical rule is necessarily irrational or inefficient.

in his "The Bureaucratic Model and the Nature of the Soviet System," *Journal of Comparative Administration,* Vol. 5, No. 2 (August 1973), pp. 134–167.

39. See H. Gordon Skilling and F. Griffiths (eds.), *Interest Groups in Soviet Politics* (Princeton: Princeton University Press, 1971), pp. 37 et seq. David Lane, *Politics and Society,* Ch. 8, pp. 234 et seq., adopts the Skilling usage and adds " amorphous groupings," " unincorporated," and " estranged " groups to the growing, undisciplined typology.

40. Meyer, " Communist Revolutions," p. 345.

41. Harasymiw, " Application of the Concepts," p. 53.

42. See Giovanni Sartori, " Concept Misformation in Comparative Politics," *American Political Science Review,* LXIV, 4 (December 1970), pp. 1033–1053. Sartori specifically cites the frequent use of a term like " interest group " as an example of this all-embracing and therefore useless variety.

43. Patrick O'Brien, " On the Adequacy of the Concept of Totalitarianism," *Studies in Comparative Communism,* Vol. 3, No. 1 (January 1970), pp. 55–60.

Noting that a reduction in the arbitrariness of government should not be confused with emergent pluralism, he says:

> To argue that the logic of rationalization leads to pluralism is to say too little if pluralism merely refers to increasing differentiation of the system, too much if pluralism means democratic pluralism, and/or not enough if it is legitimate to consider an oligarchy (as Horelick correctly defines the Soviet elite) as a pluralist elite. Pluralism is, at best, a term that demands some specification.[44]

Notes for a Research Agenda

As our stock of empirical information about Communist societies and political systems grows larger, we will no doubt have even more glaring evidence of the inadequacies of our general schemes in comparative politics. On the one hand, we can rejoice that the theoretical status of the field remains unsettled. This being so, we can join Goldstein in the surmise that it is good that the study of China (and other Communist systems) remains highly heterodox.

We must also be alert, however, to the danger that the prevailing modes of description and analysis (too often misnamed " paradigms ") will lead us away from those aspects of political systems that we must know more about if the empirical work of political scientists is ever going to produce incremental theoretical payoffs. I have said before and at great length that payoffs will be minimal if we continue to concentrate on those aspects of politics that are distant from the " black box " of government, from those institutions and processes that produce public policies and are involved in their implementation.[45] It seems to me that Goldstein has made a remarkably articulate and forceful case for a more direct approach, even as he acknowledges that the task will not be easy.

I find it astonishing, even when we discount for the problems of data availability, that the textbooks reviewed by Hoffmann, Jancar, and Goldstein devote so little attention to the governmental institutions of Communist societies. This is particularly frustrating because

44. K. J. Jowitt, " The Changing Character of European Communism," *Studies in Comparative Communism,* Vol. 2, No. 3 & 4 (July/October 1969), pp. 386–403, 394. Cf. William Taubman, " The Change to Change in Communist Systems: Modernization, Postmodernization and Soviet Politics," in H. W. Morton and R. L. Tőkés (eds.), *Soviet Politics and Society in the 1970s,* (New York: Free Press, 1974), pp. 369–390.

45. See n. 5, above.

some of the books (as well as other writing in the field) reveal that there is more information available than is often imagined. Those clusters of interests inside Communist systems that we read about are overwhelmingly centered in institutions. We require greater illumination about how the latter work, in what specific ways those who occupy key roles in them affect the public policy process. The most encouraging thing about some of the recent research is that it seems to be headed in the right direction, which for me means trying to understand better the *parts* of a political system before making sweeping, largely untestable generalizations about the whole.

Research ventures of this type need not, and must not, proceed in a theoretical vacuum. Chinese elites, for example, are involved in mind-boggling problems of administering an immense, variegated territory. The organizational experimentation described by several textbook authors cries out for middle-range theorizing, as opposed to trying to decide which whole-systems typology China does or does not fit. Why is it that speculation on so-called schemes of decentralization sees them as affecting "inputs," as opposed to the quite obvious hypothesis (too often missed by democratic pluralists) that administrative decentralization may actually *increase* the ability of centralized elites to penetrate a given territory with the policies *they* wish to pursue.

One of the textbook writers reviewed describes the dominant Communist Party as a gigantic public opinion processing machine. Another assures us that those theorists who believe "mobilization systems" to be low on information gathering and diffusion are simply wrong. Others note that elections in countries like China are really carefully honed instruments of controlled education and compliant behavior. Many of those who identify sectors of interest and of deliberate intervention in the policy process add that these interventions are carefully and by and large successfully held within bounds established by the Party. We learn, too, that rational decision-making is not necessarily fatally impeded by ideology, and that processes of development can well occur without the degree of structural differentiation or "subsystem autonomy" that some writers claim.

All of this implies what may very well be organizational innovations of truly revolutionary implications—not merely for the societies involved but for the social sciences as well. Growing information about Communist systems is intellectually exciting precisely because it may help us to test, to sharpen, and to recast the theories we have about the processes of government and the basic institutions involved in them.

Consider the problem of bureaucratization. As a pathological symptom in public administration it may refer to heavy-handed treatment of citizens, to extremely serious distortions or blocks in the flow of information, or to institutionalized conservatism and the consequent frustration of the most cherished policies a goal-setting elite may wish to implement. In the limiting case, bureaucratization would mean the transfer of *de facto* control over policies to the bureaucratic apparatus itself.

Now if, as I have said above, large-scale societies confronting large-scale problems cannot proceed without large-scale organization, devices will have to be found to limit at least the last aspects of pathology mentioned in the preceding paragraph. Communist systems seem to confront this problem by creating *a parallel Party administrative structure at every level at which governmental authority is exercised*. In principle this is not an invention of Communist parties. It was attempted by the Fascist party under Mussolini and by Hitler's National Socialists. The Soviet Union has now had more than a half-century's experience in refining this method.[46] The Chinese, like the Yugoslavs, have added some additional twists, in some measure designed to combat " bureaucratic petrification " within the Party.

It seems to me self-evident that this area of institutional analysis requires both more research and more theorizing. In his magistral study of administration, Bertram Gross identifies a number of *fallacies about bureaucratic organization*: (1) The manager is the man on top; (2) authority and power flow down from the top; (3) efficiency is the sole goal of administration; (4) technical skill equals good administration; (5) rank-and-file members of administrative organizations should be free of outside pressure; (6) administrators should execute policy, not make it; (7) in good administration, things run smoothly and easily; (8) evading formal rules violates administrative theory; and (9) the principles of administration provide answers to administrative problems.[47]

I would suggest that the genius of Party elites in many Communist societies is that they understand these fallacies and have taken steps to adapt to existential conditions that bear the closest scholarly scrutiny. The most lamentable aspect of theories of " convergence,"

46. J. F. Hough, *The Soviet Prefects: The Local Party Organs in Decision-Making* (Cambridge, Mass.: Harvard University Press, 1969), seems to me to make a more important contribution here than he does in his more recent writing on " institutional pluralism." Cf. P. D. Stewart, *Political Power in the Soviet Union* (Bloomington, Ind.: Bobb Merrill, 1968).

47. B. M. Gross, *The Managing of Organization*, 2 vols. (New York: Free Press, 1964), Ch. 13, p. 307.

or of the "requisites of modernity and development," is that they assume that Communist systems, at least in the area of making and administering public policies, have been moving toward a point where non-Communist systems have never been located in the first place. In any event, my reading of certain organizational developments in Communist systems—including certain "liberal" reforms of legislatures, broadening of electoral competition, experiments with popular involvement in developmental and other administrative programs—is that the elites of such systems understand Gross better than we do in the West.

Consider, too, the matter of inequality and of public policies and institutional arrangements designed to impinge on this universal condition. It is typical of our jaded view of Communist systems that we underscore how unsuccessful Communist systems have been in lessening or removing various kinds of inequality. We are told that discrimination against women persists, that certain privileges attached to status tend to reemerge and are transmitted intergenerationally, that specialized work in industrial society requires differential rewards, that a "New Class" of Communist Party-bureaucratic elites is apparent, and that the "structural-functional theory" of social stratification is vindicated. We are even reminded that the Bolsheviks, and Stalin himself, were never so foolish or simple-minded as to accept the notions of equality advocated by left radicals.[48]

Some or all of these claims may be true. It is equally true, however, that Communist systems everywhere, and along many dimensions, have made remarkable progress in reducing inequalities.[49] This progress has involved entirely fascinating debates over public policies, important institutional transformations, and important interactions among the institutions of government, strategic elites, and the Party apparatus in Communist countries. My assumption is that political scientists have much to learn from all of this, which, in a comparative framework, will add a healthy leavening to the profession's new-found concerns with questions of distributive justice, "public choice," and the vagaries of administering planned change.

In countries now ruled by Communist parties, such changes do indeed involve assaults on history, on the traditional cultures that

48. See David Lane, *The End of Inequality? Stratification Under State Socialism* (Baltimore: Penguin Books, 1971).

49. See the fascinating study, for all of its defects an extraordinary effort in comparative analysis, by Harold Lydall, *The Structure of Earnings* (London: Clarendon Press, 1968). Cf. LaPalombara, *Politics Within Nations*, Ch. 14.

Communist elites are to some degree committed to replacing. We would do well, I believe, to heed Alfred Meyer's advice that we take a more "naturalistic" approach to the study of Communist systems.[50] That approach will permit us to identify what seems to be unique in such systems, and perhaps better to understand the persistence of certain "national" cultural patterns in such places. This might give us one important empirical basis for determining whether these systems are or are not a logical subset of nations among which comparisons can fruitfully be made. More important, I would add, is the prospect that the findings of such research would greatly enrich the storehouse of empirical knowledge that is a necessary condition for further progress in comparative politics.

50. Meyer, "Communist Revolutions," esp. pp. 359–367.

THE CHINA QUARTERLY

An international journal for the study of China

DECEMBER 1975 **ISSUE NO. 64**

Taiwan in Transition: Prospects for Socio-Political Change — *Hung-mao Tien*
The Radical Students in Kwangtung in the Cultural Revolution — *Hong Yung Lee*
Inequality and Stratification in China — *Martin King Whyte*
The Production and Application of Chemical Fertilizers in China — *Kang Chao*

Reports from China
Wu Kuei-hsien: Labour Heroine to Vice-Premier — *Roxane Witke*
Science and the Open-Doors Educational Movement — *C. K. Jen*

BOOK REVIEWS

QUARTERLY CHRONICLE AND DOCUMENTATION

Editorial Office: School of Oriental and African Studies, Malet Street, London WC1E 7HP.

Subscriptions: Research Publications Ltd. Victoria Hall, East Greenwich, London SE10 0RF.

Subscription Rates: £6·00 or US $15.00 a year
For full-time students: £3·00 or US $7.50 a year
Individual Copies: £1·50 or US $3.75 a year

SOVIET STUDIES

A Quarterly Journal on the USSR and Eastern Europe

VOL. XXVII **OCTOBER 1975** **NO. 4**

CONTENTS

Flexible Pricing and New Products in the USSR — *Joseph S. Berliner*
An Educational Experiment: Soviet Mathematics and Physics Boarding Schools — *John Dunstan*
Methods of Deriving Data on Bilingualism from the 1970 Soviet Census — *Brian D. Silver*
History and Analysis of Soviet Domestic Bond Policy — *James R. Millar*
Is There a Ruling Class in the USSR? — *A. Nove*
Comment on Whalley and Flakierski — *Barbara G. Katz*
REVIEWS

Annual subscription £6 or $18; single issues £1·75 or $5.

Joint annual subscription to *Soviet Studies* and *ABSEES* is £10 or $30.

Communications dealing with subscriptions to *Soviet Studies* and advertising space should be addressed to Publications Officer, University of Glasgow, Glasgow G12 8QG. Cheques should be made payable to the University of Glasgow.

Articles, reviews and all editorial correspondence should be addressed to The Editor, *Soviet Studies*, 10 Southpark Terrace, Glasgow G12 8LQ.

CONTRIBUTORS

VERNON V. ASPATURIAN is Evan Pugh Professor of Political Science and Director, Slavic and Soviet Language and Area Center, Pennsylvania State University. He is the author of *Process and Power in Soviet Foreign Policy* (1971) and *The Soviet Union in the World Communist System* (1966) and co-author of *Modern Political Systems: Europe* (1963, 1968, 1972) and *Foreign Policy in World Politics* (1958, 1962, 1967, 1972). He has contributed papers to several volumes on international politics, comparative politics, and East European and Soviet affairs, as well as to numerous scholarly journals. He has held visiting appointments at Columbia, Johns Hopkins, UCLA, and the Institute of Advanced Studies in Vienna, and a Smith-Mudt Professorship with the Graduate Institute of International Studies in Geneva, Switzerland. He is currently working on book-length projects on "Soviet and Chinese Images of the Kennedy Administration" and "Factional Politics and Soviet Foreign Policy."

THOMAS P. BERNSTEIN taught at Indiana and Yale before coming to Columbia University in 1975 as Associate Professor of Political Science. His fields of interest are Chinese politics and comparative Communism. Professor Bernstein has written on agricultural collectivization in China and the Soviet Union, and has contributed to A. Doak Barnett (ed.), *Chinese Communist Politics in Action* (1969), to John W. Lewis (ed.), *Party Leadership and Revolutionary Power in China* (1970), and to John C. Wahlke and Alex N. Dragnich (eds.), *Government and Politics: An Introduction to Political Science* (2nd ed., 1971). His book on the transfer of urban youth to the countryside in China will be published by Yale University Press in 1976.

ALEXANDER DALLIN is Professor of History and Political Science at Stanford University and Senior Research Fellow at the Hoover Institution. He was Director of the Russian Institute at Columbia University, 1962–1967, and Adlai E. Stevenson Professor of International Relations there, 1966–1971. He is the author of *German Rule in Russia, 1941–45* (1957), *The Soviet Union at the United Nations* (1962), *The Soviet Union and Disarmament* (1964), and *Political Terror in Communist Systems* (1970); and editor of *Soviet Conduct in World Affairs* (1960), *Diversity in International Communism* (1963), *Politics in the Soviet Union* (1966), *Soviet Politics Since Khrushchev* (1968), and other volumes.

STEVEN GOLDSTEIN is Associate Professor of Government at Smith College. He received his Ph.D. from Columbia University. Professor Goldstein has co-authored with Michel Oksenberg "The Chinese Political Spectrum" in *Problems of Communism*, and is completing a study of Chinese Communist perspectives on international affairs during the years 1937–1941.

ERIK P. HOFFMANN, Associate Professor of Political Science at the State University of New York at Albany, received his Ph.D. from Indiana University. He is Contributing Editor and Managing Editor for Political Science of the new journal, *Soviet Union*, and is Secretary-Treasurer of the Communist Studies Group of the American Political Science Association. Co-editor of *The Conduct of Soviet Foreign Policy* (1971), Professor Hoffmann has contributed articles to *World Politics, Journal of Comparative Administration,* and *Canadian-American Slavic Studies,* and to other journals and books. His current research focuses on Soviet domestic politics, particularly the impact of technological change of policymaking and administration. During the academic year 1975–1976 he will be a Senior Research Fellow at the Research Institute on International Change and the Russian Institute of Columbia University.

BARBARA JANCAR is Associate Professor of Political Science at the State University of New York at Brockport and Executive Director of International Science Exchange, a private consulting firm. She was formerly on the faculty of Union College, Skidmore College, and also taught at the George Washington University Center at Newport, Rhode Island. Her publications include *The Philosophy of Aristotle* (1963, 1966), *Czechoslovakia 1971* (1970), and *Czechoslovakia and the Absolute Monopoly of Power* (1971); chapters in volumes on Soviet politics, Soviet dissent, and modernization in Eastern Europe; and several articles in *Orbis*, *East Europe*, and other journals. At present she is completing a book tentatively entitled *Women Under Communism: A Comparative Analysis.*

JOSEPH LaPALOMBARA is Arnold Wolfers Professor of Political Science and, since 1974, Chairman of the Political Science Department at Yale University. His research has taken him to several countries in Europe and Asia, and he has served as consultant to the Department of State, the Agency for International Development, the Ford Foundation, and other organizations. He has also served on the SSRC Committee on Comparative Politics and the ACLS-SSRC Planning Group for Comparative Communist Studies. His books and articles lie in the field of comparative politics, comparative administration, comparative interest groups and political parties, and political development. His most recent book is *Politics Within Nations* (1974).

RUDOLF L. TŐKÉS is Professor of Political Science at the University of Connecticut and Associate Editor of this journal. His most recent publication is *Dissent in the USSR: Politics, Ideology and People* (1975).

TO PROSPECTIVE CONTRIBUTORS

The editors invite the submission of articles and other communications on all aspects of comparative Communism. Priority will be given to articles attempting comparative analyses of historical as well as current developments in the Communist world and problems of Marxist ideology. Studies may be comparative with respect to other Communist states (or parties) or to non-Communist societies. Special attention will be paid to analyses of the divided countries (East and West Germany, North and South Korea, North and South Vietnam, Communist and Nationalist China), as well as of Outer and Inner Mongolia and the various republics, regions, and nationalities. In view of the difficulty of comparative analysis and the paucity of scholars specializing in more than one country, the editors will attempt to provide comparative foci on a given subject (e.g., education in China) by inviting or soliciting comments of a comparative character from scholars specializing in the same subject matter but on different Communist countries (e.g., education in Yugoslavia, the U.S.S.R., etc.). Through multiple assignments, book reviews and review articles will also be utilized as vehicles for comparative analysis. Thus, a book on Rumanian agriculture may be reviewed by an economist specializing in Polish agriculture, a sociologist specializing on Rumania, and a general expert on agriculture who does not profess any particular knowledge of Communist affairs. The journal will attempt to extend coverage to underdeveloped disciplines such as education, geography, religion, aesthetics, etc. in addition to the traditional strongholds of history, political science, economics, and international relations. Authors are encouraged, wherever appropriate, to accompany their articles with a list of primary documents, some of which may be reproduced in the journal's documentary section.

Advanced graduate students in the social sciences are encouraged to submit manuscripts of article and research-note length to: Graduate Students Essays (a new section of the journal which will feature studies by young predoctoral scholars). Correspondence about graduate essays, review articles and research notes should be sent directly to the Associate Editor:

Professor Rudolf L. Tőkés, Department of Political Science
University of Connecticut, Storrs, Connecticut 06268

Manuscripts should be double-spaced throughout, including footnotes, and submitted in triplicate. Since manuscripts are sent out anonymously for editorial evaluation, the author's name and affiliation should appear only on a separate covering page. No responsibility can be assumed for loss of or injury to unsolicited manuscripts.

The editors assume no responsibility for statements of fact or opinion made by contributors, nor do they vouch for the accuracy of translation.

SUBSCRIPTION INFORMATION

All mail (except as noted above), including correspondence about subscriptions, should be sent to the Editorial and Business Offices, VKC 330, School of International Relations, University of Southern California, University Park, Los Angeles, California 90007.

Subscriptions: Institutions $16.00 a year, individuals $10.00 a year, foreign and domestic postage included.

Printed in Great Britain by The Eastern Press, Ltd., London and Reading

50th Year

1924 — 1974

SCHOOL OF INTERNATIONAL RELATIONS

Studies in COMPARATIVE COMMUNISM

An International Interdisciplinary Journal

Winter 1975

Studies in Comparative Communism is published quarterly by the
Von KleinSmid Institute of International Affairs
School of International Relations
University of Southern California

Studies in Comparative Communism is indexed in the *Social Sciences Index; Public Affairs Information Service; ABC POL SCI; Social Science Citation Index;* and *Current Contents, Behavioral, Social & Management Sciences.* Articles are listed in the *American Historical Review* and abstracted in *Historical Abstracts* and *International Political Science Abstracts,* abstracted and indexed in the *Universal Reference System,* and analyzed in the computer-based *United States Political Science Information System.* US ISSN 0039-3592

Studies in

COMPARATIVE COMMUNISM

An International Interdisciplinary Journal

Vol. VIII, No. 4
Winter 1975

CONTENTS

SOCIO-POLITICAL CHANGE

The Role of Ethnic Politics in the Czechoslovak Crisis of 1968 and the Yugoslav Crisis of 1971
George Klein 339

Soviet Sociology and Its Critics
John Fraser 370

REVIEW ARTICLES

The Politics of Modernization in Eastern Europe: Testing the Soviet Model by Charles Gati, ed.; *Becoming Modern: Individual Change in Six Developing Countries* by Alex Inkeles and David H. Smith; *Political Undercurrents in Soviet Economic Debates: From Bukharin to the Modern Reformers* by Moshe Lewin; *The Social Prelude to Stalinism* by Roger Pethybridge; *Between Ideals and Reality: A Critique of Socialism and Its Future* by Svetozar Stojanović; *Beyond Marx and Tito: Theory and Practice in Yugoslav Socialism* by Sharon Zukin.

Revolution, Modernization, and Communism
Walter D. Connor 389

The End of Inequality? Stratification Under State Socialism by David Lane; *Class and Society in Soviet Russia* by Mervyn Matthews; *Handbook of Soviet Social Science Data* by Ellen Mickiewicz; *The Career Plans of Youth* by M. N. Rutkevich, ed.; *Social Stratification and Mobility in the U.S.S.R.* by Murray Yanowitch and W. A. Fisher, eds.

Social Stratification in the Soviet Union: Equality, Excellence, and Other Issues
Barbara A. Anderson 397

The Czechoslovak Reform Movement: Communism in Crisis, 1962–1968 by Galia Golan; *Reform Rule in Czechoslovakia: The Dubcek Era* by Galia Golan; *Social Change and Stratification in Postwar Czechoslovakia* by Jaroslav Krejci; *Political Grouping in the Czechoslovak Reform Movement* by Vladimir V. Kusin; *Public Opinion Polling in Czechoslovakia, 1968–69: Results and Analysis of Surveys Conducted During The Dubcek Era* by Jaroslaw A. Piekalkiewicz; *Winter in Prague: Documents on Czechoslovak Communism in Crisis* by Robin Alison Remington, ed.; *Civilization at the Crossroads: Social and Human Implications of the Scientific and Technological Revolution,* by Radovan Richta, *et al.*; *The Slovak Dilemma* by Eugen Steiner; *The Human Face of Socialism: The Political Economy of Change in Czechoslovakia* by George Shaw Wheeler.

Why Czechoslovakia? And Why 1968?
Susan Bridge 413

Comment: Reform Movements and the Problem of Prediction
Galia Golan 430

Comment
Jaroslav Krejci 436

Comment
Vladimir V. Kusin 439

Comment
Robin Alison Remington 441

Comment
George Shaw Wheeler 443

Rejoinder by *Susan Bridge* 444

CONTRIBUTORS 445

GENERAL INDEX TO VOLUME VIII (1975) 446

George Klein

The Role of Ethnic Politics in the Czechoslovak Crisis of 1968 and the Yugoslav Crisis of 1971

Yugoslavia and Czechoslovakia are multinational states where the ethnic question has been and is intertwined with almost all political issues. The Croat and Slovak questions have been the focus of political concern for both states since their formation in the aftermath of World War I. The political dynamics of ethnicity differ in the two states, however.

Essentially, the Czech and the Slovak involvements are bilateral. The issues that separate the two nationalities can be settled between them even though the Czechs are the majority and constitute 65 percent of the population.

Group relationships in Yugoslavia are infinitely more complex because the federal government is subjected to the multilateral demands of seven major nationalities, of which the leading nationality, the Serbs, represents only a plurality of 42 percent. Therefore, the analysis of the Yugoslav situation is more complex than that of Czechoslovakia.

The atmosphere of ferment which permeated Czechoslovakia in 1968 and Yugoslavia in 1971 reached far beyond the problems of ethnic demands, but ethnicity played a vital role in all the events in both states. Had it not been for the Slovak withdrawal of support from Antonin Novotný, President of the Republic and First Secretary of the Czechoslovak Communist Party, the Prague Spring of 1968 might not have occurred. Since the ouster of Novotný in December 1967, the post of First Secretary has been occupied by a Slovak. Similarly, the Croats exercised a decisive influence over the decentralization of power in Yugoslavia. Decentralization reached a twenty-year apex in 1971 when the amended constitutional structure of the Yugoslav state appeared to legitimize the overt expression of nationalism, including the nationalist movement in Croatia aimed at gaining ever-greater concessions from the federal government. The Prague Spring and the November 1971 Croat crisis in Yugoslavia represent the culmination of many separate events that had agitated the political environment of both states.

The Czechoslovak and Yugoslav events resulted from the activities of reforming coalitions, which had been instrumental in changing the quality of political life in both states over a period of years. In the aftermath of liberalism in both states, the respective Communist parties moved toward greater orthodoxy. Because the status quo had been far more conservative in Czechoslovakia than in Yugoslavia during the previous two decades, the Party discipline reimposed there has been quite different from that in Yugoslavia. In Yugoslavia, a federal government intervened in the political life of one of the constituent republics. There were no breaches of international legality, and the Yugoslav events remained a purely internal matter. In Czechoslovakia, the termination of the Prague Spring by Soviet intervention was in clear contempt of Czechoslovak sovereignty. The manner of termination, however, is not under examination here. Both the similarities and the dissimilarities in the two situations should be closely examined in view of the thesis expressed by some writers that an alliance between liberal Communists and nationalists is a key to the liberalization of Communist systems.[1]

In both states, the political processes were not permitted to run their full course; the democratization of the existing system was by no means the only possible outcome. The federal leadership of Yugoslavia obviously feared for the integrity of the state and for the continued role of the League of Communists within it. Ultimately, the

1. For a sophisticated discussion of this thesis, see Paul Shoup's chapter, "The National Question and the Political Systems of Eastern Europe," in Sylva Sinanian, Istvan Deak, and Peter C. Ludz (eds.), *Eastern Europe in the 1970's* (New York: Praeger, 1972), pp. 121–170, and the subsequent discussion by Stephen Fischer-Galati, Paul Shapiro, Georg W. Strobel, Kenneth Jowitt, and Paul E. Zinner, pp. 171–184.

Soviet leadership justified the Soviet entry into Czechoslovakia on a very similar basis.[2]

Ethnicity and the Organization of Czechoslovakia and Yugoslavia

Yugoslavia has been a federation since 1945, when the Partisan leadership carried out its wartime pledge to create a federal state.[3] Czechoslovakia, on the other hand, a unitary state since its inception in 1918, has rendered only token recognition to Slovak autonomy. Until Novotný's surrender of power in 1968, the Czechoslovak Communists followed the established centralist tradition. The leaders of the 1944 Slovak National Uprising against the occupation forces aspired to a federal solution, but their aims were derailed in the re-creation of the Czechoslovak Republic. Although their provisional political organ, the Slovak National Council (Slovenská Národní Rada), was permitted to exist, its functions were ill-defined; after the 1948 Communist Party coup, it atrophied politically. Because in many eyes Slovak nationalism was profoundly tainted with "clero-fascism," the Slovaks were in a poor bargaining position at the end of the war. In view of the Communists' promise to honor greater self-determination for the nationalities, it is ironic that, after a brief flurry of activity, the Slovak National Council was shorn of its remaining power in 1948. The Czechoslovak Communists instituted an all-pervasive centralism, which affected all aspects of national life and subordinated all institutions to the Party. There were Slovaks within the ruling elite, but none of them was permitted to express any particularistic aspirations.[4]

The Yugoslav tradition under Communism has been substantially different. The Yugoslav Constitution of 1946 established a federal state based on Soviet practice and the Soviet Constitution of 1936.

2. *K událostem v Československu: Fakta, dokumenty, svědectví tisku a očitých svědků* (Moskva: Tisková skupina sovětských novinářů, 1968).

3. In 1943, the Anti-Fascist Council of Liberation (AVNOJ) established a National Liberation Committee as a provisional government. AVNOJ represented a coalition of forces and stressed a future federative arrangement for the state.

4. Viliam Široký, Deputy Prime Minister, and Karol Bacílek, Minister of National Security during the purge era and Czech by birth although active in the Slovak Party most of his life, were the leading lights of the Slovak Communist Party and, unlike the Slovak intellectuals purged during the 1950s for "bourgeois nationalism," exhibited no sympathy for Slovak autonomy. Robert W. Dean, *Nationalism and Political Change in Eastern Europe: The Slovak Question and the Czechoslovak Reform Movement*, University of Denver Monograph Series in World Affairs, Vol. 10, No. 1 (Denver, 1972–73), p. 6.

The Yugoslav leadership implemented federalism only after the promulgation of workers' self-management in June 1950.[5] To justify Yugoslavia's existence outside the Cominform, the Yugoslav leadership presented self-management and the subsequent decentralization as being in accord with the principles of Marxism-Leninism. The " withering " of power at the center was hailed as the prelude to the withering of the state.

In Czechoslovakia, by contrast, centralism was the universally proclaimed policy, subscribed to by all, including the secretaries of the Slovak Communist Party. All deviations from this centralist position were persecuted as bourgeois nationalism. Only the ascent of Alexander Dubček to the post of Secretary of the Slovak Communist Party changed substantive policy in Bratislava.

The Czechoslovak and Yugoslav events shared certain common political characteristics:

1. The liberal Communists of the major nationality, who in general favored pluralization and decentralization, formed alliances with the political leaderships representing the minority nationalities within the state.
2. The liberals within the Communist Party who favored pluralization and decentralization gained influence over their Party in the mid-1960s and used their positions to reverse previously established trends.
3. The liberalizing leaderships used similar techniques to mobilize public support for their cause. In the process of building a broader power base, they involved non-party publics in the political process by appealing over the heads of the ruling party.
4. The leaderships of the Croat and Slovak minority nationalities used the liberalized political climate to advance nationalistic and sectional aims.
5. The sense of grievance of minority nationalists toward the major nationality was expressed in the liberalized atmosphere of the period. These demands consisted of federalization, greater economic autonomy, and regional self-determination.

Apart from these generalized factors, vast differences between the Czechoslovak and Yugoslav situations also must be considered.

Ethnic Conflict in Perspective

The fundamental psychological orientation of the Croats and Slovaks toward their respective major nationalities differed vastly.

5. Josip Broz Tito, *Workers Manage Factories in Yugoslavia* (Belgrade: Jugostampa, 1950).

Slovakia joined the Czechoslovak Republic in 1918 at a far less developed stage than the Czech lands and became a fertile field for directed development. The Czechs cultivated colonial attitudes toward the Slovaks, while the Slovaks suffered from inferiority feelings vis-à-vis the Czechs. On the other hand, the Croats' self-image as part of the Hapsburg domains was one of cultural superiority toward the Serbs and they viewed themselves as the carriers of superior Western culture. The ideal of Yugoslavia and Yugoslavism had wide currency among the South Slavs of the Austro-Hungarian Empire but was far less a part of the political culture of the Slavs of Ottoman territories. Misconceptions originated with the very formation of the Kingdom of Serbs, Croats, and Slovenes. The Croat leaders believed that they were joining an enlightened South Slavic federation, while the Serbs thought that the other nationalities should welcome their inclusion in an expanded Serbian state. This fundamental misunderstanding, which afflicted the leaders of both nationalities, created the conflict that remained unsettled until the collapse of the Yugoslav Kingdom in 1941. The Croats developed and nurtured a siege mentality based on both real and imagined exploitation by the Belgrade politicians, whom they held responsible for all the political and economic ills that befell interwar Croatia. The Serbs in turn resented the Croats' legalistic obstructionism.

The Croat case has been complicated by the presence of a substantial Serbian minority within the borders of Croatia, constituting 14 percent of the population of the republic. The Serbs of Croatia were subject to forceful conversion or extermination in the Independent State of Croatia set up under the aegis of the German occupation. Since World War II, the Serbian population of Croatia has ardently supported the present system. The question of the Serbian minority in Croatia has agitated both the Serbs and the Croats—the Serbs because they were unwilling to see their co-nationals in Croatia treated as a minority in a republic where nationalism was in ascendance, the Croats because the presence of the Serbian minority has given Serb leaders cause for legitimate concern.

In contrast to the relatively high development of Croatia within the Yugoslav state, Slovakia and Ruthenia were the most undeveloped portions of the Czechoslovak Republic. The Slovaks emerged out of feudalism only after World War I. The record of the First Republic in Slovakia was quite positive, if viewed in terms of nation-building. For the first time, Slovakia was endowed with a viable system of public education and, until the advent of the Great Depression, industrialization made modest economic gains.[6] Czechoslovakia carried out extensive land reform, which altered the feudalistic social structure in the Slovak countryside and wrought changes ranging from electrification to improved sanitation. In the process of development, Czechs came to Slovakia as businessmen, administrators, and teachers and held most of the key positions in civil service. Thus, the Czechs came to develop a paternalistic attitude toward the Slovaks, a characteristic common to majority-minority relationships.

During the interwar period Croat and Slovak politics tended to be centered on, and mobilized around, the ethnic problem. In Slovakia, the People's Party of Father Hlinka gained substantial support with its demands for Slovak autonomy. In Croatia, Pavle and Stjepan Radic organized the Croat Peasant Party as the main parliamentary vehicle for the articulation of Croat grievances. The outlawed Ustasha movement advocated the destruction of the Yugoslav state and the establishment of an independent Croatia. Both the Hlinkists and Ustasha accelerated nationalist trends in Slovakia and Croatia, and both used Roman Catholicism as a rallying point. In Croatia, religion was the major cultural distinction between Croat and Serb and the nationalist movement received its special edge of fanaticism by proclaiming Croatia a bastion of Western culture against the "Byzantine" Orthodox Serbs. In Slovakia, the principal leaders of the People's Party were Catholic clergymen, who borrowed some of their techniques and ideology from fascism. These two movements eventually provided the governments of the Slovak and Croat puppet states, which the Axis occupation created after the dismemberment of the Czechoslovak and Yugoslav states. Both puppet states dealt harshly with their former majority nationality. This was especially true in Croatia, where the Ustasha regime led by Ante Pavelič concentrated on creating a purely Croat state by subjecting the Serb population to forceful conversion to Catholicism or sporadic exterminations.[7] Slovak atrocities never reached that depth, although

6. This is the generally accepted view; some Slovak nationalist writers deny that Slovakia made any economic gains during the interwar Republic and even state that it retrogressed. See Joseph A. Mikuš, *Slovakia: A Political History: 1918–1950* (Milwaukee, Wis.: Marquette University Press, 1963), pp. 31–39. For a more charitable interpretation of the record of the First Republic in Slovakia, see Eugen Steiner, *The Slovak Dilemma* (Cambridge: Cambridge University Press, 1973), pp. 17–32.

7. Fitzroy Maclean, *The Heretic* (New York: Harper, 1957), pp. 125–130; and Mathew Spinka, "Modern Ecclesiastical Development" in Robert Kerner (ed.), *Yugoslavia* (Berkeley and Los Angeles: University of California Press, 1949), p. 254.

the Slovak "state" handed over its Jews to the Germans for extermination.[8] At the end of World War II, both Slovakia and Croatia were integrated into a reestablished Czechoslovakia and Yugoslavia. Thereafter, in both states, Slovak and Croat nationalism was held in low esteem. No Slovak or Croat political leader, regardless of political origins, could stress the nationality issue lest he be compromised by association with the recent past.

Administrative Socialism

The period extending from 1945 to 1950 in Yugoslavia is frequently described in official writings as the era of administrative socialism. It is characterized as a time of tight-fisted Party dictatorship during which the revolution stabilized and transformed its multitude of wartime local committees into governmental institutions. These were subordinated to the Party, and decisionmaking was accomplished by administrative fiat. Administrative socialism came to a theoretical end in 1950 with the proclamation of workers' self-management, although the influences of administrative socialism persist to the present time. With the passage of the 1953 Fundamental Law replacing the 1946 Constitution, however, the Yugoslavs made a serious effort to decentralize the government and other institutions and to circumscribe the arbitrary role of the Party. The Sixth Party Congress in 1952 renamed the Party the League of Communists of Yugoslavia and mandated a more limited role for the League than was customary in other Communist states.[9]

In Czechoslovakia, administrative socialism was never seriously questioned until the mid-1960s. Party dominance was the official doctrine from the inception of the Communist state until the fall of Novotný. The Communist Party of Czechoslovakia had a relatively large membership and thus did not possess the character of a tightly knit Leninist avant-garde. Although its rank and file was without

8. In "independent" Slovakia, Czechs were rigorously purged from all government positions. About 60,000 Jews were forcibly evacuated and handed over to the Germans for extermination. Eugen Steiner, *The Slovak Dilemma*, p. 54.

9. The Sixth Congress initiated extensive reforms in the Yugoslav Party. These included open Party meetings, encouraging the participation of non-Communists, basing of Party units solely on production and territorial units (which meant dismantling the cell system in various quasi-governmental bodies such as trade unions), and the delegation of responsibility for admissions and expulsions to local Party units. See *Sixth Congress of the Communist Party of Yugoslavia* (Belgrade, 1953).

major influence on Party policy, the concentration of power within the top leadership gave administrative socialism in Czechoslovakia its cutting edge.[10] The exclusive nature of the Party elite came under criticism in the mid-1960s, mainly in academic quarters.

In Yugoslavia, centralism swept the nationality problem under the carpet by claiming that it had been " solved " in the Soviet manner. The doctrinaire Communists who subscribed to this notion denied that the nationality question had any importance and maintained that national distinctions were merely a bourgeois survival that would " wither " as the state reached a higher stage of socialism. Characteristically, most of the centralists, as they are called in Yugoslavia, belong to the majority nationality. Their views are supported by some of the most anti-socialist elements among the Serbs who support a strong centralistic regime because they cannot envision a strong state that is not dominated by their majority nationality. These elements may be either hostile or indifferent to the prevailing social philosophy, but they support Serbian dominance, whatever ideological garb it may wear. It is widely believed that Aleksandr Rankovič, Minister of Interior, enjoyed great popularity among Serb nationalist elements after his ouster as Vice President in 1966 because he was viewed as a defender of Serb dominance.[11]

Both states have important Party factions that still view administrative socialism and tight centralism as the ideal form of political organization. These factions tend to attack any proponents of reform. In Czechoslovakia, the pre-Dubček power elites owed their positions in some sense to the purge trials in the 1950s. The Novotný leadership, which was deeply involved in the purge trials, found it next to impossible to reopen the issue of Party orthodoxy without being hopelessly compromised. During the trials, a number of eminent Party leaders, including First Secretary Rudolph Slánský, were imprisoned or sentenced to death. Also among the victims were several popular Slovak leaders and intellectuals, such as Vlado Clementis, Vávro Hajdů, Ladislav Novoméský, and Gustav Husák, who were persecuted for " bourgeois nationalism."

Those who wielded power during the period of administrative socialism did not constitute a monolith. With liberalization, deepening fissures in both parties gradually formed into overt factions. This

10. In August 1948, Party membership stood at 2,674,838. Jaroslav Krejčí, *Social Change and Stratification in Postwar Czechoslovakia* (New York: Columbia University Press, 1972), p. 145; citing *Dějiny Československa v datech*, p. 379.

11. Paul Shoup, *Communism and the Yugoslav National Question* (New York: Columbia University Press, 1968), p. 210.

process shattered the appearance of monolithic unity and raised new issues for public discussion. In essence, the Communist parties were no longer monolithic but had evolved into overt coalitions of diverse interests. This process was carried much further in Yugoslavia because it was supported by the institutional framework of Yugoslav federalism.

The revival of the nationality issue in both states during the 1960s was the direct result of the increasingly tolerant political atmosphere within both societies. Both parties made an effort to draw wide publics into the political process. The point of origin of liberalization in both societies differed widely. Czechoslovakia did not effectively emerge from monolithism until January 1968. From 1948 to 1968, the Czechoslovak leadership clung stubbornly to the ideological bequests of the Stalinist era. Czechoslovakia did not experience major changes of leadership as the result of Khrushchev's de-Stalinization. The only other East European State with a similar continuity in institutions was Walter Ulbricht's German Democratic Republic. The cohesion of the old guard was reinforced because of their shared guilt in the purge trials of the early 1950s. When they came under assault, it was from all the elements that had opposed the trials, most particularly the Slovaks, many of whom were the rehabilitated victims of the 1950s. The trials became the vehicle through which the group in power was forced on the defensive. The demand for the rehabilitation of the victims was also a means of compromising the old guard.[12]

The Slovak Party leaders played a very active role in the events preceding the Prague Spring. In general, they remembered and resented Novotný's attitudes toward the Slovaks, most particularly Novotný's contention that any assertion of a separate Slovak identity was a manifestation of bourgeois nationalism. Gustav Husák and other Slovak Party intellectuals felt that they had been singled out for special attention in the trials, which led at least indirectly to Novotný's ascent. Some observers contended that Slovak nationalism and Jewish zionism had been linked in the hope that the unpopularity of the Jews would extend to the popular Slovaks.

12. The investigation of the purge trials by the Czechoslovak Communist Party extended from 1957 until 1968. There were, in all, three separate official reports on the trials. The first was presented in September 1957 by Rudolf Barák, the Minister of Interior, and basically reaffirmed the guilt of those tried. In April 1963, a commission presided over by Drahomír Kolder partially exonerated the victims. The final report of the 1968 Piller Commission exonerated the victims but was repressed in the wake of the Soviet intervention. *Potlačená zpráva (Zpráva komise Ú V KSČ o politických procesech a rehabilitacích v Československu 1948–68)* (Wien: Europa-Verlag, 1970).

The more liberal atmosphere that prevailed in Slovakia in the mid-1960s could be traced to the emergence of Alexander Dubček as First Secretary of the Slovak Communist Party in 1963. Dubček's success in liberalizing Slovakia gave the Slovak Party leadership an entrée into the ranks of the reformers, who were becoming increasingly active on the Czechoslovak political scene. The reforming intellectuals could be found in all spheres of scientific and political activity. In coalition with the Slovaks, they engineered the coup that overthrew Novotný in December 1967. The coalition was the direct result of the economic stagnation of the early 1960s which forced the Novotný leadership to seek solutions from intellectuals and intellectual institutions. This brought the intellectuals a status that had been denied to them during the previous era. As a result, many intellectuals moved into positions of strategic importance from which they could influence public opinion and gradually erode the position of the existing leadership. By contrast, Yugoslav liberalization policies evolved gradually in accordance with the processes established by the League. Liberalization in Yugoslavia was not a consistent unilinear movement; rather, it proceeded by fits and starts and accelerated rapidly after the dismissal of Vice-President Aleksandr Rankovič in 1966. Nevertheless, the general course toward liberalization was fairly consistent over a twenty-year period and was brought to a peak by the constitutional amendments of 1971.

The devolution of power at the center encouraged the growth of grass-roots politics in Yugoslavia and entrenched the principles of federalism. The republics became the constituencies of active, regionally based politicians who owed little of their career either to the federal government or to central League organs. The Yugoslav Constitution of 1963 provided for contested elections, which further diluted League control over politics. The mass-based Socialist Alliance retained a measure of control over nominations, but it could not easily thwart the nominations of popular candidates, nor was it able to control the outcome of the final contests on both republic and federal levels. Although Party control was loosened at the federal and republic levels, it was even more diluted in the communes and workers' councils.[13] Local politicians derived their legitimacy from the support of their home constituencies, which were in general bounded by ethnic identifications. Given these political dynamics, the efforts of the political leaderships to broaden their support within their constituencies were quite logical. Thus, they increasingly turned

13. The commune (opština) is the basic territorial subdivision of a republic and also a unit of local government.

to non-Party sources for support and drew on non-Party publics outside the accepted scheme of Yugoslav politics. The Croat crisis was the logical outcome of weakened League authority coupled with the involvement of non-Party groupings in a political process that rested more and more on local bases of power.

Economic Factors

Croatia and Slovakia occupied very different economic positions in their respective states. Croatia ranks second in per capita income within the Yugoslav federation, following Slovenia. Both republics are more developed than Serbia and the other republics. By contrast, Slovakia has always lagged economically behind the Czech lands. Both Croatia and Slovenia received a substantial portion of the available Yugoslav investment capital because their more developed infrastructure was more efficient. The early theories of Boris Kidrič, which aimed at the equalization of living standards in Yugoslavia, were sidetracked by the harsh realities of postwar reconstruction. The Yugoslav planners hoped that once the economy recovered they could reverse the flow of capital to the less developed republics. This hope never materialized because the introduction of workers' self-management permitted enterprises and communes to retain locally earned surpluses. The more developed republics grew at a faster rate than the less developed areas of Yugoslavia, and the economic gap between the developed and less developed areas widened.[14] In theory, this state of affairs should have been satisfactory to the Croats, but many felt that the price exacted by the federal government for the maintenance of Yugoslavia was too high. Although the developed republics fought for the maximum retention of funds, the underdeveloped areas, where most Yugoslavs live, demanded that the federal government assume a more active role in the distribution of development money. Intense competition among the republics for investment funds led to a growth of regional nationalism, and the rhetoric of politics and economics tended to merge.

In 1971, the since-deposed Croat leadership demanded that foreign currency earned within each republic be controlled at the republic level. The Federal National Bank of Yugoslavia was one of the few

14. In 1946 Boris Kidrič, the first chairman of the State Planning Commission, proposed a bold plan for the equalization of income between the republics by 1964. However, the needs of reconstructing a war-torn economy dictated more practical strategies, which led to increasing gaps in income between regions. Fredy Perlman, "Conditions for the Development of a Backward Region" (Ph.D. diss., University of Belgrade, 1966), p. 14.

remaining means of implementing a national investment policy, and the Croat demand brought this role into question. The Croats charged that republic reserves were converted into dinars at unfavorable rates and that this benefited the headquarters of the national banking system in Belgrade.[15] The Croat sense of being exploited economically is as old as Yugoslavia. Croat economic complaints have frequently been advanced for the purpose of achieving political ends. In November 1971, the economic and political issues merged into a demand for Croat autonomy. In socialist states, economic issues are more legitimate topics for discussion than purely political matters, such as nationalism. Thus, many arguments couched in the language of economics thinly concealed nationalistic particularism.

In Czechoslovakia, the economy did not emerge from rigid central planning until 1968, despite some cautious experimentation in the mid-1960s.[16] As Czechoslovak economists have pointed out, the planners applied the Soviet model with little regard for the highly industrialized nature of the Czech lands.[17] The Soviet model tended to work far better in Slovakia, where conditions were more appropriate. The relative success of industrialization in Slovakia is borne out by the statistics; the high rate of Slovak growth has been a source of national pride.[18] The complaints of the Slovak leaders centered far more on the methods used in the industrialization of Slovakia than on the results; published criticisms were largely directed at the paternalism of the Czechs. In the later 1960s Slovak economists demanded that the plans for Slovak development be generated within Slovakia and be managed by Slovaks. These complaints were first voiced cautiously in academic publications during the mid-1960s, but after January 1968 they received prominent attention in the mass media. The economic issue was less intense for the Czechs and Slovaks than for the Croats and Serbs.

15. A strong attack on the policy of the National Bank can be found in Šime Djodan, "Evolucija gospodarskog sustava SFRJ i ekonomski položaj Hrvatske," *Hrvatski Književni Zborník*, Vol. 2 (Fall 1971), pp. 82–85.

16. Ota Šik, *Czechoslovakia: The Bureaucratic Economy* (White Plains, N.Y.: International Arts and Sciences Press, 1972), pp. 11–14.

17. Radoslav Selucký, *Czechoslovakia: The Plan That Failed* (London: Thomas Nelson, 1970), pp. 13–19, 26–31.

18. Steiner, *The Slovak Dilemma*, p. 132, quotes Lubomir Lipták as the source of the following statistics: "231,000 were employed in Slovak industry in 1948; by 1960 the number had increased to 400,000; in the building industry the increase has been from 93,000 to 142,000. Industrial production has increased by 587 percent. Agricultural output has grown 40 percent, in comparison with the situation before the war." Quoted from L. Lipták, *Slovensko v 20. storoči* (Bratislava, 1968), p. 314.

Both Slovakia and Croatia have experienced an outflow of labor during the last decades. Although Croat labor could migrate freely to Western Europe, the Slovak outflow was a purely internal migration to Czech areas. Thus, the main concern of the Slovaks was with the assimilation of their co-nationals in the Czech lands. Interrepublic mobility of labor is notoriously low in Yugoslavia. The members of the Croat middle class are usually unwilling to move to less developed portions of Yugoslavia, even if the material rewards are attractive. The outflow of Croat labor, coupled with the dissatisfaction over Croatia's share of investment funds, made ethnic tensions sharper in Yugoslavia than was the case in Czechoslovakia. For the Slovaks, it was an open question if local autonomy would have served the cause of industrialization as well as the centralism of the redistributive Novotný regime. On the other hand, the Croats generally felt that any redistribution within the Yugoslav state was at their expense. Greater autonomy for Croatia would have enabled the Croat leadership, which based its strength on the support of a politicized nationalistic constituency, to erode further the power of the central authorities to reallocate investment capital. Thus, the questions posed by nationalism in Croatia and nationalism in Slovakia differed vastly in content and depth of feeling.

The Political Crisis: Czechoslovakia, 1968, and Yugoslavia, 1971

With the removal of Rankovič in 1966, the pace of change in Yugoslavia accelerated. The subsequent curbing of the secret police removed a very persuasive threat system, and the political consequences were soon felt. The Serb-Croat linguistic dispute, the 1968 student riots, and the disturbances in the Albanian areas of Serbia can all be at least partially traced to a loosening of authority. With the blessings of the League, the foci of power had shifted from federal to republic institutions. The revised League Statutes of 1969 prohibited the traditional overlap between Party and government institutions which is the norm in Communist states. As a result, the Party lost influence over federal and regional governmental institutions. Important decisionmaking was increasingly delegated to expert bodies, which further depoliticized the governmental decisionmaking process. The 1969 Party Statutes permitted Party members the right to dissent from majority decisions so long as they did not actively oppose the officially proclaimed policies. The weakening of Party discipline in a changed political environment permitted the Croat crisis to occur. The reformers sought to equalize the political status of all the republics and provinces, and thus to defuse the charges of

Serbian dominance. Increased republic autonomy tended to institutionalize strong regional Party machines at the expense of the federal government and Party organs. Once regional leaders were freed from Party discipline, they were able to develop virtually independent bases of power within their respective areas. Decentralization and a reversed flow of power were therefore the direct result of choices made at the highest Party levels.

By contrast, the Prague Spring took place within perhaps the most centralized and egalitarian state in the Communist bloc and the period of liberalization was compressed into eight months. Despite the tentative loosening of the Czechoslovak system during the mid-1960s, there were no structural changes corresponding to the Yugoslav evolution. Democratic centralism and Party discipline remained the capstone of Party practice until December 1967. The ouster of Novotný more closely resembled a palace coup carried out within the framework of Communist legality than evolutionary change. It triggered precipitous changes in institutions and personnel, which enabled the reformers to mobilize mass support. The reform leadership lacked the institutions and resources that would have enabled them to direct the changes in a rational way. Consequently, the major changes in Czechoslovakia took place within cultural institutions and other agencies over which neither Party nor government exercised direct control. In Czechoslovakia, unlike Yugoslavia, there was no charismatic figure who could control the processes that so frightened the Soviet leaders. The legitimacy of Dubček's leadership was based on his ability to satisfy the pent-up demand for change. The reformers could not resort to arbitrary actions, lest they be accused of reverting to past discredited methods. Thus, they could not exercise adequate control over most institutions, including the secret police, many of whom opposed the reform movement.[19] Pockets of conservatism in many areas plotted against the leadership they supposedly served. These factions were not strong enough to initiate domestic countermeasures, but their existence provided a rationale for the Soviet intervention.[20]

The Yugoslav situation is in sharp contrast; once Tito decided to intervene in Croatia, he did not lack the means to implement his

19. Ladislav Bittman, *The Deception Game: Czechoslovak Intelligence in Soviet Political Warfare* (Syracuse, N.Y.: Syracuse University Press, 1972), pp. 189–196.

20. John Erickson, "International and Strategic Implications of the Czechoslovak Reform Movement," in V. V. Kusin (ed.), *The Czechoslovak Reform Movement 1968: Proceedings of the Seminar held at the University of Reading on 17–21 July 1971* (Santa Barbara: ABC-Clio, 1973), pp. 31–49.

policies. The state security organs and the army supported his policy and could be mobilized to back the federal position. The Croat events cast a disturbing shadow in a number of republics, and the intervention had few opponents outside of Croatia.[21]

Within Czechoslovakia, however, the reform movement enjoyed the overwhelming support of all sections of the country, a state of affairs acknowledged even by the Soviet White Paper, which attempted to provide an *ex post facto* rationale for the Soviet action. In the Czechoslovak instance, the government was moving fast to implement the changes outlined by the April Program,[22] although the extent to which it was in charge of the process is not clear. The abolition of censorship, the complete freedom granted to the press, including the freedom to be irresponsible, and statements by the military leaders all strengthened hard-line elements in the Soviet leadership and contributed to the Soviet decision to intervene. In Czechoslovakia, unorthodox liberalization was a truly national movement uniting the more nationalist elements within the Slovak Party with those voicing the almost universal demand for liberalization.

In Yugoslavia, the Croat events did not possess such a national character. The Croat drive for greater autonomy was a divisive issue. Although decentralization was initially supported by Serb intellectuals within and outside the League, the Croat events divided the Serb community and eventually even the Serb liberals become alarmed at the vehemence of the Croat demands.[23] The Croatian political leaders

21. Repercussions from the events in Croatia spread to other republics and served as a pretext for the removal of liberal politicians with powerful local bases. The victims outside Croatia included Koča Popovič, Serbian representative in the State Presidency; Mirko Tepavač, State Secretary of Foreign Affairs (a Slovene); Dr. S. Milosavlevski, Secretary of the Macedonian Party; Stane Kavčič, Prime Minister (a Slovene); Marko Nikezič, President of the Serbian Central Committee; Latinka Perovič, Secretary of the Serbian Central Committee; and many others in lesser positions. *Vjesnik u Srijedu*, November 8, 1972, pp. 4, 56, 58.

22. The Action Program of April 1968 was unanimously approved by the Central Committee of the Czechoslovak Party. By and large, it proposed the reforms that had been previously implemented in Yugoslavia. It stressed the Czechoslovak version of workers' self-management (enterprise councils) and the depoliticization of the economy. The program proposed to guarantee civil liberties without permitting the formation of a multi-party system.

23. This division is typified by the acrimonious debate over the 1971 constitutional amendments at the Belgrade University Faculty of Law, where a non-Communist like Mihajlo Djurič advocated in effect an expansion of Serbia at the expense of Croatia and a stronger central policy. In the aftermath of the debate, he was prosecuted and sentenced for " hostile propaganda " and " inflaming chauvinist passions." The court found that " his concern for

hoped for a sympathetic echo in Slovenia, but, as in Serbia, Slovene opinion about the Croat position was divided. Many Slovenes viewed the Croat position as the prelude to disintegration, which might end the favorable economic and political status of Slovenes within the Yugoslav state. Many Slovene intellectuals were deeply disturbed by the assimilation of the Slovene in Austria and feared change in the status of a federated Yugoslav state. It is not surprising that a Slovene politician, Stane Dolanc, emerged as the prime spokesman for "normalization" in Yugoslavia, proclaiming that the evils of disintegration might bring forth a Stalinist-type reaction.[24] The effectiveness of the federal intervention in Croatia was ensured by the loyalty of the army and the secret police. As the various discussions prior to the passage of the 1971 constitutional amendments revealed, many Serbs felt that the state had gone much too far in the direction of decentralization.

In Czechoslovakia, there was no public opinion of comparable weight to oppose the triumphant liberals and their Slovak allies.[25] The secret police resented the new situation, but there was no group of political leaders with whom they could coalesce to overthrow the widely accepted Dubček regime. Their only hope for reversal lay in outside intervention. Thus, during the period of upheavals, Yugoslav and Czechoslovak politics were constituted quite differently. In Czechoslovakia, a Slovak occupied the top federal Party post; in Yugoslavia, most major Croat politicians avoided service in the federal government. The Croat leadership operated separately and outside the direction of the federal government. In Czechoslovakia, the reform leadership constituted both the regional government and

Serbs, who were allegedly being imperiled by other Yugoslav peoples, could not be otherwise interpreted." *Borba*, July 18, 1972, p. 5. Several speakers at the debate characterized the amendments as "a monstrous Croatian plot." *Studentski List*, April 20, 1971, p, 4.

24. See "Interview of the Secretary of the Executive Bureau of the League of Communists of Yugoslavia with the correspondent of the West German Review *Die Neue Gesellschaft*, L. Bauer," *Socialist Thought and Practice*, No. 46 (January–March 1972), pp. 123–130.

25. The results of public opinion surveys taken during 1968–1969 showed a remarkable degree of unity and support for the direction of the Prague Spring. See Jaroslaw A. Piekalkiewicz, *Public-Opinion Polling in Czechoslovakia, 1968–69: Results and Analysis of Surveys Conducted During the Dubček Era* (New York: Praeger, 1972). For example, Piekalkiewicz cites a poll taken in Slovakia in September 1968, after the Soviet intervention, in which 61·5 percent of the respondents reaffirmed their support for the policy of the Czechoslovak Communist Party; 24·5 percent stated that their support of the Party had not changed; and only 4·8 percent reported that their support had been weakened. *Ibid.*, p. 65.

the federal authorities. Croats who supported a more centralistic line, such as Vladimír Bakarič, found themselves under attack at home and at least temporarily lost ground to the forces of nationalism.[26]

The mass support in Croatia expressed by student movements, religious actions, and the media at least partially articulated separatist aims.[27] In Czechoslovakia, both the Slovaks and the mass organizations were dedicated to the support of the federal authorities. The demand for Slovak autonomy within a federal state was a minor movement within the general wave of reform. In Yugoslavia, federal-regional conflict was at the heart of the issue.

The Involvement of Cultural Institutions

Both the Yugoslav and the Czechoslovak Communist parties have sizable memberships. Because both parties are composed of diverse elements from differing socio-economic and professional backgrounds, the mere fact of Party membership has never been a reliable index to an individual's political position. During the early period of administrative socialism, Party discipline temporarily submerged the differences among individuals and factions. In both societies, the Communist Party manifested a measure of pluralization and factionalization during the 1960s. In Czechoslovakia, the Party hierarchy contained conservatives like Vasil Bilák, Oldřich Svestka, and Alois Indra, along with liberals like the late Josef Smrkovský and Ota Šik. In Yugoslavia, despite the official anti-Stalinism of the League of Communists, conservatives remained and coexisted uneasily with the more liberal elements. In both parties there was a constant tug-of-war between the intellectual establishments and the representatives of the working class.[28] The divisions were also regionalized. The strong-

26. Denison I. Rusinow, "Crisis in Croatia: Part II: Facilis Decensus Averno," *American Universities Field Staff Reports*, Southeast Europe Series, XIX, 5 (September 1972), pp. 12–15.

27. At a Zagreb students' meeting called to discuss the 1971 constitutional amendments, the President of the Student Union, with the unanimous support of the 2000 students in attendance, requested that Croat sovereignty be more precisely defined; that Croats working abroad be allowed to take part in the discussion of the amendments; that Croatian be proclaimed the official language of Croatia; that the Admiralty be moved to Split; and that citizens of Croatia be permitted to do their military service in Croatia, with Croatian the official language for all military on Croatian territory. *Borba*, November 23, 1971, p. 5.

28. In the two states, the intellectual-worker conflict took different forms. In Czechoslovakia, the key positions in the Party were held by individuals who rose through the prewar trade union movement; after the purge of Slansky, these individuals were dominant within the Party until the mid-1960s. In

holds of conservative Communism in Yugoslavia were located in the most undeveloped areas of the country, because the Communists from the poorer southern portion of Yugoslavia favored redistribution of wealth within the country. In contrast, in Czechoslovakia the strongholds of conservatism were in the most developed parts of the country —in Czech lands where a large working class dominated the Party at the expense of the intellectuals until the early 1960s. Slovakia was a peasant society. Its Party representatives were mostly intellectuals who played the political game within a relatively confined circle. They did not have to compete against the trade union officials and working class representatives who dominated the Party in the Czech lands. The Prague Spring was a movement of broad national consensus linking all Czechs and Slovaks who favored reform.

In Yugoslavia, where politics were bounded by republic lines, the Croat leadership never acquired a national following. Its particularistic nationalist appeals won little support outside of Croatia. On the contrary, they created substantial apprehension in the other republics, where even non-Party members feared for the future of Yugoslavia should the demands of the then-Croat leadership be granted.

The Croat crisis of 1971 had a profoundly divisive effect. By contrast, in Czechoslovakia the broad national consensus of 1968 healed any rifts between the nationalities. Within both the Czechoslovak Communist Party and the Yugoslav League of Communists there were individuals who although nationalist in orientation were not particularly liberal on economic or cultural issues. In Czechoslovakia, men like Vasil Bilák, Gustav Husák, and Ladislav Novoméský supported greater Slovak autonomy but were not necessarily in favor of increased political participation in the democratic sense of the term. In Croatia during the months of nationalist euphoria, many very disparate groupings united in their quest for liberalization. This included the Marxist humanists of *Praxis*, who favored liberalization but were profoundly uneasy about Croat nationalism, and elements within the Matica Hrvatská, who had little interest in Marxism but used it as a vehicle to institutionalize nationalist politics.

It would be a prime mistake to equate either Croat or Slovak nationalism with liberalism. Historically, East Europe has been rife with nationalist movements that have been the very antithesis of liberalism. At the end of World War II, nationalists found their way

Yugoslavia, this conflict has had a more regional character. The representatives of the underdeveloped republics tend to be less well educated than the leaderships of Slovenia and Croatia, which gives a special edge to the many discussions about future directions.

into both parties via the resistance movements. Serbian chauvinism or assimilative Czech nationalism could be easily disguised under the cloak of Stalinist orthodoxy. The factions within the respective Communist parties could be easily recognized by the organs through which they published their criticisms. In Yugoslavia, the liberals published their polemics in *Borba* and the conservatives replied in *Komunist.* In Czechoslovakia, the conservative intellectuals aired their grievances in *Rudé Právo* while the liberals turned *to Literární Noviny.*

In Croatia, the reform leadership did not exhibit a high degree of tolerance for those elements within the Croat League which opposed them. The struggle was ruthless on both sides, and the methods used did not inspire confidence that nationalism would usher in a new period of socialist democracy. The actions of the Slovak Communists during the brief period when they achieved autonomy parallel Croat experiences. The Slovak reformers moved to restrict freedom of expression almost immediately after winning their demands for autonomy.[29] Ideology was the thin strand uniting the various factions. It is difficult to predict what would happen should that strand disappear with the triumph of particularistic nationalism.

Groupings in the Conflict

Matica Hrvatská, a nineteenth century Croat cultural organization, became the main focus of Croat nationalism.[30] In the Croat crisis of 1971, Matica Hrvatská assumed a political role by mobilizing non-Party elements and providing the Communist leadership with a means of integrating non-Communists into the Croat political process, thereby increasing their political leverage on the central authorities. In Czechoslovakia, the only similar non-Party organizations were KAN (Klub angazovaných nestraníku, the Club of Committed Non-Party Members) and K-231 (the organization of former political prisoners). Neither was constituted along ethnic lines, nor did either espouse nationalism. The Croat leadership, headed by Mika Tripalo and Savka Dabčevic-Kučar, used and were used by the leadership of the Matica. The immediate aims of the liberal Croat Communist

29. Dean, *Nationalism and Political Change*, p. 36.

30. Ironically, Novotný's downfall was at least partially triggered by his insulting behavior toward the Slovak counterpart of Matica Hrvatská, the Matica Slovenská, in August 1967. Speaking at Martin, the traditional home of Matica Slovenská, Novotný tactlessly denied that there was any problem in Slovak-Czech relations and, with a singular lack of sensitivity, refused to accept the official gift Matica Slovenská gave him.

leaders and Matica Hrvatská coincided on the demand for greater autonomy from Belgrade. It is highly doubtful that this coalition would have long endured even if Matica Hrvatská had become a mass movement with a mass press.[31] In the final analysis, it is not clear whether the Croat League commanded the controlling heights, as its leaders insisted, or whether it was being swept along by a nationalist tide which its leaders could no longer control.[32]

One of the more interesting phenomena common to the Yugoslav and Czechoslovak situations was the relative passivity and uninvolvement of the working class. Their interests tended to center on bread-and-butter demands, which they were content to articulate through established channels. The thrust of the Czechoslovak demands was toward the establishment of workers' self-management along the lines of the Yugoslav model. In Yugoslavia, most changes were adopted in the name of workers' self-management and the opposing factions were always described as the opponents of workers' self-management. Both the nationalist leaders and the supporters of the intervention waved the flag of workers' self-management. In both countries, the principal actors in the events could be found among the intelligentsia. The principal target seemed to be the arbitrariness of the central authorities rather than the Party or economic systems per se. The two main issues in the Yugoslav crisis were the status of Croatia within the Yugoslav federation and the degree of citizen participation in the democratization of the system. These issues were prominent in the Czechoslovak situation as well. Even such incipient oppositional organizations as KAN supported the Dubček reforms enthusiastically. In Yugoslavia, the Croat Communist leadership had the support of most segments of Croat society. In so far as the Croat leadership was Communist, the issue viewed from some Western perspectives as Communism versus anti-Communism never arose. Both the Slovak and Croat leaders acknowledged implicitly the leading role of the Party by operating from positions of highest Party authority.

The New Elites and the Rise of Overt Ethnic Politics

The dynamics of change in Yugoslavia produced a new generation of leaders who emerged from within the republics and tried to push

31. In 1971, membership in Matica Hrvatská increased from 12,000 to 30,000 and the number of its branches from 24 to 56. Its paper, *Hrvatski tjednik*, published 100,000 copies. *Vjesnik*, January 21, 1972, p. 45.

32. Rusinow, "Crisis in Croatia," p. 12.

the federal leadership farther down the road of decentralization than it was ultimately willing to go. The Croat leaders represented a younger group who had been socialized within the system and were not in the top leadership of the wartime Partisan movement.[33] The federal leadership was still largely in the hands of the tightly knit group who constituted the Partisan high command during World War II. Under Tito's guidance, this group tried to open its ranks to the younger generation in the aftermath of the 1968 student strike. These efforts were formalized by the Ninth Party Congress in March 1969, which injected the younger generation into top League bodies. Thereafter, all top bodies of the League were staffed by representatives of the various republic parties, and a new generation of leaders thus emerged in the League Presidium. The Presidium was expanded from 35 to 52 members, selected according to the principle of nationality. Each republic was allotted six seats, each province three. The enlarged body became the refuge of older leadership, but it also contained younger representatives from the republics. Although the old generation, with the support of Tito, was still dominant, it no longer held a monopoly on the top Party and government posts. The republics played an eminent role in so far as republic prime ministers were members of the Federal Executive Council. The changed character of Party and government bodies was a contributing factor in the precipitous institutional changes in Yugoslavia in 1971.

This situation had some analogy in changes in Czechoslovakia. The Novotný leadership, and that of Zápotocký and Gottwald before him, had its roots in the parliamentary politics of prewar Czechoslovakia. Most of the reforming leaders under Dubček had not played a major role in prewar Czechoslovak politics but had risen to prominence under the postwar system. There were some exceptions, but by and large the Czechoslovak events also reflected generational politics.

In both instances, the reform leaderships were better educated and represented the technical-managerial talent within their respective parties. Their positions were not legitimized by charisma derived from Partisan struggles but were based in current politics. In Czechoslovakia, this generation achieved power through Dubček and they co-opted members of the older generation on their merits. In Yugoslavia, the new generation of leaders consisted largely of republic politicians who were left free to implement their policies in their respective republics. Yet, once they came into conflict with the older

33. Mika Tripalo was born in 1926; Savka Dabčevič-Kučar in 1923; Alexander Dubček in 1921. During World War II, they were the soldiers of the revolution rather than its leaders.

generation, personified by Tito, they were forced to yield. The levers of power were still firmly in the hands of those who had constituted the Partisan top command. In contrast to the case in Czechoslovakia, the new generation in Yugoslavia never captured the top post in League or government. As a result, Tito's intervention was swift and final.

Yugoslavia was the first Communist state to develop a viable system of grass-roots politics. The limits of participation and expression are still set by the League and its representatives in the Socialist Alliance, but there are literally thousands of quasi-public bodies with elective offices for which League members compete with non-members on an equal basis.[34] With the dilution of League ideology and the injection of thousands of non-League members into the political process, particularism reappeared in a setting where institutional arrangements favored it. Communists, non-Communists, and anti-Communists could all coalesce around commonly held values such as the support of Croatian as a separate language, the retention of foreign exchange earnings, or a special status for Croatia. Economic and cultural nationalism came to embrace such crucial issues as the constitutional order of the state. The new generation of political leaders accurately reflected the positions of their constituencies. They no longer based their positions on League imperatives but rather assumed the role of representatives in a parliamentary democracy.

In both Czechoslovakia and Yugoslavia, liberalization was accompanied by a rise of the social sciences. In both societies, the new generation of leaders wanted to ascertain "the general will" of their constituencies and to be guided by public opinion. In Yugoslavia, various institutes conducted extensive surveys of public preferences and few subjects were taboo, including such sensitive matters as youth attitudes toward League membership.[35] In Czechoslovakia, the revival of scientific economics brought on a renaissance in sociology and a plethora of studies in the social sciences. These tended to dilute ideology and contributed to pluralization. If the political establish-

34. By 1972, the network of local organizations included 7,574 communal councils enrolling 93,000 members and averaging more than 50,000 meetings per year. Standing committees of local communities totalled 58,084; ad hoc committees 8,623. In 1970, more than 20 percent of these councils called for a referendum on local matters, most frequently in Croatia and Slovenia. "Local Communities—Development and Results," *Yugoslav Survey* XIII (August 1972), pp. 1–14.

35. See such surveys as *Organizacije Saveza Komunista i Mladi Komunisti* (The Organization of the League of Communists and Young Communists) (Zagreb: Istraživački i Izdavački Centar "Naše Teme," 1969).

ment gave primacy to public opinion, they had of necessity to abandon some ideologically " correct " solutions. No one has made a more forceful analysis of the decline of the League as a powerful political influence than the Slovene sociologist Jože Goričar.[36] He attributed the decline to the changing composition of the League, pointing out that the League membership has aged greatly and that most of the membership hold bureaucratic positions. He also pointed out that there has been a significant erosion of working class representation in the League and its elective bodies. Goričar has stated that the League scarcely constitutes a revolutionary working class force. Under the circumstances, particularistic nationalism filled a void left by the erosion of ideological, working-class-oriented values.

In Czechoslovakia, the enforced egalitarianism never permitted the embourgeoisement of the Party. By and large, Party intellectuals supported the Dubček reforms, as demonstrated by the wholesale dismissals of intellectuals in the wake of the Soviet invasion. Yet, within the Party, there was also a substantial proportion of working class members who acutely felt their lack of political efficacy. Managers who did not meet the educational requirements for their posts owed their positions to Party loyalty rather than to their professional skills.[37] To this element, the economic reforms were a direct threat. In a system in which performance became the chief criterion for success, their positions were in jeopardy. In Yugoslavia, class origins were never an important requisite for entrance into the League. Therefore, the League was more pragmatic and, by analogy, also more open to bourgeois influences. The influence of nationalism was to be felt in both reform movements.

Policies in Transition

The Ninth Party Congress of the Yugoslav League drafted revised Party statutes that provided for the toleration of individual opinions. This action opened the door to the possibility of group opposition and the legitimization of existing factions within the League as quasi-legal opposition. The result was increased factionalism, both ethnic

36. Jože Goričar, " Žarišta globalnih konfliktú u Jugoslovenskom društvu," *Društveni konflikti i socijalistički razvoj Jugoslavije, Referati, Portorož,* 10–13. 1T.1972, p. 143.

37. For example, of the 420,000 white-collar posts in Slovakia which require a specialized education, only 55 percent (230,000) of the holders of these posts have the requisite qualifications. In Slovak posts requiring post-secondary training, there are 4,097 people with only a primary education. *Nové Slovo,* October 26, 1962, p. 5.

and political. Understandably, the Croat leaders thought that their position had been legitimized by the revised Party statutes. The changed situation was anathema to the more doctrinaire Communists and to public opinion in the less developed republics. The toleration of the Croat situation opened the door to similar trends in other regions. Previous events had demonstrated such potential. In 1971, the top leadership of the League realized that they had either to abdicate the monopoly position of the League or to reassert it. Predictably, they chose the latter course.

Ultimately, the crucial question revolved around the intended role of the Czechoslovak Communist Party and the Yugoslav League of Communists. In the reform period, both were caught between nascent pluralism and near anarchy. The aim of the reformers was to abolish the monistic role of the respective parties. In this regard, both experiments failed because they failed to provide a substitute for the leading role of the Party. Yet any recentralization would necessitate a return to reliance on the very elements that had been discredited during the previous era. Neither the Soviet leaders nor the remnants of the Czechoslovak reform leadership wanted to turn the clock that far back. The Yugoslav leaders also wished to preserve the substance of many of the reforms. Whether these efforts will succeed remains to be seen.

While most of the reformers were content to liberalize the existing systems, there were also many who participated in the reform movement in the hope of eliminating the role of the Party. These opponents viewed reform as a transitory stage toward the eventual abolition of the Party monopoly. The existence of a viable substitute for the role of the Yugoslav League or the Czechoslovak Communist Party remains in question. In Yugoslavia, the League remains the only political organization that transcends the boundaries of narrow ethnic nationalism. Bourgeois democracy has not established an enviable record in the Balkans, and it is not a foregone conclusion that the alternative to Communist Party rule is some form of Western liberal democracy. The splintering of Yugoslavia into intensely nationalistic petty states would be a far more likely outcome. Some Serb nationalists apparently hoped that in the next stage of evolution in Yugoslavia a military regime might come to power. It is very unlikely that such a regime would bestow democracy on a truncated Serbian state, let alone the entire Yugoslav state. The exile Croat nationalist organizations do not inspire confidence in their dedication to the principles of democracy; much of their activity has been confined to senseless terrorism for which they seem to find little support within the country.[38]

Czechoslovak political culture is far more propitious for the development of democratic institutions. Interwar Czechoslovakia was a functioning parliamentary democracy, and its nationality problem never loomed so large as the ethnic complexities of Yugoslavia. During the Prague Spring, the differences between the Slovaks and the Czechs were worked out on a mutually satisfactory basis. There is little reason to believe that this could not be accomplished again if all outside pressures were removed.

The termination of both crises was marked by an attempt to restore Party influence. In Yugoslavia, Tito publicly repudiated the long path travelled by the League of Communists since 1952.[39] The Tenth Party Congress of May 1974 restored democratic centralism and Party discipline. In Czechoslovakia, a similar course was dictated by post-entry realities. In view of the differential points of departure of both societies on the scale of liberalization, the Yugoslav recentralization is still behind Czechoslovakia's.

The people who backed the Soviet intervention in Czechoslovakia were those least capable of mobilizing community support. It is not certain that a new generation will exhibit the same devotion and enthusiasm for the cause that made Party monism acceptable.[40] Yet, both parties have some assets on which they can capitalize. They have remained in power, and they have brought about substantial social changes in each society. It has been assumed that the forces of liberal Communism and nationalism could cooperate in the liberalization of the existing system. Yet, opposition to the existing systems is fragmented, ranging from systemic opposition to various levels of critical accommodation. In the process of articulating nationalist and other reformist aims, a coalition was forged which pluralized both societies.

The cost of returning to administrative socialism would be great.

38. For a systematic classification of oppositional types, see Vladimír V. Kusín, "Typology of Opposition," *Soviet Studies* XXV, 3 (July 1973), pp. 125–129.

39. In December 1971, Tito criticized the actions taken at the Sixth Party Congress in 1952 and charged that the roots of the present crisis lay in the Sixth Congress, which altered the role of the Party from commanding to educating and guiding. For the first time, he indicated that he was displeased with the outcome of the 1952 Congress, which took the "first step towards a more passive Party." *Borba*, December 12, 1971, pp. 1, 7.

40. Otto Ulč, "The Communist Party of Czechoslovakia and the Young Generation," *East European Quarterly* VI, 2 (July 1972), pp. 206–229.

In Yugoslavia, most intellectuals, Party and non-Party alike, would oppose such a move. If the restoration of the Party's position were followed to its logical end, positions would again be staffed on the basis of *partijnost* rather than merit. This would curtail the free-wheeling decisionmaking of self-managing organizations and would sacrifice economic efficiency to Party control. It would entail profound changes in the Yugoslav economic system and would affect Yugoslavia's position as a trading partner of the West. Any domestic tightening and increased internal controls might well decrease tourist traffic and erode the balance of payments in an economy already suffering from a high rate of inflation.[41]

In the wake of the crises, both states cleansed Party ranks. In Yugoslavia, the purge was far less drastic than in Czechoslovakia, where the number of those cast out of the Party may number 500,000.[42] The Czechoslovak Party was much larger, however, especially considering the smaller population base, and the effect of the purge on the political atmosphere of the country was far more drastic. Most of the intellectuals who participated in the Prague Spring were forced out of politics. For both parties, the ability to attract young talent into Party ranks remains the ultimate test.

The proclamation of new constitutions and the revisions of the liberalized Party statutes marked the end of the Yugoslav and Czechoslovak crises. The new Czechoslovak Constitution of October 26, 1968, proclaimed after the Soviet entry, is still in force. It remains the last expression of the Prague Spring of 1968. The document reconstituted the Czechoslovak state into a federation and created two republics, one Czech and one Slovak, which are equally represented in the upper chamber of the National Assembly. Originally, the ministries were to be headed by a binational leadership, but in practice this requirement has since been abolished. The ministries again possess the power of executive decisionmaking throughout both republics.

41. Inflation for the year 1973 jumped to 18 percent, but wages did not keep pace. Yugoslavia suffered from a persistent imbalance of payments. In 1973, exports totaled $2,853 million and imports $4,511 million. *Borba*, January 7, 1974, p. 6; *Privredni vjesnik*, January 17, 1974, pp. 2–3.

42. Since 1969, 50,370 League members have been expelled and 92,386 have been crossed off the Party rolls. *The New York Times*, May 28, 1974, p. 5. In Croatia, 23 primary Party organizations have been disbanded. *Nin*, May 14, 1972, pp. 52–60. In Serbia, between January and July 1973, 578 officials in enterprises and political organizations were replaced, 222 were recalled, and 519 resigned. *Borba*, January 16, 1974, pp. 1, 7.

Rudé Právo stated that by December 1969 membership in the Czechoslovak Communist Party had declined by 473,731. *Rudé Právo*, December 15, 1969.

Yugoslavia's federalism is still far more institutionalized than Czechoslovakia's, and no Yugoslav political leader would propose abolishing the federal system. The 1974 Constitution still rests on the principle of equal representation for each republic, regardless of size of population, and most Party and government organs are constituted on the same basis. The Yugoslav legislative system has been rationalized through the elimination of the pentacameral legislature. The delegates to the lower chamber of the new bicameral legislature are elected in equal proportion from all republics through indirect election by the Communal Assemblies. The upper chamber is also delegated equally from the republican and provincial assemblies. This indirect electoral system marks a retreat from the popular participation provided for by the 1963 Constitution. The new constitution also facilitates increased League control.[43]

The central problem for those seeking to federalize governmental institutions lies in the relationship between Party and state. In Czechoslovakia, normalization has revived many elements of the past. Initially, it was hoped that the Party would be federalized in the same way that the 1968 Constitution federalized the governmental organs: namely, the Czechoslovak Communist Party would be reconstituted into separate Czech and Slovak parties. Previously, the Czechoslovak Communist Party had served as the Czech Communist Party with a subordinate Slovak Communist Party. The initial proposals for federalization of the Party were watered down, first, by the introduction of the Czech Bureau within the Communist Party of Czechoslovakia, then, by abolition of the Czech Bureau and restoration of the *status quo ante*—a Czechoslovak Party without a subordinate Slovak Party and no special entity for the Czech lands.[44] The regional Party committees are subordinate to the Czechoslovak Party, so the evolution initiated by the reforms has come full circle.

In Yugoslavia, there has been a serious rethinking of the role of the League of Communists. Tito also has publicly regretted the infusion of new blood into the top League leadership. He stated,

43. A recent commentator hailed the new 1974 Yugoslav Constitution: "the classical representative system and traditional electoral system no longer corresponded to the system of more advanced type of self-management socialist democracy." Pavle Nikolić, "Basic Characteristics of the System of Delegates," *Review of International Affairs* (Belgrade), XXV (April 5, 1974), p. 2.

44. Until 1971, the only manifestation of the existence of the Czech Party Bureau was the publication of its weekly, *Tribuna*. Since May 1971, the Central Committee has published *Tribuna*, thus indicating that the Czech Bureau is nonfunctional, if not dead.

"Many capable older men have been removed from office and even more serious, cadres of the Revolution have been kept out of office."[45] He further expressed distrust of the younger generation by calling for their political education.

Both the Czechoslovak and the Yugoslav experiments have been halted, at least temporarily, by an effort to reintroduce Party discipline. It has been amply demonstrated that nationalism and Party liberalism can erode the power of the Party. It is not at all clear that these political forces can provide a viable means of governing the two states in question without dissolving the existing system. While the pendulum is at present swinging toward centralism, the issue of nationalism has not been laid to rest. In Yugoslavia, with its many ethnic complexities and wide participation, the issues of balance between centralist and particularist forces will be a continuing source of debate. Tito's resort to the older generation will not solve any of the present problems. It is likely that the stifling of popular participation is a temporary phenomenon in Czechoslovakia as well. Eventually the present leadership may wish to build support by increased participation, as did the Hungarian leadership after 1956. All the forces that created the crises of 1968 and 1971 are still represented in both societies.

Conclusions

The various Communist states have developed diverse institutional patterns. If there were polar opposites in the pre-1968 period, they were Yugoslavia and Czechoslovakia. While Yugoslavia had by far the more liberal and decentralized system, Czechoslovakia was perhaps the most centralized of the multinational states with the greatest proportion of nationalized industry. In order not to obscure these differences, the conclusions are grouped under three subheadings: conclusions applicable to Yugoslavia and Czechoslovakia separately, and general conclusions about both states.

Yugoslavia

1. The crisis in Yugoslavia developed as a result of a nationalistic movement in the Republic of Croatia, which appeared to have support outside the League of Communists. The federal authorities were uncertain whether the Croatian League retained control of the

45. *The New York Times*, May 28, 1974, p. 5.

republic's policy. The primary focus of the Croat crisis was on nationalism.

2. The Croat crisis was brought about by a coalition of reforming Communist liberals and nationalist elements. This combination was inherently unstable because the nationalist elements in the Matica Hrvatská thinly concealed particularistic aims; their version of reform would have brought a radical change in the system. The liberalizing elements in the League merely wanted some limited reforms within the framework of the system. Without federal intervention, these disparate elements would surely have clashed.

3. In Yugoslavia, federalism was legally established and institutionalized through the continuous evolution of the system. Republic and local organs control their own funds. Thus, the central organs had few institutional means of curbing nationalism short of the drastic measure they took—namely, dismissing the reformist leadership of the Croat League.

4. The Croat situation brought about a crisis in the relationship between the federal organs of the Yugoslav government, on the one hand, and the League, on the other. Subsequent dismissals of Party personnel affected most republics, as the central government paved the way for the reestablishment of a more centralist regime. It remains to be seen what effect the effort to revitalize the role of the League will have on League quality. One matter remains clear: there are no proposals to revoke the present federal structure.

5. Yugoslav federal institutions and the emphasis on legally sanctioned ethnic particularism has had the effect of economically benefiting the more prosperous republics of Yugoslavia to the detriment of the poorer. The ideology of Communism does not easily accommodate to the fact of income differences among the republics; this will be a continuing source of interethnic dissension as long as present constitutional arrangements are maintained.

Czechoslovakia

1. Slovak nationalism played a relatively minor role in the broad national movement known as the Prague Spring. Slovak nationalism was the catalyst for the ouster of the Novotný regime, but the goals of the nationally supported movement ranged far beyond the Slovak nationality question. The naming of a Slovak to the post of First Secretary of the Party and his leadership of the liberalization created broad binational support for the movement and a general sense of euphoria. The Czech liberals did not see the federalization of the state as a threat and therefore supported it actively.

2. The Slovak issue developed out of the lack of governmental or Party institutions capable of articulating Slovak national aspirations. Many Slovak Communists therefore participated in the reform movement for narrow nationalist reasons, with the specific aim of establishing parity between Slovaks and Czechs within the state. These Slovak Communists did not share the liberal leanings of their Czech counterparts. Once their demands for autonomy had been fulfilled, they broke the solid front of the reform movement by advocating a return to greater orthodoxy.

3. The Czechoslovak events were not the result of a continuous and planned political evolution toward liberalization but originated in a political coup within the central leadership.

4. The forces led by Dubček never fully controlled the events of the Prague Spring. The state security forces remained a Novotný stronghold. Dubček's resolution not to use forceful or extralegal methods against his opponents left important areas in the hands of the opposition. The army was disorganized by a series of internal scandals. Thus, the new regime lacked the capacity to defend itself from internal and external challenges.

General Conclusions

1. In comparison with Yugoslavia, Federal authorities in Czechoslovakia can mediate interethnic disputes far more easily because the disputes can be settled on a bilateral basis. The political dynamics of Yugoslavia are intrinsically more complex because they involve six republics and two autonomous provinces. The Croat problem cannot be isolated from the entire complex facing this multinational state.

2. The alliance between nationalism and liberal Communism was by its very nature unstable. Leaders like Dr. Gustav Husák and Alois Indra were completely fearless in fighting for the autonomy of Slovakia in a federalized Czechoslovakia, but they were equally determined to preserve the Party monopoly in the political sphere as well as its right to curb the freedom of expression. In that sense they were orthodox and devoted Communists, as their subsequent record discloses. The Czech liberals, such as Josef Smrkovský, Ota Šika, Jiří Hájek, and others, were essentially libertarians to whom as Communists the national question was of secondary importance. Similar coalitions existed in Croatia between the top leadership of the Croatian League and elements for whom the national issue had an overriding primacy. Such coalitions are inherently unstable because of the divergent aims they seek to implement. The Yugoslav federal

solution was not enough to satisfy many of the nationalists, while federalization in Czechoslovakia seemed to satisfy most of the Slovaks.

3. Both movements offended Communist orthodoxy by enlisting mass support for their cause. This had the effect of revitalizing both the Yugoslav and Czechoslovak Communist parties, but it also diluted them ideologically. They adapted libertarian ideology to accommodate the enthusiasm of their new clientele. The result was a change in the traditional character of the parties.

4. Both parties paid a heavy price for the suppression of the experiments. The subsequent expulsions deprived both of some of their most popular and talented leaders. The heavy rate of Party expulsions in both countries attests to this; expulsions were far heavier in Czechoslovakia, which had the larger Party in relationship to its population. The leaderships of both states are now trying to revive a measure of monolithism by the reintroduction of Party discipline. Yet monolithism in the 1950s was based on a younger, more dynamic membership which believed in the Party. It is doubtful that the same results can be achieved at a time when the Party has become the defender of vested positions.

John Fraser

Soviet Sociology and Its Critics

Marxists have frequently been accused of failing to relate Marxism to the historical development of the sciences in socialist societies. They either admit scientific knowledge to " Marxist terrain " for reasons of political expediency, or else make Marxism a static categorical system, an idealism wholly indifferent to the multiplicity of scientific knowledge and to its own scientific nature. Of late, sections of the " New Left " and the " New Right " have made such criticisms from a neo-Marxist or " critical " vantage point to press an anti-socialist and specifically anti-Soviet case.

The introduction into the Soviet Union of some techniques and methods of Western academic sociology has led to attacks from several quarters. For polemical reasons, two kinds of transition and transformation have been confused and intermingled. The first issue concerns the transition from pre-scientific categories to scientific concepts. Critics of bourgeois, ideological, " American functionalism " have simply transferred their hostility to " functionalist " claims to scientific status to Soviet sociology. Second, the transformation and transposition of sciences, or scientific concepts, from one mode of production to another have been treated simplistically and dogmatically. Soviet Marxists are aware of the implications of and the distinctions between these orders of problem; they have no intention of replacing Marxism with a " bourgeois sociology." They do not assume that a Western concept is by definition ideological. This

Studies in Comparative Communism Vol. VIII, No. 4, Winter 1975, 370-388 would imply that " science " can be appropriated only as a commodity that must reproduce, identify, or reconstitute capitalist relations in a socialist society, that scientific production is equivalent to commodity production.

Merely because " structural-functionalists " established their vocabulary and method as dominant in certain American academic milieux, and asserted their pseudo-science as a dominant ideology, Marxists should not exclude " structure " and " function " from their discourse along with " model " and " axiom."[1] North American functionalism is compounded of a heterogeneous and often incoherent jumble of quantitative methods, infantile science, reactionary philosophy, and parochialism. It coheres only in its specific institutional context; but if its pretension to completeness is punctured, its component parts are not valueless. Soviet sociologists are properly engaged in concerns central to creative Marxists. These include the avowed attempt to eliminate bureaucratic relations in the U.S.S.R. (through the subdiscipline *nauchnoe upravlenie obshchestvom*, or scientific administration of society) and the investigation of authority relations in production. The intention is clearly to counterpose scientific rationality to dogmatic, arbitrary, and wasteful relations. This would not seem an unconscious or philistine capitulation to bourgeois ideology. Indeed, the typical mass survey by structured questionnaire reveals the deficiencies of planning, the local failure to harmonize the forces and relations of production—it does not produce a manual for technocrats.

The critics of Soviet sociology raise important questions. Gouldner, for example, argues that the Soviet Union has accepted and institutionalized a unilateral, conservative sociology, an apparatus of American ideology and means of social manipulation. In his view, such an importation harms the growth of critical—that is, dialectically negating—theory.[2] In fact, Gouldner misunderstands the relationship between science and ideology. In the case of a non- or pre-science like American functionalism, he confuses a system of concepts with ideology. Marxism itself insists on the positive character of " negation "; it does not and cannot stand aside from ideas and defend the purity—and emptiness—of the moment of negation. His

1. Cf. Alfred Schmidt's *Storia e struttura* (Bari: De Donato, 1972) (*Geschichte und Struktur* (Munich: Carl Hanser, 1971)), which attempts a reconciliation of " structure " and " history " in the context of the history of Marxist theory.

2. A Gouldner, *The Coming Crisis of Western Sociology* (New York: Basic Books, 1970), especially Chap. 12. Professor Gouldner has declined to respond to the author's criticisms. (*Ed.*)

critical theory is simply the philosophical, idealist negation of the positive nature of science—it does not belong in Marxism.

Other critics have drawn a parallel between the " new sociology " and Bukharin's " Historical Materialism " (" A system of sociology "), arguing that Lenin's and Gramsci's strictures [3] on the latter's lifeless eclecticism and scientistic utopianism apply also to the former. While the attacks on Bukharin were well taken in their time, there is at present no suggestion that the new Soviet sociology is a redefinition or authoritative revision of Marxism. Finally, some have hypostasized Sartre's philosophical attempt to re-start a stalled and dogmatic Marxism.[4] In the name of Sartre's subjective ontology, they make Soviet sociology the target for their hostility to quantification, positivism, and empiricism. The political point of Sartre's work is lost in a mish-mash of irrationalism, existentialism, transcendentalism, and anarchism. The tone of the attack is anti-Soviet, but instead of analysis there is merely advocacy of an etiolated branch of Western idealism.

The notion that sociology is the master-science and excludes or subsumes Marxism, political economy, and philosophy is held and bemoaned by radical-conservative North American academics. This view, however, is a travesty of a situation where the arrogant, time-serving reactionaries who passed off a shoddy, pseudo-scientific justification of " imperialism as stability " are themselves increasingly challenged. These academic tyrants, proscribers of intellect, have been notoriously arbitrary and unlettered guardians of ideas. Soviet scholars, indeed, evidently fought shy of intervening in what may have seemed so much gaseous and unnecessary justification of quantitative policy, and market, research. The relation between functionalist concepts and quantitative, mathematical, method was not brought into question because of the special ideological function of American sociology. Under such tutelage, it was hardly surprising that even axioms should appear ideological and reactionary!

3. See N. Bukharin, *Historical Materialism* (New York: Russell and Russell, 1965 [1925 edn.]), and Z. Bauman's criticism of Bukharin in *Lineamenti di una sociologia marxista* (Rome: Editori Riuniti, 1971 [Warsaw, 1964]), pp. 89–96 and 458. See also A. Gramsci, *Il materialismo storico e la filosofia di Benedetto Croce* (Turin: Einaudi, 1966), p. 84, discussed in Bruno Cermignani, " 'Dialettica scientifica' e dialettica della scienza," *Critica marxista*, Quaderni 6 (1972), p. 96. On the trends in Marxism, note V. Gerratana, *Ricerche di storia del marxismo* (Rome: Editori Riuniti, 1972); and, on Gramsci and the sciences, Giuseppe Prestipino, " Momenti e 'modelli' della dialettica marxista," in *Critica marxista*, Quaderni 6 (1972).

4. Cf. the relevant passages in Jean-Paul Sartre, " Questions de méthode " in *Critique de la raison dialectique*, 1 (Paris: Gallimard, 1960). Englished as *Search for a Method*.

Contact with " functionalist " currents was slow to develop in the U.S.S.R. The scientific value of academic sociology seemed outweighed by its ideological trappings. Both philosophers and historical materialists warned of the implications of functionalist *theory*, though willing to accept quantitative techniques and other means of disseminating and de-mystifying information as already an integral part of classical Marxism. Given the climate of debate which preceded and has continued since the " re-joining " of the Marxist and revisionist provinces of sociology, it is hard to accept Gouldner's easy assumption that functionalism attracts and wins over " conservatives " in the Soviet context. These ethnocentric assumptions are, of course, typical of American scholarship on Soviet sociologists.

Marxists will be surprised by Simirenko's suggestion [5] that commitment to science is incompatible with commitment to socialism, because socialism is not disinterested. If Simirenko's conception of professionalization includes the dimension of autonomy, he then faces the paradox of " real " autonomy, which is that it ends by demanding domination of the political power (in the Soviet case, the Party) which seeks to control it. On the other hand, relative autonomies come to seem simply parochial in relation to the evidently political aims of professional autonomy. If he argues that the stultifying effect of professionalism (and the irrelevance of its political ambition as regards its knowledge function) stands in opposition to science proper, then science would seem to be conceived of as in essence critical or negating. This may be reminiscent of Gouldner's *à priori* " reflexive theory," which incidentally is in principle destructive of theory. In fact, Simirenko situates science and scientific knowledge as far as possible independent of and indeterminate by the social means of its production. This formulation, in the context of a history of science, indicates that Simirenko conceives of " science " as being an activity ideally to be abstracted from the professionalism and the politics that constantly seek its resorption.

Without rehearsing the well-worn critiques of methodological individualism and its universalizing self-justifications, one might recall Marx's characterization of the world of truth and inquiry, of the " philosopher and dogmatist " and the " sceptic and empiricist." His conclusions may be a more precise indication of the actual conditions in which scientific debate proceeds than an idealization of science.

5. Cf. Alex Simirenko, " Soviet and American Sociology in the Seventies," *Studies in Comparative Communism*, VI, 1 & 2 (Spring/Summer 1973).

> The sceptic and empiricist who holds nature to be subjective illusion considers it from the point of view of necessity and endeavours to explain and to understand the real existence of things. On the other hand, the philosopher and dogmatist who considers the appearance real sees only chance everywhere, and his manner of explanation tends rather to destroy all the objective reality of nature. . . . But one can hardly expect that these men, contradicting each other in everything, will become disciples of one and the same teaching. And yet they seem to be firmly chained to one another (doctoral thesis).

We have to question in such a context whether, for example, " the scientific administration of society " is inevitably to become the practical means of turning super-bureaucrats into super-technocrats. On the plane of ideology, the Soviet discussion of " scientific administration " is markedly divergent from the more bureaucratic, East European formula of " socialism with a human face." A deeper analysis of the tensions and conflicts in Soviet state and society is required before unequivocal declarations (on the basis of analogies with American intellectual establishments) of the allegiance of Soviet sociologists can be proposed.

Soviet sociology in its new form is of such recent date that this factor alone helps to explain its somewhat precarious character and its weakness as an undergraduate teaching subject, to which Gouldner draws attention. It is an importation, rather than a revival of earlier Soviet or pre-revolutionary sociology. In order to train researchers, and as a result of the Soviet practice of associating research institutes with administrative and productive units rather than universities, sociology has initially developed within a community of specialists. The structure of Soviet higher education itself gives the lie to Gouldner's suggestion that such specialization is a form of sequestration—of a special discrimination aimed at removing sociology from the attention of critical students. Indeed, within the specialist community, internal differentiation of its organizational units has made for a lack of theoretical focus, even diffuseness. At the same time, however, it is not fair to argue that the separation of Party and general research leads to a disciplinary schism. As V. G. Afanas'ev's discussion of organizational matters indicates, there are close institutional links between Party and general research.[6] Indeed, one might

6. Cf. esp. Vol. 3 of the series *Nauchnoe upravlenie obschestvom* (Moscow: Mysl', 1969) edited by Afanas'ev and devoted to the administration of social science and its relation to political management. Note particularly L. V. Golovanov on the structure of scientific research.

argue that the typical Soviet field research of the sixties[7]—mass opinion and attitude surveys, with relatively unsophisticated mathematical criteria—inhibited theoretical elaboration. Specialized agencies saw sociologists as gatherers of a mass of data, rather than as theorists. This tendency makes it likely that it is through the general literature, rather than Party surveys, that broad conceptual and methodological questions will be raised.

The theoretical discussion has tended to concentrate on the relation between the new sociology and sociological concepts of historical materialism, and to conclude that the new concepts serve specific problems, enriching Marxism's synchronic analysis without changing its form. Such a position is certainly consistent with the picture of the infancy of Soviet sociology. Likewise, the discussion on the transportation and utility concepts taken from information theory, cybernetics and systems analysis, to social relations of the socialist societies shows a discipline in the process of self-definition and orientation. Much research is actually testing the technique, not the properties of the real object; and while there is no doubt that popular demand for such sociological information is high, it is too early to see how that information may be used either as an encouragement to further research or as an agent of transformation. In comparison with the Polish school, for example, Soviet sociology lacks historical continuity, major theoretical innovations, and an established place on the map of the disciplines. Its subordination, however, and the necessity of importing the study from alien soil tend to reinforce the contention that it is misleading to characterize the theoretical institutional setting of Soviet sociology as " American."

While it would be wrong to assume that the theory of convergence is valid because some concepts " fit " specific Soviet problems that also " function " in the analysis of capitalist societies, there are points of similarity between the equilibrium models of some systems analysis and Bukharin's sociology. Indeed, it was Gramsci's concern to protest against Bukharin's replacement of Marxist philosophy by pseudo-scientific concepts, an Aristotelian system based on stable equilibrium. This criticism formed part of Gramsci's charge that " orthodox " Marxism tended to destroy itself by such negative (and scientific) insertions.[8] Gramsci, however, argues that it is possible for one social group to absorb the science (*scienza*) of another without

7. See, for example, G. V. Osipov and M. Hookham (eds.), *Industry and Labour in the USSR* (London: Tavistock, 1966) and *Town, Country and People* (London: Tavistock, 1969), and the journal of translations *Soviet Sociology.*

8. Gramsci, *op. cit.*, p. 134.

ingesting its ideology, or indeed neutralizing the relation of science to Marxism.[9] Perception of class struggle, and the need for a dialectical Marxism in the process of appropriating knowledge, establish the primacy of philosophy as the knowledge (or *scienza*) that constitutes the objectivity of the world.[10] Some sciences may masquerade as philosophy,[11] and the struggle for the supremacy of Marxist philosophy over such challengers is clearly and properly a political one.[12]

Gramsci's remarks, however, are concerned with opposing the attempt to substitute a non-science for the Marxism that he conceived of as a philosophy. He was not discussing the form of particular sciences, nor the logical structure of scientific thought. The remarks against Bukharin cannot apply to the relation between historical materialism and its acquisition of, and generation of, concepts. Neither Engels nor Lenin appears to have conceived of an opposition between science and ideology in socialist society, with philosophy mediating between them.[13] A definition of Marxism as philosophy which opposes its own scientific nature is as worthless as the Zhdanov-style distinction between bourgeois and proletarian science.

There are limited advantages in rigidly distinguishing between science, ideology, and philosophy, especially when opposing a sloppy, spontaneous, and subjectivist "Marxism" that reduces Marxism to a formless element in thought. Brewster, for instance, makes the struggle for science political, but disadvantageously at the cost of reducing Marxism to materialism. Class struggle is reduced to a

9. *Ibid.*, pp. 56 and 132. Note Lukács's attempt to define ideology in relation to science:

> The economic development of society raises certain problems, and ideology exists in order to make these problems conscious and to fight them out. There is no opposition between ideology and science. Ideology can be scientific and it can be non-scientific: science can in certain circumstances be ideological, or it can be non-ideological.

In "Lukács on Futurology," *New Hungarian Quarterly*, Vol. 13, No. 47 (Autumn 1972), p. 105. Reprinted from *Futurum*, 4 (1970).

10. Gramsci, *op. cit.*, p. 54.

11. Cf. Ben Brewster, "Althusser and Bachelard," *Theoretical Practice*, 3–4 (Autumn 1971), on those "apparently unphilosophical philosophies" empiricism and positivism, p. 24.

12. E.g., Brewster, *op. cit.*, p. 33, on the political danger of a science's "ideological resorption."

13. Cf. Nicola Badaloni, "Scienza e filosofia in Engels e Lenin," *Critica marxista*, Quaderni 4 (1970), pp. 109–110, and Manuel Sacristan, "Lenin e la filosofia," *Critica marxista*, Vol. 9, No. 1 (January–February 1971), p. 110.

battle of philosophies, materialism pitted against idealism, with each science considered as a neutral and inert totality at the moment of its delivery.[14] Hirst separates the " production " of science from relations and mode of production—eliminating, for example, the problem of " class " mathematics. " Science is not the property of a class subject." [15] However, the relation of science to Marxism remains obscure, and Marxist philosophy takes on a positivized form along with that of particular " knowledges " that appear to be self-moving, independent, and estranged universes of practice.

Gramsci's warning against a premature (or arguably, *any*) liquidation of Marxist philosophy can be extended to Bukharin's case as a warning against turning a system of categories into a science. Gramsci perceived that " orthodoxy " saw the relative autonomy of the sciences as both practical necessity and pragmatic opportunity. Bukharin ignored this, and produced eclecticism. Its " rightist " tendency to adialectical and aphilosophical positions was peculiarly inappropriate to the period of compromise, the New Economic Policy. However, Bukharin committed an error against science as well as against philosophy, because his method of converting categories to concepts was essentially that of idealism. It is the combination of apriorism with eclecticism which completes the criticism of Bukharin. It is precisely this mixture that current Soviet sociology, in discussion both with philosophy and with the sciences, is most anxious to avoid. If its concentration on given, concrete problems, its resolute deflation of universal concepts to the immediate and phenomenal, disappoints the idealists, it marks a proper scientific scepticism.

The dangers of taking the scientific nature of Marx's concepts as formalized and fixed for all epochs is exemplified by Charles Bettelheim's analysis of the mode, or combination of modes, of production in the U.S.S.R. Using Marx's categories to investigate the Soviet Union, he finds capitalism.[16] Marx's observation that

> there are categories which are common to all stages of production and are established by reasoning as general categories: the

14. Brewster, *op. cit.*, p. 33: a struggle for science is " a struggle for materialism against idealism."

15. Paul Hirst, " Althusser and Philosophy," *Theoretical Practice*, 2 (April 1971), p. 25.

16. Cf. Charles Bettelheim, *Calcul économique et formes de propriété* (Paris: Maspero, 1971), discussed in Paul M. Sweezy and Charles Bettelheim, *Lettres sur quelques problèmes actuels du socialisme* (Paris: Maspero, 1972) (Englished as *On the Transition to Socialism* (New York: Monthly Review Press, 1971)), and, critically, in *La Nature des Pays de l'Est, Critiques de l'Economie Politique*, 7/8 (April–September 1972), especially E. Germain, " Les réformes Liberman-Trapeznikov de la gestion des entreprises soviétiques."

> so-called *general conditions* of all and any production, however, are nothing but abstract conceptions which do not define any of the actual historical stages of production [17]

is not the equivalent of saying that these abstract categories are the concepts of the science of a specific mode.

The "new" Soviet sociology does not yet provide the new concepts—still less claims to supply the method—for a science of "socialist administration." Indeed, it has been organized more as an array of subdisciplines than as a unified science of the social totality. However, it does recognize the political, rather than the economic, character of the problems of the social formation in the U.S.S.R. In the current preliminary, exploratory phase, a "pre-science" comments on and challenges not Marxist philosophy but the deficiencies of socialist political science. It does not depart from the uncritical and equilibrated assumptions of functionalism. Its concern is with the political superstructure, and not with re-casting a political economy after the manner of Bettelheim. Soviet sociology is engaged at present in the aggregation, rather than the analysis, of phenomena. Far from emanating from "capitalist relations" in the U.S.S.R., it has as its aim rescuing Marxism from the history it has made, a factitious imprisonment that can lead to dogmatism and a positivistic self-defense.

Gouldner's epistemology refers back not to political economy but to classical German idealism, to the critical theory in which a transcendental subject "rescues" others from science. Gouldner makes little of the modalities of argument *within* Marxism, despite the foreign debate among Soviet philosophers from the mid-fifties to the late sixties, which joins part of the general European discussion of the links between idealism, dogmatism, and scientism. Indeed, his opposition to functionalism is so embracing that he implies that Marxists cravenly abandoned socialism for the keypunch with no thought for the implications. Actually, it is Gouldner himself who counterposes critical thought to Marxism, a subjective eclecticism to principle. The very principle of reflexive sociology, its rejection and negation of the positive, makes his condemnation of Soviet sociology as revisionism or neo-Machism appear to emerge from a position of "orthodoxy." Yet he is equally opposed to orthodoxy. What is primarily a methodical objection to empiricism becomes a two-edged sword against Soviet science and Soviet philosophy. Gouldner's trans-

17. Karl Marx, "Introduction," in Maurice Dobb (ed.), *A Contribution to the Critique of Political Economy* (London: Lawrence and Wishart, 1971), p. 193.

cendental subject appears as the product of a revolutionary hiring policy in American sociology departments, and the reflexive mode replaces analysis of the political and methodical issues involved in the Soviet context.

To Gouldner, Soviet Marxism seems substantially the caricature in Marcuse's book of that title. A critical current of thought is threatened by functionalism, a loosely defined, conservative, status-quo, ideologically bourgeois doctrine. Inconsistently, however, he sees its applications as directed to technical, rather than to technocratic, problems.[18] He appears to assume that Soviet Marxism is already moribund, and that knowledge is forever in the hands of an elite that uses its cutting edge on the necks of the proletariat. Again, Gouldner's desire to make an anti-Soviet point leads him to inconsistency with regard to the differential knowledge-effect of "functionalism." In Eastern Europe, he argues, it will aid liberalism; in the U.S.S.R., the more conservative—and Communist—elements![19] "Functionalism" is simultaneously bourgeois, technical, instrumental, conservative, and Communist. Instead of a discussion of class politics, we have an unsupported speculation on the policies of intellectuals.

Unfortunately, Gouldner's frame of reference is the American university as interpreted by Wright Mills—the battleground between business and philosophy. He assumes that social science institutes in the U.S.S.R. remove research from the populist influence of students and radical faculty.[20] The class relations of Soviet intellectuals, the relation of empirical research to empiricism, the significance of axiomatization, and the significance especially of the transposition of engineering and cybernetic concepts to other sciences and pseudo-sciences are all seen in terms of American class society.

To Gouldner, sociology *is* the master science, and hence must threaten Marxism. To functionalism, however, he opposes not Marxism but the non-science of reflexive, critically negating theory. The "problem" of science is forever that of its destruction *as ideology*. The destructive power of critical sociology at once is political and transcends politics: "all the powers that be are inimical

18. Gouldner: "Functionalism" is seen as concerned with "problems of integrating and managing the Soviet form of industrialization" (p. 467).

19. *Ibid.* Sociology seems liberal in Eastern Europe and "more communist-controlled and less liberal" in the U.S.S.R. (pp. 447 and 467).

20. Cf. C. Wright Mills, *Sociology and Pragmatism : The Higher Learning in America* (New York: Oxford University Press, 1966), p. 35; "The professionalization of philosophy within American institutions of higher learning is the most obvious social anchorage of the field" (i.e., between pragmatism and the American social structure).

to the highest ideals of sociology." [21] Ultimately, however, the paradox collapses on Gouldner, for sociology itself is a power-that-is.[22] Currents within neo-Marxism, from Lefebvre's resistance to mathematization to existentialist-humanism, are combined into a radicalism whose essence is its anti-Marxism. To Gouldner, positivism did not recover a " rational kernel " from fideism—it is our task to discover positivism's rational kernel.[23] By analogy and implication, then, Marx did not retrieve Hegel's " rational kernel "—it is for the critical sociologist to expose Marx's rationality and dispose of the mystical shell. Marx thus is made to stand with, perhaps, Comte as another in the line-up of great thinkers who unwittingly enshrine the principle of critical negativity!

In order critically to negate bourgeois categories, the reflexive sociologist must assume their universal substantiality. His opposition to the bourgeoisie becomes indistinguishable from his opposition to science. The known world and the bourgeois world become synonymous. Marxism does not battle the substance of bourgeois society, by this argument, because the positive nature of its very categories—or rather the very instrumental knowledge of Marxists—delivers them to the universe of their opponents. For this reason, Gouldner is compelled to make Soviet sociologists " really " economists, concerned with forces rather than relations of production.[24] The problem is after all one of industrialization, not of socialism. Soviet society is merely another American colony.

Gouldner's conceptions concerning Soviet sociology are widely held. They attract those who see Marxism as a philosophy impervious to science, fully stocked with categories—a dinosaur stuffed with its own obsolescence. In fact, the introduction of the " new sociology "

21. Gouldner, *op. cit.*, p. 499.
22. *Ibid.*, p. 497.
23. A Gouldner, " A Reply to Martin Shaw: Whose Crisis? " *New Left Review*, 71 (January–February 1972), p. 91:

> Even classical sociological positivism at its crassest was not a totally reactionary standpoint. In its opposition to the proliferation of metaphysical invisibles, positivism placed itself in abrasive opposition to established religions, and, in this, even positivism had its own rational kernel.

Shortly after (p. 95), Gouldner contrives to shift his criticism from functionalism more squarely onto the U.S.S.R.

> In the context of certain Eastern European countries which are massively controlled from a separate political centre, this same equilibrium [Parsonian] analysis has liberative potentialities. It provides certain theoretical clues as to how a socialist society may be organized with a minimum of bureaucracy and state control.

24. Gouldner, *The Coming Crisis*, p. 467.

stimulated a lively response in the U.S.S.R. In contrast to its development in North America, the discussion of " functionalist " sociology, information theory, and cybernetics took place in intellectual milieux dominated by Marxist-Leninists.[25] The loss of distinction between subject and object in information theory has been criticized as leading to a dogmatic metaphysics, a tautological and sterile pedagogy.[26] There is no agreement as to the line of continuity of Soviet sociology —whether it should be regarded as an outgrowth of pre-revolutionary sociology or of a Western tradition, or as a legitimate offspring of historical materialism.[27] The new sociology raised the question of the relation between philosophical categories and the general-abstract concepts of " scientific " functionalism.[28] This in turn drew attention to Engels's allegedly metaphysical use of dialectics as a method of science,[29] and of changes in the form of Marxism-Leninism.[30] Far from institutionalizing a body of reactionary and conventional wisdom, the importation of sociology was the occasion for a keenly contested and much-popularized debate in the " new cultural climate " of the post-Stalin period.

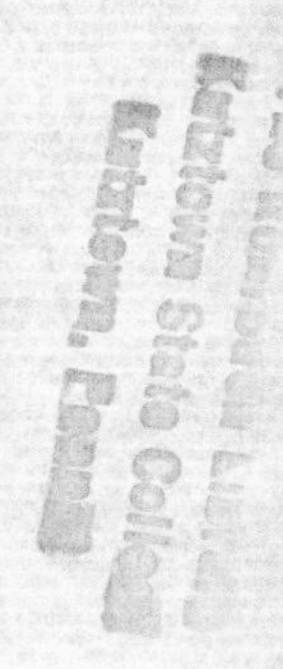

The debate took place within a body of Marxist intellectuals; but though it lacked the bitterness of the *querelles* in which Marxist and bourgeois intellectuals have been engaged in Europe, it was not confined to professional intellectuals. The proletariat, far from being the passive object of social administrators, could see the language of scientific rationality used against the bureaucrat and the irrational.

25. Cf. Erich Hahn, *Istoricheskii materializm i marksistskaya sotsiologiya* (Moscow: Progress 1971), translation of *Historische Materialismus und marxistische Soziologie* (Berlin: Dietz Verlag, 1968).

26. For a rebuttal of cybernetics as a resolution of problems of consciousness and pedagogy, see E. V. Il'enkov, *Ob idolakh i idealakh* (Moscow: Politizdat, 1968).

27. See, e.g., B. A. Chagin (ed.), *Ocherk istorii sotsiologicheskoi mysli v SSSR* (Leningrad: Nauka, 1971).

28. Cf. *Ocherki metodologii poznaniya sotsial'nykh yavlenii* (Moscow: Mysl', 1970), and the authoritative works by V. Yadov, *Metodologiya i protsedury sotsiologicheskikh isseldovanii* (Tartu, 1968), and A. G. Zdravomyslov, *Sotsiologicheskoe issledovanie: Metodologiya, Programma, Metody* (Moscow: Mysl', 1969). These questions have been discussed from the standpoint of " scientific Communism " by, e.g., L. N. Suvorov, *Nauchnyi kommunizm i upravlenie sotsial'nymi protsessami* (Moscow: Znanie, 1967), and N. E. Artyukhin, *Nauchnyi kommunizm—teoriya postroeniya sotsializma i kommunizma* (Ryazan', 1965).

29. E.g., in B. M. Kedrov, *Engel's i dialektika estestvoznaniya* (Moscow: Politizdat, 1970).

30. On what constitutes a world-view, and whether Marxism-Leninism is one, see *Marksistko-leninskaya filosofiya kak metodologiya obshchestvennykh i estestvennykh nauk* (Moscow: Moscow UP, 1972), p. 11ff.

In capitalist societies where the technocrat's scepter is a slide rule, the methodical and political implications of "scientific administration" are evident. Where man is not confronted with hostility by science and the machine, systematic study of bureaucracy is a blow against irrational authority.

The aim of the new sociology is not to replace Marxism, nor to represent "bourgeois theory" and a phantom bourgeoisie. In any case, the basis and claims of the new theories are too vapid and ill-formulated, its object too ill-defined, to permit that interpretation.[31] Much of the work on cybernetics and information theory is concerned with the transfer of concepts and their application in different "systems"—that is, with the production of a scientific terminology. In this sense, it reacts against the utopian, speculative discussions of the "new Soviet man." It seeks to forestall the separation of man from science, and especially the mystifying separation of the language of technical rationality from political systems.

The new sociology endeavors to analyze and close the gap between the sciences of the productive forces and the sciences, or pseudo-sciences, of relations of production. Certainly, there are dangers in this—scientism, reductionism, mechanistic transfers from engineering systems to social relations. However, one can only deal with the context of the debate and its origins to date, and should not speculate on the outcome of struggles to come. First, Soviet sociology at the outset was closely identified with the ending of restrictions on concrete social research during the period of the "cult of personality."[32] This point was especially stressed by Osipov's important collections, published in 1965.

Second, the founding generation of Soviet sociology has emphasized the novelty of the process of transition in the movement from socialism to Communism. This specific and uncharted phase, it is argued, requires special and immediate study. New techniques do not require a defense against revisionism, since they are applied to a transformed object. In fact, the first problem faced by the new sociology was not one of fragmentation of heterodoxy but one of separation of empirical and theoretical, and of macro- and micro-

31. Cf. Ivan Kuvavic, "Marxisme et fonctionnalisme," *L'Homme et la Société*, 23 (January–March 1972), and Piotr Sztompka, "The Logic of Functional Analysis in Sociology and Social Anthropology," *Polish Sociological Bulletin*, Vol. 2, No. 22 (1970).

32. In *Sotsiologiya v SSSR*. See also G. N. Osipov's *Sotsiologiya i konkretnye sotsial'nye issledovaniya v SSSR* (Moscow, 1970) and *Amerikanskaya sotsiologiya: Perspektivy, Problemy* (Moscow, 1972).

sociology.[33] The training of certain younger methodologues in large-scale survey research (for instance, the distinguished scholars Zdravomyslov and Yadov) led some to suppose that sociology might split up not even into subdisciplines, but into an assortment of techniques.[34] This suspicion proved unjustified, especially as a result of the efforts made by the first generation of sociologists to gain internal unity and that recognition from other disciplines which might permit theoretical as well as technical development. The political imperatives were from the outset entwined with the necessity for maintaining an intellectually rigorous and consistently innovative stance.

These political concerns and origins are evident in the subdiscipline and the forceful popularization of *Nauchnoe upravlenie obshchestvom*, especially in the work of its chief spokesman V. G. Afanas'ev. Though involved in the general discussion of quantitative research, this study is concerned with the use of systems analysis and information theory to analyze the structure and dissemination of public policy. It should again be noted in this context that the "equilibrated" properties of administrative systems are goals, not initial assumptions. Nor is this administrative science to be institutionalized in a Communist society, as it provides a means to the understanding only of the period of transition.

The earlier phases of the discussion of mathematical and engineering methods were often overoptimistic and overambitious. Greater concern is now shown to examine basic categories more closely, to avoid premature axiomatization, and to re-examine the implications of Lenin's perspective on philosophy and the sciences.[35] Some authors have suggested that the new abstractions—from cybernetics and functional and structural analysis—could be accommodated without adjustment or debate within the concrete framework of

33. This has been a particular concern of G. M. Andreeva. See her recent *Lektsii po metodike konkretnykh sotsial'nykh issledovanii* (Moscow: Moscow UP, 1972).

34. Examples of popular works that stress the need to synthesize quantitative data with discussion of the historical development of Soviet society include A. A. Ambrosov, *Ot klassovoi differentsiatsii k sotsial'noi odnorodnosti obshchestva* (Moscow: Mysl', 1972), B. I. Syusyukalov, *Sotsialisticheskoe obshchestvo: problemy dialektiki razvitiya* (Moscow: Mysl', 1973), and D. I. Chesnokov, *Istoricheskii materializm kak sotsiologiya marksizma-leninizma* (Moscow: Mysl', 1973).

35. V. V. Varchuk and V. I. Razin, "Issledovaniya v oblasti politicheskoi organizatsii sotsialisticheskogo obshchestva," *Voprosy filisofii*, 4 (1967), and B. M. Kedrov, "Ob osobennostyakh leninskikh zapisei v 'Filosofskikh tetradyakh'," *Voprosy filosofii*, 12 (1969), on Lenin's notebooks, materialist in one margin, idealist in the other, pp. 44–45.

historical materialism. As labels applied to tested engineering techniques, their scientific status was held to be assured. They could become the concepts of social science, or any other form of science. However, this simplistic and scientistic approach, which equated model and theory and used information theory to "prove" Lenin's reflection theory, has been recognized as theoretically inadequate.[36] The political implications of taking information to be synonymous with direction were resisted. These positions carried the marks of arbitrary and dogmatic experimentation, and reduced a complexly determined social formation to an idealized and simple engineering model.

More judicious observers have suggested that, for example, structure and function belong to different levels of analysis.[37] The early mechanical materialist desire to "model thought" has been replaced by a sceptical suspension of the notion of consciousness from cybernetics and a division between model and theory.[38] The danger of endowing structures with internal logic divorced from intentionality and determination from without, and of defining function as the activity of the structure's immanent logic, has also been noted. Indeed, it is precisely these bourgeois connotations—the logical justification of managerial capitalism, and the unity of structure and function—which have created dismay among Soviet sociologists.

It has been argued that "scientific administration" simply strengthens and interposes a technically knowledgeable bureaucracy at the point of production. Other subdisciplines, such as "scientific Communism" and "scientific organization of labor," are the targets of similar charges. Are these not, it is asked, means of replacing "politics" by administration, and of using the "neutral" terms of system, structure and function to persuade Soviet workers that society is an equilibrated system? Does this not turn Marxism into a new glossary intended to conceal decisionmakers' "choices," using mathematical tautologies to reinforce the objectionable features of formalism and elitism?[39]

36. A. N. Kochergin, *Modelirovanie myshleniya* (series *Nad chem rabotayut, o chem sporyat filosofy*), (Moscow: Politizdat, 1969), p. 109.

37. Yu. V. Orfeev, "Umstvennyi trud cheloveka i 'mashinnoe myshlenie'," in V. G. Afanas'ev (ed.), *Nauchnoe upravlenie obshchestvom*, 4 (Moscow: Mysl', 1970), p. 322.

38. Cf. V. P. Tugarinov, "Eshche o mashinnom myshlenii," *Vestnik Leningradskogo Universiteta*, Vol. 17, No. 3 (1966), and T. V. Kerimova, "Metodologicheskie predposylki issledovaniya sotsial'nogo upravleniya," *Voprosy filosofii*, 1 (1972). Note too J. Guillaumaud, *Cybernétique et matérialisme dialectique* (Paris: Editions Sociales, 1965).

39. See, e.g., the critical and sceptical roundtable on Soviet politics in the

In fact, Afanas'ev has stressed the need to examine the conditions under which scientific work is organized in the U.S.S.R.[40] The social scientist must reduce the distance between himself and the social object of his research. No doubt this can lead to the loss of the observer in his object, to the subsumption of analytical thought in empirical reality.[41] However, the possible confusion of scientist with science is of less immediate moment than the specific areas into which the observer is to penetrate. Afanas'ev's concern is to show the political relationships and domains to be thus intimately explored. First, "scientific administration" is to evaluate the institutions endowed with state power in terms of their performance as "information systems." Second, he proposes an inquiry into Soviet production relations from the perspective of technical and administrative division of labor. This may indicate the extent to which hierarchical (class, status, political) divisions of labor run counter to the technical rationale of specialization. Third, he suggests an examination of the Party as organizer both of political and of scientific work. As an immediate example, an analysis of the quality of the Party's political information is a project that may employ both intra-Party and general-social researchers.[42]

In these areas—proper terrain for socialist social scientists—the very vagueness and generality of functionalist concepts constitute an advantage as well as a methodical limitation.[43] A "systematic" study may deal with the equilibrium of personal relations in a production

Italian Party journal "Vent' anni dopo Stalin," *Rinascita*, No. 8 (February 23, 1973).

40. V. G. Afanas'ev (ed.), *Nauchnoe upravlenie obshchestvom*, (Moscow: Mysl', 1969).

41. O. V. Elchaninova in *ibid.*, "Rol' sotsial'noi informatsii i matematicheskikh metodov v vyrabotke upravlencheskikh reshenii," esp. on Baibakov's hope that Gosplan could be automated (1968), p. 241.

42. On tentative inquiries into state and party roles in government, see B. A. Kerimov, *Leninizm i problemy gosudarstvennogo obshchestva* (Leningrad: Lenizdat, 1969), and V. G. Afanas'ev, *Ob intensifikatsii razvitiya sotsialisticheskogo obshchestva* (Moscow: Mysl', 1969). Factory authority relations and political participation are discussed in *Nauchnoe upravlenie obshchestvom*, 4 (Moscow: Mysl', 1970), in articles by Ya. E. Stul' and I. O. Tishchenko (Chelyabinsk study) and Yu. E. Volkov (Sverdlovsk and Urals material). More general questions are raised by V. G. Afanas'ev, *Nauchnoe upravlenie obshchestvom: Opyt sistemnogo issledovaniya* (Moscow: Politizdat, 1968).

43. E.g., in the limits of the models analyzed in I. V. Blauberg, V. N. Sadovskii, and E. G. Yudin (eds.), *Problemy metodologii sistemnogo issledovaniya* (Moscow: Mysl', 1970), and V. A. Lektorskii and V. S. Shvyrev's review of the literature in *Voprosy filosofii*, 1 (1971).

team or brigade, of a regional labor force, or of an administrative structure in which scientific rationality intervenes. Certainly the questions raised remain as general as the very notion of the scientific approach—scientific rationality—but the principle raised is nonetheless one of the employment of the hypothetico-deductive method.

The old dogmatic separation of political and scientific endeavors, and the antagonistic relation between Party and scientific community which distorted and frustrated both political and scientific innovation, may now be ending. Research can now penetrate Party and production. "Functionalism" itself, where not simply a mystifying term for pragmatism, investigates the properties and interdependence of units in a complex productive system. Where the structural contradiction of class has been resolved, functionalism may be a preliminary means of restoring that analytical totality which in capitalist society is mystifyingly provided by metaphysics and idealism.

It may be objected, however, that Soviet functionalism, influenced more by systems theory than vitalism or organicism, links different problems by metaphor disguised as theory. For example, it is possible to speak of harmony between workers engaged in, and defined by, the same productive process. However, the same phenomenal, commonsense approach does not transpose to the level of the complex determinatedness of a transitional society. Systems of actors whose relations can analytically be assumed to be momentary and abstract are not analogous to the historically determinate elements of a state system. Historical materialism has not been exhausted by functionalism, though there is no reason for Marxist sociologists to be depressed by this!

The crucial notion of dysfunction is significant in that it implies not the conceptual negation of "function," but a limit to functionalism, a restriction on the scope of the theory itself. The common properties of systems, as in the case of the abstract-general categories of productive systems in Marx's analysis, are not scientific concepts. They are speculative and metaphysical, historically determined at the phenomenal, not the analytical, level. "Dysfunction" implies an extrinsic logic and intentionality which both in theory and practice determines the capacity of the function. In other words, the function is mathematical; the dysfunction belongs to the domain of practice, not to dialectical negativity. Not only, then, is functionalism a limited method of conceptualization, which resists many of the logical criteria of the hypothetico-deductive method, but it has so far resisted the movement from abstract to concrete. It is, then, on these grounds of the logical deficiency of functionalism and failure, to date, to complete the process of concrete conversion outlined in Marx's " Introduction " that we must discount its theoretical and analytical self-sufficiency.

The new sociology is a moment in the development of Soviet social theory, not a new foundation. Its limitations make it not a threat to historical materialism, but a sign of the growth of systematic inquiry, of intellectual vigor and maturity. The subsumption of " scientific Communism " under the disciplinary protection of Party history and historical materialism was a direct and serious result of the " cult."[44] This certainly frustrated one of the moments of the process of articulating the method of a science, the moment of abstraction from the concrete. Where bourgeois sociologists remain in the abstract, Soviet sociologists were for too long denied access to the concrete.

With public interest in sociology, too, come not only stimulus for Party activity, but initiatives " from below."[45] In a socialist society the demand for knowledge is distinct from the question of whether the science available is " good " or " bad." Soviet workers have a present as well as a past and a future, and Shkaratan's preliminary work on synchronic and diachronic comparisons of class structure broadens the perspective, rather than reducing it to the every-day.[46] The scale of the mass surveys—for instance, that in Leningrad—implies an historical stocktaking, not an hermetic experiment.[47] The investigation by questionnaire of the political and cultural attitudes of *kolkhoz* workers is evidence of qualitatively different social concerns, as well as of a desire to live up to the Leninist imperative of concrete social research.[48] It would seem merely perverse to conclude that this empirical work leads either to empiricism or to the tyranny of the academic sociologist.

Relations between intellectuals and their society, and the method of appropriation of knowledge in the U.S.S.R., are of course more complex than is suggested in this paper. Certainly, too, Soviet sociologists are not the neo-Bolsheviks of whom some Western radicals dream. However, it is wrong to regard a science, or would-be science,

44. Pointed out by V. D. Demidenko, *Osnovy nauchnogo kommunizma* (L'vov: L'vovskii Lesotekhn. Inst., 1964), p. 3.

45. Described in A. S. Shakir-Zade, *Obshchestvennye nachala v sozdanii kultury kommunizma* (Baku: AN Azerb. SSR, 1969).

46. O. I. Shkaratan, *Problemy sotsial'noi struktury rabochego klassa SSSR* (Moscow: Mysl', 1970).

47. A. G. Zdravomyslov, V. P. Rozhin, and V. A. Yadov (eds.), *Chelovek i ego rabota : Sotsiologicheskoe issledovanie* (Moscow: Mysl', 1967).

48. E.g., N. I. Matyash, " O razvitii vnutrikolkhoznoi demokratii v sovremennykh usloviyakh," in *Nauchnyi kommunizm : problemy i issledovaniya*, Pt. 2 (Moscow: Moscow UP, 1969). See also *Kollektiv kolkhoznikov : Sotsial'no-psikhologicheskoe issledovanie* (Moscow: Mysl', 1970).

as bourgeois ideology, when in the Soviet case it seeks to debureaucratize and demystify Soviet social and political relations. Marxists must be alive to the context of each others' political and theoretical debates. In the last resort, the level of scientific awareness of the Soviet working class will determine the correctness of their perception of the real objects of the " new sociology." It should be encouraging that in a period of transition there should be so many to take the path of materialism, notwithstanding its demands, rather than that of idealism.

REVIEW ARTICLES

WALTER D. CONNOR

Revolution, Modernization, and Communism

Charles Gati (ed.), *The Politics of Modernization in Eastern Europe: Testing the Soviet Model* (New York: Praeger, 1974).

Alex Inkeles and David H. Smith, *Becoming Modern: Individual Change in Six Developing Countries* (Cambridge: Harvard University Press, 1974).

Moshe Lewin, *Political Undercurrents in Soviet Economic Debates: From Bukharin to the Modern Reformers* (Princeton: Princeton University Press, 1974).

Roger Pethybridge, *The Social Prelude to Stalinism* (New York: St. Martin's Press, 1974).

Svetozar Stojanović, *Between Ideals and Reality: A Critique of Socialism and Its Future* (New York: Oxford University Press, 1973).

Sharon Zukin, *Beyond Marx and Tito: Theory and Practice in Yugoslav Socialism* (New York and London: Cambridge University Press, 1974).

The marriage of Marxian socialism and modernization has been one either of convenience or of necessity. Although modernizing nationalist elites of the Third World fly, more frequently than not,

Marxist banners, they could probably make do with alternative ideologies, were any others so readily available. They are not, and " Marxism " is convenient. For the Bolsheviks in the Russia of the 1920s, however, and for their followers in most of post-World War II Eastern Europe, the commitment to an ideology—by then " Marxism-Leninism "—meant a vision, even if a rough one, of a society that could only be achieved on the basis of the transformation we call modernization. *This* marriage was necessary, for Marx, as we know, looked for the future revolution in the " modern " Europe where it did not come, and saw little chance for it where it did in fact arise. The process of socialist modernization, then, with many variations and little direct guidance from the " holy writ " of the nineteenth century has been an attempt to supply the " basis " of a socialist society after the fact of political revolution.

Nowhere has the process of modernization (in its " minimal " accepted meaning—industrialization, urbanization, the development of general literacy) been so convulsive as in the Soviet Union. Much thought, and no doubt an equal amount of foolishness, has gone into analyzing those convulsions. Was the human toll of the First Five-Year Plan, to say nothing of the purges, " necessary " to transform traditional Russia? Was there a viable gradualist solution? In *The Social Prelude to Stalinism*, Pethybridge confronts these questions, at least implicitly, in examining the recalcitrant social realities with which the Bolshevik modernizers were forced to deal. The dealing amounted to a confrontation between the large-scale organizational goals and visions of the Bolsheviks (who, isolated from political participation under the Tsarist regime and urban-bred for the most part, knew little of the realities of Russia despite their plans for its transformation) and the human material of change—the peasant mass of the population. Illiterate, " silent," and parochial, its characteristic modes of social organization local, small-scale, and fitted to small objectives, the mass became a millstone " hung round the neck of the Bolsheviks."

Forward motion under such a weight is difficult, motion without collision impossible. The ten-year prelude to Stalinism saw the early postrevolutionary " utopianism " fall victim to the exigencies of the civil war, which devastated the countryside without transforming it and consumed the resources necessary to any transformation. With the civil war, however, came the first coercive militarization and mobilization of the population—a foretaste of the plan era. The New Economic Policy (NEP) provided *material* restoration but was neither capable of nor aimed at the realization of transformational goals. Over the whole decade, holding the society together was for the elite a matter of concentrating power at the center, ramifying state and Party organizations outward according to a quasi-military model (the only one with which, by way of the civil war, it had any real experience) and thus tolerating little local or regional deviation—all this in a social setting where literacy was a scarce value and its lack barred most of the population from meaningful inputs into or feed-back from the governing process.

So was the stage set. With the "great break," Stalin's move toward transformation, began a process whose outcome seems, in Pethybridge's narrative, almost overdetermined. Maximalist goals were pursued through centralized, coercive organization—what else, when no effective bridge had ever been built to the small-scale, "spontaneous," and historically rooted organizational forms of the countryside? Literacy was achieved. But along with it, because the commitment to a particular *kind* of social and political transformation had been made and would brook no questioning, came "one of the most efficient systems of censorship known in the history of man since he became a language-using animal." Verbal literacy and *political* literacy, of the sort that allows the formation of critical positions, the development of independent thought, were sundered. The bureaucratic means of transformation were frozen into ends in themselves, and the economic progress achieved came at the cost of locking the masses into a permanent political backwardness.

Russia, thus, became "modern" but with those differences that have made it a "special case" in the discussion of industrial societies. While Pethybridge limits himself to exploring the route to Stalinism, Lewin examines some similar issues but from a different angle and with a temporal perspective that takes us from War Communism to the present. *Political Undercurrents in Soviet Economic Debates* adds little to the historical record but does cast history in a new and provocative light. Lewin's basic theme is one of an interrupted continuity between the positions adopted by Bukharin and his adherents late in the economic debates of the 1920s and the positions of well-known and not-so-well-known Soviet reform economists since the late 1950s; more critically, a continuity between the political ideas underlying these positions. The NEP, in Lewin's view, was a developing entity; initially a sop to the peasants, it became, by the end of its eight years, a pattern, a program that could have constituted the base for a very different form of economic development. Stalin and Stalin's "command economy" triumphed, leading Russia toward a peculiar sort of modernity whose chronic problems in many economic sectors were at least as notable as its triumphs.

In the decompression of the post-1953 period and the subsequent critiques of various economic distortions, Lewin sees the emergence of Bukharin's "ghost." For many of the reformists' ideas aimed at remedying the dysfunctions of resource overcommitment, *dirigiste* planning, the permanent and uneconomic subjection of the peasantry, and the absence of an adequate substitute for the "market" parallel were in fact Bukharin's (given their different historical context). His ideas represented "the road not taken," an unadopted alternative to the system on which the reformers trained their guns in the Khrushchev period. The chronic economic problems of that system were consequences, in large part, of political decisions. Hence, even in the sanitized language of economics, the reformers found themselves addressing a major political question: how are the costs of a monolithic state-Party apparatus' running of the economy and the society to be borne? In cautious words, the reformers were saying, it seems, that they could *not* be; that the state *à la* Soviet cannot run a complex modern economy without taking account of economics; that in fact the state can run nothing well if, in the last analysis, it is captive to the Party in a monocratic system. The problems remain; the reformers have grown reluctant to press their claims against an elite that sees its privileges and power rooted in business as usual and is not afraid to tar even moderate critics with the brush of Bukharinism. Lewin is balanced in his parting glance at the future, perceiving the development of autonomous forces for economic and political change, which are, however, still held in check by a leadership for whom the recipe of the 1930s remains "valid." Which way the Soviet Union moves may be largely a function of whether the renewal of its leadership in the next decade brings new minds, or simply new faces, to the task of continuing modernization.

If the Soviet pattern of development is taken as one extreme, producing political and social structures of extraordinary stability (however unattractive to liberal democrats and democratic socialists), the other extreme among the outcomes of socialist development policies must be Yugoslavia. Out of the legacy of a civil war perhaps as fierce, and an underdevelopment as severe, as that of Russia came a very different type of socialist society—a one-Party state that in some real measure made the Party an arena for competing interests, tolerated relatively free discussion, let its citizens taste of the pleasures and corruptions of the West, and was, seemingly, quite serious about encouraging a real participation by the common man in the decisions that determined a good deal of his daily life.

How, then, has the singularity of the Yugoslav experience been reflected in the minds of Yugoslav citizens? In *Beyond Marx and Tito*, Sharon Zukin provides some answers, frequently in the directly quoted words of members of ten Belgrade families, repeatedly interviewed in the course of a year. The answers are diverse (as are the social levels of the families), but some common threads run through most of them. " Socialism " is understood by most people as the benefits of modernization, rather than as a particular doctrine or mode of organizing political and economic life. Because of those benefits—increased living standards, opportunities for educational and occupational advancement, a new and easier life beyond the imagining of those who underwent the rigors of partisan warfare and the postwar reconstruction—" socialism " is accorded a nearly universal legitimacy.

But this is a very " secular " legitimacy, tied to an ability to deliver the goods. The unique system of self-management is not very salient to the masses. Indeed, those most likely to perceive themselves as " active " in self-management are those who hold managerial positions in organizations. Similarly, the most positive and supportive attitudes towards the current configuration of the system are held by those whose qualities, drives, and luck have allowed them to " make it " in a post-1965 market socialism that has de-emphasized egalitarianism in favor of spurring individual and collective enterprise in pursuit of gain. Many of those who have not " made it " are puzzled by large and obvious income and consumption differentials and by the fact that effective power continues to be the preserve of upper-level political actors who owe their " clout " to political experience and skill or technical expertise. By and large, power still flows downward.

Yet, as Zukin observes, the population is not " cowering and fearful." That is no mean thing in the twentieth century. The apoliticism of many of her informants may dissatisfy those who expect more of the " Yugoslav experiment " in the way of participatory democracy, but a tolerated apoliticism is scarcely the worst conceivable outcome for a population whose road to modernity has been risky and unsure. It is indeed true, as the author argues, that " self-management " has become a *means* toward the goal of industrialization, and that industrialization *as* goal has replaced a " socialization of consciousness." If the ruling elite has not managed to solve the problems of ethnic tensions, and if much still remains to do in equalizing levels of economic development across the country, it should at least not be faulted for striving for concrete goals desired, as Zukin's interviews indicate, by the average Yugoslav citizen.

Svetozar Stojanović's book, rooted just as deeply in the peculiarities of Yugoslav socialism, goes well beyond them in its attempt to deal with the persisting gap between the liberating promise of socialism and its flawed concrete realizations. If Yugoslav socialism's particular recipe for the good society—a self-management within the enterprise gradually transforming itself into a broader social self-government—remains as yet unrealized, the Soviet Union is not a "socialist" country at all, not even any longer a perverted one. Stojanović sees the beginnings of the "statist perversion" in the fact that the Bolsheviks faced the tasks of modernization, evidenced by the "absence of a large, developed industrial proletariat." In such a situation, centralized power, "state socialism," was necessary, and acceptable in Stojanović's view, *provided* the state did represent mass interests. The tendency of the state apparatus to emancipate itself from those interests and to pursue its own brought about the Soviet transformation to statism—first of a "primitive politocratic" sort, now increasingly "technocratic" but in neither case socialist or "liberating."

Stojanović fears the loss of the impetus toward liberation in the day-to-day business of "building," against opposition, a new social order—in effect, the already demonstrated risk that a revolutionary movement "can come to prefer its organizations, activities and institutions, which it had originally conceived only as revolutionary means, to its goals." So we are back again to the means-ends dilemma. And on this and other aspects of the awesome task (which capitalism and socialism both face) of preserving freedom within large-scale organization, Stojanović has little new to offer except exhortations to be wary, to struggle, to fight "statist" tendencies. It would no doubt be unfair to fault Stojanović for his commitment to a "pure" socialism, for this is an open, sincere, and even courageous one. But, in the end one wonders about the logic of commitment to socialism, when the author can assert:

> Programmatically, socialism is a system which yields more pluralism and democracy than the most highly developed capitalist systems. In practice, however, socialism has not yet even reached the level of the developed political democracy of bourgeois society because it has been subordinated to and has relied upon the absolute state monopoly of power (p. 107).

But by what does one make political judgments except by observation of systems "in practice"? *Between Ideals and Reality* is rich in examples of the perversion of "programs." And if history does not prove that full-blown socialism must rely on an absolute state monopoly of power, it must be said, in honesty and with full appreciation of the sincerity of those who hold socialist ideals, that it has not yet proven that it can survive *without* that monopoly.

Between the extremes represented by the Soviet Union and Yugoslavia lie the rest of the states of Eastern Europe, where the socialist regimes are not the products of indigenous revolution. In *The Politics of Modernization in Eastern Europe: Testing the Soviet Model*, Charles Gati brings together a number of original papers. They address peculiarities and commonalities of most of these states, which made their various transitions to modernity according to the "command model" of development generated by the Soviet experience.

Collections, especially one as stimulating as this book (which emerged from a conference at Columbia's Institute on East Central Europe in 1973), are not easily summarized. The contents are diverse, ranging from Otto Ulč's analysis of the consequences of applying a "modernization" strategy in an already modern Czechoslovakia (the "great leap backward") to Gyorgy Ranki's eloquent discussion of the balance of traditional and modern elements in East European societies and Vernon Aspaturian's attempt to measure the specifically "socialist" impact by using Austria, Finland, and Greece as non-socialist controls. The contributions underline the diversity that is still all too frequently de-emphasized rhetorically by the use of the term "Eastern Europe." To the degree that the Soviet model has taken hold, that diversity has been moderated, but the degree differs from nation to nation and is in all of them incomplete enough to allow the persistence of national peculiarities. The process of modernization is not yet complete in any of the socialist countries. This is necessarily so, insofar as the "gap" in development between West and East continues to be a salient indicator of what remains to be done. Perhaps the most important lesson that this book conveys is that socialist modernization is likely to continue along distinct lines in the different states, creating, destroying, and re-creating a series of outcomes, which will always combine traditional and modern elements in different sorts of mixes—successive approximations of an "ideal" state of modernity as elusive in the West as in the East.

A very different focus shapes Inkeles and Smith's *Becoming Modern*, the culmination of a six-nation (Argentina, Chile, East Pakistan [now Bangladesh], India, Israel, and Nigeria) study, which began more than ten years ago. Beyond its massive and sophisticated research, this book might also serve as an agenda for research in socialist societies—research, unfortunately, that will probably remain undone.

Lengthy interviewing of nearly 6000 working-class and peasant respondents in the six countries provided the base for a set of conclusions, which can be stated summarily. (1) There is an individual syndrome of attitude and orientation identifiable as personal "modernity," which is (2) possessed by concrete individuals, and lacking in others, in underdeveloped and transitional societies, and which is (3) produced by education, work in factories (and in rationally organized agricultural enterprises that emphasize planning and participation), exposure to the mass media, and other factors, each of which has independent effects when the influence of other variables is controlled. This modernity is manifested not only in attitudes and orientations but also in (4) the tendency of men to act upon these inner states in a way consistent with them. Modern man says he is rational, oriented toward the world beyond the village and family, ambitious, and more tolerant of diversity than his traditional cousin, and he behaves in like manner.

These findings in nonsocialist societies raise many interesting questions about the patterns that one might anticipate in the generally better-developed socialist states. "Socialist man," in large measure, has been through those institutions and settings—school, factory, a world of mass communications media—which Inkeles and Smith identify as schools in modernity. Is he, then, a modern man? If so, does his socialist environment, interacting with persisting national peculiarities, make him a modern man of a somewhat different type from those found in the six nations of the Inkeles-Smith study?

One hazards the answer that he *is* modern, given the experiences and environments that he shares with modern men elsewhere: modern at least in many attitudes and orientations. But what of translating these into action? If limitations of resources and development levels constrain the opportunities of modern men in the Third World, do the political structures of state socialism similarly constrain the modern men subordinate to them? Most writing on modernization, including the books reviewed here, focuses on institutions and institution-building; Inkeles and Smith focus on the individual and argue that modernization requires modern men, without whom transplanted institutions, whether the factory or the voting booth, will falter. Is there as well reason to ask whether, given populations of modern men, certain socialist political institutions seemingly impervious to change and characterized by a tight monopoly of power at the center can continue to operate without the constant increase in cost and inefficiency that arises from their poor "fit" with modern society and modern men? These are questions worth asking, even if we must wait long for the answers.

Barbara A. Anderson

Social Stratification in the Soviet Union: Equality, Excellence, and Other Issues

David Lane, *The End of Inequality? Stratification Under State Socialism* (Middlesex, England: Penguin, 1971).

Mervyn Matthews, *Class and Society in Soviet Russia* (New York: Walker, 1972).

Ellen Mickiewicz (ed.), *Handbook of Soviet Social Science Data* (New York: Free Press, 1973).

M. N. Rutkevich (ed.), *The Career Plans of Youth* (White Plains, N.Y.: International Arts and Sciences Press, 1969).

Murray Yanowitch and W. A. Fisher (eds.), *Social Stratification and Mobility in the U.S.S.R.* (White Plains, N.Y.: International Arts and Sciences Press, 1973).

Aside from its intrinsic interest, the particular characteristics of the Soviet Union have generated a great deal of curiosity about Soviet social stratification. Its status as the first country with a successful Communist revolution and its shared status with Japan as a latecomer to modernization have raised many questions about the extent to which these characteristics can explain the forms of inequality in the Soviet Union.

Until recently, answers to such questions have had to be based on scanty and inadequate information, often extrapolated from official policy statements or fragmentary reports of émigrés. Although more work might have been based on statistical publications, there has been a real lack of information about attitudes and other matters, which could best be ascertained by interviews. Until the appearance of recent Soviet empirical work on social stratification, the major source of information was the Harvard Project on the Soviet Social System directed by Alex Inkeles and Raymond Bauer, in which post-World War II émigrés were interviewed.[1]

In the past ten years, there has been a surge of Soviet empirical work on social stratification, which can greatly add to our knowledge and understanding of the Soviet system. The edited works by Rutkevich and by Yanowitch and Fisher are the most direct results of this research. The Rutkevich book is a translation of a group of empirical studies done at Urals State University, which appeared in book form in the Soviet Union. The Yanowitch and Fisher volume brings together both theoretical and empirical Soviet studies of social stratification. Also included are a helpful introduction by the editors and some interesting conclusions by Seymour Martin Lipset. The books by Matthews and Lane are attempts to integrate all available information on Soviet stratification in order to address general topics such as the effectiveness of social policy in structuring social reality and the changing status of the collective farm. The Mickiewicz book is a collection of data on a variety of socio-economic topics; it is intended to facilitate quantitative comparison of the Soviet Union with other societies and comparison of various areas within the Soviet Union. Although the reviewed works present interesting material on several topics, this discussion will relate only to their bearing on questions of the structure of and long-term changes in the Soviet social stratificational system.

The Harvard Project produced many interesting results, and the work of which the current volumes are a part provides an opportunity to investigate the extent to which the structure and trends found in the Harvard Project have continued. From the Harvard Project, two important trends emerged. One was the decreasing importance of political reliability—as determined by social origins and education—since the Revolution. The other was the growing importance of technical competence—as determined by education—in the allocation of prestige and increasingly of power and property. The first trend may be related to the passage of time, which has contributed to the regime's sense of self-confidence and diminished fear of counter-

1. Alex Inkeles and Raymond Bauer, *The Soviet Citizen* (New York: Atheneum, 1965). This contains the major results of the Harvard Project.

revolution. The second trend is reasonable and typical of an increasingly modern society.[2]

Soviet Social Stratification, 1917–1935

Social stratification can be studied by examining what determines the allocation of such rewards as prestige, power, and property.[3] Although other kinds of rewards, such as security and sense of well-being, have been important in the Soviet Union, only these three rewards will be discussed.

Throughout the history of the Soviet Union, the main determinants of the allocation of these rewards have been technical competence and political reliability. Both the causes and the relative importance of these factors have changed over time, however. In the Soviet Union, unlike China, the major determinant of technical competence has always been formal education, rather than skill acquired through experience. In the Soviet Union, self-taught experts, such as agricultural managers and unschooled entrepreneurs, have never gained the official recognition and support that their counterparts have received in China.[4]

The determinants of political reliability have also differed from those of China. In China after its revolution, the major determinant in the assessment of a person's political reliability was social origins or prerevolutionary occupation, with assessed loyalty being inversely related to prerevolutionary social status.[5] Although social origins and prerevolutionary occupation had generally the same relationship to judgments concerning political reliability in the Soviet Union shortly after the Revolution, this relationship was never so strong as in China.

2. Talcott Parsons, " A Functional Theory of Change," in Amitai and Eva Etzioni (eds.), *Social Change* (New York: Basic Books, 1964), pp. 83–97. This is a case of the increasing importance of the adaptive subsystem with modernization. The relative importance of technical competence and political reliability can be seen in Parsons's terms as the relative importance of the adaptive and goal attainment subsystems. Technical competence is the ability to do things successfully, regardless of the purpose. Political reliability is the estimation of an individual's support of the normal paths of power distribution in the system.

3. Melvin M. Tumin, *Social Stratification: The Forms and Functions of Inequality* (Englewood Cliffs, N.J.: Prentice-Hall, 1967).

4. Isabel and David Crook, *The First Years of Yangyi Commune* (London: Routledge and Kegan Paul, 1966).

5. Michel Oksenberg, " Getting Ahead and Getting Along in Communist China: The Ladder of Success on the Eve of the Cultural Revolution," in John Wilson Lewis (ed.), *Party Leadership and Revolutionary Power in China* (London: Cambridge University Press, 1970), pp. 304–347.

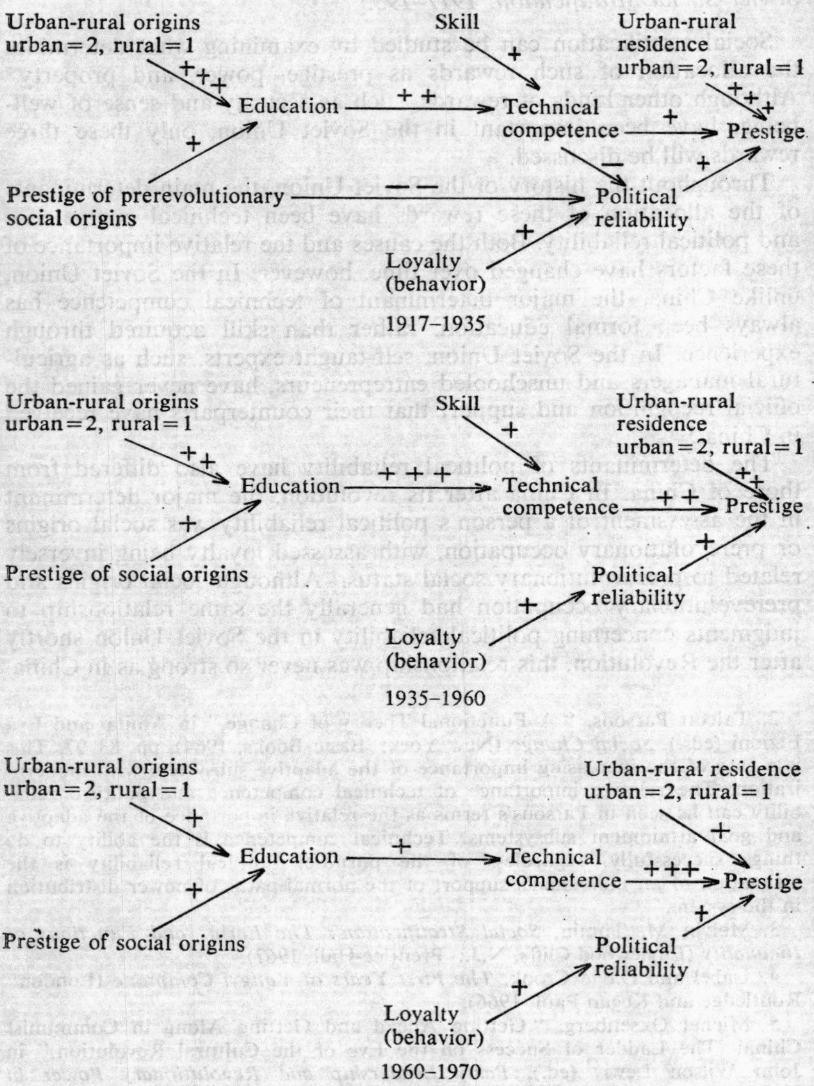
Determinants of Prestige in Three Periods in the Soviet Union
Urban-rural origins urban=2, rural=1
Skill
Urban-rural residence urban=2, rural=1
+++
+
++
+++
Education
Technical competence
Prestige
+
+
−
+
Prestige of prerevolutionary social origins
− −
Political reliability
+
Loyalty (behavior)
1917–1935
Urban-rural origins urban=2, rural=1
Skill
Urban-rural residence urban=2, rural=1
++
+
+++
++
Education
Technical competence
Prestige
+
++
+
Prestige of social origins
Political reliability
+
Loyalty (behavior)
1935–1960
Urban-rural origins urban=2, rural=1
Urban-rural residence urban=2, rural=1
+
+
+
Education
Technical competence
+++
Prestige
+
+
Prestige of social origins
Political reliability
+
Loyalty (behavior)
1960–1970
Fig. 1

Inkeles and Bauer note that the primary determinant of assessed loyalty was always overt *behaviour*. Individuals were generally considered loyal unless their actions indicated otherwise.[6] In China, persons with high prerevolutionary status were legally barred from rural power positions, although this was not always enforced.[7] In the Soviet Union, especially in the early 1930s when technically trained workers' cadres became available for managerial positions, there was some negative association between technical competence and political reliability, but technical competence, as befits a system committed to programs of rapid industrialization, also had a positive direct effect on prestige. A schematic representation of the major determinants of the allocation of prestige in the Soviet Union in 1917–1935 is shown at the top of Fig. 1. In the figure, a "+" indicates a positive causal relationship, a "−" a negative causal relationship. The number of "+"s or "−"s indicates the relative strength of the relationship. In statistical terms, the figure gives the expected sign and relative strength of standardized regression coefficients.

According to the reports of émigrés, the prestige ordering after the revolution was [8]:

Party-Soviet apparatus
Intelligentsia
Employees (white-collar workers)
Skilled workers
Rank-and-file workers
Artisans
Peasants
Others

According to reports of émigrés about the jobs that their fathers held before and after the Revolution, 79 percent of the fathers who had been nonmanual bourgeoisie before the Revolution were either employees or members of the intelligentsia.[9] This indicates that there was no large-scale, effective program to place persons with high prerevolutionary status in low-status jobs. This pattern was somewhat different from that of China, whose revolution seems to have resulted

6. Inkeles and Bauer, *op. cit.*, p. 282.
7. Crook and Crook, *op. cit.*, p. 184.
8. Robert Allen Feldmesser, "Aspects of Social Mobility in the Soviet Union" (Ph.D. diss., Harvard University, 1955), pp. 106–107. This was based on work in the Harvard Project.
9. Feldmesser, *op. cit.*, p. 111.

in greater status changes. The relative stability of Soviet social stratification may be indicative of a greater reluctance of the Soviet leaders to jeopardize production for the sake of ideological goals. This has been observed by others for the New Economic Policy (NEP) period.

Prestigious positions not requiring advanced training were usually filled by persons with little education who were politically attractive to the Party. In 1927, 80 percent of the secretaries of local Party cells were workers or peasants. Perhaps some suspicion of persons with advanced training is shown in Fig. 2.[10] Although in the 1920s peasants were the most underrepresented group among members of the Communist Party, workers were represented more heavily than employees.

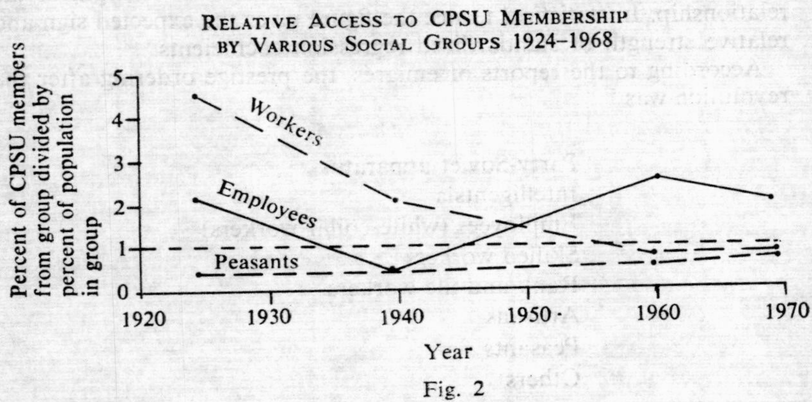

Fig. 2

There was a continuing problem of allocating power to rural residents. Figures 2 and 3 show the low representation of peasants in the

10. Matthews, *op. cit.*, p. 218; T. H. Rigby, *Communist Party Membership in the Soviet Union 1917–1967* (Princeton: Princeton University Press, 1968), pp. 85, 162, 199, 325. Rigby presents an excellent treatment of the changing determinants of CPSU membership. In Figs. 2 and 4, the measure of access is the proportion of the group (such as peasants) in the CPSU or in higher education divided by the proportion of the population in the group (such as peasants). If every group had representation proportionate to size, the graphs would all be horizontal lines at the value 1. Although Party membership is not related in a simple way to power, for brevity it is considered as an indicator in this discussion. For some problems with this approach, see Cyril Black (ed.), *Rewriting Russian History* (New York: Praeger, 1956), Chap. 1.

Party.[11] Rural underrepresentation stemmed from the urban origins of the Party,[12] from fear of counterrevolutionary tendencies among the peasantry, and from the practical difficulty of maintaining Party centers in rural areas. Even China, whose Party originated in the countryside, faced a similar difficulty and had only moderate success in locating regional Party centers outside of major cities.[13]

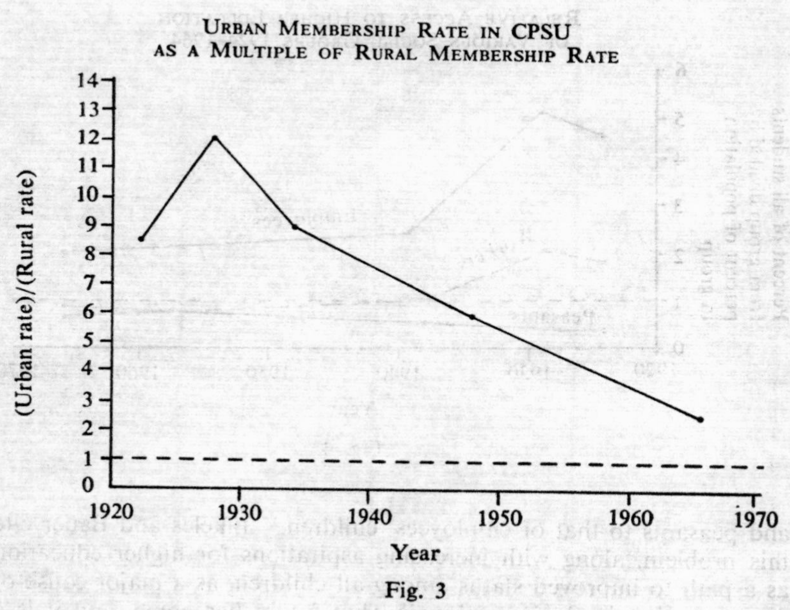

Fig. 3

Even in this early period, despite governmental efforts to recruit children of workers and peasants for higher education,[14] parental prestige bore a strongly positive relationship to the attainment of any level of education. Measures such as the *rabfak* program, which sought to educate selected workers, failed because of the reluctance of foremen to send their best workers to the program and the inability of the workers to meet academic standards. Figure 4 shows the large

11. Rigby, *op. cit.*, p. 491.
12. Rigby, *op. cit.*, pp. 486–487.
13. Oksenberg, *op. cit.*, pp. 316–317.
14. Feldmesser, *op. cit.*, pp. 77–94.

differentials in educational access.[15] Inkeles and Bauer attributed the difficulty to differential orientations to education according to socialization.[16] This circumstance, coupled with some Soviet reluctance to disregard performance, perpetuated educational inheritance. This is another deviation from the Chinese case, where more extreme steps were taken to raise the educational level of the children of workers

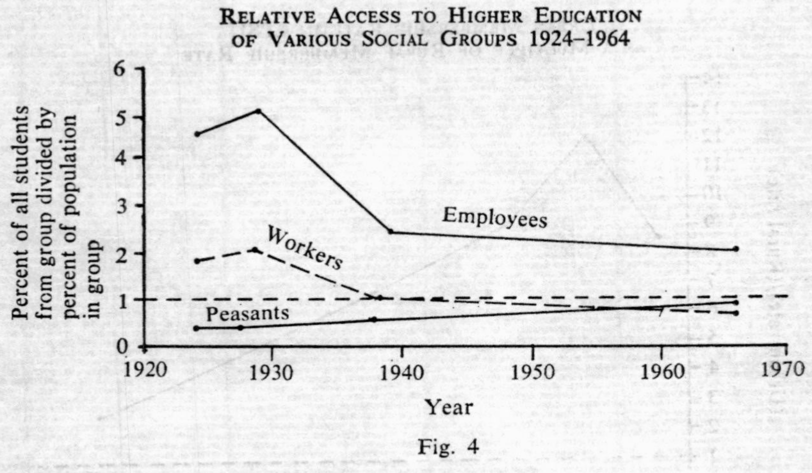

Fig. 4

and peasants to that of employees' children.[17] Inkeles and Bauer cite this problem, along with increasing aspirations for higher education as a path to improved status among all children, as a major cause of future tension in Soviet society.[18] That future has come, and it is a major theme of many of the studies by Soviet scholars which appear in the Rutkevich and the Yanowitch and Fisher volumes.

Changes in Soviet Social Stratification, 1935–1960

After 1935, partly because of the Party purges, technical competence gained in importance relative to political reliability in the

15. Feldmesser, *op. cit.*, p. 80; Matthews, *op. cit.*, pp. 291, 297.

16. Inkeles and Bauer, pp. 149–152. Ability to pay tuition was also a factor, but it alone could not explain the differentials.

17. Barry Richman, *Industrial Society in Communist China* (New York: Random House, 1969), p. 298.

18. Inkeles and Bauer, *op. cit.*, pp. 156–158.

determination of prestige.[19] The Harvard Project émigrés reported the prestige ordering at the time they left the Soviet Union as [20]:

Doctor
Scientific worker
Engineer
Factory manager
Foreman
Accountant
Officer in armed forces
Teacher
Rank-and-file worker
Farm brigade leader
Party secretary
Collective farm chairman
Rank-and-file collective farmer

The importance of technical competence is apparent. The low prestige of a Party secretary is somewhat suspect and may reflect the nature of the sample. The middle section of Fig. 1 shows the determinants of prestige in this period. By this time, political reliability was completely determined by overt behavior, and skill unrelated to educational training had become even less important in the determination of technical competence. Figure 4 shows some leveling in educational attainment according to social origins. Perhaps some degree of standardization in the education system led to more uniformity in educational orientation across social backgrounds. There were still strong effects of social origins, however.

Figures 2 and 3 also show some equalization of opportunity in terms of access to CPSU membership according both to social group and to rural-urban residence. This trend was accompanied, however, by increasing recruitment of persons of very high status. In 1947,

19. Rigby notes (pp. 221–227) that one of the major effects of the purges, especially the Ezhovshchina of the late 1930s, was to clear the ranks of the Party for recruitment into the Party of "the best people," especially those with high formal education and technical competence. For instance, in 1929, 2 percent of the Party recruits were employees, while in the late 1930s, 44 percent were employees.

20. Alex Inkeles, *Social Change in Soviet Russia* (Cambridge: Harvard University Press, 1968), pp. 194–196. Actually the question used referred to preferability rather than to prestige. Prestige is the amount of honor attached to a role, while preferability is a measure of how frequently persons wish to occupy the role.

16 percent of all teachers and 38 percent of all engineers were Party members.[21] These are very high percentages because only about 8 percent of the population over the age of twenty were members. In 1964, the percentages for teachers and engineers were 25 percent and 42 percent respectively. This may be interpreted as indicating both the disappearance of the negative relationship between occupational prestige and political reliability and the increased importance of technical competence, which had become a major political asset.

The available information on income indicates that it was positively related to both technical competence and political reliability, though more strongly to the latter.[22]

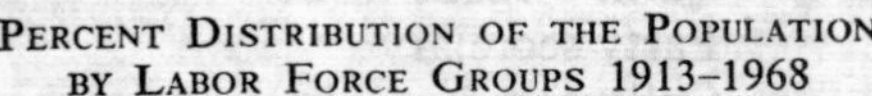

PERCENT DISTRIBUTION OF THE POPULATION BY LABOR FORCE GROUPS 1913–1968

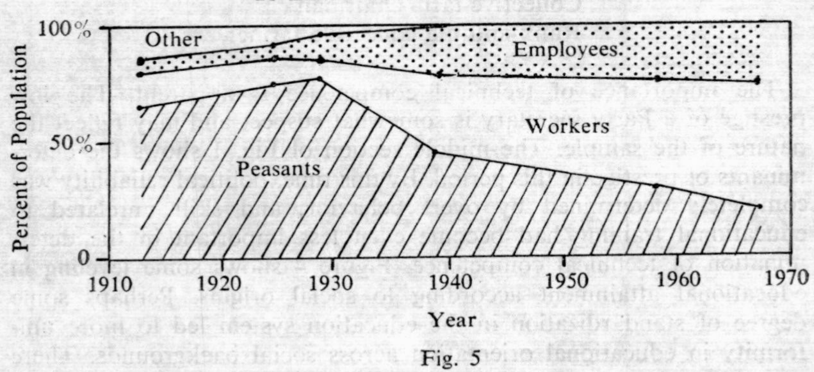

Fig. 5

Over time, the proportion of the population who were peasants decreased, while the proportion of workers and employees increased, as shown in Fig. 5.[23] Since peasants had a lower average prestige than persons in the other two social groups, the shift in the structure of the population resulted in an average increase in the level of prestige in the society. Such a change in average prestige through a shift in

21. Rigby, *op. cit.*, p. 439.

22. Inkeles, *op. cit.*, p. 206. The émigrés rated occupations on material position, lack of safety, and general desirability. According to Inkeles, it seems that lack of safety was an indication of the political reliability needed for the job. Material position has a correlation of +·818 with lack of safety, and +·670 with general desirability.

23. Matthews, *op. cit.*, p. 35. "Others" included bourgeoisie, landowners, traders, and kulaks.

population distribution among categories differing in prestige is termed "structural mobility." Throughout the studies in the 1960s, this change in population composition remained a constant theme in discussions about the reduction of dissatisfaction with status.[24]

Changes in the Social Stratificational System, 1960–1970

The lower section of Fig. 1 shows the determinants of prestige during the 1960–1970 decade. In comparison with the 1935–1960 period, rural-urban origins have become somewhat less important relative to the prestige of social origins in the acquisition of education. Technical competence has become even more important in the determination of prestige, while the importance of rural-urban residence may have decreased.

The effects of social origins on the acquisition of education are shown as operating in three different ways: (1) through orientation toward education,[25] (2) through performance on entrance examinations,[26] and (3) through choice of specialty according to the prestige of the specialty.[27] Higher aspirations and more successful performance were positively related to the social status of parents whether measured by education or by occupation. These differences were found in the future plans of eighth grade children,[28] in the choice of specialty of secondary school graduates,[29] and in the assessment of the relative desirability of occupations.[30]

The situation for rural youth was somewhat different from that for urban youth. It appears that a major disadvantage of rural origins was limited access to higher-status urban jobs. Once rural youth, even from collective farms, reached the city, they often did well.[31] The

24. In V. Arutiunian, "Social Mobility in the Countryside," in Yanowitch and Fisher, *op. cit.*, pp. 320–353; also L. I. Sennikova, "Higher Education as a Factor in Social Mobility," in Rutkevich, *op. cit.*, pp. 142–150.

25. V. V. Ksenofontova, "Career Plans of 8th and 9th Grade Students and Their Realization," in Rutkevich, *op. cit.*, pp. 46–55.

26. M. N. Rutkevich and F. R. Filoppov, "Social Sources of Recruitment of the Intelligentsia," in Yanowitch and Fisher, *op. cit.*, pp. 241–274; also L. F. Liss, "The Social Conditioning of Occupational Choice," in *ibid.*, pp. 275–288.

27. M. Tkach, "Career Plans of Graduates of Complete Secondary Schools," in Rutkevich, *op. cit.*, pp. 56–63.

28. Ksenofontova, *op. cit.*, pp. 46–49.

29. Tkach, *op. cit.*, pp. 60–63.

30. V. V. Vodzinskaia, "Orientations Toward Occupations," in Yanowitch and Fisher, *op. cit.*, pp. 153–186.

31. Arutiunian, *op. cit.*, pp. 320–353.

generally low quality of rural education was also mentioned, however, as an obstacle to the mobility of rural youth.[32]

This rural-urban differential in educational quality and aspirations is cited by Soviet scholars as a reason for nationality differentials in education and occupational prestige.[33] Although it is certainly one reason, more study is necessary to determine whether other factors are involved. In the comparison of Ukrainians with Russians, Inkeles and Bauer found little evidence of discrimination against Ukrainians in the acquisition of education or, given educational level, in obtaining jobs.[34]

Figure 4 shows that access to education of social groups has been growing more equal in the 1930–1970 period. The relative deterioration in the positions of persons with "worker" social origins may stem from the inclusion of state farmers in the worker category. It is significant, however, that by 1964 peasants had as high an educational access level as workers, even as defined.

The improved position of peasants may be linked to the educational reform of 1958, which lasted until 1965. One aim of the reform was preferential admission to higher educational institutions for rural youth. The purposes of the 1958 educational reform may be likened to those of some of the educational programs of the 1920s. Like these earlier programs, however, the 1958 reform was abandoned because of the falling quality of students.[35] Sennikova points out that, during the period of the reform, the social origins of students more nearly reflected those of the general population than they did before the reform or after its repeal.[36] Similar nationality quotas should be studied more than they have been. Again, the Soviets, unlike the Chinese, were relatively unwilling to compromise educational standards and, like the Americans, have the continuing problem of trying to be equal and excellent.

As in other parts of his book, Matthews offers an interesting discussion of the intent and results of this and other Khrushchev reforms. He skillfully combines quantitative data with analysis and reflection.

The Lane volume discusses these and other issues, but without the range of materials which Matthews employed. Rather than seeking out Soviet data on many questions, Lane turned instead to Eastern

32. Matthews, *op. cit.*, pp. 262–263. Also Arutiunian, *op. cit.*, p. 348.

33. Arutiunian, *op. cit.*, p. 348.

34. Inkeles and Bauer, *op. cit.*, pp. 341–347; also see Ralph Scott Clem, "The Impact of Demographic and Socio-Economic Forces Upon the Nationality Question in Central Asia," in Edward Allworth (ed.), *The Nationality Question in Soviet Central Asia* (New York: Praeger, 1973), pp. 35–44.

35. Matthews, *op. cit.*, pp. 288–305.

36. Sennikova, *op. cit.*, pp. 145–150.

European sources, as if they were interchangeable. For instance, rather than using the data from the Vodzinskaia study, cited below, he used only the results of the Harvard Project and some Eastern European studies in his discussion of occupational prestige.[37] His examination of various aspects of social stratification in Czechoslovakia[38] could also have been related to the Leningrad study of Shkaratan, which was not done. Such discussions could have led to a worthwhile integration of available information about both the Soviet Union and Eastern Europe. Instead, we are presented with a combination of noncomparable materials, which is not very enlightening about either the Soviet Union or Eastern Europe.

The Yanowitch and Fisher volume does include the Vodzinskaia survey of male secondary school students in Leningrad in 1968. According to this survey, the prestige ordering of occupations was[39]:

Mathematician
Scientific worker
Physicist
Worker in literature and art
Pilot
Physician
Higher education teacher
Construction engineer
Shipbuilder
Agronomist
Tailor
Clerical worker

The importance of technical competence is still apparent. There were not enough rural occupations on the list to ascertain much about rural-urban prestige differentials.

By this period, the Party had become an even higher status group, as shown in Fig. 2. Also, the recruitment of professionals continued strongly. In 1968, 36 percent of all persons with higher education were Party members.[40]

Until the death of Stalin, Soviet politics was seen by most scholars as relatively monolithic. The only political differences of importance was between those perceived as politically reliable and those thought to be politically unreliable. After Stalin's death, the amount of dis-

37. Lane, *op. cit.*, pp. 79–86.
38. *Ibid.* pp. 84–86.
39. Vodzinskaia, *op. cit.*, pp. 169–170.
40. Rigby, *op. cit.*, p. 439; Matthews, *op. cit.*, pp. 220, 223.

agreement *within* the Party, and thus within the politically reliable group, was surprising to many observers. By the 1960s, these differences had hardened along particular lines, especially within professional groups. According to Skilling and Griffiths, the distinction was generally between the older, less technically trained, and more conservative persons in each profession and the younger, more technically trained, more liberal persons.[41] This is seen in the military as the difference between the older officers with combat experience and the younger ones with more technical knowledge of sophisticated weapons. The rising importance of this younger group is reason to eliminate skill from the determinants of technical competence in this period, although it may still be somewhat premature to do so. The emergence of different groups *within* the politically reliable group may be a major change that occurs at some point in modernization. Apparently it has not yet happened in China.

On both elite recruitment and education, the Mickiewicz volume presents some interesting data, which are especially useful to those unable to use Russian language primary sources. The volume would have been more useful, however, if a more consistent set of dates and of territorial units had been chosen for data presentation. Also, although the percentage in various social groups at different educational levels and in the CPSU is provided, the breakdown of the population into these groups is not given for any date, which makes it impossible to use this source to compute any rates of participation by social group. The distribution of the population among social groups is available for most years in the Soviet yearbook *Narodnoe khoziaistvo SSSR*. Such oversights prevent the book from being as useful a research aid as it might be.

The Matthews volume presents some interesting data on wages which were not available for earlier periods. A possible effect of Khrushchev's wage equalization programs was improvement of the position of collective farmers.[42] Figure 6 shows changes in the wages of industrial workers, collective farmers, and state farmers on an index where industrial wages in 1958 equal 100.[43] Clearly, the lot of collective farmers has improved relative to that of other groups. This was important for the Soviet Union because the collective farmers were probably the most economically underprivileged group in Soviet society.

One of the most interesting studies reviewed in the Matthews

41. H. Gordon Skilling and Franklin Griffiths (eds.), *Interest Groups in Soviet Politics* (Princeton: Princeton University Press, 1971), esp. pp. 4–12.

42. Lazar Volin, *A Century of Russian Agriculture* (Cambridge: Harvard University Press, 1970), pp. 413–428.

43. Matthews, *op. cit.*, p. 65.

volume, although unfortunately a work not appearing in the volumes of translation, was O. I. Shkaratan's 1965 study of 2888 workers in Leningrad. Although it shows a direct relationship between CPSU membership and prestige, it also notes two overlapping hierarchies with respect to education and wages: a nonmanual and a manual hierarchy. Within each hierarchy, education and income increase with

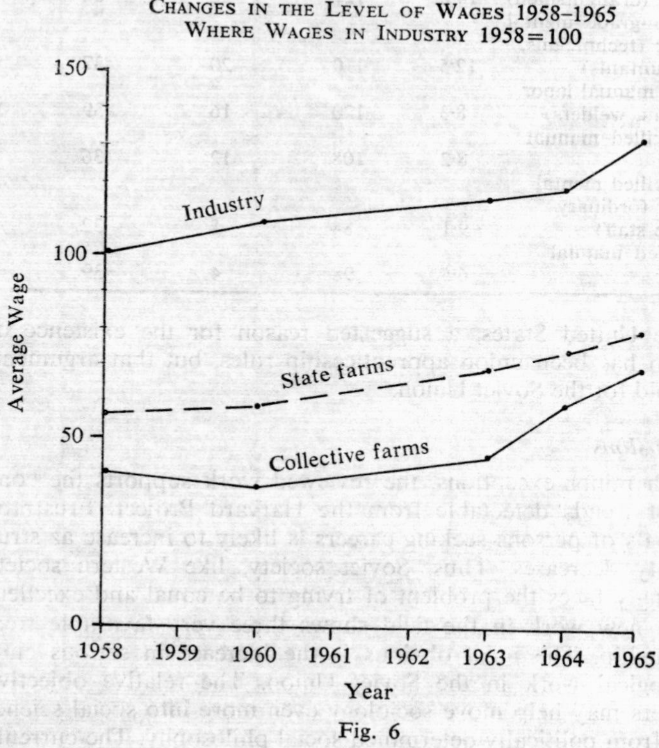

Fig. 6

prestige but the bottom of the nonmanual hierarchy overlaps the top of the manual hierarchy, as shown in Table 1.[44] This is similar to findings in the United States[45] and may reflect another aspect of the socialization of children. Children from nonmanual families may prefer a low-paying nonmanual job to a higher paying manual job.

44. *Ibid.* pp. 134–135.

45. Peter Blau and Otis Dudley Duncan, *The American Occupational Structure* (New York: Wiley, 1967), p. 27.

Table 1. Characteristics of Various Labor Force Groups in Leningrad, 1965

Profession	*Years of general training*	*Rubles per Month*	*% CPSU members*	*Average Age*	*Number*
Managers, directors	13·6	173	55	42	92
High-grade mental labor (draughtsmen)	14·0	127	20	36	135
Medium-grade mental labor (technicians, accountants)	12·5	110	20	37	287
Skilled manual labor (fitters, welders)	8·3	120	16	39	1002
Semi-skilled manual labor	8·2	108	12	36	837
Semi-skilled mental labor (ordinary office staff)	9·1	84	8	32	353
Unskilled manual labor	6·5	98	4	39	115

In the United States, a suggested reason for the existence of this pattern has been union apprenticeship rules, but that argument does not hold for the Soviet Union.

Conclusions

With minor exceptions, the reviewed work supports the continuation of trends detectable from the Harvard Project. Frustration of the goals of persons seeking careers is likely to increase as structural mobility decreases. Thus, Soviet society, like Western society, increasingly faces the problem of trying to be equal and excellent too.

The new work in the field shows three very favorable trends in scholarship. The most obvious is the increase in serious empirical sociological work in the Soviet Union. The relative objectivity of numbers may help move sociology even more into social science and away from politically determined social philosophy. The current work on social stratification is only a part of a general empirical trend in areas of great interest to Soviet leaders, including work motivation and methods of attracting persons to work in undesirable locations. Many remaining questions about Soviet structure can only be answered through more work of this type. The second good sign is the skillful use of Soviet results as shown in the Matthews book. The appearance of the Mickiewicz volume indicates that in the future students of the Soviet Union may take quantitative data more seriously in their work on social questions about Soviet society.

Susan Bridge

Why Czechoslovakia? And Why 1968? *

Galia Golan, *The Czechoslovak Reform Movement: Communism in Crisis, 1962–1968* (Cambridge: Cambridge University Press, 1971).

Galia Golan, *Reform Rule in Czechoslovakia: The Dubcek Era, 1968–1969* (Cambridge: Cambridge University Press, 1973).

Jaroslav Krejci, *Social Change and Stratification in Postwar Czechoslovakia* (New York: Columbia University Press, 1972).

Vladimir V. Kusin, *Political Grouping in the Czechoslovak Reform Movement* (New York: Columbia University Press, 1972).

Jaroslaw A. Piekalkiewicz, *Public Opinion Polling in Czechoslovakia, 1968–69: Results and Analysis of Surveys Conducted During the Dubcek Era* (New York: Praeger, 1972).

Robin Alison Remington (ed.), *Winter in Prague: Documents on Czechoslovak Communism in Crisis* (Cambridge: MIT Press, 1969).

Radovan Richta et al., *Civilization at the Crossroads: Social and Human Implications of the Scientific and Technological Revolution*, 3rd ed. (White Plains, N.Y.: International Arts and Sciences Press, 1968).

* I should like to thank my friend and colleague Professor John W. Sweeney for a very helpful conversation, in which he assured me that I was on relatively firm theoretical ground with regard to the choice of method introduced here.

Eugen Steiner, *The Slovak Dilemma* (Cambridge: Cambridge University Press, 1973).

George Shaw Wheeler, *The Human Face of Socialism: The Political Economy of Change in Czechoslovakia* (New York: Lawrence Hill, 1973).

> *Science must start with facts and end with facts, no matter what theoretical structures it builds in between. First of all the scientist is an observer. Next he tries to describe in complete generality what he saw, and what he expects to see in the future. Next he makes predictions on the basis of his theories, which he checks against the facts.*
>
> *The most characteristic feature of the method is its cyclic nature. It starts with facts, ends in facts, and the facts ending one cycle are the beginning of the next cycle.*
>
> *. . . In order to be a good scientist, one must never lose the childish urge of asking " Why."*
>
> John G. Kemeny, *A Philosopher Looks at Science*

The political drama that unfolded in Czechoslovakia in the first eight months of 1968 was many years in the making, and it ended as swiftly as it did tragically. These extraordinary events have been documented and interpreted in detail by a rich and still growing literature. Nine books will be discussed here.

The question the reviewer has been asked to address is, *have these materials contributed to political science?* One therefore owes the authors of several of these works a respectful apology in advance. What they have published will be considered in relation to criteria that most of them did not have in mind as they wrote and compiled—criteria that some might declare, even in retrospect, to be irrelevant to their scholarly purposes.

These nine books do not duplicate each other. Those that deal specifically with 1967 and 1968 include translations of primary documents first put out by some of the principal actors (Remington); the results of public opinion polls taken in Czechoslovakia during 1968 and early 1969 (Piekalkiewicz); one book that describes the non-Party, nongovernmental components of the 1967–1968 reform movement (Kusin); and another that concentrates on the conduct of reform politics in Party and government circles (Golan). Among those that trace change over longer periods of time are an account of the reform movement's gradual growth after 1962 (Golan); three reconstructions of the preceding twenty years or more—one emphasizing the economic aspect (Wheeler), another the sociological (Krejci), a third the Slovak perspective (Steiner); and, finally, a theoretical work that seeks to locate the Czechoslovak experience in a broad, generalizable historical framework (Richta et al.).

Five of these books were written by participant-observers—a most valuable type of commentator on socio-political events. A sixth and a seventh largely confine themselves to reporting the declared views of participants.

It is rare, if not unique, for a major political event in a Communist-run country to be reported and analyzed in such detail and from so many informed perspectives. The proximity of many of the reporters to the events ensures a fidelity to fact which is of no small moment. Clearly these books, taken together, form the core of an important literature. And because a reliable, many-stranded account of a complex political reality is the *sine qua non* of serious political analysis, then in this most primary sense, yes: we have here an invaluable contribution to political science.

Facts and Explanations : Focus on 1968

The Remington collection of 72 translated documents provides access to the political thinking of prominent Czechs, Slovaks, and others just before and during the Dubcek era. This volume is sensitively compiled and edited and well indexed, and includes short biographies of some two dozen prominent Czech and Slovak participants. The paragraph of editor's comments that precedes each chronologically ordered group of documents notes the immediate circumstances that surrounded their original publication. Even those who read Czech and Slovak will find this volume an essential addition to their personal libraries, for some of the originals were published in Russian, German, Serbocroatian, Albanian, Rumanian, French, Italian, and Spanish.

The Piekalkiewicz presentation of twenty public opinion polls taken during the same period provides a companion-piece in a sense; it reports the thinking of Czechoslovakia's general public on a wide variety of politically sensitive topics. Potentially, it is an equally useful research tool. It suffers, however, from two handicaps: one that could not have been avoided entirely, perhaps, and a second that was avoidable.

First, Piekalkiewicz is concerned to protect the Czechoslovak social scientists who gathered these data, while nevertheless wanting to disseminate their findings to the international scholarly community in as complete a form as possible. As he puts the difficulty,

> In order to protect the original sources, the surveys are identified only by number and date, and by brief description of the methods employed (see Appendix A). No further information can be given, and the original materials cannot be published even in the United States. . . .
>
> It was decided to include in this study all available data without any attempt at selection in terms of . . . significance. . . . The unique nature of the materials justif[ies] inclusion of all the information. The study was designed as a possible tool in further research. . . .[1]

If the book includes all of the survey results, the dates when the surveys were taken, and descriptions of the nature of the various samples, then is the identity of the researchers the *only* missing information? Or is there some other difference—besides the fact of translation into English—between the original surveys and "all available data," published here? Perhaps this ambiguity, which is not trivial, could be cleared up easily.

Second, the organization of this volume will diminish its usefulness for some readers. Piekalkiewicz groups results from surveys taken at various times and from various segments of the population under eleven main topics and numerous subtopics according to the subject matter of each individual question. There is no index and no cross-reference by chronological order. Trying to use the volume to trace trends over time will be very cumbersome.

Kusin similarly states that he intends his book to be a contribution to further research.[2] True to his stated intention, he supplies an impeccably compiled catalogue of the nuanced responses, the non-responses, and the pace of response to the new political climate observed in 1967–1968 among workers, farmers, the intelligentsia, youth and students, nationalities, the new non-Communist political organizations, and societies and churches.

1. Piekalkiewicz, *op. cit.*, p. xxix.
2. "This book proposes to tell the story of non-governmental political organisations in 1968. . . . The subject of this book is thus narrowly defined. So is the method. No political theories of any range can be formulated without the developments in the governmental structure (in the wide sociological sense, i.e., including above all the Communist Party) and the outside world being taken into account. For such an exercise this book may hopefully serve as a supplier of a part of the requisite background information." Kusin, *op. cit.*, pp. 7–8.

But Kusin is overly modest in his statement of intention. Three slender threads of explanation run through his factual presentation. Even taken alone, these partial, tentative explanations have important ramifications if they are true.

1. *Role of the intelligentsia*: The Czechoslovak intelligentsia, particularly those who were Party members, convinced the politically powerful of the need for socio-economic change.[3]

2. *Role of institutionalization*: Socio-economic liberalization, once set in motion, was accelerated and made political by the high degree of organization typical of Communist-run societies *plus* the "traditional disposition to political organization and the requisite levels of political sophistication in the Czech lands."[4]

3. *Qualification of the role of institutionalization*: Interest groups as they are frequently identified by observers of Communist-run societies (e.g., "the army, the police, the Party machinery, the planners, and the managers") did *not* play a major role in precipitating accelerated political change or in determining its direction once it was under way. Rather, Kusin writes,

> I seem to discern a more conventional group behavior asserting itself as a corollary of that relatively recent phenomenon in Eastern Europe—the economic and political reform movement.[5]

He suggests that something more inchoate, less pre-emptive, than interest groups representing officially institutionalized groupings was at work—a "budding assortment of lobbies," which are predominantly associational, became an important causal factor.

Golan's *Reform Rule in Czechoslovakia* is a truly impressive piece of scholarship. It seems likely to remain the definitive general account of what happened in Czechoslovakia in 1967–1968. More narrowly focused studies as well as any generalizations from the Czechoslovak experience will both have to be judged against this book for plausibility. The author has a special talent for weaving ideological questions into a complex political context. Ideology is made an intelligible contributing factor to political events, rather than the improbable *deus ex machina* that it still too often is in both Marxist and non-Marxist writing on politics in Communist-run societies.

Golan is a gifted, even a brilliant, chronicler. Three short pages also suggest that the author believes that generalizable patterns of political behavior are discernible in the particular.[6] Here she

3. See esp. *ibid.*, Chap. 3.
4. See esp. *ibid.*, pp. 5, 164.
5. *Ibid.*, p. 211.
6. Golan, *Reform Rule in Czechoslovakia*, pp. 236ff.

remarks that the history of Czechoslovak-Soviet Party relations has repeated variations of the same events: in 1929, in 1947, and now again in 1968. This is true, and it is important. The Soviet Party has indeed intervened frequently in the affairs of other Communist parties. These interventions have become particularly dramatic (perhaps because more public) when the other Communist parties in question have been in power, and when the intervention has involved the use (or the threatened use) of the Soviet Union's awesome armed might.

But why Czechoslovakia? And why 1968? We are still left with our deceptively simple original questions.

Given the Remington, Piekalkiewicz, Kusin, and Golan contributions discussed so far, it is evident that the events under consideration have been described skillfully and with an abundance of fact. It is curiously difficult, however, to move from these several highly professional *descriptions* to the most rudimentary *explanation* of the abrupt political discontinuities that occurred in Czechoslovakia in 1968.

Perhaps this is not so surprising. Complex socio-political causes can take a long time combining and transmuting themselves into effects. If time is the missing dimension, then it is more realistic to expect the task of explaining to be undertaken by the five remaining books being reviewed here. These trace the longer-term developments that eventually led to the remarkable events of the Prague Spring—events that few knowledgeable observers except Walter Ulbricht and his associates predicted.[7]

Narrative and Analysis: Political Change in the Longer Term

It is doubtful that readers of this review believe that political events occur at random. Quite the contrary: we are likely to believe that politics at our local city hall or in our provincial, republic, or state capital are being conducted on this day more or less as they were conducted yesterday—perhaps with small differences that even the participants do not notice. We believe that patterns of past political interaction are, in this case, good predictors of present ones. Cause-and-effect relationships are expected to remain constant. Even if we reflect for a moment on how multifarious the causes of a given day's politics are and on how many of the facts are unknown to us, still, in the absence of other information, we assume overwhelming

7. Golan reminds us that the East Germans expressed great unease about the turn that politics was taking in Czechoslovakia as early as 1963 and 1964; *ibid.*, p. 222.

continuity. This manner of reasoning is so routine that we scarcely appreciate it for what it is: a complex, assumption-ridden *prediction.*

Explanation after the fact is similar: it is *postdiction.* To continue our politics-as-usual illustration, if tomorrow we learn that our prediction of continuity was correct, we will not think that we *guessed* the single correct outcome in an infinite series of possible outcomes. Nor was this successful prediction a remarkable intellectual feat, we will explain, because nothing happened to cause the conduct of politics to change. To put it more formally, we will assert that the complex cause-and-effect sequence we predicted, even though it had to be made on the basis of very incomplete information, was essentially correct. The outcome—in this case, virtually complete continuity—is our " proof."

If, on the other hand, we learn tomorrow that today an important and surprising change occurred in the conduct of politics in our city, province, republic, or state, we will still not believe that this happened at random. We will seek an adjusted explanation (postdiction) to replace our incorrect prediction of great continuity. Perhaps some additional facts will satisfy us that we have a believable alternative explanation. Or we may revise our earlier ideas about how politics worked in the first place in the arena in question, assigning more weight or less, or a different kind of influence, to one or more factors until we arrive at an explanation (postdiction) that seems congruent with the unexpected discontinuity. Our new explanation, had it been a prediction, would have been correct. We know this because the validating events have already taken place.

The logical form of explanation and prediction is therefore the same: it is just that the former is made after the right-hand side of the equation or " proof "—the outcome—is already known. This useful truism of general scientific theory has been slow to penetrate the social sciences.

The remaining five books to be reviewed here are explanations (validated predictions) of extraordinary events that have already taken place. Each book is well worth reading on its own terms. I hope, however, that it is not playing fast and loose with these various scholarly works to consider them also as complex, thoughtful postdictions, which may usefully be discussed in terms of their predictive power. That is, can we extract analyses from these narratives that will give us an improved ability to anticipate in Czechoslovakia or elsewhere similar dramatic changes (or their absence)? And if not, why not?

In 1962, the conservative Czechoslovak Communist Party leadership began deliberately but reluctantly to initiate change in that country's political economy. Golan, in *The Czechoslovak Reform Movement: Communism in Crisis, 1962–1968*, identifies jarring economic failure in the early 1960s as the principal impetus for economic reorganization, or reform.[8] In order to regain political authority in Party circles in Czechoslovakia and abroad, and probably in order just to stay in power, the Novotný regime had to reverse a disastrous downward trend in Czechoslovakia's growth rate. The simultaneous decision to begin a cautious, belated de-Stalinization campaign, apparently at the prompting of the Soviet Union, widened the scope of these early modest moves toward reform.[9] Both the economic crisis and de-Stalinization helped legitimize preferences of those Party members who actively favored change and convinced others within the Party of the general correctness of pro-reform reasoning.

The conservative leadership undertook both economic and political reforms half-heartedly. The reforms were effectively undermined by those within the Party who felt that they stood to lose from change in the direction of liberalization. The expectations of the growing number who favored reform were raised and then disappointed at several junctures. Economic decentralization and other economic reforms were implemented so partially that they were mildly disruptive, rather than salutary; only a token number of the thousands of victims of the 1953–1956 purges were rehabilitated. By 1964, Party intellectuals—economists, other social scientists, and jurists—had responded to the crisis by undertaking a number of thorough studies of their society. Many of these studies produced practical and detailed suggestions for change.

At this point, according to Golan, pressures from Slovaks within the Party for an upgrading of the nationality's status may have been "decisive."[10] Slovak national interests coincided with the changes urged for other reasons by both Czech and Slovak reformers.

The first chapter of Golan's *Reform Rule in Czechoslovakia* (reviewed above) summarizes this earlier work and sets its conceptual outlines in bolder relief than does the original. In this chapter, she speaks of the "confluence" of circumstances that caused the discontinuities of Czechoslovakia in 1968.[11] The format of Golan's earlier book, *The Czechoslovak Reform Movement*, also suggests just such a convergence of several factors, each amplifying and accelerating the

8. See Golan, *The Czechoslovak Reform Movement*, especially pp. 4, 11–15, and 268.
9. *Ibid.*, pp. 9, 278, and elsewhere.
10. *Ibid.*, p. 20.
11. Golan, *Reform Rule in Czechoslovakia*, p. 4.

effects of the other—none, perhaps, sufficient in and of itself to precipitate dramatic change. A crucial moment, both Golan books contend, was the Party's decision in January 1968 to seek support for the reforms from the public.

This retelling of Golan's account is, of course, radically simplified. Still, it will be instructive to see how the author's explanations look when stated as seven predictions.

1. If there is a severe economic crisis, then there will be a political crisis.

2. If there is an economically caused political crisis, then political conservatives will consider partial economic reform in order to salvage their political influence.

3. If a conservative leadership acquiesces to adaptive changes it does not like, then the leadership and like-minded subordinates will prevent the changes from being well executed.

4. If special interests feel that the attempted changes would be beneficial to them, then the pressure for well-executed change will further increase.

5. If this sequence of failed reform is repeated several times, then the political crisis will deepen with each iteration.

6. If the politically knowledgeable are a small group within society, then such economic and political crises will nevertheless not cause precipitous change.

7. If, under circumstances of economic and political crisis, a small group of politically knowledgeable people abruptly informs society at large of the crisis and of the group's intentions to initiate significant change, then the pace of change will be amplified and accelerated by public response.

These explanations of what led to Czechoslovakia, 1968, are now in a form that allows one to see whether they are generalizable. In other words, if they are correct, they will help one to judge the probability of a similar major discontinuity at another time or in another society—all other things being equal. How social scientists can deal with this forbidding *ceteris paribus* assumption will be discussed briefly below.

Many other predictions can be extrapolated from Golan's narrative, but these seven rephrase the broad outlines of her account. Without pausing at this point to reflect on their correctness or completeness, let us simply add to them from the narrative explanations of other authors.

George Shaw Wheeler is an American-born economist who lived in Czechoslovakia from 1947 to 1970. During most of that time, he was a member of the Economic Institute of the Czechoslovak

Academy of Sciences in Prague. *The Human Face of Socialism : The Political Economy of Change in Czechoslovakia* covers the years when Wheeler was involved on a day-to-day basis in the matters about which he writes. This book is a sound case study of the Czechoslovak experience. It is also a first-rate general primer on the interplay of politics, economics, and human nature in much of East Europe. Illustrations from the author's own experiences will give readers who have not lived for any length of time in East Germany, Poland, Hungary, Rumania, Bulgaria, or Czechoslovakia some feeling for the special texture of these societies.

The following are predictive statements about political change which, I believe, accurately summarize Wheeler's explanation of the changes he observed in Communist-run Czechoslovakia:

8. If a centrally planned economy does not move to a less centralized arrangement when it has become too complex to run effectively from the center, then the economy will become increasingly inefficient.[12]

9. If responsibility for economic outcomes is not vested in those who ultimately make economic decisions, then the economy will become increasingly inefficient.[13]

10. If a well-educated and well-informed population perceives its society's economy to be stagnant, even if only stagnant relative to other economies, then this population will become increasingly disaffected, both with the personnel who ultimately make economic decisions and with the society's institutional arrangements.[14]

11. If a self-identified leadership group has inflicted massive suffering on a large subset of its own membership for reasons not accepted as legitimate by a large proportion of the general membership, then the leadership group will eventually be required to account further for these past actions, either by justifying them more convincingly or by condemning them.[15]

12. If this group of self-identified leaders (and thus the large subset of its membership widely felt to have been wronged) in turn makes up a large portion of the population, then the general population will feel that the wrong is " pervasive."[16]

13. If a country's population has a tradition of " experience with revolution, democracy, and struggle for sovereignty " in the past,

12. See Wheeler, *op. cit.*, Chap. 4 and elsewhere.
13. *Ibid.*, pp. 108ff.
14. *Ibid.*, pp. 4, 5, 8, 58, and elsewhere.
15. *Ibid.*, pp. 121–125.
16. *Ibid.*, pp. 121–125.

then it will be more likely to act forcefully in favor of these values in the present.[17]

Wheeler's view of political change over the very long term is essentially Marxian. This involves the implicit periodization of political change and assumptions about its direction toward a final goal-state which are the traditional hallmarks of the Marxian theory of history. The broad theoretical framework was neither falsified nor validated by the Czechoslovak events: they could have happened as they did whether or not the Marxian view of history is in its broad outlines correct.

To explain the Czechoslovak experience, Marxist observers have felt it necessary—as have non-Marxist observers—to supplement their general notions about change in the conduct of politics in such a society with *new* explanations. These explanations tend to be more complex and detailed than earlier ones, and they generalize most easily not into new "models," but into much lower-level theoretical statements, or predictive propositions.[18] In their analytical response to the challenge of discontinuity in Czechoslovak politics, there is little difference between those scholars who favor the Marxian model and those who reject it.

Social Change and Stratification in Postwar Czechoslovakia by Jaroslav Krejci is a valuable contribution to the remarkable collection of books being reviewed here. Krejci had broad training in the social sciences before he left his native Czechoslovakia in August 1968. His reader benefits both from the sheer mass of important facts he has pulled together and from the sensitive insights with which he informs their presentation.

Krejci documents the deliberate, radical socio-economic homogenization of Czechoslovak society under Communist rule. This policy left a residual heterogeneity in which each individual had three salient attributes that distinguished him from others: first, Communist Party membership or lack of it and, within the Party, degree of influence; second, level and type of education; and, finally, nationality—Czech, Slovak, or other.[19]

Each of these three major residual differences among Czechoslovak citizens divides the people in the other two categories. There is a pattern of cross-cutting cleavages that might be used as a sample paradigm of predicted socio-political stability in an introductory

17. *Ibid.*, pp. 6, 58, and elsewhere.

18. Wheeler does set forth six analytical variables explicitly; *ibid.*, pp. 6–7. This is not a carefully done exercise (variables two through five are logically subcategories of the first, for example), but it does not affect the usefulness of the rest of the book.

19. Krejci, *op. cit.*, pp. 3, 7.

democratic theory course. But we have the advantage of hindsight. We know that in fact the outcome was political instability.

Why? The most striking theme in Krejci's account is the emergence of a new elite within the new, economically homogeneous society, and this group's gradual disillusionment with its own rule. He challenges the assertion that economic crisis precipitated political crisis, yet much of his information invites that inference. From the wealth of material the author presents, the following rephrased predictive insights, based on what produced political discontinuity in 1968, seem especially useful:

14. If social heterogeneity is radically decreased, then the remaining distinctions will be proportionately more decisive in determining the nature and the pace of political change.[20]

15. If those groups that enjoy the most power and prestige in a given society are also chronically the most socially and politically insecure, then they will eventually seek to change at least those features of the existing socio-political structure which they believe cause their extreme insecurity.[21]

16. If the best educated members of a new elite lose confidence in the elite's ability to run the political economy well, then impulses to change the nature of existing rule will be further strengthened.[22]

Anyone who wants to understand fully what we now call the Prague Spring must read Eugen Steiner's book *The Slovak Dilemma*, for the view from Bratislava. Steiner identifies himself as a Slovak of Jewish descent, and a member of the Communist Party since before World War II. He left Czechoslovakia in the summer of 1968 when the armed forces of five Warsaw Pact countries invaded.

The Slovak dilemma is identical in its general outlines to that of many of the world's peoples:

> The sense of frustration felt by many Slovaks springs in large measure from the fact that other, bigger nations, including the Czechs, have often let them down. Promises made in solemn terms on solemn occasions have repeatedly been followed by disappointments.
>
> [But] . . . as a small nation, the Slovaks have always had to choose which larger grouping they shall belong to or support.[23]

While the Czechs face this sort of dilemma when they in turn deal with "other, bigger nations," they can be critical or condescending

20. *Ibid.*, Chap. 4.
21. *Ibid.*, pp. 101, 103, 104, 144, 145, 150, 170; Chap. 4 generally.
22. *Ibid.*, esp. pp. 187, 192, 193.
23. Steiner, *op. cit.*, p. 3.

toward the alleged political opportunism of their Slovak kin. The majority of commentators on Czechoslovak affairs—both Czech and foreign—adopt the Czech perspective in matters concerning differences between the two nationalities, with varying degrees of partisanship. Steiner's mildly polemical rejoinder should be welcomed not only as a source of some information not readily available elsewhere, but as a corrective to any Czech (or foreign) bias in other sources.

Steiner's book furnishes a number of predictive insights into the Slovak role in the events of 1968, which may also be of interest to students of multinational societies in general:

17. If an ethnic minority's most salient political grievance is its lack of autonomy, then its members will tend to support (or not oppose) political change in either a " reformist " or a " conservative " direction if such change seems likely to give that minority more autonomy.[24]

18. If such a minority is at a given point deprived of even what is merely a formal vestige of institutional autonomy, it will feel further aggrieved.[25]

19. If such a minority has merely formal institutional autonomy when change toward real autonomy begins, these institutions will be activated with the intention, likely to be effective, of accelerating such change.[26]

20. If such a minority additionally feels that it is being economically or culturally disadvantaged by majority policy with the passage of time, its initial preference for autonomy will be strengthened.[27]

21. If there is more than one political-administrative center in a given country, the likelihood that a political leadership favoring substantial political change will eventually emerge in one of these centers is greater, the more such centers exist.

22. If political-administrative units are demarcated territorially in a manner that coincides with ethnic or other differences, distinguishing their populations from the general population in a politically important way, then the possibility that a political elite favoring substantial political change will eventually emerge in one of these units will be even more likely.

24. *Ibid.* This theme appears throughout the book; it is essentially " the dilemma " rephrased as a program for action.

25. *Ibid.*, pp. 70, 93, 113.

26. *Ibid.*, p. 5 and elsewhere. There is a Slovak Party within the Czechoslovak Communist Party structure, but there is no separate Czech component, the Czechs apparently being assumed to be dominant in the whole and therefore not in need of a second forum.

27. *Ibid.*, esp. Chap. 12.

Much of *Civilization at the Crossroads: Social and Human Implications of the Scientific and Technological Revolution* by Radovan Richta and a team of sixty Czechoslovak social scientists was completed by 1966. This research was itself a major contributor to the intellectual ferment which widened and deepened belief within the Party that major socio-economic and political change should be instituted. The third, expanded edition, published in October 1968, is reviewed here.

This book is an eloquent and elegantly argued case for socialist humanism. Its approach is sophisticated and pan-Marxist. The authors seem thoroughly conversant with non-Marxist social science but find it inadequate to their task:

> [Western social scientists, particularly Americans] . . . tend to lack the synthetic approach for interpreting the substance of revolutions in the structure of productive forces and in the social and anthropological dimensions. . . .[28]

In other words, the Richta team does not wish to describe and count the trees: they feel it is urgent, in order to ensure rational, humanist decisionmaking, to step back at this point and take stock of the changing nature of the forest as a whole.

The authors put forward three major propositions. First, the world is in transition into a new era, the era of scientific and technological revolution. Second, this new era differs in very fundamental ways from the previous historical stage, the era of industrial revolution, about which Marx wrote. Finally, if there is to be technical-economic advancement, these fundamental differences *necessitate* greater development of human potential through a satisfactorily " rational, aesthetic, and emotional life " for the individual.[29]

> In an advanced socialist country such as Czechoslovakia, the main barrier in approaching the scientific and technological revolution is placed by some elements of immaturity in the economic structure. . . .[30]

Richta and his associates hold that a major cause of these " elements of immaturity " is the excessively centralized and politically controlled direction of the Czechoslovak economy.

28. Richta et al., p. 14.
29. *Ibid.*, p. 285.
30. *Ibid.*, p. 280.

> ... and there is a growing need to solve the difficult problem of participation in civilization, to develop democratic forms of social life and so on.[31]
>
> The time will soon be ripe for a major intervention in the structure of the nation's work. ...[32]

It is irrelevant to the specific purposes of this review to consider whether or to what degree the three propositions on which this argument is based are true.[33] What is important in explaining Czechoslovakia, 1968, might be put as follows:

23. If the overwhelming majority of the most respected social scientists within a powerful ruling group asserts that a significant reorganization of society is necessary for further economic progress, then the confidence that the political leadership within that group has in its present mode of organization will be diminished.

24. If under such circumstances the economy is in fact not progressing as well as the political leadership had expected it to, the arguments of the reformers for radical change will have additional impact.

25. If such a reform-minded group within a ruling elite asserts that greater individual freedom of action and generally more satisfying living conditions are necessary to ensure further economic progress, then the likelihood that a large portion of the political leadership will eventually favor some change in that direction will be increased.

Conclusions

These twenty-five partial explanations of what contributed to a sudden change in the conduct of Czechoslovak politics are a deliberately abbreviated list. The list is meant simply to illustrate how a body of literature of this sort can be used to move from factual description and explanation to explanation's logical homologue, a potentially falsifiable prediction.

The approach is inductive. That is, to predict change one does not refer to an overarching model of politics in a given society or type

31. *Ibid.*, p. 19.

32. *Ibid.*, p. 283.

33. All three are properly empirical questions. The third seems most likely to be vulnerable on close inspection. It would be nice, of course, if what is good for human freedom and dignity turns out to be what is good for scientific and cultural advance. But under many circumstances these values may conflict.

of society. Predictive statements extrapolated from postdictive explanations of specific events constitute a low level of abstraction. The analytical terminology used at this level of abstraction (economy, minority, nationality, and so on) is more susceptible to careful empirical definition than is the language used in more abstract constructions. And this approach does permit us to creep a bit further out of the swamp of "vulgar factology." [34]

Approaching theory in this manner has drawbacks, not the least of which is the lack of drama it affords. A model with a dashing name and immediate intuitive appeal would probably emerge only eventually, if at all. Moreover, some problems that are also present both in factual descriptions and in overarching models remain: adequate definition of terms is one.

Another difficulty is the *actual* falsification of this kind of potentially falsifiable generalization. Plodding, day-dreaming, trying null hypotheses, and systematically preferring generalizations that are likely to be applicable to a large number of situations and hence will be tested frequently—all this will help. Consider Proposition 13:

> If a country's population has a tradition of "experience with revolution, democracy, and struggle for sovereignty" in the past, then it will be more likely to act forcefully in favor of these values in the present.

Wheeler's postdiction of Czechoslovakia, 1968, appears in some form or another in many of the other works reviewed here. It may be correct.

Until the mid-1960s, however, Czechoslovak history was almost as routinely cited to explain and predict something approaching the opposite case. It was said that accommodation to foreign domination had been a national way of life since the battle of White Mountain; that Czechoslovak citizens had no penchant for quixotic gestures of the sort that Poles and Hungarians would indulge in; and so forth. Had they been stated as predictions, of course, explanations of that country's political docility based on its historical experience would have been falsified. One suspects that the alternative proposition could bear more scrutiny, too, as could some of the other explana-

34. The term "vulgar factology" has been part of my vocabulary for years, and I was long under the impression that I had invented it. I recently learned that others attribute it to Wolfgang Leonhard, however, and it is quite possible that the invention is his. Simultaneous discovery cannot be ruled out, but it seems unlikely.

tions presented as illustrations above. But they cannot be scrutinized unless they are stated plainly.

Finally, how can one hope to falsify probabilistic statements about relationships among three or four factors, when many other factors are also present, some of which might actually be decisive in any given instance? Here one faces the logical need to make a *ceteris paribus* assumption, on the one hand, and the logical difficulty of making one meaningfully, on the other. If " one-party systems " or any other complex political phenomena multiplied as quickly as fruit flies, political scientists—like geneticists before microscopes were developed which allowed them to see genes—could deal fairly systematically with the probabilistic nature of their explanations-predictions, incomplete information notwithstanding. And, as a matter of fact, those phenomena that we call " one-party systems " *have* multiplied very rapidly since World War II.

Prospects for a more scientific political science are not dim. We have an immense body of factual information at our disposal, and we readily accept the assumption that important variables interact in regular if complicated patterns, rather than at random. Moreover, those of us who have specialized in the study of Communist-run societies can take advantage of a unique opportunity. Twelve of the thirteen Communist-run states that existed in the early 1950s were probably as similar as political systems at the national level have ever been. Elite political culture was nearly uniform from country to country, and the several political elites seemed determined to increase the institutional similarities among them. Forms of internal political and economic organization were in fact rapidly becoming virtually identical. Twenty-odd years later we observe that the outcome is growing diversity.

The experiences of these countries may be the closest approximation to a controlled experiment at the macro-societal level that has ever existed, and they can be an especially rich source of insight into the causes of political continuity and change. The books reviewed here are indeed a contribution to political science in and of themselves. The authors' and editors' careful collation of facts and their insights also provide the raw material for contributions of another sort to political science: contributions to empirical theory of long-term political change. Perhaps we cannot predict idiosyncratic political storms, but we are not so very far from being able to predict something analogous to the changing seasons.

Comment by Galia Golan:

Reform Movements and the Problem of Prediction

The questions "Why Czechoslovakia? And why 1968?" would seem to be amply answered by the books reviewed, and Professor Susan Bridge would seem to have gleaned some of the principles relevant to these questions from the wealth of material presented by the nine efforts. Yet the basic question that Bridge raises may be the one connected most directly with the problem of prediction: what signs, conditions, forces, or phenomena make for change in a Communist society, and most particularly for "liberal" change or what might be called reform? To sharpen this a bit further, one might ask: what are the necessary and sufficient factors leading to reform? If one can answer this question, one might be able to provide a model for prediction wherein certain factors appear as essentials, others merely as variables, the existence of which does not necessarily predicate reform, the absence of which does not prevent it—thereby providing a basis for understanding why similar sets of conditions in different countries do not always produce the same phenomena. From this point of view, one might analyze, for example, the principle abstracted from one of my books: "If there is a severe economic crisis, then there will be a political crisis." When is this true, why is it true? That is, in what set of circumstances or conditions will this be the case? Proposition 17, derived from Steiner's book might be analyzed similarly:

> If an ethnic minority's most salient political grievance is its lack of autonomy, then its members will tend to support (or not oppose) political change in either a "reformist" or a "conservative" direction if such change seems likely to give that minority more autonomy.

The truth of this "principle" is probably obvious, but when does such a phenomenon become significant or operative? I find it hard to believe, for example, that propositions 8 through 12 from Wheeler's book, or 14 through 16 from Krejci's book, were unique to Czechoslovakia, whatever their validity. What, then, made their appearance in Czechoslovakia, at that time, a catalyst of reform?

Are they perhaps necessary but not sufficient factors? These are, I suspect, the real questions that Bridge raises in her thought-provoking essay; they are not squarely faced by any of the studies under review. Even the Richta team's thesis that the " scientific-technological revolution " produces both the requirement and the necessary conditions for reform does not explain why the same set of circumstances led to different actions and policies in Czechoslovakia of the 1960s from those in the Soviet Union, which also acknowledges this " revolution."

In my own efforts to generalize from the Czechoslovak experience, without necessarily devising a model, I have tried to work from two starting points. First, certain signs prompted me in 1963, but even more intensely in 1964 and 1965, to watch Czechoslovakia (and to begin to gather material for a book on it) in expectation of highly significant events—significant, I believed, not only for Czechoslovakia but for the whole Communist world. These signs were described in my first book (*The Czechoslovak Reform Movement*), which was completed before 1968 and which was to call attention to a potentially explosive " movement " that was already making serious efforts at innovation and reform of the Soviet system of rule. As Bridge points out, however, Czechoslovakia was perceived in those years as the model satellite; few in the academic world were willing to concede my claims, and so events turned me into an historian.[1] The signs included an economic crisis of serious enough dimensions to bear the potential for political crisis, minority dissatisfaction, which provided a type of built-in factionalism, and many others that Bridge has pointed out. My abstraction from those signs, which led me to my conclusions, was approximately as follows: a case of grave political instability within the higher levels of the Party, caused largely by external pressures (i.e., Khrushchev's de-Stalinization revelations and drives in 1956 and 1961) but also by internal conflict (i.e., the Party-splitting struggle between Novotny and Barak in 1961–1962), had created the opportunity or conditions for political exploitation of an economic crisis by various dissatisfied forces inside the Party. Because these forces *were* within the Party, they could sanction—if not actually provide—criticism and new ideas. This contributed to the political instability, permitting further exploitation or " spill over " of albeit reluctant change, which moved from one sphere to another and still another, with an inner logic

1. A notable exception was J. M. Montias, who as early as 1963 shared my enthusiasm and fascination for what appeared to be afoot in Czechoslovakia.

that could not be halted because of the political instability and division within the Party. With each concession, the blow to the Party *apparat* strengthened the questioning about the validity of the regime. The whittling away of this supreme authority could be seen as the continuous broadening of the original breach in the political monolith. The response necessary to stop the whole process either had to be so drastic as to be intolerable or had to be impossible to implement, given the corrosive nature of what had gone before.

A second starting point would be the comparison of the Czechoslovak experience (and the above generalization) with other reform movements and events in Eastern Europe, particularly in Poland and Hungary in both the 1950s and the 1960s. Here a model emerges which is similar to that posited by Zbigniew Brzezinski [2] on the basis of 1956 Poland and Hungary, with modifications and additions suggested by the analysis of subsequent events. What Brzezinski calls the existence of an alternative leader could be enlarged to division within the ruling (Party) elite. The conflict need not be of the "liberal" versus "conservative" variety; it is probably sufficient that the split be serious enough to cause a break in the monolithic nature of the supreme Party organ, making it possible for dissidents within the Party—of whatever origin (e.g., minorities, the disillusioned, the basically more liberal-leaning or honest who might be but are not necessarily younger members)—to press their demands. This division within the ruling elite can come about by external as well as, or even instead of, internal factors (viz. the elevation of Imre Nagy in 1953), but it in turn creates a thaw (or loosening of the line or policies in certain spheres), which cannot come only from external factors. One might speculate that the division could appear even in the total absence of external factors, although one would have to posit at least acquiescence or tolerance from outside (i.e., from the Soviet Union).

The necessary conditions, then, would be political instability within the ruling elite and a thaw. The thaw makes it possible to express criticism and ideas; it is a period in which ideas can be worked out *and* presented so as to gain broader support. This is done by the intellectuals, primarily those within the Party, for they have both the protection and the legitimacy to exploit the situation. Unless they exploit it, however, the political split may go no further, for want either of substantive policy alternatives or of broader support aroused by the promulgation of such views. The creation and promulgation of alternative views or policies by the intellectuals, rendered

2. In *The Soviet Bloc* (Cambridge, Mass.: Harvard University Press, 1967).

possible by the support and activities of dissident forces highly placed in the Party hierarchy who provide the thaw, constitute what could be called a reform movement. Without these elements, as was the case in East Germany in 1953 and in Poland's 1970 worker insurrection, conditions will not be sufficient to bring about thoroughgoing reform. In Poland, there was a Party split, but because there had been no thaw (the intellectuals had been effectively neutralized after 1968) and therefore no reform movement, the split could only bring about a personnel (not an overall policy) change. Thus, worker action cannot be considered sufficient for reform, but is it necessary? This is in fact another way of asking the question, are the intellectuals, albeit a necessary factor, also a sufficient one? Both Poland of 1968 and Czechoslovakia of 1963–1968 tend to demonstrate that at some point mass support (the workers) must be forthcoming both to exert pressure on the shaken conservatives and to implement the envisaged changes. Even if a reform movement can come to power without worker (mass) participation or support (as was the case in Czechoslovakia in 1968), it is highly unlikely that it can stay in power (and implement its ideas) without this element.

The division within the ruling elite and the thaw create another phenomenon, which must also be taken into account: the struggle for the Party *apparat*. The natural tendency of the *apparat* is to oppose reform, but the growing insecurity of its members during the thaw can make for defections as well as for staunch conservatism. The result of this struggle for the *apparat*—i.e., success or failure in winning over at least the more salient elements of the *apparat*—will determine the nature of the shift to reform: whether it will be a peaceful transferral of power as in Poland in 1956 and Czechoslovakia in 1968, or a revolution as in Hungary in 1956. With this last element, the *apparat*, the following pyramid could be drawn:

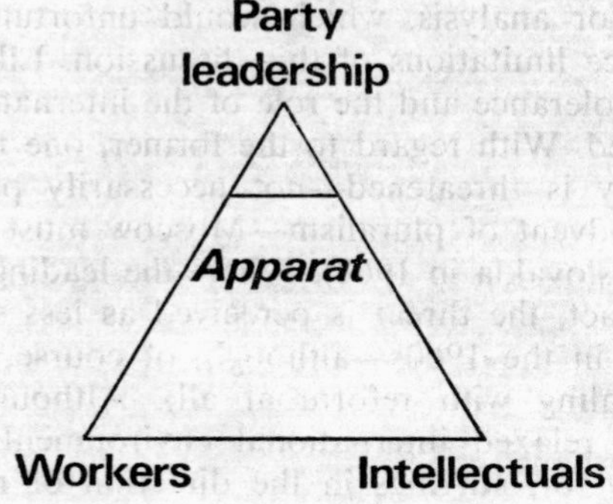

Two other forces enter in, possibly as variables. The first is the students. In all three reform movements (Poland and Hungary in 1956, Czechoslovakia in 1968), the students both provided platforms for the intellectuals and served as a bridge between the intellectuals and the workers. Although the former role may not be crucial (necessary), as the intellectuals have access to other platforms, the latter may be. The students are generally more acceptable to the workers than the intellectuals and more successful in engaging them. Because the workers are vital to the outcome of the struggle, the students' role may be indispensable. It is difficult, however, to gauge this, for in all cases where the intellectuals were involved, the students were also involved (Poland in 1956 and 1968, Hungary in 1956, and Czechoslovakia in 1968).

The second additional force is that of nationalism, defined not as minority grievances (which are not a necessary factor) but as aspirations for independence from the Soviet Union. Nationalism was indeed an important factor in both Poland and Hungary of 1956; that it is not a sufficient factor is amply proven by the case of Rumania in the 1960s; that it is a necessary factor is rendered doubtful by its absence from the Czechoslovak reform movement throughout most of its existence. It may be, however, that nationalism ultimately engages and unites mass support, as in the last stages of the reform period in Czechoslovakia in 1968 and 1969, in which case it would at some point become a necessary factor.

Many additional variables, such as the political culture or traditions of each country, may influence both the content and methods of the reform movement. These in turn may well affect the outcome, for they may determine, for example, the degree of threat to certain norms, such as the concept of the leading role of the Party. Indeed, the comparison of content and methods, and in particular the *differences* between the movements from this point of view, provides extremely fertile ground for analysis, which would unfortunately take us far beyond the space limitations of this discussion. Likewise, the limitations of Soviet tolerance and the role of the international environment must be analyzed. With regard to the former, one may conclude that where the Party is threatened—not necessarily physically but primarily by the advent of pluralism—Moscow must step in (Hungary in 1956, Czechoslovakia in 1968). Where the leading role of the Party is preserved intact, the threat is perceived as less serious (Poland in 1956, Rumania in the 1960s—although, of course, in the latter case we are not dealing with reform at all). Although it is generally believed that a relaxed international environment is conducive to, if not necessary for, stirrings in the direction of reform, it may be that Moscow's very fear of a repetition of the past has lowered its level of tolerance in the era of détente. The question then would be: can such a level (i.e., a tightening of Soviet control and intensified integration of the Soviet bloc) be implemented under conditions of détente, with increasing East-West contacts in the economic sphere at least?

The importance of the economic sphere brings us to one last problem: how does Hungary in the 1960s, with its radical economic reform, fit into the generalized framework outlined above? A tentative answer may be that, while Czechoslovakia demonstrated the spill-over principle (as did Poland and Hungary in 1956), the absence of an acute political struggle—or, positively put, the relative stability of the Hungarian political elite—may account for the apparent absence of general reform. A thorough study of the Hungarian example from the point of view of the above principles would in my opinion be worth undertaking, for the purpose both of testing them and perhaps of adding to them.

Comment by Jaroslav Krejci

Professor Susan Bridge's attempt to draw general conclusions from material supplied by the nine reviewed books should be highly appreciated. She did very well, though, in my opinion, the reviewed narratives and structural analyses provide good grounds for further, more specific explanations or generalizations, such as the following.

1. In a society where the means of production become state-owned and one political party assumes exclusive domination of the state, there is, according to Marxian concepts, scope for exploitation and alienation. It is not so much the formal ownership as the concentration of power that matters.

2. As soon as those strata who were the main supporters of the revolutionary change and the recruiting ground for the leaders of the postrevolutionary regime realize that the promise of participation in decisionmaking is not being honored and that the allocation of resources is disadvantageous to them (productivity grows much faster than real wages), they lose interest in supporting that regime and become apathetic.

3. The recruitment of the elite from a certain social group does not in itself assure the full loyalty of that group; a more positive attitude of those above toward those below is required.

4. Interest in political development can be regained (a) if there is a loosening of the Party and government power grip, (b) if the rank and file become convinced that the leadership envisages a genuine reform of the status quo, or (c) if the government takes some drastic measures or permits acute deficiencies (such as the 1953 monetary reform in Czechoslovakia or the 1970 drop in workers' living standard in Poland). Then outbursts of discontent can even assume violent forms.

5. In a political system with highly concentrated and extended power at the top, only a cleavage within the ruling elite can bring about real reform.

6. As the theorists of reform and revolution have already indicated, the change within the Communist system also starts with the " defection of intellectuals."

7. In a political system where the power monopoly depends largely on another country, a change can occur if either (a) there is a previous

change in the governing country, or (b) the ruling group in that country becomes less apprehensive about the possible change in the dependent country.

8. A voluntary abandonment of terror by the ruling group requires not only a personal change in top leadership but also a new evaluation of individuals' positions within the polity. Whatever reason there might be, such a change has an impact on public ethos and morality.

My qualifications of Bridge's explanatory suggestions mainly concern the relevance of economic and moral issues. During the " stormy " growth in the early 1950s, the Czechoslovak living standard declined and the general public considered it a crisis phenomenon. On the other hand, during the stagnation of production in the early 1960s, the living standard moderately increased. The situation then was considered a crisis by those above. Moreover, the crisis of the early 1950s occurred in an atmosphere of political terror; no publicity was given to the unfavorable features of the development. The stagnation of 1962–1964 happened in a more relaxed atmosphere; the unfavorable features of the development were broadly publicized. The preceding de-Stalinization in the Soviet Union put the political leadership in Czechoslovakia in an awkward position and resulted in a cleavage within the ruling elite. In positive terms, de-Stalinization meant a certain humanization. It awakened the consciences of some important individuals (this was my direct observation), and it also produced a favorable climate for reformist thought. Such tendencies had already emerged in the late 1950s, but they remained latent until acknowledgment of the failure of economic growth (considered as the main test of socialist superiority over capitalism). Meanwhile, the political crisis was contained within the Communist Party activists. It assumed a nationwide dimension only when the reformist stream within the Party started to talk to the public and eventually gain its confidence. This, however, was a gradual process and the manual workers were the last to become de-alienated.

Regarding the question whether the Czech tradition was democratic and revolutionary or more inclined to accommodation and docility (Bridge's comment to Proposition 13), the following has to be said: neither national tradition nor political culture is one, uniform variable; there is rather a structured pattern of tendencies and subcultures. Their relative importance changes in relationship to other variables, such as shifts in social stratification and foreign influences. So contradictory attitudes and value judgments, which coexist within a community, may acquire a different relative strength and consequently play a different role according to the constellation of other circumstances. Appropriate elaboration of this point would require more space than is reserved for this rejoinder. Here it should be stressed only that the assessment of the role of tradition and its possible ambiguity cannot be conceived in a simple, more or less static, dichotomy.

Comment by Vladimir V. Kusin

I have recently compiled a full bibliography of books on the Prague Spring published in the West, and it is flattering to see one of my contributions rated among the select few out of 600 or so. Of course, this is Professor Susan Bridge's choice. Were I to repair to a desolate island with a small bookshelf, four of the nine would stay behind. Naturally, I am not saying which.

But would another selector infer the same 25 predictions, always assuming that he or she does not look for them in journalistic or ideologically opportunistic volumes? Not necessarily, although a consensus is likely. One huge question-mark hangs over the list: what measure of validity is there in drawing general conclusions from an event aggregated in one particular country within a certain period on the time scale? One has the feeling that the *ceteris paribus* assumption simply will not hold. Admittedly, the societies of the area had been standardized to a large extent, but Bridge must allow for progress from " virtual identity " to " growing diversity." We ought to seek to establish wherein lies the divide between possible (and even then only tentative) prediction on a general level and impermissible (because insufficiently supported) specific forecast. Few things that were true about Czechoslovakia in the late 1960s need be true about any East European country, including Czechoslovakia, in the 1970s.

Nevertheless, some general conclusions do emerge from observation of the East European scene over the past 20 years. Lumping together several for the sake of brevity in this hurried comment, I would summarize them as follows:

1. Change-orientation, as against conservation of the status quo, has *on the whole* (i.e., not everywhere, all the time) become a policy.

2. Its basic motivation is a search for economic and political efficiency in response to grievance, dysfunction, and systemic failure.

3. In the process, some groups inside the political structure, as well as outside it, have reached the conclusion that a systemic reform is required, rather than just an improvement or a devolution of decisionmaking powers.

4. These trends of systemic reform coalesce or clash with the surviving elements of pre-Communist political cultures (nationalism,

pluralism, religion, and the like), with pragmatic conflicts generated within the Communist system (power struggle, checks and balances, vested interests), and with foreign " factors for change " (developments in the West *and* the East, including the *Dreispaltung* of Marxism).

5. Out of this configuration (change–efficiency–systemic overhaul–externalities), there seem to emerge a theory and a method, an alternative to Communism as it has been known to date. The theory is that of democratic socialism achieved from the positions of Communism, not " capitalism." The method is that of gradualism, with emphasis on action through the ruling Party and political elite.

Finally, the correctness of several of the inferences that Professor Bridge isolated from the books under review is highly questionable *per se*, and almost all can be contested in one respect or another. Perhaps the authors are more responsible than the reviewer, who is in any case the first to acknowledge the multiplicity of factors at play and to expose the one-cause-one-effect fallacy.

Contrary to the role in which I cast myself for the purpose of *Political Grouping*, may I endorse Bridge's call for an interpretative approach to the body of factual information already assembled, while raising the historian's warning finger? There are still dark patches alongside the lit-up corners.

Comment by Robin Alison Remington

Professor Susan Bridge's essay on a representative segment of the ever-increasing literature on the ill-starred Czechoslovak experiment in political change and the military intervention that aborted that process is a thoughtful, provocative analysis. More importantly, it is useful to students and scholars to whom the subject she deals with is irrelevant. This review gives its reader not only information and evaluation needed by potential users of the books but a method for grappling with the growing number of books and articles in the field by establishing theoretical order from a chaos of often hotly disputed and at best partially presented fact. The issue is not so much one of agreeing or disagreeing with Bridge's approach. To follow her reasoning is a valuable intellectual exercise.

The questions that remain in my mind are potential research spinoffs not dealt with in the review and only lightly touched on in the books used as the reviewer's starting point.

To what extent did what I will call the " bandwagon " phenomenon in Czechoslovak political culture—so aptly illustrated by the gripping, now forbidden film *Report on the Party and the Guests*—influence events?

What do the methods by which Novotny tried but failed to save himself tell us about the relationship between Party organization and policy change? Had Novotny turned his energies to a controlled elimination of the worst grievances, rather than simply jettisoning his most tarnished followers so slowly that some of those most ideologically inclined to support him jumped ship, he might have played a role much more like that of Kadar. Czechoslovakia might then have been a " second Hungary " in a very different sense.

For those who were making the decision to invade, how important was the perception that the Czechoslovaks would not fight? Although I agree with Bridge that the myth of the Battle of the White Mountain in 1620, with its resulting stereotype of Czechoslovak national character, has little refined predictive value, the fact remains that resistance stopped short of battle by the armed forces of Czechoslovakia or sustained guerrilla underground activity. The quiet heroism of the populace—described in the one book that I was truly sorry to see omitted from this review, Philip Windsor and Adam

Roberts, *Czechoslovakia 1968 Reform, Repression, and Resistance*,[1] —might have formed the basis for a different type of psychological deterrence had the Czechoslovak leadership been able to hold together.

In politics and history, the lines between when events are impossible, possible but not likely, probable, and virtually inevitable are ever blurred. Nonetheless, I would be fascinated to see attention shift from the international issue of the inevitability of the 1968 intervention to its domestic counterpart. Was Husak inevitable? There is no doubt that the KSC was besieged. Was its downhill slide into political corruption and decline a response to Soviet pressure, a genetic organizational weakness of that particular Communist Party—as some would have it—or the result of that still understudied constellation of political forces at work in Czechoslovakia during the Prague Spring, not of 1968 but of 1969?

1. London: International Institute of Strategic Studies, 1969.

Comment by George Shaw Wheeler

It seems to me that Professor Susan Bridge is correct in trying to discern in the Czechoslovak events a pattern of forces and events that may have some predictive validity. Every branch of knowledge, if it is to be useful for policymaking, must attempt valid generalizations. I am leery of "economic laws," because these are often used as substitutes for thinking and tend to be applied in a dogmatic fashion to new situations for which they have no validity. I have in mind the "Law of Planned Proportional Development of Socialism"—as an example of a phrase expressing the realization for some years that socialist planning could be subject to serious errors and distortions. Nevertheless, we should try to learn from experience and we can only do so if we can discern patterns of development and trends that may be repeated, even if, necessarily and always, under modified conditions. In my new book *Capitalism, Socialism and Innovation*, I have tried to show that many of the objective forces that were operating in Czechoslovakia, particularly the advances and increasing use of high-technology capital, necessarily involve certain types of problems, such as a proliferation of the number and variety of commodities made, and these problems also require certain patterns of solution. For example, there is more need for planning, yet more need for decentralization of decisionmaking. Often the forces will be so contradictory and strong that it will seem to the policymakers like trying to walk a tight rope in a hurricane.

Because I believe that we can see some trends of development, I think the term "discontinuity" is misleading. There is often abrupt change, as in Czechoslovakia in 1967–1968, but the process is continuous, just as when a fluid changes to a solid, in the sense of many of the factors involved. I think that the concept of dialectic change is more useful here. It is not the discontinuity that makes prediction so devilishly difficult, but rather the very great complexity of the forces at work and the fact that history does not permit exact repetitions. We should not complain—this is what makes political economy exciting and worthwhile.

Rejoinder by Susan Bridge

I have enjoyed reading these responses to my review article. The authors' tone is generous, and several have answered by adding still further insights to our understanding of the conduct of politics in Czechoslovakia, 1968.

Two points should be discussed briefly. The first was raised by Professor Vladimir Kusin, who addressed himself to the *ceteris paribus* assumption necessary to this type of undertaking. He questions—quite correctly—whether in the world of politics such an assumption can ever be made. The fact is that the assumption cannot be made outright either in the social sciences or in many of the messier natural sciences, except when the questions investigated are so obvious as to be trivial. It seems to me that the assumption, like the propositions it allows one to infer from observation of fact, must be probabilistic. That is, " all things are probably more or less equal " in the judgment of the researcher: two situations seem sufficiently similar that the researcher predicts that the relationship thought to have been observed previously will hold again this time.

It is precisely for this reason that, eventually, " some general conclusions do emerge," and that, to quote myself, " they cannot be scrutinized unless they are stated plainly."

Second, some responses imply that the review contributes to a better understanding of Czechoslovakia, 1968. I trust that this is simple collegial courtesy. I should be very uneasy if the compliment were meant literally.

No important insights in the review article about Czechoslovakia, 1968, are original with me. What I have done is to formalize and to state in general terms, as best I could, what other scholars have proposed. My intention in the review is to describe a strategy for building a low-level theory that would be useful in analyzing these and similar events. The substantive content of the causal relationships stated is not based on my own observations or intuitions.

CONTRIBUTORS

BARBARA A. ANDERSON is Assistant Professor of Sociology at Yale University, affiliated with the Economic Growth Center. In 1974, she was a Visiting Member at the Institute for Advanced Study and a Research Associate at the Office of Population Research, Princeton University. Her dissertation at Princeton University was on "Internal Migration in a Modernizing Society: The Case of Late Nineteenth Century European Russia." Her current research includes migration in Japan 1870–1930 and the relationships between marital fertility and nutrition in Zaire, as well as work with Ansley J. Coale on a book about fertility changes in Russia since the nineteenth century.

SUSAN BRIDGE is Lecturer in Government at Wesleyan University and is completing her doctoral dissertation in political science at Yale on "The Evolution of the Yugoslav Electoral System: A Case Study in Comparative and Theoretical Perspective." She worked for two years for the Yugoslav Mission to the United Nations and spent a year on a Wellesley College Traveling Fellowship in Rumania, Bulgaria, and Yugoslavia. Her current research includes a chapter on Yugoslavia in a forthcoming volume edited by Milton Erman on ethnic conflict, and a book on theories of political change and political ethics as applied to one-party systems.

WALTER D. CONNOR is Assistant Professor of Sociology and Research Associate of the Center for Russian and East European Studies, University of Michigan. His previous works include *Deviance in Soviet Society* (1972), contributions to several edited volumes, and articles in *American Sociological Review*, *Law and Society Review*, *Comparative Studies in Society and History*, *Problems of Communism*, and other journals here and abroad. He is currently working on a major comparative study of social stratification and mobility patterns in the U.S.S.R. and Eastern Europe.

JOHN FRASER is Assistant Professor of Political Science at the University of Waterloo, Ontario, Canada. He received his Ph.D. from the University of Leicester in 1968 with a dissertation on syndicalism in Britain. Professor Fraser has contributed articles to *Science and Society* and *The Sociological Review* on the relation between Marxist theory and the intelligentsia of socialist societies, and has just completed a study of the philosophy of the Italian Marxist, Galvano della Volpe. Preparation of the present article involved numerous field trips to the Lenin Library, Moscow. His current research concerns policies of the Italian Communist Party toward the Italian intellectual community since 1944.

GEORGE KLEIN is Professor of Political Science at Western Michigan University. He has served as the chairman of WMU's Slavic Studies Program and is currently Chairman of the European Studies Program. He has contributed a chapter on "Yugoslavia: The Process of Democratization" to Peter A. Toma (ed.), *The Changing Face of Communism in Eastern Europe* (1970), and on "The United States and Yugoslavia" to Chester L. Hunt and Lewis Walker, *Ethnic Dynamics* (1974), as well as several journal articles. Professor Klein has been the recipient of a number of travel grants and awards, taking him to Burma in 1961 and repeatedly to Yugoslavia.

GENERAL INDEX TO STUDIES IN COMPARATIVE COMMUNISM VOLUME VIII (1975)

Articles and Comments

ANDERSON, BARBARA A., "Social Stratification in the Soviet Union: Equality, Excellence and Other Issues," VIII: 4, 397–412.

ASPATURIAN, VERNON V., "Comment," VIII: 3, 300–304.

BARAS, VICTOR, "China and the Rise of Khrushchev," VIII: 1 & 2, 183–191.

BERNSTEIN, THOMAS P., "Comment," VIII: 3, 274–277.

BRIDGE, SUSAN, "Rejoinder," VIII: 4, 444.

BRIDGE, SUSAN, "Why Czechoslovakia? And Why 1968?" VIII: 4, 413–429.

CONNOR, WALTER D., "Revolution, Modernization, and Communism," VIII: 4, 389–396.

DALLIN, ALEXANDER, "Comment," VIII: 3, 245–247.

FINLEY, DAVID D., "Détente and Soviet-American Trade: An Approach to a Political Balance Sheet," VIII: 1 & 2, 66–97.

FINLEY, DAVID D., "What Should We Compare, Why, and How?" VIII: 1 & 2, 12–19.

FRASER, JOHN, "Soviet Sociology and Its Critics," VIII: 4, 370–388.

GATI, CHARLES, "Area Studies and International Relations: Introductory Remarks," VIII: 1 & 2, 5–11.

GOLAN, GALIA, "Comment: Reform Movements and the Problem of Prediction," VIII: 4, 430–435.

GOLDSTEIN, STEVEN, "China: Four Explanations," VIII: 3, 248–274.

HOFFMANN, Erik P., "The Soviet Union: Consensus or Debate?" VIII: 3, 230–244.

HORELICK, ARNOLD L., "Does the Comparative Approach Merit High Priority?" VIII: 1 & 2, 36–41.

JANCAR, BARBARA, "Eastern Europe: Toward a New Paradigm?" VIII: 3, 278–300.

KANET, ROGER E., "Is Comparison Useful or Possible?" VIII: 1 & 2, 20–27.

KLEIN, GEORGE, "The Role of Ethnic Politics in the Czechoslovak Crisis of 1968 and the Yugoslav Crisis of 1971," VIII: 4, 339–369.

KREJCI, JAROSLAV, "Comment," VIII: 4, 436–438.

KRISCH, HENRY, "Some Undone Jobs," VIII: 1 & 2, 28–35.

KUSIN, VLADIMIR V., "Comment," VIII: 4, 439–440.

LAPALOMBARA, JOSEPH, "Monoliths or Plural Systems: Through Conceptual Lenses Darkly," VIII: 3, 305–332.

LAUX, JEANNE KIRK, "Intra-Alliance Politics and European Detente: The Case of Poland and Rumania," VIII: 1 & 2, 98–122.

P.B. (Peter Berton), "Level and Context of Analysis: Concluding Remarks," VIII: 1 & 2, 62–65.

REMINGTON, ROBIN ALISON, "Comment," VIII: 4, 441–442.

ROSENAU, JAMES N., "Comparison as a State of Mind," VIII: 1 & 2, 57–61.

RUBINSTEIN, ALVIN Z., "Comparison or Confusion?" VIII: 1 & 2, 42–46.

SERFATY, SIMON, "An International Anomaly: The United States and the Communist Parties in France and Italy, 1945–1947," VIII: 1 & 2, 123–146.

SIMES, DIMITRI K., "The Soviet Invasion of Czechoslovakia and the Limits of Kremlinology," VIII: 1 & 2, 174–180.

TAUBMAN, WILLIAM, "*Political Power: USA/USSR* Ten Years Later—Comparative Foreign Policy:" VIII: 1 & 2, 192–203.
TÖKÉS, RUDOLF L., "Comparative Communism: The Elusive Target," VIII: 3, 211–229.
TRISKA, JAN F., "Foreign Policy Issues Within Conceptual Frameworks," VIII: 1 & 2, 47–51.
VALENTA, JIRI, "Rejoinder," VIII: 1 & 2, 181–182.
VALENTA, JIRI, "Soviet Decisionmaking and the Czechoslovak Crisis of 1968," VIII: 1 & 2, 147–173.
WHEELER, GEORGE SHAW, "Comment," VIII: 4, 443.
WHETTEN, LAWRENCE L., "The Plausibility and Utility of the Study of Comparative Communist Foreign Policies," VIII: 1 & 2, 52–56.

Review Articles

ARMSTRONG, JOHN A., *Ideology, Politics, and Government in the Soviet Union* (Erik P. Hoffman), VIII: 3, 230–244.
BARGHOORN, FREDERICK, *Politics in the USSR* (Erik P. Hoffmann), VIII: 3, 230–244.
BROMKE, ADAM (ed.), *The Communist States at the Crossroads Between Moscow and Peking* (Barbara Jancar), VIII: 3, 278–300.
BROWN, J. F., *The New Eastern Europe: The Khrushchev Era and After* (Barbara Jancar), VIII: 3, 278–300,
BRZEZINSKI, ZBIGNIEW and HUNTINGTON, SAMUEL P., *Political Power USA/USSR* (William Taubman), VIII: 1 & 2, 192–203.
FEJTO, FRANÇOIS, *A History of the People's Democracies* (*Barbara Jancar*), VIII: 3, 278–300.
FISCHER-GALATI, STEPHEN (ed.), *Eastern Europe in the Sixties* (Barbara Jancar), VIII: 3, 278–300.
FISHER, W. A., see Yanowitch, Murray.
GATI, CHARLES (ed.), *The Politics of Modernization in Eastern Europe: Testing the Soviet Model* (Walter D. Connor), VIII: 4, 389–396.
GOLAN, GALIA, *The Czechoslovak Reform Movement: Communism in Crisis, 1962–1968* (Susan Bridge), VIII: 4, 413–429.
GOLAN, GALIA, *Reform Rule in Czechoslovakia: The Dubcek Era* (Susan Bridge), VIII: 4, 413–429.
GOULDNER, A., *The Coming Crisis of Western Sociology* (John Fraser), VIII, 4, 370–388.
HAMMER, DARRELL, *USSR: The Politics of Oligarchy* (Erik P. Hoffmann), VIII: 3, 230–244.
HINTON, HAROLD C., *An Introduction to Chinese Politics* (Steven Goldstein), VIII: 3, 248–274.
HUNTINGTON, SAMUEL P., see Brzezinski, Zbigniew.
INKELES, ALEX and SMITH, DAVID H., *Becoming Modern: Individual Change in Six Developing Countries* (Walter D. Connor), VIII: 4, 389–396.
IONESCU, GHITA, *The Politics of the European Communist States* (Barbara Jancar), VIII: 3, 278–300.
KREJCI, JAROSLAV, *Social Change and Stratification in Postwar Czechoslovakia* (Susan Bridge), VIII: 4, 413–429.
KUSIN, VLADIMIR V., *Political Grouping in the Czechoslovak Reform Movement* (Susan Bridge), VIII: 4, 413–429.
LANE, DAVID, *The End of Inequality? Stratification Under State Socialism* (Barbara A. Anderson), VIII: 4, 397–412.
LANE, DAVID S., *Politics and Society in the USSR* (Erik P. Hoffmann), VIII: 3, 230–244.

LEWIN, MOSHE, *Political Undercurrents in Soviet Economic Debates: From Bukharin to the Modern Reformers* (Walter D. Connor), VIII: 4, 389–396.
MATTHEWS, MERVYN, *Class and Society in Soviet Russia* (Barbara A. Anderson), VIII: 4, 397–412.
MICKIEWICZ, ELLEN, *Handbook of Soviet Social Science Data* (Barbara A. Anderson), VIII: 4, 397–412.
OSBORN, ROBERT J., *The Evolution of Soviet Politics* (Erik P. Hoffmann), VIII: 3, 230–244.
PETHYBRIDGE, ROGER, *The Social Prelude to Stalinism* (Walter D. Connor), VIII: 4, 389–396.
PIEKALKIEWICZ, JAROSLAW A., *Public Opinion Polling in Czechoslovakia, 1968–69: Results and Analysis of Surveys Conducted During the Dubcek Era* (Susan Bridge), VIII: 4, 413–429.
PYE, LUCIAN W., *China: An Introduction* (Steven Goldstein), VIII: 3, 248–274.
REMINGTON, ROBIN ALISON (ed.), *Winter in Prague: Documents on Czechoslovak Communism in Crisis* (Susan Bridge), VIII: 4, 413–429.
RESHETAR, JOHN, Jr., *The Soviet Polity: Government and Politics in the U.S.S.R.* (Erik P. Hoffmann), VIII: 3, 230–244.
RICHTA, RADOVAN, *et al.*, *Civilization at the Crossroads: Social and Human Implications of the Scientific and Technological Revolution* (Susan Bridge), VIII: 4, 413–429.
RUTKEVICH, M. N. (ed.), *The Career Plans of Youth* (Barbara A. Anderson), VIII: 4, 397–412.
SKILLING, H. GORDON, *The Governments of Communist East Europe* (Barbara Jancar), VIII: 3, 278–300.
SMITH, DAVID H., see Inkeles, Alex.
STARR, JOHN BRYAN, *Ideology and Culture: An Introduction to the Dialectic of Contemporary Chinese Politics* (Steven Goldstein), VIII: 3, 248–274.
STEINER, EUGEN, *The Slovak Dilemma* (Susan Bridge), VIII: 4, 413–429.
STOJANOVIC, SVETOZAR, *Between Ideals and Reality: A Critique of Socialism and its Future* (Walter D. Connor), VIII: 4, 389–396.
TOMA, PETER A. (ed.), *The Changing Face of Communism in Eastern Europe* (Barbara Jancar), VIII: 3, 278–300.
TOWNSEND, JAMES R., *Politics in China* (Steven Goldstein), VIII: 3, 248–274.
TRISKA, JAN F. (ed.), *Integration and Community Building in Eastern Europe* (Barbara Jancar), VIII: 3, 278–300.
WHEELER, GEORGE SHAW, *The Human Face of Socialism: The Political Economy of Change in Czechoslovakia* (Susan Bridge), VIII: 4, 413–429.
YANOWITCH, MURRAY and FISHER, W. A. (eds.), *Social Stratification and Mobility in the U.S.S.R.* (Barbara A. Anderson), VIII: 4, 397–412.
ZUKIN, SHARON, *Beyond Marx and Tito: Theory and Practice in Yugoslav Socialism* (Walter D. Connor), VIII: 4, 389–396.